Sixteenth Century Europe

Expansion and Conflict

HISTORY OF EUROPE

PUBLISHED

Early Medieval Europe 300–1000
Roger Collins

Sixteenth Century Europe
Expansion and Conflict
Richard Mackenney

Seventeenth Century Europe 1598–1700
Thomas Munck

Eighteenth Century Europe 1700–1789
Jeremy Black

FORTHCOMING

Medieval Europe 1000–1250
Randall Rogers

Nineteenth Century Europe 1789–1914
Alan Sked

Series Standing Order

If you would like to receive future titles in this series as they are published, you can make use of our standing order facility. To place a standing order please contact your bookseller or, in case of difficulty, write to us at the address below with your name and address and the name of the series. Please state with which title you wish to begin your standing order. (If you live outside the United Kingdom we may not have the rights for your area, in which case we will forward your order to the publisher concerned.)

Standing Order Service, Macmillan Distribution Ltd,
Houndmills, Basingstoke, Hampshire, RG21 2XS, England

Sixteenth Century Europe

Expansion and Conflict

Richard Mackenney

First published 1993 by
MACMILLAN PRESS LTD
Houndmills, Basingstoke, Hampshire RG21 6XS
and London
Companies and representatives
throughout the world

ISBN 0–333–36923–8 hardcover
ISBN 0–333–36924–6 paperback

A catalogue record for this book is available
from the British Library.

11 10   9   8   7   6   5   4   3
04 03 02 01 00 99 98 97 96

Printed in Hong Kong

For Linda

Contents

List of maps

List of figures and table

Figures

Table

List of plates

Section I – High Renaissance

The High Renaissance is most obviously associated with the achievements of three artists of genius: Leonardo (1452–1519), Michelangelo (1475–1564), and Raphael (1483–1520). These three very different illustrations [plates 1–3] of very different subjects show how the supreme expressions of the artistic imagination were underpinned by the most rigorous application of the science of perspective: the understanding of space.

1. Leonardo, Study for the *Adoration of the Magi*, 1481 (Florence, Uffizi)
2. Michelangelo, *The Crucifixion of Haman*, c.1511 (Rome, Sistine Chapel: Mansell/Alinari)
3. Raphael, *School of Athens*, 1511 (Rome, Vatican: Mansell/Alinari)

Section II – The art of science

Leonardo's drawings [4–5] capture the force of vitality in plants and the awesome destructive power of nature. Accurate drawing was to make possible the systematic classification of animal life – as Dürer's (1471–1528) study of a hare [6] demonstrates. Simultaneously, the study of human anatomy was to revolutionise the understanding of the human body [7]. Some leading modern authorities see the hand of Titian himself (c.1487/90–1576) in the illustrations to the text of Vesalius.

4. Leonardo, *Star of Bethlehem*, c.1505–8 (Windsor, Royal Collection)
5. Leonardo, *Cloudburst*, after 1513 (Windsor, Royal Collection no. 12, 377)
6. Dürer, *The Hare*, 1502 (Vienna, Albertina: Mansell/Alinari)
7. Engraving from Vesalius, *De humani corporis fabrica*, 1543 (Bridgeman Art Library/ Fratelli Fibri, Milan)

Section III – The crisis of sensibility

The confidence in the artist's creative powers which the High Renaissance embodied easily and quickly gave way to anxiety and despair.

The futility of endeavour is captured in Dürer's incomparable engraving [8] and his fear for the future in his terrifying vision of the world consumed in flood [9], which he sketched after a nightmare. Grünewald (1470/80–1528) expressed the spiritual anguish of the period in his crucifixion [10], which depicts with compelling immediacy Christ's suffering as God made Man. While it is easy to connect German art with the spiritual turmoil of the Reformation, there was plenty of pessimism in the art of the Catholic world, as shown by Michelangelo's self-portraits as the flayed skin of St Bartholomew [11] and as St Paul on the Road to Damascus [12].

8. Dürer, *Melancholia I*, 1514 (Mansell Collection)
9. Dürer, *The Deluge*, 1525 (Kunsthistorisches Museum, Vienna: Bridgeman Art Library)
10. Grünewald, *Crucifixion* from the *Isenheim Altar*, c.1515 (Colmar Museum: Unterlinden/Zimmerman)
11. Michelangelo, *St Bartholomew*, c.1541 (Rome, Sistine Chapel: Mansell/Alinari)
12. Michelangelo, *Conversion of St Paul*, 1545 (Rome, Vatican: Mansell/Anderson)

Section IV – Renaissance art and the Counter-Reformation

It is perhaps a measure of how severe was the spiritual upheaval represented in Section III that the art of the Renaissance adapted so swiftly to the spirituality of the Counter-Reformation. Titian's *Assumption* [13] dates from 1518, yet seems to articulate the religious and artistic principles of the post-Tridentine era. The works of Tintoretto (1518–94) express the new Catholicism with extraordinary power, advertising the efficacy of works [14] and extolling the splendour of holiness [15], the latter a quality which separates this crucifixion from Grünewald's depiction of the same subject [10]. It was not always possible for artists to avoid conflict with ecclesiastical authority. Veronese's *Last Supper* had to be renamed *The Banquet in the House of Levi* [16] to conform to the requirements of the Inquisition. All the same, some of the later works of Titian [e.g. 17 and 18] show the surprising but harmonious synthesis of Renaissance art and Spanish Catholicism.

13. Titian, *Assumption of the Virgin*, 1518 (Venice, Santa Maria Gloriosa dei Frari: Mansell/Anderson)
14. Tintoretto, *Last Supper*, late 1560s (Venice, San Polo: Mansell Collection)

Section V – The art of politics

Artists sought to become beneficaries of the patronage systems which centred at court, most obviously in the form of commissions. However, the close relationship of political and cultural patronage meant that those same commissions provide something of a political record. Holbein (1497/8–1543) painted More as Chancellor [19], and the portrait of More's successor, Thomas Cromwell, here shown in his office as Keeper of the King's Jewels [20], is often attributed to him. Holbein's painting of Anne of Cleves [21] helped persuade the King [22] to a match which might have formed the basis of a European alliance against Charles V: both Henry and Anne are shown in wedding clothes. Henry's displeasure on meeting his 'Flanders mare' led to Cromwell's disgrace.

Section VI – Emblems of an age

The paintings of Bruegel impress upon us the way in which violent physical brutality was part of everyday life. The gallows were no deterrent to merry making [23], mock battles – which were not always mock – were part of popular festivities [24] and everyday life in any form at any moment might be overwhelmed by ever-present, omnipresent Death [25]. On such a social scene first fell the grim shadows of the cages at Münster in which the tortured corpses of the Anabaptist leaders were left to rot [26]. In such a social context, the close association of the true Word with fire and sword – memorably depicted in Farel's emblem [27] – could only intensify the conflicts of the era. Over these conflicts presided Charles V, here shown at his moment of triumph after Mühlberg [28], while the defeated John Frederick of Saxony looks every inch a prisoner [29]. Philip II [30] looks much more awkward in armour than did his father, but then the age of the warrior king was in many ways passed. It is part of the 'black legend' to see the man wrestling with the problems of Europe's first global empire as 'the spider of the Escorial'. His agent, Alba [31], shown in all his pride by Antoniis Mor (1517/21–1576/7), looks much more the part of the Spanish tyrant, but the contradictions of the Spanish position are encapsulated in the career of Philip's half-brother, Don John [32]. It is curious that he should be remembered as both the hero of Christendom for his victory at Lepanto, and the instrument of Spanish oppression in the Netherlands.

Some chronological landmarks, 1500–99

1500: Cabral discovered Brazilian coast and claimed it for Portugal.
Vincente Pinzon (Spanish) reached the mouth of the Amazon.
Louis XII of France conquered Milan.
Treaty of Granada: France and Spain agreed on the partition of Italy.
Pope Alexander VI proclaimed a crusade against the Turks.
Aldus Manutius founded the Venice Academy for the study of the Greek classics.

1501: France and Spain conquered Naples.
Aldine press published an edition of Vergil.
Prince Arthur married Catherine of Aragon.

1502: Fourth voyage of Columbus to the West Indies.
Forcible conversion of Moors of Castile.
Vespucci and Coelho sailed south down eastern seaboard of South America.

1503: Piero de' Medici drowned at the Garigliano (Spanish victory over French).
Death of Alexander VI; Pius III died after less than a month; Julius II became pope.
Leonardo began the *Mona Lisa*.
Michelangelo sculpted the *David*.

1504: Death of Isabella; accession of Joanna the Mad in Castile.
Treaty of Lyon: France ceded Naples to Spain.

1505: Luther entered the monastery at Erfurt.
Decree *Nihil novi* in Poland gave full legislative power to noble assembly.
Portuguese established trading posts in east Africa.

1506: Death of Columbus.
Ferdinand of Aragon regent for grandson Charles.

1507: Julius II proclaimed an indulgence to help to pay for the building of St Peter's.
Waldseemüller's map of the world makes first use of the name 'America'.

1508: League of Cambrai: European coalition against Venice.
Michelangelo began frescoes on Sistine Ceiling.

1509: Battle of Agnadello: League of Cambrai defeated the Venetians.
Death of Henry VII, accession of Henry VIII, who married
Catherine of Aragon, his brother's widow.
Portuguese naval victory over Egyptians at Diu.
Portuguese the first European settlers in Sumatra.
Erasmus, *In Praise of Folly*.

1510: Albuquerque takes Goa for the Portuguese.

1511: Albert of Hohenzollern became Grand Master of the Teutonic
Order.
Earliest known record of the Bermudas.
Peter Martyr, *De orbe novo* (history of Spanish exploration).
Raphael began *School of Athens* in the Vatican.

1512: Battle of Ravenna: French victory over Spanish and papal
forces.
Medici restored to power in Florence.
Swiss took Milan.

1513: Battle of the Spurs: victory of Henry VIII's army over French at
Guinegate.
Battle of Flodden: victory of English over Scots.
Giovanni de' Medici became Pope Leo X.
(*c.* 1513) Machiavelli, *The Prince*; *The Discourses*.
Ponce de Leon explored the coast of Florida; discovery of Gulf
Stream.
Vasco Balboa crossed the Isthmus of Panama and discovered
the Pacific.
Portuguese established a trading factory at Diu.

1514: Johann Tetzel began sale of Indulgences.
Moldavia became a Turkish province.
Battle of Tchaldiran: Turkish victory over Persians.

1515: Cardinal Wolsey chancellor of England.
Death of Louis XII; accession of Francis I.
Battle of Marignano: French victory over Swiss; French
recovered Milan.
Diaz de Solis (Spanish) reached River Plate.
Matthias Grünewald, *Isenheim Altarpiece*.

1516: Death of Ferdinand of Aragon; accession of Charles I (Emperor
Charles V in 1519).
Concordat of Bologna confirmed 'Gallican' liberties.
More, *Utopia*.
Ludovico Ariosto, *Orlando Furioso*.
Erasmus published New Testament in Greek.
Barbarossa captured Algiers.
Spanish reached Yucatan from Cuba.
(*c.* 1516) Portuguese reached China.

1517: Luther produced the Ninety-Five Theses.
Turks conquered Mamluk empire; then at war with Portuguese.
'Evil May Day' in London: apprentices rioted against alien merchants.

1518: Peace of London: Wolsey engineered European alliance against the Turks.
Luther refused to recant at Augsburg.
Titian, *Assumption of the Virgin.*

1519: Death of Maximilian, election of Charles V.
Rising of the *germanía* in Valencia.
Leipzig disputations between Luther and Eck.
Cortés landed in Mexico.
Seyssel, *La monarchie de France.*

1520: Field of the Cloth of Gold (Francis I and Henry VIII).
Revolt of the *comuneros.*
Excommunication of Luther.
Luther, *Address to the Christian Nobility; Babylonian Captivity; On the Freedom of a Christian.*
Accession of Suleiman the Magnificent as sultan.
Magellan reached Chile, discovered the strait named after him, entered Pacific.

1521: Suleiman captured Belgrade.
Cortés took Mexico City.
Luther condemned as a heretic at the Diet of Worms.
Death of Magellan in the Philippines.
Portuguese traded in the Moluccas.
Gustavus Vasa led Swedish revolt against Denmark.

1522: Battle of Bicocca: victory of Spanish and Germans over French and Swiss.
Return of Magellan's expedition under Sebastian del Cano completed first circumnavigation.
Reformation teachings introduced to Bremen.
Luther published his New Testament.
Order of St John driven from Rhodes by Turks.

1523: Philip of Hesse joined Reformation.
Knights Revolt defeated.
End of Union of Kalmar: Gustavus Vasa elected king of Sweden.
Lefèvre d'Etaples produced New Testament in French.
Europeans expelled from China.

1524: Establishment of Council of the Indies.
Spanish conquered Guatemala, Honduras, Nicaragua.
Pizarro sailed from Panama, explored South American coast, landed in what is now Ecuador.
German peasants began revolt.

1525: Battle of Frankenhausen: Swabian League crushed German peasants.

Battle of Pavia: Imperialist victory over French; Francis I captured.

Secularisation of the Teutonic Order in Prussia (East Prussia became a vassal state of Poland).

Tyndale completed translation of Bible into English.

1526: Treaty of Madrid between Francis I and Charles V.

League of Cognac (France, Florence, Venice, Milan, papacy) against Charles V.

Adult re-baptism made a capital offence in Zurich.

First Diet of Speyer.

Battle of Mohács: Turkish victory over Hungarian armies; death of Ladislas II; succession disputed between Ferdinand of Habsburg and John Zapolyai.

Pizarro reached Peru.

1527: Henry VIII sought annulment of marriage to Catherine of Aragon.

Sack of Rome by the imperial armies.

Medici expelled from Florence.

Death of Machiavelli.

Reformation adopted in Sweden (Diet of Våsteras).

Paracelsus lectured on 'new medicine' at the university of Basel.

1528: Hubmaier, leader of Austrian anabaptists, burned at Vienna.

Castiglione, *The Book of the Courtier.*

1529: Fall of Wolsey; More became chancellor.

Reformation accepted in Hamburg.

Colloquy of Marburg failed to resolve differences between Luther and Zwingli on the Eucharist.

Second Diet of Speyer: 'protest' lodged against imperial religious policy.

1530: German Protestant states formed League of Schmalkalden.

Melanchthon prepared Augsburg Confession.

Return of the Medici to Florence.

Death of Wolsey.

Infectious venereal disease named as syphilis.

1531: Zwingli killed at the battle of Kappel.

Unlicensed beggars to be whipped in England.

Charles V prohibited reformed teachings in the Netherlands.

Ferdinand of Bohemia became king of the Romans (now heir to imperial title).

Inquisition established in Portugal.

Diego de Ordas's expedition to the Orinoco.

Pizarro crossed Andes.

Elyot, *The Boke named the Governour.*

1532: Suleiman invaded Hungary; failed to take the fortress of Güns.
Religious peace of Nuremberg: Protestants pledge military support to Empire in return for toleration until a general council is convened.
Act of Annates (against episcopal payments to Rome); submission of English clergy.
Pizarro captured and killed Inca king Atahuallpa; took Cuzco.
Rabelais, *Pantagruel.*

1533: Act of Appeals forbidding appeals to Rome.
Secret marriage of Henry VIII and Anne Boleyn.
Ivan IV acceded to throne of Muscovy at 3 years of age: later became 'the Terrible'.
Holbein, *The Ambassadors.*

1534: Henry VIII became head of Church of England.
Day of the Placards in Paris.
Ignatius Loyola founded the Society of Jesus.
Anabaptist 'kingdom' in Münster.
Suleiman captured Baghdad.
Jacques Cartier sailed to Gulf of St Lawrence.
Rabelais, *Gargantua.*

1535: Milan under Spanish rule.
Thomas Cromwell became Vicar General; executions of Bishop Fisher and More.
Almagro's march to Chile.
Pizarro founded Lima.

1536: Death of Catherine of Aragon; execution of Anne Boleyn; Henry VIII married Jane Seymour; dissolution of monasteries; Pilgrimage of Grace.
Menno Simons established anabaptism in Friesland.
Calvin, *Institutes*, published in Latin.
Cartier's second voyage: claimed Canada for France.
Guicciardini began his *History of Italy.*

1537: Lutheran church established in Denmark.
Francisco César's expedition to Antioquia, foundation of Asunción.
Birth of Prince Edward; death of Jane Seymour.

1538: Calvin and Farel expelled from Geneva.
Benalcazar's expedition to Bogota; beginning of El Dorado myth.

1539: Holbein, *Anne of Cleves.*
Rebellion against Charles V in Ghent.
Coverdale's Great Bible was produced in the name of Henry VIII.

1540: Foundation of the Jesuit order.
Suleiman invaded Hungary.

Failure of Henry VIII's marriage to Anne of Cleves; fall of Cromwell.

Henry VIII married Catherine Howard.

John III of Portugal sent Jesuit missionaries to the Far East.

Spaniards reached California.

1541: Diet of Regensburg sought to restore unity of the Church.

Henry VIII took title of King of Ireland.

Michelangelo, *Last Judgement*.

Calvin returned to establish theocracy in Geneva; Knox began Reformation in Scotland.

Hungary fell to the Turks.

Valdivia explored Chile: foundation of Santiago.

1542: Battle of Solway Moss: English victory over Scots.

Execution of Catherine Howard; Henry VIII married Catherine Parr.

Paul III re-established Inquisition in Rome.

Abolition of Indian slavery in Spain's American colonies.

Las Casas, *Brief Account of the Ruines of the Indies*.

1543: Copernicus, *On the Revolutions of the Celestial Spheres*.

Vesalius, *On the Fabric of the Human Body*.

Portuguese reached Japan.

1544: Discovery of silver mines at Potosí in Peru.

1545: Opening of the Council of Trent.

Palatinate adopted Protestantism.

1546: Death of Luther.

Silver mines discovered at Zacatecas in Mexico.

1547: Death of Henry VIII; accession of Edward VI.

Death of Francis I; accession of Henry II.

John Knox exiled to France.

Battle of Mühlberg: victory of Charles V over League of Schmalkalden.

1548: Augsburg Interim: Charles V attempted religious settlement.

Ignatius Loyola, *Spiritual Exercises*.

1549: New Prayer Book; Kett's rebellion (Norfolk).

Francis Xavier arrived in Japan.

1550: Protector Somerset overthrown by Northumberland.

1551: Council of Trent began second session.

Maurice of Saxony deserted the imperial cause.

Palestrina choir master at St Peter's.

1552: Treaty of Chambord between Henry II and German Protestants.

Ivan IV (the Terrible) conquered Kazan from Tartars.

1553: Charles V's siege of Metz failed.

Death of Edward VI; Lady Jane Grey's nine-days reign; accession of Mary.

Willoughby and Chancellor sought north-east passage.

1554: Wyatt's rebellion; execution of Lady Jane Grey; Mary married Philip of Spain; Act of Supremacy repealed; Cardinal Pole papal legate to England.

Chancellor received in Moscow by Ivan the Terrible.

1555: Paul IV became pope.

Beginning of Marian persecutions; Ridley and Latimer bùrned at Oxford.

Peace of Augsburg: '*cuius regio, eius religio*' in the Empire.

Formation of the Muscovy Company.

1556: Cranmer burned.

Abdication of Charles V.

Death of Ignatius Loyola.

Annexation of Astrakhan by Ivan IV.

1557: Bankruptcy of Spanish crown.

Battle of St Quentin: Spanish victory over French.

First venture of Muscovy Company under Anthony Jenkinson.

Portuguese merchants settled in Macao.

1558: French recovered Calais; Henry II abandoned alliance with German Protestants.

Dauphin of France married Mary, Queen of Scots.

Béza issued Calvinist Confession of Faith.

Death of Mary Tudor; accession of Elizabeth I.

Death of Charles V.

Jenkinson reached Bokhara.

1559: Treaty of Cateau-Cambrésis ended Habsburg-Valois wars.

Acts of Supremacy and Uniformity severed England from Rome, established Protestantism.

Death of Henry II; accession of Dauphin as Francis II. Mary Queen of Scots now queen of France.

Margaret of Parma became regent in the Netherlands.

Paul IV published *Index of Prohibited Books*.

1560: Reformed Church established in Scotland.

Failure of Calvinist Conspiracy of Amboise.

Death of Melanchthon.

Death of Francis II, accession of Charles IX, with Catherine de' Medici as regent.

1561: Philip II transferred his capital to Madrid.

Mary, Queen of Scots, widowed, returned to Scotland.

Colloquy of Poissy: attempted reconciliation of Catholics and Protestants in France.

1562: Edict of St Germain recognised French Protestants; massacre of Huguenots at Vassy; civil war in France.

Council of Trent re-opened.

Cellini, *Autobiography*.

Trade in West African slaves began.

First of Hawkins's voyages to the West Indies.

1563: Closure of Council of Trent.

Assassination of Duke of Guise; Edict of Amboise ended fighting.

Philip II ordered the building of the Escorial.

1564: Death of Calvin.

Death of Emperor Ferdinand; succession of Maximilian II.

Dismissal of Granvelle.

1565: Mary, Queen of Scots married Lord Darnley.

Siege of Malta: Turks repulsed by Knights of St John.

Bruegel, *Autumn* and *Winter*.

1566: Death of Suleiman.

Iconoclastic riots in the Netherlands.

Carlo Borromeo became archbishop of Milan.

Murder of Rizzio at Holyrood on Darnley's orders.

Sir Thomas Gresham founded the Royal Exchange.

1567: Rebellion in the Netherlands; Alba sent to crush it; established Council of Troubles.

Murder of Darnley.

Mary, Queen of Scots married Bothwell, forced to abdicate.

1568: Treaty of Longjumeau to end hostilities in France.

Spanish Inquisition condemned all inhabitants of the Netherlands to death as heretics; execution of Egmont and Hoorn.

Pay-ships meant for Alba's army seized by Elizabeth I.

Arrest and death of Philip II's heir, Don Carlos.

Revolt of the Moriscos in Granada.

Jesuits given friendly reception in Japan.

Hawkins's slaver fleet attacked by Spaniards at San Juan de Ulúa.

Sebastian of Portugal abolished Indian slavery in Brazil.

1569: Catholic victories in France at Jarnac (death of Condé) and Moncontour.

Rebellion of the Northern Earls.

Rebellion of Fitzmaurice in Ireland (lasted until 1574).

Ottomans took the Yemen.

1570: Ottomans took Cyprus.

Elizabeth I excommunicated and declared a usurper.

Drake's first voyage to the West Indies.

Cosimo I became Grand Duke of Tuscany.

Ortelius, *Theatrum Orbis Terrarum* (first modern atlas).

1571: Battle of Lepanto: victory of Holy League (formed by Pius V) over Turks.

Huguenot Synod at La Rochelle; Dutch Calvinist Synod at Emden.

Ridolfi plot against Elizabeth I.

Spanish conquered Philippines, founded Manila.

Portuguese created colony in Angola.

1572: Assassination of Coligny; Massacre of St Bartholomew.

Seizure of Brill by Sea Beggars.

Drake's first sight of the Pacific.

1573: Withdrawal of Venice from Holy League against Turks.

Pacification of Boulogne to end wars in France.

Hotman, *Francogallia.*

Alba replaced by Requesens.

1574: Death of Charles IX, accession of Henry III.

Portuguese colonised Angola.

1575: Spanish crown bankrupt.

Foundation of University of Leyden by William of Orange.

1576: Sack of Antwerp by Spaniards; Pacification of Ghent; death of Requesens.

Peace of Monsieur ended Catholic rebellion under Alençon.

Death of Maximilian II, accession of Rudolf II.

Tycho Brahe, Danish astronomer, established observatory at Uraniborg.

Frobisher sought north-west passage.

Portuguese founded Luanda.

Bodin, *Six Books of the Commonwealth.*

1577: Don John Governor-General in the Netherlands.

Drake began voyage which became circumnavigation.

1578: Battle of Gembloux: victory of Don John and Alessandro Farnese over Dutch rebels.

Death of Sebastian of Portugal on crusade in Morocco.

Gilbert set out for north-west passage; reached Frobisher Bay on Baffin Island.

1579: Rebellion of Earl of Desmond in Ireland.

Union of Utrecht created 'United Provinces'.

1580: Philip II's army (under Alba) invaded Portugal to assert his claim to the throne.

Montaigne, *Essays.*

1581: Drake reurned to complete circumnavigation.

William of Orange, *Apology.*

1582: Gilbert founded first English colony in Newfoundland.

1583: Galileo discovered parabolic nature of trajectories.

1584: Assassination of William of Orange; Bruges and Ghent capitulated to Parma (Farnese).

Treaty of Joineville between Philip II and Guise.

Death of Ivan the Terrible; regency of Boris Godunov; beginning of Muscovy's 'Time of Troubles'.

Raleigh claimed Virginia.

1585: Treaty of Nonsuch: Elizabeth pledged help to the Dutch rebels; sent Leicester to Netherlands and he became Lieutenant-General.

Farnese conquered Brabant and Flanders.

Rebellion of the Catholic League in France (Henry III capitulated in Treaty of Nemours).

1586: Philip II began plans for Armada.

Leicester 'absolute governor and general' in the Netherlands.

Babington Plot against Elizabeth I; Mary, Queen of Scots, allegedly involved.

El Greco, *Burial of Count Orgaz.*

1587: Execution of Mary, Queen of Scots.

Discontent in the Netherlands – Leicester recalled to England.

Drake raided Cadiz.

Monteverdi composed his first book of madrigals.

1588: Defeat of the Spanish Armada.

Day of the Barricades in Paris; murder of Duke of Guise at the King's orders.

Accession of Shah Abbas I in Persia.

1589: Death of Catherine de' Medici; murder of Henry III; disputed accession of Henry IV.

Maurice of Nassau assumed leadership of United Provinces.

Hakluyt, *Principal Navigations.*

1590: Battle of Ivry: Henry IV defeated League of Joineville; Parma invaded France to relieve siege of Paris.

The last fight of Grenville's *Revenge.*

Galileo, *De motu*, on experiments on falling bodies.

Spenser, *Faerie Queen.*

1591: Philip II suppressed revolt in Aragon.

1592: Parma relieved Rouen from Anglo-French siege; death of Parma.

Shakespeare, *Henry VI; Richard III.*

Marlowe, *Doctor Faustus.*

Mariana, *Historia general de Espana.*

1593: Henry IV abjured Calvinism, became a Catholic: 'Paris is worth a mass'.

Murad III planned war on Rudolf II.

Shakespeare, *Richard II.*

1594: Lyon, Rouen and Paris surrendered to Henry IV; Henry IV entered Paris; crowned at Chartres; Jesuits expelled from France.

Barents sailed from Amsterdam and reached the Kara Sea.

1595:   Henry IV declared war on Spain.
        Accession of Sultan Mehmed III.
        Rebellion of the Earl of Tyrone in Ireland.
        Shakespeare, *A Midsummer Night's Dream.*
        Dutch began trading in East Indies.
1596:   Bankruptcy of Spanish crown.
        Magnates of Catholic League submit to Henry IV.
        Archduke Albert became Governor-General in the Netherlands.
        Death of Drake.
1597:   Huguenots failed to assist Henry IV in siege of Amiens, which
        was in Spanish hands.
        Bacon, *Essays.*
        Hooker, *Laws of Ecclesiastical Polity.*
1598:   Edict of Nantes.
        Treaty of Vervins.
        Death of Philip II.
        Rebellion in Ireland under O'Neill and Tyrone.
        Spenser, *View of the Present State of Ireland.*
        Boris Godunov elected Tsar.
1599:   Earl of Essex banished after failing to crush Tyrone's rebellion.
        James VI, *Basilikon Doron.*
        Shakespeare, *As You Like It, Henry V, Much Ado,*
        Twelfth Night.

Major European rulers of the sixteenth century

Popes

Alexander VI (Rodrigo Borgia) 1492–1503
Pius III (Francesco Todeschini-Piccolomini) Sept.–Oct. 1503
Julius II (Giuliano della Rovere) 1503–13
Leo X (Giovanni de' Medici) 1513–21
Hadrian VI (Adrian Dedel) 1522–23
Clement VII (Giulio de' Medici) 1523–34
Paul III (Alessandro Farnese) 1534–49
Julius III (Giovanni Maria Ciocchi del Monte) 1550–55
Marcellus II (Marcello Cervini) April 1555
Paul IV (Gian Pietro Carafa) 1555–59
Pius IV (Giovanni Angelo Medici) 1559–65
Pius V (Michele Ghislieri) 1566–72
Gregory XIII (Ugo Buoncompagni) 1572–85
Sixtus V (Felice Peretti) 1585–90
Urban VII (Giambattista Castagna) Sept. 1590
Gregory XIV (Niccolo Sfondrati) 1590–91
Innocent IX (Giovanni Antonio Facchinetti) Oct.–Dec. 1591
Clement VIII (Ippolito Aldobrandini) 1592–1605

Holy Roman Emperors

Maximilian I, 1493–1519
Charles V, 1519–56
Ferdinand I, 1556–64
Maximilian II, 1564–76
Rudolf II, 1576–1612

Monarchs of Spain

Isabella, 1474–1504 and Ferdinand, 1479–1516
Charles I (Emperor Charles V from 1519) 1516–56
Philip II, 1556–98

Monarchs of France

Charles VIII, 1483–98
Louis XII, 1498–1515
Francis I, 1515–47
Henry II, 1547–59
Francis II, 1559–60
Charles IX, 1560–74
Henry III, 1574–89
Henry IV, 1589–1610

Monarchs of England

Henry VII, 1485–1509
Henry VIII, 1509–47
Edward VI, 1547–53
Mary I, 1553–58
Elizabeth I, 1558–1603

Sultans

Bayezid II, 1481–1512
Selim I, 'the Grim', 1512–20
Suleiman I, 'the Magnificent', 1520–66
Selim II, 'the Sot', 1566–74
Murad III, 1574–95
Mehmet III, 1595–1603

Acknowledgements

This book has taken a tenth of a century to write, and in that time, its author has incurred innumerable debts to friends and students. I have learned an enormous amount from the work of other scholars, and I hope that none of them feels upset by the way in which I have used their work. The splendid libraries of Edinburgh – the National Library of Scotland, New College Library and above all the University of Edinburgh Library – and their staff have given me the opportunity to read the widest possible range of materials, and the incomparable facilities of the Cambridge University Library enabled me to consult a few elusive titles in the summer of 1992. Many of the ideas in this book derive from discussions with a large number of lively students, whom I thank most warmly for their stimulus. I would like to thank Rob Bartlett and John Stephens for their scrutiny of the project in its early stages, and Maurice Larkin for his comments on what was close to the final version. On specific aspects of the book, I owe a special debt to Professor G. R. Elton for his telling advice on Chapter 3. For encouragement and advice on the Irish experience, I thank Owen Dudley Edwards, and I received important help from Michael Lynch and John Durkan on Scotland. I am very grateful to Michael Bury for all his advice on the plates and on artistic matters in general. The Spanish focus of the book owes an enormous amount to the conversation and friendship of Angus MacKay and Geoffrey Parker. The readers of successive drafts were thorough and meticulous in matters great and small, and in some ways Brian Pullan and Bob Scribner have become something close to joint authors. I am very grateful for all their help. I must record a separate long-term debt to Brian, for that debt is very great. For the final revisions, I thank the Master and fellows of St Catharine's College, Cambridge, for a visiting fellowship which provided perfect conditions for study and reflection. I record a particular debt to my friends, Paul and Wendy Hartle and Stephen Lees. Sarah Mahaffy and Vanessa Couchman were patient editors, and Bruce Hunter has relieved me of any burden of negotiation. I am particularly grateful to Vanessa Graham for tolerating a string of revised deadlines with such kindness and understanding. She inspired a tremendous team effort in the final stages of production, and I am very grateful to Elizabeth Black, Keith Povey and Nancy Williams for working with me rather than telling me a schedule. All the errors which remain are mine.

It is shaming to have to acknowledge how much George and Francesca have had to put up with over the last six and three years respectively. Linda has devoted herself to them at the expense of her own writing, which has enabled me to sustain the project. Work on this book has been going on almost as long as our marriage – and it may at times have looked more enduring. My recognition of all Linda's help is lovingly but inadequately recorded in the dedication.

University of Edinburgh   RICHARD MACKENNEY
November 1992

The author and publishers wish to thank the following for kindly giving permission for the use of copyright material:

The Lutterworth Press for extracts from *Reformation Writings of Martin Luther King*, Vol. 1, trans. S. L. Woolf, 1952–6.

Every effort has been made to trace all the copyright-holders, but if any have been inadvertently overlooked the publishers will be pleased to make the necessary arrangement at the first opportunity.

A note for students and teachers

This book was written with the earnest hope that the reader may enjoy it: that point cannot be emphasised too strongly. Yet it is the author's responsibility to bear in mind that for many readers this will be a first contact with the sixteenth century, and for some it may well be the only such contact. There is no reason why an academic book should be exclusive in intellectual terms and I hope that the work will be as useful to the general reader and to students who do not intend to specialise in history as it will to those who have chosen history as their chief subject at university. Equally, I hope that the book will be useful to history teachers at all levels who are not necessarily specialists in this specific period. With those considerations in mind, the themes identified in the following pages are intended to focus concentration on basic questions which demonstrate why the sixteenth century is so important to the way we are now: What was society like? What were the most distinctive ideas of the age? What were the major wars about, and what decided their outcome? As far as possible, specialist debate is avoided, and frequent reference to contemporary sources is intended to stimulate discussion and conclusions which may well be at variance with those which I have expressed. Some of the passages will seem difficult because contemporary translations are used whenever possible. This is a deliberate choice intended to bring the reader closer to the realities of the sixteenth century by studying the age literally on its own terms.

Since many readers will be working systematically through the text, I have endeavoured to keep the coverage as even as possible: twelve chapters of similar size with the Introduction and Conclusion forming the equivalent of a thirteenth. It should be possible to work through the topics at an even pace throughout the school or university year. The bibliography is consciously designed to encourage further investigation by the reader rather than to justify what I have said.

Introduction

The shape of the century: expansion and conflict

Themes, chronologies, regions

Any period of a hundred years, arbitrarily defined, provides the working historian of Europe with three fundamental problems – or rather sets of problems – problems of theme, chronology, and region.[1] What are the main subjects for discussion? How do events mark the beginning and end of a historical process? Which countries should be the focus of attention? For the sixteenth century, the balance of organisational emphasis can never be steady, for the age is altogether lacking in focus and repose. No single region provides a cultural focus – as Italy provides for the fifteenth century. No stable pattern of society takes shape – as that of the *ancien régime* takes shape in the seventeenth. This is not to say that the history of the sixteenth century is any more difficult to present than that of the centuries which stand before it and after it, merely to emphasise that the people who lived all or part of their lives some time between 1500 and 1600 faced a particularly pressing complex of instabilities and uncertainties. New ideas about the world and man's place in it, ideas which had matured in Italy in the fifteenth century, spread to other parts of the continent, sometimes lubricating social change, sometimes jamming its mechanisms, here articulating a desire for spiritual succour, there ranting against priests. For Europeans, the world itself changed shape as the Mediterranean ceased to be the 'middle of the earth': 'Indians' in Mexico and Peru toiled at the point of swords made in Toledo, guns cast in Flanders for the Portuguese commanded the harbours at Goa and Macao.[2]

In a few lines, one uncovers the four great themes of the sixteenth century. The first is the Renaissance, that extraordinary revival of classical values in the visual arts and in letters which had its origins in fifteenth-century Florence. Later, as the courts rather than the cities became the nuclei of creativity, so the values and culture of an urban milieu became adapted to the needs and aspirations of monarchs, and this eased the transmission of Italian culture beyond the Alps after 1500. Moreover, scholarly research techniques – Kenneth Clark once compared the libraries of Florence to the great laboratories of the

3

nuclear age[3] – which stripped away the encrustations of medieval learning to expose the harmonious lines of the classical world, were applied to the Bible, in which was found no mention of monks and abbots, of the paraphernalia which made the Church such a burdensome institution.

Here of course, is the second of our themes, the Reformation, but we must be wary of any necessary connection between the achievements of the humanists and the advent of Protestantism. Erasmus was minded to remove some of the Church's furniture, not burn down the entire building. The Reformation was, initially and at bottom, a German phenomenon, and it was the legacy of the Middle Ages as much as the innovations of the Renaissance which had made Germany combustible. Since the fourteenth century, new philosophical directions had encouraged new political directions. William of Ockham, Marsilius of Padua, John Wyclif and John Hus had engendered unease about the hierarchy of Christendom and the location of power in its structures. The burdens of the Church on the laity had been eased in England by Edward I's stand against papal taxation, in France by Philip the Fair, whose lawyers presumed in one mocking draft – it was never actually sent – to address the Pope as 'Your Utter Fatuity'.[4] More recently and most importantly, the burden had eased in Spain, where the Catholic monarchs had established the Inquisition which functioned as a national institution under the orders of the Crown.

But the burden had not been eased in Germany: the imperial power had withered, and lay society had no champion. This is what Luther changed. He attacked the papacy and he attacked the monasteries with an armoury of ideas which spoke for Germany against the impositions of alien Latins. The ideas connected electrically with social unrest: if priests did not perform miracles in transforming the Eucharist, why should they enjoy tithes? In such ways, the remote abstractions of theological debate reached the people via a bridge of material grievances against the Roman Church.

The response of the Latin world to changes in the north is generally referred to, somewhat misleadingly, as the Counter-Reformation, the third dominant theme of the historians. The movement for reform in the south stemmed from changes in religious sensibility in the fifteenth century. It took on a new character with the systematic rebuttal of Protestant doctrine at the Council of Trent, and the association of spiritual revival with the might of the Spanish monarchy.

Potent as this alliance was in Europe, its impact was still greater in lands beyond the seas, for where the *conquistadores* went, so too did the Church. The fourth theme of the century is overseas discovery. The process began with the zealous campaigns of the Portuguese in the fifteenth century, and in the sixteenth, Spanish imperialism was fuelled by silver from the mines of Peru. The foundations of European dominion were laid by crusaders, not capitalists, and this perspective helps us to understand social and political change in Europe itself.

Each of these themes has its own vast literature, and any one of them could act as the organising principle for a book on the sixteenth century. But themes do not fit neatly into the span of a hundred years, and we cannot discern the shape of the century without some recognition of its chronological complexity. How does the significance of these themes vary over time? Whilst the Renaissance may be said to have spread from Italy in the sixteenth century, Italy itself endured political eclipse. During the wars which raged in the peninsula from 1494 to 1559, the 'backward' or 'barbarous' monarchies of 'feudal' Europe showed that they had overtaken the Italian princes in terms of military power. This is one of the lessons which Machiavelli drives home in *The Prince*.[5] The opportunity to form some federation of the Italian states led by the Medici from their bases in Florence and Rome was missed, and Machiavelli died in 1527, the year that the Sack of Rome demonstrated the military superiority of the Empire. The sack appeared to some as a disaster comparable to the destruction of the city by the Goths a thousand years before, and in many ways it brought the Renaissance to an end (see below, p. 239).

By then, the Reformation had been under way for a decade, and it might be appropriate to bring the 'age of humanism' to a close in 1517, when Luther published the Ninety-Five Theses.[6] But that action was not in itself revolutionary, and there was no clear threat to the universal Church before the Diet of Worms in 1521.[7] The survival of the new heresy may be explained in part by the simple fact that the Emperor Maximilian died at a crucial moment in 1518, and his young successor was too preoccupied with the French and the Turks to concentrate on the affairs of Germany (see below, chs. 11 and 12).

Charles had insisted on the convocation of a council to reform the Church, but the assault on heresy known as the Counter-Reformation is more obviously connected with the reign of Philip II (1555–98) and the power of his Spanish monarchy. Philip's wars with the Dutch and the Turks, and the threat which his power posed to the dynasties of England and France dominated the latter part of the century, before a bankrupt Philip departed this world in 1598. The power of Spain can be measured in its vast overseas territories, and the European discovery of other parts of the world needs the broadest chronology of all the themes, looking back to the crusades and forward to the imperialism of the nineteenth century.[8]

Unsurprisingly, in some of the most important available writing on the sixteenth century, themes give way to a carefully nuanced period-isation. One standard work of reference requires three huge volumes to move from 1493 to 1610, but it needs a parallel series to make sense of economic change. Another distinguished series moves from 1480 to 1598 in three brilliant studies, but it too is supplemented by another set devoted to economic history, and it excludes the history of the British Isles, creating space for volumes which cover the sixteenth century in a third collection addressing the history of English politics, the English economy and the English Church.[9] Then again, there are several superlative studies which suggest the unity of the period from the middle of the sixteenth century to the middle of the seventeenth, which forms variously a 'Golden Age', an 'Iron Century', an age of 'Transformation'. Another approach subsumes the sixteenth century into the 'early modern' period, which may or may not include the eighteenth century, depending somewhat on how far the authors draw on the idea of a 'long' sixteenth century running from about 1450 to about 1620, an attractive periodisation in terms of economic development.[10]

The themes of the century, then, are not easily defined by the most obvious and significant dates, and vice versa. One explanation of this is that themes and turning-points take on different proportions when viewed from Europe's different regions. Put another way, Europe is as hard to define as the period of a hundred years with which we are concerned.

The number of books covering different countries and different regions of those countries has increased dramatically in the past three decades: England, Scotland, Ireland, Italy and Russia all have their own series, there are durable classics on France, Spain, Germany and Sweden in periods which embrace or even subdivide the sixteenth century, and a recent masterpiece has at last introduced us to the peculiarities of the history of the Swiss.[11] The obvious gap, central Europe – eastern, as it used to be called – will no doubt soon be filled as its historians expose the roots of the national consciousness which proved too much for the 'Iron Curtain'.

In the Mediterranean world, the experience of Italy might be dealt with before and after the Sack of Rome, while the destiny of Spain must be seen in relation to the union of the *reyes catolicos* in 1469, itself the culmination of centuries of frontier wars in which the tide had turned in favour of the Christians at Las Navas de Tolosa as long ago as 1212. In the first half of the century, Spain was tied to the Habsburg lands of central Europe in the inheritance of Charles V, but after his abdication, the two different wings of the family were not always linked by common interests. There is a similar break at mid-century in France, where the power of the monarchy, which had burgeoned since the Hundred Years' War, abruptly collapsed in civil strife after 1559. Tudor England is often treated as a separate case, for its machinery of government gave a measure of stability despite its dynastic uncertainties and fundamental changes in religion. However, its apparent political precocity was counterbalanced by a sluggish economy which showed few signs of shaking off its torpor before about 1570. The separateness of the

English experience, which historians have tended to emphasise, is paralleled in other cases – Scotland, Scandinavia, Russia. The Turks, on the other hand, are often relegated to the margins of European history when their presence was in fact central and imperious.

These regions themselves dissolve as the historian clutches at them, fragmenting first into a thousand case histories of larger or smaller localities which make a nonsense of 'national' histories. 'Germany' consisted of some 300 semi-autonomous states, and stood in uncertain relation to the Swiss Confederation. 'Holland' was only one province ruled as part of the Spanish Netherlands. 'Italy' comprised five major states (Milan, Venice, Florence, Rome, Naples) and many other smaller entities, 'France' was a mish-mash of administrative divisions (see Map I.1), and the complexity of the provincial patchwork was compounded by the power bases of religious parties – the Huguenots in the south and west, the Catholics in the north and east.

Map I.1   France, c.1500

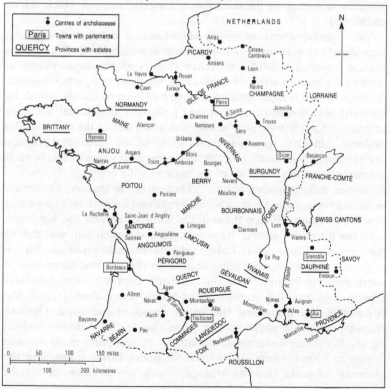

Source: J. H. M. Salmon, *Society in Crisis: France in the Sixteenth Century* (London: Methuen & Co., 1979) p.282.

A glance at a map of Europe produced in the sixteenth century shows that national boundaries – though not national types – were all but invisible, and this means that generalisation is fraught with danger . . .[12]

Given such a complicated subject, and given the remarkable field of writing which covers it, what on earth justifies another contribution?

Expansion and conflict, 1500–98: the century of Spain

Should one come clean at this point and speak of a publisher's flattering invitation – made an embarrassingly long time ago – and a young historian's ambition, both of which are more easily acknowledged now that the undertaking has aged and humbled the author? Certainly, a book of this nature by this author cannot hope to replace works which concentrate on a narrower period or a specific historiographical theme, nor does it seek to offer the volume of information available in a book of the same scope, the reputation of which is long established.[13]

Yet – perhaps because of the abundance of detail and nuance – something has been lost, and much remains to be said. What is the general importance of the sixteenth century in the development of modern Europe? In terms of the way we are now, two facts stand out. As the sixteenth century opened, no one had been round the world. By the early seventeenth century, it was possible – though certainly not common – for a merchant to make such a journey in the course of his business.[14] In 1500, hardly anybody spoke of the 'state' as a political reality – even Machiavelli uses the term somewhat vaguely. By the early seventeenth century, the idea of the state was the common currency of tradesmen talking in their shops.[15] Thus, over the century, Europeans increased their contact with a wider world and became more aware of it, while divisions between the states of Europe clarified and hardened.

In the fifteenth century, the most significant expansion was that of the horizons of the mind in Italy; in the seventeenth, expansion was an economic phenomenon largely confined to the Atlantic economies of north-western Europe.[16] In the sixteenth century, expansion was general, and it took a multiplicity of forms. It was demographic: the population rise dislocated the social world of the south German peasant, or made sense of the price rise to Jean Bodin (below, pp. 26, 38). There were more vagrants to be seen, and more of them drifted to towns, where the market for grain, cloth, spices, and the materials to build ships to transport such commodities linked the Mediterranean, Baltic and Atlantic zones in one vast emporium full of goods paid for in ever increasing quantities of silver coin (below, pp. 53–4, and ch. 4). In political life, the medieval monarch donned the robes of the Renaissance prince, and the magnificence of his court awed his subjects while the power of his armies stamped his authority on his neighbours (below, ch. 3). New voyages of reason and imagination expanded intellectual and spiritual life beyond the bounds of medieval Christendom, and the larger, more complicated Europe became divided against itself.

What was new about the conflict of the sixteenth century? Violence and war are the constants of the European experience. In the sixteenth century, however, fuelled by the expansion itself, they attained a new and tremendous scale. Dynastic disputes could still cause wars, but never before had foot-soldiers and guns been used as they were in the savagery of Habsburg and Valois in Italy, which makes Francis I's chivalrous challenge to Charles V to settle their dispute in personal combat in 1528 look all the more quixotic.[17] People still fought as crusaders, but the Middle Ages had seen no battles on the scale of the naval engagement at Lepanto in 1571, when more than 200 galleys manned by Christians smashed a still larger Ottoman fleet at a cost of 15,000 Christian lives and of 30,000 Turks (below, pp. 261–2). The unprecedented demands for the mobilisation of human and material resources bore heavily on societies experiencing their own localised conflicts – not those of classes, but of Catholics and Protestants, landholders and the landless, masters and journeymen.

Expansion – economic, intellectual and spiritual as well as purely geographical – and conflict – social and religious as well as international – move through these hundred years, connecting the changes associated with Renaissance, Reformation, Counter-Reformation and overseas discovery. As the century opened, Europe's population was growing, at a time when the Spaniards, following the Portuguese, were beginning their great overseas venture. The major theatre of conflict was Italy, its Renaissance states ripped to pieces by the wars of Habsburg and Valois. This struggle overlapped with the wars in Germany which began as the Reformation gathered pace in the 1520s, and which were settled – with some success – by the Peace of Augsburg in 1555. The idea generally described as '*cuius regio, eius religio*' allowed the prince to decide whether his dominions should be Lutheran or Catholic. There was no place for Calvinism, which began to spread from Geneva and which adapted to local aspirations in France, Scotland and the Netherlands, especially among the urban population. Although Calvinism was not a monolithic phenomenon, there were obvious reasons why its opponents might perceive it as such. (The fact that there are many factions of terrorists in the modern world does not invalidate discussion of terrorism as a general problem.) The attempts of Philip II to obliterate the Protestant heresy as a social and political force were financed by silver from the New World, and fired by the authoritarian ideology of the Counter-Reformation. The ensuing battle for hearts and minds lasted until the end of the century, but in the 1590s, economic exhaustion made the combatants falter, and that grim decade brought an atmosphere of *fin de siècle* which passed into the early 1600s, a period of disorientation and unease before the conflict was renewed as the Thirty Years' War, by which time the expansion had ceased.

If we take expansion and conflict as our themes, then solutions to the problems of chronology and region present themselves. In terms of chronology, the decisive fact which opens the century in 1500 itself was an instruction from King Manuel of Portugal to one of his exploring sea-captains, Pedro Alvares Cabral, on how to engage Muslim fleets in the Indian Ocean: 'You are not to come to close quarters with them if you can avoid it, but you are to compel them with your artillery alone to strike sail.' In such a way 'this war may be waged with greater safety and less loss'.

The document establishes that by 1500, European explorers were using the tactics of line ahead and stand-off artillery bombardment which proved crucial to Europe's relations with other parts of the world.[18] Europe is not large in territorial terms, but such tactics were to make Europeans masters of the two-thirds of the world's surface which are covered by the sea. In the vanguard of this process were the Iberian powers, and their efforts were united – albeit uncomfortably – after 1578, when Philip II laid claim to the vacant throne of Portugal. For a decade, the world seemed to be at Spain's feet. However, with the failure of the Armada and what that meant for Spanish prospects in the Netherlands, Philip's later years were haunted by bankruptcy and depression. In 1598, with the death of the ruler who had it within his grasp to make Castile the head of the world, we may genuinely affirm that an era had come to an end, though the dream of global dominion only finally ended in 1640.

Thus, the power which led European expansion and which generated European conflict was Spain, and in many ways, Spain provides the regional focus. Spain itself was a complex of different regions under the dominance of Castile, yet some general comments are permissible. The Spaniards – so often stigmatised as doomed to decline through their incapacity to change – appear in this book in a rather different light. Precocious as explorers because they never stopped being crusaders, the authors at an early stage of Church–state relations which made unnecessary an open break with Rome, apparently capable of endless military enterprise, the Spaniards were changing the shape of the European world, spreading a purified word, wielding a merciless sword. That the character of their overseas dominion was blackened and disowned by other Europeans has distorted perceptions of Europe's impact on the rest of the world, implying that Spanish tyranny had been replaced by something better. Spanish 'tyranny' was in many ways more self-questioning and more conscious of local interests in Europe and overseas than was the imperialism of the compact sovereignties which were to supersede Spanish power. The clumsy composite *monarquía* may yet be hailed as one of Europe's most successful experiments in federalism.

Of course, this is not a book about Spain alone. Its purpose is to make sense of what happened in Europe and to Europe in the sixteenth century in relation to three sections with different regional emphases.[19] Part I is not concerned with territory so much as with water, for European power can only be understood in relation to the great trading zones of the Middle Ages – the Baltic and the Mediterranean – and to the new possibilities which opened endlessly to the west, south and north in the Atlantic. Part II sees the advance of Protestantism southwards from Germany checked and then thrust back on itself by the Catholic resurgence, a process which almost literally bisects France and Poland. The regional focus of Part III is determined by the involvement of the various European states in activity overseas and in the great religious upheavals. Here, the emphasis falls on Spain and Italy in the south, France and Germany in the north, with the British Isles, Scandinavia and central Europe providing the margins. Muscovy acts as a remote onlooker, the Ottoman Empire as a powerful and menacing intruder, and both are used to emphasise the distinctiveness of social and political structures in more western regions.

Compared with the microscopic study of a locality or the vigorous reconstruction of the work of a magistracy, this may seem schematic. But I have tried above all else to recreate a world which not only has meaning for us, but which contemporaries would understand as their own. They would not have slipped their judgements into pigeon-holes labelled 'economic', 'social', 'political' and 'cultural', but they knew that their world craved the Word, and they knew it feared the sword. As so often, Luther provides our best introduction:

> God has established two kinds of rule among men, namely, the spiritual, the true Word and without the sword, that man might become pious and just . . . and the handling of such righteousness he has entrusted to preachers, the other is worldly rule, by the sword, to the end that all those who do not desire to become pious and just through the Word, will nevertheless be forced by the worldly rule to be pious and just before the world.[20]

The conflicts which intensified in the aftermath of Luther's protest engendered and exposed deep divisions between the Protestant north and the Catholic south. Yet, however deep those divisions were, an awareness was growing of the common characteristics of 'the west'. That awareness gives some justification for this book's concentration on the more westerly regions. If we are to understand Europe's impact on the rest of the world then our starting-point must be the most western region, Iberia. What defined the west in the east was the dominion of the Turk, and the colossal power of the Ottoman Empire has been chosen to provide an eastern focus (ch. 11) in preference to a survey of eastern Europe as though it were a congeries of autonomous regions. These are the terms which the English puritan, Sir Edwyn Sandys, was using in *A Relation of the State of Religion* which he wrote in 1599 and which referred specifically in its title to 'the severall States of these Westerne partes of the world'.

Spain, 'the new planet of the west' was 'a Nation that aimeth so apparantly at the Monarchy of the whole west'. In the east, the lands of the Orthodox Church can be excluded from Sandys's survey:

> though it bee granted, that they excede any other, yet are they so oppressed under Turkish tyrannie, or removed so farre off, as the Muscovite, and some others, that they come not to any account in the surveigh of the strength which nowe wee speake of.

Similarly, he set aside central Europe – 'Poland and Transilvania, with Valachia and the remains of Hungarie' – 'by reason of ther neere and daungerous confining with the Turke'. However, still more perplexing in these regions was:

> the multitude of Religions which are swarming in them, in Poland especially, of which it is sayd by way of by-word, That if a man hath lost his Religion, let him go seeke it in Poland, and hee shall bee sure to finde it, or else make account that it is vanished out of the worlde.

And he concludes of these lands that 'there is no great reckoning to be made of their force either way'.[21]

That may be contentious, but coming from an English puritan, it suggests an underlying unity of outlook and interest in the relations of those 'Westerne partes' with the rest of the planet. The World, the Word and the Sword in western regions – Teutonic and Latin – across the full span of the century: this is the book's general rationale. The three sections into which the book falls deal successively with the features of expansion, with intellectual and spiritual development, and with war. In terms of coverage, this approach is quite conventional, examining features readily identified with the sixteenth century: 'the rise of capitalism', the Reformation, and the Wars of Religion. More surprising, perhaps, are the relationships between social change, religion and war which suggest themselves. In Part I, it is argued that the expansion did not break the social mould. As a complex of values and as a body of law, 'feudalism' remained firm, it did not give way to 'capitalism'. 'Feudal' values in frontier war were to make the European expansion inseparable from conflict once the frontier began to move. This is critical to an understanding of the Reformation's social context. As Part II argues, new versions of the Word posed no threat to the power of the nobility, but they did shake the first estate, the clergy, whose social predominance was decisively questioned. However, while the pope trembled and the monasteries dissolved, a council (Trent) and the new order of Jesuits turned the tide against Protestantism. Their success in the missionary conflict in Europe itself made them an integral part of the expansion overseas. Thus opens a new perspective on the wars of the sixteenth century which are the subject of Part III. It is not the efforts of Protestants and capitalists which draw attention but those of the 'feudal' and intensely Catholic Spaniards. Their capacity to sustain an awesome war effort at any cost provides yet another link between the themes of expansion and conflict.

It seems appropriate to explain the organisation of the chapters in more detail. Part I deals with the social and economic realities of the age. It opens with a discussion of one of the sixteenth century's rare constants: the social predominance enjoyed by nobles (ch. 1). This is then related to the symptoms of expansion in that social world, overseas exploration and population growth (ch. 2). These topics are dealt with at this point because the explorations take us back some way into the fifteenth century and the population rise is fundamental to the sixteenth century as a whole. Chronologically and methodologically these subjects therefore precede a survey of political development, which focuses on the theory of the state and the practical manifestations of state power (ch. 3). The towns (ch. 4), which were so important in nursing the Reformation, also provide a natural bridge to Part II which is intended to set an exposition of what the major religious reformers said in the context of the Renaissance. Such an approach may not be the height of fashion, but some recent writing, in deploying concepts such as 'confessionalisation', seems to underplay somewhat the role of ideas themselves or to assume that the reader is already familiar with those ideas.[22] On the other hand, it is undesirable and misleading to isolate ideas altogether from their social context. Accordingly, the chapters of Part II cover the Renaissance with reference to humanism and the visual arts (ch. 5), the anti-monastic sentiments of the early Reformation (ch. 6), the progress – or lack of it – of reform (ch. 7) and the Catholic revival (ch. 8). Each of these chapters has four parts, and in each case the fourth is a set of suggestions about the social implications of new ideas and the ways in which ideas compromised with and were modified by the social environment. The subjects so treated are the relationship of education to humanist thinking (ch. 5), the significance of the Reformation to the sacrament of marriage (ch. 6), what forces reduced the social impact of

Protestant doctrine (ch. 7) and what served, by contrast, to increase the impact of the Catholic revival (ch. 8). The ideological struggle within society at large is then linked to the major military conflicts of the age, which are the subject of Part III. The wars themselves are set in a violent and hazardous social milieu, its uncertainties intensified by political centralisation (ch. 9). The dynastic wars of the first half of the century (ch. 10) are presented as a bridge between the papal-imperial struggles of the Middle Ages and the Wars of Religion. Before the latter are discussed, the emergence of the modern West as an identifiable entity is examined through a set of conflicts with the Ottoman Turks and the cultural contrasts which these suggest (ch. 11). The final chapter (12) concentrates on the civil wars in Christendom itself, and the Conclusion emphasises the immensity of the Spanish achievement and its paradoxical implications for the future of Europe as a global civilisation.

To speak in such terms does not imply some triumphal progress of European civilisation since 1500. There is no determinism in the presentation of the sixteenth century which follows. Social structures were not bound to move in a particular direction, ideas were not of necessity to make a social impact, above all perhaps, the outcome of wars was never preordained. The chapters which follow are animated by two concerns: first, that the past should speak for itself to the historian, and second, that the historian should help the past to speak to his own time. To this end, there is frequent quotation from contemporary sources. These are the best evidence of the topicality of the sixteenth century at the end of the twentieth, and the topicality of all history at all times.

Part I
The World

1 The power of lords

Material life

The great complex of changes which took place between 1500 and 1600 is sometimes seen as a critical phase in Europe's transition from 'feudalism' to 'capitalism'. That is to say, a society dominated by a nobility whose supremacy was justified by its ownership of land and its provision of military protection became, or was on the way to becoming, a society dominated by the mercantile wealth of the bourgeoisie. The symptoms of this momentous evolution are taken to be the commercialisation of agriculture and the growth of towns, developments which laid the foundations of Europe's colonial empires. According to this thesis, the development of a 'capitalist world system' was accompanied by the 'rise of the bourgeoisie'. In this light, the sixteenth century witnessed a partial progression from a society of orders to a society of classes. Put another way, the change was from a rural and seigneurial world in which status was defined by function – prayer, warfare or toil – to a world of cities in which class was defined by relationship to the means of production.[1]

There can be little doubt that the century experienced dramatic economic change, and there are powerful contemporary examples to support the case. Thomas More spoke of the commonwealth as 'a certain conspiracy of rich men'. As enclosures drove people from the land, he used the graphic description of how docile sheep 'be become so great devowrers and so wylde, that they eate up, and swallow downe the very men them selfes' to sum up the process of land enclosure and the plight of smallholders. One of More's contemporaries, Jack of Newberry, established an enterprise in cloth production which by the 1530s had acquired the proportions of a factory:

> Within one room being large and long
> There stood two hundred looms full strong;
> Two hundred men the truth is so
> Wrought in these looms all in a row.
> By every one a pretty boy,
> Sat making quills with mickle joy:
> And in another place hard by,
> A hundred women merrily,

Were carding hard with joyful cheer,
Who singing sat with voices clear.
And in a chamber close beside,
Two hundred maidens did abide
In petticoats of stammel red,
And milk-white kerchiefs on their head . . .

According to the poem at least, apart from the weavers, carders and spinners, there were 150 children who picked wool, 50 shearmen, 80 rowers, 40 dyers, 20 fullers.

In Germany, the Fuggers of Augsburg made a spectacular fortune. Jakob Fugger, the son of a weaver, made money from spices, silks and woollens, then began to use it to make loans to improvident emperors. Between 1511 and 1527, his profit rate was 927 per cent. In that time he provided the cash which Charles I of Castile used to bribe his way to becoming the Emperor Charles V. In 1523, the weaver's son reminded the ruler of half the earth that 'it is also well known and clear as day that Your Imperial Majesty could not have acquired the Roman Crown without my help'. Moreover, 'if I had remained aloof from the House of Austria and had served France, I would have obtained much profit and money, which was then offered to me'. He requested that 'the interest should be discharged and paid to me without further delay'. There may be a touch of irony in the concluding commendation that 'I humbly remain at all times your Imperial Majesty's to command'.[2] The fortunes of the Fuggers crashed with the Castilian bankruptcy of 1557, but their place was filled by the Grimaldi of Genoa, who took command of the reserves of Charles's son, Philip II, expanding their own wealth from 80,000 ducats in 1515 to 5 million in 1575. In that year, they cut off the cash supply to the hard-pressed Philip, whose troops in the Netherlands reacted to their consequent lack of pay by sacking Antwerp.

Extraordinary stories of financial success such as these may be contrasted with what are alleged to be the falling fortunes of the nobility – their social supremacy undermined by agrarian change, their wealth diminishing through mismanagement, with the result that in England and France the traditional leaders of society plunged into 'crisis'.

We should be wary, however, of equating changes in the character of economic life with changes in the pattern of society. It is important to understand that there existed definite hierarchies of status within each of the three orders of 'feudal' society', that is to say those who prayed, those who fought and those who worked. In the first estate, there was a world of difference separating the rich cardinal from the poor parish priest, the worldly prince-bishop from the spiritually dissatisfied monk. The term 'noble' covers poor robber knights, great local landlords, climbing courtiers, some of them *arrivistes*, and princes of the blood royal. Within the huge third estate, the complexity was correspondingly magnified. Practitioners of the liberal arts in the towns stood apart, merchants were more important than mere tradesmen, some trades were more skilled than others. In Rouen in 1549, a procession to receive Henry II gave a profile of the city's social hierarchy. The archers of the admiralty led the way and they were followed by the clergy (led by the four Mendicant Orders followed by the deacons, chaplains and the parish clergy). Then came royal and municipal officials and trade supervisors. There were several hundred 'notables' and bourgeois. The guard of honour was formed by 627 artisans from no fewer than 72 occupations – the spurriers strictly separated from the bitmakers. In the Baltic town of Reval in the early sixteenth century, the guild of St Knud was the charitable organisation for artisans, that of St Olai for the semi-skilled. The merchants organised their own exclusive Great Guild, kept non-members out of the trade in salt and grain, and prevented them from engaging in brewing. While we might classify the merchants as 'bourgeois', it would be misleading to see either master craftsmen or even journeymen as a dependent proletariat. In the countryside the term 'peasant' might apply to a small landowner or to a landless labourer – in other words it is a term which might include both the capitalist who owned the means of production and the proletarian who owned only his own labour, and this is a distinction which certainly endures to the end of the seventeenth century. Between the landowning peasant and the landless labourer lay a blurred spectrum of rural status containing tenants, cottagers, lodgers, innkeepers, millers, farmers, craftsmen and servants.[3] Wealth alone did not bring status, the latter was identified with the adoption of a set of values which denoted gentility. And people who made a fortune in the sixteenth century used it to buy their way into the nobility.

The historian's quest for the origins of capitalism has perhaps distorted our understanding of where the areas of pressure and strain lay in sixteenth-century society. The Reformation involved a fierce attack – not wholly successful – on the separateness of the first estate, the clergy, an assault which the nobility often supported. On the other hand, concentrations of labour dependent upon a single employer who owned the means of production are perhaps most obvious in backward, 'feudal' Europe, east of the River Elbe, where serfs laboured on the manors of noble landlords. And curiously enough, if we seek the real capitalist of the sixteenth century, accumulating and spending unprecedented sums of money in order to employ a workforce of unheard-of proportions, then the obvious example is the state and its armies. The roaming proletariat was first formed by Swiss mercenaries, and if they were not paid, then they went on strike: '*Point d'argent, point de Suisse*'. The most familiar confrontations of management and unions are found not in the workshops of Jack of Newberry, or even in the printing houses of Lyon, but in the Army of Flanders, where industrial action took the form of mutiny. Because this form of capital accumulation – control of the means of destruction rather than production – necessitated high levels of taxation, then it was the urban 'bourgeois' who tended to resist it. In 1508 the republic of Venice raised almost a quarter of a million ducats for the military – 100,000 of them earmarked for a single *condottiere*. The following year, the merchant, Martino Merlini, grumpily recorded:

> It seems to me if this damned war lasts for another year, we shall have lost everything and be ruined because of what we have to pay for our food and then what we have to pay in taxes.[4]

Indeed, were we able to visit the sixteenth century, as we shall try to do in these pages, then rather than finding an era clearly connected to our own in its economic and social life, we would be impressed by its distinctiveness. Rather than signs of nascent modernity, what would strike the twentieth-century visitor to the sixteenth century would be the extraordinarily slow pace of economic and social life. This was an inertia of anxiety, not repose. For most people in most countries, the fundamental realities of material life and social structure remained the same. We would be struck by the virtual absence of anything mass-produced in the fabric of everyday life. Coins and books were each produced in large numbers in exact copies, but while these would be familiar to us, they were rarities to many members of sixteenth-century society. In both town and countryside, the main preoccupation was for the harvest. Would there be enough grain for the peasant family? This was the local question at harvest time in June. In September, prices reflected general shortage or surplus. The full effects of dearth would hit in the period of 'tiding over' between December and March. More often than not, supplies were insufficient. In Languedoc after 1526 a 'tragedy of wheat' began: the following year the entire harvest was lost to bad weather, and the cycle of shortage lasted a full ten years. The general trend of deteriorating material conditions in the area worsened dramatically in the 1580s. In 1585–6 in Vivarais, bread was unobtainable at any price, and local people were:

> forced to eat acorns, wild roots, bracken, marc and bark and the bark of other trees, walnut and almond shells, broken tiles and bricks mixed with a few handfuls of barley, oats or bran flour.

What would be the cost of bread – or the size of a loaf – for the artisan and his dependents? Even in a prosperous city such as Venice, in crisis years such as 1575 or 1591, there almost certainly were not enough working days in the year to enable a builder's journeyman to buy sufficient bread for a family of four. In Lyon, prices rose steeply after 1560, they climbed in the 1570s and soared between 1585 and 1600.

Apart from grain, other raw materials which society required in quantity were wood (for fuel, building and utensils – barrels, tubs, spoons and furniture) leather (there were about 3,000 shoemakers in London by 1600) and wool (there were almost certainly more sheep than people in the England of Henry VIII). The mining of metals concentrated unusually large numbers of workers, perhaps 7,500 in the copper mines at Falkenstein, but this must be contrasted with the small-scale enterprises which transformed raw materials into finished products. Workshops had yet to yield to factories. 'Industry' meant 'hard work', 'science' meant 'knowledge'.[5]

This world, so insecure in its supply of life's basic needs, would be almost dream-like to us in terms of the slowness of its movement of goods and information from place to place, and in terms of the youth of its inhabitants. This made for a relationship between space, time and life-span quite different from our own. Some regions were so remote that they seemed untouched by Christianity: why go to the Indies when missionaries were needed in Cornwall or the Alps, or the Asturias, the latter '*unas Indias que tenemos dentro en Espana*'? Business letters from the period sometimes read as a transcript of someone shouting down the telephone, but there was nothing immediate about the exchanges of merchants and factors. It took a minimum of four weeks for a letter to reach Venice from Lisbon, and the same from Damascus. Venice, at the heart of the Mediterranean economy, was a month away from its periphery. Philip II's insistence on running an empire by himself may have compounded the difficulties of distance, but in any event a letter sent from Castile to Peru needed about eight months. Eternity seemed to separate the Viceroyalty of Naples from the Escorial, and 'if death came from Spain we would live for ever'.[6]

Tanning a hide or replying to a letter could take an age: life itself was short, precarious at every stage. Survival at birth was uncertain – maybe 200 babies per 1,000 died before the end of their first year, perhaps half the population would not reach 20. Childhood was hardly recognised, and only for the offspring of nobles, merchants and wealthy artisans was it likely to involve schooling. Work started as soon as possible, either within the family, or as an apprentice in the household of a master craftsman. Marriage was probably late – Shakespeare's Juliet, who is to be married at 14, is no guide to the parish registers. However, the century did see an increase in domestic privacy and family solidarity, perhaps because of a new paternal authority which replaced that of the priest. In a sense, at least in Protestant Europe, 'home' superseded the monastery and the convent. Within the domestic milieu, the possibility of a more equal secular relationship between men and women faded, and the man's patriarchal authority appears to have strengthened.

The struggle for survival was punctuated by religious observance, by sobriety on the Protestant sabbath, inebriation during Catholic carnival.[7] Death the reaper never had a bad harvest, for his scythe had three blades: war, famine and plague. Wars were fought on a hitherto unprecedented scale (below, ch.9), and direct damage was spectacular enough. The wars in Italy between 1494 and 1529 saw not just the Sack of Rome, but a host of others (below, p. 237). Antwerp never recovered from the devastation of 1576. And in addition there were the burdens of billeting and taxation. These French peasants complained as early as 1484 of:

> the continual going and coming of armed men, living off the poor people, now the standing companies, now the feudal levies of nobles, now the free archers, sometimes the halberdiers and at other times the Swiss and pikemen, all of whom have done infinite harm to the people . . . It is necessary for the poor labourer to pay and hire those who beat him, dislodge him from his house, make him sleep on the ground, deprive him of his substance . . . And as for the intolerable burden of tallage and taxes which the poor people of this kingdom have not carried, to be sure, for that would have been impossible, but under which they have died and perished from hunger and poverty, the mere description of the grievousness of these imposts would cause infinite sadness . . .

Even allowing for the rhetoric of misfortune, the picture is not a happy one, yet it predates the mobilisation of much greater resources for the Italian Wars by some ten years. Since high politics and ideological abstraction tend to dominate discussion of the Wars of Religion in France, it is perhaps worth dwelling on the suffering of rural society in that troubled country. In 1578, Claude Haton saw the duke of Anjou's troops assembling at Montereau before their expedition to Flanders:

> They were all vagabonds, thieves, and murderers – men who renounced God along with the worldly debts they owed. These slaughtermen were the flotsam of war, riddled with the pox and fit for the gibbet. Dying of hunger, they took to the roads and fields to pillage, assault, and ruin the people of the towns and villages, who fell into their clutches in the places where they lodged.

When the *croquants* rebelled against the dominion of the Catholic League in Perigord in 1594, there was no doubt as to the cause:

The *plat pays* has been completely ruined by a vast horde of bandits. The poor farmers, who time after time have suffered from the quartering of the soldiery upon them by one side or the other, have been reduced to famine. Their wives and daughters have been raped and their livestock stolen. They have had to leave their lands untilled and die of starvation, while great numbers of them languish in prison for failure to meet the enormous tailles and subsidies both parties have levied upon them.

It is striking that the state was nowhere to be seen, and that the two warring confessions lived off the peasantry in a manner which foreshadows the devastations in Germany in the Thirty Years' War. The end of a war did not bring peace, it merely unleashed a disbanded soldiery on the peasantry. In Paris in 1525 there were fears that 'the foot soldiers and others back from the said army and under their shadow various bad lads, thieves, vagabonds and vagrants are forming large gangs'.[8]

The presence of soldiers or the imposition of taxes to pay for them intensified shortages in the countryside – there was virtually uninterrupted famine in parts of Germany in the years leading up to the peasants' war of 1525. In the cities, in years of famine, people simply starved in the streets. Empty stomachs were all the more vulnerable to disease: plague, which struck on average every ten years, could affect the lymph glands (bubonic), the lungs (pneumonic) or poison the blood (septicaemic); measles, typhus, smallpox, and in addition there was the scourge of syphilis from the New World. Medical science offered many explanations but few reliable cures, and it is understandable that people made sense of their predicament in terms of the hostility of the supernatural. The environment worked by magic. Misfortune was God's punishment, or the Devil's work which had drawn people into heresy: either way, earthly life's weak frontiers were constantly forced back by eternity. Luther affirmed that God 'intends to bring heaven and earth into one heap and make a new world'. Calvin – master of a city in which life expectancy was a mere 23 years – and his wife had to endure the loss of three infants. It is surely not facetious to suggest that a belief in predestination might almost have been necessary to keep him sane, that such bitter losses would otherwise raise doubts as to God's purpose in bringing life into the world merely to take it away so suddenly:

> God shows as in a mirror the frequent and sudden changes in the world which ought to awaken us from our torpor so that none of us will dare to promise himself another day, or even another hour, or another moment.[9]

Amid all the insecurity, one principle of the social order remained fixed and certain: lords were in command. True, the greatest changes of the century saw the power of some clerical lords questioned, even overthrown, but lordship, identified with nobility, was something to which people deferred or aspired. The power of the noble was rarely resisted, and it was never displaced, it was a power which society acknowledged and which the state had to respect. The social supremacy of lords was time-honoured, and it is worth pausing to measure the weight of the tradition, not least because this dominance is not so much the dominance of a coherent class as the dominance of a way of life.

Since the eleventh century, ecclesiastics had promulgated a vision of a society in which those who fought offered protection to those who worked in a relationship sanctioned by those who prayed. Gradually, the cost of military hardware – notably horse and armour – meant that the function of the warrior was reserved for the rich. Vassals became knights, knights nobles: those who fought became a social order defined by birth.

The social pattern of three orders, distinguished from power structures elsewhere in the world by fealty and the manor, is usually referred to as 'feudal'.[10] Whether or not we choose to use that controversial term – and historians of the early Middle Ages now tend to avoid it altogether – we need to acknowledge that the formative centuries of European development saw the emergence of a set of relationships founded upon the acknowledgement of lordship over land in the form of fiefs organised around manors, justified by the lord's role as warrior and protector. The structure was to prove remarkably resilient. It survived the crises of the fourteenth century when the Black Death loosened the bonds of serfdom by reducing both the number of tenants (which in turn reduced the value of rents) and the size of the workforce, which raised the cost of labour. The lords put down the associated rebellions – such as the English Peasant Revolt of 1381 – and profited from the reversal of conditions which set in after the middle of the fifteenth century. From about that time, population growth increased demand and raised prices, and it produced a surplus of labour which brought down wages. Wherever we look in Europe, east, centre or west, we find lords in the ascendant. Sometimes the control was local and economic, sometimes it was central and cultural. Universally it was legal. Different forms of dominion must never obscure the fact of dominion.

Noble landlords in eastern Europe

The clearest and most emphatic advantages of economic change accrued to nobles in the east.[11] By the late fifteenth century, the growth in population in western Europe had necessitated a search for new sources of grain. A partial solution to the shortage was offered by the Baltic territories. In the 1460s, Poland and Lithuania were exporting about 2,500 lasts of rye a year. By the 1560s, the figure had risen to 40,000, about 35 per cent of the total production of those regions. The volume of shipping in the Baltic increased equally dramatically. In 1497, 795 ships were recorded passing through the Danish Sound, in 1557 the figure was 2,251, by the end of the century 5,500. In 1565, 90,000 tonnes of rye were shipped out of Danzig. In 1593, 16,000 tonnes were imported from the Baltic to Livorno. That was a particularly bad year in a terrible decade, but it was becoming clearer that Sicily and Andalusia could not be the bread-baskets of the Mediterranean for ever. In Prussia, western demand caused prices to double in the second half of the century – rye was up 247 per cent, barley 187 per cent, oats 185 per cent. Nor was demand limited to grain. Hungary supplied cattle to Vienna and even Venice, and between 1548 and 1558 some 550,000 head were herded westward, accounting for maybe 90 per cent of Hungary's exports.

And let us be quite clear that the suppliers were not eastern merchants but eastern landlords. Since this does not fit very happily with the idea of a 'transition from feudalism to capitalism', the process has been described by the cumbersome term 'capitalism in a feudal framework'. This is not helpful because feudalism as military service in return for land was by no means universal: it may not have operated at all in the vast territory of Lithuania, for instance. The new phenomenon – and it did not go back into the mists of the Middle Ages in these regions – was the imposition of serfdom. Peasants were tied to the land in the Czech regions in 1487, Poland in 1495, Hungary in 1514, Prussia in 1526, Silesia and Brandenburg in 1528, Upper Austria in 1539, Livonia in 1561. What is striking about the advance of seigneurial power is that the law provided the dynamic, and this was possible because the nobility enjoyed such enormous political leverage. In the east, the major assertions of seigneurial power – the extension of the demesne (land under the lord's direct control) and the robot (labour services owed by the peasantry), restriction of the movements and property rights of tenants, the appropriation of holdings – were usually accomplished by decrees duly approved and duly enforced. In Hungary, Poland, Brandenburg, Prussia and Bohemia, local diets – representative institutions – were exclusively noble: there was no challenge from the state or the towns. Nobles had a virtual monopoly of public office in Prussia from the 1540s, in Pomerania from 1560, in Bohemia from 1564. In Poland, nobles had held a similar monopoly since the late fourteenth century. In 1505, the decree '*nihil novi*' forbade the king to legislate on matters concerning the nobility, in 1565, the Sejm, the nobles' parliament, forbade Polish merchants to travel abroad for goods, and indeed in Danzig the transit trade to Atlantic ports was controlled by the Dutch. In Brandenburg, there were decrees restricting peasant movement in 1518 and 1536, in Prussia in 1526, 1540 and again in 1577. The landlords' right to dispossess peasants in these regions was confirmed in laws of 1540, 1550 and 1572, and the sixteenth century saw not the rise of the bourgeoisie but the 'gradual feudalisation of the territory of the state' by the Junkers. In Hungary, the nobles removed the peasant's right of inheritance in 1514. In the same year, the labour requirement on a grain-producing estate was one day, but by 1570, the lord of Krasnahorka 'forces them to do as much work as there is'. The nobles enjoyed privileges in the production of wine, which became their exclusive right in 1570, and they could even use forced labour to build fortifications against the Turk. The noble commonwealths of eastern Europe were 'stateless societies' in which peasant resistance was all but impossible. The net result was a set of colonial economies which exported raw materials and imported finished goods, curiously fuelling western progress by their own increasing backwardness, making the River Elbe, for some historians, 'the most significant socio-economic divide in Europe'.

Lords and peasants in Reformation Germany

However, one must be careful not to exaggerate the distinction, for west of the Elbe the growth of the towns and the development of the state did not overturn noble predominance, they merely ensured that it took a greater variety of forms. This is clear from the experience of the Holy Roman Empire, which of course straddles the two zones which historians are so insistent on separating. Some western areas of the Empire do offer a contrast with the chilly manorial estates further east. In the north-west, landlords had power over property rather than persons, in the Rhine the clusters of towns with their traditions of freedom shrank the possibilities of any reimposition of serfdom, in central Germany, personal freedom and free tenure were the bulwarks of prosperity and therefore the assurance of healthy tax revenues: tampering with these structures was not in the lordly interest. In the south-west, however, in Thuringia, Swabia and Franconia, the picture was more complicated.

After the Black Death, these areas had experienced the reduction of lordly power and then its reassertion. In the course of the fifteenth century, the peasants of Upper Swabia lost their rights to common land, to wood, to hunting. They had been burdened with labour services and taxes. Serfdom had been extended, movement restricted, and many noble estates were taking on the character of petty absolutisms ruled arbitrarily by landlords – as in the lands east of the Elbe.[12]

However, in contrast to the eastern lands, in south-west Germany there was a tradition of peasant resistance, and of course in the nearby Swiss Confederation there was a tradition of peasant victory. Unrest had gathered momentum in the last quarter of the fifteenth century. In 1476, in Würzburg, which had perhaps been touched by the influence of Hussite protest from neighbouring Bohemia, peasants had marched in a pilgrimage of protest in support of the mysterious 'Piper of Niklasshausen' against the extortions of the prince-bishop. The century closed with ten years of unrest associated with peasants led by Joss Fritz marching under a banner which bore their laced leather boot or *Bundschuh* as its device. There was another outbreak at Speyer in 1502 – again against episcopal extortions. Then in 1514, poverty and oppression produced an uprising in Württemberg in the name of 'poor Conrad' – which also revealed the level of discontent in the towns. Between 1517 and 1524 there was relentless famine, and the storm broke in 1525. As in the late fourteenth century, the unrest was perceived to be general, and the unsympathetic chronicler, Sebastian Franck, lamented 'the great peasant rebellion which seems to be spreading all over Europe'. Even he had to acknowledge the root cause: 'this particular insurrection grew out of a protest against oppressive tithes, death duties, forced labour, tributes, interest payments, and serious grievances'. This general uprising of 'the common man' was to meet a ferocious reaction, 'for the rest of their days our peasants will have to bear conditions worse than those against which they protested'.

It may be tempting to describe such conflict as class war – one peasant slogan ran, 'Nobleman, may a cow shit on you' – but it is better understood as hatred of the privileged estates. The social protest was underpinned by a more positive ideology, which drew inspiration from the ideas of Luther. 'The freedom of a Christian', 'the priesthood of all believers', the importance of God's Word in the Scriptures as the basis for social renewal, these were tenets which touched the material grievances of the peasants and gave them a language of dissent. The Bible does not make mention of serfdom, for instance. The visionary leader, Thomas Müntzer, went so far as to argue that lordship itself was anti-Christian, and Michael Gaismair preached an egalitarian millennium. The peasants themselves, however, relied on something more solid than wild rhetoric. They formulated clear petitions which systematically listed their grievances – and which foreshadow the *cahiers* of 1789. From Stühlingen and Lupfen, Allgäu and Kempten the complaints are the same: the injustices of serfdom and the heriot or death-tax, new labour services, restrictions of hunting and fishing rights, the removal of rights on common land, the failure of lords to offer protection in the courts. Moreover, the peasants' complaints against the impositions of churchmen who were also lords gave specific focus to general anti-clerical feeling. In a fury against the tyranny of bishops, cathedral chapters and abbeys, the rebels plundered 70 cloisters in Thuringia, 52 in Franconia. The uprising can be seen as a great mass movement, perhaps the greatest in Europe before 1789.

And the lords – clerical and lay – crushed it. In the battle of Frankenhausen and its aftermath, it is said that some 100,000 peasants were slain. The lords enjoyed enormous military superiority, and the professionalisation of war since the late fifteenth century meant that untrained masses could not confront full-time soldiers with any prospect of success. At Frankenhausen, Müntzer could only oppose the firepower of the noble army by offering to catch its cannon-balls in the sleeves of his cloak.[13] Military power is only part of the explanation for the lords' overwhelming victory. Luther's attitude to lords and his reaction to the rebellion illustrate very clearly that whilst the sixteenth century witnessed an unprecedented attack on the separate privileges of the first estate – those who pray – there was no question of a dissolution of the second – those who fight – and their privileges seemed the guarantee of order itself. Luther's anti-clericalism was violent, bludgeoning. We should perhaps consider what fuel there was for peasant grievance in one of his manifestos of 1520:

> To call popes, bishops, priests, monks, and nuns, the religious order, but princes, lords, artisans, and farm-workers the secular estate, is a specious device invented by certain time-servers; but no one ought to be frightened by it, and for good reason. For all Christians whatsoever really and truly belong to the religious order, and there is no difference among them except in so far as they do different work . . . Hence we deduce that there is, at bottom, really no other difference between laymen, priests, princes, bishops, or, in Romanist terminology, between religious and secular, than that of office and occupation, and not that of Christian status . . . A shoemaker, a smith, a farmer, each has his manual occupation and work; and yet, at the same time, all are eligible to act as priests and bishops . . .

There is even a direct reference to merging the three orders of society – followed by a sudden retraction:

> Hence one says to the pope and his adherents, '*Tu ora*', Thou shalt pray; but to the emperor and his minister, '*Tu protege*', Thou shalt protect; and to the ordinary man, '*Tu labora*', Thou shalt work. Not as if praying and protecting and working were not each man's duty, for he who fulfils his own task, prays, protects and labours; but to each should be assigned a special function . . .

But was a first estate really necessary?: 'it is better to do without a cloister unless, at its head, is a spiritually-minded prelate versed in the Christian faith'.

Yet the writer so fierce in his attacks on the clergy would have nothing to do with rebellion:

> any man against whom it can be proved that he is a maker of sedition is outside the law of God and Empire, so that the first who can slay him is doing right and well. For as when a fire starts, the first to put it out is the best man. For rebellion is not a simple murder, but is like a great fire, which attacks and lays waste a whole land . . . Therefore let everyone who can, smite, slay and stab, secretly or openly, remembering that nothing can be more poisonous, hurtful or devilish than a rebel. It is just as when one must kill a mad dog; if you do not strike him, he will strike you, and a whole land with you . . .
>
> I will not oppose a ruler who, even though he does not tolerate the Gospel, will smite and punish these peasants without offering to submit the case to judgement . . . If he can punish and does not – even though the punishment consist in the taking of life and the shedding of blood – then he is guilty of all the murder and all the evil which these fellows commit, because, by wilful neglect of the divine command, he permits them to practise their wickedness, though he can prevent it, and is in duty bound to do so. Here, then, there is no time for sleeping; no place for patience or mercy. It is the time of the sword, not the day of grace.
>
> The rulers, then should go on unconcerned, and with a good conscience lay about them as long as their hearts still beat . . . Stab, smite, slay, whoever can . . .

The quotations which show Luther's ferocious anti-clericalism were addressed *To the Christian Nobility of the German Nation*. His exhortations to slaughter rebels are taken from his tract *Against the Robbing and Murdering Hordes of Peasants*.[14] Luther's revolution – and let us have no doubts about the magnitude of his achievement – lay in attacking a social vision which separated the clergy from the laity, it did not involve the removal of the distinction between nobles and commoners. Luther's condemnation of the peasants makes painful reading, but it is misleading to condemn these ranting exhortations as indicative of social and political 'conservatism'. Luther's ideas were revolutionary, but he recognised that the only way to undermine the status of the first estate was an alliance with the second. He perceived that power in society lay with lords. We can confirm the accuracy of this perception by detaching the discussion from considerations of serfdom in the east or the Reformation in Germany and concentrating on countries further west. In these regions neither the 'rise of the bourgeoisie' nor the expansion of the state was a threat to the social predominance of nobles. Their supremacy was more variegated, perhaps, but it was no less emphatic.

Lordly dominion in the west: economic, political, cultural

In economic terms, lordly power in rural areas of the west was advancing throughout the century. In southern Italy, a world away from the urbanised north of the peninsula, the exploitation of the land through the subjugation of the peasantry – the extortion of a grain surplus through low wages and repressive conditions by barons possessing vast latifundia – produced under Mediterranean skies social conditions which can be compared to those in the lands east of the Elbe. Economically, the region was more inefficiently handled than the eastern manors because of the peculiarly western habit of 'conspicuous consumption' amongst the nobility. In the early seventeenth century, Tommaso Campanella described a vicious circle of exploitation and profligacy:

> The barons . . . come to Naples, and to the court, and there spending their money profusely and lavishly, they make a great show for a while . . . and at length having spent all, they return poor home, and make prey of whatsoever they can, so that they make themselves whole again, and then they return to Court again; running round still, as it were in the same Circle; in so much that we see these men's territories much more desert, and naked, than the King's in Italy; all through the default of the barons themselves.[15]

In Languedoc in the south of France, the new operation of the wage-price 'scissors' in favour of landlords was dramatic. In 1480, a farm labourer could expect to earn about 20 *livres* per year, the equivalent of some 30 *setiers* (468 litres) of wheat. A hundred years later, the labourer's wages had risen to 30 *livres*, but by this stage such a sum would buy only 8 or 10 *setiers* of wheat. Moreover, the quality of bread and the quantity of payments in kind had both declined. At the same time, there is evidence of improved estate management by nobles of long pedigree in Béarn. The growth of Pau as the provincial capital of that region owed nothing to thrusting capitalists. It was merely a fairly large market town amid a patchwork of lands controlled by *sénéchaux* and viscounts. It seems that in France, noble landholdings increased (though to a degree as yet unclear) by the sale of church lands. The effects of that phenomenon in England are more familiar, and irrespective of whether the fortunes of the gentry were rising or falling:

> the Elizabethan aristocracy, in general, retained their lands, and these lands, reduced perhaps in compass but often correspondingly improved in value, were for their descendants the basis of long-continued wealth and power.

This helps to explain why the impulse to live an aristocratic life was to persist into the Victorian era and beyond.[16]

In France, both urban growth and urban wealth reinforced the noble ethic. In the case of Toulouse, it can be argued that the migration of urban capital to the countryside meant that the rural population exchanged 'aristocratic protectors' for 'bourgeois masters', but such a juxtaposition seems too sharp when set against the case of Lyon. Between 1554 and 1561, there were some 87 acquisitions of land in the neighbouring countryside, and lawyers and merchants made 61 of these purchases. But these representatives of the 'bourgeoisie', then proceeded to employ domestic servants and to live like nobles. Lyon was one of the sixteenth century's most spectacular examples of urban growth, yet in the event, it was 'capitalism' which proved a fleeting phenomenon, while the attractions of the noble life-style never weakened. Even if pedigree or monarchy had not bestowed nobility, then if one lived nobly, who was to know? At the meeting of the Estates General at Orléans in 1560, François Grimaudet sarcastically remarked:

There are an infinite number of such false nobles whose fathers and ancestors performed their feats of arms and deeds of chivalry by trading in grain, wine, and drapery or managing the mills and estates of the seigneurs; and yet, when they come to speak of their lineage, it seems they are all descended from the blood royal, from Charlemagne, Pompey, or Caesar.

In any case, it is misleading to see all the traffic of influence moving from the town to the countryside. Whilst there are no obvious examples of noble entrepreneurialism in western towns – as there are in, say, Kiel – if we examine the pattern of production in the high-quality high-cost luxuries which guilds fostered and protected, we find it geared to the tastes of nobles: enjoying the London season, perhaps, consuming conspicuously in Paris or Madrid. Rich townsmen who stayed in the towns pursued the same ideal – though sumptuary làws restricting extravagance in dress were designed to prevent people from following fashions which were above their station. And there are significant cases of noblemen tapping new sources of wealth rather than losing out to the entrepreneurial instincts of a new bourgeoisie. Thus, in Holstein, noble businessmen were active in production, marketing and even money-lending. In Lucca, traders became aristocrats, in Barcelona, citizenship conferred tax exemption and the status of 'knight of the city-state'. Men who could afford to lend Philip II 8,000 ducats free of interest for a year had the privilege of wearing a sword and dagger in the city hall. In Seville, as Tomas de Mercado wrote in 1587:

the discovery of the Indies had presented such opportunities to acquire great wealth that the nobility of Seville had been lured into trade when they saw what great profits could be made.

In southern German towns, there is evidence of the 'feudalisation of urban merchants' and the 'embourgeoisement of the nobility'. Like the growth of the towns, the development of the state tends to impress upon us the durability of lordly power, not its decline. In the localities, public power remained essentially in private hands. The link between a peasant and his lord was stronger than any link between the peasant and the state. Noble predominance was 'natural', the protective function extending from the defence of the realm to the well-being of the countryside: the lord was the source of justice and mercy. The gentleman was expected to '*soutenir les autres états*', or, as Symphorien Champier put it in his awkward poetry of 1510:

> An order is not allocated to a man so that he may love
> his order alone, but that he must love the other orders.
> For to love one order and hate the other is not to love
> an order, for God does not produce an order which is
> at odds with another order.[17]

In some ways, the development of the state itself depended on a concentration of bonds of personal loyalty rather than the creation of an abstract entity to be loved and served or the systematic construction of new governmental institutions. The nucleus of political power in the sixteenth-century state was the court, and the court was held together with the bonds of chivalry. Court culture and court politics provide a particularly effective illustration of noble dominance because they show that noble values operated at the apex of the state even though those who espoused and promoted such values were not necessarily great landowners in the localities. The connection between traditional feudal power and the government of the state was often cemented – as Castiglione himself recognised – in the exclusive knightly orders which gave the European nobility its own international brotherhood, 'for these knights in great Courtes are alwaies highly esteemed'. The Order of the Garter in England, the Star in France, the Austrian Salamander, the Sash in Castile, the Cross in Sicily, these badges of distinction symbolised the importance of noble cooperation in the maintenance of the state and were 'an integral part of the mystique surrounding sixteenth-century monarchy'. Perhaps the most celebrated was the Burgundian Order of the Golden Fleece. A measure of the international brotherhood amongst nobles which the knightly orders created is provided by the gathering of members of the Golden Fleece at Utrecht in 1546, prior to the Emperor's campaign against German Protestantism. At Utrecht assembled Cosimo de' Medici, Grand Duke of Tuscany, Emmanuel Philibert of Savoy, the Duke of Alba, and his subsequent sworn enemy, Count Egmont. The campaign culminated in the destruction of the Protestant armies at Mühlberg. The imperial triumph is celebrated in Titian's magnificent equestrian portrait – and Charles V wears the insignia of the Golden Fleece. Indeed, membership of the Orders could perform an important role in diplomatic relations: when Charles IX of France was awarded the Garter in 1564, he reciprocated by giving the Order of Saint Michel to the Earl of Leicester and the Duke of Norfolk.[18]

Even though the 'military revolution' (below, ch. 3) was tending to reduce the independent military power of the nobles, pushing them into country houses rather than castles, duels rather than civil wars, its full implications were not apparent until the later seventeenth century. In the sixteenth, traditional habits of violence could still operate on a scale which could threaten the state itself, especially in a religious cause.

In northern England, local lords gave the lead to the Pilgrimage of Grace, and northern earls gave their name to a rebellion. Those involved were the old gangster families of the Wars of the Roses – Percy, Neville, Dacre, Darcy – and the local power bases were linked to the cause of the universal Church by the figure of Cardinal Pole. In France, although the historian's language has forsaken the phrase 'lord and vassal' for 'patron and client', the reality of independent military power remained the same. The Prince de Condé's followers attached themselves to his cause by the collective indenture of 1562. As late as 1595, the Tremouïlles could raise 500 gentlemen and 2,000 infantry at their own expense. The civil wars themselves saw the great feudatories bursting out of their reservations: the Montmorency from Languedoc, the Guise from Burgundy. The Wars of Religion are often seen as creating the ideology of revolution and of the modern state. Yet in the crisis year of 1572, the year of the Massacre of St Bartholomew, just before the Huguenot Synod of La Rochelle, the Protestants gave a clear signal of their new unity of purpose when, with ostentatious formality, Gaspard de Coligny paid homage to Henry of Navarre, thus becoming 'his man' – not his client or his creature – for which he received not a book on resistance theory but a golden helmet and spurs. In the Netherlands, often the exception to general tendencies, the revolt which overthrew the power of Spain drew strength, at least in its early stages, from the withdrawal of allegiance by nobles protesting that Philip II had failed to fulfil his side of the feudal bargain in providing good lordship. When the Estates of Holland and Zeeland protested against taxation in 1574, they did so in the following terms:

Our ancestors have left us laws of investiture which specify that if the king, being here in person, continues in the present kind of government, he would no longer justly be sovereign, and the subjects would be absolved from their duties and their oath, until he gave up this way of governing as unreasonable and entirely contrary to his promises, and be prepared to reign reasonably, and in accordance with his promises. Our ancestors displayed exceptional prudence when as a condition for his solemn recognition they made the sovereign agree that he would be refused service in the event of bad government.

To emphasise that the Netherlands were not an exception in this regard at least, we should remember that Philip could face similar obstacles in his Spanish kingdoms outside Castile. This is the grudging oath of allegiance traditionally ascribed to the nobility of Aragon:

> We who are as good as you swear to you who are no better than we to accept you as our king and sovereign lord, provided you observe all our liberties and laws; but if not, not.[19]

Of all the symptoms of lordly power in sixteenth-century Europe, perhaps the most revealing is the most abstract: their cultural dominance. Everywhere except Switzerland and the Balkans, we find a set of attitudes and assumptions which looked up to the noble way of life as superior. It needs to be spelled out that 'absorption into the nobility' is not the same as 'the rise of the bourgeoisie'. Moreover, noble predominance gave the west a restricted measure of social mobility which contrasts with the meritocratic status groupings of the Ottoman Empire (below, p. 249) and with the totally motionless social structure of Muscovy. Of the latter, Giles Fletcher remarked that a commoner 'hath no means to aspire any higher', for there would be 'no farther reward nor preferment whereunto they may bend their endeavours and employ themselves to advance their estate'.[20]

In Europe, people sought honour and reputation because these were the hallmarks of nobility, and they were to be maintained at all costs. Castiglione's handbook for toadies, *The Book of the Courtier* (1517) reveals some inclination to give more room to merit as grounds for promotion in the service of the prince – but the same book emphasises the need for the courtier to separate himself from society at large through his speech, dress, manners and accomplishments, to cultivate an air of nonchalance and disdain: in short to be uncommon.

> in men of base degree may raign the very same vertues that are in Gentlemen. But ... for so much as our intent is to fashion a Courtier without any maner default or lack in him, and heaped with all praise, me thinke it a necessary matter to make him a Gentleman, as well for many other respects, as also for the common opinion, which by and by doeth leane to noblenes.

The original function of the warrior must be preserved and refined:

> I judge the principall and true profession of a Courtier ought to bee in feates of armes, the which above all I will have him to practise

lively, and to bee knowne among other of his hardines, for his atchieving of enterprises, and for his fidelitie towarde him whom he serveth.

And the opponents must be worthy, 'for it were not meet that a gentleman should be present in person and a doer in such a matter in the countrey,'where the lookers on and the doers were of a base sort', so taking on a common opponent must be done with nonchalant assurance of winning:

> and a man ought (in a manner) to be assured to get the upper hand, else let him not meddle withall, for it is too ill a sight and too foule a matter and without estimation, to see a gentleman overcome by a carter, and especially in wrastling.[21]

The most unassailable stronghold of noble values was Castile, the centre of the Spanish *monarquía*, the most powerful political entity of the age. This was an area which, like Lithuania, did not know 'feudalism' in the Middle Ages as land in exchange for military service, yet once again there is no questioning the social predominance of lords and their values. As the servant boy observed in the picaresque novel, *Lazarillo de Tormes*:

> you have great secrets, O Lord, unknown to common people. Who would not be deceived by his demeanour and by his smart cloak and jacket, and who would think that the noble gentleman spent all day yesterday without taking a bite of food except that crumb of bread which his servant Lazaro had carried for a day and a half under his shirt and where it couldn't have kept very clean, and today, when he washed his hands and face and didn't have a towel, he used his shirt-tail? Nobody would dream that was the case. And how many men like him must be scattered throughout the world, suffering for the sake of their ridiculous honour what they certainly wouldn't suffer for Your sake?

However, honour was far from ridiculous. For Charles V, war was in some ways conducted as a form of conspicuous consumption: pursued as a duty with no vulgar calculation of financial cost. We might also remember that Philip II's sense of honour overrode considerations of political prudence which might have delayed the sending of the Armada until it was better prepared:

> If the fleet remains in Corunna, it will do nothing to enhance our prestige in any peace negotiations, if there are any . . . To leave our fleet bottled up and ineffective would be a disgrace . . . by which we would lose both advantage and reputation.

Francis I was captured at the battle of Pavia in 1525, having refused to withdraw because of the 'shame and infamie' which this would bring. In France in the sixteenth century, it was the mark of a parvenu that he had 'no idea how to conduct himself to preserve his reputation'.[22] Reputation, in short, was more important than peace, or even life itself. And reputation was the mark of the noble. For all the changes it witnessed, the sixteenth century saw the power of lords resurgent and resplendent. In subsequent chapters, we shall trace many complicated and exhausting processes of change: lordly power as a social fact transcends them all. The social dominance of this principle survived a considerable growth in the size of the general population and unnerving changes in the value of money, and the traditional habits of violence of the order of warriors provided the mainsprings of European expansion overseas.

2 The symptoms of expansion

Contemporary perceptions

In the course of the sixteenth century, the fundamental principle of social organisation – that lords were supreme – remained unchanged, but its representatives came to establish themselves in a much wider area of the globe. In Europe itself, the social framework had to accommodate many more people, increasingly divided amongst rich and poor. Thus we identify the three obvious symptoms of European expansion in the age: overseas discovery, population growth, price inflation. The combination of these phenomena eventually shifted the balance of European economic power away from the south to the north-west, from the Mediterranean to the Atlantic.[1] Some of the implications were surprisingly clear to contemporaries. The Florentine historian, Francesco Guicciardini, writing in about 1540, was well aware of the significance of the discovery of the Cape route to the east for the Mediterranean spice trade which the Venetians had traditionally dominated:

> But the Portugalls going by sea from Lyshbone the capitall Citie of the Realme, into regions farre removed, and having confederation with the kings of Calicut & other regions neare, they pearsed by degrees further, and buylded with time fortresses in places convenient, by whose opportunities making them selves friendship with certayne cities of the countreis, and reducing others to obedience by their armes and oppression, they have appropriate to them selves the trafficke of the spices which the marchauntes of Alexandria were wont to have afore: and bringing them by sea into Portugall, they distributed them also by sea into the selfe same Realmes and countreys, where the Venetians at the first had custom and vent for them.

With regard to developments in Europe itself, by 1568, the French philosopher, Jean Bodin, had made a clear connection between price inflation and the amount of bullion in circulation, between burgeoning wealth and the rise in population:

> I conclude that the high prices we see today have four or five causes. The principal and almost the only one (which no one has hitherto

made reference to) is the abundance of gold and silver, much greater today in this kingdom than it was 400 years ago, to go no further back . . . The other cause of the vast amount of wealth which has come to us in the last hundred and twenty or thirty years is the huge population which has grown up in the realm.

There was a clear consciousness that the world was changing shape and that society was expanding its proportions, as the price rise suggested. The interrelationship of the three phenomena is complicated and controversial. Overseas discovery certainly seems the odd phenomenon out. The discoveries pre-date the population rise, the price increases seem to have been due to population pressure on foodstuffs, not on manufactured goods, and this discrepancy suggests that the influx of treasure from the New World was not all that significant as an inflationary pressure. However, taken together as symptoms of a general process rather than dealt with separately in terms of their causes, what is striking – and rather perplexing – is that the expanding society acquired an extraordinary unity in its attitude to the expanding world. However, the sense that the pearls of the world were in a European oyster owed as much to continuities in the attitudes of the remote past as to changed conditions in the sixteenth century.

New horizons

The importance of the arrival of Europeans in other parts of the world can scarcely be overrated, yet its origins are obscure, its place in conventional history courses uncertain. This ambiguity was already apparent in the sixteenth century. Lopez de Gómara wrote to his master Charles V in 1552 that the discovery of the East and West Indies was 'the greatest event since the creation of the world, apart from the incarnation and death of Him who created it'.[2] Charles V wrote his own autobiography in the same year, yet he never mentions the Americas. Perhaps there is a sense in which startling novelty and obvious tradition operated in harness, for while the frontiers of Europe were shifted in a new direction, the motivation for extending frontiers remained substantially the same.

Exploration in the Middle Ages was, on the whole, eastward and overland – we need think only of Marco Polo – while in our period, the most significant discoveries were westward and oceanic, even when they sought a route to the east – the Portuguese explored Atlantic sea routes which came to extend as far east as Nagasaki. Not all the Atlantic powers were involved, however, least of all those in the north-western region which was to advance so dramatically in the seventeenth century. The English achievement was patchy and half-hearted before the 1570s, the French, dragging out their own entrails in wars first dynastic and then domestic, had little time for a world outside themselves, the Dutch were yet to involve themselves in colonial rivalry. Imperial conquest in the sixteenth century was an Iberian phenomenon – yes, Iberian, for we must endeavour always to take note of the achievements of the Portuguese as well as those of the Spaniards. The Iberian impact on other parts of the world was uneven. In the Far East, the Portuguese were just one team of competitors among many, especially in Japan and China, and their dominion in Africa was by no means deep-rooted. In 1585–6, the Mir Ali Bey swept the Portuguese from the coast of west Africa, leaving Malindi as their only stronghold. In other ways, too, there was a sense that the sudden changes might prove impermanent. When the Cape was rounded, the Venetians, fearing the competition in the spice trade, opened negotiations with a view to cutting a canal at Suez to preserve the Mediterranean trade link. In the event, the spice trade along the traditional Mediterranean sea route experienced a revival in the middle of the sixteenth century.[3] Nevertheless, the Portuguese stations in the East were important footholds, and the significance of Europe in the wider world was underlined by the decisive impact of the Spaniards in Central and South America.

The people of Iberia were unlikely leaders of what turned into Europe's domination of the world. Portugal was poor by European standards – a population of maybe a million, no flourishing urban centres (apart from Lisbon), an empire which at its most extensive scattered only about 10,000 Portuguese in outposts between Brazil and Japan. The Spanish monarchy was more populous, certainly, but its maritime traditions were more obvious in the Mediterranean world, for instance in the port of Barcelona, than in those of its regions that looked to the west. Neither place was alight with the intellectual curiosity of the Renaissance, even though some of the most famous of Spain's early captains were Italians – Christopher Columbus the Genoese, Amerigo Vespucci the Florentine. There is no profit in pursuing the origins of the imperialist impulse in terms of hard-nosed entrepreneurialism, for Portugal was scarcely a centre of precocious capitalism, Castilian merchants looked north to Antwerp and it was the Genoese who ensured the prosperity of Seville. And yet . . . Beginning with the conquest of Ceuta in North Africa in 1415, the Portuguese pushed south along the west coast of Africa in adventures of unflagging excitement, led by individuals whose daring and ingenuity can never be subsumed into a general socio-economic process. With the mysterious inspiration of Prince Henry 'the Navigator' (d.1460), they reached Cape Bojador in 1434, and ten years later, via Madeira and the Azores, they touched Cape Verde. There were astounding leaps forward at the end of the century: to the western Sudan in 1482, the Congo the following year. In 1487, Bartolomeu Diaz rounded the Cape of Good Hope. A decade later Vasco da Gama's voyage was to take him as far as Calicut. Guicciardini again provides a summary of the impact barely forty years afterwards:

> Sure this navigation is right wonderfull, for that it conteynes a course of eyght thousand french leagues, through seas altogether unknowen, under other starres, under other firmament, and with other instrumentes: for, the lyne Equinoctiall being passed, they are no more guided by the northstar, and stand altogether deprived of the service and use of the Adamant stone, and for that they can not take harbour in so long a way, but in regions unknowen, differing in language, in religion, in customes, and alogether barbarous and enemies to straungers. And yet notwithstanding so many difficulties, they have in time made this navigation so familiar, that where afore they had wont to consume ten months in the voyage, they runne it nowe commonly in lesse than sixe, their daungers being lesse, and all things in more securitie. But farre more marveylous is the navigation of the Spaniards . . .

The Spaniards had sailed west to seek the Indies: Columbus's two voyages of 1492 and 1493 were a prelude to the foundation of Santo Domingo in Hispaniola in 1496–7. By now, Pope Alexander VI had divided the world between the two empires at the Treaty of Tordesillas in 1493. This concentrated the energies of the explorers in a way which produced an astonishing surge of activity in the early part of the sixteenth century. By 1510 Albuquerque's expedition was safeguarding the spice monopoly for Portugal with a fort at Goa: two more at Malacca (1511) and Ormuz (1515) were soon to follow, the last-mentioned opening the way to Macao and thence Japan. By now the Portuguese were dealing in 70,000 quintals of spices a year – 20,000 or 30,000 of these the pepper so essential to the preservation and flavouring of European meat.

One of Albuquerque's subordinates, restless with his prospects, took service with Spain in 1517. His five ships sailed ever westward, rounding Cape Horn and, with the loss of one ship wrecked and another which deserted, the others pitched and tossed through straits that still bear the commander's name. In the Pacific, the privations for the crew were intense:

> Wednesday, November 28, 1520, we debouched from that strait, engulfing ourselves in the Pacific Sea. We were three months and twenty days without getting any kind of fresh food. We ate biscuit, which was no longer biscuit, but powder of biscuits swarming with worms, for they had eaten the good. It stank strongly of the urine of

rats. We drank yellow water that had been putrid for many days. We also ate some ox hides that covered the top of the mainyard to prevent the yard from chafing the shrouds, and which had become exceedingly hard because of the sun, rain and wind. We left them in the sea for four or five days, and then placed them for a few moments on top of the embers, and so ate them; and often we ate sawdust from the boards. Rats were sold for one-half ducado apiece, and even then we could not get them. But above all the other misfortunes the following was the worst. The gums of both the lower and upper teeth of some of our men swelled, so that they could not eat under any circumstances and therefore died.[4]

The arrival in the islands which became the Philippines – the first landfall since Patagonia – brought some relief from scurvy, but the commander became involved in a local war and was killed, along with forty of his crewmen. Sebastian del Cano brought the remnants home. And thus, by sailing round it, Magellan's expedition brought the world within the European compass. Magellan, the Portuguese in the service of Spain, had essentially completed a circle which joined the eastward exploration of his countrymen with the drive west of his employer. The permanence of the European presence was confirmed when, in 1519, Hernán Cortés sailed from Cuba to conquer Mexico: discovery was giving way to dominion.

What made this possible were various combinations of quite specific pieces of naval and military hardware and their alliance with a conviction of the essential righteousness of boundless conquest. In short, the foundations of European dominance were technological and ideological. It needs to be stressed that there is no question of a general cultural superiority: who could argue that Iberia boasted a civilisation to match the elaborate world of Islam, the sophistication of the majestically condescending Chinese, the imperial splendour of the Aztecs? For the Portuguese in the east the reality of power was a combination of guns and sails. The use of portholes gave the galleons and carracks of the Portuguese great advantages of manoeuvrable fire power, as they demonstrated against Muslim fleets at Diu in 1509, and in defending Goa and Chaul in 1571. Much the same was true further east. In 1584, a Portuguese factor in Macao, Geronimo Roman, noted the inferiority of Chinese warships. The junks, he observed:

> have some small iron guns, but none of bronze; their powder is bad
> . . . Their arquebuses are so badly made that the ball would not
> pierce an ordinary cuirass, especially as they do not know how to
> aim. Their arms are bamboo pikes, some pointed with iron, others
> hardened by fire, short and heavy scimitars, and cuirasses of iron
> and tin. Sometimes a hundred vessels are seen to surround a single

corsair, those which are to windward throw out powdered lime to blind the enemy, and, as they are very numerous, it produces some effect. This is one of their principal warlike stratagems.

The Chinese came to acknowledge the specific sphere of European superiority:

The most unparalleled anger which has ever existed since the creation of heaven and earth is exciting all those who are conscious in their minds and have spirit in their blood: their hats are raised by their hair standing on end. This is because the largest country on the globe today . . . is yet controlled by small barbarians . . . Why are they small and yet strong? Why are we large and yet weak? . . . What we have to learn from the barbarians is only one thing, solid ships and effective guns.

This is not a complaint against exploitative capitalist merchants but against superior sea power. The intriguing point in terms of what guns and sails meant to European dominance is that the Chinese complaint dates not from the sixteenth century, but from the middle of the nineteenth.

We find similarly specific sources of superiority in the land-based Mexican campaigns of Cortés. There is no question of Aztec inferiority in the matter of material opulence. As Cortés himself wrote to Charles V concerning the riches of Montezuma's capital, Tenochtitlan:

The city itself is as large as Seville or Córdoba . . . One square in particular is twice as big as that of Salamanca and completely surrounded by arcades where there are daily more than sixty thousand folk buying and selling . . . what could be more astonishing than that a barbarous monarch such as he [Montezuma] should have reproductions made in gold, silver, precious stones and feathers of all things to be found in his land, and so perfectly reproduced that there is no goldsmith or silversmith in the world who could better them, nor can one understand what instrument could have been used for fashioning the jewels; as for the featherwork its like is not to be seen in either wax or embroidery, it is so marvellously delicate . . . I think that not even the sultans themselves or other eastern potentates were surrounded by such pomp and display.

His opinions were shared by his subordinate and critic, Bernal Díaz, who found among the Aztecs, 'such magnificent painters and carvers that, had they lived in the age of Apelles of old, or of Michelangelo, or Berruguete in our own day, they would be counted in the same rank'. It is noteworthy too that Aztec resources of weaponry and courage made them formidable opponents. Díaz saw in Montezuma's stores:

> two-handed swords set with flint blades that cut much better than our swords, and lances longer than ours with five-foot blades consisting of many knives . . . They had very good bows and arrows, and double and single-pointed javelins as well as their throwing sticks and many slings and round stones shaped by hand, and another sort of shield that can be rolled up when they are not fighting, so that it does not get in the way, but which can be opened when they need it in battle and covers their bodies from head to foot . . . I do not know why I am writing so calmly, for some three or four soldiers of our company who had served in Italy swore to God many times that they had never seen such fierce fighting, not even in Christian wars [!] or against the French king's artillery, or the Great Turk; nor had they ever seen men so courageous as those Indians at charging with closed ranks.

What made the difference was the genius of Cortés in seeing early on the advantages which his tiny army enjoyed, a combination not of guns and sails, but of guns and horses:

> 'Do you know, gentlemen, I believe it is the horses that the Indians are most frightened of. They probably think that it is just they and the cannon that they have been fighting, and I've thought of a way of confirming their belief.'. . .

The Indians' ambassadors were told that if they refused to cooperate, something would jump out of the Spaniards' iron demons, which were angry with them. At this point a heavily charged cannon was fired, and then a stallion was given a scent of a mare and began to create an uproar. Cortés made it seem he had power over both, and the Indians were duly intimidated.[5]

However, the capacity to turn the technology to maximum advantage despite vastly inferior manpower – Cortés had no more than 600 troops – lies in the mentality of the *conquistadores*. The roots of both discovery and dominion lie in the common history of the Iberian powers: frontier war, with the aim of establishing Christian rule over Muslims and heathens. The Portuguese victory at Ceuta in 1415 had been unusual, but in many ways their exploration of West Africa was the result of their being deflected from a direct southward thrust by Muslim strength in the north of the continent and the subsequent pursuit of a weakness in the flank, an assault spearheaded by the Order of Christ, founded to replace the Templars in 1319, and sanctioned by papal bulls of 1452, 1455 and 1456. The empire of Islam was by no means passive or sluggish, and its hold on North Africa extended and strengthened from about 1520 to about 1590 (see Map 2.1). From this point of view, the disastrous Saharan campaign of Sebastian of Portugal, which ended in his death at Alcázarquivir in 1578, was, paradoxically, the work of the heir of Henry the Navigator rather than the futile pursuit of an anachronistic dream.[6]

In the case of the Spaniards, too, the westward enterprise was an extension of centuries of war against Islam. For 700 years, the Spaniards had known no purpose other than the defeat of the Moors. Seville, the gateway to the Americas, had once been part of Muslim rule in Andalusia – or Al-Andalus. The western frontier of Christian Iberia in the Middle Ages and the focus of crusading aspirations had been Santiago di Compostella. By 1541, the extension of that frontier was marked by the foundation of Santiago del Nuevo Estremo, now the capital of Chile. Grubby adventurers such as Cortés and Pizarro were the heirs of the *caballeros villanos*, the serf knights who had fought in the wars of Rodrigo de Bivar, known to tradition as El Cid. They sought booty and fiefs, and as in medieval holy war, they did so with the sanction of the Church. Cortés took Franciscan missionaries with him, and projected himself as God's instrument in the matter of conversion. He conquered under the banner of Christ, as is recorded in the eye-witness acount of Bernal Díaz:

> He then had two standards and banners made, worked in gold with the royal arms and a cross on each side and a legend that read: 'Brothers and comrades, let us follow the sign of the Holy Cross in true faith, for under this sign we shall conquer.'

According to Díaz, Cortés insisted that 'ever since we entered this country we have preached the holy doctrine to the best of our ability in every town through which we have passed, and have induced the natives to destroy their idols'. In Mexico City, once it was established that Montezuma would not allow a cross to be set up in the temples of his gods, the Spaniards had a church built in two days, and even though wine for the mass had been consumed for medicinal purposes:

> we still went to church every day and prayed on our knees before the altar and images, firstly because it was our obligation as Christians and a good habit, and secondly so that Montezuma and all his captains should observe us and, seeing us worshipping on our knees before the cross – especially when we intoned the Ave Maria – might be inclined to imitate us.

From what Díaz tells us, the Spaniards clung to their faith and fought like men possessed to save themselves from the terror of capture

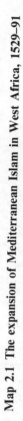

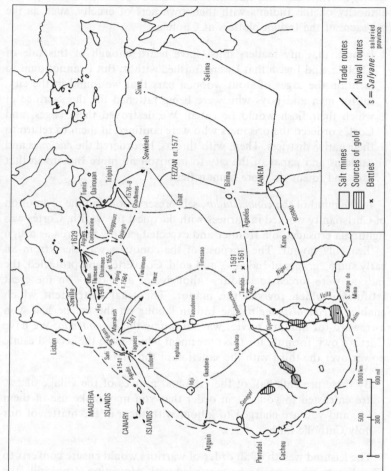

Map 2.1 The expansion of Mediterranean Islam in West Africa, 1529–91

Trade routes

Naval routes

s = *Salyane*: salaried province

☐ Salt mines

▦ Sources of gold

× Battles

Source: Andrew C. Hess, *The Forgotten Frontier: A History of the Sixteenth-Century Ibero-African Frontier* (Chicago: Chicago University Press, 1978), p.117.

and sacrifice. The stench of Montezuma's great abattoir temples was clearly horrific, and may have encouraged the Spaniards to stamp their authority on the Indians with their own acts of cruelty, such as the massacre of the Indian plotters at Cholula:

> I think that my readers must have heard enough of this tale of Cholula, and I wish that I were finished with it. But I cannot omit to mention the cages of stout wooden bars that we found in the city, full of men and boys who were being fattened for the sacrifice at which their flesh would be eaten. We destroyed these cages, and Cortés ordered the prisoners who were confined in them to return to their native districts. Then, with threats, he ordered the *caciques* and captains and papas of the city to imprison no more Indians in that way and to eat no more human flesh.[7]

In the mind of the *conquistador*, self-preservation and the promotion of Christianity worked in harness with the quest for wealth. Cortés was fighting a crusade on a frontier and expected earthly rewards as a sign of heavenly favour. The purpose of the conquest was clear from an early stage, 'grants of Indians', and gold. Converted and protected, the Indians were forced to labour – though not as slaves – in the great latifundia which revived the manor. The legal instrument which enabled a *conquistador* to use Indian labour on the fief he had won as reward for military service was known as the *encomienda*. We have Cortés's own formula for this agreement which gave the second estate power over the third with the sanction of the first:

> By these presents half of the land and natives of the village of . . . are entrusted to you . . . in order that you may make use of them . . . and you are charged to labour with them in the matter of our holy Catholic faith.

The leisured wealth of an order of warriors would ensure converts to Christianity who were to be rewarded with protection. Ironically, the frontier's opportunities encouraged social mobility, and the upwardly mobile sought to fix the social order. 'In the Indies, everyone is a gentleman', said the Viceroy of Peru in 1582. In this 'feudal paradise', fealty to the Church was underpinned with control of the manor. The great jurist, Juan Lopez de Palacios Rubios, put together the ominously titled 'Requirement' of 1513, which set down that Indians were to work for the Spaniards willingly – or be forced to do so. In 1544, one Dominican view was that:

> in a well-ordered commonwealth, it is necessary that there be rich men who can resist the enemy in order that the poor of the earth may be able to live under their guardianship.[8]

There can be few darker corners of European history than that in which the *conquistadores* indulged their distaste for manual labour with a ruthless and inefficient exploitation of the Indians, which appears to have sent the native population of Mexico plunging from 27 million in 1500 to 1 million in 1600. Yet by mid-century, the Crown had begun to bridle the *encomenderos* in New Spain, converting their lordship to a pension for their lifetime only, installing an instrument of public authority in the shape of a court of appeal, the *audiencia*. The case of Peru, however, conquered gradually between 1531 and 1572 after Francisco Pizarro's initial intrusion, shows the crown to be as ferocious as the *conquistadores* in its exploitation. When we read of the silver that poured into Seville in the later part of the century, we should remember that Indians dug it out of mountains, placed it in sacks which weighed 23 kilograms when full and then hauled it out of shafts often 250 metres deep, onto mountainsides where the thin air of the Andes brought further exhaustion. And then more Indians carried the silver from the mountains to the sea. The native population of Peru is said to have fallen from 7 million in 1500 to 500,000 in 1620.

As the Indian population collapsed under the strain, some of the silver had to be paid to the Portuguese to supply black slaves: 50,000 went from Africa via Portugal to Spanish America in the sixteenth century, and similar numbers were transported to the sugar plantations which the Portuguese ran for themselves in Brazil, which they had taken from the French in 1565. The Portuguese had fewer qualms about slavery, and the Church sanctified *As conquistas* in terms such as those of Padre Jose da Anchieta in Brazil in 1563: 'for this kind of people, there is no better way of preaching than with the sword and the rod of iron'. As late as 1587, a Franciscan missionary in Goa wrote that 'this is a frontier land of conquest'.[9] The great humanitarian bishop, Bartolomé de Las Casas, championed the cause of the Indians, disputing the idea that one part of mankind was set apart for labour, but he won no clear victory in the debate with his opponent, Juan Ginés de Sepúlveda, at Valladolíd in 1550. Las Casas accused Sepúlveda of arguing a case for natural slavery, and of perverting Aristotelian philosophy and medieval notions of the just war borrowed from St Thomas Aquinas.

In the latter part of the century, opponents of Spain in England and the Netherlands used Sepúlveda's apparent victory to demonstrate that Spanish dominion meant tyranny and slavery, and so was born the 'black legend' of Spanish imperialism. Las Casas's work was translated into French and then English 'to serve as a president and warning to the xii provinces of the Lowe Countries'. Las Casas recorded the cruelty of 'certayne Dutch Marchauntes' in Venezuela and in Peru, though this was rather ignored amid all the polemic.[10] The English railed against the wickedness of the devil dons of Spain with a shrillness born of insecurity as the Armada threatened. It is easily forgotten that the sea-dog defender of English liberty, John Hawkins, was on a slaving expedition when he was cornered and gored by a Spanish fleet off San Juan de Ulúa in 1568. And Elizabethan colonisation in Ireland offers a horrible example of mistreatment on the grounds of racial inferiority. The 'gentle poet', Edmund Spenser, offered the Irish – polluted by their Gaulish, Spanish and Scythian ancestries – only one remedy: 'it is in vaine to speake of plantinge of lawes and plottinge of pollycies, till they be altogeather subdued'. And there should be

> noe remorse or drawing backe for the sight of any such rufull objectes as must thereupon followe, nor for compassion of theyr calamityes, seeing that by no other meanes it is possible to secure them, and that these are not of will but of very urgent necessity.

Sir Humphrey Gilbert, an Elizabethan adventurer better known for his maritime exploits, ensured that 'none should come into his tent for any cause but commonly he must pass through a lane of heads'. In the Netherlands, William of Orange, with a raucousness unbefitting his nickname of 'the Silent' warned that Spanish victory would result in a servitude such as the Indies had to endure:

> I have seene (my Lordes) their doings, I have hearde their wordes, I have bin a witnes of their advise, by which they adjudged you all to death, making no more account of you than of beastes, if they had power to have murthered you, as they do in the Indies, where they have miserablie put to death more than twentie millions of people, and have made desolate & waste, thirtie tymes as much lande in quantitie and greatnes, as the lowe countrie is, with such horrible excesses and ryottes that all the barbarousnesses, cruelties, and tyrannies, whiche have ever bin committed, are but sport, in respect of that, which hath fallen out upon the poore Indians, which thing, even by their owne Bishoppes and Doctours, hath bin left in writing . . .

The colossal numbers of slaves whom the Dutch employed in their households in Batavia or the plantations of Surinam in the seventeenth century show scant regard for humanity. We might narrow the gap between Spanish 'tyranny' and its opponents still further by pointing to Sepúlveda's strenuous attempts to deny that he was advocating expropriation and enslavement. He argued that the gospel must be preached without let or hindrance, and that the obedience which the Spaniards should command was that of the son to his father:

> I must repeat that I do not argue in favour of despoiling the barbarians or reducing them to slavery. I advocate instead that

they be subjected to *Christianorum imperio* to prevent them from impeding the propagation of the faith, persecuting preachers, and insulting God with their idols and other things: and this for the benefit of the barbarians themselves.

The fact that many peoples of the world acknowledge their Hispanic origins is perhaps a reminder that the Spaniards offered assimilation while the Dutch opted for apartheid. Sir Humphrey Gilbert, along with Sir Thomas Smith, Sir Richard Grenville, Sir Walter Raleigh and Martin Frobisher all indulged in colonial experiment in Ireland. For the Irish it was the English who were 'the greatest murderers and the proudest people in all Europe'. This is not to say that any European power's treatment of native populations was better or worse than another's. Far more significant for our present purpose is the disturbing unity of approach in terms of assumptions of an inherent superiority, much of which derived from Christianity. Europeans took the fact of their superiority for granted, even though they differed over the form their superiority should take.

Had Philip II remained king of England, then the English might have acknowledged overtly that they were content to follow a Spanish lead. Indeed, this appeared the likelier course in 1555. As Richard Eden said of the Indians in his translation of the works of Peter Martyr, the Spanish had set an example by enlarging the Christian world:

> Their bondage [under the Spanish] is such as is much rather to be desired than their former liberty which was to the cruel cannibals rather a horrible licentiousness than a liberty, and to the innocent so terrible a bondage, that in the midst of their fearful idleness, they were ever a danger to be prey to these manhunting wolves. But the Spaniards as ministers of grace and liberty, brought unto these new gentiles the victory of Christ's death whereby they being subdued by the worldly sword, are now made free from the bondage of Satan's tyranny.[11]

The distortion in the writings of Las Casas is not that he exaggerated the enormities of Spanish cruelty, but that he implied that they were unique. In any case, even in his earnest desire that the Indians be converted but not oppressed, we find an attitude to non-Europeans which is disquietingly superior. And throughout the century, one wonders whether the liberal conscience ever freed itself from the feudal vision. Even when they tried to forsake the idea of Indians as serfs labouring for a leisured warrior order, Europeans found a new conviction of their own superiority. This was to find expression in the condescension of one of the most enlightened minds of the age, the French philosopher, Michel de Montaigne (1533–92). Writing 'Of

Cannibals', he argues persuasively that eating a dead person is better than torturing them while they are alive. Yet he shows little of the respect for martial valour and artistic skill which Cortés and Díaz had shown. In his essay 'Of Coaches', the Indians appear as savage innocents, helpless before the cunning violence of European technology. The conquerors had all the advantages:

> mounted upon great and unknowen monsters, against those who had never so much as seene any horse, and lesse any beast whatsoever apt to beare, or taught to carry either man or burden; covered with a shining and harde skinne, and armed with slicing-keene weapons and glittering armour . . .

The Indians, on the other hand:

> for the wonder of the glistring of a looking-glasse or of a plaine knife would have changed or given inestimable riches in gold, precious stones and pearles; and who had neither the skill nor the matter wherewith at any leasure they could have peerced our steele . . . silly-naked people . . . for the most altogether unarmed . . . unsuspecting poore people . . .

By the beginning of the next century, a Europe utterly divided within itself still enjoyed a unity in its superiority over all other peoples, not just Indians. As Samuel Purchas expressed it, Europe's mission to the rest of the world was still a crusade:

> Europe is taught the way to scale Heaven, not by Mathematicall principles, but by Divine veritie. Jesus Christ is their way, their truth, their life; who hath long since given a Bill of Divorce to ingratefull Asia where hee was borne, and Africa the place of his flight and refuge, and is become almost wholly and onely Europaean. For little doe wee find of this name in Asia, lesse in Africa, and nothing at all in America, but later European gleanings.[12]

In their dealings with other parts of the world, then, Europeans created and preserved a curious unity, and while they recognised that there was much to gain, they gave less thought to what they might learn. The wealth of the New World was a fearful burden to the dwindling native populations. It brought few obvious benefits to the growing numbers of people in Europe itself. While economic stagnation reduced demand, depressed prices and lowered incentives to improve productivity, expansion took the price of bread beyond the purses of many and emphasised the limitations of the productive mechanisms.

People and money

The general growth of the European population in the sixteenth century has been described as 'the most important fact' of the age. Alas, the fact is hard to substantiate with figures. Table 2.1 is one set of statistics from a standard work on European economic history.

Another authority, Professor Braudel, collected information suggesting that around 1600 there was, in addition, an Islamic population of 22 million in the Ottoman Empire and North Africa. Unfortunately, his figures for 1600 suggest 9 million for Spain and Portugal, 16 million for France. Only his 13 million for Italy in 1600 corresponds to any degree with the figures in Table 2.1. Yet a third set of statistics presents a population of 69 million in 1500 and 89 million in 1600. These are Professor Miskimin's figures, and he suggests an increase of some 50 per cent in the population in the period 1450–1600, at the same time acknowledging a margin of error in the data of the same magnitude.[13] Such variations emphasise that it is specious to present figures drawn from the records of a pre-statistical age with any confidence of their accuracy.

For our purposes, perhaps we should work with the idea that the Europe of the sixteenth century had a population which grew to no

Table 2.1 The European population in the sixteenth century (millions)

	1500	1600
Spain and Portugal	9.3	11.3
Italy	10.5	13.3
France	16.4	18.5
Benelux countries	1.9	2.9
British Isles	4.4	6.8
Scandinavia	1.5	2.4
Germany	12.0	15.0
Switzerland	0.8	1.0
Danubian countries	5.5	7.0
Balkans	7.0	8.0
Poland	3.5	5.0
Russia	9.0	15.5

Source: R. Mols, 'Population in Europe, 1500–1700', in Carlo M. Cipolla (ed.) *Fontana Economic History of Europe* (London: Harper-Collins Ltd (Fontana), 1974), vol.2, p. 38.

more than about 100 million. (This compares with a figure of some 350 million for the EC in 1992.) Such data as we possess strongly suggest growth, though its origins are obscure. If we consider the traditional sources of mortality, then we find that in the sixteenth century, these were more savage than ever: wars were more destructive, plague cut great swathes through the population, and the more mouths there were to feed, the greater the likelihood of famine. There may be some substance in the idea that the key to the new cycle of growth lay in the mid-fifteenth century when the level of population and the resources of the rural economy achieved some kind of balance. As usual, the evidence is hard to find.

However, while the fact of growth is hard to explain or measure, its impact is clear enough: there was pressure on the land and what it could produce, which led to a radically different distribution of the population, and the new level of demand contributed to startling rises in the cost of living, or, more appropriately, the cost of staying alive. There are two aspects of the new distribution which indicate the new stresses and strains which population growth had induced, and they endured beyond the chronological limits of the expansion itself. More people began to live in urban centres, and more people were destitute. So, as towns grew, so too did poverty.

The growth of the urban population is but one aspect of the enormous impact of towns on European life in the sixteenth century, and we must set aside the construction of a typology in terms of function and historical significance for another chapter (below, ch. 4). For the time being, we should concentrate on the question of scale. In the area which excludes Russia, the Ottoman Empire and Hungary (which the Turks occupied) the available statistics suggest an overall population increase from 61.6 million people in 1500 to 78 million in 1600. In 1500 in the same area, we have evidence of 154 towns of more than 10,000 inhabitants. By 1600, there is evidence of 220 of them. In 1500, their total population amounted to about 3.4 million people; in 1600 about 5.9 million. Thus, while the general population had risen by 25 per cent, the urban population rose by almost 75 per cent. There are some spectacular examples of growth: Amsterdam from 14,000 to 65,000, London from 40,000 to 200,000, Paris from 100,000 to 220,000.

All the same, there is no suggestion in the course of the century that urbanisation had become a phenomenon of the north-west of the continent, laying the foundations for the economic take-off of that region in the next century. Between 1500 and 1600, the distribution of the towns themselves remained in consistent proportions: about 50 per cent of the urban population lived in Italy and Iberia, 33 per cent in France, Germany and Switzerland, and about 16 per cent in Scandinavia, the British Isles and the Low Countries. It is significant that the growth was particularly marked in Iberia. This would be hard to explain if the social structure, as so often assumed, had been 'backward' and 'ossified'. In Spain, the total population grew from about 6.8 million to about 8.1 million. The number of towns with more than 10,000 people almost doubled, from 20 to 37. The total population of such centres more than doubled, from 414,000 to 923,000, with growth particularly marked in Burgos, Madrid, Córdoba, and of course Seville. This marks an increase in the percentage of the total population living in such towns from 6.1 to 8.6. The population of Lisbon more than trebled, from 30,000 to 100,000 over the century. Yet if we approach Iberian urbanisation in terms of the establishment of dumping grounds for crusader booty rather than homes of bourgeois capitalism, then overseas exploration and urban growth in the Iberian experience can be more convincingly linked.

There can be little doubt that the European economy as a whole had had its ligaments significantly strengthened. Indeed, the process of urbanisation, certainly in northern Europe, outlived the end of the great demographic expansion of the sixteenth century. This is a reminder that we must not be dogmatic about the connections between population growth and urbanisation. However, while the connection of the phenomena may be less secure than used to be thought, convincing alternative hypotheses have yet to be formulated. With those qualifications in mind, we might still find the following model serviceable. The growth of the urban population was not, for the most part, due to an increase in the number of stable urban inhabitants. The major demographic reality of the pre-industrial city was that conditions which were dirty and overcrowded hastened the spread of virulent disease. In any year, more people died than were born, and a net increase – at least on the scale achieved in the sixteenth century – depended heavily, though not absolutely, on the arrival of immigrants. Probably 5 or 6 per cent of people born in the countryside were destined to move to the towns, a total of about 70,000 people over the century as a whole, a figure which in turn represents about 66 per cent of the 'surplus' rural population.[14] The 'rural surplus' of migrants did not bring wealth with them. Europe's rural population could be either pushed or pulled to the towns: pushed to escape shortage, pulled in the hope of plenty. Either way, their presence often worsened conditions in the cities themselves. The nightmare poor began to haunt the streets of the Renaissance city. The famine in Venice in 1528 produced horrible scenes, as the diarist, Sanudo, recorded:

20 February 1528. I must record a notable thing, which I want to be a perpetual memorial of the great famine in this city. Apart from the poor who belong to Venice and are crying in the streets, they have come from the island of Burano, mostly with their clothes upon their

heads and children in their arms, asking for charity. And many have
come from the provinces of Vicenza and Brescia – a shocking thing.
You cannot hear mass without ten paupers coming to beg for alms,
or open your purse to buy something without the poor asking for a
farthing. Late in the evening they go knocking at the doors, and
crying through the streets, 'I am dying of hunger!' yet no public
measures are taken against this.

A month later, Luigi da Porto recorded similar scenes in Vicenza
itself, emphasising the plight of the regions to which Sanudo had
alluded:

> Give alms to two hundred people, and as many again will appear;
> you cannot walk down the street or stop in a square or church
> without multitudes surrounding you to beg for charity: you see
> hunger written on their faces, their eyes like gemless rings, the
> wretchedness of their bodies with the skins shaped only by bones.

In Lyon, three years later, the streets echoed with the cries of the
starving poor: 'overwhelming us' as one citizen put it.

The new spectre of widespread material want raised urgent and
unsettling questions which touched the great social issues of the era.
Humanists were forced to reconsider the nature of Christian duty in
society, for how could one extol the virtues of a return to the Scriptures
and then ignore what the Gospels said about charity? And if charity
was to have any meaning, how could one tolerate wasteful ritual when
the poor stood in need? The renowned Spanish humanist, Juan Luis
Vives, provided a forthright answer:

> Surely it is a shame and disgrace to us Christians, to whom nothing
> has been more explicitly commanded than charity – and I am
> inclined to think that is the one injunction – that we meet every-
> where in our cities so many poor men and beggars. Whithersoever
> you turn you encounter poverty and distress and those who are
> compelled to hold out their hands for alms. Why is it not true that,
> just as everything in the state is restored which is subject to the
> ravages of time and fortune – such as walls, ditches, ramparts,
> streams, institutions, customs and the laws themselves – so it would
> be suitable to aid in meeting that primary obligation of giving, which
> has suffered damage in many ways?[15]

Action to remedy the problem of the poor became a priority for
Protestants and Catholics, the work of godly magistrates and new
religious orders, part of the great battle for hearts and minds which
gave the religious conflicts of the age their powerful social dimension

(below, chs. 7 and 8). New initiatives to deal with the growing problem were outlined in Nuremberg in 1522, Strasbourg and Leisnig in 1523–4, Zurich, Mons and Ypres in 1525, Venice in 1528–9, Lyon, Rome and Geneva between 1531 and 1535, Paris, Madrid, Toledo and London in the 1540s. The poor were a challenge for the state, too, as Vives pointed out, though public order was usually more significant than Christian duty in the calculations of authority. Rebellion such as the one in Lyon in 1529 was, according to contemporaries, the work of those who had 'scarcely anything to gain and still less to lose'. Poor laws were proclaimed in the Netherlands in 1531, in France in 1536 and in Brandenburg in 1540. The driftwood vagrants of Tudor England were similarly regarded as a public menace. The removal of monastic charity is a reminder that the assault on the clergy was institutional as well as spiritual, the savagery of the Poor Law a reminder of what people might have to endure if driven from the land by rack-renting, enclosure, harvest failure and all the other causes of grim, ragged, dearth. In the Act of 1531, the government of Henry VIII made a convenient connection between poverty and idleness:

and be it further enacted . . . that if any man or woman being whole and mighty in body and able to labour having no land, master, nor using any lawful merchandise, craft, or mystery, whereby he might get his living . . . be vagrant and can give none reckoning how he doth lawfully get his living, that then it shall be lawful to the constables and all the King's officers, ministers, and subjects of every town, parish, and hamlet, to arrest the said vagabonds and idle persons and to bring them to any of the Justices of Peace of the same shire or liberty . . . and that every such Justice of Peace . . . shall cause every such idle person so to him brought to be had to the next market town or other place where the said Justices of Peace . . . shall think most convenient . . . and there to be tied to the end of a cart naked and be beaten with whips throughout the same market town or other place till his body be bloody by reason of such whipping; and after such punishment and whipping had, the person so punished . . . shall be enjoined upon his oath to return forthwith without delay in the next straight way to the place where he was born, or where he last dwelled before the same punishment by the space of three years, and there put himself to labour like as a true man oweth to.

Shakespeare had presumably not read the Act, but he knew the social reality of Poor Tom, 'whipp'd from tithing to tithing, stock-punish'd and imprison'd'. And everywhere the price rise worsened the condition of the poor and swelled their numbers. In the middle of the sixteenth century, for every 1,000 producers there may have been as many as 780 dependents. And the line between the two groups was easily breached by economic circumstances. According to one homily during the dearth of 1596:

> Though they do labour and take pains in their vocation and trade, yet by reason of the extremity of the world, for that their rents are so great, the prices of all necessities so dear, and the hearts of men so hardened, they cannot live by their labour, nor maintain their charge, but suffer want and are poor.

The task of providing enough bread grew more impossible as the century wore on. Taking grain prices at a level of 100 index points in the first decade, by 1600 the figure had risen two and a half times in Germany, had tripled in Austria and the Northern Netherlands, quadrupled in the Southern Netherlands, Spain, England and Poland, and the figure for France had risen to about 650. In Paris, between 1542 and 1566, grain prices rose more than four times, from 2.55 *livres* per *setier* to 10.70.

It would appear that the amount of money required for bread left little for other wares: the returns on manufactured goods could not keep pace with the inflation in the cost of foodstuffs. With labour plentiful and prices so high, the value of wages collapsed. In Augsburg, for instance, where the population rose from 20,000 to 40,000 in the first half of the century, figures from the 1560s onwards suggest that a building-worker's pay simply could not ensure the subsistence of his family. In Strasbourg at the end of the fifteenth century, 60 hours work would pay for 50 kilograms of wheat. By the end of the sixteenth century a similar quantity cost the equivalent of 200 hours. There may have been some lifelines. Sometimes alternatives to wheat – such as millet, rye or barley – may have been available. Perhaps people exchanged goods and services rather than seeking payment for them – the extent of barter remains unclear. Shopkeepers and artisans may have extended credit facilities. Government intervention (as in Venice) reduced the size of a loaf as wheat prices rose, rather than letting bread move beyond the realms of possibility for the working populace.[16]

After a 'bullion famine' in the late Middle Ages, coin itself became more abundant and less valuable, which also tends to exaggerate the upward tendency of prices. There was more gold and silver in circulation. Not all of it came from overseas. The mines of central Europe produced about 90,000 kilograms of silver a year, and Spanish imports from the New World did not overtake this figure until the 1570s. Yet the growth in the imports of treasure is startling. In the first decade of the century, some 5,000 kilos of gold arrived from the Americas; in the 1550s, over 42,000. No silver was arriving before the 1520s, but then it became a flood – more than 85,000 kilos in the 1530s, more than 300,000 in the 1550s. After 1560, the amount of gold declined rapidly in relation to the quantities of silver, though there was a recovery to a level of about 20,000 kilos in the 1590s. But by now, the supplies of silver had reached astonishing levels: more than 300,000 kilos in the 1550s, over a million in the 1570s, 2.7 million in the 1590s. The precise contribution of American treasure to European prices remains a matter of some debate.[17] It is perhaps an advantage in this chapter to be concerned with symptoms rather than causes. What is important in our discussion is that the symptoms of expansion did not operate in step. However much treasure arrived from the New World, it was never enough to meet the needs of Europe itself. Unsurprisingly, it never reached the poor, and this was partly because governments spent it, often before they had it, which helps to explain why monarchs had to use other metals for coins. Debasements – such as those of Henry VIII (throughout the 1540s) or Francis I (1533 and 1541) may not have caused much inflation, but they were symptomatic of the needs of states for more money. This was obvious by the early seventeenth century. In a scene from Traiano Boccalini's *Advertisements from Parnassus*, a shopkeeper is imprisoned for daring to sell 'meer smoke', a terrible threat to the monarchs of the world:

> for meer smoke serving Princes upon many occasions instead of ready money, all their richest Treasure would soon be exhausted when the so current money of meer smoke becoming of no reputation amongst people, Princes should be forced like common people, to pay their debts in ready coin.[18]

Throughout the century, princes needed ever-increasing amounts of money to conduct their business, which was mainly the business of war.

3   The shaping of statehood

The obstacles: universalism and localism

The development of the state is surely one of the most significant themes in modern history, yet its definition is elusive. Perhaps the following list of characteristics might be generally acceptable in our own times:

- The state is a complex of political institutions embodying a principle of sovereignty.
- The operation of those institutions is governed by a body of law.
- The law is supreme within defined territorial boundaries.
- The supremacy is generally recognised by a group of people usually referred to as a nation.[1]

Roughly speaking, then, the principal elements of statehood in the modern world are these: sovereignty, law, consent, territoriality, nationhood. The emergence of the contours of this form of statehood was a long and difficult process, certainly not one confined to the sixteenth century. In the Middle Ages, the major obstacles to the advance of such a political entity lay in the power structures of the society of orders. The power of the first estate, the clergy, lay in its attachment to the universal authority of the Church. The power of lords was a combination of landed wealth, military resources and social deference which pervaded local society. Even in the sixteenth century, universalism and localism operated as great millstones which threatened to grind emergent states to powder. Political power lay in a wide variety of political forms which, as in the case of, say, empires and city-states, bore little resemblance to the modern state as we would recognise it. In any territorial entity larger than the Venetian Republic, and in many smaller than that, the idea that the state existed as an abstraction separate from the personal relations of ruler and ruled emerged only at the very end of the century. And although the growth of the state tends to focus attention on the western monarchies, the particular and quirky rather than general and inevitable character of the process is sharply illustrated by examples from more eastern regions. The Habsburg monarchy in central Europe, for instance, had all the regalia of the medieval empire, yet found itself compromised by local traditions in

Hungary, where a local warlord, John Zapolyai, became king with Ottoman support, and in the elective monarchy of Bohemia. In Poland, the local power of the nobles overwhelmed the notion of centralised sovereignty – and acquired a fierce attachment to the universal Catholic cause. The weakness of Polish statehood, and the peculiarities of state development in Europe are thrown into still sharper relief by the power of Poland's autocratic neighbours, Russia and the Ottoman Empire. In the west itself, dynastic and religious considerations were the major constraints on political development, and exercised far more influence on the character of political configurations than did notions of the secular nation-state (below, chs.10 and 12). Religious liberty or the claim to an inheritance provided ample grounds for a dispute of sovereignty, law did not easily override local custom; consent was largely a question of noble cooperation; territoriality was compromised by separate inheritances which belonged to the same ruler; laws of succession or religious affiliation overrode considerations of nationhood. Moreover, it should be emphasised that the sense of nationhood in the sixteenth century was not like the romantic nationalism of the nineteenth. Liberal and democratic aspirations had no part to play in sixteenth-century politics. Freedom was usually a question of liberty in religion guaranteed by privileges granted to a locality. Most people lived in social worlds which were simply too local to enable them to think in terms of the 'nation'. There was, however, a sense of fatherland which was defined not by territory but by a particular form of worship – a point which the example of the Netherlands makes clear. In 'national' terms, the Low Countries were neither really '*Germania*' nor yet '*Gallia*': what gave them unity was the notion of the '*patria*' whose prerogatives the king of Spain sought to subvert on the grounds of religion.[2] Amid all the qualifications and complexity, what needs to be borne in mind is that the development of statehood in different national contexts was, from the perspective of the sixteenth century, neither uniform nor inevitable.

The concept of universal sovereignty was the legacy of the Roman Empire. In the Middle Ages, the papacy appropriated concepts of Roman law as the foundation and elaboration of its own authority. In 1302, in the bull, *Unam Sanctam*, Boniface VIII made the subjection to the pope of all living things 'utterly necessary for salvation'. Such arrogations crumbled in the schism and conciliarism of the fourteenth and fifteenth centuries.[3] This did not make way for nation-states. In the sixteenth century, the tradition of universal sovereignty revived in a different guise – the territorial power of the Emperor Charles V. Guicciardini observed that:

the fundacions of the greatnes of Charles were such and so mighty, that adding that dignity Imperiall, there was great hope, that he

Local Particularism

might reduce into one monarchie all Italie and a great part of Christendom.

From Charles's father came the Duchy of Burgundy (1506) – itself never a state since the duke in theory acknowledged the sovereignty of the King of France. His mother, from the Castilian royal house, was mad – a weakness which was to re-emerge in Charles's grandson, Don Carlos – and this made her own succession in Spain impossible on the death of Isabella in 1504. Ferdinand of Aragon ruled as regent on Charles's behalf. At Ferdinand's death in 1516, Charles therefore became Charles I of Castile – with all its American possessions – and of Aragon – with its Italian territories. To the Spanish inheritance were added the lands of the House of Habsburg which belonged to Charles's grandfather, the Emperor Maximilian, who died in 1519. At Maximilian's death, the imperial title beckoned, and at the time the imperial election seemed much more significant than the intemperate words of a monk in Wittenberg uttered a year earlier. The matter was settled with a bribe provided by the bank of the Fuggers (above, p. 18) to the electors responsible for choosing the Holy Roman Emperor. Charles's titles reflect the diversity of his inheritance, and the fact that he ruled, formally at least, in partnership with his mother:

> Charles by the grace of God Emperor *semper augusto*, King of Germany; and dona Juana, his mother, and the same Charles, by that same grace, Kings of Castile, Leon, Aragon, the two Sicilies, Jerusalem, Navarre, Granada, Toledo, Valencia, Galicia, the Mallorcas, Seville, Sardinia, Cordoba, Corsica, Murcia, Jaen, the Algarve, Algeciras, Gibraltar, the Canary Islands, the Indies, islands and *terra firma* of the Ocean Sea; Counts of Barcelona; lords of Biscay and Molina; Dukes of Athens and Neopatria; counts of Rousillion and Cerdagne; Marquises of Oristano and Gozo; archdukes of Austria; Dukes of Burgundy; Counts of Flanders, Tyrol, etc [*sic*!][4]

While this may seem a cumbersome and haphazard patchwork, the very diversity of political forms in the *monarquía* seemed to make possible an infinite extension. The federal potential of the empire lay in the fact that it was not an absolutist state – its one ruler wore different crowns in his different territories – but it promised fleetingly to bury the differences between empire and papacy. The Emperor's tutor, Adrian of Utrecht, assumed the papal tiara as Hadrian VI in 1522, and the imperial chancellor, Mercurio Gattinara (who was in power from 1518 to 1530) revived Dante's vision of a 'world monarchy' and sought to apply it to his master's dominions. In the 1520s, the Emperor's defeat of Francis I in Italy seemed to make possible the incorporation of

France. In the event, the Emperor's ambitions never stretched so far, and indeed Charles was unable to pass on his own possessions undivided. When he retired in 1555, the imperial title and the Habsburg lands went to his brother Ferdinand, with Spain and the Americas, Italy and the Netherlands going to Charles's son Philip II. The concept of a *monarquía universal* with a single head was never to be realised. However, there were plenty of theorists who kept alive the vision of Dante and Gattinara – Postel, Patrizi, Bruno and Campanella.[5] Moreover, both the *monarquía* and the Holy Roman Empire were controlled by the same Habsburg dynasty, and the western power of Philip II's Spain threatened virtually the whole of Europe with conquest in the cause of universal Catholicism. The collection of territories in Italy contained only two areas – Lombardy and the Kingdom of Naples – directly dependent on Spain, but the others were continuously vulnerable to Spanish power. The Swiss Confederation could face invasion from Spanish soldiers marching north from Italy to the Netherlands, the civil war in France might prompt the Spaniards to intervene – from the Netherlands as well as from Spain – on behalf of the Catholic party, and of course Philip II was briefly king of England (1554–58) as consort of Mary Tudor and might at some stage be expected to assert his claims against the heretic queen, Elizabeth I.[6] In some ways, these possibilities did not subside completely until the end of the Thirty Years' War. From the point of view of its territorial power and its justification for intervention in the affairs of other states in the cause of religion, the strength of the Spanish monarchy is at least as striking as signs of weakness or 'decline', and there was nothing inevitable about the emergence of more manageable territorial entities as the normal form of state. In the main, the Spanish monarchy's control of its far-flung territories was remarkable, yet it was a provincial revolt – in the Netherlands – which was to make the state totter, expressing as it did the powers of obstruction which existed in the localities.

For our purposes, 'localism' is a shorthand term for the social and political forces which operated in introverted rural societies interspersed with the occasional self-consciously independent town. Local custom and lordly power outweighed state sovereignty. Public affairs were still controlled by private hands, and what took politics out of the locality were not so much the national concerns of central government as universal and transcendent questions of religious allegiance. In the political world of the sixteenth century, there was plenty of political inertia in terms of local resistance, and there was plenty of space for debate and conflict in the main instruments of protest – that is to say, estates, and if these were ignored, rebellions.

The parliaments of different European regions in the sixteenth century existed in a bewildering variety of forms. They were essentially assemblies of notables – nobles, clergy, burghers, sometimes even free peasants – consulted by a monarch or consulting among themselves, particularly in fiscal matters. These institutions therefore demonstrate the importance of local particularism in determining the preoccupations of central government. Generalisations must be restrained, however, and our terminology must be disciplined, for the various assemblies of notables were not always representative institutions, and played different parts in different theatres of state formation. The Magyar Diet and the Polish Sejm for instance were effectively sovereign, and so was the Great Council in Venice. Such assemblies as these expressed a species of collective absolutism. In the state of Venice, however, the provinces enjoyed a measure of autonomy in institutions such as the Friulian parliament and the urban councils of Padua, Verona, Vicenza, Treviso, Bergamo and Brescia. There is some similarity with France, where the Estates General coexisted with provincial assemblies. In the case of France, however, the destinies of central and local estates diverged. The Estates General, which met in 1484, was not convened again until 1560. Its meetings during the Wars of Religion were an expression of the chaos of central government rather than the inherent vitality of the representative institution. On the other hand, provincial estates were to strengthen their political role, and those of Languedoc, Burgundy and Brittany met regularly irrespective of the fate of the Estates General. In Tudor England, Parliament came to represent the localities at the centre without a substructure of local assemblies. In the Netherlands, there was enormous variety in the composition of the estates in the provinces – the balance of power between towns and nobles was quite different in Hainaut, Brabant and Flanders – but all 17 provinces (even that figure is not fixed) were in turn represented at the States-General. Elsewhere in the Spanish monarchy, the remoteness of the central power left provincial assemblies in semi-autonomy: in Naples and Sicily, the parliaments fulfilled the role of a viceroy. Nearly all such assemblies had a traditional importance in the granting and allocation of taxes. In the sixteenth century, however, as the cost of war spiralled, taxation became a matter of supreme significance, and since the wars were often fought in the cause of religion, then estates came to play a key role in the establishment of the Reformation, if only in formally acknowledging the will of the prince. This was the case in Sweden, where the Riksdag was instrumental in the installation of Lutheranism (at the Diet of Våsteras in 1527), and in the Habsburg lands, where the nobility made gains at the expense of princely prelates. The Tudor supremacy in the Church owed its durability to the ratification by law of the sovereignty of the king in Parliament. In the Netherlands, the power of the States-General blocked Philip II's innovations in taxation and religion, and, in contrast to the English Parliament, rather than binding themselves to the Crown, the assembly formally abolished the monarchy in 1581.[7] Thus, the estates enabled the localities to gain some influence upon central government – by petitioning the monarchy or by passing statutes. However, representative government in the democratic sense was unthinkable, and local discontent – as in the case of the Netherlands – might take the form of armed revolt.

The Dutch Revolt drew ideological strength and political organisation from religious conviction. Elsewhere in the Spanish monarchy, threats to local autonomy were sufficient in themselves to spark revolt. Rather than being distractions from greater problems (such as the Turks and heresy) uprisings are perhaps better understood as an integral part of a whole complex of social and political forces which challenged the power of the state from the localities. There had been a rebellion in Flanders well before the Revolt of the Netherlands, in the shape of the great guild uprising in Ghent in 1539, and in the Mediterranean, the power of Spain was shaken by the *germanía* of Valencia in 1519 and by the *comuneros* of Castile in 1521. In 1568 the Moorish uprising, the revolt of the Alpujarras, seemed to forge a chain of heresy between the Turks, the Moors of Iberia and the rebels in the north. And Aragon rebelled in the early 1590s. More compact states were just as vulnerable as the composite monarchy of Spain. The 'images of revolt and flying off' which plagued King Lear were scarcely less menacing in England, where the innovations in central government were not guaranteed by a standing army. The Pilgrimage of Grace (1536) mixed the dangerous ingredients of resistance to taxation and religious discontent. A revolt in the west country and Kett's rebellion shook the fabric of the state in 1549, Sir Thomas Wyatt led an uprising in 1553–4, the northern earls cut loose in the cause of Catholicism in 1569. In the aftermath of Luther's protest, the promotion of new religious practices in the localities inspired peasant revolt, and the defence of the reform led to war between some of the German princes and the German emperor. While the situation in Germany stabilised after 1555, it was to deteriorate in France, and in the second half of the century, conflict between Calvinists, Catholics and central authority turned rebellion into civil war.[8] These were not the death-throes of outdated feudalism: rebellion in the localities provoked towering crises at the seat of government. Indeed, in Germany and France, local power and a religious cause combined to make a significant contribution to modern political thought. The League of Schmalkalden in Germany, Huguenot propaganda and the Catholic League in France – these were the powerful articulation of a right to resist the tyranny of a prince, which broke a link in the traditional political hierarchy and cut its way through old ties of obedience to the royal majesty.

These words of caution and qualification are of the utmost importance if we are to understand the complexity and the significance of state development in the sixteenth century. Perhaps the chief problem is the need to operate within two chronological frameworks, one particular, the other general. The sixteenth century experienced a crisis of state formation, for its history shows how easily the process of European political development could have been pushed in directions other than that of the nation-state, and this crisis must be discussed later in the context of the wars of religion (below, ch.12). In the long perspective, the sixteenth century witnessed significant advances both in the theory of the state and in the practical manifestations of its power, and such advances form the subject of the rest of this chapter.

The theory of the state

By the seventeenth century, the state – and reason of state – were commonplace terms, the currency of barbers and artisans, according to one commentator.[9] The language of politics had changed, and although the obstacles to secular sovereign entities recognisable to our eyes remained colossal, as we have laboured to emphasise, there were enormous advances in political theory. The many contributions of writers whose texts helped to change the context in which they were written have been the subject of authoritative analysis.[10] Of all of them, one name stands out in fame and infamy: Niccolò Machiavelli (1469–1527). What were the ideas which make him the most significant political theorist between Plato and Marx? What was so special about a short piece of writing – perhaps not even intended for publication – written in exile, probably in 1513, in an effort to regain favour in the eyes of the Medicean regime, as the author lived out the fantasies of power in insignificant Tuscany? For the twentieth century, the answer probably lies in the sheer modernity of expression. For a generation accustomed to the cynicism of dictators and presidents an excellent modern translation of *The Prince* reads as natural and obvious. While we might not wish to espouse Machiavelli's ideas overtly, we are not shocked by them either:

> because it is difficult to combine them, it is far better to be feared than loved if you cannot be both. One can make this generalisation about men: they are ungrateful, fickle, liars and deceivers, they shun danger and are greedy for profit; while you treat them well, they are yours. They would shed their blood for you, risk their property, their lives, their children, so long, as I said above, as danger is remote; but when you are in danger they turn against you.[11]

Section I – High Renaissance

The High Renaissance is most obviously associated with the achievements of three artists of genius: Leonardo (1452–1519), Michelangelo (1475–1564), and Raphael (1483–1520). These three very different illustrations [plates 1–3] of very different subjects show how the supreme expressions of the artistic imagination were underpinned by the most rigorous application of the science of perspective: the understanding of space.

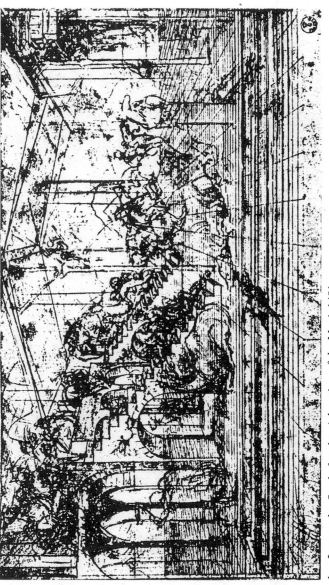

1. Leonardo, Study for the *Adoration of the Magi*, 1481

2. Michelangelo, *The Crucifixion of Haman*, c. 1511

3. Raphael, *School of Athens*, 1511

Section II – The Art of Science

Leonardo's drawings [4–5] capture the force of vitality in plants and the awesome destructive power of nature. Accurate drawing was to make possible the systematic classification of animal life–as Dürer's (1471–1528) study of a hare [6] demonstrates. Simultaneously, the study of human anatomy was to revolutionise the understanding of the human body [7]. Some leading modern authorities see the hand of Titian himself (*c*. 1487/90–1576) in the illustrations to the text of Vesalius.

4. Leonardo, *Star of Bethlehem*, *c*. 1505–8

5. Leonardo, *Cloudburst*, after 1513

7. Engraving from Vesalius, *De humani corporis fabrica*, 1543

6. Dürer, *The Hare*, 1502

Section III – The Crisis of Sensibility

The confidence in the artist's creative powers which the High Renaissance embodied easily and quickly gave way to anxiety and despair. The futility of endeavour is captured in Dürer's incomparable engraving [8] and his fear for the future in his terrifying vision of the world consumed in flood [9], which he sketched after a nightmare. Grünewald (1470/80–1528) expressed the spiritual anguish of the period in his Crucifixion [10], which depicts with compelling immediacy Christ's suffering as God-made Man. While it is easy to connect German art with the spiritual turmoil of the Reformation, there was plenty of pessimism in the art of the Catholic world, as shown by Michelangelo's self-portraits as the flayed skin of St Bartholomew [11] and as St Paul on the Road to Damascus [12].

8. Dürer, *Melancholia I*, 1514

9. Dürer, *The Deluge*, 1525

10. (*below*) Grünewald, *Crucifixion* from the *Isenheim Altar*, *c*. 1515

11. (*left*)
Michelangelo,
St Bartholomew,
c. 1541

12. (*below*)
Michelangelo,
*Conversion of
St Paul*, 1545

Section IV – Renaissance Art and the Counter-Reformation

It is perhaps a measure of how severe was the spiritual upheaval represented in Section III that the art of the Renaissance adapted so swiftly to the spirituality of the Counter-Reformation. Titian's *Assumption* [13] dates from 1518, yet seems to articulate the religious and artistic principles of the post-Tridentine era. The works of Tintoretto (1518–94) express the new Catholicism with extraordinary power, advertising the efficacy of works [14] and extolling the splendour of holiness [15], the latter a quality which separates this crucifixion from Grünewald's depiction of the same subject [10]. It was not always possible for artists to avoid conflict with ecclesiastical authority. Veronese's 'Last Supper' had to be renamed *The Banquet in the House of Levi* [16] to conform to the requirements of the Inquisition. All the same, some of the later works of Titian [e.g. 17 and 18] show the surprising but harmonious synthesis of Renaissance art and Spanish Catholicism.

13.   Titian, *Assumption of the Virgin*, 1518

14. Tintoretto, *Last Supper*, late 1560s

15. Tintoretto, *Crucifixion*, 1565

16.   Veronese, *Banquet in the House of Levi*, 1573

17.   Titian, *Martyrdom of St Lawrence*, 1564–7

18.   Titian, *Spain coming to the Aid of Religion*, c. 1570

Section V – The Art of Politics

Artists sought to become beneficiaries of the patronage systems which centred at court, most obviously in the form of commissions. However, the close relationship of political and cultural patronage meant that those same commissions provide something of a political record. Holbein (1497/8–1543) painted More as Chancellor [19], and the portrait of More's successor, Thomas Cromwell, here shown in his office as Keeper of the King's Jewels [20] is often attributed to him. Holbein's painting of Anne of Cleves [21] helped persuade the King [22] to a match which might have formed the basis of a European alliance against Charles V: both Henry and Anne are shown in wedding clothes. Henry's displeasure on meeting his 'Flanders mare' led to Cromwell's disgrace.

Next page

19. Holbein, *Sir Thomas More*, 1527

20. Holbein [?], *Thomas Cromwell*, 1534

21. Holbein, *Anne of Cleves*, 1539–40

22. Holbein, *Henry VIII*, 1539–40 (replica)

Section VI – Emblems of an Age

The paintings of Bruegel impress upon us the way in which violent physical brutality was part of everyday life. The gallows were no deterrent to merry making [23], mock battles–which were not always mock–were part of popular festivities [24] and everyday life in any form at any moment might be overwhelmed by ever-present, omni-present Death [25]. On such a social scene first fell the grim shadows of the cages at Münster in which the tortured corpses of the Anabaptist leaders were left to rot [26]. In such a social context, the close association of the true Word with fire and sword – memorably depicted in Farel's emblem [27]–could only intensify the conflicts of the era. Over these conflicts presided Charles V, here shown at his moment of triumph after Mühlberg [28], while the defeated John Frederick of Saxony looks every inch a prisoner [29]. Philip II [30] looks much more awkward in armour than did his father, but then the age of the warrior king was in many ways passed. It is part of the 'black legend' to see the man wrestling with the problems of Europe's first global empire as 'the spider of the Escorial'. His agent, Alba [31], shown in all his pride by Antoniis Mor (1517/21–1576/7), looks much more the part of the Spanish tyrant, but the contradictions of the Spanish position are encapsulated in the career of Philip's half-brother, Don John [32]. It is curious that he should be remembered as both the hero of Christendom for his victory at Lepanto, and the instrument of Spanish oppression in the Netherlands.

23. Bruegel, *Magpie on the Gallows* (*Peasants Dancing*), 1568

24. Bruegel, *Battle of Carnival and Lent*, 1559

25. Bruegel, *Triumph of Death*, c. 1562

26. (*left*) The Anabaptists' cages
    on the tower of the
    Lambertkirche in Münster

27. (*above*) The emblem of
    Calvin's friend Guillaume
    Farel: 'the sword of the true
    word' surrounded by flames

28.   Titian, *Charles V at Mühlberg*, 1548

29. Titian, *The Elector John Frederick of Saxony*, 1550

30. Titian, *Philip II in Armour*, 1550–1

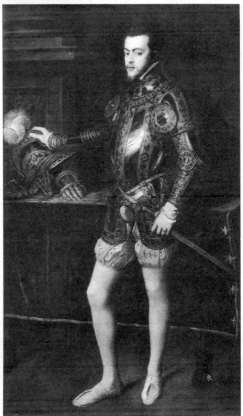

31. Antoniis Mor, *Alba*, 1559

32. Anon., *Don John of Austria*

So easily do such words cut through to the present that it is difficult to grasp how startling they were in the sixteenth century. Perhaps we can come closer to the enormity of Machiavelli's moral challenge in a translation of 1640 – the first English version to be published even though manuscripts in English had been in circulation well before then. Here is the same passage:

> but because hardly can they subsist both together, it is much safer to be feard than be lov'd; being that one of the two must needs fail; for touching men, wee may say this in generall, they are unthankfull, unconstant, dissemblers, they avoid dangers, and are covetous of gaine; and whilst thou doest them good, they are wholly thine; their blood, their fortunes, lives and children are at thy service, as is said before, when the danger is remote; but when it approaches, they revolt.[12]

Even this may seem like a script for the stock villain of the Jacobean stage rather than the reflections of a great political theorist. A view of human nature as immoral was not new, but the idea that this made humans irredeemable and therefore worthy of immoral treatment marked an extraordinary, inadmissible departure. It was a rejection of scholastic Christianity, and it was a rejection of Renaissance humanism. To prize earthly glory above the rewards of the hereafter broke with the scholastic requirement – expressed by authors such as St Thomas Aquinas – that the Christian prince should show contempt for the things of the world. In a sense, that was at least compatible with Renaissance ideas of fame. On the other hand, the humanists of the Renaissance, basing their ideas on the works of the Romans, could see fame as attainable through virtue, which raised man above all the other beings in creation. For Machiavelli, glory was to be attained by a different sort of *virtù*, brute force and animal instinct combining the lion and the fox, seeking the favour of capricious and merciless fortune. What is disturbing is the clarity of his examples. He plucks them from the Bible – David as a guide to the correct choice of weapons – to shock those convinced that Christian morality must govern political behaviour, and from the classics – the Romans as soldiers, not rhetoricians – to show his knowledge of history and the pedigree of what he advises. Most effectively of all, he supports his case with examples from the world around him to demonstrate that he is an observer rather than an innovator. Machiavelli's defence is that he writes about real politics, not ideal states, about what is done rather than what ought to be done. In terms of how politics were to unfold in the sixteenth century, the tension between the descriptive and the normative is most revealing of his determined separation of religion and politics. On this he is as lucid as he is ruthless: Savonarola had no political sense, the papacy had no religion. The implications of this for the liberation of the laity through the exercise of political power were enormous, unthinkable, and we shall need to pursue them in greater detail in the context of the assault on the institutional Church identified with the Reformation (below, ch. 5). For the time being, let us be more specific. As we have seen, the emergence of modern nation-states was hindered by two great obstacles: universalism and localism. In two key chapters of *The Prince*, these are Machiavelli's targets.

In his typology of states, he includes ecclesiastical principalities – and it is a wicked inclusion, which seems to confirm Marlowe's idea that for Machiavelli, religion was 'but a childish toy'. Ecclesiastical principalities, according to Machiavelli:

> are maintained by orders inveterated in the religion, all which are so powerfull and of such nature, that they maintaine their Princes in their dominions in what manner soever they proceed and live. These only have an Estate and defend it not; have subjects and governe them not; and yet their States because undefended, are not taken from them; nor subjects, though not govern'd, care not, think not, neither are able to aliene themselves from them. These Principalities then are only happy and secure.

Apparently, he makes of them an exception:

> but they being sustained by superiour causes, whereunto humane understanding reaches not, I will not meddle with them: for being set up and maintaind by God; it would be the part of a presumptuous and rash man to enter into discourse of them.

There is a telling irony in the 'yet' which begins the next part of the same passage:

> Yet if any man should aske mee whence it proceeds, that the Church in temporall power hath attaind to such greatnesse, seeing that till the time of Alexander the sixt, the Italian potentates . . . in regard of the temporality made but small account of it, and now a King of France trembles at the power thereof, and it hath been able to drive him out of Italy, and ruine the Venetians and however this bee well known, me thinks it is not superfluous in some part to recall it to memory . . .

Thus the papacy is located in the scheming, dirty business of secular politics.[13] If Alexander VI – the spiritual head of Christendom – can be openly described as 'a great liar and deceiver' in secular politics, what moral restraints are there for anyone else? Moreover, if the aim is to establish an integrated, orderly state, then local power networks must be smashed, and without mercy. This is exactly the work which, according to Machiavelli, Cesare Borgia, the pope's son, had accomplished in his pacification of the Romagna, which forms the notorious subject of the seventh chapter:

And because this part is worthy to bee taken notice of, and to be imitated by others, I will not let it scape. The Duke, when he had taken Romania [the Romagna], finding it had been under the hands of poor Lords, who had rather pillag'd their subjects, than chastis'd or amended them, giving them more cause of discord, than of peace and union, so that the whole country was fraught with robberies, quarrels, and all other sorts of insolencies; thought the best way to reduce them to terms of pacification and obedience to a Princely power, was, to give them some good government.

His instrument was Remiro de Orco, 'a cruel haughty man', rendered superfluous by his own success:

the Duke [Cesare] thought such excessive authority serv'd not so well to his purpose. and doubting it would grow odious, he erected a civill Iudicature in the midst of the countrey, where one excellent Iudge did precide, and thither every City sent their Advocate: and because he knew the rigours past had bred some hatred against him, to purge the minds of those people, and to gain them wholly to himselfe, he purposed to shew, that if there was any cruelty used, it proceeded not from any order of his, but from the harsh disposition of his Officer. Whereupon laying hold on him, at this occasion, hee caused his head to bee struck off one morning early in the market place at Cesena, where he was left upon a gibbet, with a bloodie sword by his side; the cruelty of which spectacle for a while satisfied and amaz'd those people.[14]

In many ways, Machiavelli's ideas are still more shocking in his *Discourses*. The genre which Machiavelli uses perhaps cushioned his audience a little: after all, the *Discourses* are a reputable piece of humanist scholarship in that they are a careful commentary on a classical text, (the first ten books of the histories of Livy). In addition, the discussion of imperialism could be conducted in a zone of moral neutrality in that Christianity was obviously irrelevant to pagan Romans. Yet the idea of the state as something more than a single sovereign and with war as its main business was coupled with a startling cynicism in terms of how the Romans used religion. In his discourse on this subject, Machiavelli departs from the specific sphere of Roman history:

The rulers of a republic or of a kingdom, therefore, should uphold the basic principles of the religion which they practise in, and, if this be done, it will be easy for them to keep their commonwealth religious, and, in consequence, good and united. They should also foster and encourage everything likely to be of help to this end, even though they be convinced that it is quite fallacious.[15]

These were not precepts for a Christian prince: the immorality was too vivid. No one would own up to following Machiavelli's principles, not necessarily through shame, but because self-exposure would spoil the deceit. Indeed, commentators such as Stephen Gardiner thought this insidiousness was the chief menace of the book, and such a reaction induced a kind of paranoia. Direct imitation is hard to trace, though there were plenty of accusations against prominent politicians – Thomas Cromwell or Catherine de' Medici – identified with deviousness in the business of government, and therefore as 'pupils of Machiavelli'. Such denunciations may have been insubstantial in terms of Machiavelli's direct influence, but without looking for Machiavellis under every sixteenth-century bed, could we not expect the governors of Tudor England to see the saintly Henry VI as a classic example of the inappropriateness of Christian principles in the business of government? Did not his piety fail to control the power-hungry lords in the localities? Was not the result civil war? When Giles Fletcher commented on the role of religion in the Rus commonwealth, he observed that the Tsar knew 'superstition and false religion best to agree with a tyrannical state and to be a special means to uphold and maintain the same'. The assessment is coloured with the words 'false' and 'tyrannical', but if those are lifted out, then the message is surely Machiavellian. Machiavelli had pointed out in the *Discourses* as in *The Prince* that men 'are frequently influenced more by appearances than by reality': and in Spanish political vocabulary the term '*dissimular*' was often employed.

Yet Machiavelli had, publicly at least, to be disowned. Other commentators refused to see the world he described. Erasmus clung to the concept of the Christian prince, Thomas More's thoughts fled to the ideal society – which Machiavelli had set aside – and for others too the impossible dream was more attractive than the unthinkable reality.[16] The accuracy of Machiavelli's vision was confirmed all too emphatically as the century wore on and religion and politics became embroiled. Paradoxically, however, in an age of religious conflict, the state was freeing itself from religious considerations, and the concept of sovereignty became increasingly a secular matter. Indeed, there was a sense in which religious war hastened the recognition of a need for the assertion of secular authority in the interests of stability. It was in France, torn by the wars of Huguenots and Catholics, that Jean Bodin

(1529–96) developed the argument which underlies his *Six Books of the Commonwealth*, published in 1576. Bodin sought to give religious sanction to an authority which had encountered resistance in the name of religion. In this respect, the book is an answer to Machiavelli and to theorists of resistance – of whom more in due course (below, ch. 12). In the first of the six books, Bodin dismantles feudal obligations as inimical to princely power, distinguishing quite clearly between the obligations of a vassal and those of a subject:

> For the vassal . . . if he be not a subiect, oweth but the service and homage expressed in his investiture, from which hee may not without fraud exempt himself, by yeelding up his fee: but the naturall subiect, which holds in fee, in farm, or fee simple, or be it that he hold nothing at all that he can call his owne, yet can hee not by any meanes without the consent of his prince exempt himselfe from the personall obligation wherewith he is unto him bound . . .

He then attacks the medieval papacy for its temporal power-mongering. The popes:

> after turning the spirituall power into the temporall, by little and little still encreased their power . . . howsoever the Bishop of Rome pretended to have a soveraigntie over all Christian princes, not only in spirituall, but also in temporall affaires.

Feudal power and papal supremacy: once again, the targets were localism and universalism. However, whereas Machiavelli attacked both of these with a new political immorality, Bodin sets them against each other, appropriating to the secular state the trappings of universal power as a means of demolishing local particularism, and asserting that no sovereign could have a feudal relationship with the pope or the emperor.

Significantly, Bodin had disclaimed any intention to discuss religion: 'I here speake not but of temporall soveraigntie . . . to the end it may be understood, who be absolute soveraigne princes'. Bodin's secular sovereigns however, enjoy a power of which Boniface VIII would have been proud:

> Seeing that nothing upon earth is greater or higher, next unto God, than the maiestie of kings and soveraigne princes; for that they are in a sort created his lieutenants for the welfare of other men: it is meet diligently to consider of their maiestie and power, as also who and of what sort they be; that so we may in all obedience respect and reverence their maiestie, and not to thinke or speake of them otherwise than of the lieutenants of the most mightie and immortall

God: for that he which speaketh evill of his prince unto whome he
oweth all dutie, doth injurie unto the majestie of God himselfe,
whose lively image he is upon earth.

In this way, secular sovereignty forced its way into political thought
in alliance with papal tradition as divine right. Roman law, a universal
scheme, became the means to assert the equality of all subjects under
the sovereign, thus flattening the local bonds of personal allegiance:

Wherefore let this be the first and chief marke of a soveraigne
prince, to bee of power to give lawes to all his subjects in generall,
and to everie one of them in particular . . . without consent of any
other greater, equall, or lesser than himselfe.[17]

The emergence of the state as an abstraction rather than an entity
identified with a ruler, the emphasis on secular power, these ideas,
reformulated by Bodin without the moral departures of Machiavelli,
laid the 'foundations of modern political thought'. The implications
were virtually invisible in sixteenth-century France, and only a few
states, notably England and Venice, separated the rule of law from the
will of the ruler. In practice, the power of the state generally found less
secure and more primitive expression.

Assertion and struggle: force, favour and the faith

The embodiment in law of a lay sovereignty independent of the papacy
and of power networks in the localities was rare in sixteenth-century
Europe. Curiously, the principal example of the application of the
imperial theme to a territorial nation-state is that of England, and this
is the achievement of Thomas Cromwell. Yes, Cromwell, the visionary
pragmatist. Without plunging into the morass of controversy concerning Tudor government, it is important to reassert the significance of the
Act of Supremacy and the Act in Restraint of Appeals to Rome as
formidable practical expressions of the sovereignty of the king in
Parliament over an independent state (see also below, ch. 12). This
was an extraordinary feat without the sanction of a standing army,
foreshadowing Bodin by four decades and superseding him in realising
ideas about the nature of the state and giving them practical form,
virtually before the ideas themselves had been formulated.[18] Yet
making an exception of Tudor England must not produce the
assumption that all other states were in some sense inherently more
sluggish, less adaptable. Cromwell's career shows the importance of the
individual in determining political structures. Elsewhere, there were
enormous variations in the size of the state's personnel, the balance of

power between different institutions, the strength of the estates, the whims of princes, and the timing of their death. That said, by the middle of the seventeenth century, the power of the state had begun to crystallise as military might, court patronage, and control of religion. In the sixteenth century, these areas – force, favour and the faith – were theatres in which the state asserted itself and then struggled: the commitments of states to war induced financial panic and the inflation of the elaborate, inefficient and insubstantial structures of patronage and religious interference risked civil war. The state's increased military commitments, the expansion of the court, and arrogations of power formerly reserved to the Church were often causes of weakness rather than symptoms of strength.

In the long term, the sixteenth century can be seen as part of a process by which the state came to hold supreme coercive authority: what sociologists have called 'the monopoly of legitimate violence'. Certainly, the century saw significant changes in the character of warfare. In the fifteenth century, international war was barely distinguishable from the habits of violence of local magnates. The battles of the Hundred Years' War were fought out by great mercenary contingents, the involvement or aloofness of the Duke of Burgundy – that greatest of feudatories, a king-*un*maker – could make sovereigns tremble, and England's eventual defeat led to the fragmentation of the realm and the confrontation of jagged retinues in the Wars of the Roses. The pervasiveness of violence we need to examine in more detail (below, ch. 9). Local power networks are not to be discounted in the sixteenth century, and the state had yet to mobilise an army for domestic policing, as happened in the seventeenth. Nevertheless, the scale, duration and cost of expeditions which furthered international ambitions were changing decisively. What we have to grasp in terms of the power of the state is that there were critical changes in the character of fortification, guns came to play a crucial part, and the numbers of foot-soldiers increased dramatically.

Oddly enough, the development of more durable defensive fortification was the achievement of the Italians, but their feuding states were eclipsed by the invasions of the French and the Imperialists. The wars of the *condottieri* in the fifteenth century were feeble affairs compared with what engulfed the peninsula from outside in 1494, yet by that time, the Italian states were sponsoring designs of low, thick walls which could absorb bombardment and thwart frontal assault. Yet those states were small, and the scale of the Italian Wars overwhelmed and consumed their elaborate designs and their cautious mercenaries in a conflict of unremitting destructiveness. In it, the balance of cavalry and infantry changed dramatically. In 1494, Charles VIII's army of 18,000 consisted of 9,000 infantry and 9,000 horse. The army of Francis I in 1525 was much larger, 30,000 strong, and the balance of horse and foot was quite different for now there were 24,000 foot-soldiers. By this stage of the century, France and the Empire could muster 30,000 men each, by mid-century 50,000, and by the 1590s the Spaniards had more than 80,000 men in the single theatre of the Netherlands.

Larger armies engaged in longer wars demanded new apparatus of maintenance and supply: the expansion of war in the business of state exerted unprecedented financial pressure. The Spaniards could field 16 cannon in 1480 – and these had toppled the high towers of Granada's strongholds. Their use was extended: by 1482, the Spanish monarchs had 66 pieces at their disposal, by 1495 there were 77, and Spanish armies in the age of the Italian Wars could call upon the fire power of no fewer than 162 such pieces. By that stage, field armies of 30,000 men were commonplace. Every day, each soldier needed about 1½ pounds of bread, 6 pints of beer and a pound of meat, fish or cheese.[19] Every prince knew he had to fight wars, and no prince knew how to pay for them. It was the need to raise enormous sums of money at short notice which made the state suddenly bulk much larger as a burden upon society at large. Preparing for wars and fighting them came to demand a much greater proportion of human and material resources. The costs of war outstripped the general expansion of the European economy. These costs were met not by the planned extension of machinery of government but by expedients of often desperate short-sightedness. As the Jesuit commentator, Giovanni Botero, said of war in 1589:

> to pay for it you use ordinary income, so it is necessary to find extraordinary sources which become ordinary and thus seeking to remedy one evil with a greater one, states fall from one disorder to another and eventually are ruined and lost.

The Republic of Siena collapsed under the strain of paying for a fort; the much-debated 'decline of Venice' needs to be seen in relation to the cost of sustaining a formidable land army as well as a reserve fleet of 100 galleys.

England was exceptional in not developing a standing army to underpin central power. Yet, curiously enough, it provides one of the best-documented case histories of rising costs – caused by the familiar ingredients of cannon, ships, fortifications and mercenaries – met by recklessness. In the 1540s, extraordinary expenditure was running at roughly double the value of ordinary revenue. Between the Scots War of 1541 and the death of Henry VIII in 1547, war costs amounted to some £2 million. Perhaps a tenth of this sum was necessary to upgrade fortifications. But in 1545, when a French attack threatened, Henry raised an army of 100,000 men and put 90 ships in the Channel. In the event, there was no great battle because of outbreaks of sickness on both sides. Yet the subsequent Boulogne campaign absorbed about

£600,000, fortifying the town and maintaining a garrison for two years cost a further £425,000. Mercenaries had to be hired, not just because they were better soldiers than militia men but also in order to deny the enemy access to them. These developments were financed in part by the increase of subsidies granted to the Crown by Parliament, which raised about £430,000 in the period 1542–6. A further £220,000 was raised through forced loans in 1542 and 1545. That was still nothing like enough, and Henry proceeded to the sale of crown lands – an irrecoverable alienation which raised about £1.2 million between 1539 and 1558 – and monastic lands, half of which had been disposed of by Henry's death. Even more irresponsible was the debasement of the currency – calling in the traditionally fine English coinage and exchanging it for money containing less silver at a greater face value. This wild and crude tactic brought in about £450,000 between 1542 and 1547, with economic results, particularly in terms of inflation, whch can only be guessed. Between 1538 and 1552, the English crown spent about £3.5 million on wars against France and Scotland, surpassing by £0.5 million the regular annual income of £200,000 on which it could more or less rely, a debt which was only paid off in 1578. It is hardly surprising that Elizabeth I had such difficulty in squeezing extra war subsidies from Parliament later in the century.[20] Such was the case in the compact sovereign space of England. The sprawling monarchies of Spain and France took on greater debts and resorted to an even wider range of clumsy but expedient depredations.

Charles V was only too well aware of his different commitments – which, in his own words, account for his failure to stamp out heresy in Germany. In 1532, he entered Germany 'to see whether he could not hit upon some means of putting a stop to the heresies that were spreading there', but the Turks advanced and 'religious matters were therefore left aside, as there was not time to discuss them'.

In the case of the Spanish monarchy, war was financed by vast loans based on optimistic assumptions about tax revenues. Charles's wars crippled his treasury. To cover imperial policy, he borrowed roughly 30 million ducats – which cost over 37 million including interest. The lack of political integration in his domains forced the burden increasingly onto the one kingdom in which he exercised an assured authority: Castile. Charles V, fighting Turks and Lutherans, had to put pressure on the *cortes* of Castile – those of Aragon were not so pliant – to increase their emergency grants or *servicios* to the Crown. These extraordinary grants eventually became part of his regular income, as Botero was to observe – and an increasingly important part as the value of the *alcabala*, a general sales tax, declined because its assessment was fixed and did not rise with inflation. This was in any case a cumbersome business, and it did not yield the hard cash to be placed in the palm of the serving soldier. This was contributed by individuals who received in return the value of tax revenues from future years. When Philip II came to the throne in 1556, he found that his income from taxes in Spain had been mortgaged in this way for the next five years. Thereafter, Philip needed an average of some 5.5 million florins a year for his soldiers in the Netherlands. Some of this was raised by issuing bonds, or *juros*, which promised a regular income – usually 5 per cent per year – in return for cash. Fleetingly, it looked as though there might be a rational solution in the establishment of the *Casa de Contratación* (1557) in Seville. In effect, the *juros* became shares in the national debt guaranteed by the in-flow of treasure to the Casa from the New World. But there was no time for such a system to mature: by the 1570s, the costs of war accounted for some 75 per cent of Philip's revenue, and money was not set aside for the repayments on the bonds. Instead, more were issued, with promises of increased interest. There were discouraging bankruptcies in 1575 and 1596, and when Philip died in 1598, his monarchy was 85 million ducats in debt.

Charles V's great rival, Francis I, was just as extravagant in his bellicosity. In 1536, his expenditure on war amounted to about 4.5 million *livres*, falling to 1 million in the following year. The campaigns beginning in 1542 cost around 16 million, 3 million more in 1545, another 2 million in 1546. Through the agency of the *Hotel de Ville* in Paris (which he rightly assumed inspired more confidence than the monarch himself) he sold annuities comparable to the Castilian *juros*, known as *rentes*, from 1522 onwards, and by 1550 the tactic had raised 7 million *livres*. By the mid-1560s, the French monarchy was issuing bonds worth some 1.7 million *livres* every year. Henry II offered bonds to a total of 6.8 million *livres*, Charles IX to almost 26 million. More notorious – and also much more important in the case of France than anywhere else in the sixteenth century – was the expedient of playing on society's desire for nobility by selling office and title to those prepared to pay. Ennoblement was obtainable in return for a payment to the Exchequer, 'in order to subsidise, satisfy and provide for the great, costly and pressing affairs which we must bear or direct', as one directive stated in 1522, or as in 1544, to meet:

> the excessive and extreme expenditure that we are constrained to make for the maintenance and governance of the great forces which we have mustered on land and sea . . . in order to resist the hostile intentions of our enemies.

In 1554, for instance, 80 posts of secretary to the king were for sale at 6,000 *livres* each.[21]

The sale of office and title emphasised the Crown's role as the fount of honours, the source of all patronage, the competition for which centred at court. What a spectacle the courts offer! The shadowy mechanisms of their politics are brilliantly illuminated by Shakespeare's Prospero as he explains to Miranda how he had lost Milan to his brother by handing over control of appointments. Antonio:

> Being once perfected how to grant suits,
> How to deny them, who t'advance and who
> To trash for over-topping, new created
> The creatures that were mine, I say, or chang'd 'em,
> Or else new form'd 'em: having both the key
> Of officer and office, set all hearts i' the state
> To what tune pleas'd his ear; that now he was
> The ivy which had hid my princely trunk,
> And suck'd my verdure out on't.
>
> (*The Tempest*, 1613, I.i.79–87)

This was a dangerous game for high stakes. The prince could advance favourites who lacked aristocratic pedigree – Wolsey, Cromwell, Perez – but any apparent exclusion of the hereditary nobility would generate alienation and resentment. This proved one of the chief fractures in the power of the French monarchy. Professional secretaries such as those of Henry II, de Laubespine and Villeroy, were one thing, the personal creatures of Henry III were quite another. The king was apparently incapable of controlling the excesses of his *mignons*. The disillusion was irretrievable within two years:

> There is now much talk about the *mignons*, who are greatly loathed and despised by the people, as much for their haughty ways as for their effeminate and immodest appearance, but most of all for the excessive liberalities of the king towards them. It is generally said that this is the cause of the ruin of the kingdom . . . These nice *mignons* wear their hair long curled and recurled, and surmounted by little velvet caps like those of the women of the streets. Their collars are wide and loose so that their heads resemble St John's upon the platter . . . Their pursuits are gambling, blasphemy, leaping, dancing, quarreling, seducing, and attending the king everywhere. They do everything to please him, giving no thought to honour or to God, contenting themselves with the grace of their master.

The importance of favour shown or obtained at court is an expression of the looseness of the structures of the state. Of course, the stiff ritual of rulership had its own rigidity, but the court was, at bottom, no more than the extended royal household, and the exercise of power, though hedged by formality and mystique, was surprisingly personal. In the court of Archduke Ernest of Austria in 1593, for example, chamberlains and high stewards were part of the same retinue as were *dapifers*, carvers and silver cleaners to a total of 480 persons and 486 horses. Ministers were often favourites, dependent – like Oswald in *King Lear* – on the 'gale and vary' of their masters. Wolsey rose and fell like Lucifer, Cromwell encountered displeasure and the axe, disgrace amounted to the removal of favour for Alba and Farnese. The court of Philip II embodied some 1,500 appointments. Although the Habsburgs were much less prone to resort to sale of titles than the Valois or, later, the Stuarts, the possibilities for corruption and intrigue were apparently endless, as the Duke of Alba was to discover. The king's secretaries had ample networks of their own. As *mayordomo*, or royal steward, Alba encountered the opposition of Ruy Gomez, the *camerero mayor*, or senior chamberlain. Antonio Perez, whose father had been an ally of Alba's, turned against the Duke, inherited the mantle of Gomez and through his control of finance undermined Alba in the Netherlands by blocking release of his funds.

Intrigue bred instability, and venality of office and title hindered the development of trained bureaucracies which the universities were now able to provide with manpower (below, ch. 5). For all that, it is possible to discern within the courts those figures who were genuine servants of the state – as legal authorities (for example, Thomas More) as secretaries, as in the case of Thomas Cromwell, as people who might extend bureaucracy and the law to increase the regulation of society's relations with the state and of the subjects' relations with each other. Moreover, negotiators and observers from the court became Europe's first *corps diplomatiques*.

As we shall see, artists such as Holbein and later Rubens were to form part of this cadre, and the patronage of artists was as important as the promotion of other officers in the life of the court. Indeed, the patronage networks of the court – dependent as they were on the chance of princely whim – are probably best understood in cultural terms. They bound the aristocracy to the monarch, emphasising their separateness and aloofness by weaving chivalry into the fabric of princely magnificence to bedazzle the commonalty, and if service to the prince brought honour, then opposition would bring shame. The cultivation of magnificence proved a strikingly effective counterweight to the checks on real power. If eyes could be drawn to the splendours of the prince, so could hearts. The art of the Renaissance proved one of the most effective servants of the state.

Princely magnificence, with its badges and triumphal arches, its elaborate symbolism and obscure intellectual substructures, can seem wholly alien to us as an instrument of political power. Perhaps one way of understanding it, however, is as the combination of images and celebrations – works of art and festivals – in a theatre of rulership which was the nearest the sixteenth century got to state-controlled broadcasting. A literary form, the fête book, developed to list all the performances, and whenever a ruler entered a city, held court or died, he or she was on stage.

As usual in cultural matters, the prototypes were worked out in Italy. Machiavelli observed that one of Lorenzo the Magnificent's chief skills as a ruler was that 'he entertained the city with festivals at which were displayed tournaments and representations of ancient deeds and triumphs'. Some of the floats incorporated the designs of the Pollaiuolo and Botticelli, and the first European experiments in opera in the sixteenth century worked in all sorts of subtle references to the benefits of Medicean rule. Indeed, Florentine art provides one of the most thunderous depictions of divine-right absolutism in the *Apotheosis of the Grand Duke Cosimo* by Vasari, which looks forward to Rubens's depiction of James VI and I on the ceiling of the banqueting house at Whitehall. But even by 1500, princely magnificence had begun to take shape outside Florence: in the palatial refinement of Urbino, or in the court of the Gonzaga at Mantua. The 'splendours of the Gonzaga' entered every detail of everyday life: ceramics, devices, buttons, and a salt cellar designed by an artist of the stature of Giulio Romano (c.1492–1546), Raphael's chief assistant. Raphael himself (1483–1520) pursued in Rome a career as a courtier which at one stage looked as though it might win him a cardinal's hat, and his contemporary Benvenuto Cellini (1500–71) made palaces showrooms of luxuries. His boastful autobiography makes no apology for making plate, chalices, jugs, medallions, rings, seals and coins which were as much a part of his work as the casting of *Perseus*. The courtiers of Rudolf II stood in fear of the Emperor's bouts of melancholy, but those who could provide objects of gold and silver might extend the stay of his favour.

Artists were often responsible not just for the props but also for the sets and costumes of the princely stage. Leonardo offered his services to the Duke of Milan as architect, painter and sculptor, but he devoted much of his time and effort to the devising of entertainments. What genius he expended on costume design! In 1490, he himself judged his theatrical devices for the weddings of his patron and Beatrice d'Este, and of Caterina Sforza with Alfonso d'Este as his greatest triumph. Leonardo himself and then Catherine de' Medici were to take their designs and productions to France, and that curious figure, Arcimboldo, fulfilled similar functions for Rudolf II in Prague.

Charles V derived much of the splendour of his own imperialism from the culture he inherited with his Burgundian title, but his public appearances were 'great compilations of imperial mythology on a scale unknown since the Roman Empire'. The increasing emphasis on the stature of the prince was something in which Charles himself came to believe. At the siege of Metz in 1552, he compared poor soldiers 'to caterpillars, insects and grubs which eat buds and other fruits of the earth'. Henry VIII's efforts to compete with the great powers involved the elaboration of the court as 'a political institution, a cultural centre, and a market-place of patronage and profit'. As a cultural centre, Henry's court appropriated the trappings of the Renaissance in order to compete with Francis I. In their meeting near Calais in 1520, a complicated amalgam of politics and culture was used to dazzle the world. At the Field of the Cloth of Gold, the English pavilion, according to an Italian observer, was worthy of Leonardo, the French tents were said to have cost 300,000 ducats, and the jousts, bouts of wrestling – and drinking – continued for three weeks.

Some of the images of power dimmed in France as the century wore on, but the pull of the Tudor court strengthened under Elizabeth. Moreover, her progresses proclaimed the imperial rule of the Virgin Queen, another instance of the application of a universal ideology to the territorial state. Philip II was not of a temperament to project himself as one who 'doth bestride the narrow world like a colossus', and confined himself to the monastic chambers of the Escorial. Yet, on his funeral monument at Naples, he was depicted as a rather unlikely Hercules, carrying the earth 'that Atlas may rest', a reference to his assuming the role of world-bearer from Charles V, the ultimate 'tired Caesar'. His Habsburg cousins in Vienna developed a court which 'exerted an attraction on all levels of political society, so that estates, aristocracy, towns, Church, intellectuals in fact conformed'. 'Austria' was the dynasty, the dynasty was the court, the court was the state.[22] All over Europe, however, imperial power – derived from the classical past and expressed in its motifs – involved new interventions in the affairs of the Christian Church.

In some ways, the involvement of the state in the ordering of the Church resulted – as Machiavelli observed – from the involvement of the papacy in secular politics. In fact, in the pages of *The Prince* there may be a measure of envy in the animus against the popes, envy of the success with which they had curbed their universalist ambitions and shaped a compact territorial state in Italy itself. The taming of the barons of the Romagna was the achievement of Cesare Borgia, bureaucratic and financial restructuring was the work of Julius II. Earlier popes seemed precocious models for Machiavelli's 'secular' ruler. By the end of the fifteenth century, the papacy had forsaken even the appearance of Christian justification for its actions. When the Pazzi faction plotted the assassination of Lorenzo de' Medici in 1478, as Guicciardini observed, 'His Holiness the pope [Sixtus IV] was aware of it and approved of it'. Venice challenged the secular power of the papacy in the War of Ferrara (1482), and suffered excommunication as a result. Savonarola undertook the regeneration of a Christian society in Florence in part at least because of the worldliness of the Church's present concerns. In 1475, he had written a poem 'On the Ruin of the Church', lamenting the decay of 'the learning, love, and purity of olden times'.

However, by the late fifteenth century, princes had begun to learn – perhaps from the popes themselves – how to use religion for their own ends. The Inquisition established in Spain in 1479 was an instrument of the monarchy. It was the only institution which was genuinely Spanish in that it operated in the same way throughout the different kingdoms of the peninsula. It proved so effective in the attack on heresy, that the Spanish Church seemed well ahead of that of Rome in the business of reform. As we shall see, even after the Council of Trent, Spanish Catholicism and Roman Catholicism did not always enjoy harmonious relations. We should remember that the expansion of papal power in the Middle Ages involved control of ecclesiastical appointments – the great revolution associated with the pontificate of Gregory VII (1073–1085) known as the Investiture Contest, was a dispute about who could invest bishops with the symbols of their office. Yet the French monarchy came to enjoy considerable power in such matters, confirmed in the Pragmatic Sanction of Bourges of 1438. This was superseded in 1516 by the Concordat of Bologna in which the papacy formally conceded that the King of France would nominate the bishops of France:

> In future, when any cathedrals or metropolitan sees in the said kingdom . . . shall fall vacant . . . their chapters and canons shall not be entitled to proceed to the election or postulation of the new prelate. In the event of such a vacancy the King of France for the time being shall within six months . . . present and nominate to us and our successors as bishops of Rome, or to the Holy See, a sober and knowledgeable master or graduate in theology, or a doctor or graduate of both or either laws, taught and rigorously examined at a reputable university, who must be at least twenty-seven years old and otherwise suitable. And the person so nominated by the king shall be provided by us and our successors, or by the Holy See.

There were qualifications, and it can be argued that the Concordat found Francis caught between the impulses of the Parlement of Paris, which wanted a tougher line on the reform of abuses in the church, and the papacy, which reasserted its power by annulling the Pragmatic Sanction. All the same, the papal statement is a clear enough definition of the power of the Crown, even though France never adopted Protestantism: the Church was part of the clientage system. As Pope Julius III put it to Henry II in 1551:

> You give elective benefices, which I do not . . . You place tithes on the churches as you please. You order the cardinals and bishops as

you think fit and as it pleases you. No matrimonial cases, benefices, or spiritual cases ever come into this court. Finally, you are more than pope in your kingdoms.

In 1563, the council and the Parlement agreed that the equivalent of 3 million *livres* of church property should be confiscated to pay royal debts after the first civil war. All this in a state which did not break with Rome! In that he chose to make such a break, the ecclesiastical power of Henry VIII was markedly greater, more uncompromisingly sovereign, as the Act in Restraint of Annates made abundantly clear in 1532:

> be it ordained and established by the authority aforesaid that at every avoidance of any archbishopric or bishopric within this realm or in any other the King's dominions, the King our sovereign lord, his heirs and successors, may grant unto the prior and convent or the dean and chapter of the cathedral churches or monasteries where the see of such archbishopric or bishopric shall happen to be void, a licence under the great seal, as of old time hath been accustomed, to proceed to election of an archbishop or bishop of the see so being void, with a letter missive containing the name of the person which they shall elect and choose; by virtue of which licence the said dean and chapter or prior and convent to whom any such licence and letters missives shall be directed, shall with all speed and celerity in due form elect and choose the said person named in the said letters missives to the dignity and office of the archbishopric or bishopric so being void, and none other; and if they do defer or delay their election above 12 days next after such licence and letters missives to them delivered, that then for every such default the King's Highness, his heirs and successors, at their liberty and pleasure shall nominate and present, by their letters patents under their great seal, such a person to the said office and dignity so being void as they shall think able and convenient for the same . . .

Princely power in ecclesiastical matters enjoyed a similar extension in the Empire. Although Charles V seemed to have Protestantism at his mercy after his victory over the League of Schmalkalden at Mühlberg (1547), the princes were to triumph a few years later. The Peace of Augsburg (1555) enabled the local ruler to determine whether his state should be Catholic or Lutheran. The settlement later summed up in the formula *cuius regio, eius religio* destroyed the Empire as an entity holy and Roman. The abdication of the Emperor Charles V, the heir of Charlemagne and the defender of Christendom, was the natural outcome: 'within the territorial boundaries it was the will of the absolutist ruler which alone prevailed'.[23]

The foregoing gives the sixteenth century its place in the long-term development of the European state between the Renaissance states of the fifteenth century and the absolutisms of the seventeenth. If we now concentrate on the span of the sixteenth century alone, we become aware of a dangerous teleology driven by two questionable assumptions. These are, first that the nation-state is the natural unit of European political organisation, and second that the modern state is a secular state. All those features which we attribute to the absolutism of the *ancien régime*, all the paraphernalia of central power – docile nobles and dormant parliaments, uniformed dragoons and armies of tax collectors, a clear distinction between domestic and foreign affairs, objectives pursued without the spurs of religious fervour – all this lay in the remote future.

In the sixteenth century, the obstacles to sovereign national entities, universalism and localism, took new forms and indeed acquired new vigour – and in their novelty became more recognisably modern as political forces precisely because of the expanding importance of religion as an ideological and social force. After all, the Reformation itself began as a local phenomenon which then confronted the universal power of the Holy Roman Emperor. The Reformation was also in its initial stages an urban phenomenon, and the growth of cities brought much else that was distinctive and novel to the social world of the sixteenth century.

4 Cities and citizens

The pattern of urban expansion

In virtually any period of European history, towns in their different forms can be described as 'the motors of change': the city-state of the Greeks and Romans gave birth to modern politics; medieval towns, 'islands in a feudal sea', were the nuclei of the revolutionary phenomenon which we call commercial capitalism; the sprawling conurbations of the nineteenth century were both causes and symptoms of the gigantic process of industrialisation.[1]

Yet in trying to understand the city in the specific context of the sixteenth century, we must remember not only those features which connect the contemporary world to its remote past, but also the characteristics which separate and distinguish the pre-industrial age from our own. In particular, we might emphasise that there is no necessary connection between the religious changes which towns fostered and the 'rise of capitalism'.

The contrasts between then and now are often stark. In the modern world, most people live in cities. Historically, they were drawn there by the prospects of work in an age of mass production, and other opportunities arose from the provision of goods and services for the industrial workforce. This was a pattern of development established in the nineteenth century, as coal, iron and railways transformed the structures of everyday life and material culture. The working day came to be determined by clocks rather than by seasons, by the factory siren rather than by light and dark, people travelled on trams and read newspapers where once superstitious illiterates had trudged to the fields. In the sixteenth century, towns undoubtedly played a dynamic role in opening new material and cultural possibilities, but they occupied a quite different place in the social landscape. The power of lords was underpinned by the deference and subjection of the nine people in ten who worked as peasants in rural areas (above, ch. 1).

Something in the order of 2 per cent of the people of Europe lived in towns with a population of more than 40,000 in 1500, about 3.5 per cent a century later. If we classify settlements of over 5,000 people as towns, then the corresponding figures are 9.6 per cent in 1500 and 10.8 per cent in 1600.

With one or two significant exceptions – such as the Arsenal in Venice – there was no industry in the sense of concentrations of labour in urban factories. Enterprise was a commercial phenomenon concerned with unprocessed bulk commodities – grain, salt, fish, timber – not with mass-produced finished goods. Manufactures were produced in small-scale enterprises by a highly skilled labour force operating from workshops governed by guild regulations, and the products are often described – rather misleadingly – as 'luxuries'.

Larger-scale networks of production were not entirely unknown, and large numbers of people were engaged in the production of textiles, in mining and in building. However, some stages of textile production – sometimes the entire process – were based in rural areas, while the small workshop remained the focus of urban cloth production. Mines – from the Harz mountains to Peru – were not associated with 'mining towns' as they were to be in the nineteenth century in Scotland or Wales or in the American gold rushes. Building certainly was an urban phenomenon, yet in some ways it was subordinated to activities of more fundamental importance already mentioned. The building of ships in Venice concentrated several thousand workers in the Arsenal, which was probably the largest industrial enterprise in the pre-industrial world. Yet the hulls were destined to carry bulk commodities such as salt, and luxuries such as silk in overseas trade, and in that sense industrial power served commercial enterprise rather than being an end in itself.

The construction of great churches and palaces in the cities might also require large numbers of workers: 2,000 laboured on site to build St Peter's in Rome. On the other hand, the engineering and technical skills involved in such construction depended on traditional training supervised by guilds which allowed a surprising degree of open-endedness and flexibility in the organisation of labour. Moreover, the palaces and churches themselves were filled with high-quality goods wrought with great skill in small urban workshops. The training which ensured the quality of the end-product remained the province of the guild system: a 'masterpiece' was, after all, what one had to produce to be acknowledged as a master by other practitioners of a trade. From that point of view, what are sometimes referred to as 'works of art' in the period were attached to typical patterns of urban production which served courtiers, churchmen and nobles.[2]

That élite dominated the social structure of the towns. According to the rough model of social structure which historians of the early modern town have established, the 'rich' – that is to say, those with some reserves of grain – made up 10 to 15 per cent of the population. They were a material world away from the permanently poor. Widows, orphans, lunatics and beggars remained poor whatever the condition of the economy – they were 'structural' in that their misery was built in to the natural order of things, and they probably accounted for some 5 per cent of the urban population.

What of the other 80 per cent? In times of plenty when the economy boomed, the labour force enjoyed some security, but they were vulnerable to crisis. In England, thousands were thrown out of work in slumps in 1562–4, 1571–3 and 1586–7 and became 'masterless men', adding to the ranks of the vagrant population. Even in prosperous cities such as Antwerp or Lyon, 75 per cent of a craftsman's income would have to be used to buy food. Bread shortages would drive prices high and leave no surplus for manufactured goods, falling prices for manufactured goods widened the gap between day-wages and the cost of bread, the recovery of the manufacturing sector was slow because production was part of a more intricate network of supply and demand than the simple fact of an abundant harvest or a meagre one. Economic crises swelled the numbers of the poor in sudden and spectacular fashion: the *Aumône Générale* in Lyon had to cope with a queue of 6,000 people – that in a population of 70,000 – seeking food in 1586.

Famine was one source of mortality, plague another. In Augsburg, a city which more than doubled in size from 20,000 to 45,000 people, there were eight years of plague in the first half of the century and in those years a total of nearly 40,000 people died. The death rate in London in 1563 was 27 per cent; in 1593, 18 per cent. A total of about 50,000 people died in those two years, as many as 40,000 of them died of plague – and still the population climbed from 80,000 to 200,000 in the second half of the century. In the great outbreak of pestilence which struck Italy in 1575–7, some 50,000 people died in Venice (a city of almost 170,000 people), more than 17,000 in Milan (a city which recovered to a population of about 120,000 in about 1600), nearly 30,000 in Genoa, a city of about 70,000 inhabitants. In 1597, more than 6,000 people died of plague in Hamburg when the city's total population was no more than 40,000, nearly 8,000 in Lübeck, which was probably a third of all inhabitants of the city at the time.

Urban society was divided, then, between rich and poor – those who had grain reserves and those who did not. The latter group was in turn divided. There were those who enjoyed a measure of protection in work and social life within the corporate structures of urban guilds. Many day-labourers hung on at the fringes of the world of the guilds, others were completely dependent on charity. The overall population level was periodically determined by savage bouts of mortality. Such was the unpromising social framework of urban expansion in the sixteenth century, yet the fact of expansion is inescapable.[3]

Urban growth was not unprecedented. The development of cities in the sixteenth century had been foreshadowed in the period from the twelfth to the early fourteenth century. In that phase, a general growth in population was accompanied by the development of trade and the establishment of markets which needed recognition of their separate legal identity. Such centres formed the spinal column of the European economy in a complicated formation of vertebrae stretching from London to Rome. In the north, the Hanseatic zone combined London with the trade of Lübeck and Danzig and with the cloth towns of Flanders, such as Bruges, Ghent and Ypres. The network extended through south Germany via centres such as Cologne and Nuremberg and the fairs of Champagne into northern Italy. This last, the most urbanised area in Europe, can be defined as Lombardy with its centre at Milan, and Tuscany, its centre in Florence, and these areas were flanked by ports – in the west Genoa and in the east Venice. There were signs of strain in the European economy by about 1300, but urban growth had come to a decisive end in the mid-fourteenth century as a result of the Black Death.

The subsequent stagnation lasted about a century, but the renewed growth of the sixteenth century bore the same hallmarks as the growth of the earlier period: population increase and the expansion of trade. While many of the older centres experienced substantial growth, more striking still is the spectacular emergence of new boom towns, which dramatically changed the balance between western and eastern Europe. In the Middle Ages, the dominant form of social organisation in the west was feudal, and its economic underpinning was the manor and the unfree peasant who laboured on it. The eastward colonisation (the *Drang nach Osten*) of the twelfth and thirteenth centuries offered a greater measure of liberty both to fief-holders and to peasants. From about the middle of the fifteenth century onwards, increasing demand in the west, particularly in urban centres, was met by labour-intensive manorial cultivation in eastern lands, which, as we have seen (above, pp. 24–6), stunted the possibilities of social diversification and urban growth east of the Elbe.

Moving through the old urban heartland of Europe, we see in the Hanseatic zone London growing enormously from maybe 40,000 in the age of Caxton to as many as 200,000 in the age of Shakespeare. The population of Ghent remained steady at around 50,000, as did that of Lübeck, but at its lower level of maybe 25,000, while Danzig experienced substantial growth to at least 60,000. However, Danzig had acquired a new importance outside the traditional Hanseatic framework as an exporter of grain. The trading centres of Germany tended to hover at their medieval levels, but in northern Italy, there was marked growth in Venice, Milan, Florence and Genoa, and if Bologna tended to fade, then Verona had become a very large city, and likewise within Venetian dominions, there were considerable concentrations of population in Brescia (42,000) and Bergamo (23,000).

Of the new centres, Antwerp moved from maybe 40,000 to 90,000 in the first half of the century, and at its demise in the last quarter of our period, then Amsterdam took command of the northern economy, growing from about 13,500 people in 1520 to a city of well over 60,000 people by 1600. In the south, Seville expanded as a result of its new importance in dealing with the influx of silver from the New World, from about 65,000 in the 1550s to at least 90,000 in the 1590s. Lyon, an inland city, but heavily dependent on river traffic on the Rhône, rivalled both Antwerp and Seville in an enormous surge of growth from about 1520 to 1580, its population growing to around 70,000.

Great fortunes were to be made in banking in Lyon, and its sudden prosperity did not altogether eclipse traditional centres, for some of these acquired a novel importance in linking their fortunes to the new Atlantic opportunities, which helps to explain the importance of Augsburg. For the first three decades of the sixteenth century, the branches of the House of Fugger embraced the entire European economy. From the German base, the bank spread north and east to Cracow, Breslau and Danzig, north and west via Nuremberg, Leipzig, Frankfurt, Cologne and of course Antwerp, south to Innsbruck, Venice and Rome, south-west to Lisbon and Seville.[4]

This typology, however, needs refinement, and we need to take account of those towns which – without necessarily experiencing dramatic growth – provided the Reformation with its social foundations. In other words, the economic and political significance of towns should not distract attention from their dynamism as centres of new ideas.

Boom towns

No part of the peninsula of Asia referred to as Europe is very far from the sea.[5] In some ways, urban expansion in the sixteenth century is a reminder of the importance of this basic fact. The towns of the Middle Ages were service centres for the trade of the Baltic in the north and the Mediterranean in the south, and landlocked towns linked the two zones overland. In the sixteenth century, the pull westward of the Atlantic broke the north–south chain, and the sudden importance of the new axis is emphasised by increased maritime activity in and from specific ports, a reminder that the mature structures of commercial enterprise were of infinitely greater significance than the occasional weak embryo of industrial capitalism. That said, the sixteenth century witnessed an extraordinary reorientation of its commercial perspective. The Baltic and the Mediterranean have to be seen not just in relation to each other, but in relation to the Atlantic (see Map 4.1). While the importance of towns in the Middle Ages can be seen in terms of their capacity to grow in clusters, in the sixteenth century we can identify several centres which formed a coherent commercial network even though they were widely separated geographically.

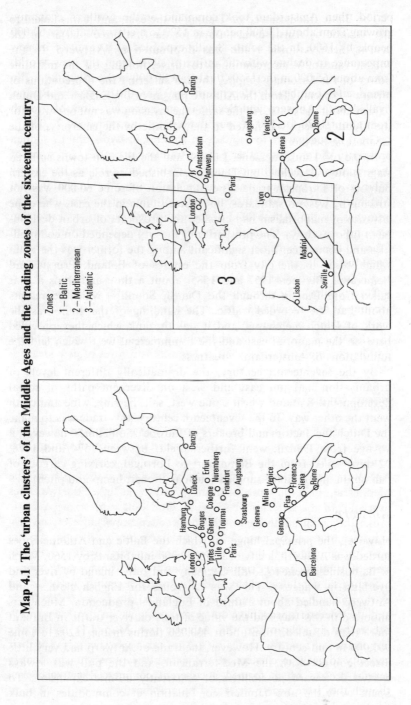

Map 4.1 The 'urban clusters' of the Middle Ages and the trading zones of the sixteenth century

Zones
1 – Baltic
2 – Mediterranean
3 – Atlantic

The Baltic trade centred on Danzig in the east, and it was linked to the Atlantic by Amsterdam, though for the first three-quarters of the century, the Atlantic trade was dominated by Antwerp. In the Mediterranean, Venice continued to thrive, holding off the maritime power of the Ottoman Empire, though suffering the depredations of pirates – especially from the Atlantic powers of the English and Dutch – from about the 1580s. All the same, the invasion was not one-way, for the Mediterranean was linked to the Atlantic by the enterprise of the Genoese in Seville.

In the old Hanseatic zone, Lübeck and the Flemish towns suffered stagnation and decline, but Danzig refurbished its role as the eastern outpost of European trade. The population of some 60,000 was not striking by western standards, but it was titanic in the east, where the advance of manorialism had crushed the prospects of urban development (above, ch. 1). The prosperity of the city depended on commodities and commerce. Most significant among the former was the grain which came to the city from the estates of Poland, Prussia and Pomerania. Between 1557 and 1585, about a thousand ships a year sailed from Danzig through the Danish Sound – which represents about half the recorded traffic. The handling of the grain was the work of Dutch merchants, and it was the link which they provided between the manorial east and the commmercial west which laid the foundations of Amsterdam's greatness.

By the seventeenth century, the dramatically different levels of urbanisation had put east and west on divergent paths of social development. Rye and wheat came west; salt, herring, wine and cloth went the other way. In the seventeenth century, this trade was to make the Dutch the 'factors and brokers of Europe'. Sometimes, however, a voyage from Danzig went further afield. Between 1574 and 1578, 92 ships sailed from the Baltic port to Portugal, carrying cargoes of fish, grain and military supplies (such as timber, hemp and pitch).

Antwerp

However, the principal hinge on which the Baltic and Atlantic zones turned was Antwerp, a city of some 90,000 inhabitants by 1560. Much of its business went to south Germany and Italy, inland by river and overland in waggons. This was the route for English cloth – and Antwerp handled about a third of England's production. Much was imported in this way and the value of tolls on river traffic in Brabant more than doubled, from about 400,000 florins in the 1520s to some 900,000 in mid-century. However, the trade of Antwerp had very little direct contact with the Mediterranean, and the pull was always westward, toward possibilities of apparently infinite expansion. To Spain went the now familiar combination of commodities in bulk and luxuries. What a staggering variety the bald terms conceal! The Ruiz firm had factors and correspondents in Lisbon, Seville, Madrid, Florence, Lyon, Nantes, Rouen and Mexico as well as Antwerp. To Iberia they exported wax (especially for candles for the great religious festivals between February and Easter), corn, textiles, metal (copper and mercury as well as iron), tapestries, books from Antwerp's 56 printing houses, furs, amber. In return, from Biscay came salt vital to the Baltic fishing industry, oil for soap-makers, dried fruit and saffron. Yet it is the Atlantic dimension of the Iberian trade which is most significant in terms of Antwerp's economic supremacy. Antwerp enjoyed a world monopoly on the spices which Atlantic exploration had brought to Iberia: pepper, ginger, cloves, cinnamon, mace, plus the sugar grown in the Canaries, Madeira and the Azores. There were alum and dyestuffs (such as indigo and cochineal) for producers of textiles, and cotton which came from India and Brazil. Merchants in Antwerp handled some 10 million florins of exports per year in the mid-1540s – 33 per cent of them by sea – about 75 per cent of the total exports of the Netherlands.

The wheels of commerce were oiled by credit, and although there were more than a hundred different types of coin in circulation in the city in the mid-century, very little of it needed to change hands in the conduct of business. A new Exchange, the *Beurs*, was built in 1531 to house the money market. Interest rates on short-term loans halved from 20 per cent to 10 between about 1510 and 1550. No doubt this attracted the colonies of foreign merchants – German, English, Portuguese and Italian – and perhaps it fuelled a species of 'popular capitalism' – the individual and collective enterprise of small-scale investors – which linked the world of high finance and international trade to craft-based manufactures. There was much retail credit – which might extend for two years – and there were high profits even in small-scale enterprises such as those run by members of the mercers' guild, one of the three corporations (the other two were boatmen and textile workers) which controlled the organisation of labour.

Sculptors, painters, glaziers, makers of majolica, of harpsichords, of buttons, all worked for export. In the first three-quarters of the century, Antwerp prospered on pepper from the Portuguese discoveries, then silver from the New World controlled by Spain, and then on peace: the Treaty of Cateau-Cambrésis (1559) ended the wars of Habsburg and Valois which had dominated international politics for so long (below, ch. 10). In 1568, just as the storm broke in Flanders, an Italian observer, Lodovico Guicciardini, beheld Antwerp at the height of its power. He observed that, historically speaking, Portuguese spices had been the great stimulus to growth, attracting investment from the great German banks, those of Fugger, Welser and Hochstätter, and trade and finance were tied to an extraordinary multiplicity of manufactures:

Now as to the kind and number of crafts exercised in this city, one can almost say in a single word – all. For here they make cloth, linens of every kind, tapestry, Turkish carpets and fustians; armour and all other munitions of war; they carry on tanning, painting, dyeing, colour-making, gilding, silvering, glass-making in the Venetian style; they make every kind of mercery, of gold, of silver, of silk, of thread, of wool, and small wares of metals of all kinds and other things beyond number. They also make here all kinds of silk cloth, such as velvet, satin, damask, sarsenet, taffeta, and others; but what is more, from their own silkworms, and contrary almost to nature and to the climate of this country, they produce and weave silk itself, although in small quantity. This, in addition to what comes to them from outside (which is of inestimable value), they work up in all ways and manners. They refine in quantity, with great industry and skill, metals, wax, sugar, and other merchandise. And it is only here that vermilion, which we call 'cinnabar', is made.

Letters from Portuguese merchants confirm the picture, and a Venetian, Giovanni Zonca, found the social atmosphere far more liberated than his native city, and his letters home enthuse about skating, oysters, girls and free speech. Zonca's letters also register a note of disquiet concerning rumours of Spain's intention to introduce the Inquisition. This would have been a threat to Portuguese merchants of Jewish descent trading in Antwerp. In the event, however, the good times were consumed by fire and sword in the infamous sack of 1576 and the debilitating siege of 1585 in which Parma starved the city into submission.[6]

Venice

While Antwerp rose and fell in the north, Venice endured in the south. As an antidote to talk of the 'decline' of the Mediterranean, we might recall that the population of Venice in the 1560s was probably close to 170,000 – nearly double that of Antwerp. Losses from frequent bouts of plague were made good by immigrants from the mainland, where the various provinces of the Venetian state each had a population of between 150,000 and 300,000. There was a remarkable recovery even after the dreadful plague of 1575–7. Only with the devastation of the plague of 1630 did it become clear that the population of the metropolis could only be sustained by the demographic ruin of the mainland provinces.

Despite the competition from the Portuguese Atlantic route and the pressure of the Turkish advance, Venice was to benefit from the revival of the Mediterranean spice trade in mid-century, causing a drop in prices in Antwerp. In the 1560s, some 4.5 million pounds of spices –

mostly pepper – arrived in the market at Alexandria, and the Venetians continued to play a key role in bringing it west. One young nobleman, Alessandro Magno, loaded a single cargo of some 500,000 pounds in 1561. As a manufacturing centre, Venice remained the envy of Europe. The Arsenal supplied more than half the fleet of the Holy League at Lepanto in 1571 (below, ch. 11). Opportunities lost to the Turks in the Levant were made good by the disruption of the Italian mainland by war, which enabled the Venetians to establish a powerful woollen industry, with production growing from a bare 1,300 pieces of cloth in 1513 to more than 27,000 in 1592. In other respects too, Venice remained at least the equal of Antwerp: glassware, jewellery and lace abounded, so too did wax and sugar. Northerners – including the Fuggers – still came to Venice to learn business techniques, capitalism was most definitely a popular phenomenon, and in 1568 the 400 or so masters of the mercers' guild could command resources of at least 500,000 ducats.

The last quarter of the century was less happy for the Venetians. The effects of the plague of 1575 were compounded by bank failures, by the depredations of pirates and wrecks – there were some 250 losses to privateers, 350 to rocks in the period 1592 to 1609, and by the early seventeenth century, insurance costs had rocketed to around 50 per cent of the value of the cargo. Yet in 1600, Venice was still the centre of a territorial state of about 1.5 million people, and – unlike Antwerp – the city itself had remained peaceful and unconquered. In 1499, the French ambassador, Philippe de Commynes, had warned that the Venetians were 'on the road to future greatness', ten years later another ambassador had fulminated extravagantly against their design to subjugate the whole of Europe. That these predictions were not ultimately fulfilled is not necessarily a symptom of Venice's decline. More remarkable is that in 1499, the Venetians suffered a damaging naval defeat at Zonchio at the hands of the Turks, and in 1509 lost the whole of the mainland state to the armies of the League of Cambrai. Yet the Venetians continued to fight off the Turks throughout the century, contributed hugely to the victory of the Holy League at Lepanto, and recovered the mainland state within four short years of its loss. Of course, the Venetian economy, tied to the established markets of the Mediterranean, could not in the long term compete with the Atlantic powers, but that long term goes beyond the confines of the century.[7]

Genoa and Seville

Genoa, the city which linked the Mediterranean to the Atlantic, did not preserve its political independence. Braudel has described the period from about 1557 to about 1627 as 'the age of the Genoese'. They had already given proof of their adaptability. After the defeat by Venice at the end of the fourteenth century, the Genoese concentrated their energies in their own city and – as was to happen in the cases of Antwerp and Venice – the populace at large became involved in the creation of commercial profits. Despite the sack of 1522 – scarcely less horrendous than what Rome was to experience five years later – the city's population remained buoyant at 60,000–70,000. The city, however, was much less significant than its citizens, who were dispersed. By 1500, they had already established themselves in Iberia at Lisbon, Medina del Campo, Valladolíd, and, most important, at Seville. From this centre – a port 54 miles from the sea – the Genoese effectively opened up the New World for the Spaniards. They had helped to fill the gaps left in Castilian enterprise by the expulsion of the Jews in 1492. The founding charter of the Genoese colony dates from the very next year, by which time Francesco Pinelo had invested the first instalment of some 1.4 million *maravedis* in the voyages of another Genoese businessman, the agent of the Centurione firm, one Christopher Columbus. By 1534, Seville had a population of about 50,000, and this had practically doubled by the last decade of the century. Contemporaries were well aware of the explanation, and as Father Tomas de Mercado put it:

> Was not Seville and all Andalusia before this event the utmost point and end of all land, and now it is the middle to which come the best and most esteemed of the Old World . . . to be carried to the New.

Over the same period in which the population doubled, 1530 to 1590, the value of precious metals imported to the city from the New World had risen from 1 million *pesos* to 30 million. Through the *Casa de Contratación*, the Genoese handled the treasure which was mortgaged to them in return for loans. The other bulk commodity imported was sugar. Obligingly, the Genoese helped to sustain the productivity of the plantations by sending black slaves in the other direction, taking advantage of prices in Mexico which rose from about 45 ducats per head in 1528 to 100 ducats in 1559.

However, by the second half of the century, the Genoese had clearly begun to separate financial services from trade in goods. Between 1519 and 1556, the Spanish crown had borrowed about 39 million *ducados* – nearly 40 per cent of it from the Genoese. From 1550, the Cataro bank was providing some 200,000 *maravedis* a year – to be repaid at 13 per cent interest. In 1554, Charles V borrowed about 200,000 *maravedis* from the partnership of Negron and Lercaro; the Gentil company supplied a further 315,000.

One reason for the Genoese concentration on high finance was the development of a spirited enterprise among the Sevillians themselves.

Unusually in an Iberian context, aristocrats traded and traders became aristocrats. As in Antwerp, the small investor was prominent; as in Antwerp, manufactures in Seville met the demands for luxuries amongst the rich. Of the city's 60 guilds, the largest were those of the embroiderers, the silversmiths, the engravers, and the painters – soap-making was one of the larger-scale enterprises. But amidst the fountains and coaches were the poor: according to Cervantes, Seville was 'the refuge of the outcast' and the outcasts – Jews, Moriscos, slaves, those to whom the guilds were closed – often sought work in the port or stole in the Arenal. In terms of two economic worlds, one of banking services and the other of luxury manufactures, in terms of the popular capitalism which linked them, Seville was a typical boom town. Yet it had no political freedom. The Genoese tied Seville to the Crown by a silver thread. The port city, Seville, depended on the capital city, Madrid. The banks in the port were ruined by the monarchy in the capital.[8]

Lyon

The major inland beneficiary of the great urban expansion of the sixteenth century was Lyon. The city was linked to the Atlantic by the interests of its merchants in spices, and in silver – the king of France regarded Lyon as his 'Peru'. Lyon was a society which retained its 'medieval' character through the survival of groups long familiar on the urban scene – shopkeepers, artisans, lawyers and clerics. Beyond this spectrum, however, were new extremes of wealth and poverty, especially in the city's new industries, printing and silk manufacture, which depended on merchant capital rather than artisan production. Unlike some previous examples, Lyon's fortunes depended on 'big business' rather than on 'popular capitalism'. Two silk merchants, Voisin and Durier, were said to employ between 800 and 1,000 people. Yet the boom did not last. Lyon's prosperity faded as civil war raged.[9]

The survival of Danzig and Venice, and the future greatness of Amsterdam and London, owed much to the tight interaction of economic and political power. Antwerp, Genoa and Seville had little say in their own political destinies. Too many political considerations were beyond the cities' control. Increasingly, European political life centred on capitals.

Capitals

The emergence of capital cities is a clear reflection of a long-term process of political centralisation. In this regard, Florence retained its precocity, emerging as a clearly defined capital, the seat of sovereign institutions. A splendid court surrounded the Medici and out of the aristocratic establishment grew a bureaucracy comfortably housed in purpose-built offices (the Uffizi).[10] The duchy established in Florence in 1530 (a grand duchy from 1569) was not a power to tilt the scales in sixteenth-century Europe, or even in Italy where Naples and Milan were the nerve centres of Spanish power. Indeed, for much of the sixteenth century, the character of political centres often reflected the composite nature of states: the Baroque capitals of absolute monarchy were to be a seventeenth-century phenomenon. Charles V was essentially an itinerant ruler, and his autobiography records his movements from Valladolíd to Augsburg to Regensburg to Monzon, Toledo, Worms, Bruges, Utrecht. Vienna, on the other hand, was not to become the seat of the Austrian Habsburgs until Leopold I made it so in 1658.

However, the three case-histories which most clearly illustrate the importance of the capital in a territorial state are Madrid, London, and Paris, and it is worth examining each in turn.

Madrid

In the 1540s, Madrid was a city of no more than 30,000 people. By 1597, its population had more than doubled to around 65,000. This is because it had become the political centre of Philip II's monarchy. In 1561, Philip moved his court there. The claims of Valladolíd or Toledo were ignored, and although Madrid is the geographical centre of Spain, the establishment of the capital there appears to have been an otherwise arbitrary choice. It marked the end of the peripatetic style of rulership which had so exhausted Charles V, and, fittingly, the Emperor was laid to rest in the Escorial, which Philip began in 1563. Indeed, the Escorial seems a somewhat bizarre political centre for a metropolis. It was a place in which to escape from the world rather than involve oneself in its affairs. For Charles, it was a mausoleum, for Philip a palace and a monastery. Indeed, its unworldly concerns were reflected in its layout, 207 metres by 161, planned according to the proportions of the grid on which St Lawrence met his martyrdom. Here dwelt the royal family with a household of some 2,000 servants and counsellors, though few of them influenced the remote mental world of the king, whose maxim of government was 'trust none but yourself'. The asphyxiatingly detached world of the court was reflected in the entirely parasitic city nearby. It is as though Madrid was a city in which people stood around waiting to live off the court, and in the meantime lived off the country. Madrid consumed without producing, and periodic appropriations of all wheat, wine and bread within a radius of 50 miles were the ruin of other centres, sucking the life-blood out of Toledo. The economy of the city existed only to serve a set of political residents. A few people made coaches, many more watched them roll by, luxury services for the court contrasted with the poverty of the urban population, yet there was a curious harmony between the unproductive world of the élite and its parody, the unproductive world of the *picarós*.[11]

London

What a contrast with London, where the economy fed the state and vice versa. And what a strident reminder that industrialisation is by no means the only explanation of massive urban growth. With good reason, Thomas Platter remarked in 1599 that 'London is the capital of England and so superior to other English towns that London is not said to be in England, but rather England to be in London'. In terms of sheer population growth, London seemed far more important than England. The single city accounts for half the increase in the population of Britain in the sixteenth and seventeenth centuries. In our period, the most striking phase of growth would appear to be from 1550 to 1600, during which time, the number of people in the city rose from 80,000 to a staggering 200,000. This perhaps reflects a change in the pattern of the city's economic life. Until the 1540s, London's trade was essentially wool exported by the Merchant Adventurers to Antwerp: one commodity, one company, one market. Ninety per cent of England's wool was marketed in this way. In the latter half of the century, especially when Antwerp's supremacy was shaken, there was considerable diversification. The formation of the Muscovy Company opened a broader commercial horizon and showed the penetrative power of European maritime enterprise, while in 1569, the Adventurers, with some reluctance, moved their staple from Antwerp to Hamburg. By the 1570s, London was the basis of England's impact on the wider world, which was much more noticeable after this date as the city emerged from the shadow of Antwerp.

By the end of the century, the commercial dynamism of London had apparently sent other ports into decay, and the attractions of the metropolis had drawn people from all walks of life and skills and wares of all sorts into its orbit. As John Stow remarked, the capital was rather a stimulus than a parasite:

> I have shortly to answer the accusation of those men which charge London with the loss and decay of many or most of the ancient cities, corporate towns and markets within this realm by drawing from them to herself alone, say they, both all trade of traffic by sea and the retailing of wares and exercise of manual arts also. Touching navigation, which (I must confess) is apparently decayed in many port towns and flourisheth only or chiefly at London, I impute that partly to the fall of the Staple [a decline in the wool trade] . . . As for retailers . . . and handicraftsmen, it is no marvel if they abandon the country towns and resort to London; for not only the court (which is

nowadays much greater and more gallant than in former times, and which was wont to be contented to remain with a small company sometimes at an abbey or priory, sometimes at a bishop's house, and sometimes at some mean manor of the king's own) is now for the most part either abiding at London, or else so near unto it, that the provision of things most fit for it may easily be fetched from thence; but also by occasion thereof the gentlemen of all shires do fly and flock to this city, the younger sort of them to see and show vanity, and the elder to save the cost and charge of hospitality and housekeeping. For hereby it cometh to pass that the gentlemen being either for a good portion of the year out of the country, or playing the farmers, graziers, brewers or such like more than gentlemen were wont to do within the country, retailers and artificers, at the least of such things as pertain to the back or belly, do leave the country towns where there is no vent and do fly to London, where they be sure to find ready and quick market.

The passage shows London consuming to a purpose: a great centre of demand, a social nucleus, but also thriving on production. London imported in quantity raw materials, food and manufactures, but unlike Madrid, its own productive sector proved immensely energetic. There were plenty of opportunities in domestic service or delivery, but a quarter of the London labour force was employed in the building trades, in clothing, leather and metal. In the 1550s, the city's trades were absorbing as many as 1,500 apprentices a year, by the end of the century as many as 5,000. The economy was tied to the business of government through public finance, and government itself was more businesslike than in Madrid or Paris. There was a courtly establishment of about a thousand people under Elizabeth, and by 1600, the London season was generating a good deal of conspicuous consumption along continental lines. Yet the attractions of another type of court were stronger, more positive. The courts of Chancery, Augmentations and King's Bench all expanded their activites, and young men flocked to the Inns of Court to train as lawyers. About 750 young gentlemen took up the profession every year – about 10 per cent of the capital's annual immigration. Thus – for all the crime and poverty – London was the point at which political and economic life intersected and advanced. A sovereign state which governed by the rule of law was supported by the prosperity generated in the metropolitan economy.[12] The relationship between the capital and the state was nothing like so stable in France.

Paris

Paris, by contrast with Madrid, was the traditional seat of government in France, so its rise to prominence was not a phenomenon of the sixteenth century. Its population grew to around 200,000, though in 1549 there were apparently only 10,000 houses, which – unless twenty people were living in each – seems to indicate a substantial 'floating' population. Like Madrid, Paris was a parasite, dominating the river traffic and food resources of the surrounding area within a radius of about 40 kilometres. The economic energies of Paris were consumed in supplying itself, and it was too busy in that pursuit to act as a market for the rest of the country. Some 2,000 horses delivered vast quantities of meat twice a week: poultry, boar, pork, venison, teal, duck, lark. According to one estimate, dating from 1599, the city consumed 200 bulls, 2,000 sheep and 70,000 chickens and pigeons every day. There were 5,000 porters delivering food and carrying wares, and production was almost exclusively concerned with luxury and ostentation: gloves, scabbards, playing cards, furniture, pictures, tapestries. There may have been as many as 1,800 tennis courts, and these and other pleasures such as drinking and brawling, were among the pastimes of a university population which may have been as high as 30,000.

Paris was a capital city, but the state could not control it. Only in the seventeenth century did the absolutist state stamp its character on the city's buildings. Lawlessness in the sixteenth century was often a symptom of political contempt as well as a product of poverty and overcrowding. In 1533, a *prévot* expressed to the Paris Parlement the king's concern about the lack of order in the city – which had evidently threatened the royal person:

> He said that every night in this city some unknown persons gather in various troops and bands, who do nothing else than brawl during the night, and they have had the temerity to enter the king's chamber at the Louvre and that three, carrying weapons under their cloaks, had been caught, who might inform on their fellows and that it was necessary to strengthen the watch of this city so as to avoid all seditions, tumults and scandals. To this effect the king had commanded him to confer with the governors of the city concerning the problem of the poor, because a large number were to be found within it and even around the king's lodging in spite of the fact that the court had offered good and holy provision and that the king had instructed it to take such action as it would deem necessary regarding the said poor, notwithstanding any oppositions or appeals.

As the century wore on, the collapse of royal authority amid civil war was nowhere more obvious than in Paris itself. In the case of Spain, the problems of government were in the peripheral territories, not in Madrid. In France, the monarchy had little authority in Paris itself. In February 1573 – a few months after the Massacre of St Bartholomew

– Catherine de' Medici set off for vespers with her daughter, the Queen of Navarre, and an entourage:

> The students of Paris, who are wont to indulge in scuffles with the servants of the court, had collected in bands outside the College [of Jesuits], where they began quarrelling and brawling with the muleteers. When the courtiers and the Princes came out of the College and were about to bestride their horses and enter their coaches, the students attacked them with rapiers and cudgels, surrounded the carriages with great turbulence, thrust their hands into the bosom of the Queen of Navarre and mockingly stroked her plumes. The Cardinal de Lorraine they pushed into the deepest hole in the deepest mud. The aged Queen they not only assaulted with unsheathed foils, but also insulted in obscene, foul and lewd terms, which it would be shameful to repeat.

What made the disorder of Paris so disturbing to the public weal was its association with religious unrest. In 1534, when the monarchy of Francis I was still secure, placards were posted up throughout the city – and on the door of the king's chamber – denouncing 'the great and insufferable papal mass'. By 1558, a Protestant gathering might involve 4,000 people. Henry II's death in 1559 prevented his embarking on the war on heresy he had sworn to undertake in the Treaty of Cateau-Cambrésis. The king himself, Charles IX, was involved in the Massacre of St Bartholomew in 1572, and thereafter disorder became chaos. In 1588, Catholics built barricades which excluded Henry III from his own capital – and the University of the Sorbonne pronounced that the king's subjects were absolved from their obedience to him. Only when Parisians were sure of their king's allegiance to the Catholic cause could he expect an acknowledgement of his authority, and this was what forced Henry IV to acknowledge that Paris was 'worth a mass'.[13]

In the case of Madrid, a capital took shape in accordance with purely political functions. London, on the other hand, combined its role as the seat of sovereignty with a concentration of the economic power of the kingdom. Paris was a parasitic and political capital like Madrid, but it was more disorderly, paralysed by religious violence in the later sixteenth century. From that point of view, it points toward another urban type: the town whose importance was determined by the vigour of its religious life.

Religious centres

In a fundamental sense, all pre-industrial towns were religious centres, for churches governed time and space. The day's routine was punctuated by church bells – look at the towers which dominate contemporary depictions of Nuremberg or Venice. Market-places were often located in church squares – in Venice at San Marco, Santi Apostoli, San Giacomo dell'Orio, San Polo. The church's calendar was the point of reference for fairs – two of those held at Lyon took place at Easter and All Saints'. And of course those days when work was forbidden were religious holidays – 90 or so in most places, a staggering 161 in pre-Reformation Germany. On such occasions, the urban space was often dominated by civic processions which celebrated a city's special relationship with its patron saint – St Mark in Venice, St John the Baptist in Florence – and though godly cities in the north did away with saints' days, they always sought to observe the sabbath.

Indeed, the identification of a city with religious life could determine its economic and political significance. Here there is a paradox, for, as we shall see, the towns most closely associated with religious reform were also the most remote from economic and political change, retaining their 'medieval' character.[14] On the other hand, the city most closely associated with the decadence of traditional religious forms would probably have been the least alien to a visitor from the twentieth century.

Rome was as grand a capital as Madrid, Paris or London. It was not so large, though its population grew from around 54,000 in 1527 to about 105,000 by 1600. Montaigne, who visited the city in 1581 – and felt compelled to remain several months – observed nothing but leisure: 'the town hardly changes its character for a working day or a holiday'. There were about 70 cardinals in the city, and their households employed over 10,000 people. This made Rome 'a city all court and nobility: everybody takes his share in the ecclesiastical idleness'. He was struck that there were 'no trading streets . . . nothing but palaces and gardens', and 'usually the effort of leaving the house is made solely to go from street to street without any fixed object' – and there were about 900 coaches in the city to ease the strain of such excursions. This much would have been familiar in Madrid, yet Rome had its own distinctive bustle, and it excelled all the cities of Europe in its modernity. This was manifest in a variety of ways. Rome was a genuinely international city in its communications with other places. The traditional networks of papal power involved couriers who sped to Florence, Genoa and Milan, Fano, Rimini, Venice and Bologna, and then on to Lyon, Spain, Flanders, Sicily. Moreover, according to Montaigne, Rome was 'the most cosmopolitan city in the world', and he specified that it surpassed even Venice in this regard, for in Venice foreigners 'were like people living in somebody else's home'. Cosmopolitanism was not just a question of residence, for what made Rome so important as a city was the number of visitors. In 1575, there were about 400,000 pilgrims to the city, more than 500,000 in 1600. This raised problems of accommodation and traffic familiar to the twentieth century. Rome was noted for the excellence of its hotels – one for every 230 inhabitants. Building programmes in the city – unlike anywhere else in Europe before the seventeenth century – involved palaces and churches not in isolation but in relation to each other. All roads led to Rome, and Rome was unique for its thoroughfares. The popes took this so seriously that nearly all of them are commemorated in the name of the street which each had built: the *Via Alessandrina* of Alexander VI (about 1500), the *Via Giulia* of Julius II (1503–13), the *Via Leonina* of Leo X, the *Via Paolina* of Paul III. The *Via Pia* of Pius IV (1561–2) opened Europe's first 'axial city vista', which took John Evelyn's breath away almost a hundred years later. Sixtus V made his mark with fountains, and in all 35 were built between 1575 and the end of the century. Even though the Reformation is sometimes considered symptomatic of economic and social change, no Protestant city could compete with the size and splendour of the Rome of the Counter-Reformation.[15]

As the example of Catholic Rome makes clear, one of the central features of the century is that the impulse for religious reform cannot be explained in terms of any simple relationship between urban life and economic or political change. Put another way, boom towns and capitals were not the breeding ground of Protestantism. Here the thesis – misleadingly identified with Max Weber[16] – which connects Protestantism with the rise of capitalism breaks down irredeemably. The port of Hamburg opted for the Lutheran confession, but Augsburg wavered – and we should always remember that an agent of the Fuggers, the greatest capitalists of the age, accompanied the infamous hawker of papal indulgences, Johann Tetzel. Curiously – and what a contrast with the modern, cosmopolitan Rome of the sixteenth century – the most convincing explanation of the impulse of German and Swiss cities to opt for religious reform is not their modernity but their archaism. Their social structures and their cultural life reflected the solidarity of medieval corporate institutions – guilds, confraternities, patrician families – rather than new patterns of economic organisation. And even this needs to be set in a limited chronological context – the first three decades of the century – when other sources of support for reform were less secure.

The towns of Germany with a population of more than 10,000 accounted for a total of less than 400,000 people, in turn less than 5 per cent of the German population of something between 12 and 14 million. The defeat of the peasants in 1526 led to religious indifference in rural areas by the 1540s; and what gave the reformed churches large numbers of at least nominal members were the decisions of princes to adopt Lutheranism, as the Peace of Augsburg recognised. At one level, nothing could be more fragmentary than the pattern of urban reform. According to one recent survey, of some 2,000 towns, only about fourscore have been studied in detail, and even those have revealed a bewildering variety of historical experience, explicable only through strict attention to local circumstances.

Even concentration on a clearly defined type of town, the imperial free cities (which recognised the superior authority of the emperor alone and not that of a local territorial prince), reveals enormous diversity. Of these 85 cities, 65 of them directly subject to the Empire, the most important in terms of size and function were Nuremberg, Augsburg, Ulm and Frankfurt am Main. Of middling proportions were Worms, Constance, Heilbronn, Reutlingen, Esslingen and Nördlingen. But Zell am Harmesbach enjoyed the status of a free city, even though its population was probably no more than a few hundred. In addition, the size of the urban population alone is no indication of the extent of the city's territorial authority: Ulm controlled an area of some 500 square miles, Augsburg, which was a larger city, controlled virtually none.

Broadening the discussion to take account of other towns, shows that the relationship to other political authorities becomes paramount – but no more illuminating. The weakness of episcopal power might have spurred some citizens towards reform in Bremen (18,000 people) where the bishop was an absentee, but the very presence of prince-bishops in Mainz (6,000), Erfurt (15,000), Worms (less than 10,000) and Regensburg (only 23,000 in 1800) may have increased the impatience of some sectors of the local populations. The power and inclinations of secular princes would also influence the course of reform. The Wittelsbachs had designs on Regensburg and Augsburg, the Hohenzollern on Nuremberg. Pragmatic considerations of political and economic self-interest help to explain why Cologne did not opt for the reform, and why the authorities hesitated in Regensburg in 1534 or Speyer in 1538. Augsburg wavered before opting for a reform along Zwinglian lines in 1537 – though Charles V insisted on a reversion to Catholicism in 1548.

It would be misleading to speak of 'towns' opting to support the Reformation when the option was made only by certain influential categories of people: patrician rulers who might be pressed by dissatisfied artisans, with some trades more likely to agitate than others. That said, and hazardous though any generalisation may be, it seems possible to identify two geographical areas responding to two different spiritual fields of force (see Map 4.2). The first of these is a group of free cities where the authorities opted for a reform in accordance with the ideas of Luther. These were Lübeck, Goslar, Bremen, Hamburg, Lüneberg, Braunschweig and Göttingen. Luther's influence extended as far south as Franconia, where the major centres of Lutheranism were Nuremberg, Windesheim and Weissenberg, with secondary nuclei in Dunkelsbühl, Schwäbisch Hall and Heilbronn. In the 1540s, Regensburg, Schweinfurt, Rothenberg and Donauwörth were to follow suit. Further south, in Swabia, the inspiration was Swiss. The limits of this field of force are marked by a northern line running eastward from Strasbourg through Esslingen to Augsburg, with a southern boundary in the city of Constance. In that area, Reutlingen is the sole exception to a pattern of Swiss-inspired reform.

These two zones shared a common heritage of political independence: this links Nuremberg, Augsburg, Strasbourg and Constance, for instance. Here was the 'archaic' scenario of clusters of small towns capable of asserting civic autonomy in the communal tradition of the Middle Ages. In recent history, the cities of Switzerland had asserted their independence in the most dramatic manner. The war of the Swabian League in 1499–1500 resulted in the effective withdrawal from the Empire of Zurich, Lucerne, Berne, Schaffhausen and Solothurn. Basel did likewise in 1501. This was partly due to sheer military power. The Swiss had a tradition of defeating the Austrians. In 1477, their pikemen had brought about the destruction of Burgundian power, and at the end of the century they triumphed over the imperial armies. At a crucial phase of the reform, Nuremberg showed it could stand up to Frederick V of Brandenburg-Ansbach, the citizens of Worms and Speyer refused to be cowed by their bishops.

Urban independence made the Edict of Worms, condemning Luther, unenforceable, for the towns refused to recognise any imperial edict designed 'to forbid us in any way the Word of God'. It was that sort of independence which Charles V recognised as the chief threat to the unity of his Empire, for in his years of triumph between 1547 and 1552 he abolished the constitutions of about thirty cities.[17]

Sometimes perhaps, historians have concentrated too heavily on why urban authorities did or did not opt for one type of religious reform or another, neglecting the importance of their capacity to exercise a choice. Luther laid greater emphasis on individual spirituality, Zwingli on corporate solidarity. Both appealed to the townspeople of Germany not because the towns had changed, but rather because they had stayed the same: manageable political entities, face-to-face societies with a political shell resistant to alien tyranny. Once the tyranny was identified as absentee bishops – Montaigne speaks of one in Constance drawing 40,000 crowns from the see even though he resided in Rome – confessors who sought to find out the intimate details of sex life, a calendar which interfered with dietary habits and work practices, indulgences better used 'to wipe one's arse', the self-contained, introverted world of small towns was the obvious place to experiment with spiritual self-sufficiency. However, to understand why certain ideas might prove attractive in a particular social milieu does not explain the power of the ideas themselves. Having examined the context of religious reform, we need to examine the texts of the reformers, turning our attention from the world to the Word.

Map 4.2 The urban Reformation, *c*.1520-*c*.1550

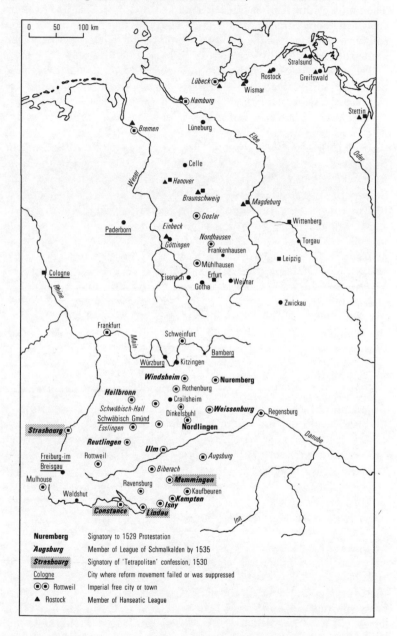

Source: Euan Cameron, *The European Reformation* (Oxford: Oxford University Press, 1991), p. 211.

Part II
The Word

5 New dimensions

Humanism and its implications

The first part of this book examined some of the sources of change in sixteenth-century society within the flexible framework of lordly power. Having identified the potentiality of movement, however, we need to explain why change took a particular direction, and in this regard it is necessary to examine the corpus of ideas current in Europe in 1500 and the implications of those ideas for subsequent European development. If such a discussion is to have any meaning at all, then we must establish a working definition of the term which is used to encapsulate the ideas of the Renaissance: humanism.

The spread of humanism from Italy to other parts of Europe is one of the principal sources of historical change in the sixteenth century, yet the term 'humanism' itself remains loose, vague and elusive. Distressingly, Renaissance humanism is difficult to define in positive terms, because it is so encrusted with the distorting glosses of subsequent eras – something, by the way, which the humanists themselves would have abhorred. Sometimes, our notions of humanism are shaped by nineteenth-century ideas of 'humanitarianism', the application of humane values to the way in which human beings relate to each other. Sometimes, humanism is identified with a secular philosophy which gives emphasis to man rather than God. This spectrum of ideas is too wide to be serviceable, for the first interpretation tends to emphasise the realisation of Christian values, while the other looks toward atheism. Both definitions are useful in that they show how momentous were the implications of humanism, but neither explains how a new way of thinking could produce such contradictions, and neither does justice to the tremendous diversity of ideas which humanism generated. To appreciate this point, we need to dispense with the idea of humanism as a set of values, still less as coherent philosophy. It is an advantage to bear. in mind the startling new possibilities which humanist ideas opened up, but we must be careful not to assume that these were realised within the more limited compass of the sixteenth century.

To appreciate what humanism was about, we might do worse than imitate the humanists themselves: return to the sources, strip away obfuscation and reveal the true nature of the original. In what follows, we shall be working with a narrow definition of humanism which, by exploring the potential of language, gave man a new place in time, and with a parallel set of developments in the visual arts which gave him a new sense of space. Both these modes of perception were fully mature in Italy by the end of the fifteenth century: what is distinctive about their spread to other parts of Europe in the sixteenth is their interaction in new contexts, and this process in many ways fertilised what is called the 'Scientific Revolution' of the seventeenth. At the same time, that initial distinction between humanist letters and the visual arts was sustained, for the application of humanist techniques to the study of the Bible was to prove influential amongst those who called for ecclesiastical reform in the north, while the visual arts played an equally large part in the Catholic revival in the Latin world.

The dynamism of humanist thought is all the more remarkable because humanism was not a broad programme of fixed principles which might make up a 'movement'. Even when defined narrowly, the most striking characteristic of humanism is its capacity for change. What 'humanists' had in common was not a philosophy, but a specific technical skill: the ability to understand and imitate the words of the ancient world, first those of the Romans and later those of the Greeks. The discovery – or recovery – of a delight in eloquence, in that capacity for speech which elevated man above the rest of creation – this was the humanist achievement. The possibilities which it opened up seemed endless, and this helps to explain those changes in the concerns of the humanists themselves which can be so hard to follow.[1]

It is possible to map out some of the most significant discoveries of the intellectual voyage. We set out from Italy, not purely because of the Renaissance of the fifteenth century, but also because Italy had never entirely lost contact with its Roman past. The ruins of Rome littered the cities of the peninsula, useful pieces of the wreckage had been used to build churches and palaces. In the middle of the twelfth century, Bishop Otto of Freising, the uncle of the Emperor Frederick Barbarossa, observed in some perplexity that the Lombards 'retained something of the Roman gentleness in their manners and speech'. That gentleness was conspicuously absent from the treatment which the Lombard communes gave the Emperor, and their victory at the battle of Legnano in 1176 secured what the Lombards had begun to refer to as the *libertas italica*. The Lombard League expressed its political aspirations in the language of classical republicanism – which helps to account for the strong links between humanism and politics in the Renaissance of the fifteenth century.[2]

However, the humanism of the Renaissance was a narrower phenomenon, and should be defined as such if we are to appreciate its significance. The term derives from the *studia humanitatis* of the Latin curriculum of the Middle Ages, which centred on seven subjects: four in the *quadrivium* (arithmetic, geometry, astronomy and music), which was the basic arts degree, and three in the *trivium* (that is to say grammar, rhetoric and logic). The humanist scholars reorganised priorities: they gave new emphasis to the importance of grammar and rhetoric, and applied them to the writing of history and poetry. The scholastic emphasis on logic, particularly when applied to metaphysics and moral philosophy, was something they derided as sterile – but for the time being we may set aside the educational aspirations of the humanists, for they need separate treatment in the context of educational institutions and social change (below, pp. 124–8), and examine instead the key stages in the development of humanist thinking. This involves a digression from the confines of the sixteenth century, but it would be misleading to summarise the complex of ideas known as the Renaissance as a period. Rather, it is important to emphasise the profundity of the cultural changes which had occurred since the fourteenth century and therefore the weight of their impact on Europe as a whole in the course of the sixteenth.

Given the cultural and political durability of the Roman tradition in Italy, it is misleading to think of Francesco Petrarca (Petrarch) (1304–1374) as the 'father of humanism', for he made less of a break with the medieval past than he himself assumed. He was an admirer of the Latin used by the ancient Romans, and of classical republicanism (he supported the experiments of Cola di Rienzo in Rome in 1347) yet in some ways his own modes of thought were typical of his time – the crisis and depression of the later fourteenth century. What could be more tied to its own age than the feelings of transience and despair which he expressed in the aftermath of the Black Death?

I had reached this point in my letter, and I was wondering what I should say further or what I should not say, and meanwhile, as is my custom, I was tapping the blank paper with my pen top. My action brought me a subject, for I reflected how in that brief interval time was flowing on, and I was flowing with it, slipping down, departing, or to use the right word, dying. We are continually dying: I while I am writing these words, you while you are reading them, others when they hear them or fail to hear them, we are all dying. I shall be dying when you read this, you die while I write, we both are dying, we all are dying, we are dying forever.

Yet it is this very sense of time which makes Petrarch's thinking so original. He had an attitude to the past which was quite new – so new that he helped to create our modern sense of periodisation. He did not develop a systematic philosophy to be compared with the universal vision of the scholastics, but in rethinking the relationship between his own world and the ancient world, he relocated man in history. He sought to return to the true texts of Roman authors, Cicero (106–43

BC) in particular, and to imitate their Latin. To achieve this, he had to remove the assumptions and corruptions of those who had copied the original manuscripts – many of them monks, we might remember. The period of conservation and corruption was, for Petrarch, an age of darkness which obscured the originals, and eventually it was described as an 'age which came between', or, in Latin, a *medium aevum*. And thus Petrarch's notion of what separated him from the classical past was to give us our concept of the 'Middle Ages'. Sometimes, he went so far as to remove that vast tract of time altogether, writing letters to Cicero and Socrates as though they were his contemporaries. In the Middle Ages, time was something which belonged to God (which was why ecclesiastics abhorred the taking of interest on sums of money purely because of the duration of the loan). Petrarch and the humanists who followed him gave man a new freedom in the exploration of the past, and since the remote past was also pagan, the concept of time became more secular.[3]

One of Petrarch's assumptions about the classical world was that thought itself needed time, time uncluttered with worldly concerns, what the Romans called *otium*, what we might call leisure. However, as the momentous process of scholarly research went ahead, more – and different – texts were collected. Petrarch's perceptions of Ancient Rome changed when Cicero's letters to Atticus came to light, for these showed the unworldly philosopher as a power-conscious lawyer deeply embedded in the dirty business of politics. The next generation of humanists had to take account of the possibilities of the active life rather than those of the contemplative life, of *negotium* rather than *otium*. By 1400, humanists were using the words of Cicero in politics rather than poetry, and they applied their knowledge of the shape and substance of Roman politics to the life of their own Florentine Republic. Thus opened that phase of humanist thinking identified with the 'civic life'. Leonardo Bruni (c.1370–1444) used the skills of Cicero – a lawyer, the strength of whose case depends on the persuasive powers of his oratory or rhetoric – to produce the propaganda of Florentine republicanism, extolling the virtues of freedom and warning of the dangers of tyranny. Bruni wrote a *Laudatio* of the Florentine Republic, and his target, Giangaleazzo Visconti, Duke of Milan, thought Bruni's words were worth a hundred lances.

Hitherto, the models to imitate – Seneca (c.5 BC–65 AD) and Quintilian (c.35–100 AD) as well as Cicero – were all Latin authors. Bruni, however, learned Greek, and the other half of the classical heritage came to occupy an increasingly prominent place in the interests of the humanists. This was especially so as the Turks threatened Constantinople, which pushed more Greek scholars – and more Greek texts – to the west. Some of the scholars came to the Council of Florence of 1439, and a meeting designed to heal divisions in the

Christian Church had more positive results in transforming once more the character of Florentine humanism. Amongst the scholars were Cardinal Bessarion and George Gemisthus Plethon and amongst the texts towered the works of Plato. What Aristotle had been to the schoolmen of the Middle Ages, Plato became for the humanists of the Renaissance: the essential point of reference. Indeed, he was the quintessential, for Plato's ideas helped to elevate the dignity of man to a position scarcely lower than that of God Himself. This quest for the sublime led to a renewed emphasis on the value of the contemplative life at the expense of the active. On the one hand, Plato taught men to seek God through the progressive refinement of the soul, and on the other he taught them to think in ideal terms in their relations with each other. European man in the sixteenth century was equipped both to abandon externals in his religious life and to seek Utopia in politics. Moreover, attempts to understand the workings of nature in platonic terms helped to build a long and not always steady bridge between magic and science, between 'mysticism' and 'rigorous observational technique'.[4]

The historical development of Renaissance humanism which we have so far mapped out is diffuse: a specific research technique, a potential for political involvement, a philosophical quest for the sublime, an inspiration to scientific inquiry. Yet these tendencies were like unstable elements in poorly sealed containers, and as the temperature of the environment rose in the sixteenth century, their combustion became ever more imminent. The first glow can be located in the career of a Roman humanist, Lorenzo Valla (1405/7–1457). He was a brilliant technician, most celebrated in his own time as the author of a work on the eloquence of Latin. He turned these skills to the service of a secular ruler when, in 1439, under the patronage of Alfonso of Naples, he wrote a book on the *Donation of Constantine*. The *Donation* was a document in which the first Christian emperor had, so it was alleged, granted Pope Sylvester I primacy over other patriarchs and an imperial authority in the western empire. People had for centuries thought it to be a fake. Valla proved that this was so through systematic criticism of the language used. Constantine was not a king, the author of the *Donation* clearly had no idea about the imperial insignia: no one in the fourth century would have used the word *phrygium* to mean the imperial tiara. Such distortions damn the author as a phony, and Valla exults in his rhetorical condemnation: 'May God destroy you, most depraved of mortals who attribute barbarous language to a cultured age!' To his eloquence and political service, Valla added speculations on the nature of the soul, particularly in a work on free will, which was an attack on medieval scholasticism. He went further still and applied his technique to another ancient text: the Bible. His *Adnotationes in Novum Testamentum* laid the foundations of 'Christian

humanism', which attempted to reform the Church by returning to its
first principles, thus providing a link between Renaissance learning and
the Reformation.

By the 1490s, John Colet, lecturing at Oxford, was comparing St
Paul's Epistle to the Romans with Suetonius's *Life* of the Emperor
Claudius. In 1504, a scholar already influenced by Valla's quest for
pure Latin came across a manuscript of the *Adnotationes* in the library
of a monastery near Louvain. In a previous visit to England, he had
made contact with Colet's enthusiasm for Plato: Desiderius Erasmus
(1467–1536) now had a model for his exploration of the text of the
Bible. Christianity too must return to its sources, and the corruptions
of the Vulgate text must be removed to reveal the Word of God.

With the introduction of Colet and Erasmus, we must be clear that
the spread of humanist ideas from Italy was not a question of slavish
imitation. Rather, we should understand humanism as liberating local
energies and combining with them. The piety of Erasmus drew its
strength from the devotional traditions of the Netherlands, especially
from the *devotio moderna*, that revolutionary effort to laicise the
monastery. The most famous product of this movement was a book
second only to the Bible in popularity in the late fifteenth century, *The
Imitation of Christ*, by Thomas à Kempis. Erasmus was to propagate
the ideal. What could be a more stirring call to lay self-discipline than
the injunction of Erasmus in *The Handbook of the Militant Christian*?:

> What I say about money also applies to honours, pleasure, health –
> in fact to the life of the body itself. Our determination to imitate
> Christ should be of such a nature that we have no time for these
> matters.

To imitate Christ, however, one needed to understand His message, the
good news spread by good messengers or 'evangelists':

> You must believe me when I say that there is really no attack from
> the enemy, no temptation so violent, that a sincere resort to Holy
> Writ will not easily get rid of it. There is no misfortune so sad that a
> reading of the Scriptures does not render bearable. Therefore, if you
> will but dedicate yourself entirely to the study of the Scriptures, if
> you meditate day and night on the divine law, nothing will ever
> terrorise you.

The closer one came to the words of those who knew Christ, the closer
one came to the Word of God:

> You must maintain at all times a high regard for the revealed word.
> It is genuine because it has its origins in the very mind of God. If
> you approach the Scriptures in all humility and with regulated

caution, you will perceive that you have been breathed upon by the Holy Will.

Humanism as a scholarly exercise was beginning to equip people to strip away externals, and remove centuries of accumulated rubbish, not just in terms of what they read, but in terms of how they behaved:

> But to place the whole of religion in external ceremonies is sublime stupidity. This amounts to revolt against the spirit of the Gospel and is a reversion to the superstitions of Judaism . . . Charity does not consist in many visits to churches, in mass prostrations before the statues of saints, in the lighting of candles, or in the repetition of designated prayers. Of all these things God has no need. Paul declares charity to be the edification of one's neighbour, the attempt to integrate all men into one body so that all men may become one in Christ, the loving of one's neighbour as one's self. Charity for Paul has many facets; he is charitable who rebukes the erring, who teaches the ignorant, who lifts up the fallen, who consoles the downhearted, who supports the needy.

His ridicule of ecclesiastical power structures continued and intensified in *The Praise of Folly*, which he completed in 1514. As is well-known, the Latin title, *Encomium Moriae*, was a pun on the name of his friend and admirer, Sir Thomas More, yet in the attack on the Church's fund-raising activities as an encouragement for superstition, it is easy to see why Erasmus could later be accused of Lutheranism:

> Then what shall we say about those who happily delude themselves with false pardons for their sins? They calculate the time to be spent in Purgatory down to the year, month, day, and hour as if it were a container that could be measured accurately with a mathematical formula. There are also those who think there is nothing they cannot obtain by relying on the magical prayers and charms thought up by some charlatan for the sake of his soul or for profit.[5]

Yet Erasmus was consistent in seeking the reform of a united church, not its division, and it is important to remember that after Luther's protest, and even until about 1530, Erasmus's ideas seemed to find almost universal approval. Henry VIII, Philip of Burgundy, the Prince-Bishop of Liège, the Archbishop of Mainz, the Duke of Bavaria, Charles V, the Archduke Ferdinand – all expressed their admiration, offering employment, or pensions, or benefices, and in the case of Francis I 'mountains of gold'.

Francis had wanted Erasmus to come to his new Collège de France, and French intellectual life had been buzzing with Erasmian ideas since the great man's visit to Paris in 1488. However, Frenchmen had already established direct contact with Italian humanists. Jacques Lefèvre d'Etaples (1450–1536) had visited Pico and Ficino in the 1480s. Like Erasmus, he sought to add wisdom and piety to eloquence, and he urged Christians to acquaint themselves with Scripture – his most important work was a translation of the New Testament into French (1523). However, discussion with the Venetian, Ermolao Barbaro, had made him more receptive to Aristotelianism than was Erasmus himself, and he prized medieval mystics as well as the Church fathers, an attitude which kept Christ quite definitely divine.

For François Rabelais (1490–1553), however, Erasmus was 'my spiritual father and mother'. As we shall see, the two men shared an aversion to contemporary monasticism (below, ch. 6), and Rabelais's full-blooded anti-clericalism can be interpreted as drawing strength from the traditions of popular culture. Yet Rabelais's most famous works, the adventures of *Gargantua* and *Pantagruel*, are so bizarre that they lend themselves to any interpretation – and then defeat it. The titles of the books are better known than the texts, which are virtually incomprehensible. This was probably the author's intention. They are not systematic, but their ramblings and ribaldry could be identified as humanist in their sheer delight in the possibilities of words, not those relating to the intellectual life of man, but to his physical being. The genius of Rabelais must be identified with copulation rather than contemplation, excrement rather than exegesis, and in his preoccupation with man as a physical being – he was, after all, trained in medicine – he links humanist ideas with some of the achievements of Renaissance artists.[6]

However, before we turn to the visual arts, we must highlight another episode in the history of that phase of humanist thinking identified with Erasmus. In the light of subsequent developments, the most intriguing of all the offers of advancement made to Erasmus was that which came from Cardinal Ximenes, proposing that Erasmus take up a bishopric in Spain. That Erasmus, the champion of reason and tolerance, might take up a post in the Church engaged in an inquisitorial war on heresy, the Church which was to spearhead the Counter-Reformation – what an incredible thought! Yet, before 1530, Erasmus's ideas of a harmonious Christendom appealed to those who entertained notions of universal rule in the reign of Charles V (above, ch.3), and his idea of tolerance as an expression of Christian love was attractive to the *conversos*, those Jews who had been baptised, but whose suspected lapses were the main object of the investigations which the Spanish Inquisition pursued. By 1530, with Charles once again occupied in war against France in Italy, the aggressive opponents of Erasmus were in the ascendant, and Erasmianism was linked with heresy. Those identified as supporters of Erasmus were to suffer for it.

The Valdes brothers – one of whom had been secretary to the Emperor – were prosecuted, as was Miguel de Eguía, the printer who had produced Erasmus's works at Alcalá.[7] It is a reminder of differences between writers and artists that Charles V and Philip II could suppress the works of 'Renaissance' authors such as Erasmus yet continue to patronise 'Renaissance' painters such as Titian. There is an irony in this, since there were dynamic points of contact between humanist letters and the visual arts, and in trying to understand the importance of the Italian Renaissance to sixteenth-century Europe, we must take account of the vision of man spread abroad by artists as well as by humanists.

Humanism and anthropocentrism

The Renaissance of the fifteenth century provided not just new ways of seeing, but also new ways of depicting what one saw. Humanism narrowly defined was the technical skill of an intellectual élite. Before making the obvious connection between humanist ideas and the new technology of printing, it is important to remember that the implications of humanism in terms of man's place in the world were first given more generally accessible form in the visual arts. The artistic achievement articulated at once the most general, profound and comprehensible results of humanist scholarship: that man stood at the centre and the apex of the natural world. With a very few exceptions, the great artists of the Renaissance were not humanists in the sense of being trained as philologists, yet they gave expression to its man-centred view, and we might complement our narrow definition of 'humanism' with the broader consequence, 'anthropocentrism'. By 1500, artists had complemented the humanists' exploration of historical time by providing a new sense of man's location in space (see plates, section I). The Florentine painter, Giorgio Vasari, (1511–74) catalogued the achievements of Renaissance art in his *Lives of the Most Excellent Painters, Sculptors and Architects of Italy* (1550), and in so doing became Europe's first art-historian.

Essentially, Vasari concentrates on three great leaps in the pulse rate of creativity. The first he identifies with Giotto da Bondone (1266/7–1337), who gave new realism and new drama to the art of painting by forsaking the two-dimensional iconographic tradition and creating the illusion of three dimensions in only two. Even the figures of his master, Cimabúe (1240–c.1302), look awkward and wooden by comparison, piling up in two planes rather than standing firmly in three. Giotto could create the illusion of depth on any figure or object by foreshortening in his drawing. However, the relationship of objects and figures to each other was geometrically insecure. That problem was solved during what Vasari saw as the next great period of vitality, in the early fifteenth century, which he identified with the painter Masaccio (1401–28), the sculptor Donatello (c.1386–1466) and Donatello's great friend, the architect, Brunelleschi (1377–1446). In this period, the realistic representation of objects in space reached a new perfection. The reason was the application of the rules of linear perspective: the fixing of a single 'vanishing point' on the horizon at which all parallel lines converged to create the appearance of systematically ordered depth. This was probably the invention of Brunelleschi, and learning its rules and how to apply them remained the basis of the training available in European schools of art until 1945.

Yet, according to Vasari, artistic achievement had only reached its apogee in a third stage in his own time when Michelangelo (1475–1564) became the greatest painter, sculptor and architect of his day. Contemporaries regarded him as a unique genius, '*il divino*', and in terms of his exploration of the relationship of mass and space he had certainly demonstrated capacities as a draughtsman which have never been equalled. He could create the illusion of three dimensions on two, as we can see in the swirling figures which thrust out of the Sistine ceiling. This was a reflection of his sculptor's understanding of the human figure and how to recreate it in marble. His grasp of the laws of perspective gave his architectural designs all the harmony, proportion and symmetry which classical motifs could offer. He could show God creating the universe, he could plunge the beholder into a terrifying vision of hell, and he could reshape the dimensions of life on earth.[8]

Michelangelo's genius was and remains unique, yet other artists enjoyed something of his fame. This change in status – the result of competition among artists and among patrons – inflated the honours accorded to artists and the esteem in which they were held. No longer were artists expressing the narrow requirements of a local church, a guild or a city: instead they had become international celebrities, part of the recognised structures of power and prestige. Charles V is said to have stooped before Titian to retrieve the painter's brush from the floor, and the Venetian's plump nudes delighted – perhaps even tempted – the monkish eye of Philip II. Titian rarely left Venice, for his patrons came to him, and this was unusual, for the age of the courtier-artist had dawned (see above, pp. 76–7). Had Raphael (1483–1520) not died so young, he might have hoped for high ecclesiastical office. Leonardo was fêted by Francis I and died in his service. Hans Holbein the Younger (1497/8–1543) increased the stature of Henry VIII – in so far as that was possible – and was sent abroad to paint prospective brides. The famous portrait of Anne of Cleves is said to have deceived Henry, who quickly disowned his 'Flanders mare' when he saw her in the flesh, but we should not dismiss the anecdote merely as an instance of Henry's famous lust and bad temper, for this is to underestimate the seriousness of Holbein's mission and its political implications. In the Low Countries, it was thought that Francis I approved of the match, and that Henry was seeking to bind up an alliance with France, Cleves and the rebels of Ghent against Charles V (see plates, section V). Conversely, Rudolf II used his diplomats to expand his collection of works of art.[9]

For all that the status of the artist was changing, the range of talents which he could offer was not a development which we can view in purely social or political terms. We might develop at this point the notion of Renaissance art as the exploration of space: however many horizons opened up, the imagination could expand to take them in. Knowing how to make parallel lines converge produced a new control over the idea of infinity. The intimidating barriers which the modern world has established between 'arts' and 'sciences' did not exist in the sixteenth century. Indeed, the terms themselves carried a Latin meaning which was almost the reverse of modern English usage: 'art' was a skill or craft, 'science' was abstract knowledge. And they were complementary. One of the greatest monuments to the Renaissance imagination is surely Raphael's fresco, the *School of Athens* (plate 3) painted in the Vatican between 1509 and 1511. Everyone is busy: deep in contemplation, hurriedly scribbling without time to sit down, disputing, instructing. At the centre stand the philosophers, Plato and Aristotle. The figure of Plato is perhaps a portrait of Leonardo, and in the foreground the architect, Bramante, appears as the Greek geometrician, Euclid, while Raphael has added a self-portrait in a group to the right. All is contained beneath a great barrel vault which powers back toward infinity. The art of the Renaissance created a new awareness of space which laid the basis for a scientific understanding of the universe.

The man-centred universe

The seventeenth century was to witness advances in science made possible by new mathematics (Newton, Leibniz), a new inductive philosophical method (Bacon, Descartes) and new instruments such as the telescope (Galileo), the microscope, the thermometer, the barometer, the pendulum clock, the air pump (Galileo, Boyle, Huygens). These spectacular advances should not overshadow the intellectual achievements of the sixteenth century. In terms of advances in scientific method we might note the astronomer, Gemma Frisius, who wrote an exposition on triangulation in surveying in 1533, and the mathematician, John Napier, who, between about 1595 and 1614, developed logarithms. However, these examples are but symptoms of much more profound cultural changes. In 1500, the universe was still understood in Ptolemaic terms, the human body through the formulations of Galen. During the next hundred years, the development of modern science began with the intersection of humanist letters and anthropocentric art.

Drawing was to the artists what language was to the humanists: it created a new concept of the natural world, and indeed of where that world might end (plates, section II). Leonardo da Vinci used his chalk to capture the forces of growth and change in plants and animals, winds and waves: what could be more 'scientifically' precise than Albrecht Dürer's famous drawing of a hare? While these drawings were not published, we should remember that in the writings of Otto Brunfels on herbs, 'the illustrations alone revolutionised the study of plant life'. These were tendencies which Rudolf II encouraged among his courtier-artists. The implications of the accurate depiction of the human body were equally momentous. From his studies at Padua, the Netherlander, Andreas Vesalius (1514–64) produced in 1543 his *On the Structure of the Human Body*. He never quite freed anatomy from the framework provided by Galen, but he gave the subject a new practical emphasis by conducting his own dissections instead of lecturing from a text while an assistant did the cutting, which was the previous practice. In our present context, it is also important to bear in mind that the success of Vesalius's book owed as much to the brilliant illustrative drawings (by unknown artists, though Vesalius's earlier work had been illustrated by a pupil of Titian) as to its wider availability made possible by printing. While anatomical elaboration made man a micro-universe, the universe was becoming a macro-man, and the connection of the two was one of the supreme sources of universal harmony whose secrets intellectuals strove to understand. Fittingly, the same year – 1543 – that Vesalius published his findings on the universe which was within man saw the publication of a work which was to revolutionise the relationship of man to the universe beyond him. Nicholas Copernicus (1473–1543) combined a sound grounding in Latin literature with a degree in law from Ferrara and the study of anatomy in Padua – where he also learned Greek, which gave him access to ancient writings on mathematics and astronomy. When he returned to Prussia, to the cathedral of Frauenburg, he took up quarters in a turret, from which, through some observation and much more reflection he produced the ideas underpinning his great work (which he probably saw only on his death-bed): *On the Revolutions of the Celestial Spheres*. This book, the first expansive propagation of the idea that the earth revolved around the static sun, drew strength from Pythagoras and modified Ptolemy and in that sense was a humanist work. Its author had a training in anatomy, a study which had taken on a new significance thanks to the rules of drawing established by Renaissance artists. In that sense, Copernicus shared an anthropocentric vision. He operated within a notion of eight spheres, yet he made the spheres superfluous to an understanding of the universe by putting forward the idea of the fixity and remoteness of the stars. The immeasurable distances which separated them from the earth made the universe infinite. In that sense, his humanism and anthropocentrism had made a huge contribution to a scientific vision of the cosmos. Its impact was not as immediate or as sensational as was the work of Vesalius. It was to be Galileo's telescope which made possible the type of observation from which accurate drawings could be made.

It would be dangerous to speak of Vesalius or Copernicus as 'typical', yet the interaction of the investigation of the ancient past which the humanists had inspired, the observation of the natural world, which Renaissance art could accurately record, and the broader questions of how the universe itself functioned was among the most important intellectual tendencies of the age, and it continued, without sustaining the same level of creative energy, through the later part of the century. We think of the flourishing court of the Emperor Rudolf II (who ruled from 1576 to 1612) which employed the Italian antiquary, Jacopo Strada, the Flemish artist, Peter-Paul Rubens and, in 1599, the Danish astronomer, Tycho Brahe (1546–1601). The latter had extended Copernicus's work, particularly the idea of infinity, through the observation of a new star in 1572, and his brief stay at Rudolf's court brought him into contact with one of the great scientific minds of the next century, Johann Kepler.[10] Such figures can be identified as the forerunners of modern science, but there was another intellect whose ideas and attitudes might seem still closer to our own time.

Michel de Montaigne (1533–92), one of the transcendent minds of our period, defies categorisation, and yet that makes him a helpful guide to the categories which the historian needs to understand the ideas of the era. In his attitudes and interests, though not in his training, he was a humanist, delighting in the works of Horace, Lucretius, Seneca and Plutarch. He was active in public service and served as a magistrate in Bordeaux from 1557 to 1570. Thereafter, he pursued the contemplative life, retiring from the world to his famous tower. He shared the humanists' preoccupation with history and poetry ('Historie is my chief studie, Poesie my only delight'), and he had a sense of the inconstancy of human affairs rather akin to Machiavelli's, and wrote of 'the uncertaintie and vicissitude of humane things, which by a very light motive, and slight occasion, are often changed from one to another cleane contrary state and degree'. Like Machiavelli, too, he had a distaste for rhetoric. At times, he found Plato and Cicero boring, and he followed Rabelais in his sense of the ridiculousness of man, which enables him to speak freely of impotence, urinating, the filthiness of a handkerchief.

He quotes Augustine on the power of the will in relation to the saint's observation of a man who could break wind musically, 'who could command his posterior', 'who could let tunable and organised ones, following the tune of any voice propounded into his eares'. And he had a detached view of the smallness of man. These ideas were put forward in a quite new literary form, the essay, a deliberately exploratory and speculative vehicle which proceeded in its investigations without preconditions. People were prisoners of custom. Some societies exist 'where men may lawfully get their mothers with childe: where fathers may lie with their daughters and with their sonnes'. His approach opened up all kinds of new questions about the acceptability of social structures, and indeed the desirability of eternity ('Imagine truly how much an ever-enduring life would be less tolerable and more painfull to a man'). Human affairs were of infinite diversity ('man is a wonderfull, vaine, divers, and wavering subject') and from that point of view the finite character of life was itself a reassurance – a theme which Shakespeare was to take up with more passion and anxiety. Montaigne's detachment enabled him to ask one single searching question, '*Que sais-je?*', 'What do I know?', and this was one of the first symptoms of that intellectual scepticism which was to prove so profound a force of change in the eighteenth century.[11]

It is tempting, therefore, to see the great intellectual advances of the sixteenth century as an important step towards the Enlightenment: the search for a reasonable, harmonious, tolerant world which functioned according to certain comprehensible rules. This is to ignore the enormous conflagration which consumed Europe in religious war for a hundred years from the middle of the sixteenth century onwards – a series of conflicts to which the last part of this book is devoted. Montaigne withdrew to his tower 'to rest myself from wars', the glittering culture of Rudolf's court did not survive the Thirty Years' War. Indeed, the lateness of that flowering was exceptional, for the vision of excitement and endeavour which the *School of Athens* seems to propound had begun to fade much earlier, almost as soon as it was articulated, its confidence faltering amid wars of an unprecedented scale and of a ferocity which religious protest intensified. Artists and writers had loaded man with new responsibilities, and he was not equal to them (plates, section III). His infinite potential might be for ill rather than good, for cruelty rather than kindness:

Creatures shall be seen upon the earth who will always be fighting one with another with very great losses and frequent deaths on either side. These shall set no bounds to their malice; by their fierce limbs a great number of the trees of the immense forests of the world shall be laid level with the ground; and when they have crammed themselves with food it shall gratify their desire to deal out death, affliction, labours, terrors, and banishment to every living thing. And by reason of their boundless pride they shall wish to rise towards heaven, but the excessive weight of their limbs shall hold

them down. There shall be nothing remaining on the earth or under
the earth or in the waters that shall not be pursued and molested and
destroyed, and that which is in one country taken away to another;
and their own bodies shall be made the tomb and means of transit of
all the living bodies which they have slain. O Earth! what delays thee
to open and hurl them headlong into the deep fissures of thy huge
abysses and caverns, and no longer to display in the sight of heaven
so savage and ruthless a monster?

What a pessimistic view of fallen man those lines embody! Yet they
are taken from the notebooks of Leonardo, the essential 'universal man'
of the Renaissance, for whom all things seemed possible. Similarly,
Dürer's *Melancholia I* (1514) shows how narrow was the boundary
between exhilaration and despair. The female figure – paralysed by her
own energy, in Panofsky's memorable analysis – sits with fixed, sleepless
gaze amid unconcluded works of architecture and science which
ultimately give no satisfaction. We might interpret this as the depressive
disposition of an individual artist, but, like Leonardo, Dürer's pessimism seems to reflect a general unease about the state of the world
rather than the state of mind of an introvert. In this regard, we could
adduce the vision of upheaval in the engraving of the *Four Horsemen of
the Apocalypse*, and in the watercolour he painted to depict a nightmare
of the destruction of the world in flood. Dürer's *Deluge* (plate 9) was a
long grey column and mushroom cloud: terrifyingly prophetic. Yet this
was the work of a well-informed neo-platonist, the associate of the
humanists, Conrad Celtis and Willibald Pirckheimer, the artist for
whom Erasmus sat. There was a detectable 'failure of nerve' among
Italian painters after about 1520, a mood which intensified after the
Sack of Rome in 1527 (below, pp. 239–40), affecting Pontormo and
Lotto, and taken to France by Rosso Fiorentino. Whatever the grounds
for hope, whatever the reassurance which the capacities of great minds
seemed to offer, there were other obvious symptoms of the malaise. The
harmony breaks down in Holbein's *Ambassadors*. What could be more
confident and assertive than these two earthly power-brokers, a world to
divide between them, the elongated skull in the foreground concealed by
the artist's consummate skill in twisting the demands of perspective: and
yet one string on the lute which is part of the opulent setting has
snapped. Somehow, there is no concealing spiritual discord. Michelangelo himself had been among the followers of Savonarola, and he
lamented the condition of the Church in a sonnet:

> They make a sword or helmet from a chalice,
> And sell the blood of Christ here by the load
> And cross, and thorn, become a shield, a blade,
> And even Christ is being stripped of patience.

The poem ends with the line 'What is there in our state that can restore us?', a theme of uncertainty reflected in Michelangelo's paintings. While so much of his work celebrates the glory of the human form, he is only too aware of his own inadequacies: one self-portrait appears on the formless flayed skin held by St Bartholomew in the *Last Judgement* (1541), another gropes blindly as St Paul on the road to Damascus (1550) (plates 11 and 12), a third in sculpture, an unfinished grizzled Nicodemus, supporting a broken, one-legged Christ in the *Pietà* of about 1550.[12] Shakespeare comes to share the same vision of potential and failure, of excitement and despair. In the *Comedy of Errors*, we find:

> Man, more divine, the master of all these,
> Lord of the wide world and wild wat'ry seas
> Indued with intellectual sense and souls
>
> (II.i.20–2)

By the time he wrote *Hamlet*, man had become no more than the 'quintessence of dust'.

The mentality caught between comfort and despair was not simply the product of intellectual tendencies, it was the symptom of that general spiritual crisis to which Luther first gave expression, and which is identified with the shorthand term 'Reformation'. Luther stood at an explosive point of contact between the refined culture of the humanists and the spiritual thirst of society at large. His protest certainly drew strength from German humanism. In particular, Luther could speak to a society which, thanks to humanism, had a dramatically new sense of its own history, and he could convey a message whose conviction was based on a commitment to the proper understanding of the words of a given text: the Bible. It is worth examining each in turn.

While in Italy humanism had traced the roots of civilisation back to Rome, the discovery of German scholars was their traditional independence of Latin culture – a point emphasised by the *Germania* of the Roman historian, Tacitus, a text discovered in a monastery in the fifteenth century. When crowned as poet-laureate in 1501, the scholar, Heinrich Bebel, included these words in his celebratory oration before the Emperor Maximilian:

> The books of rhetoricians, poets, historians and philosophers are replete with the deeds of Romans and Greeks, whom they hold up as very paradigms for posterity. But who speaks of Frederick, of Charles, of Otto? No one does, and yet no finer examples could be given, and none worthier of emulation. For this neglect there is no reason except the oblivion into which the deeds of our ancestors have fallen. Whoever wishes to praise Germany as she should be

praised will find that our history has no shortage of praiseworthy and virtuous deeds. Indeed he will realise that the German past can hold its own not only with attainments considered excellent in our own day but also with the greatest of the feats of antiquity.[13]

Such ideas of a separate historical tradition made the impositions of an alien Latin church all the more intolerable, as Luther himself emphasised in a characteristically bludgeoning assault on the infiltration of Germany by Italian clergy:

> Already we have a few cardinals. They think the drunken Germans will not understand what the game is, till there is not a single bishopric, monastery, parish or benefice, not a cent or farthing, left for them . . . and then they proceed to justify it all by saying, 'We are Christ's agents and the shepherds of Christ's sheep. The silly drunken Germans must put up with it'.

In this way, 'the Romanists make fools and apes of us' and in so doing they debase 'the Word of God'. In his urgent desire to place man in closer contact with his Maker, Luther emphasises – as Erasmus did – the importance of direct access to the Word, unvarnished, untarnished. His *Preface to the New Testament*, written in the seclusion of the Wartburg, but with Erasmus's work on Valla's *Adnotationes* to hand, makes the point at the outset, almost apologising for any words of introduction as superfluous:

> It would only be right and proper if this volume were published without any preface, or without any name on the title page, but simply with its own name to speak for itself. However, many unscholarly expositions and introductions have perverted the understanding of Christian people till they have not an inkling of the meaning of the gospel as distinct from the law, the New Testament as distinct from the Old Testament.[14]

In many ways, of course, Luther's whole theology came to depend on what the words of the New Testament really meant. How did one 'do penance' (*agere poenitentiam*)? What was Christ's purpose at the Last Supper in raising the bread with the words 'This is my body' (*hoc est corpus meum*) (Matthew 26:26)? And how did one understand the idea that 'If anyone eats of this bread, he will live forever' (John 6:51)?

The new direct contact between the Christian and God made the offices of a priestly intermediary superfluous – an exhilarating possibility which had something in common with the platonism of the Christian humanists. On the other hand, the removal of the spiritual broker imposed awesome new responsibilities on the Christian and made him only too aware of his own shortcomings. In that sense,

Luther shared both the confidence and the pessimism of the greatest minds of the era. However, he went further than any of his contemporaries in his efforts to communicate his ideas to society at large.

The clarity of the relationship between intellectual and spiritual tendencies, between ideas and their implications for the life of Christians in society, is in part to be explained by the travels of writers and artists – Leonardo, Erasmus, Dürer – and their influence in different milieux. However, the sudden topicality of new ideas and the vigour of their initial impact must also be understood in relation to a speed of circulation increased by new educational programmes and the new technology of the printing press.

Humanism, education, and printing

On the surface, the connections between humanism, education and printing look quite simple. Many of the humanists were, after all, professional teachers. Understandably, their influence could be expected to achieve a measure of reform in educational institutions, and theory was spread and practice facilitated by printed books. With the qualification that this was not the only chain of causality in the communications revolution of the sixteenth century, the model remains serviceable enough.

Certainly, the training of the young was among the highest of humanist priorities. Pier Paolo Vergerio, writing as early as 1404, emphasised the importance of education to the public weal:

> For the education of children is a matter of more than private interest; it concerns the state, which indeed regards the right training of the young as, in certain aspects, within its proper sphere. I would wish to see this responsibility extended.

The rhetorician, Bruni, encouraged the study of classical literature for women as well as men. The curriculum was extended and redefined, laying the foundations in grammar on which were built poetry, history and rhetoric, moral and natural philosophy, the study of the Church Fathers, mathematics, astrology, natural history, music and physical training. Such thinking left its imprint on Erasmus, who extended its implications for the Christian life:

> All knowledge falls into one of two divisions: the knowledge of 'truths' and the knowledge of 'words': and if the former is first in importance the latter is acquired first in time.

Latin and Greek were essential, for 'a man ignorant of letters is no man at all'.[15]

As though in response to such calls, there was in the fifteenth and sixteenth centuries an enormous expansion of educational institutions. There were new university foundations in Scotland (St Andrews in 1411, Glasgow in 1451, Edinburgh in 1582). The Empire had a mere 5 universities in 1400, but 18 in 1520 – including the new foundation at Wittenberg – and more still in the second half of the century, amongst them Dillingen and Würzburg. Tübingen educated the clergy for Württemberg, Jena for Ernestine Saxony, Leipzig as well as Wittenberg for Heidelberg and the Palatinate. Between 1475 and 1520, 18 new universities were founded in Castile. The traditional centres of Salamanca and Valladolíd expanded to accommodate about 7,000 students each. Of the new universities, Alcalá was easily the most significant with up to 4,000 students. Both Vesalius and Copernicus studied at Padua, Colet lectured at Oxford, and of course the central importance of one of its academic disputes brought the university of Wittenberg to prominence.

The 'overthrow of the ancient clerical monopoly of culture', according to Professor Stone, brought about an 'educational revolution' in England. There were about 1,200 students at Cambridge in the 1560s, more than 3,000 half a century later. In the case of England, such an increase was fuelled by the growth in the number of schools. Education attracted as much as a quarter of all charitable giving in one sample, and, in the ten counties of one notable study, more than 400 new schools – mostly grammar schools – were established. In the cities of the continent, compulsory education was seen as the means of implanting the Word of God in the young. In Strasbourg, for instance, under the guidance of Johann Sturm, the *Gymnasium* combined the civic consciousness of the Roman republic with the lessons of the gospel, and the magistrates elected a public schoolmaster to give Christian instruction in 1524. Along with poor relief, education became the means by which both Protestants and Catholics sought to 'reach the people' (below, chs. 6–8).[16]

Accompanying and strengthening the new initiatives was the printed book. Printing with moveable type – which had been known in China for centuries – remained in its infancy (hence the 'incunable' or 'cot' period) in the second half of the fifteenth century. The technology spread from Mainz to Bamberg and then Strasbourg, to Subiaco, Rome and Venice, to Valencia and London. By 1500, it had 'grown up', and there were printing presses in nearly 200 towns. The valuable commodities which they produced were sold at fairs in Frankfurt, Leipzig and Lyon. The new accessibility was to prove decisive in the propagation of reformist ideas. Erasmus owed much of his fame to Aldus Manutius in Venice – who pioneered the pocket edition and italic script – and to Johann Froben in Basel. Within a month of publication (September 1522), the first edition of Luther's German New Testament was sold out: all 3,000 copies had gone. More than a million copies of his New Testament and complete Bible were sold in his lifetime, many of these produced by the printer, Spalatin, and this was the means by which Luther's ideas reached the likes of Coverdale and Foxe. While the sixteenth century was, in general, an era of price inflation, the cost of books fell dramatically in real terms, increasing the accessibility of God's word and the ideas of the reformers. In Strasbourg in 1480, a Bible cost the equivalent of two months of a craftsman's wages. Forty years later, a copy could be had for the cost of two rabbits. No wonder, then, that some felt threatened: as one English clergyman put it in the Henrician era, 'either we must root out printing, or printing will root us out'.[17]

In these ways, humanism had opened up new educational prospects for the laity. There was a great institutional expansion, and printing increased immeasurably the audience for new ideas: this much is clear. Far less straightforward are the interconnections of these developments, and in many ways the tendencies have to be seen as separate.

First, humanists did not necessarily see their ideas about the training of the young in institutional terms. Once again, we must avoid seeing the sixteenth century as 'modern' because we recognise in schools and universities institutions with which we are familiar. It is important to remember that one of the most refreshing aspects of the Renaissance is its independence of institutional ties. There was no great academic tradition in Florence in the fifteenth century, and education had a purpose but it was not an end in itself:

> for the man who has surrendered himself absolutely to the attractions of letters or of speculative thought follows, perhaps, a self-regarding end and is useless as a citizen or as prince.

Erasmus was never a teacher, avoided offers of university posts, and indeed had a miserable time at Queens' College, Cambridge. The beer was foul, the academics dull and conceited. He savaged bad teaching in the colloquy 'A Meeting of the Philological Society', and Luther ridiculed his opponents at the Sorbonne as 'the moles and bats of Paris'. Montaigne, whose withdrawal from the world did not mark him out as an especially practical person, had a horror of pedantry, on which subject he wrote an acidic essay, arguing that formal instruction could stifle rather than liberate. Montaigne's was never an ivory tower, his speculations, however abstract, were never merely academic:

> Except our mind be the better, unless our judgement be the sounder, I had rather my scholler had imployed his time in playing at tennis: I am sure his bodie would be the nimbler. See but one of these our universitie men or bookish schollers returne from schoole, after he

hath spent ten or twelve years under a pedant's charge: who is so
inapt for any matter? who so unfit for any companie? who so to
seeke if he come into the world? all the advantage you discover in
him is that his Latine and Greeke have made him more sottish, more
stupid, and more presumptuous, than before he went from home.

'These letter-puft pedants', he continues 'knowe the theorike of all
things, but you must seeke who shall put it in practice'.[18]

It seems doubtful that either Erasmus or Montaigne sought any
vehicle for the general transmission of their ideas. Erasmus's writings
on education are dominated by the figure of the tutor in a comfortable
household, Montaigne had grave doubts about a vernacular Bible,
'which is not for everyone to study', and in any case, who could check
the translation into Basque or Breton? Both seemed implicitly to accept
the social distinctions which Castiglione's notions of aristocratic
education reinforced.[19]

As for the universities themselves, their expansion owed more to the
demands of the state for officers than to the intellectual awakening of
the laity (above, ch. 3). This was what made the Inns of Court so
attractive to the gentry of Tudor England. Law dominated the
curriculum in Castile, princes determined the acceptability of profes-
sors in the universities of the Empire. Renaissance foundations did not
always survive into the modern era, and many institutions of learning
in our society do not have a history before 1945. In the sixteenth
century, schools and universities affected only a tiny proportion of the
European population. Apprenticeship remained far more common
than schooling as a way of training the young, and shops were often
the scene of more original debate than classrooms.

The humanists' social vision was not always terribly broad, the
expansion of educational institutions more striking quantitatively than
qualitatively. While it is tempting to see the spread of the Reformation
as a combination of humanist ideas and educational reforms, this serves
to detract from the thunderous impact of Luther and printing.

One of the most striking aspects of the early history of European
printing is what we learn about the culture of the unlearned. Rather
than being a vehicle for the ideas of the humanist élite, the press
articulated ideas and circulated materials which expressed the feelings
of ordinary lay people. One of Erasmus's most brilliant attacks on the
superficiality of external observances is a long colloquy 'On the Eating
of Fish', conducted by a butcher and a fishmonger. In Venice, a
goldsmith called Alessandro Caravia produced a brilliantly witty poem
about the excessive pomp of the charitable institutions of the city,
admonishing them to spend their money not on self-glorifying building
projects, but on the relief of those who stood in real need. In Germany,
images from woodcuts were important in propagating the Reformation

amongst the semi-literate and illiterate, attacking monks and popes. In Strasbourg, the presses produced novels, biblical dramas and journalism as well as learned works. In Venice and Lyon, the printing industry was in the hands of a skilled and self-confident workforce, and shops were often the setting for the exchange of ideas as well as the production of books.[20] This great diversity helps to explain the limitations of printing as a means of spreading the Reformation. There was no coherent programme systematically fed to a passive populace. Print culture did not carry all before it, because it was not advancing in one single direction but on many different fronts. As we shall see, this gave the established Church the opportunity to regroup its resources and replan its strategies.

What then was the overall importance of new ideas in the history of the sixteenth century? This chapter has examined the implications of the Renaissance in terms of humanist learning and the visual arts, and it has sketched the features of the context in which ideas were circulating in terms of religious unease, new technology and a vigorous popular culture. The influence of ideas is readily identifiable – we need think only of Luther's debt to humanism and to the press – yet what did those ideas change? Humanism asserted the intellectual and ultimately the spiritual independence of the laity. Printing brought that assertion into contact with a popular culture of immense vitality and it gave expression to both. Learning was no longer the preserve of a separate social order. True, the Counter-Reformation was to reassert the ideal of the priesthood as an order of missionaries to the flotsam and jetsam of society, but the idea of a life spent in the cloister as the ultimate goal of the religious was gone forever. The monastic ideal, the supreme expression of medieval Christianity, was finished.

6 The dissolution of monasticism

The Reformation in historical thought

Broadly speaking, historians have given the Reformation two great contexts. The final break-up of Christendom in the rapids of revolution has to be related first to the stagnant waters of the late-medieval Church and second to the new springs of intellectual and spiritual sustenance to be found amongst the laity. In many ways, the achievement of historians of the Reformation has been to set Luther's protest in relation to the chronic weaknesses of the institutional church and those techniques of humanism which exposed the failings so clearly and so ruthlessly to a dissatisfied laity desperately seeking spiritual solace. In the fourteenth and fifteenth centuries, there were plenty of assertions that popes, bishops, priests, monks, nuns and friars were in no fit state to meet the spiritual needs of the Christian laity. Their detachment made their worldliness more obvious and more burdensome, observance of the religion they purveyed had become mechanical, superficial and thoughtless. What made the internal division of the Church among rival councils and popes all the more lamentable was the increasing pressure of external criticism from those powerful intellects who anticipated Luther's ideas.

John Wyclif (d.1384), the revolutionary English heresiarch, advocated a vernacular Bible accessible to the laity, formulated a theology of predestination, and he rejected transubstantiation – the Catholic doctrine which sets down that during the mass, the bread and wine of the sacrament are transformed into the body and blood of Christ. Moreover, he advocated clerical marriage, held the worldly power of the papacy in contempt, and like Marsilius of Padua (above, p. 4) saw the secular state as supreme in Church affairs. His ideas remained influential in England at the time of the Reformation, when Lollardy experienced something of a revival. Contacts between England and the flourishing civilisation of Bohemia – one of the few areas of Europe untouched by the Black Death – had been strengthened by the marriage of Richard II to Anne of Bohemia, and it was from central Europe that the next great challenge stemmed.

John Hus (c.1369–1415) spoke out against the corruption of the Church and advocated that the laity receive communion in both kinds. This was a fundamental attack on the separateness of the clergy, who administered the sacrament to the congregation only in the form of the bread which became Christ's body, and reserved the taking of the wine which became Christ's blood as a privilege for the priesthood. The Hussite doctrine of 'utraquism', communion in both kinds for the entire congregation, was a practical expression of what Luther later called the priesthood of all believers. Hus went to the Council of Constance to defend his views, but, in spite of an imperial safe conduct, he was condemned and burned as a heretic. However, despite the loss of its leader, the Hussite Church remained secure in its national setting. Gunfire from covered waggons – Europe's first tanks – drawn up under banners proudly flaunting the chalice from which the laity took the wine of the Eucharist, hurled back the crusaders sent against the heretic kingdom.[1]

The great tide of resentment known as anti-clericalism found sharp expression amongst those scholars and intellectuals who had placed so much more learning at the disposal of the laity.[2] They urged reform through a return to the ancient sources of Christianity, the removal of those cluttering structures of the medieval Church which formed a great misleading gloss on the pure Word of God.

Yet the industry of modern scholars in their books, their journals and their conferences has failed to do more than skirt two fundamental problems. First, why did a church in such a manifestly appalling condition endure so long? What circumstances or ideas made Luther more significant than Wyclif or Hus? Second, what did the humanists contribute to the break-up of Christendom when the greatest of them, Erasmus, as well as others such as More, devoted their energies to the preservation of its unity? This raises the broader question of how to link the Renaissance – one of a series of revivals of classical values which hold together the European experience – to the Reformation, a unique divide which cuts across that experience. There are no simple answers, and probably no final answers to such questions, but it seems worth trying to recast our problem in the light of them.

In the first place, there is a risk that concentrating on the state of the late medieval Church produces a view of its condition before then which is both idealised and static. Complaints about the lax morals of monks and nuns were not new in the sixteenth century, but they preceded the fourteenth as well. Consider the condition of a tottering church through the evidence from a penitential which made specific provision for the atonement to be made for fornication, which was the first category of sin, detailing 42 types of liaison and allowing many variations on what might happen between monks and nuns, or between laypeople and clergy. Examine the records of a general council which met twenty years later and sought to initiate a system of annual visits by the bishop to ensure that monastic discipline was observed, particularly in the matter of drunkenness. These apparently desperate efforts to control monastic morals and improve pastoral care come from the eighth century. The author of the penitential was not Gerson, but probably Bede; the Council met, not at Constance in 1414, but at Clovesho in 747. Two centuries later, the papacy was the plaything of the empire, lacking all moral authority, sometimes involved in open conflict.

Consider a pope elected to office at 18 years of age, soon debauching the widow of one of his vassals, siring a child on his own father's mistress, turning the Lateran palace into 'a harlot's brothel'. The emperor was forced to write to him over charges of 'homicide, perjury, sacrilege and of the sin of unchastity with your own kinswoman and with two sisters', to elaborate no further, since there were 'such filthy tales about you that we should be ashamed of them, even if they were told about actors'. The pope was so lacking in education that his own reply amounted to 'you ain't got no power to depose no one', and the emperor had to correct the crude triple negative. The pope was prepared to take the field 'equipped with helmet and cuirass', and was eventually deposed by a council of bishops, who elected a successor, soon to be challenged by a usurper. Here we have a precursor of John XXIII, the wanton fighting man, of the scandalous roué Alexander VI, of the bellicose Julius II, challenged by conciliar power. Yet the year of the three popes was 964, which saw the deposition of John XII in favour of Leo VIII, challenged in turn by Benedict V.

Even after the Gregorian reform of the late eleventh century, examples of laxity are readily found if we choose to look. What could be more symptomatic of the loose morals of the convent than Abelard's admission that he had his wife, Heloise, disguised as a nun and had sex with her in a corner of the refectory – during Lent, too, which was a season of abstinence? Such examples are scattered, but we should avoid the assumption that the late medieval Church was necessarily more corrupt or less capable of reform than it had been before 1250. After all, there was a vigorous religious revival in fifteenth-century Italy – led by figures such as San Bernardino of Siena, Sant'Antonino, and Savonarola – to accompany the classical Renaissance of the humanists.[3]

With regard to humanism itself, before linking its energies inexorably to the Reformation and, beyond, to the Enlightenment, we should remember that the revival of traditional doctrine and the rebuttal of lay criticism which we call the Counter-Reformation obliterated humanism in southern Europe: humanism was reabsorbed by scholasticism. Free speculation without preconditions gave way to a world view insistent upon the role of philosophy as a means of proving the existence of God by induction or deduction. This is not to say that humanists did not believe in the existence of God, but they studied the classical world as a pagan world, and they were prepared, on occasion, to abandon certainties. Galileo's crime was that he could not say he was sure, which was unacceptable in an age when the faithful were called to believe what the Church taught as the unchallengeable and authoritative truth: if the Church decreed that black was white, then this was not to be questioned, as St Ignatius asserted. The enormous success of Catholic reform – its massive reassertion of traditional dogma, its revamping of traditional power structures – in reclaiming the souls of Europe from Protestantism (and humanism) suggests sources of enormous energy within structures which are easily dismissed at the eve of the Reformation as 'ossified', 'burdensome', 'lacking in spirituality'. One is drawn to reflect on how quickly 'Renaissance popes' adapted to 'the Counter-Reformation' Church. A partial explanation may lie in the Church's adaptability to changing circumstances, a characteristic which stereotypes of 'obsolescence' have obscured.

As we have seen (above, pp. 99–100) Rome was a modern city, and the papacy was a modern institution: worldly, cynical and hungry for money in order to run a territorial state which as a political entity was a brilliant managerial adjustment to the decay of papal claims to universal authority. In that sense, it may have been too far ahead of its times to survive, rather than too obsolete – in some respects the papacy was dragged backwards rather than forwards by the Counter-Reformation (above, pp. 66–7; below, pp. 185–8).[4]

Leo X renewed the sale of indulgences in 1517 because he was short of money, especially for the great project of St Peter's. This cynical but lucrative practice offered for sale the pope's power to shorten a soul's time in purgatory – the punishment chamber for earthly misdeeds which preceded entry into paradise – providing that the sinner expressed his contrition through confession. It constituted a sort of private insurance for souls, guaranteeing quick treatment, and the application of the funds raised to the rebuilding of St Peter's had begun under Sixtus IV in 1476. The company managing the sale for Leo was run by Albrecht of Brandenburg, Archbishop of Magdeburg and Mainz, and the advertising consultancy was given to the Fuggers of Augsburg. The Dominican, Johann Tetzel, was a brilliant salesman who used the jingle:

> As soon as the coin in the coffer rings
> A soul from purgatory springs.

The parallels with modern marketing are not anachronistic: rather, they show how sophisticated was the machinery of papal fund-raising. It may be significant in terms of the sources of institutional vitality in the Roman Church that St Peter's, the great project of the Renaissance papacy, so naturally came to symbolise the authority of the Counter-Reformation Church. In the early sixteenth century, such expedients offered nothing in religious terms to those whose fear of God's judgement was so great that they needed in equal measure the reassurance of His mercy on their eternal souls.

There is no question of the importance of weaknesses in the late-medieval Church, and of the new intellectual possibilities opened up by humanism. What is missing, however, is a sense of why Christendom split precisely when it did, and why the split became irreparable. In other words, we lack some sense of the shock of the Reformation's initial impact. Volcanoes are a permanent feature of the earth's surface, but they do not erupt every day. The Reformation was not the inevitable culmination of centuries and it did not 'develop and spread' in any simple way. On the contrary, it was soon in difficulties, often compromised, frequently defeated, and it took root where the secular power wished it to do so. However vast the landscape, Luther cannot be allowed altogether to disappear from view, and nor can those secular rulers who gave the Reformation their decisive support. What then, were the sources of power in Luther's initial onslaught? When, in about 1520, Erasmus was asked why there were objections to Luther's ideas, he said that the cause lay in Luther's attack on 'the crown of the pope and the bellies of the monks'.[5] And indeed, these were the two great fields of force: an attack on the papacy as an institution – on the *papacy* rather than *a* pope – and an attack on the traditional bonding force which held together the structures of western Christendom under papal supremacy: monasticism.

'It is all over with the Holy See of Rome'

The events of Luther's life and the formation of his ideas are, at bottom, relatively straightforward. However, the influence of the former upon the latter has so preoccupied commentators that both the career and the ideas tend to obscure each other. What follows is an attempt to separate the two, offering first a simple sketch of the main developments in Luther's life and thought and then a summary of his critique of the papacy gleaned from his own writings.

In many ways, the Reformation began quite literally with a bolt from the blue. In 1505, Luther, a 21-year-old student returning from a visit to his parents to school at Erfurt, was struck to the ground by lightning. In terror, he called upon St Anne, the patron saint of his father's trade, mining, and promised that if he were delivered from death, he would become a monk. Barely two weeks later, he entered the Augustinian cloister at Erfurt. His studies progressed, and between 1510 and 1513, he began to respond with unease but conviction to the texts of the Psalms and of St Paul's letter to the Romans. In the latter, chapter I, verse 17, he read:

Justitia enim Dei in eo revelatur ex fide in fidem: sicut scriptum est:
Justus autem ex fide vivit.

This was later rendered in English as:

For therein is the righteousness of God revealed from faith to faith:
as it is written, The just shall live by faith.

This was to inspire his doctrine of Justification by Faith, the idea that
the Christian's inner self found solace in the certainty of salvation
which only complete abandonment to God's will could achieve. This
notion of spiritual self-sufficiency through an admission of helplessness
owed much to the German mystical tradition of the thirteenth century
as represented by figures such as Meister Eckhart and Johann Tauler.
Yet the demands for concentrated introspection had never before
subverted the external rituals of the Church or the spiritual authority
of the papacy.

This is what Luther brought to bear on the specific question of the
validity of indulgences. The reassurance of salvation could not be
bought from Tetzel, as Luther recognised. The support of the secular
ruler was immediately necessary, and the Elector, Frederick of Saxony,
forbade the hawking of indulgences in his territories, but Luther's
parishioners in Wittenberg were not far from the border, and it became
imperative to offer them a more meaningful path to salvation than was
available from the agents of the pope. Luther chose to engage in public
debate about the relationship of such superficial practices to the life of
the Christian soul. He did so in the conventional manner by setting out
his own ideas – it is not certain that he nailed a version to the door of
the local church – and inviting responses. These ideas were the Ninety-
Five Theses. He sent a copy to Albrecht of Mainz, with the covering
note that 'If you will look over my theses, you will see how dubious is
the doctrine of indulgences, which is so confidently proclaimed'.
Albrecht sent them on to Rome, where Pope Leo (it is said), in words
that Luther himself might have predicted, commented that 'Luther is a
drunken German. He will feel different when he is sober.' Luther took
the opportunity of an appearance before the cathedral chapter at
Heidelberg the next year to defend his position, which had attracted
the support of his secular master, Frederick the Wise, as well as two
other academics at Wittenberg, Andreas Karlstadt and Philip Melanchthon.

Later in 1518, at Augsburg, Cardinal Cajetan tried to correct
Luther's stance to accord with papal teaching on indulgences. Luther
stood firm and Frederick of Saxony refused to banish him in
accordance with the Church's instructions. In 1519 – the year Charles
V succeeded Maximilian as Holy Roman Emperor after a hotly

contested election – a professor from Ingolstadt, well-versed in theology and the classics, Johann Eck, worsted Luther in debate at Leipzig and pushed him close to admissions of heresy. At this point, Luther received an offer of help from two rebellious knights, Ulrich von Hutten and Franz von Sickingen. In 1520, under increasing pressure to submit to Rome, Luther retreated into a stronghold identified with the interests of the German nation and, having regrouped his ideas, burst forth in magnificent attack. The papal bull, *Exsurge Domine*, had given him 60 days to recant. He burnt it, and in reply, he wrote an *Address to the Christian Nobility of the German Nation*, attacked the *Execrable Bull of Anti-Christ*, and in the same month wrote the soaring restatement *On the Freedom of the Christian Man*. The following year, Luther appealed to the Emperor and appeared before him at the Diet of Worms. In the face of another attack of tremendous intellectual power from Eck, questioning his right to challenge traditional orthodoxy, and implying that his simple humility was a mask for arrogance and presumption, Luther closed his own case – as he could easily have sealed his fate – with the ringing assertion:

> Unless I am convicted by Scripture and plain reason – I do not accept the authority of popes and councils, for they have contradicted each other – my conscience is captive to the Word of God. I cannot and I will not recant anything, for to go against conscience is neither right nor safe. God help me. Amen.

The first printed edition added the words which everyone knows, which could easily be genuine, and which have to be repeated: 'Here I stand. I can no other.' The Emperor decided to proceed against him as a 'notorious heretic', but at least honoured the safe conduct.[6] Frederick whisked Luther into hiding in Wartburg Castle, where he suffered from constipation and insomnia, but not, apparently, writer's cramp, for here he completed his translation of the New Testament into German, and a host of other works, including *On Monastic Vows*, of which more in due course. He also became detached from what he himself had started, and in redefining his own position, he exposed painful divisions within the movement for reform. By 1522 his ideas had been taken up and distorted by Hutten and Sickingen, who were in revolt against the bishop of Trier. Luther dissociated himself from Karlstadt in particular and from unrest in general in a manner which was forceful to the point of cruelty (above, p. 29).[7]

However, while distancing himself from social revolution, he also severed his links with Christian humanism, and engaged his talents in writing against Erasmus on the matter of free will, in which exchange his conviction became the crude self-righteousness which Eck had so nearly exposed. As Luther expressed it in his own conclusion:

And it is not difficult to suppose that you, since you are human, may not have rightly understood or observed with due care the Scriptures or the sayings of the Fathers under whose guidance you think you are attaining your goal; and of this there is more than a hint in your statement that you are asserting nothing, but have only 'discoursed'. No one writes like that who has a thorough insight into the subject and rightly understands it. I for my part in this book have not discoursed, but have asserted and do assert, and I am unwilling to submit the matter to anyone's judgement, but advise everyone to yield assent.[8]

Equally, his fierce individualism could not compromise with the practical urban evangelicalism of the Swiss reformer, Huldrich Zwingli (1484–1531), who had established his own brand of the new religion in Zurich. Zwingli – an intriguing figure who claimed to have formulated his own version of the doctrine of Justification by Faith – rejected transubstantiation altogether, holding quite firmly to the notion of the mass as a symbol and a memorial of Christ's sacrifice. Luther always believed in the doctrine of Christ's real presence in the Eucharist, and the meeting with Zwingli in 1529 (the Colloquy of Marburg) failed to unite the Swiss and German currents of reform, despite the efforts of the moderate Martin Bucer of Strasbourg to join them in a common stream. By now, however, the politics of the reform had begun to outstrip its theology. The Emperor convened the Diet of Speyer in 1529 with a view to withdrawing all concessions to Lutherans, whose formal protest against such measures gave them the name of Protestants (see below, p. 270). In 1540, the movement for reform lost its footing on the moral high ground when Luther privately sanctioned the bigamy of Philip of Hesse. By the time Luther died in 1546, the movement for Christian freedom which he had begun had been pressed into the northeast of Europe. Elsewhere it was hardening into an alternative world-system: Calvinism.

Such, in brief outline, were the events in Luther's career to which historians and theologians relate his character and his ideas. What was his significance? The compromises, disappointments, frustrations and, yes, the tantrums of the years after 1525 must be set aside, for the work of liberation was done by then. The early career of Luther the reformer is an illustration of the seismic power of ideas in influencing human history.

The doctrine of Justification by Faith (above, p. 134) involved an overwhelmingly demanding concentration on the inner self, on the soul, a concentration so powerful that the soul had to become the mainspring of human action. Action without such awesome motivation was worthless as a means to achieving salvation. In 1517, Luther used this idea to attack indulgences, and in so doing, he questioned the power of the pope to forgive sins. Only God could do this, and the pope could not command the performance of externals because Christ alone could ascertain the purity of the motivation, the humility of the just believer. The commands of the pope and the intermediary role of the clergy were rendered superfluous to salvation.

Dramatic as this may sound, it does not establish what components of Luther's thinking set him apart from his predecessors and from his contemporaries. Both Wyclif and Hus had challenged the whole notion of a separate order of priests. And in the matter of the mass, Luther was much less of a revolutionary than Zwingli. Yet the nature of his protest was new. He attacked a system, rather than abuses within a system – which distinguishes him from his precursors – and he set the individual Christian free from sin, eternal doom and the burdensome law of the Old Testament rather than creating an alternative system – which sets him apart from Calvin.

In this regard, *On the Freedom of the Christian Man* is of critical importance. Significantly, the piece is dedicated to Leo X, and is preceded by an open letter to the Pope. The tone is reasoned and conciliatory, though the language is uncompromisingly critical. It would be superficial to put this down to mere arrogance and insolence, for what Luther sets out is a clear distinction between the pope's person and his office. Traditionally, the ideology of papal power rested on the idea of the inviolable sanctity of the office, even though the incumbent might prove unworthy. The torrents of criticism in the late Middle Ages concentrate on the failures of individuals. Luther turned the tide in a new direction, making no criticism of the personal life of the pope, but shattering the notion that the papacy was somehow always to be preserved.

So, he addressed the pope in terms of 'the fame of your blameless life'. All the same, even a saintly man would be helpless amid the corruption of papal power structures:

It cannot have been hidden from you yourself what has been happening now and for many years in Rome, and extending everywhere. There has grown to be a corruption of body, soul and goods; every kind of wickedness has seized upon and overwhelmed all men alike. All of this is open to the day and known to everyone. Thereby the Roman Church, which in past ages was the holiest of all, has now become a den of murderers beyond all other dens of murderers, a thieves' castle beyond all other thieves' castles, the head and empire of every sin, as well as of death and damnation.

Luther remains respectful towards the Pope himself:

Holy Father Leo, you seem like a sheep among the wolves . . . What can you do alone among so much that is vile and shocking? Even if three or four learned and pious cardinals came to your aid, what is that among such a multitude? You would certainly all be poisoned before you could begin to mend matters. It is all over with the Holy See of Rome; God's anger has fallen upon it, and will not relent. That see is hostile to the general councils; it will let itself be neither taught nor reformed, and is not even able to restrain its own rankly unchristian nature . . .

Herein was Luther's revolution: he does not criticise a pope, but the papacy, as Antichrist:

The Evil One is the veritable pope, for he certainly rules in this Babylon more truly than you . . . Is it not true that nothing under heaven is more wicked, more poisonous, more hateful than the court of Rome? It has surpassed the immorality of the Turks so far, indeed, that Rome, formerly a gate of heaven, is now the wide-open throat of hell, and, unhappily, such a throat as, by the wrath of God, no man can shut . . . Lo! Holy Father, that is the final and the efficient cause why I have made such attacks upon this pestilential see. So far was I from intending to gird at you personally, that I even hoped to earn your goodwill and thanks, and be recognised as labouring for your highest good by virtue of the very lustiness and sharpness of my attack upon your prison, for your Throne must seem like hell to you.

And the letter reaches its climax by overturning the whole notion, embedded in Roman law, that the pope could be the Vicar of Christ:

Consider the dissimilarity between Christ and His vicars or representatives; if, indeed, all of them do want to represent Him. I fear it is only too true that they replace Him, for a representative only acts in a place from which his superior is absent. And the pope, unless Christ dwells in his heart, rules in the Lord's absence, and then only too truly does he replace Christ.

Yet all this precedes the offering of 'a little book', and Luther is at pains to emphasise the importance of its subject matter, for 'I send it with the lively hope that Your Holiness may discern the kind of subject on which I would spend my time and strength'.[9]

The 'little book' was *On the Freedom of the Christian Man*. In it, Luther sets out the idea that the soul is free, the body in bondage:

In as far as he possesses a soul, a Christian is a spiritual person, an inward regenerate self; and in as far as he possesses flesh and blood, he is a sensual person, an outward, unregenerate self.

For the Christian man 'no outer thing can make him free or religious', and this can only be understood through a study of God's message to mankind:

> The only means, whether in heaven or on earth, whereby the soul can live, and be religious, free, and Christian, is the holy gospel, the Word of God preached by Christ . . . all apostles, bishops, priests and the whole clergy were called and instituted only for the sake of the word; although, unfortunately, things happen differently nowadays.

Scripture is the only authority for the Christian, not the traditions of the Church. And from this stems the idea of the 'priesthood of all believers', for 'we are priests, and thus greater than mere kings, the reason being that priesthood makes us worthy to stand before God, and to pray for others'.

The outward, fleshly being must be disciplined with works, not as an end in themselves but 'in order that it [the body] may be obedient to and in harmony with, both the inner man and with faith'. It would be hopeless merely to carry out these works at the commands of men, which he elaborates as 'ecclesiastical law, or other man-made rules and doctrines'.

> The deeds are not the real essence of being good, and it is not true that they make a man dutiful and righteous before God. Rather, he does them voluntarily and freely, out of love, in order to please God.

The critique of the papacy was thus an attack on the entire notion of works, the things which had to be done to ensure salvation, here exposed as useless unless properly motivated. Thanks to printing, these ideas were circulating with unprecedented rapidity. The Ninety-Five Theses posted in October 1517, were available in German in a fortnight, and by March 1518, Erasmus had had ample time to study them and then send a copy to Thomas More.[10]

Even so, we have yet to see the implications of Luther's ideas drawn out in the everyday life of Christian Europe. Despite the attack on the papacy, that institution was to survive and, once reformed, it answered its critics in ways which stemmed and reversed the tide of Protestantism. Despite the groundswell of anti-clericalism and the enormous strength of Luther's concept of the priesthood of all believers, the Catholic clergy underwent moral refurbishment and reasserted its own separateness – and even Protestant societies preserved a distinction between clergymen and laypeople. However, papal power could never again be universal, for Luther had led an attack on vows made in accordance with the laws of men, and this was the spearhead of a general assault on the monasteries. In this, perhaps, lies the great impact of the initial attack on the Church, for the great phases of papal power had coincided with the phases of monastic renewal. Luther attacked the papacy in a new way, and he added his strident voice to general criticism of monasticism. The link between popes and monks was irreparably broken, not least because of the urgent need for the sanctification of marriage, which the monastic ideal made impossible.

The overthrow of the monastic life

By 1500, the monasteries had apparently become utterly lethargic, superfluous to social needs. However, we lack the large-scale study which could demonstrate this, and we must again avoid the notion that one limb of the Christian Church was moribund after centuries of putrefaction and was merely awaiting amputation. Much more startling is that with the decay of monasticism, the Church had lost what had been one of the chief and one of the most durable sources of renewal in the Christian life of the Middle Ages, and perhaps the most powerful instrument of papal power. Monks had carried out the initial work of conversion, the Gregorian reform was inextricably linked to the Cluniacs, the crusade launched by Urban II with the Cistercians. Perhaps most significant of all in providing a lifeline to the future was the association of the friars with Innocent III's titanic efforts to embrace the towns and define the universal limits of orthodoxy in a war on heresy, which was to link the regular clergy of the Middle Ages with the missionaries of the Counter-Reformation.

The monastic ideal had provided intellectual, spiritual and artistic leadership since the earliest days of Christianity. The demise of so powerful a spiritual ideal, so clear in its relationship to social change, so closely associated with the power of the pope in the world, can hardly be attributed to two and a half centuries of unexplained 'stagnation' before the Reformation. By 1500, the number of Cistercian monasteries had grown to nearly 750, and there were 900 or so nunneries. There is some evidence that the monasteries had shown their adaptability in land management – and even book production. In response to the competition of stationers there was a revival in scribal production in the late fourteenth and early fifteenth centuries – as at the charterhouse of St Barbara at Cologne – and some Benedictine houses even gave work to printers. At the Dissolution, the library at Canterbury contained more than 4,000 volumes. Thomas Cromwell was careful to entrust the industrious John Leland with the work of salvaging monastic libraries, a task which helped to make possible the revival of antiquarian learning in England in the later sixteenth century. Cromwell's reasoning was sound. On the continent, many of the texts which brought classical antiquity to life – such as Tacitus's *Germania* – had been found in monasteries in the course of the fifteenth century. Given the facilities which Erasmus had to hand at Steyn, which Luther enjoyed at Erfurt, which Zwingli found in the library at Einsiedeln, it would be unconvincing to pronounce that the intellectual life of the cloisters was dead in the age of the Reformation. It might be more helpful to see Renaissance humanism as the natural successor of medieval monasticism. Monastic learning had contained within a separate social order of the religious the great tensions of principle which the Renaissance identified for the laity: that between the individual and the community, between the active and the contemplative life, between opulence and puritanism – tensions articulated in classical texts which the monasteries had accidentally corrupted in the infinitely patient task of reproducing them.

Yet the great minds of the sixteenth century rejected monasticism, and often – Calvin is a notable exception – they did so in reaction to direct experience. This was a reformist idea which found clear expression in everyday social life: wherever the Reformation was established, the houses of the religious orders disappeared.[11] Erasmus remembered the cloister as a miserable phase of his life, Bucer gladly left it behind. Rabelais, drawing on his own experience, turned the monastic world upside down in a glorious lampoon. Rabelais's monk could keep pace with the guzzling of Gargantua himself, for he had 'a paved stomack as hollow as a But of malvoisie, or St Benedictus boot, and always open like a Lawyers pouch', and he offers a wonderfully obscene explanation as to why 'the thighs of a Gentlewoman are always fresh and coole'. Monks are shunned, says Gargantua:

> because they eat the ordure and excrements of the world, that is to say, the sins of the people, and like dung-chewers and excrementious eaters, they are cast into the privies and secessive places; that is the Convents and Abbeys separated from Political conversation . . . They mumble out great store of Legends and Psalmes, by them not at all understood: they say many patenotres, interlarded with ave-maries, without thinking upon or apprehending them, which truly I call mocking of God, and not prayers.

The monk remarks that 'I never sleep soundly, but when I am at Sermon or Prayers', and in the abbey of Thélème, which Gargantua endows, there was only one rule, 'the strictest tie of their order': 'Do what you like'. The superficiality of the rule, however, contrasts with what really matters, even in this libertine world:

> The Holy Sacred Word
> May it alwayes afford

T'us all in common
Both man and woman
A sp'ritual shield and sword,
The holy sacred Word.[12]

The lampoons of Rabelais and the mockery of Erasmus are satirical and their value as historical evidence of views generally held may be thought dubious. Luther launched an attack of an altogether more serious nature. Monasteries demanded vows made to the rules of men. The only rules that mattered were laid down in the Word of God. Therefore the monasteries were an affront to Christian freedom, Christian faith and Christian marriage. Erasmus had allowed that some monks were holy men and good scholars. Luther allowed for no such qualifications: concentrating on vows, he systematically dismantled the whole notion of their validity.

Luther wrote his *On Monastic Vows* in the Wartburg in 1521. He set out five main objections:

- vows are not commanded by God;
- vows conflict with faith;
- vows violate Christian freedom;
- vows go against the first commandment because the founders of the religious orders set themselves up as more important than Christ;
- vows are contrary to common sense, especially in the matter of celibacy.

Characteristically, Luther built his case on the bedrock of the Word. St Anthony was a hermit, not a monk. Monastic vows are 'without the authority and example of Scripture', and in that sense monks reject the gospel:

Is not this kind of a vow of obedience just a magnificent illusion? The gospel commands all men, always and in all situations, to yield, submit and obey. Those who have vowed to keep these counsels submit themselves neither to their equals nor to their inferiors, but to one superior only, and this not in everything, only some things. There again you see what happens to those who devise for themselves better things than Christ taught, who despise Christ and run their own lives in their own way.

As for poverty:

Evangelical poverty means to desire nothing in spirit and to serve freely for the good of others. How can they vow anything more than this unless they vow an outward use of things? . . . Under this holy vow of poverty they have become the most greedy of men and are rolling in wealth. Yet they boast that they have vowed these counsels, though no layman is more removed from poverty than they.

Chastity could not be dealt with in quite the same way:

> Because Satan could in no way turn a thing like chastity into its opposite, as he did in the case of obedience and poverty, he left it untouched, though he turned it into the greatest danger. Satan abolished its natural use, extolled it far above ordinary faith, and then he spread the error far and wide so that through the weakness of human nature he has entangled countless souls in his net and brought them to perdition.

In attacking monastic vows, Luther made an explicit – though not original – distinction between poverty as a spiritual condition and poverty as a state of material want: 'Under this holy vow of poverty they have become the most greedy of men and are rolling in wealth.'[13]

Moreover, the refutation of traditional ideas of obedience had colossal relevance to contemporary state-builders. On the one hand, freedom from obligation to the commands of men made it possible for states to become more independent of Rome. But by the same token, how did an independent secular power assert its own authority? The only answer was to acquire God's sanction. The secular prince was a divine instrument. The solution to centuries of conflict between Church and state was to make the ruler head of the Church. Within such a framework, we can accommodate both the constitutional revolution of Thomas Cromwell and the divine-right absolutism of Bodin and later Hobbes. Of course, as the history of the sixteenth century was to show, this development did not resolve the relationship of religion and politics. Rather, it heightened and intensified the conflict. A subject might disobey his prince – might even kill him – in what he perceived as lawful resistance to ungodly commands. Equally, a sovereign power sanctioned by God could not tolerate a challenge to its own authority as anything less than a challenge to God's. Heresy and rebellion were to become indistinguishable (below, ch. 12).

Luther's dismantling of the monastic ideal, then, gave voice to a new language of social and political obligation – towards the poor and towards the state. It also gave a revolutionary redefinition of the intimate relations of men and women.

The sanctification of marriage

'Every monk is a whorer either in secret or in public.' These are the words of the reformer, Urbanus Rhegius, and at one level they are typical of the great polemic against clerical immorality which often depicted the papacy as the Whore of Babylon and which gave the reform so much of its momentum. More profoundly, however, such opinions are symptomatic of the recognition that a Christian society needed a choice other than that between celibacy and fornication. Amongst the most sensitive and moving of the works of the great reformers are their words on marriage as a means of Christian renewal. Let us disclaim at once any crude notion that the Reformation was 'all to do with sex': Freudian interpretations of history consistently say more about the obsessions of the post-Freudian age than they do about the past. What must be acknowledged is that one of the most profound struggles between the Church and its critics was what to do about the celibacy of priests.

Catholic reformers revived the priestly order. In regions which the Reformation strongly affected, the removal of the identification of celibacy as a superior state entailed a corresponding elevation of marriage as something at once human and holy. Erasmus was ashamed of his own illegitimacy, and he was probably the son of a priest involved in a long-term illicit relationship. His writings prize marriage as a holy state, commanded by Scripture – unlike the celibacy of the clergy: 'What's this new religion that abrogates what the law of Nature sanctioned, the old law taught, the law of the gospel approved, and apostolic teaching confirmed?'; 'the marriage vow is unquestionably of divine ordinance and yet it is broken by taking monastic vows – a human invention.' He articulates the sentiments of human affection in terms which dispense altogether with lust. In 'Old Men's Chat', the loss of a partner is irreparable: 'My wife's death was truly the bitterest blow of my life. I had earnestly hoped she would grow old along with me, and that we would enjoy our children together.'[14]

It is highly significant that Luther explained his central doctrine of Christian freedom in terms of the union of the soul and Christ:

Faith not only gives the soul enough for her to become, like the divine word, gracious, free and blessed. It also unites the soul with Christ, like a bride with the bridegroom, and, from this marriage, Christ and the soul become one body, as St Paul says. Then the possessions of both are in common, whether fortune, misfortune, or anything else; so that what Christ has, also belongs to the believing soul, and what the soul has, will belong to Christ. If Christ has all good things, including blessedness, these will also belong to the soul. If the soul is full of trespasses and sins, these will belong to Christ. At this point a contest of happy exchanges takes place. Because Christ is God and man, and has never sinned, and because His sanctity is unconquerable, eternal, and almighty, He takes possession of the sins of the believing soul by virtue of her wedding-ring, namely faith, and acts just as if He had committed those sins Himself. They are, of course, swallowed up and drowned in Him, for His unconquerable righteousness is stronger than any sin whatever. Thus the soul is cleansed from all her sins by virtue of her dowry, i.e., for the sake of her faith. She is made free and unfettered, and endowed with the eternal righteousness of Christ, her bridegroom. Is that not a happy household, when Christ, the rich, noble, and good bridegroom, takes the poor, despised, wicked little harlot in marriage, sets her free from all evil, and decks her with all good things?

These are principles which he develops and elaborates in those letters of advice which give some clues as to the revolution in feeling which Luther's gentler words encouraged. He offers directness and certainty to Wolfgang Reissenbusch, a monk contemplating marriage. Woman is made to help man 'so that he may not be alone':

This is the Word of God, through whose power procreative seed is planted in man's body and a natural, ardent desire for woman is kindled and kept alive. This cannot be restrained by vows or by laws. For it is God's law and doing.

Luther had married a former nun, Catherine von Bora, in 1524.

One of Zwingli's initial spurs to the reform of the Christian life was a recognition of his own incontinence, his own incapacity to do without sex. He admitted that he had visited a prostitute, though his was not an exceptional lapse, and it was well-known that the Swiss clergy were often, to all intents and purposes, living as married men. In 1522 Zwingli himself married in secret. The quest to find official sanction for priestly marriage soon became a priority, and failure in this matter was one of the chief reasons for Zurich's break with Rome. In July 1522 Zwingli and ten other priests petitioned the bishop of Constance for permission to marry. The text is thoughtful, and frank, particularly in the fears expressed about promiscuity:

Therefore it appears to us most true and most right that for a Christian no third possibility besides chastity or marriage is left, and that he should live chastely if that is given unto him from above, or marry a wife if he be on fire with passion.

As in the case of Erasmus (much read by Zwingli) and Luther, the Bible provides for Zwingli the justification for change:

We have on the side of our request that Creator who made the first human beings male and female; we have the practice of the Old

Testament, which is much more strict than the New, under which, however, even the highest priests took upon their necks the gentle yoke of matrimony; we have Christ, who makes chastity free, nay, bids us marry, that his little children may not be offended.[15]

In all three cases – and we could add the thinking of Calvin to that of Erasmus, Luther and Zwingli – there is a clear concern to establish marriage as something fit and proper, an alternative to the celibacy of which so few were capable, and a safeguard against fornication.

Although no one appears to have made the specific connection in their surviving writings, what may have made the reform of marriage more urgent was the terrifying spread of syphilis. For this, the lax morals of clergymen cannot be blamed. Syphilis was probably unknown in Europe before the discovery of the New World. Some of the crewmen of the early voyages of discovery appear to have contracted the disease from the Indian populations and brought it home. There were soon plenty of famous cases. Cesare Borgia wore a mask to cover the ravages of the disease. Benvenuto Cellini needed treatment. Ulrich von Hutten, leader of the Knights' Revolt in 1522, was to die of the disease, as was the German humanist, Conrad Celtis. One reason why Luther sanctioned the bigamy of Philip of Hesse was that the prince was both promiscuous and syphilitic and a second marriage may have seemed the only way to reduce the number of women he infected. There is some evidence to suggest that Henry VIII was a sufferer, though his apothecaries never submitted bills which involve the obvious treatments.

However, what made the problem general were large armies on the move. Initially, the pox spread most rapidly in Italy in the early sixteenth century because of the wars of Habsburg and Valois (below, ch. 10). Some French soldiers contracted the disease at the siege of Naples and spread it when they were disbanded, which appears to be why the pox became known as 'the French disease'. Special hospitals for 'incurables' were established in Rome, Verona, Vicenza and Genoa. In Venice in 1522, the Commissioners of Public Health issued a proclamation seeking to provide for the 'many persons sick and afflicted with the French pox and other ills' in order to prevent its spread. By 1525, the *Incurabili* had 150 patients. The armies of the powers engaged in the Italian Wars involved a high proportion of mercenaries from Germany and Switzerland, and they clearly spread the contagion in their homelands. Zwingli, who had been a chaplain amongst Swiss companies, was a vigorous opponent of mercenary soldiering. The connection was obvious to Shakespeare's contemporaries, as is clear from *Troilus and Cressida*. Thersites denounces the doings of heroes as 'Lechery, lechery, still wars and lechery! Nothing else holds fashion.' And Pandarus the procurer ends the play with a graphic warning to pimps:

Good traders in the flesh, set this in your painted cloths:
As many as be here of Pandar's hall,
Your eyes, half out, weep out at Pandar's fall;
Or if you cannot weep, yet give some groans,
Though not for me, yet for your aching bones.

Promiscuity had made syphilis a general social problem well before
Shakespeare's day. For Erasmus, the disease was 'both more hideous
and more harmful than every kind of leprosy, for it progresses quickly,
recurs over and over again, and often kills', and it is spreading, for 'so
huge a plague has filled a large part of the globe'. It appears to be the
most deadly of all diseases: 'how much less is the peril from plague than
from this pox!'. A sure sign of contemporary fears was the paranoia
about transmission. Aside from physical contact, the sufferer might
breathe it into the air, and what of 'sheets, combs, and scissors' or the
common drinking cup? And Erasmus seems to have been aware that
prostitution invited the spread of the disease. One of his characters, a
young man, tries to persuade a harlot to change her ways:

you make yourself a public sewer that every Tom, Dick and Harry –
the dirty, the vile, the diseased – resorts to and empties his filth into!
If you haven't yet caught the new contagion called the Spanish pox,
you won't long escape it.

Luther himself posted an uncompromising warning to students
about the dangers of whoring:

I ask you in fatherly fashion, dear children, that you believe
assuredly that the evil spirit sent these whores here and that they
are dreadful, shabby, stinking, loathsome, and syphilitic [*Frantzö-
sich*] as daily experience unfortunately demonstrates. Let every good
student warn his fellows. Such a syphilitic whore can give her disease
to ten, twenty, thirty and more good people, and so she is to be
accounted a murderer, as worse than a poisoner.

Thus, the early work of reform took apart the monastic ideal, and one
of the positive creations of Erasmus, Luther and Zwingli was the
suggestion that marriage was natural, and it offered a genuine
alternative to the impossible demands of celibacy, a vital source of
reassurance to a society which stood in fear of a new and deadly
disease.

Of itself, however, the new marital ideal was not enough to fill the
void which the monasteries left, the great airy vortex at the centre of
Christendom. In the north, many of the social and spiritual experiments
of the age look like quests for substitute monasteries. More's Utopia

comes to mind with its common ownership, its contempt for money, its uniform clothing and its vigorous routine of work and contemplation, and so does More himself, a man who found the tonsure in the Tower. The mutual censure of the pastors in Calvin's Geneva recalls the monastic *culpa*, as does the duty of the elect to look to the needs of the poor at their gates. The anabaptists fled from the world, seeking to establish their independence of its laws. Perhaps the search for some alternative form of the monastic life was a symptom of the disquiet and perplexity which the figure of woman now raised. Even though reformers spoke of marriage with such warmth and gentleness, their new vision was flawed by anxiety about woman as temptress. As Luther put it to his students:

> I must speak plainly. If I were a judge, I would have such venomous, syphilitic whores broken on the wheel and flayed because one cannot estimate the harm such filthy whores do to young men who are so wretchedly ruined and whose blood is contaminated before they have achieved full manhood.

Although the reform implied and promoted a new psychology of marriage, the reformers never freed themselves from the view of woman as responsible for the fall of man through a league with the devil which made her responsible for original sin. Such thinking is clearly represented in Bosch's disturbing view of the creation of woman, which shows the fall of Lucifer in the background. It may help to explain why women were so frequently persecuted for having caused impotence, adultery and eventually even crop failure, for these were obviously the work of the witch.[16]

Such was the experience of parts of the Protestant north. In Catholic regions, the old church stabilised, reformed and fought back. Some Catholic reformers toyed with a new monasticism. A notable example is the Theatine Order, which counted the future Pope Paul IV among its members. But when we think of the Counter-Reformation, we do not think of the Theatine Order, we think of the Jesuits, and for them the cloister was irrelevant: and it is perhaps symptomatic of the great change that Catholic authorities were often at least as ferocious as Protestants in their suppression of witchcraft. It took the papacy nearly a century to come to terms with the change – Paul IV and Ignatius Loyola were always antagonists – but the great battle for hearts and minds which now ensued depended on the social involvement of the priesthood, not their seclusion. Monasteries had dissolved into missions.

7   How the Word spread

Missions

For centuries, the monasteries had represented the Christian ideal as
the realisation of spiritual potential in seclusion from the world. In the
sixteenth century, missionaries sought to give spiritual aspiration a
social form. It is a symptom of the momentous character of this change
that virtually nothing of the monastic life or the monastic ideal is now
familiar, while the mission is easily recognised as an index of Europe's
impact on the wider world. Everyone has heard of the Alamo, which
was founded in 1718 as a mission to the Comanche Indians, and
everyone knows that David Livingstone, Albert Schweitzer and
Mother Teresa are part of a tradition which offers Christian charity
and Christian education to the poor and needy in Africa and India.
Christian education, Christian charity ministered to the non-European
world: these are the modern associations, and they were forged in the
sixteenth century. However, the mission assumed the shape we
recognise not because of Europe's contact with the outside world,
but because of the deep social conflict of Protestantism and Catholicism in Europe itself. Education and charity were the areas in which
rival missions sought to demonstrate a superior capacity to meet the
needs of Christians and to regenerate Christian society.

Protestant missions were part of an attack on the idea that a separate
clerical order was the repository of godliness. By mid-century, they
were competing with a refurbished Catholic clergy which justified its
separateness by the abandonment of worldly values and involvement in
the life of the needy – those rejected as not among the elect. This was
the social dimension of the ideological struggle which is often
compressed into the terms 'Reformation' and 'Counter-Reformation'.
The Protestant experiment sought a formula which would regulate the
daily social behaviour of all Christians. Reformed Catholicism emphasised that Christians needed an example to follow, an example provided
by the clergy in the form of their work in society. Paradoxically, the
Protestant attempt to make the Christian life all-pervasive became
increasingly exclusive, while the separate clerical order of reformed
Catholicism offered a religion that was all-embracing.

A comparison of the missionary activities which the two forms of
Christianity pursued helps to explain the puzzling limitations of

149

Protestant success and the startling triumphs of the Catholic revival. That comparison is the subject of the next two chapters. While terms such as 'Protestant' and 'Catholic' or 'Reformation' and 'Counter-Reformation' immediately evoke ideological conflict, it is important to remember the common cultural roots of both missionary enterprises. Both Protestants and Catholics sought to impose 'social discipline' through a process of 'confessionalisation'. With regard to the differing strategies of social control, here too there is evidence of a shared culture. The Renaissance can be understood at bottom as a culture of humanists and artists. The sixteenth century witnessed a rift in that achievement. While the Protestants espoused the word, Catholic ideas found expression in imagery – and it was the image which proved victorious (plates, section IV).

Missions are methodologically helpful, especially with regard to new religious ideas and their social impact. The degree of interaction between ideas and context remains very obscure.[1] Missions were at once a reflection of ideas and a response to social needs. Analysed as a concept, the mission helps us to understand the agenda which sixteenth-century reformers set out in relation to perceived and real social needs. As an institution, the mission enables us to see religious ideas and their social context in dynamic equilibrium. The identification of that equilibrium helps to avoid presenting the religious ideas of the sixteenth century as abstractions, and it avoids the determinism which makes ideas the product of social environment.

The Lutheran message

The last chapter examined the explosive originality of Luther's teaching. What was its impact on the way in which people worshipped? In a sense, Wittenberg set a Saxon model, which was then copied and modified in different contexts – Franconia, central and northern Germany, the Baltic, and Strasbourg. In Switzerland, the reform progressed from Zurich to Berne, Basel, St Gallen and Schaffhausen. In terms of what happened in church, the laity, encouraged by Luther, took both bread and wine in communion, they listened to sermons preached in the language of everyday life rather than Latin, they did so in interiors from which offensive and non-Biblical images were removed (though not smashed – Luther never advocated iconoclasm), where exclusive brotherhoods ceased to meet, and where private masses were no longer said, and the congregation was expected to contribute to a common chest of funds which would be distributed amongst the poor. The new pattern of worship embodied a set of profound changes. The penitential emphasis of medieval Christianity was gone. The new emphases were on Christ, faith and scripture. The Church itself was a community of believers rather than an institution or place of worship, and sacrificing priests had given way to preachers.

From a very early stage, however, there were hesitations and lack of direction in the implementation of reformed religion. Luther for instance returned to communion in one kind only and to the Latin mass in 1523 in order to distance himself from the ideas of Andreas Karlstadt. The practical manifestations of reformed principles owed much to Luther's supporters, in particular Philip Melanchthon (1497–1560) and Johann Bugenhagen (1485–1558). Melanchthon, 'the quiet reformer', was an unlikely partner for Luther, but he harnessed his genial Erasmianism to Luther's passion and savagery. He was a professor of Greek, and the aim of his scholarship was clear and unshakeable:

for I think that the commentaries of men on sacred matters must be fled like the plague, because the teaching of the Spirit cannot be drunk in purity except from Scripture itself.

His skills in exposition enabled him to set out Luther's ideas lucidly and systematically. What a range he had to cover! Penance, baptism, the mass, sin, works, the Eucharist, clerical marriage. Above all these and central to them was a calm and reassuring insistence on the salvation which only faith – 'the hope God offers in the face of death' – could provide:

since we are justified by the mercy of God alone, and faith is clearly the recognition of that mercy by whatever promise you apprehend it, justification is attributed to faith alone.

He was the author of the Augsburg Confession (1530). This document set out to reconcile Lutheran doctrine and the universal Church. In the event, what it omitted – for example any compromise between Lutheran belief and Catholic notions of purgatory and any compromise between Catholic belief and the Lutheran priesthood of all believers – served to define what separated Lutheran ideas from Rome, and the clarity of his views on justification emphasised the distinction between Luther's followers and those of other reformers.

Melanchthon's influence as a teacher was considerable, but it was the doggedness and tenacity of Bugenhagen which translated Luther's ideas into educational practice. This tireless preacher spread the word in prolonged sermons, and following an invitation from Christian II, he was influential in the establishment of the Reformation in Denmark and its spread to other parts of the Baltic.

However, an evaluation of the establishment of Lutheranism in Denmark seems a minor episode after all the initial excitement.

Luther's volcanic spiritual energy seemed sure, as we saw in a previous chapter, to carry all before it. Yet despite the initial exhilaration of the attack, and despite the possibilities offered by intellectual circles sharing Luther's background and conclusions – such as the one at Tübingen – there is no adherence to a common core of doctrine, no integrated 'movement'. One explanation is that the reform was qualified out of existence by the particular circumstances of a local community: its political status, its economic interests, the composition of its ruling élite (above, pp. 100–2). But a substantial measure of the explanation lies in the actions and opinions of Luther himself. Indeed, the progress of the Reformation – that is to say, the installation of religious practices similar to those adopted in Wittenberg – owed very little to Luther. Here we have to accept an impenetrable paradox: the great liberator was not a great leader.

In a sense this is consistent with his initial protest. He attacked an entire world system in an effort to free Christians from the principle of spiritual constraint, and he was correspondingly wary of creating from the wreckage an alternative system which merely offered a different set of constraints. But in whatever way we choose to interpret his attitude, we must recognise that contemporaries sympathetic to Luther's ideas faced formidable problems in doing anything about their implementation. Luther was reluctant to see his ideas adapted to the needs of particular communities, and he was unreceptive to the ideas of others. The net result was that Luther often abusively disowned those he had inspired, and he left those who looked to him for leadership to their own devices. In this sense, Luther's protest was genuinely explosive: a sudden unforgettable crash which in one burst of energy consumed the fuel which might have sustained it. That stubborn conviction which enabled Luther to withstand Eck, to stand alone if necessary against 1500 years of ecclesiastical tradition, was the same force which marred his relations with Erasmus, and which urged the princes to the cruel destruction of peasant rebellion. The enormous concentration upon the spiritual problems of the isolated soul confronted with eternity seems at least partially to have blocked the development of an awareness of the Christian as a social being.

Failure rather than success emanated from Wittenberg itself. The loyalty of Melanchthon and Bugenhagen kept them close to Luther, but he disowned a small group from nearby Zwickau who raised doubts about the validity of infant baptism. A former Zwickau pastor, Thomas Müntzer, a millennial visionary who later led the peasant armies, found no favour in Luther's eyes. Another of Luther's pet hatreds, Andreas Karlstadt, a university intellectual, senior to Luther, who did not share a penchant for violence, stood for an austere puritanism in matters of sabbatarianism and images, and Luther roared him down too. To isolate these figures as too 'radical' for Luther's liking is to miss the broader problem (below, pp. 208–9). Reformers who differed with Luther on the matter of the Eucharist were all opponents: 'One side must be the devil, and God's enemy. There is no middle ground.' Consequently, there was an equal measure of venom for Oecolampadius at Basel, humanist, correspondent of Erasmus and of the Nuremberg reformers Kristof Scheurl and Willibald Pirckheimer – but then Luther hurled invective at Osiander in Nuremberg as well – and we leave aside for the moment the assaults on Zwingli and Bucer.

The problem for those who sought Luther's guidance was enormous. Luther's stated aim was to reach the people with the Word of God. In the constitution which he drew up for the town of Leisnig (in 1523) – it was never actually put into practice – he explained how this was to be achieved:

> every householder and his wife shall be duty-bound to cause the wholesome, consoling word of God to be preached to them, their children, and their domestic servants, so that the gospel may be impressed on them for their betterment.

Where evangelicals sought to establish the Reformation, they established schools: Luther himself at Wittenberg and Leisnig, Agricola at Eisleben, Melanchthon at Nuremberg, Brenz at Schwäbisch Hall, Aepinus at Stralsund and Heidelberg, Bugenhagen at Braunschweig, Hamburg and Lübeck, Bucer at Ulm and Strasbourg.[2] Yet these initiatives did not christianise society according to evangelical principles, for there was no clear statement of what such principles might be, no uniformity, no coordination.

Predestination and puritanism

Thus, while in the previous chapter we saw Luther towering above the context of his times, we need also to remember that he did not relate to that context. There is no space in a work of this nature to trace the successes and failures of evangelicalism in every tiny community.[3] The transformation of Protestantism from a set of liberating ideas to an institutional and political alternative to Rome owed its trajectory to the very closely related experiences of three leaders and three cities. Huldrich Zwingli staged a reformation in Zurich contemporary with Luther's protest but quite independent of it and very different in its ideas. In Strasbourg, Martin Bucer undoubtedly took his cue from Luther, but he owed and acknowledged a considerable debt to Zwingli, and set out decisive new organisational and political possibilities. These in turn took more expansive ideological shape in Geneva, where John

Calvin created an alternative world system which made permanent the division of Christendom.

The critical change in the character of the reform – perhaps not in theology, but certainly in terms of social and political organisation – was the elaboration of the doctrine of predestination, which was in some ways a development of justification by faith but in others a departure from it. For Luther, God offered salvation to the lonely individual who believed. For Calvin, God promised salvation to an exclusive community. We can trace how this came about by examining the course of reform in Zurich, Strasbourg and Geneva and in the minds of Zwingli, Bucer and Calvin.

The character of the reform as something more than Lutheranism was plain from the outset. Zwingli was never a disciple of Luther, and in some ways it is misleading to place him in Luther's shadow. His career shows the decisive importance of individual conviction in determining the course of the Reformation. For it was in Zurich that the Swiss reform began, not in Berne, the pre-eminent military power, not in Basel with its vibrant intellectual life, and it began in Zurich because of the ideas and personality of Zwingli.

His preoccupations were often similar to Luther's. The Word was the inspiration of Christian faith, 'so vital, strong and powerful that all things must necessarily obey it, and that fully and at such time as God Himself appoints'. Accordingly:

I undertook to devote myself entirely to the Scriptures, and the conflicting philosophy and theology of the schoolmen constantly presented difficulties. But eventually I came to a conclusion – led thereto by the scriptures and Word of God – and decided 'You must drop all that and learn God's will directly from His own word'.

The condition of the soul was fundamental and externals irrelevant, for 'all that is a show before men is gross hypocrisy and iniquity'. His own sense of mission increased enormously in the light of personal experience, most importantly his recovery from plague in 1519. Like Luther, he set out his ideas in theses (67 of them, written in 1523), which he defended in debate against Catholic opponents in Berne in 1528, a performance which was carefully stage-managed, but which established the reform in that city.

The results in Zurich display similarities to Wittenberg. The mass was abolished (1525), and the Last Supper commemorated in a dramatically simplified manner, 'appointed ministers' giving the congregation communion in both kinds. Like Luther, Zwingli placed great emphasis on the sanctity of marriage (above, pp. 145–6) and, like Luther, Zwingli fought off any association with 'radicals' such as the anabaptists.

As in Wittenberg, the Bible provided the foundations of the new religious forms and the new social behaviour. The city council made careful provision for the public to be educated in the Word, issuing a decree in 1523:

> that learned, skilful, and upright men shall lecture on, and expound the Bible publicly every day devoting one hour daily each to the Hebrew, Greek and Latin texts, very necessary for the proper understanding of the divine word . . . In addition, a schoolmaster, better paid than previously, shall be provided to be an active teacher and leader to the boys.

This was a training for missionaries, not an effort to stimulate mass literacy. Preachers were expected to read the Bible in the original languages and turn themselves into prophets. Here perhaps, there are a drive and purpose which Lutheranism somehow lacked. The Zwinglian model was copied in Strasbourg and Basel, and found parallels in England and Scotland – and in 'prophecy' surely lay the seeds of that organised ideological conviction which reached its supreme form in Calvin's Geneva.

There are other more obvious contrasts with the Lutheran reform, emphasising the importance of approaching the Reformation as a complex of movements rather than a unitary phenomenon. Zwingli was operating within the particular social and political configuration of the Swiss Confederation. There was no question of princely protection, no reference to the emperor: Zurich was a city-state, a guild republic, its social traditions definitely corporatist. In terms of the immediate circumstances of the reform, indulgences were much less significant than mercenary service. Soldiers were the chief export of the Swiss, and they often served in the armies of the pope. Zwingli had seen service in the Italian Wars, which marked a new era in the history of warfare in terms of their sheer scale (below, ch. 10), and as chaplain to the soldiers, he had been profoundly distressed by the carnage of the battle of Marignano in 1515. Rather than hawkers of indulgences, it was the papacy's recruiting agent, Cardinal Schiner, whose activities seemed so unchristian:

> Against a wolf one raised the hue and cry, but no one really opposed the wolves who destroyed most people. It was fit and proper that these latter wore red hats and cloaks; for if one shook them ducats and crowns would be scattered round about; if they were wrung out, the blood of your son, brother, father and good friends would flow.

Mercenary service was abolished, and Zwingli – 'I recognise my own sin before God and man' – renounced his papal pension. So, while

Luther broke with Rome for its involvement in the world, Zwingli was more concerned about Rome's use of the sword. More significant for the future of Protestantism were two key areas in which Zwingli developed ideas quite different from those of Luther. Zwingli was at once more rational and proposed more fundamental change in the matter of transubstantiation, and he hardened a doctrine of predestination, which, to Luther and Melanchthon, was a matter of indifference.

The importance of the debate on transubstantiation is difficult for us to grasp. To speak of the issue as 'a source of division amongst Protestants' does little to evoke the passions it raised in an atmosphere of spiritual turmoil. The re-enactment of the Last Supper was – perhaps is – as close as any Christian could come to Christ. For Luther, the mystery of Christ's omnipresence was an aspect of his divinity. If He said 'this is My body', then the words were to be taken absolutely literally. Zwingli's doctrine was that communion was a commemoration, that Christ was spiritually present in the heart of the recipient, but not real in the bread and wine: 'He is the lifegiving bread as put to death, not as pressed with the teeth or eaten.'

For Luther, such notions cut the slender cord which attached God's Son to the world. For Zwingli the 'is' in 'this is My body' meant 'represents', the bread was 'a sign and nothing more', as he put it. This may seem somewhat forced – it certainly did to Luther – but Zwingli's argument was that a clear distinction existed between Christ's spiritual presence and Christ's real presence, in the sense of being substance. He put his case with conviction and wit, pointing out, for instance, that Christ also said 'I am the vine' – were we to take that literally too? For Zwingli, to hold otherwise on the Eucharist was to endorse the superstitions with which the papists had for centuries enslaved Christians, allowing 'the common people to be deceived into thinking it is something strange and unusual'.

The division between Luther and Zwingli on this central question was to fragment Protestantism irreparably, though strenuous efforts were made to heal the rift. Philip of Hesse, anxious to expand and tighten the Protestant alliance after the Diet of Speyer, brought the two reformers together at Marburg in 1529: not a desperate gamble, but an enterprise essential to the progress of the reform. The gap proved unbridgeable. Luther ruled out compromise with people whom he regarded as 'enemies of God and His Word', and began the colloquy by chalking '*hoc est corpus meum*', 'this is My body', on the table in front of him. His intractability was to prove disastrous for Protestantism. Zwingli had paid generous tribute to Luther's achievement in 1527, 'the only faithful David', 'that one Hercules', 'Who has set forth more clearly and plainly than you from apostolic sources the hostility of body and soul?'. But in a letter reporting the colloquy, he expressed frustration as well as self-righteousness in referring to Luther's 'countless absurdities, inconsistencies and follies which he babbles out like water lapping on the shore'. In the same letter, he remarked that he found Melanchthon 'uncommonly slippery'.[4] Had Zwingli tied Melanchthon down, it is likely that a further difference would have emerged.

'Let us not allow our faith to be shaken by unreasonable discussions about predestination', Melanchthon was to write in 1532. Predestination is, literally, an unreasonable doctrine. One cannot explain it, one merely believes it. Predestination is an aspect of divine providence: the doctrine that nothing happens except as part of the divine purpose. However cruel and haphazard the vicissitudes of the world, they are part of a divine plan which is quite beyond human understanding. Predestination is part of the divine plan – that is to say, God will give salvation to some, the rest are damned. 'The elect', who are destined to be saved, cannot be sure that that is what is in store for them. For some – such as Luther and Ignatius Loyola – to inquire into God's inscrutable purpose was itself sinful. For Melanchthon, predestination for the elect went contrary to the 'universal promises of the gospel':

> when we hear that mercy is the cause of election, and yet that few are elected, we are even more distressed, and wonder whether there is respect of persons with God, and why he does not have mercy on all.

For Zwingli, predestination was the ultimate expression of God's sovereignty. To regard His purpose as anything but inscrutable was born of pride. It is a measure of the different spiritual sources of the Zwinglian reform that for him, predestination was even more fundamental than faith: 'the elect are the children of God even before they believe'.

The doctrine was to have tremendous implications for Protestantism as a social and political movement, but they were not realised in Zwingli's career. His influence was limited by a rash campaign against Catholic cantons which brought defeat and death at the battle of Kappel in 1531. It is poignant that accounts of Zwingli's end suggest that he was finished off by a mercenary captain who received a pension, 'one of those against whom he had always preached so eloquently'. Yet he had already secured Berne for the Protestant cause. And in the course of that final campaign, with imperial power resurgent after victory over France in Italy, and Protestantism in disarray after the Diet of Augsburg, he had sought to unite the anti-imperial cause of France with the Swiss reform:

> no king or people has more steadfastly resisted the power and tyranny of the Roman Empire than the most Christian kings of France and the Swiss people. It is to their activity that they owe the

fact that not only has their own freedom survived unharmed but also that of the princes, peoples and cities which have not yet submitted to imperial domination.

The military power of Zwinglian Berne was the only safeguard of the Protestant cause in Geneva, and the quest for a reformed power base in France was work taken up by Calvin.[5] Moreover, Zwingli had exerted an important influence on the director of the second great theatre of reform, the imperial city of Strasbourg. Martin Bucer (1491–1551) can seem a passive, unoriginal figure: influenced by Erasmus, won over to Luther by the latter's performance at the Heidelberg Disputation of 1518, much impressed by Zwingli. However, there is a curious dichotomy in Bucer's career. He was the chief driving force of a long process of reform in Strasbourg, a process which eventually established a Lutheran church. Yet ideologically, Bucer built on Zwinglian foundations, notably on the questions of transubstantiation and predestination, and he was the architect of institutional reforms which Calvin copied but never surpassed. There were early differences with Luther. Despite Bucer's admiration, he suffered at least two savage personal assaults. The first was the result of what Luther regarded as Bucer's inaccurate translation of his *Postil*:

> The devil saw clearly that this book was being disseminated everywhere. Therefore he seized it, and loaded and smeared it with his dung. So I, an innocent man, must now be the waggon driver of the devil's manure, whether I will or not.

At Marburg, when Bucer asked Luther what was wrong with Zwingli's doctrine on the Eucharist, it was he who bore the brunt of Luther's uncompromising rejoinder:

> I am not your master, your judge, or your teacher, but it is clear that we have not the same spirit, for there cannot be the same spirit where the plain words of Christ are implicitly believed in one place while elsewhere the same faith is criticised, turned into falsehood and treated with every kind of insolent abuse. So, as I said before, we commit you to the judgement of God and do you consider how you will answer before Him.

Bucer is usually projected as the mediator between Luther and Zwingli and there can be no doubt about his anxiety for unity amongst the reformers. He reached agreement with Luther about the Eucharist in 1536 (the Wittenberg Concord) and carried south German Protestantism with him. This perhaps is the problem with Bucer: formal agreements with Luther, personal convictions which match those of

Zwingli. Identified with the progress of the Lutheran reform, he was in fact taking it in a very different direction. In launching his reform – and again at the Colloquy of Marburg – he supported Zwingli on the question of transubstantiation. Predestination would have proved another source of division between Bucer and Luther. Justification by Faith was a doctrine which could ensure the salvation of any Christian. Predestination, on the other hand, divided the elect and the damned as sheep and goats. This was to make Protestantism much more muscular and manageable in social and political terms – and was for that reason essential if Protestantism was to survive. It helped to explain why some people could never be touched by the Word, however often they heard it. Bucer left no doubt that the wicked were part of God's purpose. Predestination meant 'the election of the saints and their separation from the remaining polluted mass of mankind'. The saints are elected 'before they are even born', 'by the pure grace of God' – salvation is in no sense a reward. For Luther – and for St Ignatius – it was pride, the sin of Lucifer, to presume that a man could interpret God's purpose. Although the divine plan was inscrutable, Bucer stated – in terms significantly more lucid and direct than those of Calvin – that the elect might know that they were to be saved, writing of 'our immutable election, the knowledge of which both immeasurably strengthens faith and actively kindles in us a zeal for purity'. And zealous puritans could expect the realisation of Christ's kingdom on earth, for 'those who persevere in manifest wickedness have no part in the kingdom of Christ', while 'the kingdom of Christ in this world is the ministry of salvation of the elect of God'. The elect had a mission:

the elect are gathered from the world into this kingdom [of Christ] through the preaching of the gospel, ministered by fit ministers chosen and sent for this very purpose by the Lord himself, with the simultaneous breathing forth of the Holy Spirit, the Spirit of faith, through whom it is given to men to have a real faith in the gospel.

The gospel would be preached unremittingly on the sabbath:

Who, therefore, would not see how salutary it is for the people of Christ that there be one day in the week so consecrated to religious services that it should not be allowable to do anything else on that day except assemble in the congregation of worship, and there hear the Word of God?

Who indeed, if not the damned? And even for the saints:

since it has to be diligently guarded against that no occasion be given to men for doing their own will on the Sabbath of the Lord, it must be a matter of special concern for those who wish the Kingdom of Christ to be restored among them that Sunday religious observance be renewed and established.

Luxuries 'and all things contributing more to the delight of the flesh than to the virtue of the spirit and the utility of the commonwealth' are to be prohibited.[6]

Zeal, sabbatarianism, worldly delights an abomination, these are the marks of the saints: in Bucer's thought took shape the austere morality of Protestant puritanism, in Bucer's Strasbourg the Gospel became law. Luther had never envisaged this, Zwingli's city-church could have proved a transient quirk of its Swiss context.

Strasbourg was in any case a managerial challenge for the reform. It was an imperial free city, and unlike Zurich, it had no rural surroundings to govern. Yet its social structure was at once more variegated and dynamic. The population of 20,000 – three times that of the city of Zurich, twice that of Geneva – was stratified into patricians, burghers and artisans, and the sources of tension in terms of social status, economic interests and political power – or the lack of them – made the realisation of a harmonious Protestant community a difficult business. In terms of evangelical propaganda, Strasbourg's thriving printing industry offered exciting possibilities. In a fundamental sense, the presses of Strasbourg had been the very first to offer a new view of the world.

As early as 1507, the Strasbourg printer, Matthias Ringmann, had worked with Martin Waldseemüller to produce a map of the world, and had produced a revision of Ptolemy's geography. Johann Schott commissioned the illustrations for Otto Brunfels's work on botany (above, p. 118), Michael Toxites worked with the humanist educator, Johann Sturm, on Cicero, and had developed skills which he was to apply to an edition of the works of Paracelsus (above, p. 125). Yet the intellectual independence of the populace made it no passive recipient of reformed ideas. There was a high literacy rate amongst artisans, who owned a wide variety of books, and who were quite capable of producing their own publications. A furrier might read Vergil, a gardener could write a pamphlet. This ensured that there would be no bland acceptance of mere novelty. Indeed, perhaps it was the challenge of the social context which concentrated so powerfully the minds and talents of reformers – Hedio, Capito and Zell as well as Bucer. Their ambitious aim, simply stated, was that evangelism should regenerate morality, and the new moral sense would be the new orthodoxy.

From the outset, there were resonances with the Lutheran reform. The first sign of radical change came in 1522, when Tilman von Lyn left a Carmelite house to preach the Word. In 1524 clerical celibacy was ended and the monasteries closed. The attack on the mass, however, was inspired by Zwinglian ideas. As early as 1523, Bucer, Capito and Zell expressed their own convictions by taking communion quite specifically as a memorial. (Luther was blasting his first criticisms of Bucer in 1524.) In 1530, at the Diet of Augsburg, Charles V sought to free himself from German problems in order to crusade against the Turks. Melanchthon had drawn up the Augsburg Confession, an effort to find and expand common ground between Protestants and Catholics. There was real will for peace on both sides. Strasbourg's reformers stood aloof. The city did not accept the Augsburg Confession until 1534, maintaining instead ties with Switzerland: 'We are using every trick against the mass', Capito wrote to Zwingli.

The institutional organisation of the reform in Strasbourg was more practical than anything Luther achieved, more complete in Strasbourg than in Zurich – or even Geneva. Education was of fundamental importance, and the celebrated *Gymnasium* established in 1538 under the dynamic direction of Johann Sturm, and with Calvin amongst its lecturers, offered an education in the Bible in both Latin and German. Reformed teaching – on penance, the Eucharist, the Christian in society, family life, education and marriage – spread in printed form as well as in the spoken word. The relief of poverty was another priority. Once again, the challenge which Strasbourg offered reformers was more considerable than in many other centres. The population grew by about 25 per cent in the course of the sixteenth century: there were some 3,000 widows and orphans in 1525; 1,500 refugees arrived in 1538 alone. Amongst the most important changes in the organisation of everyday life were that the Dominican friary became a sort of 'welfare headquarters', while that of the Franciscans was, from 1530, a refugee centre.[7]

In his quest for spiritual satisfaction, Luther had tended to neglect worldly organisation, Zwingli's achievement lay buried in its Swiss roots at Kappel. By contrast with both, Bucer offered propaganda for the reform as practical advice drawn from the experience of Strasbourg. Perhaps his most important general message was the recognition that the reform could not do without the support of the secular power. Bucer's *De Regno Christi* is addressed to Edward VI of England. It is not a particularly revolutionary document, and it is not particularly well-known. Yet this handbook on the implementation of religious reform sheds some light on the character of Bucer's programme. The mission should be the work of 'managers' (*oeconomi*). The churches should be part of the state in terms of 'their ministers, their schools and their poor'. Bucer was as passionate as Luther in advocating the indoctrination of the young, 'for unless the foundation of the Church is firmly laid in early childhood through the catechism of Christ, its upbuilding will proceed very poorly from then on'.

Luther would have agreed that 'approved evangelists must be sent out to all parts of the realm', but one wonders whether Luther could have asked the question 'who will pay the expenses for these evangelists?'. There would be returns for public investment, for if all Christian children could read and write, they would be 'better prepared for a fuller service to Church and state' – while education itself was coupled with 'the suppression of idleness'. There was high principle in matters of poor relief, for without charity 'there can be no true communion of the saints'. However, discrimination was necessary. The churches should exclude the able-bodied who 'refuse to seek the necessities of life by their own industry', and the deacons 'should keep a special written record of the names, kind of need, and behaviour of the poor'. Bucer's programme for godly reform under the auspices of a godly state was to have an influence at once profound and direct on the development of English puritanism – he lived his last years in Cambridge – particularly in matters of 'discipline', and parochial charity.[8] Yet he left on Protestantism a more general impression as a result of the influence he exerted on Calvin, whose debt to Bucer's Strasbourg was enormous.

From Calvin to Calvinism

Humour and individuality – which Luther possessed in abundance – are not necessarily sources of political inspiration. We lack a clear sense of Calvin's personality, yet there is no doubt that what he stood for provided the leadership and ideological conviction which Luther had failed to supply. And in the sense of providing a holy place of earthly pilgrimage, Calvinism created a myth of stable perfection in a world of frightening uncertainty, a myth which exceeded and simplified the workmanlike reforms of Zwingli and Bucer. While Zwinglian Zurich never freed itself from the introverted politics of the Swiss Confederation, Calvin's Geneva used the peculiarities of its cross-roads location to evangelise Europe as a whole. Calvin experienced more setbacks and achieved less in Geneva than did Bucer in Strasbourg: but we do not speak of 'Bucerism', because Bucer did not generate that powerful mythology which we identify with Calvin. What made Calvinism a world-system was that setbacks on this earth were irrelevant to God's overall pupose, an eternal plan which would not be tied to secular expectations. Man could not presume to hurry God's work.[9]

The relationship of Calvin's life to the evolution of Calvinism – an immensely complicated subject, but essential to an understanding of the 'wars of religion' – can be examined through three generally recognisable facts. Calvin's most important ideas are contained in his *Institutes of the Christian Religion*. Calvin's name is forever identified with the

Reformation in Geneva. Calvin's ideas and activities helped to inspire revolutionary activity in France and the Netherlands. We must guard against any simple model which projects the *Institutes* as a statement of ideas, Geneva as their practical expression, religious war as the result of their systematic generalisation. The ideology had to adapt dramatically to different contexts in Scotland, the Netherlands and France, for example. The *Institutes* did not take on their final form until 1559, and they are a reflection of the Reformation rather than a blueprint for it. Calvin did not enjoy absolute power in Geneva: there was plenty of opposition from theologians and magistrates. Nor can Calvin be depicted as orchestrating the political resistance of European Protestants.[10] The intermingling of religion and politics was a failure, not a success. That said, the *Institutes* in their final form remain a statement of Calvin's thought, Geneva – or the myth of Geneva – provided an important source of inspiration for Protestants in other parts of Europe, and such inspiration could destroy the fragile balance of social forces on which the stability of states depended. In order to avoid any simple connections between them, we might best proceed by examining the nature of the reform in Geneva, how it was to spread to other places, and the emergence of Calvinism as a doctrine of political revolution in relation to the final version of the *Institutes*.

Geneva's city council had opted for the reform some weeks before Calvin's arrival: Farel, not Calvin, was the prime mover. In May, 1536, the council 'made a promise before God that we should live in future according to His holy and evangelical laws and by the Word of God', and made provision for a schoolmaster.

Calvin (1509–64), an exile from persecution in France, visited Basel and Ferrara, and was on his way to Strasbourg when he halted at Geneva in August, 1536. There, Farel, one of Bucer's disciples, gave him a mission, pleading with him to stay:

> Guillaume Farel detained me in Geneva, not so much by counsel and exhortation, as by a dreadful threat, which I felt in the same way as if God had laid His mighty hand upon me from heaven to arrest me. As the most direct road to Strasbourg, to which I then intended to retire, was shut by the wars, I decided to go quickly via Geneva, not intending to spend longer than a single night in the city. A little before this, popery had been driven from the place by the exertions of that excellent man whom I have just mentioned [Farel] and Pierre Viret. But matters were not yet settled there and the city was divided into ungodly and dangerous factions . . . Farel, who was consumed with an extraordinary zeal to advance the Gospel, immediately strained every nerve to detain me . . . God would curse my retirement and the tranquillity which I sought for my studies if I withdrew and refused to help when it was so urgently needed. By

this I was so struck with terror that I gave up the journey I had planned to undertake.

Calvin's appointment as 'reader in Holy Scripture' opened a new phase in the history of Protestantism. Yet he was expelled from the city in 1538, and his ideas and their application required a further three years in gestation in Strasbourg, with Bucer's achievements before him, before they were to achieve anything like their final form. Following a change in the composition of Geneva's city council, Calvin was invited back, and – with much reluctance – he returned. It was in the period after 1541 that Calvin's Geneva took shape. At once, Calvin provided the city with a constitution. His *Ecclesiastical Ordinances* are in some ways a more accessible guide to his vision of reformed Christian society than are the *Institutes*. That vision – inspired by Bucer's work in Strasbourg – was to be realised by the policing of morals. Pastors were to preach the Word, doctors were to teach in the schools, deacons were to look after the poor. The elders were to be elected by the council, and they held the most general responsibilities. However, the central arena of collaboration between the council and the Church, and the principal instrument of moral coercion, was the Consistory. All officials were to go about their business with decorum, and their business was to impose discipline – by excommunication if necessary. As the records of enforcement show, moral supervision could enter every detail of life, and even those measures which some might regard as 'progressive' were expressions of a puritan obsession with sexual immorality. Marriage became 'a reciprocal and mutual obligation so far as conjugal rights are concerned' – a woman could ask for a divorce on the grounds of her husband's adultery, Calvin might investigate the background of a prospective partner to check for evidence of syphilis.
Some of the associated strictures were, however, inquisitorial:

the ministers should, at appointed times of year, go round all the wards of the city accompanied by an elder and a deacon to instruct the people and examine every individual briefly as to his faith.

And the burden of censorship was oppressive: certain Christian names were banned because they encouraged superstition, because they were 'absurd and stupid', because they 'do not sound harmonious'. There were vigorous laws against swearing, and responsible citizens were to tell the offender 'to kneel down and kiss the ground'. Scripts of plays were submitted to Calvin who took the decision on whether to permit the performance as 'wholesome and for the public's benefit'.
Geneva acquired a myth of godliness, propagated by the city's printing houses, and reinforced by polemical pamphlets which Calvin

himself wrote. His memorable attack on relics asked how Christ's foreskin could have disappeared for 500 years and then be venerated in three different churches, each of which claimed to have the authentic item. In calling for Protestants to declare themselves he expressed that ominous intolerance which raises doubts about his professed distaste for worldly conflict: 'what I say is so manifestly true that no one can deny it without denying the Word of God.'[11]

After 1550, propaganda was to turn Calvin's programme for reform in Geneva into international Calvinism. There were more than thirty printing houses in the city, run by Bavarians, Franconians, and by Frenchmen, especially from Lyon and Paris. We know of 37 printers who went from Lyon to Geneva between 1550 and 1564. After that, Geneva benefited from the arrival of Michel Vincent, the Senneton, Gabiano and Honorat firms. Lyon felt the loss, its printers complaining in 1583 that 'the booksellers have destroyed the printing trade of Lyon and removed it to Geneva'. From Paris came the renowned Conrad Badius, Jean Crespin and Henri Estienne. Into Italy 'flowed those endless editions of anti-Roman propaganda and evangelical theology which travelled clandestinely by the most ingenious and devious routes'. The godly city attracted immigrants as refugees, trained them in the Academy (founded in 1559) and dispersed them as missionaries. In the period 1550–62, about 7,000 immigrants are recorded. Some of them were exiles from Mary Tudor's Catholic England. French Protestants fled later, leaving their homeland after the Massacre of St Bartholomew in 1572. From Scotland came John Knox who wrote with enthusiasm of Geneva as 'the maist perfyt schoole of Chryst that ever was in the erth since the dayis of the Apostillis', and of the strength which he had drawn from seeing 'maneris and religioun so sinceirlie reformat'. Knox was already prepared to stand up to kings and emperors in defence of his faith. To the modern eye, it would appear that by the late 1550s, the Calvinist International was preparing for the revolution of the saints.[12]

The roots of this militancy lie in Calvin's most important work, the *Institutes of the Christian Religion*. Here are set out the ideological foundations of Calvinism. The significance of this enormous work lies not in its originality but in the scale of its synthesis. In a fundamental sense, Calvin integrated humanism and scholasticism. His humanism reveals Calvin as a disciple of Erasmus in terms of his acquaintance with the Word, 'the everlasting wisdom, residing with God, from which both all oracles and all prophecies go forth'. This, after all, was the foundation of the Gospel as expounded by St John:

In the beginning was the Word, and the Word was with God, and the Word was God.
The same was in the beginning with God.

All things were made by him; and without him was not
anything made that was made.

Calvin explains:

> For John at once attributes to the Word a solid and abiding essence,
> and ascribes something uniquely His own, and clearly shows how
> God, by speaking, was Creator of the universe. Therefore, inasmuch
> as all divinely uttered revelations are correctly designated by the
> term 'word of God', so this substantial word is properly placed at
> the highest level, as the wellspring of all oracles. Unchangeable, the
> Word abides everlastingly one and the same with God, and is God
> Himself [*Institutes*, bk.I.ch.xiii.sec.7. vol.1, pp. 129–30].[13]

The commentary on what the Bible says is buttressed with the work
of the Church Fathers, most notably St Augustine, who is cited about
800 times. However, this is no sprawling demonstration of learning.
The framework of the *Institutes* is contained within a scholastic
structure, that of the *summa*. Here, Calvin stands in the same tradition
as St Thomas Aquinas, offering a work which is at once a textbook, an
encyclopedia and a conspectus. The treatise is monumental and
systematic, moving from the knowledge of God to the nature of
Christ, the doctrine of grace and then the external means of entering
the society of Christ.

It is a synthesis, too, of scholastic theology and humanist history –
for human experience is an expression of the divine purpose. The Bible
speaks of the Fall and the Redemption. This is mirrored by the
corruption of the Church (i.e. the history of the papacy) and the
salvation which the elect will receive. Thus, just as the Old Testament
became law for the children of Israel, the New Testament must become
law for the elect, which helps to explain why the work ends with a
discussion of secular politics. This is in Book IV, which is concerned
with God's gift of grace, but which includes a long explanation of the
abuse of episcopal office, and sections on subjects such as 'The
Donation of Constantine fraudulent and absurd', and 'The relationship of Henry IV and Hildebrand' [IV.xi.12 and 13. vol.2, pp. 1224–6],
and which ends with the celebrated chapter on civil government.

In his successive reworkings of the text, Calvin laid increasing
emphasis on predestination, and in the 1559 edition, predestination is
the adhesive of the whole structure. Calvin summarises the doctrine as
follows:

> As Scripture, then, clearly shows we say that God once established
> by his eternal and unchangeable plan those whom he long before
> determined once for all to receive into salvation, and those whom,

on the other hand, he would devote to destruction. We assert that, with respect to the elect, this plan was founded upon his freely given mercy, without regard to human worth; but by his just and irreprehensible but incomprehensible judgement he has barred the door of life to those whom he has given over to damnation [III.xxi.7. vol.2, p. 931].

The elect were designated before creation itself. This is based upon Paul's letter to the Ephesians which speaks of those who are 'elect before the creation of the world'. For Calvin, this means that the elect are not 'confined to the age when the Gospel was proclaimed' [III.xxii.2. vol.2, p. 934].

The manifestations of election are 'call and justification'. There would be a vocation to preach the word and an effort to escape the filth of the world – one of the most basic reasons for regarding Calvin as a puritan. However, following Augustine, Calvin goes on to admit that there was another sign of God's special favour – persecution:

> Now, to suffer persecution for righteousness' sake is a singular comfort. For it ought to occur to us how much honour God bestows upon us in thus furnishing us with the special badge of his soldiery. I say that not only they who labour for the defence of the gospel but they who in any way maintain the cause of righteousness suffer persecution for righteousness [III.viii.7. vol.1, p. 707].

There is no doubt that this is a call to endure, not to resist, but the military allusion is significant. It is one symptom of the most ambitious and contradictory aspect of the whole synthesis, and it helps to explain why there is so much controversy surrounding the 'Calvinist theory of resistance' (below, pp. 283–95). At bottom, the problem of how Calvin's doctrines could translate into social terms is that on the one hand the teleology of the *Institutes* insists that the gospel must be translated into law, while on the other, Calvin insists on the separation of the spiritual and political spheres. There are plenty of instances where the latter could scarcely be stated more clearly. Here is one of the most forceful:

> Therefore, in order that none of us may stumble on that stone, let us first consider that there is a twofold government in man: one aspect is spiritual, whereby the conscience is instructed in piety and in reverencing God; the second is political, whereby man is educated for the duties of humanity and citizenship that must be maintained among men . . . the former resides in the inner mind, while the latter regulates only outward behaviour . . . Now these two, as we have divided them, must always be examined separately; and while one is being considered, we must call away and turn aside the mind from thinking about the other [III.xix.15. vol.1, p. 847].

Even when concentrating on civil government 'we must keep in mind that distinction' [IV.xx.1. vol.2, p. 1486]. Civil obedience is a necessity, and a tyrant's rule must be endured, for power itself is divine:

> In a very wicked man utterly unworthy of all honour, provided he has the public power in his hands, that noble and divine power resides which the Lord has by His Word given to the ministers of his justice and judgement. Accordingly, he should be held in the same reverence and esteem by his subjects, in so far as public obedience is concerned, in which they would hold the best of kings if he were given to them [IV.xx.25. vol.2, p. 1513].

As a logical distinction, this would be hard to fault. In addition, Calvin has the majestic support of both Paul and Augustine. In many ways, they supply Calvin's distinction between the spiritual and political spheres. Paul urges obedience in his letter to the Romans:

> Let every soul be subject unto the higher powers. For there is no power but of God: the powers that be are ordained of God.

Augustine takes all the politics out of the Christian life by concentrating upon the 'City of God' toward which the soul progresses in pilgrimage through the ultimately irrelevant tribulations of the temporal life. However, both use the terminology of military struggle to inspire the Christian towards his goal. In Ephesians, chapter 6, for example, Paul exhorts the Christian to spiritual combat:

> 11. Put on the whole armour of God, that ye may be able to stand against the wiles of the devil.
> 12. For we wrestle not against flesh and blood, but against principalities, against powers, against the rulers of the darkness of this world, against spiritual wickedness in high places.
> 13. Wherefore take unto you the whole armour of God, that ye may be able to withstand in the evil day, and having done all, to stand.
> 14. Stand therefore, having your loins girt about with truth, and having on the breastplate of righteousness;
> 15. And your feet shod with the preparation of the Gospel of peace;
> 16. Above all, taking the shield of faith, wherewith ye shall be able to quench all the fiery darts of the wicked.
> 17. And take the helmet of salvation, and the sword of the Spirit, which is the word of God.

At the outset of his book, Augustine appropriates for God's kingdom the mission which the poet Vergil had expressed for the Roman

Empire, 'to spare the conquered and to war down the proud'. In Book XIX, the pilgrim's progress towards eternal peace is fraught with 'danger of the devil's manifold ambushes', and peace itself is a 'victory'.

Unsurprisingly, Calvin's spiritual struggle is also an armed pilgrimage:

> We have been forewarned that an enemy relentlessly threatens us, an enemy who is the very embodiment of rash boldness, of military prowess, of crafty wiles, of untiring zeal and haste, of every conceivable weapon and of skill in the science of warfare. We must, then, bend our every effort to this goal: that we should not let ourselves be overwhelmed by carelessness or faintheartedness, but on the contrary, with courage rekindled stand our ground in combat. Since this military service ends only at death, let us urge ourselves to perseverance [I.xiv.13. vol.1, p. 173].

The images are of sword, and shield, and watchtower. For as long as the distinction between earthly and spiritual matters is sustained, they remain images, as they did for Paul and Augustine. However, there are moments when Calvin departs from his sources and chooses to suspend the distinction – and allows the confusion of religion and politics.

St Paul advised the Romans that 'ye must needs be subject, not only for wrath, but also for conscience sake'. This Calvin disowns:

> From this it follows that consciences are also bound by civil laws. But if this were so, all that we said a little while ago and are now going to say about spiritual government would fall [III.xix.15. vol.2, p. 848].

Conscience he defines as 'inward integrity of heart', 'a mean between God and man' which is 'without regard to other men' [III.xix.16. vol.2, p. 849]. He later admits that some 'human constitutions' are 'contrary to the Lord's Word' [IV.x.8. vol.2, p. 1186]. And the papacy's 'vain fictions' are the source of 'this sham obedience which turns away from God as much as it inclines to men' [IV.x.10. vol.2, pp. 1188–9]. 'Pious consciences are oppressed with an immense multitude' of such laws – which he then demonstrates with reference to the history of the popes.

This also marks a departure from Augustine, for while the latter charted the progression from the earthly life to the city of God, Calvin posits a divine plan for the realisation of God's kingdom on earth. In this regard the last two sections of the work were a rallying cry. The people's freedom could be defended by magistrates – 'Let the princes hear and be afraid', he trumpets. The modern editor can explain in a footnote that 'it is God that princes are to fear', but Calvin does not make this explicit, and the final chapter of the entire work reminds the reader that 'obedience to rulers . . . is never to lead us away from obedience to Him, to whose will the desires of all kings ought to be subject' [IV.xx.31–2. vol.2, pp. 1518–21].

The fundamental question remains as to whether Calvin successfully reconciles the idea of a divine plan for humanity with a strict separation of religion and politics. It is likely that he never resolved the problem in his own mind. In 1556, he wrote to French Protestants:

> I have heard that some are debating among themselves whether, if an atrocity is committed against them, they would resort to violence . . . you suffer in a righteous cause, and one in which God has promised that he will stand by you. But he has not armed you to resist those who are established by him to govern.

He was alarmed by the Conspiracy of Amboise (below, p. 287), and feared 'rivers of blood' as a consequence. Yet it is hard to depict Calvin as the troubled intellectual whose ideas were distorted by events and exploited by opportunists. He also wrote to the churches in France 'Give me wood and I will send you arrows', and his churches were 'ordained for this purpose, that as long as it is a sojourner in the world, it is to wage war under the perpetual cross'. Calvin's right-hand man, Béza, spoke at Poissy on 24 and 26 September 1561. His words were in print in Geneva – along with a section of the *Institutes* – by 6 October. Calvin's propaganda encouraged Protestants to stand up and be counted. 'Nicodemites' taking their name from the man who visited Jesus by night in order to hide his sympathy, were 'split between God and the devil':

> I ask all these people how they can say . . . that I am too extreme. For I merely tell them things that their own consciences tell them are wicked and damnable and manifest idolatry.

There was no room for conciliation with Rome. The Council of Trent was doomed to fail, 'and we cannot do better than hasten to rally round the banner which the Son of God holds out for us'. Suffering was soldiering, and, given his attitude to oppression of conscience by papal constitutions, he cannot have been entirely surprised at the violence which he helped to generate. After all, Farel's printed emblem was 'the sword of the true word' surrounded by flames (plate 27).[14]

In the Genevan reform, Word and sword were never far apart. Yet there were few converts. In the first half of the sixteenth century, before the emergence of Calvinism, Protestant efforts to evangelise society met with success – and limited success at that – in two contexts: the urban and the Swiss. In the towns of Germany, Protestantism did not become a 'popular movement'. The spirit was willing: John Frederick of Saxony ordered in 1554 that in Saxony and Thuringia:

In order to note and record the names of those pastors who have improved their parishioners and succeeded in teaching them the catechism, our visitors are to call together and interrogate these same parishioners in every place; for it matters little whether or not a pastor be a learned and accomplished man if he does not apply himself diligently and with devotion to the work of instructing his parishioners in the essentials of Christian knowledge.

Yet the dispiriting observation of a visitation report in Wolfenbüttel was that 'people do not go to church on Sundays'. Drinking was more attractive than worship. The population was 'scarcely touched' by Christian doctrine. Even when we move to the next phase of the Reformation, we find change blocked by political hostility and social indifference. Calvin was forced out of Geneva in 1538, Bucer had to leave Strasbourg in 1549, both as a result of the city councils' assertions of authority. In Lyon and Rouen, religious allegiances changed as the political struggle intensified. Even in the acre of ground which Edinburgh occupied Knox did not enjoy the support of a majority of the Protestant community.

And that was the position in the towns. In the countryside, the failure was total. Lutheranism made no impression on magic and folklore. Calvin's *Ecclesiastical Ordinances* laid down that ministers should meet once a week, but preachers from local villages should merely be urged to attend 'whenever possible'. There were no peasants among the missionaries from Geneva. Where Calvinist infiltrators scoffed at saints and mystery plays as superstition – as they did in Champagne – they sometimes reinforced superstition, intensifying the tenacity with which people clung to their local traditions. Calvinism made little progress in the Netherlands: only about one tenth of Holland could be said to be 'reformed' in 1587.[15]

By mid-century, the Protestant mission was a failure in social terms. The clergy remained a self-perpetuating order: in Württemberg in the course of the sixteenth century, of 511 ordained pastors, 323 (63 per cent) were sons of pastors. Despite Luther's revolutionary ideas and Calvin's revolutionary organisation, the reform of religion only took root in those places where the secular power thought it desirable. As Bucer and Calvin found, the support of city councils was unreliable. And, having failed to reach the people, the reformers were thrown back on the authority of princes. In the aftermath of Luther's protest, the survival of the reform was guaranteed by Saxony, Hesse and Württemberg, and the political support, generated in large measure by the energy of Philip of Hesse, was formalised with the protest of reformed states at the Diet of Speyer in 1529. Political advantages, particularly the secularisation of church property, were balanced against the serious risks involved in defying the Emperor, and princely gains are easily exaggerated. However, quarrels between secular rulers and the Roman pontiff did not of necessity lead to the espousal of the reform in national churches. In 1521, Henry VIII of England had earned the title 'Defender of the Faith' from Pope Leo X after publishing his defence of the seven sacraments against Martin Luther. In 1532, the Act in Restraint of Appeals to Rome effectively created the Church of England and cleared the way for his divorce from Catherine of Aragon. But Henry himself was not a Protestant, merely a schismatic Catholic. In France, Lutheran ideas had spread more successfully than in England – and printing was more highly developed – but the reform never received the support of the monarchy. In Denmark, Bugenhagen had worked as adviser to Christian III for two years before the Reformation came at a stroke, by princely decree. In Sweden, the Church agreed to meet King Gustavus Vasa's demand for money at the Diet of Våsteras in 1527 because he threatened to resign if it did not, and he merely enacted ordinances to promote reformed religion at the same time. This proved unpopular – and the effects on education were disastrous.[16]

Curiously, Calvinism became equally dependent on princely guarantees. In the later sixteenth century, it enjoyed some success in Bremen (1581), East Friesland (1583) and Anhalt (1596), but the most zealous Calvinist states were the Palatinate and Hungary. In the Palatinate, the Elector Frederick III, who ruled from 1559 to 1576, helped Heidelberg to become a species of princely Geneva. From there was proclaimed the Heidelberg Catechism in 1563, which in many ways provided a greater ideological coherence than what had come from Geneva itself. At the periphery of the state, however, Calvinism had to be ruthlessly imposed: there was little popular support. The Hungarian Reformed Church was full of missionary zeal, and identified closely with national culture, but it was also 'homespun', fabricated to compensate for the weakness of the Habsburgs and the Catholic Church to offer any protection against the Turk. The bloodlessness of Calvinist successes in east central Europe was symptomatic of a species of religious anaemia in society at large.[17]

At the very time when Calvinism became identified with resistance to monarchy in France and the Netherlands, it depended heavily on princely sponsorship in the Empire. Calvin had spawned an anti-monarchical ideology which failed to win popular support. The increasing militancy of Protestantism belied the fact that its mission was crumbling – and the revitalised forces of Catholicism began to close in.

8   How the Image triumphed

The Catholic offensive

As Protestantism ran into difficulties, many of its own making, changes in the Catholic Church compounded the problems which the Protestants faced. Conventionally these changes are summarised as the 'Counter-Reformation'. In deploying this concept, historians usually distinguish two main strands of Catholic history: the first is a reaction to Protestantism stimulated by the Reformation, and the second a longer-term process of reforms stemming from internally generated spiritual revival. The first strand is twisted from the dogma of the Council of Trent, which met intermittently from 1545 to 1563, and the military power of Spain, and its purpose was to choke heresy. The second strand is a continuous thread of renewal patiently spun within the Church which shares and even anticipates many of the preoccupations of Protestant reformers.[1] Yet only a little reflection is necessary to show that the history of the Catholic Church in the sixteenth century is at once more diverse and more integrated than those two strands suggest or allow.

The first of them weaves in the assumption that there was a harmony of interests between the papacy and the Spanish monarchy. For this, there is no evidence whatever. Charles V and the papacy were rarely at ease with each other; by mid-century, the tensions were tremendous. Within a few months of his election as Paul IV in 1555, the hateful Gianpietro Carafa, a Neapolitan, declared war on Charles V in an effort to drive the Spaniards from Italy, alleging, in a staggering display of hubris, that the emperor could not abdicate without papal permission. He would have nothing to do with a general council of the church, and he hated Loyola so much for his criticism of the Theatine Order that but for the death of Ignatius in 1556 and the election of Laynez as general – more of him in due course – the Jesuits could easily have faced the dissolution of their order. This antipathy went very deep in the Roman Church. The great organiser and reformer, Carlo Borromeo, seemed so determined to reduce Spanish influence in the Church that he would at times risk the whole reform programme to achieve this end. Thus the first strand twists and frays.

The second is a bonding of reforming energies within the church and of developments in Italy. It draws together the cultivated Christian

173

humanists – Sadoleto and Seripando, Contarini, Giberti – and the new orders – the Oratory of Divine Love, the Theatines, the Somaschi and the Barnabites – all working to repair the social damage of the Italian Wars. Once again, the problem is how to accommodate the Spanish experience, for what this second strand lacks is Spanish input. What of Santa Teresa of Avila insisting on her unlettered simplicity? What of the untutored quest for spiritual solace which St John of the Cross entered upon in the dark night of his soul? Above all, what of the Jesuits? The two traditional strands of the Counter-Reformation fail to tie up. The troubled relations of the papacy and the Spanish monarchy undermine the notion that both were allied in a war on heresy. The intellectual tendencies of the Italian humanist churchmen and their influence upon the new orders through the Oratory of Divine Love or the Theatines make one wonder why the Protestant reformers were not re-accommodated within the universal Church.[2]

Given these sources of disunity, perhaps it might be appropriate to dispense with the idea of the Counter-Reformation altogether. The risk then is one of failing to acknowledge the existence of deeply felt anti-Protestant sentiments which provided a genuine source of unity amongst Catholics. In what other way could we characterise the profound and intense conflicts of Protestants and Catholics in the religious wars which tore Europe apart in the later sixteenth and early seventeenth centuries? We cannot do without a term which summarises what set Protestants and Catholics at odds, and in that regard, 'Counter-Reformation' seems serviceable enough. However, this chapter experiments with a different version of the term. It takes account of the traditional elements: of both the deep-rooted quest for spiritual regeneration and the pragmatic pursuit of wordly ambitions by Spain and the papacy. But these should not obscure or preclude a third dimension. The Counter-Reformation was a sudden spiritual offensive which drew its impetus from the revolution in feeling brought about by the Jesuits, a new order recognised by Pope Paul III in 1540, and formally designated as the Society of Jesus three years later. Their revolution brought Spanish Catholicism to Rome. The result was a missionary war between the evangelical puritanism of the Calvinists and Jesuit puritanism. For the history of religion in the sixteenth century – perhaps it is more or less latent throughout the Christian centuries – is characterised by a general urge for purification. As we have seen, the Protestants sought to purify the church by removing its abuses – along with its altars, vestments, paintings and sculptures – and this is connected to the more familiar puritanism of the English Civil War. Yet James VI and I expressed his frustration with the Jesuit Cardinal Bellarmine's position on episcopal jusrisdiction by saying that 'it is no wonder he takes the Puritanes part, since Jesuits are nothing but puritan-papists'.[3]

For there was a Catholic urge for purification as well, and this purification would be achieved by the extermination of heresy. This was the puritanism of Philip II and of Carlo Borromeo; above all, it was the puritanism of the Jesuits. Authoritarianism and ideological conviction, both drawing strength from deep popular support: these are the essential characteristics of the Catholic cause, and they are the characteristics of Jesuit puritanism. They derived from the particular historical experience of the Iberian peninsula, and they were generalised through the attachment to the papal cause of Jesuit missionaries. Two questions must now occupy us if this thesis is to stand. How did Spanish religion assume its distinctive contours? And what was the nature of the Jesuit revolution?

The character of Spanish Catholicism

To emphasise the distinctiveness of Spanish Catholicism with reference to the fervour of its popular piety is not to say that Italy experienced no popular religious revival before the Reformation. Paradoxically, amid the opulence of the Renaissance we find in Italy a sober puritanism which anticipates the mood of the later sixteenth century, and which resonates with contemporary feeling in Spain. Yet there is a single profound difference: in Italy, the puritanism was anti-institutional, in Spain the puritanism was institutionalised.

The greatest of popular reformers in Italy – and a precursor of European Protestantism – was San Bernardino of Siena (1380–1444). He was an indefatigable evangelist: in a few months in 1422 he preached throughout the Veneto, giving 60 sermons in Padua alone. His most repeated themes were an attack on worldly vanity – what we would call materialism – and a consistent identification with the cause of the poor. He stressed that works should have their origin in compassion:

> If a poor man comes to your door and you give him alms with a lukewarm and unwilling heart, the merit of these alms has gone before you have reached the door.

He rejected a bishopric on three separate occasions, and he was aware that some highly placed clerics thought his teaching heretical, joking that 'some want me fried and some want me roasted'.

This he avoided, yet the stake was indeed to be the destiny of the Florentine puritan, the Dominican Girolamo Savonarola. He too urged the destruction of vanities, and bonfires consumed the luxuries of the Florentines in a sort of collective catharsis. Like San Bernardino, he lamented the condition of the Church, and urged a return to the ideals of primitive Christianity:

> In the primitive Church the chalices were of wood, the prelates of gold; in these days the Church hath chalices of gold and prelates of wood. These have introduced devilish games among us; they have no belief in God, and jeer at the mysteries of our faith! What doest Thou, O Lord? Why dost Thou slumber? Arise, and come to deliver Thy church from the hands of the devils, from the hands of tyrants, from the hands of iniquitous prelates.

Savonarola's efforts to establish a godly state in Florence ended in failure, and he was burned as a heretic at the orders of the morally corrupt Alexander VI. It is curious that a Spanish pope should have brought such infamy to the throne of St Peter, for the church in Spain had, by the end of the fifteenth century, experienced two decades of vigorous and sustained reform which had installed puritan principles at the heart of ecclesiastical life.[4]

Throughout the Middle Ages, across the Iberian peninsula, the Church had been associated with frontier war against Islam, and the war was to end in Christian success, that is to say the victory of 'true religion' over its enemies. This bare fact is highly significant. On the eastern frontier of Christendom in central Europe, the Christians were on the defensive against the infidel, and these lands were to prove vulnerable to Protestantism (above, p. 172). By contrast, the association of the Church in Spain with a Christian triumph made it the champion of Catholicism. The victory of the Catholic Monarchs, Ferdinand and Isabella, in Granada in 1492 was the culmination of centuries of conflict. Granada rapidly became the first laboratory of missionary experiment prior to the extension of such work to North Africa and then the New World. The first archbishop built a cathedral to rival the moorish Alhambra, and he set about the organisation of parochial discipline – an important anticipation of what was to happen throughout the Catholic world after the Council of Trent.

And suddenly, Spain loses the conventional landmarks which give us our sense of period in European history. The *Reconquista* was the climax of seven centuries of war against the heathen and marked the end of a protracted historical process. It is easy to see this medieval experience as an over-extended crusading era which left Spain in general and Castile in particular burdened with a set of aristocratic knightly values quite out of place amid the new developments of the early modern age: hence Spain's 'backwardness', 'ossification' and, of course 'decline' in the seventeenth century. In Part I, it was suggested that frontier war in Iberia played an important part in the expansion of Europe, Part III will argue that there was nothing 'inevitable' about

Spain's decline – on the contrary, the durability of Spanish ascendancy is far more striking.

This ascendancy might itself be seen in relation to Spain's extended 'Middle Ages', for there is a sense in which the victory of the Catholic Kings gave Spain a head start of half a century on the rest of Europe, for Ferdinand and Isabella established state control of the Church a good fifty years before Protestant princes took advantage of the Reformation, and they did so without breaking with Rome. While sixteenth-century monarchs flaunted their independence through flirtation with heresy, Spain had done so by its extirpation. At least one contemporary remarked on how advanced for its time was Ferdinand's control of the Church:

> Hee is now become for fame and glory, the first King of Christendome, and if you shall well consider his actions, you shall find them all illustrious, and every one of them extraordinary. Hee in the beginning of his reigne assaild Granada, and that exployt was the ground of his State. At first hee made that warre in security and without suspicion he should be any wayes hindred, and therein held the Barons of Castiglias minds busied, who thinking upon that warre, never minded any innovation; and in this while he gaind credit and authority with them, they not being aware of it; was able to maintaine with the Church, and the peoples mony all his souldiers, and to lay a foundation for his military ordinances with that long warre: which afterwards gaind him exceeding much honour. Besides this, to the end hee might be able here-among to undertake greater matters, serving himselfe alwaies of the colour of religion; hee gave himself to a kind of religious cruelty, chasing and despoyling those Jewes out of the kingdome; nor can this example bee more admirable and rare: under the same cloke hee invaded Africk and went through with his exployt in Italy: and last of all hath hee assaild France, and so alwaies proceeded on forwards contriving of great matters: which always have held his subjects minds in peace and admiration, and busied in attending the event what it should bee: and these his actions have thus grown, one upon another, that they have never given leysure to men so to rest, as they might ever plot anything against them.[5]

Machiavelli was writing in 1513 or thereabouts, but he was commenting upon actions which went back more than thirty years. It is worth dwelling on this subject, for it may help to explain why relations between the Spanish monarchy and the papacy were so strained in the sixteenth century.

Although Iberia is closely identified with the cause of the Counter-Reformation, the Catholic Monarchs had played a leading role in promoting reform of the Church, with little if any reference to Rome. They made particular progress in terms of establishing their own control over ecclesiastical appointments, and in stamping on priestly absenteeism – a problem over which the Council of Trent almost came to grief. One of their chief instruments was the Archbishop Francisco Cisneros de Ximenes (1436–1517), who imposed a radical programme of mass baptism on the conquered Moors of Granada. The only alternative on offer was expulsion. He pressed for the extension of the frontier through crusade, as the fervent Isabella had wished, but at her death in 1504, Ferdinand insisted on pursuing traditional Aragonese interests in Italy.

Cisneros's career illustrates not only the precocity of state–church arrangements in Spain but also the distinctive relationship between religious sentiment and institutional forms. Cisneros forced the conventual Franciscans out of their convents, and he harnessed his work to the new learning of the universities, particularly Alcalá, which he founded in 1508. Like San Bernardino an Observant Franciscan, he entertained some of the weird visions more readily associated with Savonarola. Yet in contrast to the Italians, he kept his puritanism within the institutional bounds of the Church. And in Spain, that puritanism was literal, and the state institution which tested for impurities of blood and faith was that surprisingly popular institution, the Inquisition. Cisneros became Inquisitor General in 1507. While he was head of that bastion of orthodoxy he banned the preaching of indulgences – on the grounds that they took money from Spain to fill papal coffers in Rome. This was years before the outcry against abuses in Germany, and the purification of the Spanish Church helps to explain its sense of moral superiority and the incapacity of its authorities to accept that the reform of the Church necessitated an open break with Rome.

Ironically, Cisneros, the opponent of papal exploitation through indulgences, was regent of Spain between Ferdinand's death in 1516 and the arrival of Charles I (later Charles V) the following year: head of state and head of the state–church in the year of the Ninety-Five Theses. This fact suggests the remarkable precocity of Catholic reform in Spain. Once the Lutherans had opted for a breach with the papacy, the historic question within the Catholic world was whether Rome could catch up with – and hold on to – the religion of the Spaniards.

The decisive means of doing so seemed unquestionably the establishment of an Inquisition. In Spain, the Holy Office had operated as an instrument of the state against converted Moors and Jews who were thought to have lapsed. It was to prove just as useful in the extirpation of Protestant heresy. The principal threats to the authority of the church in Spain in the early sixteenth century were perceived to be Illuminists and Erasmians. The Illuminists or *alumbrados* were a sect which practised an emotional abandonment to God, a process known as *dejamiento*. Active in centres such as Toledo and Alcalá, in the atmosphere of tension which developed in the aftermath of the Lutheran protest, the Illuminists were prosecuted for heresy. Mystical experience from now on needed the approval of the Inquisition – as Santa Teresa was to find. Erasmianism poked fun at the clergy, and it was identified with alien Flemish influence at the court of Charles V. The contacts of some intellectuals such as Juan de Valdes with Illuminist circles were unfortunate, and suppression of Erasmus's books followed (above, p. 115).

Neither the *alumbrados* nor people who enjoyed the works of Erasmus were likely to destroy the religious fabric of Spain, and these seem superfluous triumphs over insignificant enemies. Yet what appears to us as distasteful authoritarianism proved, in the context of its time, an effective means of protecting orthodoxy. Charles V – the former patron of Erasmus – knew only too well what trouble heterodoxy had caused in Germany, and he was quite clear about how Philip II should avoid such problems in Spain. Writing from his monastic retirement to his daughter in 1557, he found it 'necessary to place the greatest stress and weight on a quick remedy and exemplary punishment'. In 1559, such a policy was implemented in a series of 'acts of faith' (*autos da fe*): 56 suspected Protestants in two public burnings in Valladolíd in 1559, 40 more in Seville in the same year, another 20 Lutherans going to the stake in 1562. These events literally 'burnt out Protestantism in Spain'. A comparable institution was established in Portugal in 1547, and the Spanish model proliferated throughout the Hispanic world: to Lima in 1570, for instance, and to Mexico City the next year.[6]

More significant however, is the Roman imitation of the Spanish example. The Roman Inquisition dated back to the thirteenth century, when it had foreshadowed the later Spanish version in its popularity, meeting the demand that more heretics be eliminated. Yet its revival in 1542 had more recent inspiration. As early as 1530, the papal legate, Cardinal Campeggio, an enthusiast for the elimination of abuses – reform of the curia, the ending of absenteeism – left Charles V in no doubt as to the remedy for Germany:

> The first step in this process would be to confiscate property, civil or ecclesiastical, in Germany as well as in Hungary or Bohemia. For, with regard to heretics, this is lawful and right. The mastery over them thus obtained, then must holy inquisitors be appointed, who shall trace out every remnant of them, proceeding against them as the Spaniards did against the Moors in Spain.

This is the first of several significant associations of those advocating reform with a hard-line stance on heresy. Other examples include

Contarini, the great advocate of the Jesuits as well as the papal legate at the Diet of Regensburg, and Sadoleto, who wrote the Bull of Convocation of the Council of Trent. In 1542, at the moment when the Regensburg conference seemed to have failed, that implacable enemy of things Spanish, Cardinal Carafa (above, p. 173), called for an end to attempts at compromise with manifest heresy. Carafa railed that there was but one remedy for the evils which threatened the Church: 'As St Peter subdued the first heresiarchs in no other place than Rome, so must the successors of Peter destroy all the heresies of the whole world in Rome.' His appeal to the past was the more effective for the support it received from Juan Alvarez de Toledo, Cardinal of Burgos, and from Ignatius Loyola. Carafa and Toledo became Inquisitors General. This was among the rules that Carafa laid down, and the spirit is surely Spanish: 'No man must debase himself by showing toleration towards heretics of any kind, above all towards Calvinists.'

The Inquisition waged war on heresy throughout the Italian peninsula. Even the self-consciously independent Venetians were forced to accept this agency of Roman power (in 1547), though they managed to instal representatives of the state upon the tribunal. The handbook which Inquisitors used dated from the fourteenth century, but it was reworked by the Spanish canonist, Francesco Peña, in 1578. One of his insertions was that 'the ultimate end of the trial and condemnation to death is not to save the soul of the accused, but to maintain public order and to terrorise the people'.

It worked: at a cost, of course, at least in the mind's eye of modern liberalism. The Inquisition imposed restrictions on economic contacts with places identified with heresy, and thereby it may well have inhibited commercial enterprise. Its control of the book trade narrowed the horizons of the mind, restraining intellectual as well as commerical speculation at one and the same time. Yet the inescapable fact remains that where the Inquisition was most active – Spain, Portugal, Italy – Catholicism was most secure.

That said, it is important not to exaggerate the repressiveness of the Inquisition – Spanish, Portuguese, or Roman. Compared with secular courts, it is remarkable for its leniency. From some 150,000 trials in the period 1550–1800, about 3,000 executions resulted. Surprisingly, there was very little anti-heretical activity from the Inquisition in Spain in the sixteenth century. The psychological sophistication of the Roman Inquisitors showed a genuine concern to understand the workings of the heretical mind rather than consign it to thoughtless destruction. In Spain, the Inquisition's popularity may have owed something to forms of torture more subtle than the rack and the stake, and it appears to have played a role which combined psychiatrist and agony aunt. In short, it appears to have been a phenomenon in which we have all but ceased to believe: an effective deterrent, balancing spectacular but very infrequent punishment – which was all the more memorable for that – with a reassuring concern for the safety of society. Certainly, there is a case for saying that the Inquisition is as important for what it authorised as for what it suppressed.[7] Amongst those suspected of illuminism arrested in 1526 was a crippled ex-soldier by the name of Ignatius Loyola.

Jesuit puritanism

Institutional reform is only one aspect of Spain's contribution to sixteenth-century Catholicism. For Spain – as a Christian community, rather than as a political configuration – provided the papal cause with one great, indispensable means of harnessing the zealous spirituality of the Spaniards to the institutional authority of the Roman Church: the Jesuits.

Ignatius Loyola was a fighting man of noble blood. Too much can be made of the relevance of his experience of war for his work as a militant Christian. The Church militant is not a Jesuit innovation, it is merely the Church on earth, as opposed to the Church suffering (purgatory) or the Church triumphant (paradise). Loyola's military background is more important, however, in locating him in the Spanish tradition of the frontiersman. While the Inquisition could defend orthodoxy, it was a cumbersome means of advancing the Catholic cause in that it would depend for its establishment on the acceptance of Spanish or papal interference by the secular power. Loyola was to formulate a more effective means of reclaiming souls for Catholicism.

He was irreparably crippled during the siege of Pamplona – in the frontier kingdom of Navarre – which he was helping to defend against the French in 1521. On his sickbed, with a suddenness comparable to Luther's escape from death or Zwingli's recovery from plague, Loyola became a soldier in the service of Christ. The fitness of the soul for the struggle was ensured by that demanding process of purification through self-abandonment embodied in *The Spiritual Exercises*. The blinding flash which steeled his convictions was what made him suspicious to the Inquisition, and he was banned from preaching for three years. His puritan education advanced in Paris, at the College of Montaigu, to which he went in 1528 – not long after Calvin had left the same institution. He then travelled to Italy. Along with his half-dozen companions, he survived further charges of heresy, and dedicated himself and his followers to the service of the papacy. This was of twofold importance. First, that Jesuit puritanism which had its deepest roots in Spanish piety became institutionalised in the Roman Church. Second, his sense of blind obedience to the visible Church countered the

Lutheran attack on the papacy as an institution (above pp. 137–9), re-establishing the idea that the office of Pope demanded obedience, whatever the character of its holder. This was a reminder to the Spanish monarchy as well as to the Protestants of the supreme spiritual authority of the papacy. As we shall see, the incumbents of the papal throne did not, as personalities, mark a decisive break with their 'Renaissance' predecessors (below, pp. 185–6), but the throne itself was inviolable. This was clear from Loyola's protest at the charges of heresy levelled at him:

> What grieved us was that doctrine itself which we preached should have been declared unsound and our way of life evil, neither of which is ours but Christ's and the Church's.

He pleaded for papal recognition of the brotherhood for whom obedience was a watchword. The 'Rules for Thinking within the Church' which are contained in *The Spiritual Exercises* leave no doubt as to the institutional origins of spiritual authority:

> To arrive at the truth in all things, we ought always to be ready to believe that what seems to us white is black, if the hierarchical Church so defines it.

In this emphatic rejection of the value of individual conviction, the spirituality of Loyola embodies, in the literal sense, a 'counter-reformation'. The request for papal recognition of the society was passed on, significantly, by Cardinal Contarini, who was much impressed by what he saw of the Jesuits at work in Venice. As the humanist cardinal fumbled for compromise at Regensburg, did the eyes of his mind ever turn to the clarity of Ignatius's beliefs, with their emphasis on the superiority of the celibate life of a separate clerical order, and the obedience due to the papacy? Obedience to the Church expressed itself in taking the sacrament and in the mass, and it was a duty 'to praise greatly Religious Orders, virginity and continency, and matrimony not so much as any of these'.

The Jesuit mission, always obedient to the papacy, was transparently designed to fight to the finish a social war against heresy:

> to perform whatsoever the reigning pontiff should command them, to go forth into all lands, among Turks, heathens or heretics, wherever he might please to send them, without hesitation or delay, as without question, condition or reward.

Jesuit cells would counter those of the Calvinists, and Loyola's instructions to the Jesuit missionaries to Ireland in 1541 clearly aim to defeat Protestantism in its own chosen areas of social conflict:

If you could introduce grammar schools in some places and find efficient Catholic masters for them, it would be a great remedy for the great ignorance of the country . . . And it would be a good thing, too, to provide *monti di pietà* [cheap loan banks] for the assistance of the poor, and hospitals and other pious institutions.

Priests would offer education and poor relief as works to save souls. This was the Jesuit mission. The missionaries themselves received an education which impressed upon them not only the depth of the spiritual commitment required – by no means all aspirants stood the test of the training which Ignatius designed – but also the breadth of the front along which they must advance *ad maiorem Dei gloriam*, 'for the greater glory of God'. Jesuit colleges were rapidly attached to existing universities – attached yet set apart, for there was no lecturing in this training: '*No estudios ni lectiones en la Compania*'. Paris, Lisbon, Coimbra, Padua, Louvain and Valencia all provided hostels for the missionaries. In central Europe, the Society established training grounds for its spiritual commandos. A college was established at Cologne in 1544, Ingolstadt in 1549, Vienna in 1552, Worms in 1557, Strasbourg in 1558, Augsburg in 1559, Innsbruck in 1563. By 1630, the Holy Roman Empire had been fortified with no fewer than 2,283 seminaries, colleges and missions. When Loyola and his followers had preached in stumbling Italian, people had laughed: within a decade, Jesuit missionaries aimed to be able to preach in at least two languages, and to get by in five – in Bohemia, they impressed by learning Czech. And they took the war to the enemy. We think of the spiritual titan, Peter Canisius, the successor of the formidable Eck at Ingolstadt, who between 1555 and 1558 tramped 6,000 miles spreading his version of the Word, reclaiming the city of Augsburg in the process, or Jerome Nadal, whose career took him to 35 cities, from Regensburg in the north to Palermo in the south, from Lisbon in the west to Vienna in the east. There was princely support from Bavaria, and from the prince bishops. A college was founded at Trier in 1561; in Bamberg and Würzburg in the 1570s. In significant contrast to the Calvinists, Jesuit missionaries scored some success in rural areas, particularly in Eichstätt, where Julius Echter von Mespelbrunn (Bishop from 1573 to 1617) provided the fullest encouragement. These were charted areas, but simultaneously, the Jesuit mission took Catholicism into the jungles and over the mountains of the world, penetrating the Congo in 1548, Brazil in 1549, China in 1551.

Their revolution was to forsake monasticism yet restore papal authority. Their work was not 'in the choir', and this is what set them apart. None of the other 'new orders' abandoned the monastic tradition as did the Jesuits, none of them had so comprehensive a notion of their mission. The Theatines (founded as early as 1524), guided by the gentle Gaetano da Thiene and, of all people, the ferocious Carafa, were priests who took monastic vows, and their aim was to offer a more effective training for the priesthood while living a life of contemplation. The intention of the Somaschi, who modelled themselves on the Theatines, was to relieve the suffering of northern Italy amid the devastations of the 1520s – in Venice, Brescia, Como, Milan, Pavia, and Genoa. In Milan also were the Barnabites who offered acts of mercy to the poor of that unfortunate city. Yet none of these combined the aims to preach, to educate and to relieve with the same energy as the Jesuits, and none dispensed so totally with the cloister. It might be argued that the Jesuits were building on foundations laid by the Franciscans, but the Franciscans themselves had been divided by a bitter quarrel between the Observants and the Conventuals and the split was made official in 1517, a bad moment for overt disunity in the Catholic Church. In abandoning the monastic ideal, the Jesuits had restored society's ecclesiological framework. While the reform had attacked the separate status of the clerical estate, the Jesuits had enlisted those who pray as those who fight in the cause of Christ, the cause of the very weakest in the third estate.

Here is a description of one of Ignatius's companions in the hospital for syphilitics in Venice:

> In the hospital of the *Incurabili*, a leper, or one suffering from a form of skin disease, covered all over by a kind of pestilential mange, called one of the fathers and asked him to scratch his back. The father diligently performed this service, but whilst he was so doing he was suddenly struck with horror and nausea, and with the terror of contracting the contagious disease. But since he wanted to master himself and to suppress his own rebellious spirit rather than take thought for the future, he put into his mouth a finger covered with pus and sucked it. Another day, he told one of his companions about it, and said with a smile: 'I dreamt last night that the sick man's disease had stuck to my throat, and that I tried to expel it by coughing and spitting it up, but in vain'. But for this father, who had done this act in good faith and fervour in order to conquer himself, the words of our Lord Jesus Christ were fulfilled: 'And if they drink anything deadly, it shall not harm them'.

According to Diego Laynez, Loyola's successor as General of the Order, the young brother in question was Francis Xavier, who later took ship for India, and worked as a missionary in Goa, Malacca, and Japan. The Jesuit involvement with the dregs of humanity made them superhuman, and through what appeared to be miracles of endurance they were sublimated into sainthood – which was to be the eventual accolade of Ignatius himself, Canisius, Xavier, and even of a Duke of

Gandia. In terms of what the Jesuits had changed about the Catholic Church, perhaps this Spanish grandee is the most intriguing case of Jesuit sainthood. He set his domestic affairs in order on the death of his wife in 1546 and took Jesuit vows four years later. He had founded the first Jesuit university at Gandia in 1545, and to him is attributed the idea of the Congregation *De Propaganda Fide*, which eventually formed in 1622. He was to become General of the Jesuit armies in 1565. This Duke of Gandia was Francisco de Borja, a name more familiar in its Italian form, Borgia, and Francisco was indeed the descendant of Alexander VI. The Jesuit inspiration had ensured that at least part of the fortune acquired so corruptly by the most infamous occupant of St Peter's throne was dispensed in good works by a man who almost became a Jesuit pope.[8] What, in the meantime, had happened to the papacy itself?

Tridentine Catholicism

Calls for a General Council of the church in the fifteenth century were the result of a crisis of papal authority (above, p. 129). Such a council threatened the primacy of the pope within the Church. Throughout the fifteenth century, the conciliarists' fear was that, once elected, popes could not be relied upon to acknowledge the power of councils as superior to their own. The Council of Trent was to reinforce papal supremacy, and it is another aspect of the spiritual revolution which the Society had generated that Jesuit influence was crucial in achieving this unpredictable result.

The chief threat to the position of the papacy in the first half of the sixteenth century was in many instances, its own lethargy, which seemed to prove Luther's point that it was 'all over with the Holy See of Rome' (above, pp. 137–9). Leo X (1513–21) had been slow to wake up to the crisis. Hadrian VI (1522–3), the former tutor of Charles V, seemed to offer the hope of a stable relationship between empire and papacy – but this could easily have proved stable servility, and any hope of reform and renewal dissolved in the familiar worldliness of Clement VII (1523–34). Here was a Medici bastard, orphaned by the Pazzi conspiracy of 1478. Even his ancestry was a reminder of papal skulduggery, for the conspirators who had hacked down his father, Giuliano de' Medici, in the cathedral church of Santa Maria del Fiore had been egged on by Sixtus IV, whose papacy was also noted for its sales of indulgences to finance building projects in Rome. Clement lived as a Renaissance prince, the generous patron of Guicciardini, Cellini, Raphael and Michelangelo. His changes of allegiance in a critical phase of the Italian Wars betokened a Machiavellian disregard for moral scruple and the validity of a prince's word – Clement had all the deviousness of Julius II without the latter's brash courage. The most iniquitous results of his machinations were devastation for Rome and humiliation for the papacy with the sack of 1527 (below, pp. 234–5). After this, Clement was the prisoner of Charles V – though he was still capable of seeking an alliance with Francis I. His lack of spiritual authority proved critical to the fate of England, for Clement mishandled Henry VIII's divorce from Catherine of Aragon, seeming at first to accommodate the king, and then excommunicating him.

The advance of the state at the expense of papal authority in England came a decade after the Diet of Worms. Given the lack of papal response, it was not to be wondered at that pressure increased for the summoning of a general council as the means of effecting reform. Charles V was one of the driving forces. He recalled his own enthusiasm in his autobiography:

> For it must be known that since the year 1529, when, as already stated, he visited Italy for the first time, and had an interview with Pope Clement, he never ceased whenever he saw either Pope Clement or Pope Paul, and in every journey, and at every Diet in Germany, and at every time and opportunity, continually to solicit, either personally or through his ministers, the convocation of a general council to provide a remedy for the evils which had arisen in Germany, and for the errors which were being propagated in Christendom.

Clement's successor, Paul III (1534–49), scarcely had the credentials of a reformer. He was a Farnese prince whose career advanced under the patronage of the powermongers Alexander VI and Julius II. When, at last, he summoned a council, expediency was his inspiration, not vision. Convoking such an assembly was preferable to having one foisted upon him – and what moment could be better than 1542, as the Emperor faced a renewed war with France? Charles recalled with some bitterness that Paul's prevarication was like that of Clement, a mere sweetening feint. Clement had let him down 'despite the promise he had made to His Majesty', and his successor was another deceiver:

> Pope Paul declared at the commencement of his pontificate that he had promised to announce and convoke the council immediately, and exhibited a lively desire to provide a remedy for the evils which had befallen Christianity, and for the abuses of the Church; nevertheless those demonstrations and first zeal gradually cooled down, and, following the steps and example of Pope Clement, he temporised with soft words, and always postponed the convocation and meeting of the council, until . . . he sent to Monzon, where the King of France commenced the war in 1542 – a bull of convocation of the

said council at Trent. The time and opportunity show what his real intentions were. God knows them, and they are easily discernible in what then took place . . .

The Bull of Convocation acknowledged that there had been false starts: projected assemblies in Mantua in 1537 and Vicenza a year later had never materialised. The meeting at Trent did not take place until 1545, and in many ways it had been precipitated by the outcome of the Imperial Diet at Regensburg. There, the papal legate, Contarini, and Melanchthon reached agreement on a doctrine of 'Double Justification'. Eck and Calvin found it acceptable. The world was astonished – that was until Luther disowned Melanchthon, and the cardinals in Rome more politely refused their support. The need to define Christian doctrine comprehensively and to clarify the position of the papacy within the Church was now irresistibly urgent. In 1545, a General Council of the Church assembled at Trent.

From the outset, the Council seemed doomed to failure. Representation was, to put it mildly, patchy. Despite the efforts of moderates to attract them – especially after the progress at Regensburg – no Germans arrived. Moreover, no delegates from battlegrounds such as Ireland, Poland or Hungary materialised in 1545. In other words, the 'general' council consisted of fewer than 200 bishops from Spain and Italy – and the Spaniards and Italians were furiously divided. For a time, it seemed that the Spaniards' sense of moral superiority might lead to a political separation. Absenteeism had been widely criticised as undermining the effectiveness of pastoral supervision. In keeping with the reforms of Ferdinand and Isabella, the Spanish bishops generally supported the idea that episcopal residence was commanded by divine law and could not be dispensed with when it was convenient to do so. The papal legates, the cardinals Gonzaga and Seripando, put the matter to a vote. Sixty-seven voted that it was, 35 that it was not, with 34 referring the matter to the pope. Therefore, if the pope, as anticipated, voted against residence as *ius divinum*, his majority (35 + 34 against 67) was only two. Paul III dared not intervene directly for fear of exposing still more sharply the deep division within the Council, and merely forbade further discussion of that subject. Gonzaga and Seripando fell into disfavour, and one Spanish bishop wrote that:

They have fallen into disgrace because they refused to defend the abuses of the curia. All good men have lost hope that the Council will achieve any positive result and fear that great harm will come of it.

As the Council broke up in 1547, there were complaints that there had been no institutional reform, and no general drive to eliminate heresy. Subsequent meetings scarcely offer evidence of any unity of purpose. The next assembly, in 1551–2, did attract a few Germans – but the French were absent because of the continued war with the Emperor. Julius III (1550–5) was obliged to suspend the Council in 1552 because of the crisis of imperial authority in Germany, and the repercussions of that for papal power against the French in Italy. The rest of the 1550s lie in the unlovely shadow of Paul IV. Indeed, he all but ruined the Catholic revival with his war on the Emperor and his irascible imprisonment of Giovanni Morone (1509–80), Bishop of Modena, and ironically, the man who was to be the saviour of papal primacy at the last sessions of the Council of Trent.[9] The assembly of 1562–3 had no clear relationship to the earlier meetings. It was concerned with Calvinism in France rather than Lutheranism in Germany: Philip II urged the theme of continuity, Ferdinand I – still hoping for compromise in Germany – thought this council should be quite separate.

However, there is a sense in which the Council of Trent created the Counter-Reformation. For all the divisions and disunity, for all the backstage bargaining and hard-nosed fixing, the Council of Trent eventually provided a powerful doctrinal clarity which was, as we have seen, altogether lacking in Protestantism. To refer to the statements of what the Council declared Catholic beliefs to be as 'dogma', implies a heavy-handed authoritarianism. The lucidity was refreshing, the authority welcome to a Christian population which had come to distrust the papacy but confused by the alternatives to it. It became clear that Protestantism was a heresy to be utterly uprooted and destroyed. By 1564 – what a contrast with the Protestants! – there could be no doubt about what a Catholic Christian should believe in.

Even the initial Bull of Convocation, written by the 'moderate' Jacopo Sadoleto, and full of apologies for the state of the Church, suggests that the time for compromise had passed:

> For since, as we had previously feared, we might be petitioned by a decision of the [imperial] diet to declare that certain articles maintained by the dissenters from the Church be tolerated till they be examined and decided upon by an ecumenical council, and since neither Christian and Catholic truth, nor our own dignity nor that of the Apostolic See would permit us to yield in this, we chose rather to command that it be proposed openly that a council be held as soon as possible.

Cardinal Pole, who rationally argued that projects for reform should not be dismissed merely because they accorded with ideas held by Luther, urged the Council to concentrate its attention on three central issues: 'heresy, the decline in ecclesiastical morals, and internal and external war'. These the Jesuits cauterised into a single great cause:

peace and moral regeneration were only possible through the elimination of heresy.

In 1545, developing the language of compromise employed by Contarini at Regensburg, Cardinal Seripando offered the Council a view of Justification by Faith acceptable to Protestants. In a speech of astonishing weight and power – which must have lasted well over two hours – the Jesuit theologian, Diego Laynez, later general of the order, tore to pieces the fabric of compromise. This was no mere intellectual exercise. The text of the speech is long and learned, but its message is of almost brutal simplicity: charity is good, sin is bad, justification by faith alone takes no account of either. 'Without charity we are nothing' – what devastating use of St Paul – and works are the fruit of charity. They are the manifestations of grace, the necessary signs of faith in Christ, and therefore of merit. Not to perform works is sinful and God hates sin. For Laynez, it is impossible to argue that a manifest sinner might also be elected to salvation because of the inscrutability of God's predestination:

> For in hatred with God is the impious man and his impiety, whoever he may be, and God does not hate the reprobate because of their nature, but because of their sin, because it is hateful, wherever it is, and in that man who lapses a penalty is owed.

As if to refute Protestantism from its own sources, having quoted St Paul on charity, Laynez's punch line – in an almost literal sense – is drawn from Augustine:

> 'The things which you say are to be wondered at, the things which you say are new, the things which you say are false. We are amazed at the things which are to be wondered at, we are wary of the things which are new, we condemn the things which are false.'

His Jesuit companion Salmerón went so far as to ask whether our actions altogether lost meaning, if all were directed by Christ's justice.[10] If the Jesuits could say this to Catholic theologians, what might they blast at Protestant heretics? The Jesuits, untarnished with a history of moral laxity, with no manifest abuses of which to be ashamed, identified totally with doctrine as defined by the Church. Since criticism of the Church was disobedience to the Church, why compromise with it? What a relief such ideas brought, relief from the anxiety that somehow fifteen hundred years of the Roman Church were to be blown away by the blusterings of heretics. By 1547, the entire Council was perfectly clear about the efficacy of works:

> The sinner is justified when through the merits of the most holy passion, and through the operation of the sacred Spirit, the love of

God is implanted in his heart and abides in it; thus become the friend of God, man goes forward from virtue to virtue, and becomes renewed from day to day; whilst he walks by the commandments of God and the Church, he grows with the help of faith through good works, in the righteousness obtained through the grace of Christ, and becomes more and more justified.

By the same token, the proposition:

that justification once received is not preserved and even increased in the sight of God through good works; but that these same works are only fruits and signs of justification, not causes of its increase

was simply anathematised. The spell was broken. However haphazard the subsequent history of the Council may be, however great the conflict between Spain and the papacy, the authority of traditional doctrine was consistently restored. In 1551, for instance, on the Eucharist:

this Holy Synod now declares anew, that through consecration of the bread and wine there comes about a conversion of the whole substance of the bread into the substance of the body of Christ our Lord, and of the whole substance of the wine into the substance of his blood. And this conversion is by the Holy Catholic Church conveniently and properly called transubstantiation.

There was no longer any pressure to be self-conscious about penance (also 1551), the mass (1562), purgatory and the saints (1563). As for the matter which had kindled Luther's spirit against Rome – indulgences – the Council concluded that their use 'is greatly salutary for Christian people and has been approved by the authority of sacred councils'. When the Council finally closed, it did so with a unanimous declaration of support for the decrees, and Cardinal de Guise exclaimed in exultation:

That is the faith of all of us. We are all united in it, we embrace it and subscribe to it. That is the faith of St Peter and the apostles. That is the faith of the fathers. That is the right faith!

The articles of that faith are embodied in the Tridentine Profession, still imposed on all converts to Roman Catholicism. It is symptomatic of the new unity of interests, however, that the Profession appeared in a *papal* bull in 1564. Pius IV (1559–65) showed both courage and vision in reconvening the Council, and – along with Borromeo's organisation and the diplomatic skills of Morone – takes credit for its successful outcome. Papal monarchy had emerged supreme from a council, and it was fitting that the pope gave voice to the new doctrinal certainty which ran directly contrary to what Protestantism had preached:

I acknowledge the sacred Scripture according to that sense which Holy Mother Church has held and holds . . . I profess also that there are seven sacraments . . . in the most Holy Eucharist there are truly, really and substantially the body and blood, together with the soul and divinity of Our Lord Jesus Christ . . . I hold unswervingly that there is a purgatory . . . that the Saints who reign with Christ are to be venerated . . . that the power of indulgences has been left by Christ in the Church . . . I vow and swear true obedience to the Roman pontiff . . . I accept and profess without doubting, the traditions, definitions and declarations of the sacred Canons and Oecumenical Councils and especially those of the holy Council of Trent; and at the same time I condemn, reject and anathematise all things contrary thereto . . .[11]

In teachings which resounded with the message of *The Spiritual Exercises*, the Council of Trent had stated with absolute clarity the doctrine of the efficacy of works in the salvation of souls.

Even more remarkable than the clarity of the declaration is the vigour and effectiveness of its enforcement. What was the influence of the Council of Trent on the social life of Catholics? The contrast with Protestantism is once again stark. Perhaps the doctrine of works, which assumed the translation of feelings into action, offered a more serviceable and attractive message than the anxious abstractions of justification and predestination. And perhaps it was natural that a revival which owed so much to 'popular' religious feeling in Spain, should, through the simplicity which was inseparable from its authoritarianism, offer reassurance to groups of people untouched or unthreatened by Protestantism: country people in general and women in particular.

The words of the great mystic Santa Teresa – writing before 1565 – present the reaction of the simple believer to the miracle of transubstantiation which a priest could perform through the nature of his office, even though he were in a state of mortal sin – making him a miniature pope:

Once when I was about to take Communion, I saw with the eyes of my soul, more clearly than ever I could with my bodily eyes, two most hideous devils. Their horns seemed to be about the poor priest's throat; and when I saw my Lord, in all His majesty, held in those hands, in the form of the Host that he was about to present to me, I knew for certain that they had offended against Him, and that here was a man in mortal sin. How terrible, O my Lord, to see that beauty of Yours between two such hideous shapes! They seemed so cowed and alarmed in Your presence that I think I would gladly have fled if you had let them go. I was so upset, Lord, that I do not know how I was able to receive the Host; and afterwards I was afraid, for I thought that if the visions had been of God, His Majesty would not have allowed this in order that I might realise what power there was in the words of consecration, and that God never fails to be present however wicked the priest who pronounces them. He also wanted me to realise His great goodness in placing Himself in the hands of His enemy, only for the good of myself and of all men. This clearly showed me that priests are under an even greater obligation to be good than other men, and what a terrible thing it is to receive the Most Holy Sacrament when one is unworthy, also how completely the devil is master of a soul that is in mortal sin.

The effectiveness of Catholic magic in rural areas is attested by the success of its overseas missions, and by its remarkable achievements in the seventeenth century. It is estimated that while about half Europe lived under Protestant rule in 1590, some four-fifths of it were controlled by Catholic rulers by 1650. In still more surprising contrast to Protestant failure, however, is the extent of the success which Tridentine Catholicism achieved in the towns.

The business of the Council of Trent could scarcely have taken on such purposeful shape without careful programming. The organisation of the final sessions of the Council owed much to Carlo Borromeo, nephew of Pope Pius IV. His career shows clearly how ideas were put into practice. Papal nepotism was responsible for his nomination – at only 22 – as Cardinal and Archbishop of Milan, yet his diocese was to become a model of reformed Catholicism. The stiffening puritanism of episcopal control which Borromeo brought to his office gave purpose and point to episcopal residence: there was much more for a bishop to do. The impact of the new Catholicism in Milan can be glimpsed in the pages of a diary kept by a carpenter, Giambattista Casale. They are an unusually precise guide to the rapid transition from pronouncement to enforcement. He records at the end of August 1564 that the decrees of the Council of Trent were published throughout the diocese by Nicolo Ormaneto, a trouble-shooting bishop. On 10 December, thirty Jesuits arrived as ordered by the pope, 'in order that the said fathers establish a seminary to bring together a quantity of clerks and instruct them in the holy apostolic and divine doctrine'. There was also a new domestic routine. The prior-general of one of the devotional brotherhoods – devotional rather than lay, for the prior was a priest, Hieronimo Rabia – provided a prayer, which the whole of Casale's household every day kneeled to say, along with three Our Fathers and three Ave Marias. Borromeo himself arrived in 1565. There was a long procession of priests, friars and penitent confraternities, and 24 masters of the Company of Christian Doctrine 'which teaches Christian doctrine *gratis*' were presented to the cardinal, Giambattista among them. In 1568 'the most reverend Cardinal Carlo Borromeo laid the cornerstone for the restoration of [the church of] San Fidele . . . which was later occupied by the Jesuits'. In 1567, the authorities put discipline into carnival. The teachers of Christian doctrine were asked to take communion every day 'in order to give a good example to the people', and they of course agreed:

> Having heard the answer of our Company . . . he instantly sent to invite all the penitential confraternities in Milan to join us in such a holy gathering; and they too were prompt in obeying his request. It was then broadcast to all the people; and by the grace of God . . . 1,300 souls came to receive communion from the hand of the cardinal.

The diary shows the powerful emphasis placed on parish discipline in terms of an education in correct belief – indoctrination in the literal sense. The confraternities to which Casale so frequently refers were important vehicles of the new Catholicism – not least because such brotherhoods had been objects of scorn for reformers who saw them as symbols of mechanical, unfelt works. After the Council of Trent, taking the sacrament and believing in transubstantiation were the obvious marks of a good Catholic, and brotherhoods for the cult of the Eucharist proliferated. By the end of the sixteenth century, it was said that they existed in 556 of Borromeo's 763 parishes. Virtually every church in Venice – a city of 70 parishes – appears to have housed a *Scuola del Santissimo Sacramento*. After 1530, two dozen sacramental confraternities were founded in Florence, often linked to the arch-confraternity of Santa Maria Sopra Minerva in Rome. The devotional life of Genoa's 200 confraternities bore the impression of Borromeo, and 8 of them were under the direct control of the Jesuits. The brotherhoods had traditionally acted as agencies of poor relief in Italian cities, the new Catholicism used them to save souls as well as relieve want: to show charity to prostitutes and prisoners, or – as did Francis Xavier – to syphilitics was a demonstration that works earned salvation for those who benefited from them as well as those who performed them.[12]

The confraternities had another part to play in the Catholic revival. Their patronage of the arts made them the source of much of the 'splendour of holiness' associated with the Counter-Reformation. Many of the works of art which they sponsored communicated a powerful doctrinal message, in particular by encouraging both philanthropy and orthodoxy. The advertisement of the Church's role in charity and education in ways which could reach the illiterate was critical to the outcome of the missionary war. Tintoretto worked extensively for the *Scuole del Santissimo Sacramento* in Venice. In the emphasis he laid upon the link between the Eucharist and charity, he perhaps displays the influence of Ignatius. In one *Last Supper*, for instance – itself a celebration of the Eucharist – Christ gives bread to two disciples, another disciple passes bread to a beggar, another feeds a child. In the summary of one authority, spiritual food and succour for the poor were inseparable.

Such works were part of a much grander initiative, reaching far beyond the confraternities. The new iconography disowned the brazen nudity of the pagans for the sufferings of the saints. As the Council proclaimed:

> Let the bishops diligently teach that the story of the mysteries of our Redemption, expressed by paintings or other representations, instructs and confirms the people in remembering and assiduously rehearsing the articles of the faith; that sacred images are the source of great spiritual profit, not only because the people are thus reminded of the blessings and help which Christ has granted them, but also because the marvels and wholesome examples of God are through his saints placed before the eyes of the faithful, so that they may thank God for them, and rule their life and manners after those of the saints, and may be incited to worship and love God, and cultivate piety.

Artists were expected to observe such principles. In Venice, in contrast to Tintoretto's depiction of the same scene, Paolo Veronese produced a *Last Supper* in full Renaissance regalia, but he had to rename it *The Banquet in the House of Levi* because the Inquisition deemed its dwarves and *Landsknechts* were out of place. The orthodox message had to be unmistakable. Paintings of the Immaculate Conception reminded the congregation of the divinity of the Blessed Virgin. The martyrdom of the saints inspired their veneration: El Greco's St Maurice faces execution for his faith, Titian's St Lawrence agonises on his burning grid. Who would have thought that the greatest master of the Venetian Renaissance would in his last years produce a sincere expression of his own piety in a composition called *Spain coming to the Aid of Religion*? A picture of San Carlo Borromeo among plague victims was worth many sermons on the value of works. In an earlier chapter, it was suggested that the visual arts were at least as important in spreading the message of Renaissance humanism as was the printed word. The Counter-Reformation shows why it is dangerous to attribute too much importance to changes associated with the new technology. For books were far less important in generalising the message of the new Catholicism than pictures were, and the point is best made by the pictures themselves (plates, section IV). A section which takes 'the Word' as its title must conclude by acknowledging the triumph of the image.

Yet that triumph was only complete in the seventeenth century.[13] We might see its beginning with the defeat of the Protestants at the Battle of the White Mountain in 1621, when, in Trevor-Roper's magnificent phrase the 'powerful theological engine and proud philosophical wings' of the Calvinist world-system were left 'crumpled and burnt out, to rust at the foot of a Bohemian ravine'.[14] Thereafter the triumphal progress of Catholicism continued at once with the formation of the Congregation *De Propaganda Fide*, 'For Spreading the Faith', the very next year. In the sixteenth century, no such end result was predictable (see Map 8.1 on following page). After the Council of Trent, with Calvinism spreading from Geneva to the Palatinate and to Scotland, threatening the subversion of France and the Netherlands, Catholicism was safe only in Italy, Portugal and Spain. The two world-systems faced each other as equals in a contest for mastery of the souls of Europe. This was to be a competition not just about who offered the superior social institutions for education and welfare, but about who could demonstrate the greater effectiveness in the destruction of the enemies of truth. Both versions of the Word had to find champions who would take up the sword, and those champions were already involved in contests of their own.

Map 8.1 Religious divisions in Europe, *c.*1560

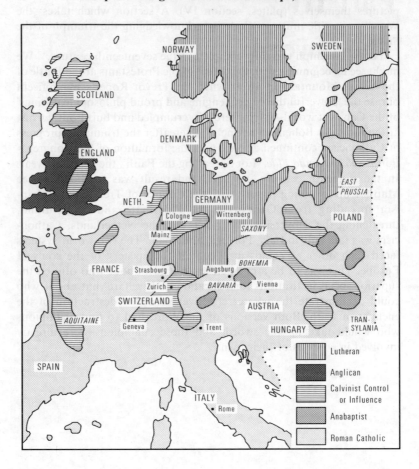

Source: Steven Ozment, *The Age of Reform, 1250–1550* (New Haven: Yale University Press, 1980), p. 373.

Part III
The Sword

9 Victims

The spectrum of violence

At the end of Part II, we examined the intensification of the ideological struggle between Protestantism and Catholicism at the social level. This, however, was only one dimension of the conflicts of the era. These final four chapters have to deal with the wars which that same ideological struggle intensified and broadened: intensified because existing antagonists – rebels as well as rulers – took up the cause of 'true religion', broadened because religion created new antagonisms. We have already seen how warfare itself was entering a new phase in terms of its scale (ch. 3). Machiavelli had insisted in his *Discourses* that war was the main business of states – much more important than the creation of wealth. 'Money is not the sinews of war': for all its riches, Venice lost its possessions on the Italian mainland in 1509 because of the inadequacy of its military institutions. For once, his views can be seen as unexceptional. However, he also warned against allowing religious passions to influence political calculation. In the second half of the sixteenth century this rarely proved possible. The larger armies engaged in longer and more costly wars were fighting in an unprecedentedly savage manner because they were fighting for different confessions. The Word was forever sharpening the edge of the sword.

However, the first task is to relate the social context and the ideological confrontations which we have already outlined to wars between the armies of states. It would be misleading to portray the Wars of Religion as some sort of aberration which scarred societies and an international complexion otherwise placid and peaceable. It is more accurate, perhaps, to see the violence which religion inspired as an extension of an already broad spectrum. Everyday life was a battle for survival which could shade rapidly into food riot, provincial rebellion and even international war. The famine in the Netherlands of 1565–6 helped to spark iconoclastic riots, and the brutally heavy-handed response of the Duke of Alba led some Dutch nobles to identify more closely with Calvinist ideology. This is not to say that the shortages of that year 'caused' the Dutch Revolt in any simple way: the shortage of 1556–7 had been more severe, and Calvinist preaching in 1565 did not create a mass movement against Spanish Catholicism. Yet in the Netherlands as elsewhere, the structures of everyday life were terrifyingly fragile, and their collapse produced a pile of combustible materials which religious passion or political ambition could easily ignite. For violence was inherent, barely contained, in those same structures. Even in the case of a state lauded for its stability, it might be said that peace was the superficial phenomenon, violence the social reality. Venice was remarkable to contemporaries because the city was never conquered by an invader and because its aristocratic government was never threatened by rebellion. Venetians still cross 'Fisticuffs Bridge' (*Ponte dei Pugni*) where inhabitants of one part of the city, the Castellani, used to meet to thump inhabitants from another, the Nicolotti. The dimensions of the peace which 'the Most Serene Republic' enjoyed dwindle still further if we move beyond the confines of the lagoon. In its mainland territories, the government wielded such feeble police authority that its famously all-seeing secret service was reduced to offering pardons to bandits who would betray other bandits. Throughout the century, the maritime commerce which was the traditional source of the city's wealth was harassed by pirates – Dutch, English and Italian as well as Barbary corsairs – who were often freebooters operating as the agents of states. In many ways, 'peaceful commerce' simply did not exist.

In rural areas of Europe a similar picture of simmering trouble presents itself. The mayhem of peasant life and the volatility of popular culture are caught in all their raw energy in the paintings of Pieter Bruegel (c.1525–69) (plates 23–5). This cultivated man is sometimes known as 'Peasant Bruegel' because of the delight he took in scenes of village life. It is striking that his depictions of merrymaking have so much in common with his representations of more serious themes. How haunting is the image *Magpie on the Gallows (Peasants Dancing)* – an awkward modern title for a composition less bizarre to sixteenth-century eyes than to our own. In the grim vision of *The Triumph of Death*, peasant folk dance again – this time with death itself in a thousand skeletal variations – amid banditry, the wheel and the gallows. In the *Battle of Carnival and Lent*, a fat man jousts with a thin woman in mock conflict amid an unruly and largely inebriated crowd divided into two camps, without any evidence of a public authority which might impose a measure of restraint. Moreover, the potential for violence of this nature might, on occasions, be realised, for example in rural France. Many rebellions seem to have occurred in the wake of *Corpus Christi* processions, and in 1580, at Romans, the carnival throng stood the social order on its head by attacking the local notables in a bloody uprising.

Many of these observations could be made for periods other than the sixteenth century. 'The violent tenor of life' is a concept which Huizinga applied to the later Middle Ages. Virtually anyone was a potential victim to war, famine or plague at any stage in the pre-industrial era –

as most people are in the non-industrial world in our own time. In any century, merriment and savagery are often close companions: gambling, brawling, drinking and blood sports are common enough social phenomena throughout history, and we should remember that the public execution of criminals has a history which stretches into the twentieth century. The grisly tortures meted out to criminals in the sixteenth century – 6 or 8 people were whipped or hanged every week in Seville, and criminals were herded to the galleys 50 at a time – were an exaggerated deterrent, a response to violence rather than a testimony to the state's capacity to terrorise society, and they must always be set against the pitiful rate of detection.

That said, the distinctive characteristics of violence in the sixteenth century are its direction and its targets. In trying to identify the victims of religious conflict (who give this chapter its title), we perhaps gain fresh insight into the peculiar relationship between religion and politics upon which so much of the historical experience of the sixteenth century depends. From this categorisation are excluded those Catholics and Protestants who regarded each other as heretics and who mobilised states in their respective causes. Many of those who went to the stake would have consigned their opponents to the same fate had they had the political upper hand.[1] This chapter is more concerned with those who had no such leverage. The chief victims of the sixteenth century were stateless.

Heretics or exiles?

The formation of armed camps in a Europe divided between Protestantism and Catholicism was heavily dependent on the religious allegiances of the principal political powers. It might even be argued that the papacy and not Luther initiated the process of definition. For in consolidating its territorial power in Italy, the papacy was exposed – as Machiavelli recognised – as one state (albeit a powerful one) amongst others, and its universal claims, particularly in the matter of heresy, looked increasingly artificial (above, pp. 79–80). This in turn was to give Protestantism a new momentum, for the heresy was new not so much in its social appeal – which was limited (above, pp. 170–2) – but in the degree of political shelter which it was afforded.

Thus, the control of ecclesiastical appointments which the French monarchy enjoyed acquired a new significance, for such powers might be used to promote a Protestant Church. In England, the Royal Supremacy enabled the monarchy to extend its power by submerging heresy in treason – as the trial of Thomas More was to demonstrate. The Catholic response to such developments drew strength from the precocity and decisiveness of state–church arrangements in the Spanish kingdoms, while the Peace of Augsburg (1555) – which ensured more than half a century of peace in the Empire – clearly acknowledged that the territorial sovereign should determine whether his subjects were to follow the Catholic or the Lutheran confession. All these would be observations not only obvious but trite had the patterns of statehood been clearly defined before the Reformation.

What gives the interaction of religion and politics in the sixteenth century its formidable complexity is that the decision to adopt a particular confession – Catholic, Lutheran or 'Reformed' (as the Calvinist Church became known) – was an act which set in motion a process of forced growth in some organs of the embryonic state. Moreover, such decisions could be disputed – as they were in the Spanish Netherlands by the subjects of Philip II – avoided – as they were by the Valois monarchs of France – or revoked – as they were in England under Mary Tudor. In other words, there was no inexorable advance of state power based upon control of the Church and through ecclesiastical institutions the religion of its subjects, and no sudden pounce – a sort of *coup d'église* – assured the state's enduring dominance in ecclesiastical affairs.

The assumption that there were no rebels in Spain because there were no heretics proved impossible to apply in the Netherlands, where Spanish greatness foundered. The failure of the French monarchy to give a clear commitment of support to Catholicism or Protestantism after 1559 proved catastrophic, and the state collapsed into four decades of civil war. Had the Peace of Augsburg offered a truly durable solution, then Germany might not have endured the horrors of the Thirty Years' War, but it had made no provision for a Calvinist Bohemia or for the militant Catholicism of a resurgent Habsburg Empire.

Resuming one theme from a previous chapter (above, ch. 3), it might be said that in the sixteenth century, state sponsorship of a particular confession was a measure of the state's new assertiveness, but that this was not of necessity symptomatic of a durable power. The experience of those unfortunate groups who were heretics to both Catholic and Protestant powers shows not just the state's new impulse to assert its control, but also its anxiety to find targets which it would have no difficulty in destroying. The most effective persecutors – Protestant or Catholic – were well-consolidated territorial states which needed to assert their authority. Superstition was rife in Ireland, but there was no central authority to being it to heel.[2]

Those whom the rival confessions sought to destroy were, of course, heretics. 'There is practically no sect which does not hold all others for heretics', wrote Sebastian Castellio in a rare plea for mercy and toleration. At bottom, a heretic was someone with whom one disagreed about religion. Toleration was not an accepted norm in the sixteenth century and the historian cannot apply an objective scale to the term. The type of toleration which allowed different views because no one could be sure who was right was all but unknown in the sixteenth century (as any other?). There are examples, however, of people who were thought to be damned but were allowed to coexist either because there was no means of destroying them, or because toleration brought economic benefits. Thus, the weakness of the state enabled the anabaptists to survive in parts of central Europe, the Venetian government allowed Jews to settle in the city because of the wealth which they helped to generate.

Generally speaking, however, views which were deemed heretical were inherently unacceptable. In the sixteenth century, the content of 'heretical views' was less significant than who deemed them heretical. Here the new assertiveness of the state is startling. The history of the 'easy targets', the victims, demonstrates that they were persecuted because they did not have the protection of the state, not because their views were in any objective sense 'extreme' or even 'radical'. From that point of view, they were stateless persons, exiles. The discussion which follows is primarily concerned with two groups within the Christian world: anabaptists and witches. In important ways, however, they shared the history of the Jews.

The Catholic Monarchs, Ferdinand and Isabella, established a new Catholicism in Spain, its personnel and institutions operating independently of the dictates of Rome (above, pp. 176–9). Perhaps the chief expression of the new relationship of the Church to the state was the Inquisition, and the Inquisition was established to ensure that *conversos*, Jews who had converted to Christianity, were not backsliders, secretly retaining their Judaism while maintaining the appearance of having become Christians. The *conversos* had been the target of popular fury in the pogroms of 1391, and a move against them was always likely to win general social approval. In 1492, within three months of the conquest of the Moorish kingdom of Granada, the monarchs issued an edict of expulsion against all practising Jews. Many opted for conversion to Christianity for the practical reason of not being expelled. At a stroke, the Catholic monarchs probably doubled the number of potentially backsliding *conversos* against whom the power of the Inquisition could be directed. And at least 100,000 Jews left. The act of expulsion was not a novelty – Edward I had ordered the Jews from England as long ago as 1290 – but what is striking is that in the case of Spain, centuries of coexistence were brought to an end, and that many other states adopted similar policies at about the same time. Many of those Jews who left Spain went to Portugal, where a similar expulsion was enacted in 1497 – and there was a whole series of expulsions from various states of the Holy Roman Empire in the period between about 1470 and about 1520.

More followed. Jews were forced to leave Saxony (1537), Thuringian towns (1540), the Duchy of Brunswick (1543), the Duchies of Hanover and Lüneberg (1553), Brandenburg (1573), the Palatinate (1575), Silesia (1582).

It can be argued that European Jewry came to enjoy greater toleration in the aftermath of the Reformation: Christianity was not so coherent, not so sure of itself.[3] This thesis is persuasive when applied to the early modern period as a whole, but within the confines of the sixteenth century, the eventual destiny of Jews who were forced to leave one state for another creates a pattern of its own. Curiously, Rome welcomed Jewish refugees, though with the establishment of an Inquisition on Spanish lines in 1542, *conversos* became common suspects, and Pius V drove the Jews from his territories in 1569. Elsewhere in northern Italy, Christian loan banks (*monti di pietà*) gave the Jews some competition as money-lenders, and the acceptance or otherwise of the Jewish social presence seems to have depended not on greater or lesser levels of toleration, but on whether the economic desirability of allowing them to remain outweighed the religious advantages of forcing them to leave.

This was certainly the case in Venice. Jews were present in the city in the fourteenth century. Venice's commercial links with the eastern Mediterranean and with northern Europe had helped to establish communities of Levantine (eastern) and German Jews. The Iberian expulsions pushed more Ponentine (western) Jews into the city, and there was a new influx of Jewish refugees from the Italian mainland during the Italian Wars. This last development resulted in the establishment of a Jewish quarter in the city: Europe's first 'ghetto' took its name from the old foundry located in that part of Venice which the government allocated to its Jewish population. In the sixteenth century, Venetian Jews negotiated a series of deals with the government, paying for licences or *condotte* which confirmed their commercial privileges. In this way, the government could exploit the economic utility of the Sephardic Jews' commercial links with the Ottoman Empire, and make use of the Germanic and Italian Jews as money-lenders. Venice had no Christian loan banks, and as the patrician diarist Sanudo put it 'the Jews are necessary for the sake of the poor'. As another nobleman pointed out, however, the Venetians could not be sure what they were missing as a result of such policies:

> it would be good to expel them from the whole world, and God would prosper this Republic as He did the King of Portugal, who, on expelling them, discovered the new route to India, and God made him the King of Gold. Even so did the King of Spain permit such great wealth to depart from his country, for the sake of exiling these devourers of Christians and enemies of Christ.

In the later sixteenth century, apparently following the trade routes, and perhaps as a result of the power vacuum, there was increasing Jewish immigration to the Netherlands, laying the foundations of their famous prosperity in a genuinely tolerant society in the Dutch Golden Age. However, Jews also settled in Austria and Bohemia, where the authorities seemed indifferent or powerless, and the other principal centres were the Balkans, Lithuania, and above all, Poland – in other words areas where the state remained comparatively weak.[4]

Vulnerable because of their beliefs, occasionally acceptable because of their economic usefulness, most secure where the state was weakest: these features of the history of the Jews in the sixteenth century are similar to those of Christian communities whose beliefs no state chose to adopt.

Like the Jews of Spain and other states, some Christians also found themselves displaced. Calvinist Geneva offered a home to some of those who fled Marian England, and to many Huguenots who fled France after the Massacre of St Bartholomew in 1572 (above, p.165). Not all refugees were secure there. Michael Servetus (1511–53) was a Spaniard who had trained in medicine and travelled in Europe. He developed views on the Trinity which he published in 1542 in a work entitled *The Restitution of Christianity*. In it, he argued that Christ was only partly human, and that since consciousness of mortal sin was impossible before the age of 20, infant baptism was absurd. His views on the Trinity disturbed Calvin, with whom he corresponded in 1547. Calvin recorded his own reaction in a letter to Farel:

Servetus has recently written to me and has included with his letter a large volume of his wild imaginings, adding with a boastful gesture that I should find some of the contents amazing and never heard of before. If it is agreeable to me, he takes it upon himself to come here. But I am unwilling to guarantee his safety, for if he does come and my authority counts for anything, I will never let him get away alive.

He was as good as his word. In 1553, with Calvin's connivance, information reached the Inquisition – yes, the Inquisition – in Lyon about Servetus's presence in the city:

A certain heretic is countenanced among you, who ought to be burned alive, wherever he is to be found. And when I say heretic, I mean a man who will be condemned by papists as readily as he is (or should be) by ourselves. For, although we differ over many things, we agree in our belief that in the one essence of God there are three persons . . .

The controversial doctor escaped, and shortly afterwards appeared in Geneva. He was arrested and burnt at the stake for his anti-trinitarian beliefs. He was subsequently described as an 'anabaptist' – a name invented by enemies to describe a variety of very different tendencies. In the Netherlands, 'anabaptist' was sometimes interchangeable with 'heretic' and between 1534 and 1536 at least 200 people were executed as anabaptists.

Amongst the thousands who shared such a fate there was a perplexing mixture of wild fundamentalists and mild pacifists, of coarse popular rationalism (for some, transubstantiation was impossible because God could not want to turn himself to excrement in human bowels) and sophisticated intellectual speculation about the mortality of the soul (which perhaps went to sleep on the death of the body and would not waken until judgement day, whenever that would be, the doctrine of psychopannichism). What united them was the conviction that the dictates of popes, princes and magistrates could not produce 'true religion'. Such views have led some historians to place these 'radicals' alongside Lutheranism, Calvinism and Anglicanism as one of the chief sources of momentum within the Reformation. Yet this 'radicalism' was unacceptable to other Protestants. Zwinglian Zurich banned anabaptist beliefs in 1524, and Zwingli himself was to denounce their 'pretext for seditions' in terms of adult baptism and the sleep of the soul. One 'catabaptist', Konrad Grebel, was expelled, and subsequently made contact with Andreas Karlstadt.

More significantly, some of Müntzer's followers, such as Hans Hut and others from Thuringia were also anabaptists, which has linked their beliefs to the leaders of the German peasants in the war of 1525. Such leaders had already been denounced by Luther as '*Schwärmer*', which means something between 'fanatics' and 'dreamers'. From Switzerland, anabaptism spread to Austria and the Tyrol, south and central Germany (notably Augsburg and Strasbourg). Apparently, anabaptism then effortlessly confirmed its own subversiveness. Jakob Hutter, with 200 or so followers, established a 'communist' society not subject to the laws of the state in Moravia after 1527. That 'communism' was itself a sign of grace – as Ulrich Stadler wrote in about 1537:

> Whoever is thus free, unhampered, and resigned in the Lord from everything, [ready] to give over all his goods and chattels, yea to lay it up for distribution among the children of God – it is God's grace in Christ which prepares men for it.[5]

And this was in the aftermath of events in Münster, where in 1534–5 the 'anabaptist kingdom' of Jan Matthiis, Bernd Rothman and Jan of Leyden, added polygamy to communism, throwing all decency and order to the winds in an orgy of visionary nonsense. The policies of extermination which all but a few states pursued against the anabaptists were apparently largely effective by 1600. After the dispersion which followed the battle of the White Mountain in 1621, such communities as survived found their haven in the New World.

There is evidence which suggests that the history of the 'radical Reformation' is more important to people in the twentieth century as a chapter in the history of intolerance than it was as a social phenomenon in the sixteenth. In central Europe, anabaptism was both insignificant and contradictory. In Switzerland, Austria, Moravia, and south and central Germany, the total number of anabaptists throughout the period 1525–1618 probably did not exceed 30,000. In Württemberg the identification of 129 anabaptists must be set against the duchy's population of almost half a million. In Augsburg, anabaptists accounted for less than 2 per cent of the city population. Yet in 1573, one observer, Georg Eder, listed no fewer than 38 different types of anabaptist. Some groups, such as those who followed Balthasar Hubmaier (1481–1528) or Menno Simons (1496–1561) appear as quiet pacifists unjustly persecuted, others – such as the amoral enemies of godlessness at Münster – seem angry threats to the social order, swift to sneer and condemn. The 'radical' Müntzer quoted the book of Matthew and preached to the Saxon princes that 'I am not come to send peace but a sword.' What a contrast with Georg Blaurock, in his criticism of Luther and Zwingli – also on the basis of Matthew:

Faith is not like that, a matter of coercion, but rather a gift of God. And Christ speaks to His disciples [Matthew 16:24]: If anyone will follow me . . . let him deny himself and take his cross upon him. He does not say the sword, for this has no place beside the cross.

Obbe Philips, sickened by the Münster débâcle, wrote more in sadness than in anger against the man who inspired the Münsterite prophets, Melchior Hofman, 'a fiery and zealous man':

I know of no one who has so much calumniated and damned in his own writings as this Melchior; whereby also we all taught many blasphemies and considered it was a true, pure and saintly thing to denounce [others] as heretics and godless and to damn those who were not receptive or disposed to our belief. As such they were all Lutherans, Zwinglians and papists; and all who did not say yes and amen were devilish and satanic spirits, godless heretics, and people damned to eternity.[6]

Given the small numbers of peasants and craftsmen involved, and given the huge variety of affiliations and beliefs, it is hard to present anabaptism as a sort of popular Reformation competing with the Reformation directed by magistrates. There is no point in trying to prove that anabaptism was a 'mass movement', because it did not involve the masses and it was not a movement.

While it is easy to overrate anabaptism as a social phenomenon, however, it is equally easy to overlook its significance as an illustration of political change. At first sight, this seems a curious assertion, for the anabaptists sought to separate themselves from the state. On the other hand, it was precisely this separation which made them so vulnerable, even though their beliefs and practices were nothing like as 'extreme' as their opponents and sympathetic historians of 'radicalism' have chosen to depict them. To grasp this point, it is essential to set anabaptism in the mainstream of those religious sentiments which advocated reform of the Church, and to forsake anachronistic judgements based on terms such as 'radical' or 'left-wing'. Although we must acknowledge the new importance of the state in religious matters, this does not mean that we should ground our analysis in terms borrowed from modern politics. It is highly inappropriate to apply the language of modern politics to the history of the state in the sixteenth century, not least because religion was so important in the political arena and party politics were all but unknown. Enormous distortion sets in, therefore, if historians apply modern political terms to describe religious groups who thought the state was irrelevant to the Christian life.

Such usage has obscured rather than clarified the development of the state in our period. For instance, talk of the 'left wing' of the Reformation perforce imposes the obligation to define the 'centre' and the 'right'. The confusion deepens when religious 'radicalism' is characterised as 'communism' and set in the context of 'class war'. This terminology does little to evoke a convincing historical reality. If the 'radicals' are to be placed on the 'left', does this mean that Luther is a 'conservative' on the 'right' because he disowned them? Was Luther's attack on the separateness of the clerical estate not 'more revolutionary' (because it was unprecedented) than the rebellion of peasants against lords (because it was not)? Is Erasmus at the 'centre' because he was more tolerant than Luther or was he a 'conservative' because he could not countenance schism within the Catholic Church? The use of such language gives the impression that religious leaders and their supporters were operating within a clearly defined political framework. The religious tendencies of the age are not to be judged by a modern scale stretching from a 'moderate centre' to different 'extremes' of 'right and left'. The critical consideration for the reform was not the degree of 'extremism', but whether the religious principles of particular leaders and groups acquired the backing of secular states. The two great contending world systems of the later sixteenth century were both strains of the same religious impulse – puritanism – the one Calvinist, the other Jesuitical (above, p. 174). The anabaptists – who did not even refer to themselves as such but as 'brethren and sisters in the Lord' –

were heretics to both sides not because of the inherent extremism of their beliefs, but because they never won political patronage. Let us try to assemble a different version of their sad history.

The idea of adult baptism was in many ways quite consistent with that general review of the sacraments – particularly marriage and the Eucharist – which gave so much momentum to calls for reform of the Church: 'for the Christian life is not child's play', as the Austrian anabaptist, Johann Schlaffer, put it. If we shift the regional focus from Germany to the Low Countries, then anabaptism displays clear links with Erasmianism and with the *devotio moderna* which stood behind it. After all, Christ was baptised as an adult, and the Christian should attempt the imitation of Christ.[7] Even Münster can be included within the orbit of such ideas. The inspiration of the anabaptists in that unfortunate city was Melchior Hofman. True, there was a millenarian vision in his thinking. He urged true believers to follow St Paul's advice and:

> make a good race for the true Mount Zion and to the city of the congregation of the living God, to the assembly of the perfectly righteous, to the company of the angels and to the blood of Jesus Christ. And one may enter into the Holy [Jerusalem], into the true new heaven of God. There they will become true newborn children. There all is new and the old wholly wasted away.

Yet the faithful would proceed there 'having routed out and laid aside the old Adam and having, through baptism, taken and put on the new Adam Christ Jesus'. Moreover 'all children of God and brothers of the Lord Jesus Christ should imitate Him', 'letting themselves be introduced by the servants of the Lord into the spiritual wilderness'. The mystical strain in anabaptism, as evidence from south Germany demonstrates, should be seen not as exceeding the bounds set down by Luther, but as sharing with Lutheranism the religious traditions of the Rhineland.

Even the communitarianism – a term less loaded than 'communism' – was not as revolutionary as is sometimes claimed. The Hutterite withdrawal from the world might be interpreted as a species of 'substitute monasticism', undermining family ties, perhaps, but no more so in some ways than the Brethren of the Common Life had done in the fifteenth century, or than Thomas More suggested in *Utopia* (above, pp.147–8). There is no evidence that this sort of communitarianism was a primary reason for the persecution of anabaptists. Indeed, the Hutterites who practised communitarianism most thoroughly also achieved the longest period of stability under the lords of Moravia. There were also clear statements from leading anabaptists which distance them from any idea of the forced community of goods. The emphasis was rather that one could not own something which must have come from God. As Hubmaier gently stated:

> we are not lords of our possessions, but stewards and distributors. There is certainly no one who says that another's goods may be seized and made common; rather, he would gladly give the coat in addition to the shirt.

Rather than being a novelty, such principles had their grounding in the Scriptures, and indeed in the corporatist principles of work-sharing and social justice which characterised many urban societies – including Leyden, whence hailed Münster's King Jan. The idea that 'a Christian should not have anything of his own, but should have all things in common with his brother' should be seen in relation to the very next phrase which Ambrose Spittelmaier then adds, 'not allow him to suffer need'.[8]

This is a far cry from the rampant modern communism of the common man which some historians have identified amongst the rebellious German peasantry and the Münsterite 'fanatics'. Contact between the anabaptist Grebel and the rebel leader, Thomas Müntzer, did not constitute collusion. Grebel warned against 'singing and tablets', the one not sanctioned by Scripture, the other idolatrous even though the tablets mentioned were the Ten Commandments. His dissociation from violence was absolute:

> Moreover, the gospel and its adherents are not to be protected by the sword, nor are they thus to protect themselves, which . . . is thy opinion and practice. True Christian believers are sheep among wolves, sheep for the slaughter; they must be baptised in anguish and affliction, tribulation, persecution, suffering and death; they must be tried with fire, and must reach the fatherland of eternal rest, not by killing their bodily, but by mortifying their spiritual enemies. Neither do they use worldly sword or war, since all killing has ceased with them . . .

With these general considerations in mind, even the anabaptist kingdom in Münster appears in a different light. First, it is important to remember that the anabaptists came to power not by slaughtering their enemies but by winning control of the town council in the elections of 1534. The anabaptists were not pacifists – though their supporters included people such as Obbe Philips who became so (above, p. 207). The rule of Jan of Leyden began after the death of Jan Mathiis in a sortie against the besiegers in August. His arbitrary rule included the death penalty for opposition – he once struck off the head of someone who had just spoken out against him in public – for blasphemy, seditious language, scolding, disobedience and lewd gossip.

However, such a draconian regime can be attributed in part to the need to maintain order under siege. The shortages which the siege induced go some way to explaining the community of goods: enforced sharing to try to ensure that there was enough to go round. The outrageous polygamy also has its explanation in the shortage of men in the city. As for the alienation of Jan's luxurious parvenu court as the rest of the population starved, this could be seen as a microcosm of general structural weakness in the Renaissance state, rather than some bizarre black comedy. That kingdom enjoyed sixteen months of military success, not least because its leaders used their superiority in cannon to considerable effect. Those same leaders showed political judgement as well. Jan of Leyden designated Philip of Hesse as the prince who would survive the destruction of Münster's godless enemies, and Philip himself was prepared to negotiate with any brand of evangelical Protestantism. Indeed, Charles V had been in contact with Bernd Rothman, for the latter seemed a serviceable counterweight to bishop Franz, who had refused to become the emperor's vassal. Ultimately, nothing came of such dealings, but had the anabaptist regime survived longer militarily, historians might be discussing Münsterite 'communism' with the same respect which they use towards the Hussites who protected their heresy so effectively at Mount Tabor in the fifteenth century, and there would be more frequent reminders that Dutch Calvinists were no less belligerent and subversive in their response to Alba's oppression – as in their seizure of Brill in 1572, for instance.

In the event, Münster was betrayed, though its 800 defenders fought to the death. King Jan gave his account of his own polygamous regime to the agents of Philip of Hesse, a syphilitic bigamist. Then, at the order of Bishop Franz, Jan, his chief minister Knipperdolling, and one other were bound in iron to stakes in front of the cathedral. Their executioners ripped out their tongues with red-hot pincers which were then used to torture them to death. Knipperdolling tried in vain to strangle himself with the iron collar as he watched the agony of Jan. The corpses were hung in cages – which are still there – and left to rot on the cathedral tower (plate 26).[9]

Such savagery was not reserved for the leaders in Münster. Many anabaptists shared a similar fate. In 1535, an anabaptist coup failed in Amsterdam. Some of the participants had persuaded the mild Obbe Philips to become one of the brethren. As a mark of respect, he went to look for them amongst the bodies after their execution in Haarlem:

> I was curious to know which in the heap those three were who had baptised us and had proclaimed such calling and promise to us. But we could not identify them, so frightfully were they changed by the fire and smoke, and those on the wheels we could not recognise either, nor tell one from the other.

In the aftermath of Münster, anabaptism acquired a new discipline with a firm commitment to pacifism and the clear separation of Church and state. Much of this transformation was the work of Menno Simons (from whom the 'Mennonites' took their name). Even though he wrote a tract against the blasphemy of Jan of Leyden, anabaptism became no more acceptable. Calvin wrote of Simons that 'nothing can be more conceited than this donkey, nor more impudent than this dog'. The catalogue of those victims of confessional power who were anabaptists is depressing. The executions in Münster and Haarlem were not the earliest. The first Protestant to be killed by Protestants was Felix Manz, drowned in the lake at Zurich in accordance with Zwingli's ordinances against re-baptism.

One of the best-reasoned defences of the century is surely that of Michael Sattler in Rottenburg in 1527. He set out his beliefs as eight points, the last of which was in favour of pacifism in the face of the Turkish threat:

> But that I said that if warring were right, I would rather take the field against so-called Christians who persecute, capture and kill pious Christians than against the Turks was for the following reason. The Turk is a true Turk, knows nothing of the Christian faith, and is a Turk after the flesh. But you who would be Christians and who make your boast of Christ persecute the pious witnesses of Christ and are Turks after the spirit!

Sattler consoled himself prior to execution with a species of spiritual immersion – *Gelassenheit* – in God's will: 'In this peril I completely surrendered myself unto the will of the Lord, and . . . prepared myself even for death for His testimony.' Balthasar Hubmaier, who had in fact urged the brethren to pay taxes for the war against the Turk in accordance with Christ's injunction 'Render unto Caesar the things which are Caesar's', was arrested in 1528 and then executed in Vienna, his end hastened by the sulphur and gunpowder which were rubbed into his hair. Jakob Hutter died in 1536: he was dipped in freezing water, his skin was lacerated, and he was rubbed with brandy which was then ignited.

His followers had found their haven in Moravia, that part of the Habsburg lands which lies to the east of Bohemia and to the north of Austria. Despite the alarm of Ferdinand of Habsburg, which he expressed at the Moravian Diet of Znaim in 1528, and despite expulsion orders in 1535 and 1545 – that is to say, after the horrors of Münster – members of the nobility allowed the Hutterite *Brüderhöfe* to remain on their estates. These communities of between 200 and 400 people acquired a high reputation for manufactures, especially textiles, which they traded conventionally in local markets, the subsequent pooling of profits apparently of no concern to the landlords. The latter made profits of their own by the arrangement, and tended to ignore royal edicts. A similar tale unfolded in Prussia where Duke Albrecht, under pressure from Luther, failed to enforce an edict of expulsion after the destruction of the anabaptists in Münster. In Danzig too, the economic utility of the anabaptists outweighed dislike for their beliefs.[10]

Like the Jews, anabaptists were most likely to find acceptance where they were useful to the local economy, though also like Jews, they remained an easy and obvious target if the authorities chose to flex their muscles in the interests of confessional conformity. More danger- ous to true religion, more vulnerable and – conveniently – more easily destroyed were those enemies of God who were allies of Satan himself.

Scapegoats

The persecution of the anabaptists shows that the choice of a Catholic or Protestant confession became, in the course of the century, so critical to the definition of statehood itself, that beliefs which asserted their independence of the state were an unacceptable menace. From about 1580 onwards, as the scale of the conflict widened, the rival confessions became engaged in the elimination of another enemy. As missionaries sought to claim the souls of Europe's rural inhabitants, they discovered that imposing Protestantism or Catholicism was something of a theological nicety, for they found that many regions lived within a matrix of beliefs which synthesised Christianity with local traditions and culture. Thus, the principles which helped the peasant to make sense of his environment became forces of darkness working against godly society. Whether the peasant lived or died was a question of the degree of hostility which the environment displayed, for upon this depended the success or failure of the harvest. Roman Inquisitors discovered a particularly well-developed set of convictions in Friuli in 1580:

> On their way home the witches go into the cellars to drink, then piss in the casks. If the benandanti [white witches] did not go along, the wine would be spoilt . . . I go with the others to fight four times a year . . . I go invisibly in spirit and the body stays behind; we go forth to serve Christ, the witches to serve the devil; we fight each other, we with bundles of fennel and they with sorghum stalks . . . and if we are the victors, that year there is abundance, but if we lose there is none.

The principles which ruled the universe then were magical, but it is important to recognise the importance of the operations – as revealed in the above quotation – of white magic as well as black.

For some time, the operations of missionaries in rural areas have been seen as a forum in which 'learned' culture encountered the 'superstition' of the peasant masses, in which the 'élite' discovered 'popular culture'.[11] This has not been altogether helpful, because there is a tendency to see 'learned' culture as somehow more 'rational' or 'scientific', therefore able to control, direct or reshape the ignorance of society at large. It seems more likely that the confrontation was between two different sorts of magic. The calculations of the judges were perhaps not so well-informed as is sometimes assumed. After all, we have already seen some of the greatest minds of the era testing themselves to breaking point over the question of transubstantiation. This institutionalised miracle was in many ways a magical transformation. Johann Eck earnestly believed that Jews were engaged in ritual murder, that they 'buy and sell the blood of innocent children, just as their fathers had bought the innocent blood of Jesus Christ from Judas with thirty pennies'.

Some sixteenth-century minds had less of a problem than have modern historians in incorporating popular belief in their own learned world. How eloquent is Shakespeare's reference to the fairy world and its repercussions for the harvest in *A Midsummer Night's Dream*, a play written during the dearth-ridden 1590s. With Oberon and Titania squabbling:

> The ox hath therefore stretch'd his yoke in vain,
> The ploughman lost his sweat, and the green corn
> Hath rotted ere his youth attain'd a beard;
> The fold stands empty in the drowned field,
> And crows are fatted with the murrion flock;
> The nine-men's morris is fill'd up with mud,
> And the quaint mazes in the wanton green
> For lack of tread are indistinguishable.
>
> (II.i.93–100)

When Marlowe's Faustus conjures devils, he uses them 'to find the secrets of astronomy',

> He views the clouds, the planets and the stars,
> The tropic zones, and quarters of the sky,

And then, riding a dragon,

> He now is gone to prove cosmography,
> That measures coasts and kingdoms of the earth
>
> (III.i.2, 7–8, 20–1)

In other words, his learned mumbo-jumbo is closely associated with rational scientific inquiry. Some cases suggest that this is not mere literary artifice. While some doubted the transformation of bread into flesh and wine into blood, many sought to turn lead into gold. We may think of John Dee and Edward Kelley as quacks, but we might also remember that Kepler was to become a fortune-teller – and rather a good one.[12]

Such considerations perhaps help our understanding of why interest in witchcraft amongst intellectuals was so strong, and why belief in witches became, in the eyes of jurists, a real crime rather than a pitiable error. The construction of the crime of witchcraft began in the 1480s. The instigators of systematic persecution were the Dominican Inquisitors, Heinrich Krämer and Jakob Sprenger, who published a book called *Malleus Maleficarum*, or 'The Hammer of Witches' in 1486. They believed that they had found in witchcraft the root of all those heresies which their order had been founded to destroy. The motives of the papacy in sanctioning the campaign remain obscure. An old-fashioned crusade against old-fashioned enemies, the Waldensians of the Alps, was launched in 1487. Were these new initiatives signs perhaps that the papacy had recognised the need to compete with the *reyes catolicos* in the extirpation of the unrighteous? Certainly, the message of the *Malleus* was widely diffused, and in the later sixteenth century found serious and distinguished support in the treatises of Nicolas Rémy (*Daemonolatrie*, 1595), Henri Boguet (*Examen des sorciers*, 1602), who offered a 'scientific' estimate that there were 1,800,000 witches in Europe, and the Jesuit, Martín del Rio, who published an encyclopedia on the subject in 1599.

Rather earlier, and much more significant, however, was the impetus which the great Bodin supplied. *De la démonomanie des sorciers* (1580) called for the burning not only of witches, but of all those who did not believe in this dreadful threat to the world.

Given the intellectual credentials of witch-hunting, the historian might feel a sense of relief that it was not more widespread. In a world in which war, famine and plague hacked down people in their hundreds of thousands, in the context of the everyday violence which we have already observed, witch-hunting – it is perhaps inappropriate to talk of a witch 'craze' – can seem rather limited in scale and scope.

This certainly applies in the south of Europe and in the north. Inquisitors pursued witches in Italy – in the famous trials in Friuli for instance, and in proceedings against soothsayers in the city of Venice. In Spain, the largest recorded outbreak of witchcraft was in 1610. There were six executions, and those only after exhaustive examination of the accused. Perhaps Inquisitors need only one stereotype, and the Inquisitors of Spain were content to proceed against Jews. In the north there was more intensity and greater violence, but scarcely a craze. In Norway and Sweden in the sixteenth and seventeenth centuries there were some 2,700 trials, none of which seems to have involved torture, and the 1,200 executions are outweighed by the 1,500 acquittals. The evidence from Lutheran areas is patchy, but in Bremen over the period 1503–1711, the records show only 62 trials, and in general, Lutheran authorities were milder than Calvinists in their approach to witchcraft. In Sweden, in Austria and in Poland, the peaks of persecution were reached only in the very late seventeenth century, in Hungary in the early eighteenth.

In central Europe, in the Alps and the Pyrenees, the story is different. In south-western Germany in the period 1560–1670, almost 3,000 executions are recorded. The sudden bursts of judicial massacre within that period are much more startling: 40 per cent of those executions involved groups of 20 or more victims at a time. In Eichstätt in one year alone, 274 witches were burned. In Quedlinburg in 1589, 133 were eliminated in a single day. And when one reads of the 'extremism' of the anabaptists in Münster, it is as well to call to mind the Archbishop of Trier, Johann von Schöneburg – an imperial elector. A devotee of the Jesuits (and they found plenty of witches outside Spain), his grim career virtually provides a pattern for this chapter: he was merciless towards Jews, then Protestants, then witches. Between 1587 and 1593, he authorised 368 executions in 22 villages.[13]

There were trials for witchcraft in Venice, and in parts of France and Switzerland which sought to root out magical beliefs, but elsewhere intellectual conviction often intensified persecution on the basis of a range of quite specific charges. What follows is a summary of the trial of Walpurga Hausmännin, who was condemned in Dillingen in 1587:

Walpurga Hausamännin [a widow] . . . has, upon kindly questioning and also torture . . . confessed her witchcraft and admitted the following . . . [31 years ago] the Evil Spirit visited her again in the same shape and whored with her. He made her many promises to help her in her poverty and need, wherefore she surrendered herself to him body and soul. Then the devil inflicted a scratch below her left shoulder, and demanded that she sell her soul to him with the blood that had flowed therefrom. To this end he gave her a quill and, whereas she could not write, the Evil One guided her hand . . . At their nightly gatherings she and her playmates had often trodden underfoot the Holy and Blessed Sacrament and the image of the Holy Cross . . . She confesses also that her paramour gave her a salve with which to hurt people and animals, and even the precious fruit of the field. He also compelled her to do away with and kill young babies at birth, even before they had been taken to Holy Baptism . . . [She lists 43 cases of infanticide] . . . Walpurga confesses further that every year since she sold herself to the devil, she has on St Leonard's day exhumed at least one or two innocent children. With her fiend-paramour she has eaten them and used their hair and their little bones for witchcraft . . . She had used the said little bones to manufacture hail . . . After all this, the Judges . . . unanimously gave the verdict that the said Walpurga Hausmännin be punished and dispatched from life to death by burning at the stake as being a maleficent and well-known witch and sorceress . . . The aforesaid Walpurga to be led, seated on a cart, to which she is tied, to the place of her execution, and her body first to be torn five times with red-hot irons. The first time outside the town hall in the left breast and the right arm, the second time at the lower gate in the right breast, the third time at the mill brook outside the hospital gate in the left arm, the fourth time at the place of execution in the left hand. But since for nineteen years she was a licensed and sworn midwife of the city of Dillingen, yet has still acted so vilely, her right hand with which she did such knavish tricks is to be cut off at the place of execution. Neither are her ashes after the burning to remain lying on the ground, but are thereafter to be carried to the nearest flowing water and thrown thereinto . . .

The 'confession' contains three notable features of a stereotype, a clear and unchanging form which we can identify in a host of other witch trials. First of all, there is the idea of a pact with the devil, a diabolic contract for evil-doing – what a macabre touch that the devil signs on the illiterate Walpurga's behalf. Second, there is the sabbath: Walpurga is part of an assembly of witches practising unspeakable anti-Christian rites as part of a coven. Third, as if to seal the bond and blaspheme to the lowest degree, the witch has sex with the devil. The same features appear in Friuli in 1649, though, as an earlier quotation has shown, none of them was familiar from the culture of the locality. The credentials of such allegations were respectable enough amongst intellectuals, however. Faustus signs his soul away to the devil in his own blood, and one kiss from the spirit of Helen of Troy will 'suck forth' his soul. Although witches were alleged to gather together, there is no evidence that a witches' sabbath took place apart from the confession of witches themselves. The authorities never discovered a coven through a surprise raid (and they did discover secret meetings of anabaptists, so the necessary machinery of policing was available).

Other details of the 'crimes' of Walpurga enhance the stereotype in social terms, make it more credible for locals. She can be blamed for hail storms or infanticide, which would make sense of crop failures or infant mortality for neighbours, and her role as midwife of course gave her unique opportunities.

Walpurga was an old widow (the 'crimes' began 31 years ago), and she was tortured to say that witchcraft was responsible for things which the judges knew to have happened. Her 'crimes' explained catastrophes in local life, thus building up social pressure against the witch once she was identified. The conclusion to draw from such a tragic and distasteful episode is this: witches who made a pact with the devil and gathered at the sabbath for acts of blasphemy to which the sexual act was central existed first and foremost in the minds of those who sought to destroy them. Moreover, the judges propagated this fearful stereotype amid circumstances which made it all the more convincing to local society.

Once more, it is important to avoid seeing the historical phenomenon as some sort of conspiracy consistently enhancing state power. On the contrary, proceedings against witches – as against Jews and anabaptists – were expressions of the insecurity of public authority rather than its new powers. Identifying a 'learned' establishment of Inquisitors, secular magistrates, intellectuals and theologians in cultural conflict with popular traditions tends to overemphasise the coherence of both. There were great tensions within the establishment, particularly between ecclesiastical and secular authorities, and if a great cultural divide existed there was such seepage of views across it as to render it invisible. The people of sixteenth-century Europe, elevated intellectuals such as Bodin or nameless Friulian peasants, lived in a world of magic and demons. Those who contested such a world picture – another intellectual such as the learned Servetus or another Friulian, such as Menocchio the rationalist miller – were burned. Let Calvin's judgement serve as a guide to the mentalities of the era: 'God expressly commands that all witches and enchantresses shall be put to death and this law of God is an universal law.'

As the confessional struggle intensified, the problems of enforcement multiplied and public authorities – secular and ecclesiastical – were reduced to creating an anti-Christian alternative to godly society, a species of phony opposition (real enough to the authorities themselves) which could then be destroyed by the forces of righteousness or by superior magic. Those who were not Jews, anabaptists or witches expressed some measure of conformity by not being so, some crudely induced awareness of the unacceptable produced a measure of group solidarity amongst those who conformed.[14]

Much of this chapter has been devoted to the theme of how states came to define themselves, and how that process induced social change, particularly with regard to the psychological boundaries of the acceptable. It may well be that the process was uncertain and poorly controlled because a long series of military struggles was simultaneously failing to resolve the material and ideological interests of the contending European powers. States encountered enormous problems in establishing effective control over social life, and they found it increasingly difficult to win decisive victories in war.

10 Habsburg and Valois

The dynastic web

In the violent, haphazard social world of the vast majority of the European population, there were many agencies which competed with kinship ties. The village or the parish could give a sense of local solidarity. While apprentices trained in a craft, they were members of a master's household and were entitled to food and shelter. Religious confraternities in commemorating dead members also made a pledge to look after their widows and orphans. It may even have been the case that such associations as these operated as substitute families for many members of the third estate. The problems of landlessness and vagabondage perhaps also suggest that kinship ties in the localities were not strong enough to withstand the pressure of population growth. Put more simply, if a household grew too large then one or some of its members might have to move on, especially if laws of inheritance bastioned primogeniture. Within the social order which ruled or aspired to rule, it was a different story. For those who governed, the interests of the family were all important. The word 'dynasty', which denotes a succession of rulers of the same family, could in itself mean 'sovereignty' or 'power'. Indeed, the survival or extinction of the dynasty was the difference between peace and war, and the accidents of inheritance shaped the power blocs of Europe. What extraordinary intricacies and fragilities this engendered in Europe as a whole![1] It is no surprise that genealogical charts figure so regularly in books on the sixteenth century, and the family trees of Habsburg and Valois are reproduced later in this chapter. The detail can be confusing, but it may be helpful to bear in mind the general point that the elaborate pattern of dynastic politics was a distinctive feature of the western regions. It contrasted with the Ottoman Empire, where a smooth succession was ensured by the practice of fratricide: the new sultan had all his brothers killed to eliminate any chance of rivalry (below p. 248). The alleged complicity of Philip II in the death of his mad son, Don Carlos, perhaps seems less shocking by comparison.

Dynastic politics were not, of course, new in the sixteenth century. The Hundred Years' War had been fought out between rival families, squabbling over laws of succession. However, the context of dynastic rivalry was to change. Narrow family interests disputed under feudal

219

law were one thing, but pursuit of those interests in a context of the 'military revolution' and religious uncertainty was to generate unprecedented instabilities. As the military narrative of the dynastic struggle unfolds, each engagement seems to confirm and increase the significance of arquebus, cannon and infantry, while the latter stages of the conflict drift into protracted sieges. Such developments set an ominous pattern of chronic destructiveness for the religious wars in the later part of the century (below, ch. 12), and it was a way of war which was to hold the Turks at bay in the east and give Europeans dominion in their maritime enterprises to the west (below, ch. 11). Either way, it was a pattern which took shape in the wars which broke out in Italy in 1494 and which were to set the House of Valois against the House of Habsburg.

When the Hundred Years' War ended, the Valois of France were supreme in reputation. In the aftermath of the defeat of the Plantagenets, England had plunged into turmoil as rival dynasties fought for the throne in the Wars of the Roses. It was no wonder that the eventual victors, the Tudors, whose claims to the crown were hardly incontestable, sought to ensure a line of succession. In this context Henry VIII's infamous obsession with siring a male heir seems rather more comprehensible – and if his daughter Mary had produced a son, then England would probably have remained a Catholic country.

At the end of the fifteenth century, secure in his homeland, Charles VIII, King of France, could turn his attention to Italy, where the House of Anjou, the old royal line of France, had a claim to Naples which went back to 1264, and which had lain dormant since the expulsion of the Angevins from Sicily in 1282 (the so-called 'Sicilian Vespers'). Valois intervention in southern Italy meant conflict with the House of Aragon, which ruled in Naples. When the Duke of Orleans succeeded Charles as Louis XII in 1499, his pretext for intervention in Italy was the Orleanist claim to the Duchy of Milan. The dynastic windfall of Spanish monarchy, Habsburg lands and imperial title which fell to Charles V in 1519 transformed the entire picture in Italy and the balance of power in Europe as a whole. Because the conflicts revolved around the material and territorial interests of secular rulers, the Italian Wars are often presented as a key phase in the development of the modern state. By the end of the fifteenth century, according to this view, secular diplomacy had become a European phenomenon, an aspect of the Italian achievement which was transmitted to other parts of Europe as the Renaissance. This transfer ended the political isolation of Italy, which exposed not only the precocious notions of statehood in the peninsula, but also the playful character of its power games. The new diplomacy was taken in harness by the military machines developed in the Hundred Years' War and in the *Reconquista*, in which Italy had not been involved. This combination became a central feature of the 'new monarchies' of France and Spain which then crushed the petty deviousness of Italian states and fought out a real, modern war on the colourful wreckage of the Renaissance. On the whole, diplomatic manoeuvre is seen as more significant than military considerations.[2]

The danger of this interpretation of the wars is twofold: first, it tends to exaggerate the coherence of the political interests involved, and second, it tends to underestimate the impact of the fighting itself. This chapter explores two different emphases. First, it will suggest that the secular struggles of dynasties tended to stunt the development of statehood rather than to promote it. Second, it will argue that the wars helped to stimulate a new complex of religious sentiments in Italy which were to widen the gulf between Latin and Teutonic Christianity once the Reformation had begun.

In this light, the conflicts of the dynasties in Italy in the first half of the sixteenth century form a bridge between the papal-imperial struggles of the Middle Ages and the Wars of Religion which erupted almost as soon as the contests of Habsburg and Valois in Italy came to a close. This interpretation becomes more persuasive when attention is focused on the fate of the Papal States, which were governed by a prince, but not a hereditary prince, and of Venice, which was governed by a hereditary aristocracy, but not by a single ruling house. The imperial triumph over the papacy was the victory of a rambling composite monarchy over a compact sovereign state; the Venetian constitution, which only just survived the crisis of the Italian Wars, became an ideal for many Europeans because it seemed to subsume the sources of conflict which ripped other European societies apart. In a Europe in turmoil – not least because of the instabilities of dynastic politics and the decline of papal authority – it was a republic without a dynastic prince which seemed to provide the only point of repose.

It is important to stress at the outset that rather than attaching 'petty states' to 'new monarchies', 'Renaissance diplomacy', attached Italian dynasties to foreign dynasties. On the eve of the French invasion of 1494, there were five major power complexes of European importance in the peninsula: the Kingdom of Naples, Medicean Florence, the Papal States, the Duchy of Milan, and the Venetian Republic. The family of the Aragonese Alfonso ruled as kings in Naples. Florentine republicanism had broken its back on family faction, the avoidance of which was guaranteed by the triumph of a single family, the Medici, who were princes in all but name. The Pope, Alexander VI, schemed to ensure the continuation of Borgia power in the Romagna: hence the campaigns of his son, Cesare. The Sforza had succeeded the Visconti in Milan and had extinguished the Ambrosian Republic to do so. The Venetian Republic apparently stood aloof, but even though there was no single ruling house in Venice, there was a hereditary ruling caste defined by

Map 10.1 Italy in about 1494

Key:
× - battle
F - Fornovo   1495
A - Agnadello   1509
N - Novara   1513
M - Marignano   1515
B - Bicocca   1522
P - Pavia   1525
L - Landriano   1529

① MARQ. of MANTUA
② MARQ. of SALUZZO
③ DUCHY of MODENA
④ DUCHY of FERRARA

Source: Richard Lodge, *The Close of the Middle Ages: European History, 1273–14* (London: The Rivington Press, 1910), endpapers.

membership of specified families. In the interstices of this power network, we find microcosmic empires, often identified with the dominion of a family: the Este in Ferrara, the Gonzaga in Mantua, the Montefeltro in Urbino, the Bentivoglio in Bologna.[3] The city-republics of Genoa and Siena were pawns rather than players. This was the world on which the Valois invasion fell.

The eclipse of Italy (1494–1530)

The timing of the French invasion was sudden, but it might have happened earlier. Foreign intervention had been possible in the affairs of Italy in 1479 in the aftermath of the Pazzi conspiracy against the Medici and again in 1482–84 as the Venetians sought to wrest Ferrara from the papacy. In the event, it was a dynastic squabble in Milan which brought in the invading dynasties.

Lodovico Sforza, known as *il Moro* because of his swarthy complexion, had been regent of the duchy during the minority of his nephew, and – in the manner of Richard III – sought to displace his brother's son and ensure the succession for his own line. His nephew was married to Isabella of Aragon, whose father was the King of Naples. She complained bitterly to her father of Lodovico's machinations and of the presumption of Lodovico's wife, Beatrice d'Este. To counter-balance the threat from Naples, Lodovico established a treaty with Charles VIII of France, who agreed to play the card of his dynastic claim to Naples should Naples threaten Lodovico in Milan. What Lodovico had not bargained for was the seriousness with which Charles VIII viewed the opportunity to intervene in Italy. When the forces of Alfonso of Naples threatened Genoa – which was defended by Louis of Orleans (later Louis XII) and was an obvious staging-post in a French invasion, Lodovico persuaded the Florentines 'that the French king should not march at all, or at least if he did passe, he shoulde with the same speede returne'. This was a significant diplomatic miscalculation.

Giangaleazzo Sforza, the true Duke of Milan, died suddenly – poisoned, it was said, by his 'wicked uncle' – which heightened the tension between Milan and Naples. As the French advanced, Piero de' Medici (would Lorenzo so have blundered?) capitulated unworthily by surrendering Florence's Tuscan fortresses – 'the king could have bene contented with farre meaner condiccions' – and was disowned by the Florentine government, which suddenly remembered that the Medici held power, but not office. Charles nevertheless entered Florence as conqueror, not as ally, 'in signe of victorie, armed himself and his horse, with his launce upon his thigh'. The speed of Charles's advance took Alfonso of Naples by surprise. Like the Medici in Florence, the dynasty's hold on its subjects was feeble, and Alfonso took flight as sympathy for the Angevin claim provoked rebellion. Charles had marched the length of Italy using weapons no more formidable than the chalk with which his officers had marked up the homes in which his troops were to be billeted. Getting back was another matter.

The French claim to Naples is a powerful example of the way in which dynastic ambition brushed aside strategic sense in determining policy. To the north, Charles's army faced a march of 400 miles across potentially hostile territory. The Venetian fleet had command of the eastern seas (in so far as the Turks permitted), the Aragonese commanded those to the west. In 1495, a Holy League (the first of several) was formed in Venice, amid great celebrations. Its ostensible purpose was the defence of Christendom against the Turk. In practice it formed a ring of steel on the French army. The latter would face harassment from the Aragonese and Venetian fleets if it stayed, and if it left it faced more layers of strength than had the shield of Ajax. The Pope, the Holy Roman Emperor, the Spaniards, the Venetians and the Milanese were pledged to oppose the retreat of Charles's army. An Italian army of Venetian and Milanese forces was due to deliver the *coup de grâce*.

The French army, decimated by syphilis which many soldiers had contracted in Naples, moved north to return to France. There was a skirmish at Parma as the French demanded passage. Then in early July, on the River Taro, the French faced the Italian coalition. It is a commonplace to argue that Fornovo showed up the military short-comings of the Italians. The French cavalry routed the Italian horse, the Swiss pikes routed the mercenaries of Venice and Mantua, we are told. Historians since Guicciardini have been quick to point out the lessons of Fornovo for the Italians. We have lost sight, however, of how easily they might have won.

The Milanese and the Venetians had a force of at least 14,000 troops. Some estimates go as high as 30,000. Even if it is the lower figure which is more accurate, then the Italians alone almost certainly outnumbered the total number of soldiers involved at Bosworth Field ten years before, a fight which had decided the fate of the English kingdom. The French at Fornovo were a depleted and exhausted 9,000.

The Italian plan, now easily dismissed as over elaborate, was to attack with heavy cavalry across the dry gulch of the Taro, a shaly bed with a sandy bank, harrying further the enemy flank with stradiots (Venetian light cavalry recruited from the Balkans). On the eve of the battle, 5 July – summer in the Mediterranean – there was a terrific rainstorm. The broad shaly bed of the Taro became like glass, the sandy bank turned to mud. Even so, the initial Italian assault went ahead, and with vigour. According to Guicciardini at least, Gonzaga's onslaught brought a response of equal ferocity from the French, and on *all* sides, units entered the fight 'pelmelle and not according to the custom of the warres of Italy'. The unexpected condition of the river-bed held back some of the Italian men-at-arms, and amid the 'incredible furie' of the battle, Ridolfo Gonzaga, uncle of the Marquis, was slain. This was critical because it was his responsibility to notify Antonio da Montefeltro to bring up his contingents from the rear. They never materialised. Despite the rain, despite the breakdown in communications, Gonzaga pressed his numerical advantage against the French. For a fleeting instant Charles VIII was isolated 'almost naked of his garde', a bastard of Bourbon was taken prisoner a few paces away from him. On Gonzaga pressed – but the battle turned. 'The danger of the king so touched and inflamed those that were left farre of, that ronning to cover with their persons, the person of the King, they susteined thItalians [sic].'

The Italians claimed victory, but their casualties were much higher than the French and in this regard Guicciardini's austere judgement on the French achievement must stand: 'they wonne their libertie to passe further, which was the controversie for the which they came to the field'. In at most an hour and in perhaps as little as fifteen minutes, the French had cut through. If Gonzaga's contingent had captured the King of France or killed him – as they so easily might have done – the modern perspective on Fornovo, and the course of Italian and European history would probably have been very different. As it is, the words on the medal which Gonzaga had struck '*Ob restitutam Italiae libertatem*' ('For the liberty of Italy now restored'), conjure the melancholy ghost of what might have been.

Political circumstances now encumbered the formation of a new and effective Italian coalition, apparently reflecting the dislocation of Italian hopes. Florence became increasingly independent and increasingly unstable. Its republican constitution was strengthened by the expulsion of Piero de' Medici, and Savonarola introduced a Great Council after the manner of Venice. Alexander VI's plans for Cesare Borgia took more defined shape, and 'Duke Valentino' was soon to embark, with French support, on the pacification of the Romagna. More than ever the Venetians found their eastern flank pressed by the Turks. In 1499 the Ottoman fleet got the better of a naval engagement at Zonchio, and Skander Beshaw, Sanjak of Bosnia, crossed the Isonzo river.

That same year, Charles VIII had a seizure while watching a tennis match. His successor was the Duke of Orleans, and the House of Orleans had a long-standing claim to Milan . . . Ferdinand of Aragon seized the opportunity to partition the Kingdom of Naples with the French King by means of the Treaty of Granada, and as French attentions switched northward Spanish soldiers claimed *de facto* power for Aragon in the south.

Louis XII's claim to Milan received papal approval, and in return Cesare got his army for the Romagna. The Venetians, this time genuinely engaged with the Turk, stood aside. In a shameful episode confirming Machiavelli's bleak view of mercenary troops, Lodovico's Swiss soldiers first deserted him and then betrayed him. The prince who had hazarded Italy's security for the duchy of Milan was to die ignominiously in a French dungeon in 1508:

> being now inclosed to one straite prison the thoughtes and ambicion of him, which earst could skarcely be contained within the limits and tearmes of all Italie.[4]

Ferdinand's apparent disregard for partition arrangements in Naples drew the French south once more. This time all that could stop them was the power of the Spaniards. Ferdinand entrusted the defence of Spanish claims to a commander of genius, '*el gran capitano*', Gonsalvo de Cordoba. The decisive year was 1503. To Gonsalvo may be attributed the opening of a new phase in European warfare. He seems to have been the first to realise the potential of the arquebus and to devise the best means of protecting those units of soldiers who were armed with that ponderous weapon. To that end he mixed pikemen and footsoldiers armed with short swords. Most devastating of all, his arquebusiers dug themselves in. At Cerignola in 1503, the French attempted a head-on charge of Gonsalvo's prepared position. The cavalry foundered in a ditch, the Swiss pikemen were shot to pieces and the rout was completed by a cavalry charge by a force held at the rear.

Louis's response was to hire another 8,000 Swiss mercenaries and repeat the attempt. The two armies met on the Garigliano at the very end of 1503. The precise date is significant. The French arrived in September. Once again Gonsalvo's men dug themselves in – and they did not abandon their position during the arduous winter months. The Spanish arquebusiers in their muddy trenches outfaced the French and Gonsalvo was able to watch his opponents' morale disintegrate in front of him. When the Spanish attack came – on 29 December, during prolonged Christmas celebrations by the French – they swept the field. Gonsalvo had won a campaign of attrition with a force of about 15,000 against some 20,000 in the ranks of the French. This was too much for Ferdinand, who recalled his great captain to Spain.

Elsewhere in the peninsula, power was shifting once again. As the French and Spaniards faced each other in the south, Cesare Borgia was carving out a Borgia principality in the Romagna (and the notorious details are found in chapter VII of *The Prince*). Fortune was against him. His father, Alexander VI, died on 18 August, and his successor, Pius III, lasted only three weeks. The new pope was Giuliano della

Rovere, sworn enemy of the Borgia. Cesare himself fell ill and his Romagnol state collapsed. Chief amongst the beneficiaries were the Venetians, also hated of the new pope. Julius II engineered an alliance against them, confirmed in the League of Cambrai in 1508. The combination of the papacy, the Emperor Maximilian and Louis XII in fact followed a defeat which the imperial forces had received at the hands of the Venetian army. But at Agnadello in 1509, after a hard fight of three hours, French forces overwhelmed Alviano's Venetian infantry – who might have fared better had they received support from the other commander, Pitigliano. Now it was the Venetian state which collapsed, and the Republic lost all its mainland possessions apart from Padua. According to Guicciardini the wars had become more burdensome. Previously, the fighting had fallen 'for the most parte upon the straungers only': now there were to be 'destructions and spoyles of cities, a libertie of warre'.

The victors of Agnadello were soon at odds. Julius feared that the combination of the Emperor and the King of France might be turned against the papacy. The Venetian recovery involved some military initiative rather than relying purely upon the divisions among the Republic's enemies. A Venetian army chased German, French and Spanish soldiers from Vicenza in 1510. That same year, Julius organised yet another Holy League, pitting his own forces, those of the Emperor, Ferdinand of Aragon and the Swiss against the French. In this campaign, the French won a great victory at Ravenna in 1512. The chief instruments of their success were their artillery, which pounded the Spanish emplacements for fully 2 hours – though there was a reply in kind which left as many as 2,000 dead among the Gascon foot – and a sweeping cavalry charge. The death of their general, the brilliant Gaston de Foix, blighted the French success, and the battle was a turning-point in terms of the scale of losses, for Ravenna was no rout. The Spaniards lost some 9,000 soldiers, the French as many as 4,000 – more than one sixth of their force. The war was assuming a new scale and fury, as the inhabitants of Ravenna found when the French sacked the town:

> In this cruell action nothing was less respected then moderation in killing and spoyling, no age spared, no sex reserved, no sorte of people nor goods pardoned, all thinges were brought into the rewardes of the victorie and nothing lefte free from the violence and furie of the souldiers.

Julius II's plans were in ruins, especially since the Venetians proceeded to recover their mainland territories. Yet with French success at its height, the Swiss, now operating in their own right, rose against them, and took Milan. The French withdrawal enabled Julius II to die 'more full of high conceites and travelling thoughts then at any time before'. It also left the Florentine Republic friendless. The Medici celebrated a double triumph with their return to Florence and the election of Giovanni, second son of Lorenzo the Magnificent, as Pope Leo X. It is intriguing to reflect that this was probably the moment at which Machiavelli conceived the idea of *The Prince*. The battle of Ravenna had exposed the divisiveness of papal policies and for the first time had shown that the interests of the Italian states were irrelevant to the real struggle, which was between the French and the imperialists (see Figures 10.1 and 10.2). '*Fortuna*' had given the Italians the perfect '*occasione*' in the election of a Medici pope who might unite the peninsula in a common cause, but speed was of the essence if the moment was to be seized. The moment was lost, and Machiavelli's vision was to melt before his own eyes.

Louis XII tried his hand once more. A surprise night attack by 8,000 pikemen at Novara gave the Swiss their last great victory in these wars, remarkable since they were 'but a fewe in number, without horsemen, and without artilleries', though they turned the French guns against the conquered army as it fled. The English success at the battle of the Spurs and the capture of Tournai in the same year cooled the ardour of French ambition in Italy. Wolsey's apparent masterpiece, the Treaty of London (1514), promised a new era of tranquillity. But the next year, the dynastic stakes were again all to play for. Louis died in 1515 – worn out, according to Guicciardini, by a new young bride. His successor was Francis d'Angoulême. Amongst the titles he claimed was that of Duke of Milan.

At 22, Francis cut a magnificent figure to contemporaries: 'Of a very long time there was none raysed up to the Crowne with a greater expectation.' In his quest for glory abroad and absolutism at home he foreshadows Louis XIV. J. H. Hexter has stripped off the king's Renaissance trappings:

> In 1515, the new young king of France, Francis I, following the precedent sanctified by his revered predecessors, Charles VIII and Louis XII, began once again to pour the human and material resources of his kingdom down the rat hole of Italy.

He took an army of 30,000 men – amongst them 2,500 of the famous *gendarmes*, 6,000 Gascon foot, and some 9,000 *Landsknechts*, in a daring crossing of the Alps. With the Venetians as his allies and with the renegade engineer, Pedro Navarro, in his train, the king's reckless ambition appeared to have some point when he faced the Swiss and smashed them at Marignano. The Swiss, numerically inferior, and with no element of surprise this time, failed to break through the French vanguard, faced a fierce bombardment when darkness brought a lull,

Figure 10.1 The Houses of Valois and Bourbon

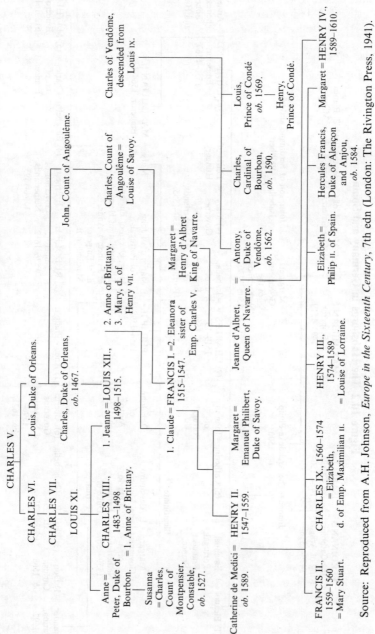

Source: Reproduced from A.H. Johnson, *Europe in the Sixteenth Century*, 7th edn (London: The Rivington Press, 1941).

Figure 10.2 The Habsburgs in Germany and Spain

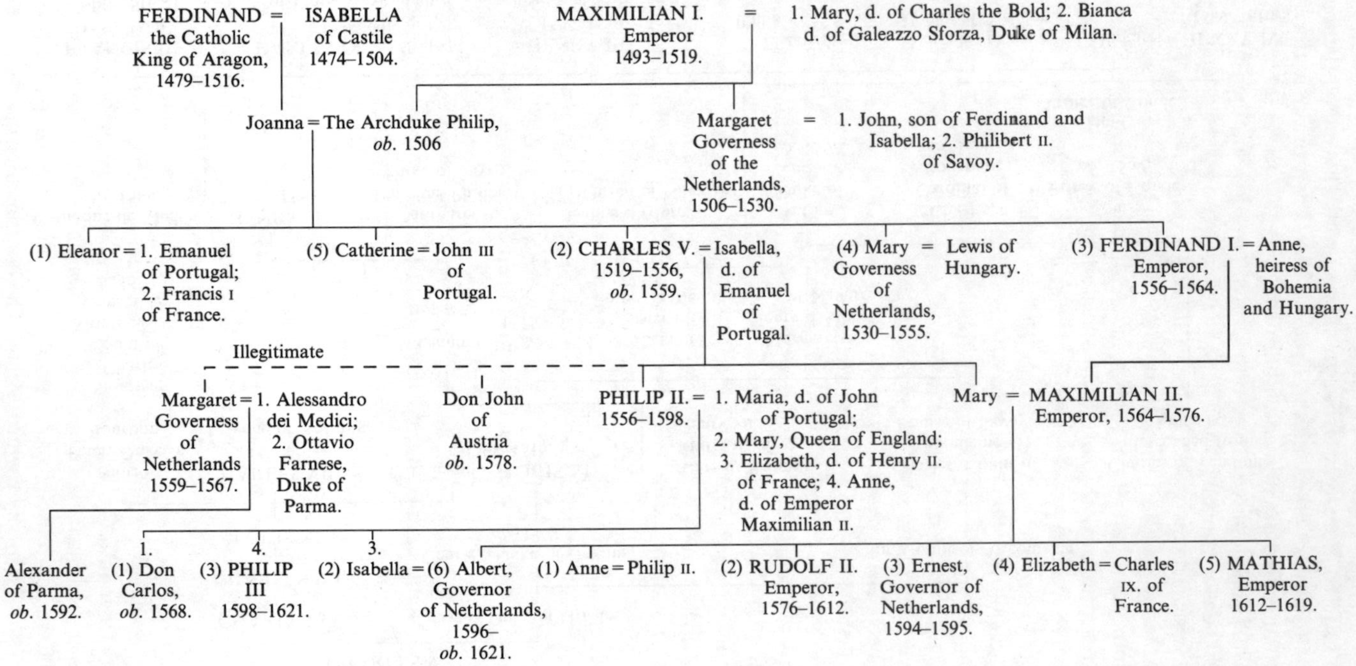

FERDINAND = ISABELLA
the Catholic | of Castile
King of Aragon, | 1474–1504.
1479–1516.

MAXIMILIAN I. = 1. Mary, d. of Charles the Bold; 2. Bianca
Emperor | d. of Galeazzo Sforza, Duke of Milan.
1493–1519.

Joanna = The Archduke Philip, ob. 1506

Margaret = 1. John, son of Ferdinand and
Governess of the | Isabella; 2. Philibert II.
Netherlands, 1506–1530. | of Savoy.

(3) FERDINAND I. = Anne, heiress of Bohemia and Hungary.
Emperor, 1556–1564.

(4) Mary = Lewis of Hungary.
Governess of Netherlands, 1530–1555.

(2) CHARLES V. = Isabella, d. of Emanuel of Portugal.
1519–1556, ob. 1559.

(5) Catherine = John III of Portugal.

(1) Eleanor = 1. Emanuel of Portugal; 2. Francis I of France.

Mary = MAXIMILIAN II. Emperor, 1564–1576.

PHILIP II. = 1. Maria, d. of John of Portugal; 2. Mary, Queen of England; 3. Elizabeth, d. of Henry II. of France; 4. Anne, d. of Emperor Maximilian II.
1556–1598.

Don John of Austria ob. 1578.

Illegitimate

Margaret = 1. Alessandro dei Medici; 2. Ottavio Farnese, Duke of Parma.
Governess of Netherlands 1559–1567.

(2) RUDOLF II. Emperor, 1576–1612.

(3) Ernest, Governor of Netherlands, 1594–1595.

(4) Elizabeth = Charles ix. of France.

(5) MATHIAS, Emperor 1612–1619.

(1) Anne = Philip II.

(6) Isabella = Albert, Governor of Netherlands, 1596– ob. 1621.

(3) PHILIP III 1598–1621.

(1) Don Carlos, ob. 1568.

Alexander of Parma, ob. 1592.

Source: Reproduced from A. H. Johnson, *Europe in the Sixteenth Century* 7th edn (London: The Rivington Press, 1941).

and suffered more losses from the cannon which played on them as they came to push of pike with the *Landsknechts*. Their pride shattered, they yet managed a disciplined withdrawal.

Thus, Milan passed from one foreign power to another, at a cost of 12,000 dead, a cost which sickened Zwingli, who served as a chaplain to the Swiss. The Swiss had lost a battle and a reputation, the French had regained ground lost since Ravenna in 1512. The Venetians had played an important part in the French success, but a subordinate one: they at least had learned that a sensible level of military collaboration could preserve the independence of an Italian state. If there had been some doubts before, it was now clear that the Italian states were no longer masters of their own destinies. Milan was in French hands, the papacy was dependent upon its French alliance, Naples was ruled by Spanish might. And Francis was soon to find – in Charles V – a rival whose power could only spur his own ambition.

The inheritance of Charles V (see Figure 10.3 and Map 10.2) is a powerful reminder of the significance of dynastic power. His territories came to him piecemeal but their extent was awesome. His mother, Juana, was mad. She could not, therefore, inherit Castile and Aragon – with their possessions in America and Italy – from her parents, Ferdinand and Isabella, and so Charles ruled in her name, at least after Ferdinand's death in 1516. From Charles's father, Duke Philip, came the Burgundian title. Philip was the only son of the Emperor Maximilian, which gave Charles the title to the Habsburg lands on Maximilian's death. More important still, it made Charles a contender to succeed Maximilian to the imperial title. With a colossal bribe to the imperial electors from the Fuggers, Charles became Holy Roman Emperor in 1519. Francis I had also been a candidate:

> It was not to be doubted that betwene these two Princes of equall youth and ambicion, and having indifferent reasons and occasions of ielousie and contencion, would not in the ende arise a great and daungerous warre.[5]

The rivalry of the kings of France and Spain in Italy now had a European dimension.

That Italy was now a cockpit without a home champion became clear as other venues presented themselves. In 1521, with Charles occupied in Germany and his regent pinned down by the revolt of the *comuneros*, Francis invaded Navarre, and besieged Pamplona (where Ignatius Loyola was among the defenders), though he was soon turned back. The next year, it was Charles's turn to threaten, and he flexed the muscles of his new power, drawing troops from Naples and from Germany toward Milan. The composite army was under the the command of the old *condottiere*, Prospero Colonna, who wore the

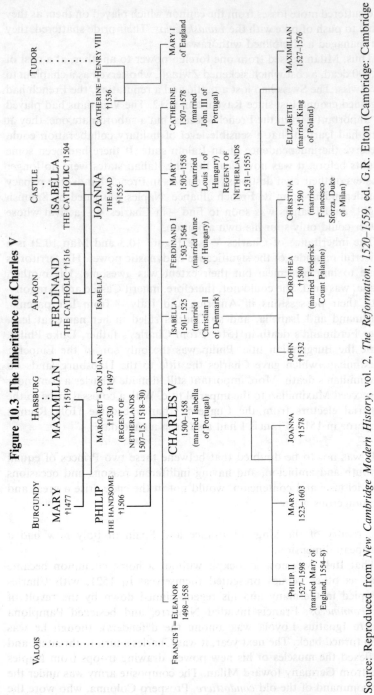

Figure 10.3 The inheritance of Charles V

Source: Reproduced from *New Cambridge Modern History*, vol. 2, *The Reformation, 1520–1559*, ed. G.R. Elton (Cambridge: Cambridge University Press, 1975), p. 302.

Map 10.2 European dominions of Charles V

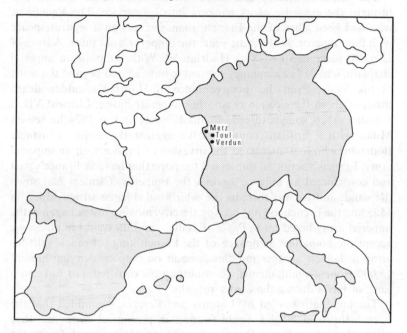

Source: Based on *The Collins Atlas of World History*, ed. Pierre Vidal-Naquet, trans. Chris Turner *et al.* (London: HarperCollins Ltd, 1987), p. 149.

French out with his Italian delaying tactics – which do not look in the slightest outdated. His manoeuvres included an ingenious river crossing worthy of the great Gonsalvo, and then the unfortunate French Viceroy, Lautrec, found his own strategy ruined by the departure of many of his Swiss. Colonna dug himself in in the grounds of a villa near Milan, and lured the French into assaulting his carefully prepared position – given the similiarities to the Garigliano, how curious is the assumption that the Italians learned nothing from the new style of war. The Swiss who remained needed little luring: they refused to halt and were mown down by Colonna's guns. Those who survived the artillery barrage had to negotiate a deep ditch in which they were slaughtered by the Spanish arquebusiers. They gave ground only against the onslaught of old Georg of Fründsberg's *Landsknechts*, but they left 3,000 dead – including 22 captains – on the field, losses which represent the equivalent of about one third of the population of Zurich. Direct losses in battle were now comparable to the devastations of the plague. Perhaps the chief explanation is gunfire. At Bicocca, small-arms fire had triumphed.

The imperial victory also gave Charles control of Genoa, and brought the expertise of its bankers into his service. The Venetians, who had been allies of the French, managed to sign a separate peace with the Emperor. In the same year, the Emperor's old tutor, Adrian of Utrecht, succeeded Leo X as Hadrian VI. With the pope an imperial chaplain, Charles's ascendancy seemed to have soared beyond the reach of his rivals. Even the inconvenience of Hadrian's sudden death brought about the election of another imperial choice, Clement VII.

Still Francis sought to redeem his honour, and in 1524 he retook Milan with a brilliant counter-strike against the traitor constable Bourbon, who had attempted the invasion of France with an imperial army. Francis's action so impressed the pope that he took France's part and constructed an alliance against the Emperor. Clement had sown the wind, and he was to reap the whirlwind. Plague struck Milan in 1525 and the French did not occupy the city, moving instead against the imperial army holed up in Pavia. Fatally – and inexplicably unless we accept the boundless arrogance of the French king – Francis split his army to launch another mindless assault on Naples, denying himself 15,000 troops, simultaneously committing his own reduced force to a siege of Pavia during the winter months.

The imperialists – led by Lannoy and Pescara – gambled that the French thrust at Naples would founder in prolonged sieges and they resolved to relieve Pavia. Despite the splitting of the French forces, the imperialists were numerically inferior to the army of Francis, and wisely avoided an early pitched battle. Six thousand troops from the Grisons deserted Francis, and he had lost his superiority. This was convenient, for the imperial army was close to mutiny for lack of pay. The pioneers achieved surprise by breaching the walls of the French position under cover of darkness, and a harrying attack launched from Pavia itself delayed the response further. The Swiss performed poorly and marched off; Francis himself fought desperately in a series of frantic cavalry charges. This time the King of France was taken prisoner, and the 'flower of French chivalry' – as at Agincourt – had perished. The withering gunfire of the Spanish arquebusiers had destroyed the cavalry.

Under the Treaty of Madrid (1525), the royal prisoner had to agree to abandon claims to Naples, Milan and Genoa, and to recognise imperial possessions in Flanders. Charles went too far in insisting that all Burgundian territories in France itself should be recognised as his. This would establish an imperial presence in the valley of the Seine, no more than 80 miles from Paris. Francis gave a solemn vow to observe all these conditions. But the next year, Charles faced emergency in Germany in the aftermath of the great Turkish victory at Mohács (below, p. 254). The Pope dispensed the King of France from his vows and he again declared war, joining with the papacy, Venice and

Florence in the League of Cognac (1526). The expedition to Naples was a catastrophe and the French rout at Landriano (back in Lombardy) in 1528 was eased only by the Emperor's preoccupations with the Turks. The Pope's treachery brought unmitigated disaster to Italy.

Charles took seriously his role as the heir to Charlemagne. The pillar of Christendom, beset by heretics in Germany and the invasions by sea and land of the infidel Turk had found himself opposed by his partner in the sustaining of Christendom. The military effort had exhausted the imperial coffers, and his army in Italy lacked pay. It is a comment on the messiness of European politics that the renegade Bourbon became leader of German mutineers – many of them Lutheran – and led them on Rome and its turncoat pope. The pontiff was Antichrist for some of them, and destroying the Babylon which was the seat of his rule would remove an abomination. Rome's fabulous wealth would, conveniently, assuage more worldly appetites. The Emperor disclaimed responsibility for what happened, but he did not seek to impose restraints on his troops. As Clement cowered in the Castel Sant'Angelo, the *Landsknechts* ran amok. Under the terms of the Treaty of Cambrai (1529), Francis again repudiated his Italian claims and recognised the imperial title to Flanders. The Emperor, anxious to free his hands for war against Lutherans and Turks, gave up his own claims to Burgundian territories in France itself. He marked his triumph with an imperial coronation at Bologna, the last to be conducted by a pope.

'A libertie of warre'

Looking back on the wars which began in 1494, Italian commentators such as Machiavelli and Guicciardini could point to the poor military performance of the Italian forces, drawing the general conclusion that mercenary troops were undesirable because they were unreliable. Guicciardini depicted the Italians as anxious to avoid coming to blows with the French. He concluded that Fornovo (1495) had not been fought 'according to the custom of the warres of Italy . . . wherein commonly died but very few people'. Italian mercenary captains, careful not to hazard their men, that is to say their capital assets, were accustomed to polite manoeuvres in which they often 'brake of without victorie certeine of either parties', retiring to pick up the money due to them under the terms of the *condotte* reached with their employers. Later historians have tended to draw a contrast between Italian forces and the 'standing armies' of the 'new monarchies' and their 'national sentiment' (above, pp. 220–1).

The battle of Fornovo (1495) is once again the obvious illustration, for the French army's success was spearheaded by the men-at-arms (*gendarmerie*). They formed the *compagnies d'ordonnance* which served the French monarchy in the very last stages of the Hundred Years' War, replacing the old feudal levy or *arrière-ban*, which continued to provide poor-quality auxiliaries.

However, it might be argued that the contemporary judgements on the Italian military performance were unfair, and that the contrast between Italian forces and the invading armies has been overdrawn. Some of the *condottieri* of the fourteenth century – Sir John Hawkwood, for instance – had learned their trade in campaigns of the Hundred Years' War, so there is no special reason for isolating Italy from military developments elsewhere in Europe. Perhaps it could be argued that the restraint and caution of the *condottieri* were among the more civilising features of Renaissance Italy. Whatever one thinks of that notion, it is important to understand that the destructiveness of the wars which broke out in 1494 cannot be attributed to effective diplomacy and sound military organisation, but rather the reverse. Diplomatic initiatives often outran military logistics, especially in the matter of pay. What was unleashed on Italy was indeed Guicciardini's 'libertie of warre', and its effects were traumatic.

Compared with the wars of Renaissance *condottieri*, the confrontations of armies of pikemen and arquebusiers were appallingly wasteful since their outcome depended on who was prepared to absorb greater casualties. The performance of the French is important here. Charles VIII brought with him a formidable army:

> it conteined (besides the two hundreth gentlemen for his guard) . . . xvi hundred men at armes, allowing to every of them according to the custom of Fraunce, two Archers, so that under every launce (for so they call their men at armes) are comprehended vi horses: of the Swyzzers vi thousand footemen, and vi thousand of the realme of Fraunce.

And he brought 'a huge proporcion' of deadly bronze cannon. 'This hell or torment of artillerie' was to be used 'both for batterie and service of the field, but of such sortes as Italy never saw the like'. But the famed *gendarmerie* did not win the Italian Wars. Indeed, one might argue that their outdated cavalry charge across their own guns at Pavia in 1525 showed how little French tactics had advanced since Agincourt. Moreover, the Valois kings scarcely commanded a 'national' army. They relied for too long on the Swiss, whose hired pike formations might also fight against the French – as in the great Swiss victory at Novara in 1513 – or choose not to fight at all. '*Point d'argent, point de Suisse*'. This could mean wholesale desertion. Francis turned this to his advantage when he bribed the captains to lead off 12,000 pikes before Marignano, fatally weakening the Milanese forces. The unquestionable bravery of the Swiss did not make them reliable. Indeed their insistence on engaging the enemy despite orders to halt at Bicocca (1522) resulted in their being mown down by Spanish gunfire. At the same fight, the old Italian *condottiere*, Prospero Colonna, refused to commit his troops precipitately and contributed hugely to the imperialist victory. The Swiss often opposed German *Landsknechts* – more mercenaries – and there is little doubt that the savagery of their combat was something of a sales drive designed to impress prospective employers. The fury which the Germans unleashed on Rome in 1527 drew much of its impetus from the fact that they had not been paid, at which point considerations of discipline evaporated.

As has already been described, the carnage was fearful in the great set pieces, but these were not confined to a single area, they raged throughout the peninsula: Fornovo (1495), Cerignola (1502), the Gargiliano (1503), Agnadello (1509), Ravenna (1512), Novara (1513), Marignano (1515), Bicocca (1522), Pavia (1525). Yet the battles often spilled into unrestrained pillaging of cities: Ravenna (1512), Fabiano (1519), Como (1521), Genoa (1522), Pavia (1525) – and Rome (1527).[6]

It is possible to trace a growing anxiety within Italy itself, an anxiety which marked a transition – and a fairly sudden one – from the worldly confidence of the Renaissance to the spiritual austerity of the Catholic revival (plates, section IV). In 1495, Savonarola explained a vision of his to the Florentines:

> The quivering sword (I wish to tell you, Florence) is the sword of the king of France, which is showing itself to all of Italy. The angels with the red cross and the white stoles and the chalice are preachers announcing this flagellation, and they give you the red cross to kiss, which is the passion of martyrdom, in order that you may sustain this flagellation which must come about for the renovation of the Church . . . And this sword has not yet turned its tip downward, but will go about showing itself throughout all of Italy, because God still waits for you to repent. Convert, Florence, for there is no other cure but repentance. Put on the white stole while there is time and do not wait any longer, for then you will have no opportunity to repent.

There were plenty of other initiatives for religious reform which are often associated with the Catholic revival, but rarely set in the context of the Italian Wars. The Oratory of St Jerome in Vicenza was inspired by Bernardino da Feltre and looked back to the principles of San Bernardino of Siena (above, p. 175). The Oratory of Divine Love was founded in Genoa in 1497, and reached Rome between 1514 and 1517 – both Thiene and Carafa became members. As we have already seen (above, pp. 183–4), the Theatines and other new religious orders sought to minister to the victims of the wars. Egidio da Viterbo, the right-hand man of the warrior pope, Julius II, was general of the Augustinian order – yes, Luther's order – and he appears to have been responsible for a surge of foundations of confraternities of the Holy Sacrament. These institutions were to become the vehicles of Tridentine Catholicism (above, pp. 193–4), but the emphasis on the Eucharistic cult, on spiritual austerity and on parochial solidarity date from the era of the wars. And there is no doubt about Egidio's opinion as to the source of the malaise and its remedy. This sermon came in the wake of the French victory over papal forces at Ravenna in 1512:

> What should I say about that most serious and most dangerous matter of all, which everyone in our days deplores? I mean the wrongs inflicted by princes, the insolence of armies, the threats of armed force. For what can be heard or thought of that is more pitiable than that the queen of heaven and earth, the Church, is forced to be a slave to might, to surrender, or to shudder before the weapons of plunderers?

And he closed the sermon with a prayer that the result of the trauma might be that the Church 'is cleansed from every stain it has received and is restored to its ancient splendour and purity'. These, then, were the sentiments expressed by an ecclesiastical lieutenant of Julius II. At the heart of the Renaissance papacy, it seems, was the life-blood of the Counter-Reformation.

There were at least 37 foundations of brotherhoods of the Holy Sacrament in Venice between 1504 and 1521, apparently following a visit by Egidio. These foundations cannot be explained in relation to the catastrophe of Agnadello, but there is no doubt that the Venetians were urged to repentance during the wars, for reverses were a punishment for sin. Prayers were to be said 'so that God would assist this republic against its enemies', priests were to be paid to beg 'the favour and assistance of all-powerful God', offerings were made so that 'God might be inclined to pity and mercifulness towards our state'.[7] Venice retained its independence as a republic amid the conquering dynasties.

Prudent exploitation of divisions among the victors of Agnadello ensured that by 1516 the Venetians had re-established their hold on their mainland territories. This narrow escape suggested to the European imagination that the Venetian state had something of a charmed life. The state seemed to preach republican austerity – such was the message of Contarini's book on the Venetian constitution – yet its public celebrations matched those of the most magnificent princes – especially when Andrea Gritti was Doge (1523–38). It remained a Catholic state, but was wary of papal claims. It withstood interdicts in 1482 and 1509 and most famously in 1606, when some observers thought that the Republic might espouse Protestantism. Venetian bookshops published the most challenging works of reformers and satirists such as Erasmus and Aretino, yet Venetian painters, such as Titian (the friend of Aretino) and Tintoretto, promoted the values of the Council of Trent. After 1527, it seemed that Venice alone in Italy was invulnerable, for in that year Rome once more fell to the barbarians:

it is not onely impossible to reaccount, but also to imagine the calamities of that Citie raysed to a wonderfull greatnes, and appointed by Gods ordinance to suffer many fortunes and directions, having bene sacked by the Gothes, within nyne hundred and foureskore yeres: It is harde to particulate the greatnes of the pray, both for the generall wealth and riches which the greedy hands of the souldiours had made up in heapes, and for other thinges more rare and precious drawne out of the store houses of Marchauntes and courtiers: But the matter which made the spoyle infinite in value, was the qualities and great number of prisoners redeemed with most riche and huge raunsomes: And to make up a full tragedie of miserie and infamie, the Launceknightes being so much the more insolent and cruell, by howe much they bare hatred to the name of the Church of Rome, took prisoners certayne Prelates, whom with great contempt and indignities they set upon Asses and leane Moyles, and with their faces reversed to the croupe of the beastes, they ledde them through the Citie of Rome apparelled with the habites and markes of their dignitie . . . no age, no sex, no dignitie or calling was free from the violation of the souldiours, in whom it was doubtfull whether bare more rule the humor of crueltie to kill, or the appetite of luste to deflowre, or lastly the rage of covetousness to robbe and spoyle.

Luther's name was scratched in graffiti in rooms decorated by Raphael. Even supporters of Luther thought it barbaric, and Melanchthon wrote in one letter:

Nothing new, except for rumours about the capture of Rome. I would wish them false for many reasons, but primarily out of fear for the libraries, which have no equal anywhere in the world. And you know, not only our soldiers and Mars despise books, but this whole age, by what fate I do not know, is more inimical to culture than any other ever was.[8]

The confident urban civilisation of the Italian Renaissance was at an end (above, p. 121; plates, section IV). A new Rome was to rise from the wreckage, but it was to be the Rome of the Baroque, of the splendour of holiness. We have seen that part of the change may be explained by the arrival of Spanish Catholicism with its spiritual opulence and its personal austerity. Perhaps the new sobriety which the wars had bred and which increased in the aftermath of the sack eased the arrival of new religious forms, made them less alien, more inviting even. Renaissance man had begun to fast in penance for his excesses (above, pp. 120–2; 193–5).

With the coronation of Charles V at Bologna in 1530, it seemed that the contest between the empire and the papacy had been settled in favour of the empire. The papacy's pretensions to headship of a secular state were in the dust. The compact, well-funded, well-informed state (above p. 78) had to retreat from leagues and armies and refurbish its spiritual weaponry.

Broadening stalemate (1536–1559)

After the imperial success, the largely Italian perspective which has hitherto been-serviceable to us becomes less satisfactory. What is now important to bear in mind is the financial and military exhaustion which the wars in Italy had bred for the Emperor, fatally weakening his chances of success in the new theatres of war to which he now found himself committed. The Treaty of Cambrai (1529) came in the same year as the Diet of Speyer (below, p. 270). No sooner had Charles gained some respite in the dynastic contest in Italy than he was forced to come to grips with a newly militant Protestantism in Germany. The struggle of Habsburg and Valois, so often discussed in terms of Italian weakness in the face of nation-states, had debilitated both the protagonists financially. The decision to increase the sale of office in France (above, p. 74) and the uncontrolled sack of Rome by the imperialists – these were symptoms of the malaise in the machinery of supplying the war effort. In the later stages of the struggle, chronic financial problems were worsened by new tactics which slowed the pace of conflict without easing its costs. As the stalemate broadened, the wars of Habsburg and Valois blurred messily into the Wars of Religion, for the latter involved the same style of war and many of the same personalities, though the intensity of the confessional strife had redrawn the patterns of allegiance.

Twice more before his death, Francis I struck at the imperialists in Italy, in 1536–8 and again in 1543–4. His excuse in 1536 was the execution of a French agent on his way to the sultan with proposals of collaboration from his master. Charles responded not in Italy, but with counter-thrusts at Provence and Picardy, a curious over-commitment given his Turkish wars. Even at this stage, we should note, the Emperor's preoccupations remained dynastic. In an interview in 1536, he asked the pope:

to take the part of the Duke of Savoy, who besides being a vassal of the empire was married to his sister-in-law and cousin-german, the Infanta Dona Beatrice of Portugal.

The Truce of Nice (1538) brought an inconclusive end to hostilities. Then, in 1543, this time in close alliance with Suleiman the Magnificent, Francis resumed the conflict, and confirmed his presence in Piedmont with victory at the battle of Ceresole (1544). Again Charles reacted in another theatre, combining with Henry VIII to strike in northern France. The Treaty of Crépy (1544) brought another truce, though the French retained Savoy and part of Piedmont.

Henry II confirmed a strategy of tying the Emperor down in theatres in which opposition to Charles could be identified with support from France. Thus, he encouraged Turkish naval activity in the Mediterranean, and a military thrust in eastern Europe. He sought an affinity with England and helped to foment rebellion in Naples and Siena, placing imperial forces in Italy under intense pressure. Having established contact with Maurice of Saxony, Henry seized Metz, Toul and Verdun in 1551. Maurice's desertion of the imperial cause all but ruined Charles, whose recovery after the Treaty of Passau (1552) ran into the sand in an unsuccessful siege of Metz. The Habsburg cause recovered under Charles's successors, however. With Germany quiet under Ferdinand after the Peace of Augsburg (1555), Philip II could take advantage of his possessions in Flanders to worry northern France. After the victories at St Quentin (1557) and Gravelines (1559), Henry was content enough to sign the Treaty of Cateau-Cambrésis (also 1559).

The new importance of siege warfare gave the 'military revolution' a new twist, prolonging the duration of campaigns beyond the endurance of royal treasuries, and even of European manpower. Architects and engineers used the designs of Italian artists – including Leonardo and Michelangelo – to strengthen the bastion, a low thick wall which could absorb artillery fire, and whose protruding strong points could send down murderous fire on any section of wall threatened by frontal assault. The enervating quality of the siege was all the greater because withdrawal would render the strung-out columns of besiegers vulnerable to counter-attack. Moreover, siege warfare drew off the men whose weight might have ensured decisive victory in the open field. The importance of successfully withstanding a siege swallowed up armies in garrison duty. Despite the long-term implications of the 'military revolution' for increased army size, the last phase of the Habsburg–Valois struggle often saw no more than 15,000 men deployed for battle. The indecisiveness of the conflicts of the 1540s and 1550s is striking, but it is explicable in terms of the smaller scale of battlefield victory and the immense reluctance to use such victories given the prospect of assembling, equipping and protecting the garrisons subsequently necessary. Thus the French did not follow victory in the carnage of Ceresole with the conquest of the Milanese, Charles overran Provence in 1536 but could not hold on to it. Landrécis (1543) might have been a decisive battle, but both sides backed off – somewhat in the manner of the Italian *condottieri* of the Renaissance. Victory in this sort of war was achieved eventually by Alessandro Farnese in the Netherlands, an important reminder (below, Conclusion) of how close the Spaniards came to success – under an Italian general.

There was little for either side to celebrate after Cateau-Cambrésis. After more than 60 years of conflict, the French kept nothing of Italy save the small Marquisate of Saluzzo, though they held Metz, Toul and Verdun further north. Habsburg fortunes had revived in a difficult period during which the depressed and defeated Charles V handed power to his son Philip and to his brother Ferdinand, who had refused to contemplate Philip's assumption of all Charles's inheritance.

The wars between the Houses of Valois and Habsburg show that the narrowness and instability of dynastic politics were all the more explosive in a context of expanding military commitment. Religion was a further source of ignition. Dynastic politics were ill-equipped to provide the kinds of institutional and legal structures which might have acted as safety precautions. Celebrations there were, however. As part of the festivities for the peace which Cateau-Cambrésis heralded, Henry II took part in a joust. An accidental but hideous eye wound was to kill him, and the succession of a minor was to plunge France into civil war. Such were the vagaries of dynastic politics. Henry II had been perhaps the most genuinely absolute monarch in Europe.[9] His sudden death and an untimely succession produced a dynastic crisis and anarchy in France. In due course, this must draw attention to the infamous and savage wars among Christians in the later sixteenth century. However, neither the dynastic wars in Italy nor the confessional wars in the north can be isolated from the struggle of the traditional champions of Christendom against the might of Islam.

11 Christians and Turks

'The shadow of the crescent'

The religious and political problems of sixteenth-century Europe – so vast, so intricate in themselves, so enmeshed in social change and cultural reorientation – were consistently rendered more complicated and more intractable by the holy war which Islam had vowed against unbelievers. This is plain from the autobiography of the monarch charged with the defence of Christendom, the Emperor Charles V. In 1527, despite his preoccupations in Italy, Charles convoked the Castilian *Cortes* 'to organise the necessary means of defence against the Turks'. In 1532 he entered Germany 'as well as to see whether he could not hit upon some means of putting a stop to the heresies that were spreading there as to oppose the invasion of the Turk', and to both ends called together the Imperial Diet at Regensburg. The Turkish threat was such that 'religious matters were therefore left aside'. Later that year, Charles met with Clement VII 'as well to consider the state of religious matters as to concert resistance to the Turk, and also to secure peace in Italy'. In 1541, he convoked the Diet at Regensburg once more, 'chiefly to establish concord and to effect a remedy in the state of religious affairs'. All the same, Charles became preoccupied with the Turk on two fronts. An invasion of Austria was expected, and the Emperor was already committed to war in the Mediterranean: he left Regensburg to pursue his projected expedition to Algiers. In 1542, the Diet met at Nuremberg 'to discuss defensive measures against the Turk, and matters of religion'. In 1545, his hopes of an 'amicable arrangement' in Germany rose 'as he was at peace with the king of France, and there was no appearance of the Turk attacking Germany'. Most significant of all perhaps, it was a precondition of his triumph over the Protestants in 1547 'that it was rumoured that the Turk was engaged in wars at home . Still, 'to make matters more sure', imperial emissaries negotiated an armistice with the sultan. From one perspective, the Turks prevented Charles from dealing with German Protestantism. However, as the Emperor's own words make plain, the war with Islam was much more than a nuisance or a distraction. His role as the chief pillar of the Christian world made war with the infidel his central preoccupation, and there can be little doubt that when his hands were free from problems in Christian Europe, Charles turned his mind to crusade. From that alternative perspective, it is perhaps more helpful to see Protestantism in Germany as a distraction from the war with the sultan rather than *vice versa*.

In Chapter 2, much emphasis was given to the influence exerted by crusading traditions in frontier war in that grand process of overseas expansion which is so prominent a feature of the age (above, pp. 43–4). While Christendom was expanding across the Atlantic, it was contracting in the Mediterranean. For the power of the sultan stretched from the borders of Muscovy to the Pillars of Hercules, and it threatened to engulf western Christendom. It was a power to be reckoned with in every sense. Its potential for intervention entered political calculation in the great Livonian war between Tsar Ivan the Terrible and his Polish foes, and this at a time when Turkish power threatened the gates of Tunis. So considerable was the might of Suni Islam that it became more than some vague external influence. Rather, it was an integral and substantial component of the mechanisms of international politics. The formal alliance of Francis I with the sultan after Pavia (1525), which generated such outrage among Christians, was no isolated renegation. The threat to the Christian frontier in Hungary looked all the more terrifying because, as already mentioned, the rulers of Poland might ally with Turkish power in their war with Muscovy. The rulers of Spain were right to be suspicious of their Moorish population, that 'Ottoman fifth column' which burst into revolt in the Alpujarras in 1568.

Protestant rebels in Germany and the Netherlands could look to the Golden Horn for encouragement and support. Unsurprisingly, the vast, alien power appeared invincible and all-conquering, its relentless might fuelled by unlimited reserves of men and wealth:

> Now shalt thou feel the force of Turkish arms,
> Which lately made all Europe quake for fear.
> I have of Turks, Arabians, Moors, and Jews,
> Enough to cover all Bithynia.
> Let thousands die: their slaughter'd carcasses
> Shall serve for walls and bulwarks to the rest;
> And as the heads of Hydra, so my power,
> Subdu'd shall stand as mighty as before.
> If they should yield their necks unto the sword,
> Thy soldiers' arms could not endure to strike
> So many blows as I have heads for thee.

What Marlowe's imagination put into the mouth of the Sultan Bajazeth in *Tamburlaine* (III.iii.134–44) was not, it seems, mere fancy. It echoes the hubris of the Grand Vizier, Mehmet Sököllü, who, in 1572 – only a year after Lepanto, the greatest victory of

Christian arms since the completion of the *Reconquista* (below, pp. 261–2) – gave forth this haughty boast:

> The Ottoman state is so powerful, if an order was issued to cast anchors from silver, to make rigging from silk, and to cut the sails from satin, it could be carried out for the entire fleet.

And indeed, the Ottoman force which anchored off Tunis in 1573 was larger even than the great armada destroyed – apparently once and for all – in the Gulf of Corinth two years before.[1]

The problem for the historian is how to convey the impact of the Ottoman Empire without forcing this great Islamic power into a westernised mould. Put another way, the impact of the Turks upon Europe should perhaps be understood in terms of those characteristics which distinguished the Ottoman Empire from the Christian powers rather than in terms of similarities which, though not necessarily superficial, do not take account of what was different about the culture whence Turkish power sprang and upon which Turkish power rested. This empire was too massive in its non-European dimensions for us to consider it in purely European terms, yet too much a part of the international political scene to be treated as some external influence. Any attempt to study the Ottoman Empire in its own right, however, is intensely difficult because of the technical complexity of matters as fundamental as historical dating or consistent transliteration into English from Turkish sources. The scope of this chapter is therefore more limited, and is built round the idea that the unchanging basis of Ottoman might in the sixteenth century is immensely revealing of changes in the nature and extent of western power in the same period. Turkish domination or the threat of it and the degree of success which the Christian powers achieved in halting the Ottoman advance were critical to the emergence of a cultural entity recognisable as the modern West.

The anatomy of Ottoman power

The origins of the Ottoman Empire provide a key to its expansion in the sixteenth century. The territorial nucleus of the empire was a frontier principality in Anatolia, caught between the Byzantine Empire in the west and the Seljuk Turks in the east. The Seljuks shook Byzantium to its foundations with their triumph at Manzikert in 1085. Their own power, however, was checked by the Mongol invasions of the thirteenth century, and the frontier zone between Byzantium and the Seljuks widened as local war lords built up their own power bases. The Osman dynasty came to power in the fourteenth century in a principality dedicated to holy war, or *gaza*, on the borders of Byzantium. However extensive its territories, the Ottoman state remained a frontier empire with *gaza* as its highest purpose – hence the importance of vassal states in frontier regions and the collaboration of voivod, khan or corsair to the imperial war machine.

Although the Ottomans made gains at the expense of Byzantium, marked at Kossovo and Adrianople in 1389 – which ensured the subjugation of Serbia until 1878 – and at Nicopolis in 1396, the extension of their territorial power was checked in the early fifteenth century by the last Mongol eruption, led by Tamburlaine – a struggle central to Marlowe's great play. But as the century progressed, Constantinople itself became more and more vulnerable. It fell in 1453 to the vast army and heavy cannon of Mehmet the Conqueror. The success of the Ottoman siege of Constantinople has perhaps obscured the significance of their subsequent failures to reduce fortified strongholds, yet there can be no doubt of the prospects of conquest which opened up for the Turks after the fall of Byzantium. Mehmet immediately changed the city's name to Istanbul, and made it the centre of a formidable autocracy. At its head was the representative of the dynasty, the sultan, who enjoyed absolute power in the appointment of ministers, the most important of whom was the grand vizier. The sultan and his advisers formed the chief law court or divan, and sought guidance, when necessary, from the ulema, that formidable body of priests whose sacred trust was the interpretation of Islamic law. The sultan's power was guaranteed by the celebrated janissaries, a military élite which formed the first standing army to be seen in Europe. Scarcely less formidable in the field, though available only during the campaigning season and not as a permanent force, were the *sipahis*. These horsemen were also known as timariots because they were holders of timars or fiefs which obliged them to do service in the sultan's wars. They answered the call of the local military governor, the sanjak bey, who in turn was responsible to his superior, the *beylerbey*, the district governor who supervised the attachment of regional musters to the sultan's army. Although there are few reliable statistics, the army was probably 80,000 strong, and equipped with fine cannon, while naval power was enhanced by the many Greeks who served as sailors in the Ottoman fleet.

Since the sultan's power so clearly depended upon the military machine, the monopoly of official appointments and the total integration of the state and a religious cause, it is tempting to see the autocracy as a realisation of the ambitions of western absolutists (above, ch. 3) – and this is also a reminder of the autocratic tendencies of western absolutism itself. However, it is more profitable to reflect on the cultural contrasts which made possible for the sultan a power which was beyond the wildest dreams of any Christian prince: even Tsar Ivan

Figure 11.1 The Islamic–Ottoman social structure

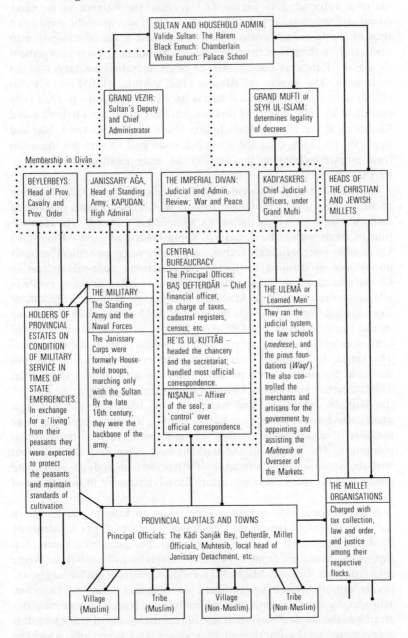

SULTAN AND HOUSEHOLD ADMIN.
Valide Sultan: The Harem
Black Eunuch: Chamberlain
White Eunuch: Palace School

GRAND VEZIR:
Sultan's Deputy
and Chief
Administrator

GRAND MUFTI or
SEYH UL-ISLAM:
determines legality
of decrees

Membership in Divãn

BEYLERBEYS:
Head of Prov.
Cavalry and
Prov. Order

JANISSARY AĞA,
Head of Standing
Army; KAPUDAN,
High Admiral

THE IMPERIAL DIVAN:
Judicial and Admin.
Review; War and Peace

KADI'ASKERS:
Chief Judicial
Officers, under
Grand Mufti

HEADS OF
THE CHRISTIAN
AND JEWISH
MILLETS

HOLDERS OF
PROVINCIAL
ESTATES ON
CONDITION
OF MILITARY
SERVICE IN
TIMES OF
STATE
EMERGENCIES.
In exchange
for a 'living'
from their
peasants they
were expected
to protect
the peasants
and maintain
standards of
cultivation.

THE MILITARY
The Standing
Army and the
Naval Forces
The Janissary
Corps were
formerly House-
hold troops,
marching only
with the Sultan.
By the late
16th century,
they were the
backbone of the
army.

CENTRAL
BUREAUCRACY
The Principal Offices:
BAŞ DEFTERDÃR – Chief
financial officer,
in charge of taxes,
cadastral registers,
census, etc.
RE'IS UL-KUTTÃB –
headed the chancery
and the secretariat;
handled most official
correspondence.
NIŞANJI – Affixer
of the seal; a
'control' over
official correspondence.

THE ULEMÃ or
'Learned Men'
They ran the
judicial system,
the law schools
(*medrese*), and
the pious foun-
dations (*Waqf*).
The also con-
trolled the
merchants and
artisans for the
government by
appointing and
assisting the
Muhtesib or
Overseer of
the Markets.

THE MILLET
ORGANISATIONS
Charged with
tax collection,
law and order,
and justice
among their
respective
flocks.

PROVINCIAL CAPITALS AND TOWNS
Principal Officials: The Kãdi Sanjãk Bey, Defterdãr, Millet
Officials, Muhtesib, local head of
Janissary Detachment, etc.

Village
(Muslim)

Tribe
(Muslim)

Village
(Non-Muslim)

Tribe
(Non-Muslim)

Source: C. Max Kortepeter, *Ottoman Imperialism during the Reformation*
(London and New York: New York University Press, 1972), p. 255.

the Terrible had to fight a fearsome struggle with his boyars to establish his own autocracy. As Figure 11.1 reveals, the balance of political, social and religious life in Ottoman civilisation was quite different from that of the Christian world. The Muslim had a sacred obligation to make war on the infidel, irrespective of whether or not it was expedient to do so. Religious considerations often dictated the target of an expedition. The attacks on Rhodes (1522), Malta (1565) and Cyprus (1570) were designed to secure access for Muslim pilgrims to their holy places. Moreover, the infidel was not just the Christian – Orthodox and Catholic – it was also the unorthodox Shiite Muslim. In the 1530s, and again in the 1550s, even the great Suleiman had to turn his attention from empire-building in the west to the extermination of heretics in Persia.

The social structure provides further evidence of the subordination of all loyalties to a commitment to holy war. The infamous practice of fratricide through which the sultan secured his power by the elimination of rivals within the dynasty is symptomatic of a world in which kinship ties were strikingly feeble – especially when we remember their importance in defining aristocracy and shaping political interest in Christendom, where the solidarity of families often explains political allegiance (above, p. 219). Machiavelli observed that the kingdom of France would be easy to seize but hard to hold on to, while the reverse would be the case in the Ottoman Empire, and the relationship of central authority to local power structures clearly made the difference. The timar, for instance, was not private property, and it was not heritable: the sultan merely passed it from one holy warrior to another. The janissaries were slaves. Many of them came from Christian areas in the Balkans, where children were given as tribute to the sultan, a practice known as *devshirme*. Paradoxically, slavery provided a large measure of social mobility: this was not the slavery of the colonial plantation. The peoples of the Balkans may often have been content with the *devshirme*, which freed their offspring from a dour, unyielding region and provided the opportunity for advancement in the service of the sultan.[2]

Many of the contrasts between the Ottoman Empire and Christian societies appear in the astute and frank letters of Ogier Ghiselin de Busbecq. He acted as ambassador for the Archduke (and then Emperor) Ferdinand from 1554 to 1562. Whilst in Istanbul, he wrote four letters to Nicholas Michault, an old friend from student days. He points out obvious but significant contrasts in terms of Ottoman attitudes to wine, women and animals in a society where rice not grain was the staple diet, camels not horses the means of transport. It is a testimony to the impression of stability and prosperity which he gained that he felt Christian societies had something to learn from the Turks. Having found out that women descended even from royalty might be married to 'ploughmen and shepherds', he remarked – with some admiration – on the 'lowly estate of nobility in the realm of Turkey', that 'no value is attached to anything but personal merit', and the ruling family was unique 'being the only family in which birth confers rank'. Even when he was received by the sultan, he noticed that in the great assembly of officials, the sultan's favour was conferred as a recognition of merit:

> no one is distinguished from the rest by his birth, and honour is paid to each man according to the nature of the duty and offices which he discharges. Thus there is no struggle for precedence, every man having his place assigned to him in virtue of the function which he performs. The sultan himself assigns to all their duties and offices, and in doing so pays no attention to wealth or the empty claims of rank, and takes no account of any influence or popularity which a candidate may possess; he only considers merit and scrutinises the character, natural ability, and disposition of each. Thus each man is rewarded according to his deserts.

He gradually builds up to a contrast with the Christian west. The 'sons of shepherds and herdsmen' may aspire to the highest positions:

> They do not consider that good qualities can be conferred by birth or handed down by inheritance, but regard them partly as the gift of heaven and partly as the product of good training and constant toil and zeal. Just as they consider that an aptitude for the arts, such as music or mathematics or geometry, is not transmitted to a son and heir, so they hold that character is not hereditary, and that a son does not necessarily resemble his father, but his qualities are divinely infused into his bodily frame. Thus, among the Turks, dignities, offices, and administrative posts are the rewards of ability and merit; those who are dishonest, lazy, and slothful never attain to distinction but remain in obscurity and contempt. This is why the Turks succeed in all that they attempt and are a dominating race and daily extend the bounds of their rule. Our method is very different; there is no room for merit, but everything depends on birth; considerations of which alone open the way to high official position. On this subject I shall perhaps say more in another place, and you must regard these remarks as intended for your ears only.

And perhaps 'a just and mild form of slavery' was preferable to poverty. Liberty exposed the individual to material want; oppression might in itself involve a measure of care. If Christian states returned to the Roman example as the Ottoman experience suggested they should, then:

there would not perhaps be need of so many gallows and gibbets to restrain those who possess nothing but their life and liberty, and whose want drives them to crime of every kind, while their freedom combined with poverty does not always lead them in the path of honesty.

This impression of central power and social discipline was perhaps most obvious while the great Suleiman was in power, however. Clearly, the system depended heavily on the personal qualities of the sultan himself, and under less able rulers there is plenty of evidence of intrigue in the harem, and factional power struggles. The other side of social stability was a lack of social change. Busbecq noted that the Turks were quick to learn:

> For no nation has shown less reluctance to adopt the useful invention of others; for example, they have appropriated to their own use large and small cannons and many other of our discoveries.

However, they were resistant to printing and to clocks on religious grounds:

> They have, however, never been able to bring themselves to print books and set up public clocks. They hold that their scriptures, that is, their sacred books, would no longer be scriptures if they were printed; and if they established public clocks, they think that the authority of their muezzins and their ancient rites would suffer diminution.

This may have affected their attitude to historical time as well: 'The Turks have no idea of chronology and dates, and make a wonderful mixture of all the epochs of history', and we have already seen what the dynamics of change in the west owed to a sense of the past and the realisation of the possibilities of specific pieces of technology (above, chs. 2 and 5).

What we should perhaps acknowledge – without a value judgement – is that the Islamic civilisation of the Ottoman Empire produced meritocracy as well as autocracy. Ottoman culture ensured that the empire did not know the struggles of church and state or of crown and aristocracy which proved so disruptive in Christian societies, but it never faced the scale and pace of change – by no means all of it progressive, or even positive – which those struggles generated.

The very low level of local turbulence – a reflection of the relative weakness of regional autonomy – emphasised the dimensions of central power. That power seemed all the greater in Istanbul itself, a city probably six times the size of Venice, five times as big as Paris, 'created by nature for the capital of the world':

It stands in Europe but looks out over Asia, and has Egypt and Africa on its right. Although these latter are not near, yet they are linked to the city owing to ease of communication by sea. On the left lie the Black Sea and the Sea of Azov, round which many nations dwell and into which many rivers flow on all sides, so that nothing useful to man is produced through the length and breadth of these countries which cannot be transported by sea to Constantinople with the utmost ease.

In strategic terms, this was the ideal base for operations in Hungary and the Mediterranean, but the weight of wealth and manpower which the state could command from so opulent a centre pushed the implications of any military action much further afield. As late as 1625, a Venetian observer remarked:

The sultan has two wings with which he flies very far. One is Barbary on the sea, and the other Tartary on the land: both are insatiable birds of prey.[3]

The predatory aspect was critical in both a military and an economic sense. Although the military machine needed more and more land to supply more and more timars, a city of the size of Constantinople needed colossal amounts of grain. Conquest and appropriation were much more likely to supply it than trade alone. So, having sketched the internal organisation of the Ottoman Empire, we should now trace the nature and scale of its impact on Christendom.

The lengthening shadow

Ottoman conquests were not complete in 1453. The dynamic of the *gaza* kept the Empire forever on the move. Its naval power soon mounted a challenge to the Venetian Republic. A long series of campaigns between 1463 and 1479 forced the Venetians to relinquish significant power bases at Coron and Modon in the Morea – the area of Greece south of the Gulf of Corinth. Suddenly, even Venice's command of its home waters in the Adriatic seemed far from secure. When the Turks landed in Otranto on the east coast of southern Italy in 1480, the commercial network which ensured Venetian prosperity looked as though it might shrink to nothing because of blockade, and the Republic's maritime confidence suffered another setback at Zonchio in 1499. The survival of Venice as an important state owes much to that vast dependence on the character of the sultan which determined the direction and thrust of Ottoman advance: why Bajazed II (1481–1512) failed to launch an assault on Venice when the Republic was poised on the brink during the Italian Wars remains a mystery.

Here perhaps we must acknowledge the incompleteness of that western perspective which a book on Europe perforce employs: we should not assume that the sultan, even a weak one such as Bajazed, was always looking toward the prize of Christendom. For the scale of the Ottoman threat to the west which became so awesome between about 1520 and about 1580 was preceded by the careful securing of the imperial frontier in the east and its dramatic extension to the south. Bajazed's inaction was to result in his deposition in favour of his son, Selim, known as 'the Grim'. To the east, Selim faced the resurgent Shiite power of Shah Ishmael of Persia, whose ideological hostility had prompted rebellion in Turkish dominions in the last years of Bajazed's reign. Selim's invasion perhaps aimed to unseat the Safavid dynasty, which was of relatively recent establishment (1501), and his armies won a decisive victory at Tchaldiran, west of Tabriz, near Lake Urmia in 1514. His conquests brought Selim to the borders of the Egypt of the Mamluks. These elected war lords he smashed at Dabik near Aleppo in 1516 and his thrust south culminated in another victory at Ridanieh near Cairo in 1517. The conquest of the Mamluk Empire doubled the tax revenues of the Ottoman sultan.

Nevertheless, while the Turks had been making gains in the east and south, significant changes were occurring in western power structures. By the time the Turks looked west again, the empire of Charles V had taken shape. Charles took the imperial title in 1519, just a year before Selim's successor, Suleiman the Magnificent, began his assault on Christendom. The momentum which Suleiman gave to the westward enterprise of Islam was to last until the truce between Philip II and Selim II in 1581.

Suleiman's strategy was to launch his most energetic strikes at times when divisions amongst the Christian powers would prevent a concerted resistance. On the other hand, the complex of Christian power was something more formidable than squabbling 'co-religionists' whose survival was merely ensured by the internal problems of the Ottoman Empire. The turmoil in the west reflected dynamism as well as division, and while the military response to Islam never united Catholics and Protestants, there is a sense in which Christian Europe – not merely the Christendom of the Middle Ages, not yet the Europe of the modern age – redefined its geographical and cultural boundaries in the face of the Turkish threat, and it did so in a series of resolute actions on sea and land. Moreover, even in military terms, Turkish power ebbed when it faced dams in the west as well as when it was drawn back by the tidal forces of the east, and the power which lay behind those dams was itself capable of flowing forth. An examination of their struggle against the Turks reveals the origins of that dependence on land-based strongholds and maritime power which was to make Europeans masters of the world until at least 1914.

That was by no means clear, however, at Suleiman's accession in 1520. The Balkans were firmly within the Ottoman sphere of influence, and the Christian frontier was seriously strained. The Turks had the military capability to invade the kingdom of Hungary, and the kingdom of Hungary was in no condition to withstand the assault, for it suffered from that lack of dynastic stability so critical to the pattern of western politics. Following the death of the native lord, Matthias Corvinus (1458–90), the nobles who dominated the Estates of Hungary had installed a member of the Lithuanian dynasty (which also ruled Poland) as Ladislas I (1490–1516). What a contrast with the Ottoman Empire! In Hungary, the local lords did as they pleased while the monarchy foundered, and deteriorating conditions engendered revolt amongst the peasantry in 1514. Strong-arm tactics from the nobles ensured suppression, and amongst the strongest arms were those of John Zapolyai, voivod, or warlord, of Transylvania. His prominence amongst the nobility and his considerable local power base made him a potential contender for the crown should its future become uncertain. The Turks were to provide first the uncertainty, and then the crown. As we have seen, however, in 1514 the Ottomans were far to the east, at Tchaldiran in Persia.

Suleiman's first foray westward came within a year of his accession, in 1521, the year of the Diet of Worms (above, p. 135). He advanced through the Balkans with a view to securing a base for operations north of the Danube. Belgrade, protected on one side by the river, was exposed and cut off to landward. The garrison was inadequate, there was no Christian army which could raise the siege by challenging the Turks in the open field. Batteries of cannon and relentless mining operations ensured that the city would fall – but direct assaults, significantly, were repulsed several times with heavy losses, and the tiny garrison still won terms which allowed its withdrawal. Belgrade was indeed to be Suleiman's base for an attack on Hungary, but this did not come for four years.

In the meantime, the sultan looked to the islands which the Christians controlled in the eastern Mediterranean. The Venetians held Cyprus and Crete, either of which could provide naval bases for operations against Muslim pilgrims travelling east, or interfere with seaborne communication between Istanbul and Cairo. The jaws of Islamic power, however, closed round Rhodes, which was held by the crusading Order of the Knights of St John, the implacable foes of the infidel. The ideology of the crusaders still endured, but their fortifications were no relic of the past. It is important to acknowledge that this was the front line of confrontation between two contending world powers, not of obsolete ideologies in an obsolete theatre of action. The Order had devoted its funds to the building of ingenious patterns of modern bastions which jutted from squat, thick walls. Yet the Grand

Master, Villiers de l'Isle Adam, commanded no more than 6,000 troops including all his auxiliaries. The Turks landed in force in June 1522. Sorties and counter-mining held their engineers at bay. The defenders repulsed a tremendous assault in October, inflicting fearful losses, and Suleiman dismissed his generals and summoned reserves. Even so, the proud might of the sultan did not prevail through storming the walls. The knights were short of powder, Suleiman saw no point in losing more troops and offered terms which allowed the withdrawal of the defenders. The evacuation – of a mere 180 knights, and 1,500 assorted mercenaries – was complete by 1 January 1523. Charles V offered the Order a new home at Malta, and the Knights of St John lived to fight another day.

Suleiman's war of conquest in the west was delayed for three more years by revolts in Egypt. This did nothing to alleviate the scale of the disaster which Suleiman inflicted on Christendom in 1526. It was as though the sultan's wrath had merely fermented. The Turkish host marched from Belgrade. The Jageillon heir, Ladislas II, stood in its path on the plains of Mohács. Hopelessly short of infantry, effectively abandoned by the neutrality of Poland and Venice, who looked to their own interests, the Christian camp descended into factious bickering over tactics. Some lords would serve only under the royal standard and refused to be part of a detachment, some urged caution until Zapolyai should arrive from Transylvania or distract the Turks by invading Wallachia, some urged withdrawal to join up with such Christian troops as were on their way from Bohemia. The crusading spirit of warrior bishops was to prevail, and was to condemn Hungary to some three centuries of subjugation. The tenacity was not outdated – as the defence of Rhodes had shown – but it was tactically misplaced. The cavalry charge which sought to save the kingdom merely ensured its destruction. It was courageous and penetrating, but the Christians were eventually mown down at point-blank range by Turkish cannon. The remains of the 20-year old Ladislas were found in a gulch in the remnants of his finery months later. Zapolyai offered his good offices to the sultan and became the client king of Islam. The dynastic web (above, pp. 219–23) provided a western competitor.

The challenge came from Ferdinand of Habsburg, Archduke of Austria, brother of Charles V – and husband of Anne, the sister of Ladislas. Ferdinand and Anne were elected King and Queen of Hungary at a diet in Pressburg (Bratislava) in October, 1526. Suleiman's withdrawal to suppress revolts in Cilicia and Karamania led to the immediate opening of hostilities between the Christian claimants. Suleiman was forced to delay his attack on Ferdinand until 1529. This time the sultan made for Vienna, brushing aside Buda and Pressburg on his imperious way. Vienna did not enjoy the defences of Rhodes. It is easy to say that the city lay just beyond the possibilities of the Ottoman campaigning season, but had it fallen, Vienna would have opened the way for a general Turkish advance against Germany. Here, the problems of penetrating the Turkish sources frustrate us. Dare one suggest that Suleiman did not show the nerve and imagination in siege warfare which he displayed on the open field? To this we shall return. For the moment, we might point out that the siege lasted two months, and by the end of it, the Turks faced the lash of their own officers more readily than the firepower of the German and Spanish arquebusiers from defensive positions. Suleiman fell back. Bad weather in the late season in 1529 eliminated the possibility of a further attack on Austria the following year. Suleiman spent 1531 assembling his power and marched west once more in 1532. He advanced on the fortress at Güns, where 700 defenders resisted him for three weeks. The eventual capitulation was a token affair: hostages were exchanged, keys given over – and the garrison was left in place. It would appear that Suleiman had no stomach for a fight with the army which Charles V had assembled at Vienna. He signed a truce with Ferdinand – whose forces had made little headway in Hungary itself – in order to concentrate on new problems in Persia. Perhaps it was a measure of his own confidence that Charles V was not a signatory to his brother's treaty with the sultan.

Such might be the inference from Suleiman's decision to open another theatre of conflict in 1533, this time in the Mediterranean. There is no particular evidence of a grand strategy, but pragmatism or even opportunism assume grander proportions in the case of the Turks because of the scale of the resources which might be mobilised. Alliance with Francis I seemed yet again advantageous, but once more it was frontier warlords – this time the corsairs – who advanced the Turkish cause. We should not assume that another phase of inexorable Turkish advance was opening, with the Christian powers waiting and quaking. The pirate ruler of Algiers, Khaireddin (known as Barbarossa), felt his own bandit realm threatened by the Spaniards in Oran. He first offered his services to Selim in 1519. In 1533, Suleiman gave him command of the fleet. He fell on Tunis the following year. He lost it to Charles V in 1535, but the extension of piratical activity was a critical influence in drawing the Venetians out of their neutrality in 1537.

Whilst historians have given much attention to the problems which governments and societies faced in raising and funding a standing army, the Venetian Republic had to experience a naval as well as a military revolution. Its fortresses were strengthened – probably because the Venetians were aware of the lesson of Rhodes – and in 1537 Corfu withstood an Ottoman siege. Let us note that in Turkish hands, Corfu could have been the base for an Ottoman invasion of Italy, cutting off the Venetian fleet from its Spanish allies. This reflection perhaps mitigates the disaster which Christian forces, using Corfu as their

base, suffered in 1538. In that year, the Venetians joined the imperial
fleet under the Genoese admiral, Andrea Doria, in operations against
the Turks at Prevesa, near what is now the island of Levkas, off the
Greek mainland. This time it was a Christian siege which failed, and
Doria chose to cut his losses. The withdrawal was untidy, and the
Christian accounts could not deny that Barbarossa's counter-attack
was a triumph:

> Passing Andrea with his fleet near Santa Maura [i.e. Levkas], which
> is an island, Barbarossa sortied from the Gulf with his fleet and
> came out against ours. Andrea was forced to stand by because the
> wind fell calm and the roundships were unable to move. And
> Barbarossa took the wind and began to bombard our roundships
> and they to reply to him. He sent to the bottom one of our ships
> with 300 Spanish soldiers. He took a galley of the pope without
> resistance. He took another of the Venetians. He destroyed another
> Vizcayan roundship in which were 400 Spanish soldiers.

Ironically, such comfort as the Christians could draw from the defeat
was yet again from their defensive showing, from a species of siege, this
time seaborne. Despite the raggedness of the retreat, the slow Great
Galleon of Venice, a floating fortress, held out all day, its powerful
guns inflicting notable damage on the Turkish assailants.

Venetian policy was the product of intelligent realism. The Venetians
acknowledged that decisive victories were unlikely and elusive. They
strengthened their forts, and they prepared for war at sea as a
permanent conflict rather than a series of temporary mobilisations.
In 1537, the Senate acknowledged that 'forever and perpetually there
will be a need to supplement the reserve fleet'. A galley required 156
oarsmen for its 19 horsepower. In 1539, the Venetian reserve fleet was
doubled to 50 galleys. The commitment of manpower and money was
colossal: while the papal galleys had 130 soldiers aboard, the Venetians
could provide only 50, the annual cost of a single galley was about
8,000 ducats. The Venetians paid two-thirds of the cost of the Lepanto
campaign in any year of 'peace' thereafter – yet the constant state of
readiness had its own unforeseen dividends. As Traiano Boccalini put it
early in the seventeenth century:

> It seemed very strange that the Senate of that commonwealth
> studied more and more the peace yet with great vigilancy and
> assiduity did perpetually prepare for war and that armed peace
> was only seen in the flourishing Venetian state.[4]

Historians are sometimes inclined to think of the 'rise of the Atlantic
economies' as spelling the decline of the Mediterranean, yet in many

ways, it was the strength of Christian bulwarks in the Mediterranean against the threat from the east that helped to make possible the continued expansion westward across the Atlantic.

Venetian preparations for the long war of attrition which was to render periods of armed conflict inseparable from periods of peaceful commerce proved entirely sensible, for the conflict of Christians and Turks gradually reached stalemate. In 1540, John Zapolyai died. What would be the fate of Hungary? The first strike on the kingdom came from the west, from Ferdinand, and the Turks repulsed it. Charles sought to return to the Mediterranean theatre and planned to take Algiers. Suleiman countered with a closer association with Francis I, but this foundered after the Peace of Crépy in 1543. Barbarossa died in 1546, to be succeeded by his scarcely less formidable subordinate, Dragut. Charles sought to concentrate on his German problems, Suleiman on Persia. The Emperor triumphed at Mühlberg in 1547, but faced humiliation in 1552. Still Suleiman was tied down in the east, and could not exploit the Emperor's misfortune, or even support and extend the hostilities which Henry II of France launched with the seizure of Metz, Toul and Verdun. Indeed, once Suleiman was free to turn west once more, the peace of Cateau-Cambrésis (1559) had halted the Habsburg–Valois conflict, and France soon plunged into civil war, making concerted international collaboration impossible.

The Habsburgs were in no position to exploit the new situation. The 1550s were a decade of painful transition within the complex of the dynasty's power. The political defeat of Charles in Germany, confirmed in the Peace of Augsburg, precipitated his retirement. The aftermath of this grand farewell was messy, to say the least. The fate of the Holy Roman Empire, the role of the retired Emperor, the relation of the Spanish and imperial inheritances were all uncertain. While the Peace of Augsburg tranquillised the empire somewhat, Suleiman's preoccupations in Persia were of small use to Spain. The value of the corsairs to the Ottoman cause at this time was inestimable. They disrupted regular trade – particularly serious as it often affected the grain supply – they launched impudent raids against Malaga, Cadiz and Gibraltar.

Salah Rais, the sultan's *beylerbey* in Algiers, took Bougie in 1555, threatening Valencia and Catalonia. In 1556, his successor, the son of Barbarossa, attacked the Spanish base at Oran. That same year, revolt flared in Aragon as doubts about the succession in Spain intensified, and as political paralysis set in: why should the Spanish fleet be moored in Italy, when Spain faced a full-scale Islamic invasion? Yes, Islamic, for the Moriscos, the corsairs, the Moors of North Africa and the Turks appeared in Iberia as a single threat. Philip faced financial ruin. His revenues in 1559 amounted to about 1.5 million ducats. He needed some 4.2 million for defence and for the servicing of his debts – and the latter stood at some 25 million ducats. Yet his reputation was at stake, and to Philip that was priceless. As soon as the Treaty of Cateau-Cambrésis was signed, he strained the reserves of gold and silver to breaking-point and equipped a fleet of about 50 galleys and a force of 5,000 troops, which gathered at Messina. He sought to recover Tripoli from Dragut. The Christian fleet achieved surprise at Djerba in 1560, and the Turkish position was overrun. Yet the pirate, Uluj Ali, escaped to warn the Ottoman fleet of Piali Pasha. As it descended, Gian Andrea Doria fled with no semblance of battle order in the Christian fleet, though he had the firepower to resist. He lost some 30 galleys in the Turkish onslaught, and he had abandoned the garrison ashore. Don Alvaro de Sande was made of sterner stuff and the resistance on land was defiant – until lack of water forced the commander to seek terms.

The loss of experienced manpower in the actions at Djerba was catastrophic for Spain, a point to be related to Spain's military commitments and ideological ambitions in Europe itself.[5] In strategic terms, the Turks now commanded the narrow seas of the Mediterranean, Malta was exposed and vulnerable. And Malta would surely fall.

The Turks gathered their strength so as to make victory a formality. A great fleet left Istanbul on 26 March and landed on Malta on 18 May 1565. Very speedily, a force of some 40,000 troops had assembled to begin an assault which could have but one outcome. They faced three forts – St Elmo, Senglea, and Birgu – as obstacles. While this meant three separate sieges for the Turks, it also forced Jean de la Valette, the Grand Master, an ex-galley slave of extraordinary hardiness, to split the apparently pitiful Christian forces – no more than 2,500 professional soldiers. He calculated that the first assault would have to fall on the stronghold of St Elmo in order to secure a harbour for the Ottoman fleet. Here 1,500 crusaders were holed up, their only lifeline a hazardous crossing of the harbour which separated them from the other forts, Senglea and Birgu. Once in place, the Turkish batteries rained destruction on St Elmo, and the arrival of Dragut early in June gave new impetus and direction to the operation. Yet the Christians in St Elmo used their 20 cannon to grim effect. Careful marksmanship repelled wave after wave of fanatical dervishes, rendered careless of life by generous distributions of hashish, their loose clothing a hindrance when climbing siege ladders, a positive danger against the whirling hoops of fire and primitive grenades which the Christians unleashed. Their steady counter-fire claimed Dragut with shrapnel, though he lingered on for days in his tent: the site of the Turkish batteries is still known as Dragut's Point. But the defenders' position worsened.

At first, Christians from the other forts came as volunteers, across the harbour in eights and tens, all that la Valette could spare. But when the dangers of the crossing cut off all hope of continuing relief, la Valette – who remained in Birgu – ordered a fight to the last man at St Elmo. When there was no wall left to defend and no one fit to defend it, on the rubble, from their chairs and on their knees, in scenes which foreshadow the Alamo, the wounded crusaders fought to the death. St Elmo fell on 29 June. The garrison had held out for an impossible four weeks. The frustration of the Turks fuelled their ardour, the grief of the Christians fuelled theirs. The only hope was a relief from Sicily. Otherwise, no quarter would be given. When St Elmo fell, la Valette executed his Turkish prisoners at Birgu and bombarded the victorious enemy camp with their heads.

St Elmo's defenders had won precious time for the other Christians, and for the viceroy of Sicily, Don García de Toledo. They had inflicted serious losses on the Turks, particularly the janissaries. Nevertheless, the momentum of the assault on Senglea and Birgu (7 July) was furious. La Valette led the crusaders for 9 hours of fighting and for a while Turkish standards waved above the walls of Birgu. Only an attack on the Turkish camp by Dom Pedro de Mezquita and a tiny force of Portuguese from Mdina forced the Turks back, for word spread that a relief force had landed. In fact, the fighting continued for another two months. Neither weight of numbers, firepower nor fervour could apparently shift the Christians, and all the time the psychological advantage was passing to the defenders. Despite devastating preparatory barrages, no Ottoman assault could overrun the compact combination of bastions, cannons, pikes and arquebuses. The effectiveness of the new military technology should not be exaggerated, for at close range, the defenders 'found it easier to lay aside our arquebuses and hurl rocks at them. In this way we could do more harm and hit them more often'. Don García – often accused of lethargy – timed his arrival to perfection. When his force of 11,000 arrived on 7 September, the Turks were in no mood to oppose him. Impossibly, Malta had held out, the Turks had yet again failed to conduct a successful siege.[6]

Rather than victory prompting the application of more pressure in a second theatre, frustration forced the move. Suleiman's rage turned northward. The impetus this time came from the death of Ferdinand in 1564. Following the failure of his generals at Malta, Suleiman – who was now 72 years of age – took the field in person for the thirteenth time and attacked Hungary. His vast land army of perhaps 100,000 advanced to the fortress of Szigeth, and its garrison of 2,300, which were under the command of the imperial governor, Count Nicholas Zriny. Szigeth provides a variation on the now familiar theme: Ottoman assault never lived up to Ottoman battery. The siege guns were effective enough, but the fort was awkwardly sited in marshland, and the Turks had to build improvised causeways for their soldiers. Szigeth held for a month. Another St Elmo. The janissaries fell in their hundreds in unsuccessful assaults against murderous gunfire. But by 8 September Zriny knew his position was hopeless. He put a match to his powder-magazine, and led a last charge. The explosion of the magazine took hundreds more of the enemy at the very moment of their triumph. What none of them knew was that Suleiman had died. Some sources suggest that his rage and frustration at the failure of his attacks brought on an apoplectic fit, though others report a prosaic bout of dysentery. In any event, the news was withheld from the troops to keep up morale for the final attack on Szigeth.

Suleiman's successor, Selim the Sot, was no warrior, but came to an undisputed throne because of the ruthlessness with which Suleiman had eliminated his other sons. Having met his father's corpse at Belgrade, Selim hurried back to Constantinople. However, the vengeful Grand Vizier, Mehmet Sököllü, kept alive the *gaza*. In 1569, Philip II faced revolt from the Protestants in the Netherlands (below, pp. 299–302), which made it still harder for him to deal with the Morisco uprising in the Alpujarras, which had begun the year before. Cyprus, which Venice held, and which – it is said in ungenerous sources – would provide the sultan with endless supplies of his favourite tipple, was near at hand, isolated and indefensible. The more serious motive was religion. Even Selim appears to have felt the need to stir himself in holy war to recover for Islam land lost to Christendom. The Venetians could not risk committing their entire fleet to an engagement so far to the east, and left the forts at Nicosia and Famagosta to face a Turkish fleet of 116 galleys and 50,000 troops, while they themselves canvassed for support among the Christian powers.

Even when Nicosia fell – after seven weeks, which was sooner than expected – it seemed that help must arrive for Famagosta. The Turks slaughtered the Nicosia garrison, and arrived at Famagosta with the head of the commander in a basket. In the event, Marc'Antonio Bragadin managed to get news to Venice of his plight, and took heart from the arrival of a Venetian fleet in Crete. As Bragadin set about strengthening his defences during the winter months, the Venetian government in turn appealed for help. Their great hope was Spain, for Philip II's half-brother, Don John of Austria, had put down the Morisco revolt. That cherished dream of Pope Pius V, the Holy League, brought the papacy, Spain and Venice together in May 1571. But the fleet of the Holy League could not be ready before the summer. By the time it was, Famagosta had fallen.

Bragadin had done all he could. The genuine prospect of relief sustained the defenders against every assault, against the mining and the bombardments. By August supplies of powder were all but spent. Lala Mustafa offered the kind of terms which Suleiman had granted at Rhodes and Güns, and the Venetians capitulated. The Turk was then guilty of the vilest treachery. He slaughtered the Venetian officers when they came to parley, and his army fell upon the transport ships which the 2,000 Christian troops had already boarded. Bragadin lost his nose and ears and was subjected to public humiliation for days. Then he was flayed alive in the town square and his skin, stuffed with straw, was sent to Constantinople for the sultan's amusement.

Don John, meanwhile, ignorant of Famagosta's fall, assembled his forces at Messina. Their target was not Cyprus or, alas, Lala Mustafa, but the Turkish fleet which had gathered to defend Turkish Cyprus against Christian relief. Don John was only 26, and a letter which he had written from Naples to Don García de Toledo, who knew the taste of disaster at Algiers as well as triumph at Malta, reveals something of the young general's inexperience, as well as his resolve:

> I would you were with me here, but as this may not be, I will set great store by such prudent counsel as you may see fit to give a youth who is about to undertake such an enterprise as I now have in hand.

Don John decided to search out and destroy the enemy. He found it in October at Lepanto near the Corinthian Gulf. On 5 October, he received news of the fall of Famagosta and the fate of Bragadin. He had probably already decided on pitched battle, but there can be little doubt that news of the atrocities in Cyprus stiffened Christian determination.

There were good reasons for avoiding an engagement: it was late in the campaigning season, and the Turks enjoyed considerable numerical advantage, some 270 ships against Don John's 208. The Turkish admiral, Ali Pasha, drew heart from this, and from the encouragement of the renegade warlord of Algiers, Uluj Ali, who took command of the left wing. Don John had made alterations to the Christian ships to ensure greater freedom of movement for soldiers and wider fields of fire for cannon. For Don John enjoyed an advantage in having some 1,800 guns against the Turks' 750. Taking the centre himself, he put the Venetians on his left and Doria on his right. Crucially, he added weight to the line with six Venetian galleasses which were to ram and then make use of their devastating fire-power at close quarters, a tactic which probably sank 70 Ottoman ships. This was not to be a battle of tactics and manoeuvre. Don John aimed at achieving a breakthrough by head-on collision, victory by close fighting. There was a crucifix on every deck, and the Christians knelt at mass in gleaming armour before battle was joined.

Mindful of Famagosta, the Venetians became lions rather than foxes and were first to engage. Don John in *La Réal* made for the *Sultana* of Ali Pasha. Turkish gunnery was poor, but the fight raged for two hours before the head of Ali Pasha – renowned for his humanity in the treatment of slaves – was raised upon a pole. Doria meanwhile had been turned by the ferocity of Uluj Ali's attack, but the pirate saw the fight going against the Turk elsewhere and sensibly made off, taking a mere five galleys with him.[7]

While the significance of Lepanto is a matter for debate, there can be no reducing the scale of the Christian victory on the day, for on their side losses were lighter. While 15,000 Christians perished, Turkish losses were double that, and 113 of their galleys had been sunk, 117 more captured. It was to be the biggest battle of the sixteenth century.

A galley arrived in Venice with the news, 'dragging the Turkish ensigns through the water', and the city went wild. Philip II praised God and Don John, and wrote to his brother that he was 'pleased to a degree which it is impossible to exaggerate'. Cervantes, the creator of Don Quixote, certainly did not regard the victory as quixotic, recalling his own role in the preface to his *Exemplary Novels*:

> He [Cervantes] lost in the naval battle of Lepanto [the use of] his left hand from a shot of an arquebus – a wound which, although it appears ugly, he holds for lovely, because he received it on the most memorable and lofty occasion that past centuries have beheld – nor do those to come hope to see the like.

The celebrations were scarcely over when the realisation dawned that Turkish recovery, under the direction of the Grand Vizier, Mehmet Sököllü, was under way. The Venetians acknowledged the loss of Cyprus, and agreed to pay an indemnity of 300,000 ducats. In 1573, Philip of Spain received a Venetian ambassador who brought the bitter news that the Republic had withdrawn from the Holy League. The following year, Tunis fell to the Turks, and pirates reigned supreme in Algiers and Tripoli. 'It was a memorable victory, but they made no progress', judged Giovanni Botero of Lepanto looking back in the year 1589, and subsequent historians on the whole have shared this view. The truce between Philip II and Selim in 1581 can easily be seen as the recognition by both sides that they faced more important problems elsewhere than the Mediterranean: Philip had to deal with Protestantism in the Netherlands, Selim with the rising power of Shah Abbas of Persia.[8] Furthermore, there were signs of strain in the political and social structures of the Ottoman Empire itself.

The shadow of the mast

There is a sense in which the Ottoman military machine had its own 'natural limits' in terms of the distances which it could travel, while maintaining lines of communication and supply. This distance was determined by the limited availability of the timariots, that is to say for the duration of a campaigning season no longer than the period from March to October – no measure of the independence of the *sipahis*, merely sensible in allowing time for their horses to rest and gather strength in between campaigns. By such reckoning, the radius of

Ottoman advance would be a maximum of around 100 days. Any extension westward, as we have seen, might also be limited by events in the east, and by the necessary presence of the sultan himself at Istanbul. The incapacity of those who governed the empire to remedy such organisational problems through institutional reform or reorganisation can also be linked to notions of social and political atrophy, which are attractive, but a trifle vague when viewed as 'internal problems'. It is important not to see internal signs of strain as the cause of some sort of 'lucky escape' for Christendom. Rather we need to take into account what had changed in the west in the course of the century. Perhaps such an approach helps to explain why the Ottoman threat, so powerful when the period opened, had receded by the time it closed.

That threat was terrifying after 1453. What could stand against an empire with bottomless resources of manpower devoted to permanent war? At its fullest extent – whatever the 'social atrophy' within it – the empire's borders were some 9,000 miles in length, and this chapter has sought to demonstrate that the shadow of the crescent stretched still further. However, the military experience of the Turks in the sixteenth century reveals an empire which assumed that continuous war meant continuous conquest. It is worth remembering that the Turks gained a massive victory over imperial forces at Keresten in Hungary in 1595, and that they laid siege to Vienna as late as 1683. The frontier empire had shown an apparently infinite capacity for territorial extension. In many ways, the conquest of land and its redistribution to client rulers who then became glorified timariots was a most efficient way of expanding the capacity of the imperial military machine for it did not necessitate the involvement of administrators or colonists.

It is true that the timariot system was not well-suited to certain key roles in sixteenth-century warfare. A cavalryman who campaigned seasonally was of small use in manning a garrison throughout the year, and his horse was of small use if the rider was required to fight on ship. While Christendom so often seemed to be on the defensive against the Turks, in the key areas of siege warfare and sea warfare it was the Christian powers that held the initiative. The obstacles which they could place in the path of conquest exposed weaknesses of Ottoman military organisation which might otherwise have been concealed. Time and again in this chapter we have seen the Turk victorious in the field but demoralised before the bastion. At Vienna in 1529, Güns in 1532, Corfu in 1537 and of course Malta in 1565, Christian garrisons remained in place after a Turkish siege. Belgrade fell in 1521, and Rhodes in 1522, but in both cases small numbers of defenders won honourable terms of withdrawal, and even the awful saga of Famagosta (1571) did not see the Turks victorious by storm.

Christian fortunes at sea in the Mediterranean were mixed, but it is notable that whatever the historian may decide about the aftermath of

Lepanto, the Turks never again risked a naval confrontation with Christendom on such a scale. Moreover, the anachronistic or even irrelevant character of the battle – crusader warfare in a theatre of declining importance – is exaggerated by failure to take proper account of the war with the Turk as part of a general process of Europe's definition, with implications far beyond the Mediterranean. Spanish power – and Spanish galleons – operated in both theatres and perhaps the assumption that the Ottoman threat came and went independent of developments in Christian Europe should be questioned. The extent of Ottoman power – its 9,000 miles of borders, its capacity to threaten Muscovy and Gibraltar simultaneously – is surely impressive (see Map 11.1).

But how much greater was the power which could outflank it! While this was never achieved by territorial power, it was achieved at sea. And western ships turned the flank of the mighty Ottoman Empire, establishing a frontier in the Indian Ocean. Whatever the internal divisions of Christendom, there is an unplanned coherence in its maritime expansion which laid the foundations of future power. In many ways, the pattern of development based on secure strongholds and powerful navies was set in the Mediterranean in the sixteenth century. While Europe's early modern empires came to control about 35 per cent of the world's land surface, let us think for a moment of the sea – two-thirds of the world's surface – and examine the growing crescent of western power (see Map 11.2).

In the sixteenth century this extended from Archangel to Mexico City to Macao. In 1553, the Tudor venturer Richard Chancellor penetrated Muscovy from Archangel and began western involvement in the trade of the Caspian. Anthony Jenkinson's journeys after 1557 established a commercial nexus which might take in the bloaters of Yarmouth and the tapestries of Samarkand. The Muscovy Company was inspired by the Venetian, Sebastian Cabot, whose westward voyages had taken him as far afield as Newfoundland. The eastward venture shifted the base of English global enterprise from Bristol to London and led London merchants to invest in a joint-stock enterprise. The one extension reinforced the other. We are apt to think of trade between eastern and western Europe in terms of grain. At the same time, the naval supplies of eastern Europe – timber, tar, potash, flax, hemp and tallow – carried through the Baltic ensured that western shipping could face the bad weather of the Atlantic's heavy seas. The Muscovy Company was a joint-stock enterprise, and many of those who served it were involved in other oceanic initiatives: to Guinea, the Caribbean and Brazil, for instance, and to Baffin Island. London was taking its place at the centre of the Atlantic economy, just as Venice had once done in the Mediterranean.

Map 11.1 The Ottoman Empire in the sixteenth century

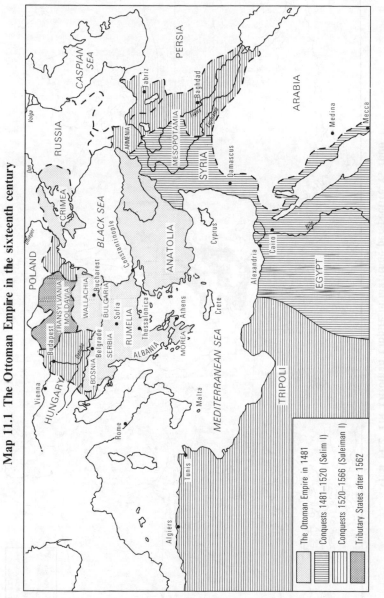

The Ottoman Empire in 1481

Conquests 1481–1520 (Selim I)

Conquests 1520–1566 (Suleiman I)

Tributary States after 1562

Source: H. G. Koenigsberger, *Early Modern Europe, 1500–1789* (London: Longman Group (UK), 1988). p. 78.

Map 11.2 The Ottoman Empire in maritime perspective, *c.* 1600

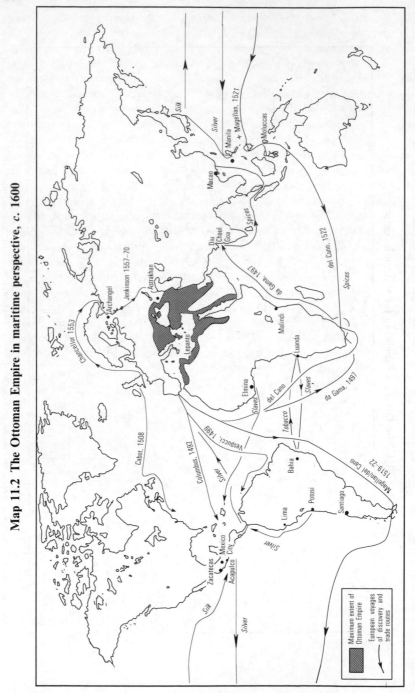

Silk

Silver

Manila + Magellan, 1521

Moluccas

Macao

Spices

Diu
Chaul
Goa

del Cano, 1522

da Gama, 1497

Spices

Jenkinson 1557–70

Astrakhan

Archangel

Chancellor 1553

Lepanto

Malindi

Luanda

da Gama, 1497

Elmina

Slaves

del Cano

Slaves

Cabot, 1508

Columbus, 1492

Silver

Vespucci, 1499

Tobacco

Magellan/del Cano
1519–22

Bahia

Potosi

Santiago

Lima

Silk

Mexico City

Zacatecas

Acapulco

Silver

Silver

Maximum extent of
Ottoman Empire

European voyages
of discovery and
trade routes

Simultaneously, the guns and sails of the Portuguese protected their dominion of the Indian Ocean. In 1571 – the year of Lepanto – 1,000 Portuguese held Chaul against a siege force of 140,000 Muslims.

How many thousand miles of borders could the western maritime empires now boast? They had girdled the earth. This is not to deny the strengths of Ottoman sea power. We have seen the corsairs at their formidable best in the Mediterranean, and they were capable of great victories in coastal fights in Arabia and Africa – but not in the open ocean. While Ottoman power rested on large armies which could be held up by small garrisons in well-built forts, western navies increased cargo space, decreased crews, and they defended themselves with cannon, thus increasing wealth and power simultaneously. The potential of this combination became much clearer in the seventeenth and eighteenth centuries: the United Provinces and then Great Britain became 'great powers' not because of their command of territory, but because of their command of the seas. The combination of sea power and the rational calculation of material advantage are characteristics of the mercantilist era, when the furtherance of commercial interest became a matter of policy.[9] The potency of the combination may already be glimpsed in the sixteenth century, and is most tellingly revealed by the contrasting fortunes of the Ottoman territorial empire and the maritime imperialism of the west. The process which combined sea power and economic gain was, however, obscured and interrupted by civil war in Christendom itself.

12 Catholics and Protestants

Religion, sovereignty and consent

The roots of conflict

The civil wars in Christendom which set Catholic and Protestant against each other form one of the great tragedies in the European experience. This has become a truism – something so obvious that it scarcely requires further discussion. The elements of the tragedy are easily rehearsed. The wars sprang from a fatal confusion of religion and politics which made blind prejudice and naked ambition the matrices of action – and contemporaries could not distinguish the two. In 1559, the Venetian ambassador in France, Giovanni Michiel, reported categorically that the power struggle which he witnessed was purely secular, comparable with that of Caesar and Pompey in ancient, pagan Rome, 'these wars are born of the wish of the Cardinal of Lorraine to have no equal, and the Admiral [Coligny] and the house of Montmorency to have no superior'. Two years later, the same ambassador was equally categorical in his assertion that religion was the cause of revolutions: 'It is common knowledge', he said, 'that, with a change of religion, there will of necessity follow changes of states'. The rational intelligence could only conclude that a religion which preached brotherly love was subject to cynical misuse. From his Olympian retreat, Montaigne lamented what he observed, that is to say, religion used irreligiously:

> Let us confess the truth; whoever should draw out from the army, even that raised by the king, those who take up arms out of pure zeal to religion (and also those who only do it to protect the laws of their country, or for the service of their prince) could hardly, out of both these put together, make one complete company of *gens-d'armes*.

It took European statesmen more than a century to conclude that confessional attachments could not be allowed to dictate international relations or domestic politics. The confusion of religion and politics was resolved – partially and impermanently – only after the insanity of the Thirty Years' War – in which, for instance, a Lutheran king fought a Catholic emperor and saved German Protestantism with the blessing of the pope and a subsidy from the cardinal who ruled France. The grim lesson was that only sovereign secular states could guarantee peace and order.

It is understandable that historians have followed Montaigne in lamenting the excruciating events which stunted the growth of toleration in the life of the state. On the other hand, this perspective provides a distortion of its own, for in many ways, the overidentification of modernity with secularism in the development of the state exaggerates the distance which separates us from a world in which religion and politics were confused. The quest for freedom of conscience in the face of burgeoning state power can appear 'modern' and 'secular', for it was a struggle between the principles of sovereignty and consent – principles at the root of representative government. Yet what we should guard against is the idea that religion was some sort of constricting dead skin, diseased tissue which had to be sloughed off before modern politics could emerge in their secular form.[1]

Previous chapters in this section have suggested that such a progression, if it took place at all, was not so linear or so direct as often implied. After all, the conflict of Habsburg and Valois was not one of religion. These Catholic powers fought each other to a standstill in Italy for power and glory. Nor was this particularly novel, as the secular strife of the Wars of the Roses or the Hundred Years' War bears witness. On the other hand, the great struggle between Christendom and Islam was between rival faiths, sworn enemies in the matter of whose God was right. It drew strength from the Spanish *Reconquista*, and behind that, from the crusade. Paradoxically, it is the secular conflict which shows the weakness of state structures, particularly the instability and caprice of dynastic politics, while the 'old-fashioned' crusade against the infidel is suggestive of the growing power of a Europe which was to exercise global dominion in the modern age.

This chapter seeks to reduce still further the historical and cultural divide between our world and the age of the Wars of Religion, emphasising the changing – and increasing – role of religion in creating both order and instability in the life of the state. Put another way, until 1555 religion helped to create territorial sovereignty, and after 1555 it almost destroyed it. In that earlier period, first in Spain, then in England, then with variations in Germany, there seemed to take shape a remarkable resolution of an ancient debate conducted in terms of Roman and feudal law – from those points of view secular in emphasis – which established territorial sovereignty by placing the monarch at the head of the Church in a given region. In a deep sense the Renaissance preoccupation with the classical world synthesised with the medieval experience as humanism and scholasticism absorbed each other. Before Calvin's faction triumphed in Geneva in 1555, and prepared the way for Calvin's ideological ascendancy, religion seemed the surest means of defining both territorial sovereignty and nationhood, and this was to prove critical in defining a relationship between state and society which became one of the most distinctive features of the congeries of countries and values which has become known as 'the modern West'.

After 1555, the subversion of territorial sovereignty in the name of universal religion first by Calvinists, and then by the militant Catholic reaction created a conflict also quite familiar to modern eyes. Insurgency and counter-insurgency, assassination, kidnap, massacre, propaganda – these are all surely part of modern politics, and few modern states can afford to ignore them. They appear for the first time in European history not at a moment of increasing secularism but at a time of religious intensification. Religion, in other words, was inescapable. To discuss its political role in the sixteenth century in terms of a fatal confusion is in many ways no more helpful than saying that ideological conviction is likely to influence policy and action. As well as looking for 'schollers of Machiavell', which was often a rhetorical term of abuse rather than a rational description, we should remember the deep religious conviction of the Reformation Parliament in Scotland, the uncompromising zeal of Gaspard de Coligny, the Huguenot troops marching to war singing psalms, the deep Catholic commitment of Philip II and the Jesuit king-slayers. Analysis of the wars reveals rather more calculation and rather less hypocrisy than is sometimes implied.

Indeed, the dynamic interaction of religious ideology and political action is inherent in the very word 'Protestant'. In 1529, the Imperial Diet assembled at Speyer. The preoccupation of Charles V – secure for the moment in his wars with the Valois and the Turk – was to re-establish the unity of the Catholic church. This is unremarkable: the Emperor wielded a sword which was the secular counterpart of the spiritual blade which the Pope controlled. That division had caused trouble within Christendom for centuries: further division had to be avoided at all costs. The Emperor urged withdrawal of all concessions made to Lutherans in the 1520s. Six princes, including John of Saxony, George of Brandenburg-Ansbach and Philip of Hesse, and 14 cities, protested against this policy – hence the identification of the protesters with Lutheranism, and hence Protestantism. Thus, though the term is identified with a set of religious beliefs, it derives from a refusal voiced by secular rulers in a secular assembly against their secular superior – in the matter of religion. The carefully legitimated resistance to imperial authority – imperial in the sense of absolute and supreme on earth – in the name of religion is the chief cause of the conflicts which bedevilled Christendom in various theatres of war – notably but not only in France, the Netherlands and Germany – for more than 100 years. To ascribe the duration and savagery of the fighting to the cynical manoeuvres of Machiavellian rulers is to miss the profundity of what was at stake, and the deep historical roots of the conflict. The many examples of short-term opportunism should not obscure the pedigree of the principles which were involved, principles transmitted from the ancient world and transmuted in the Middle Ages.

Charles's imperial authority was based on Roman-law concepts of *imperium*, the authority enjoyed by a Roman emperor, who held the title *princeps* or prince. The Roman imperial power furnished later generations with the idea of absolutism. This term derives from the idea that the *princeps* was *legibus absolutus* – not bound by the law. Indeed the will of the prince, the *voluntas principis*, was itself the law: *quidquid principi placuit legis habet vigorem*. It is surely no surprise that a sixteenth-century ruler seeking to assert his own authority – be he Henry VIII or the Duke of Cleves – would claim to be emperor in his own lands: *imperator in regno suo*. What prevented the emergence of this startling power as autocracy – the absolute authority of one person? This is an important question, for it helps to define what sets the west apart from the autocratic regimes of Muscovy and the Ottoman Empire. The obstacles were not new discoveries, political innovations, they were principles forged in the Middle Ages, principles not secular and modern but Christian and feudal.

The principles of the Roman law were kept alive after the fall of the western empire by the papacy – a sovereign princely office superior to all earthly powers, as Gregory VII asserted during the Investiture Contest of the late eleventh century. However, the canon-lawyers of the Middle Ages drew a clear distinction between the person of the pope and his office (which is why Luther's assault on the office itself constituted a revolution). The exercise of power was not personal, and a person unfit for the office could forfeit it. A pope was elected by the representatives of the community of Christians, the *ecclesia*, and these representatives assembled in council. The canonists developed the notion that what affected all members of the community had to be approved by them – *quod omnes tangit, ab omnibus approbetur* – and if the approval was not universal then, if necessary, the will of the majority, the *maior pars*, would have to carry the day. Armed with such concepts, the representatives of the *ecclesia* could enforce forfeiture of the papal office if they deemed its holder personally unsuited. Nor was this purely theoretical. In 1415 the Council of Constance had asserted its authority in this way, and proclaimed itself superior to the papacy in order to bring the Great Schism to an end.

The Christian Church then, had imposed restraints on the personal authority of its Roman-law *princeps*. The emperor, on the other hand, found his Roman-law authority checked by the body of secular Germanic custom which became known as feudalism. The most significant practice in terms of the nature of sovereignty was the elevation of the chosen leader of a war-band on the shields of his warriors: in other words, an election. If this seems somewhat remote from the Europe of the sixteenth century, then one might recall that it was precisely this practice which the Huguenot theorist, François Hotman, used to illustrate the elective character of the French monarchy:

> I think it is clear that the kings of Francogallia were constituted by the people and not by hereditary right . . . Tacitus indicates that the Caninefates, a Frankish people, placed the king-designate upon a shield and carried him high upon their shoulders, and we have noted that the same was done with our kings. Whoever had been chosen by the people was lifted to men's shoulders, seated on a shield, and carried three times around the assembly of the people or the army, while everyone applauded and shouted their approval.

Throughout the Middle Ages, the absolute authority of Roman-law sovereignty proved impossible to enforce against the fief-holders of Germany, who gained increasing power at the imperial expense. In 1356, an imperial edict known as the Golden Bull formalised arrangements for the election of the Holy Roman Emperor by a college composed of the King of Bohemia, the Dukes of Brandenburg and Saxony, the Count Palatine and the Bishops of Mainz, Cologne and Trier.

Thus, sovereignty defined in the language of the Roman law for the offices of Pope and Emperor had in the Middle Ages been modified by principles of consent embodied in the representatives of the *populus christianus* and of the German nation.[2]

From resolution to revolution

This might seem a rather laborious route to a rather trite point: that the waning of the medieval empire and the decline of the medieval papacy eventually made way, via dynasticism and absolutism, for the nation-states of the modern world. It was a long and complicated process, and what needs to be heavily underlined is that the states of the sixteenth century were not secular states. It might well be logical to see the assertion of an imperial authority in ecclesiastical matters within a given territory as a subversion of papal and imperial power by territorial monarchs, but that assertion was met by the same arguments which had checked the powers of medieval popes and emperors, arguments which drew strength from Christian principles of church government and from feudal law. The one knew no territorial bounds, the other knew only local privilege. What would become of the sovereign power if universal and local causes combined against it? Rather than producing a larger number of more manageable sovereign entities, the process of state formation multiplied the possible theatres of conflict – perhaps *ad infinitum*, as the formation of a Huguenot 'state-within-a-state' in France seemed to portend, as did William of Orange's claim that he had 'the name of an absolute and free Prince, though in deede my Princedome be not verie great'.

It is significant that the examples of France and the Netherlands bring to the fore the question of Calvinist influence. The adoption of Protestantism was not a precondition of religious sovereignty in the territorial state. Until 1555 – yes, even after Luther's assault on the papacy – the gradual creation of national churches under monarchical headship had not always necessitated a breach with Rome, and one phase of the conflict of sovereignty and consent seemed to have been resolved. Rather than putting this down to the gradual decline of the papacy's power and prestige, what took place was the resolution of the great medieval debate between sovereignty and consent in the spiritual and temporal spheres in different regional contexts, the papacy taking its place as an Italian and European state without necessarily sacrificing its spiritual supremacy.

In this perspective, perhaps resolution is a more appropriate term than revolution for what happened in Tudor government in the 1530s. Henry VIII was not a Protestant but a schismatic Catholic, and yet his headship of the Church was an imperial supremacy which nullified papal power and invalidated canon law. This is clear from the preamble of the Act in Restraint of Appeals (designed to prevent Catherine of Aragon from taking her case against divorce to Rome):

> this Realm of Englond is an Impire . . . governed by oon Supreme heede and King having the Dignitie and Roiall Estate of the Imperiall Crowne of the same, unto whome a Body politicke compacte of all sortes and degrees of people, devided in termes and by names of Spiritualtie and Temporaltie, ben bounden and owen to bere nexte to God a naturall and humble obedience.

The Act for the Punishment of Heresy (1534) made it clear that the canon law was 'mere repugnante and contrarious to the prerogatyve of your ymperyall Crowne regal jurisdiccion lawes statutes and ordynaunces of this your Realme'. The Act of Dispensations, however, contained a formulation of genius which melded the representative principle (consent) to the imperial theme (sovereignty) by placing legislative sovereignty firmly with the king in Parliament:

> In all and everey suche lawes humayne made within this Realme . . . your Royall Majestie and your Lordes Spirituall and temporall and Commons, representyng the holle state of your Realme in this your most high Courte of Parliament, have full power and auctoritie . . . the seid lawes . . . to abrogate adnull amplyfie or dymynyshe.

Such a formulation did not eliminate conflict between sovereignty and consent in religious matters – the tragedy of Thomas More is a reminder of that – but it may have reduced the possibility and certainly postponed the advent of outright civil war.

In the states of the Empire, and in Scandinavia, the sovereign declared outright for Lutheranism without lengthy consultations: such was the case in Hesse (1526), Württemberg (1535), and ducal Saxony (1539), in Denmark (1526), in Sweden (1527), and in Norway (1539). The success of the Peace of Augsburg in giving Germany half a century of relative religious peace surely lay in the clarity with which the treaty allocated sovereign power in religious matters to the territorial ruler – *cuius regio, eius religio*, as it became known.[3]

Yet 1555 was a turning-point, for it marked a transition from resolution to revolution, even though the roots of both remained in the remote past. The Peace of Augsburg allowed the ruler a choice between Lutheranism and allegiance to Rome. It made no provision for Calvin's doctrine, which consolidated its position in Geneva in that same year and subsequently threatened to wreck the principle of territorial sovereignty. This was not because of its doctrine of resistance – which the leaders of Lutheran Germany had formulated – but because of its capacity for subversion, which encouraged the violation of territorial sovereignty in the name of true religion. This helps to explain why it is impossible to confine discussion of the French Wars of Religion or the Dutch Revolt to clear national contexts.

In France and the Netherlands in the second half of the century, the struggle was evenly poised: first in Germany, then in France and the Netherlands, it is the tyrant who becomes the rebel, and it is a Christian duty to resist him, even kill him. As the century toiled to its close, one of the most creative tensions in European history, that between society and the state, seemed to have become a paralysis, and no one could meet the cost of a cure. What is most striking in view of the developments of the next hundred years is that divine-right absolutism seemed incapable of overcoming divine-right resistance. However, the first symptoms of utter powerlessness in the powerful appeared in the body politic of Charles V.

Lutheranism and resistance, 1521–55

Given the extraordinary inheritances of Charles V (above, pp. 59–61, 231–3), the chronic weakness of imperial power before his election is easily forgotten. He was enmeshed in the confusing power structures which had compromised imperial authority throughout the Middle Ages – and the Reformation had added to the interlacing. This becomes plain from an examination of the balance of power in the Empire at the start of the century and the changes in that balance which the Reformation brought about. What is remarkable is not that Charles V faced humiliation in 1552 and that this was effectively institutionalised in 1555, but that he seemed to have triumphed so utterly between 1545 and 1547 – especially given his far-from-harmonious relations with his Austrian brother, Ferdinand, who was further distracted by his wars with the Turks (above, pp. 254–5).

Within the borders of the Empire were a host of cities and principalities ecclesiastical and temporal, which had steadily gained in independence throughout the Middle Ages and in the early years of the sixteenth century. Some 85 cities claimed to acknowledge no authority but the Emperor's, which was an expression of local independence rather than loyalty to the Empire, an allegiance to a remote idea rather than a local lord, as is shown by the history of Nuremberg. The city won a victory over the Margrave of Brandenburg at the start of the century, and the Reformation was forced on the city council by popular demand in 1524. Although Nuremberg did not join the Schmalkaldic League to resist the Emperor in 1530, the city government had called for the formation of such a union and refused to enforce the Emperor's Edict of Worms outlawing Lutheranism. Might Nuremberg and other cities – such as Ulm and Strasbourg – form another confederation like that of the Swiss? The precedents for armed resistance were recent but secure. Amongst the Swiss, Charles's grandfather and predecessor, Maximilian I, had sought to reassert imperial authority and suffered military defeat in the Swabian War of 1499. Basel joined the Confederation in 1501, Mühlhausen and Rottweil followed. How many more cities might 'turn Swiss', strengthening civic autonomy with religious independence? And what would happen if, as Zwingli urged, the king of France supported such a move (above, pp. 157–8)? Such possibilities – which were genuine enough – are a reminder of the popular pressure for the Reformation in the cities which governments simply could not ignore, even at the risk of the Emperor's wrath.[4]

Such popular pressure almost pushed Cologne into the Lutheran camp – despite the fact that its prince-bishop was an elector of the Emperor (above, p. 101). Along with the other episcopal electors, at Trier and Mainz, and with the Bishops of Metz, Strasbourg and Worms, ecclesiastics dominated the upper Rhine. In the north-west were more bishoprics – Utrecht, Bremen, Münster and Paderborn – and in central Germany lay Hildesheim, Halberstadt, Magdeburg, Würzburg and Bamberg. Along with Salzburg and Trier further south, the bishoprics were agents of papal exactions and therefore rich pickings for princes who could secularise their lands.

With the cities in ferment, and the bishops the focus of much urban anti-clericalism, the religious attitudes of the princes of the Empire were decisive. If the Emperor failed in his duty to protect the German nation from the depredations of Rome, might not the representatives of the German nation withdraw their allegiance to the Empire? The indulgences which Luther denounced were part of 'the copious flow of German money' to papal coffers, against which the humanist, Jakob Wimpfeling, railed in 1515, and which figure so prominently in the grievances presented to Charles V at the Diet of Worms in 1521.

The Habsburgs' chief rivals among the German dynasties were the Houses of Wittelsbach in the south, of Hohenzollern and Wettin in the north. Each of them was divided into 'branches' occupying different territories, and for at least part of the century, the different branches held to different confessions (see Map 12.1 on pages 278–9).

The Wittelsbach dukes controlled Bavaria, which remained staunchly Catholic, though their jealousy of the Habsburgs meant that their support of the imperial cause was never energetic. But first the Wettin and then the Hohenzollern offered their formidable support to Lutheranism.

The so-called Ernestine branch of the Wettin dynasty commanded the electorate of Saxony (and therefore Wittenberg). Frederick the Wise (1486–1525) remained Catholic but sheltered Luther, and his successors, John the Steadfast (1525–32) and John Frederick (1532–54), took up and sustained the Lutheran cause. The Albertine branch, who held the title of dukes, became Protestant through Henry (1535–41). Their power is exemplified in the career of Maurice (1541–53), a Protestant who advanced the cause of Charles V from 1545 to 1547 (partly to secure the electoral title from the rival branch) and dashed it thereafter.

In effect, Frederick asserted a form of territorial sovereignty in religious matters similar to that of the Catholic Monarchs of Spain and Henry VIII. He was and remained a staunch Catholic, though he was genuinely interested in debate about doctrine, as his foundation of the University of Wittenberg confirms. In 1518, a papal representative, Cardinal Cajetan, interviewed Luther in Augsburg. He afterwards urged Frederick to expel Luther from Saxony, or even truss him up and send him to Rome. Frederick's refusal to do so was based on the fact that the Pope – who had already called Luther a 'son of iniquity' – had yet to declare him a heretic. 'His teaching has not been shown' – this from a Catholic – 'to be unjust, unchristian or heretical'. Asserting his moral responsibility as a ruler, he emphasised that 'our whole purpose is to fulfil the office of a Christian prince'. Luther's views demanded a hearing and he could not be 'condemned in advance'. There was no animus against Rome: 'We will not lightly permit ourselves to be drawn into error nor to be made disobedient to the Holy See', but the inclusion of the word 'lightly' suggests that compliance with Rome's wishes was not automatic.

But we must repeat that Frederick remained a Catholic. More positive princely support would be needed if Lutheranism was to survive the ban placed upon it by the Edict of Worms (1521). Here we must pause to reflect that with the cities in uproar and the countryside about to erupt in the war of 1525, the new religious ideas might easily have become associated with popular revolution. Unrest in the name of the new religion among artisans and peasants could easily have persuaded the authorities that their interests lay in the maintenance of the existing religion as the guarantee of the existing social order. It is one of the surest measures of genuine religious conviction that it was in 1525, the precise year of the peasant uprisings, that certain of the princes took the dangerous option. John the Steadfast, a Wettin elector of Saxony, was followed by a Hohenzollern, Albrecht of Brandenburg (1512–68). Albrecht ruled Prussia as Grand Master of the Order of Teutonic Knights. He dissolved the Order and became Duke of Prussia, and vassal of the King of Poland. The next year Landgrave Philip brought Hesse into the Lutheran faith. He was the prime mover behind the first stirrings of princely resistance in the name of religion, the League of Torgau (1526), which came to incorporate the Dukes of Brunswick and Mecklenburg, the Prince of Anhalt, and the Count of Mansfeld as well as Saxony and Hesse, and stood against implementation of the Edict of Worms in their territories. At the Diet of Speyer in 1526, they appeared to have made their point and it was agreed that urban and princely authorities were to do nothing more specific than answer to God and the emperor in their ecclesiastical arrangements. And with Charles in the ascendant at a second Diet of Speyer (1529), this was the group which made the fateful protest (above, p. 270) In the following year, the Protestants expanded and consolidated their ranks in the League of Schmalkalden, which for a time threatened to turn Catholicism out of Germany. The Schmalkaldic League consisted of 8 princes and 11 cities (including Magdeburg, Bremen, Lübeck and Strasbourg).

As early as 1529, Philip of Hesse appears to have been arguing that the states of the empire enjoyed their own *imperium*. In 1530, the theory came closer to practice when the Catholic majority at the Diet of Augsburg rejected Melanchthon's *Confession* and insisted on a return to religious unity within the empire. At this point, Luther's doubts about armed resistance dissolved. If the Emperor behaved as a tyrant then, 'in this instance it is necessary to fight back'. The Emperor's agents forfeited the respect due to their office even more comprehensively if they made war on the Protestants, indeed they came 'much closer to the name and quality which is termed rebellion'. The theme of the tyrant as rebel menaced the emergent notion of sovereignty.

It was Charles's other preoccupations with the Turk and the Valois which made him back down temporarily, but when he did so the League took positive action in the Protestant cause by restoring Ulrich to his Duchy of Württemberg, facilitated by the victory of Philip of

Map 12.1 Central Europe in the Reformation era

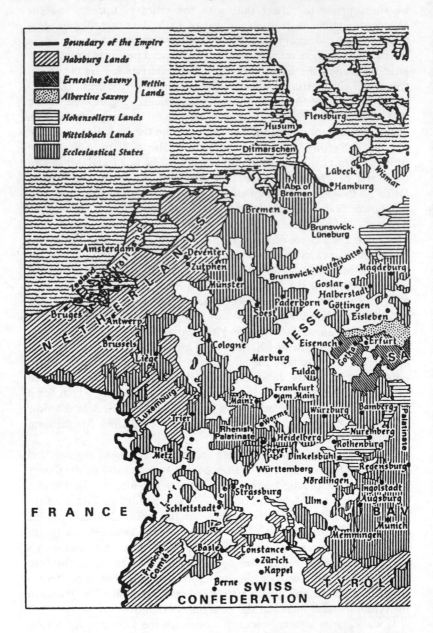

Source: A. G. Dickens, *The German Nation and Martin Luther* (London: HarperCollins Ltd (Fontana), 1976), pp. x–xi.

Stralsund
Rostock
Danzig
EAST PRUSSIA
Ermeland
POMERANIA
BRANDENBURG
Berlin
POLAND
Wittenberg
Leipzig
Mühlberg
SAXONY
Dresden
SILESIA
Zwickau
Prague
Cracow
BOHEMIA
Moravia
Upper
Passau
Vienna
HABSBURG-HUNGARY
ARIA
AUSTRIA
Salzburg
TURKISH
HUNGARY

Hesse's troops over the army of Ferdinand, the Emperor's brother, at the battle of Laufen. By 1539, of the important states of the empire, although only Saxony, Hesse and Württemberg were Lutheran, only Austria, Bavaria, the Palatinate, Brunswick-Wolfenbüttel and the three electoral bishoprics were still Catholic, and among the bishoprics, Cologne was far from steady.

Charles V is often portrayed as a worthy but slow-witted character, tied to medieval notions of the imperial office which can look quixotic in the Reformation era. Yet, in the 1540s, after twenty years of exhausting war, he used a version of 'social imperialism' – a call to sink all domestic differences in the interests of unity against a common alien foe – and a policy of divide and rule which seemed for a spell to have achieved brilliant success. At the Diet of Regensburg in 1541, Catholic and Protestant theologians reached a compromise on transubstantiation. Charles, sincerely in all likelihood, was urging the pope to call a General Council. This appeared to come to nothing when Laynez gored the compromise at Trent (above, pp. 186–9), and when the Chamber of Princes rejected it. All the same, Charles had demonstrated a capacity for conciliation which the princes appeared to disown, especially when the League of Schmalkalden drove Duke Henry out of Brunswick (1542), thus capturing for Lutheranism the last major Catholic principality in north Germany. Francis I had declared war in 1543 (above, p. 240) and Charles seemed beset by enemies without and within. In 1544, the Imperial Diet assembled yet again at Speyer. Charles revealed that Francis had offered him assistance against the Protestants (in return for the cession to him of Milan) in 1539, and reminded the assembled princes of France's alliance with the Turk. Continuing to hold out the prospect of a General Council, Charles secured support for his own war effort which brought defeat at Ceresole (above, p. 242), though a combined operation with Henry VIII threatened northern France. After the Peace of Crépy (1544), Charles had his hands free for the struggle against John Frederick of Saxony, Philip of Hesse, and the League of Schmalkalden. The General Council assembled at Trent, demonstrating his good faith. He warmed the support of the Wittelsbach by offering the prospect of transferring the electoral dignity to Bavaria itself should the Elector Palatine remain Protestant. Two of the Hohenzollern, John of Brandenburg-Küstrin and Albrecht Alcibiades, had not welcomed the restoration of Ulrich of Württemburg by the Schmalkaldic League and joined the imperial cause, persuaded that the leadership of Hesse and Electoral Saxony gave them little scope in the Protestant camp. Of the Wettin, Charles worked on Maurice of Saxony, the Albertine duke, offering him the prospect of the Saxon electoral dignity, as well as control over Saxon bishoprics which were a source of contention with the other branch of the house. Charles had split the League – for Maurice did not leave it, and other of its members had agreed to remain neutral. Moreover, he stressed that this was a secular matter – making a titanic effort, perhaps unique in the sixteenth century, and certainly beyond the capabilities of his son, Philip II – to separate heresy and rebellion. Resembling anything but the dull plodder familiar from the history books, he moved against the League by placing the imperial ban on those who did not submit to the jurisdiction of the *Reichskammer*.

The League mobilised forces provided by the princes John Frederick of Saxony, Philip of Hesse and Ulrich of Württemberg and by the cities of Augsburg, Strasbourg, Ulm and Constance. Maurice declared himself and, with Ferdinand, occupied Electoral Saxony. Charles had fought gruelling campaigns of stalemate against the Turks, he had won great victories in long wars in Italy against France. Decisive victory for one state or another in a short war had been unheard of in the century. In 1547, with a surprise attack through the fog near Mühlberg, the imperialists achieved just that. The Leaguer armies were routed.

The moment of triumph is caught in two of Titian's masterpieces. Charles is painted in the armour he wore at Mühlberg and astride the horse he rode there, serenely in control, steady in vision. He is supreme and alone. What a contrast with the awkward bulk of John Frederick, whom the Venetian painted in 1550: a mountain of fat flesh cannot reduce the psychological tension, and the beholder and the apprehensive subject look at each other as though through the peep-hole of a cell (plates 28 and 29).

Though Charles had shown energy and imagination in his conduct of the war, there was an ungracious petulance in the settlement which he imposed, and this was to cost him dear. Perhaps he regretted having granted Luther a safe conduct so many years before. Without magnanimity, Charles granted John Frederick his life. He inveigled Philip of Hesse into his presence (though the Landgrave had not taken part in the fighting) and had him arrested.

According to a famous version of the story, Maurice of Saxony, acting as the Emperor's intermediary, had instructions from Charles to promise Philip, who was his father-in-law, that there would be 'no imprisonment' (*'nicht einiges Gefängnis'*) while the Emperor maintained that the guarantee was of 'no perpetual imprisonment' (*'nicht ewiges Gefängnis'*). Even if apocryphal, the anecdote may preserve something of the pinched pettiness so inappropriate at so historic a moment, and of the breakdown of the Emperor's judgement in the 1550s. It may also suggest that something more than opportunism dictated the subsequent actions of Maurice of Saxony.

Yet for a moment Charles's victory seemed total. The Diets which met at Augsburg at the command of the victorious Emperor was compliant, and it looked as though German Protestants would attend the Council of Trent to end a schism of the Church and begin its reform. The Augsburg Interim declared the supremacy of the Pope at least as chief bishop, and deferred other matters for a meeting of the General Council of the Church. Charles seemed to favour a federal solution to the problems of the empire, along the lines of a reconstituted Swabian League, which at least suggested that he would not seek to rule in Germany as he could in Castile.

However, significant tensions remained unresolved. Trent was hit by plague and the Council transferred to the more agreeable milieu of Bologna, without concern, it seemed, that German representatives might not travel to a council held in papal territory. In Germany itself, a federal empire might be acceptable to the smaller territories, but not to those larger principalities which had laboured so hard to establish independence in religion. And that independence Charles would clearly not suffer: from that point of view adherence to ideas which he thought heretical amounted to rebellion against his imperial authority. Moreover, in fostering divisions within the German dynasties, Charles ignored that developing in his own. His brother was increasingly unhappy about arrangements for the imperial succession which might be detrimental to the interests of the Austrian Habsburgs, and in many ways Ferdinand offered the first outright opposition to Charles since Mühlberg. Placing the Netherlands outside imperial jurisdiction, perhaps with a view to allocating their wealth to Philip, was to prove a catastrophe.

At all events, fearful perhaps of the Emperor's new power and the threat that this posed to his own, Maurice of Saxony changed his allegiance. He was not the first to desert. John of Küstrin and Albrecht Alcibiades began to regroup Protestant powers in Germany – and opened negotiation with Henry II of France. This in itself was a threat to Maurice's interests, but he may well have felt resentment about Charles's treatment of his father-in-law, Philip of Hesse, and unease that since the Emperor's whim had spared John Frederick, it might also release him to reclaim his power in Saxony. Maurice, who was supposed to be imposing the Augsburg Interim on the city of Magdeburg, offered the citizens respectable terms which guaranteed their Protestantism. He then threw in his lot with Henry of France at Chambord in 1551. With Charles at Innsbruck waiting to move to Trent, Maurice joined Philip's son William of Hesse, while Henry seized Metz, Toul and Verdun. With Ferdinand anxious to come to terms with the Protestant powers of his future empire, Charles was helpless. The victor of Mühlberg, tortured by gout and unable to ride, fled in a litter from Innsbruck to Villach. In 1552, with Ferdinand counselling compliance for the sake of peace, Charles accepted that those who adhered to the Confession of Augsburg of 1530 (above, p. 151) were free to do so, and John Frederick of Saxony and Philip of Hesse were released.

Henry II was not party to the treaty, and Charles sought – unsuccessfully – to retake Metz in a siege which, by a quirk of history, set those Catholic champions the Dukes of Alba and Guise against each other. Maurice died – at only 33 – from wounds received in trying to catch his former ally, Albrecht Alcibiades.

In 1555, as Charles languished, broken in body and spirit, Ferdinand presided over the Diet of Augsburg. Its greatest success was to acknowledge the religious division of Germany, while preserving the principle of sovereignty. The ruler of a region was to choose between Catholicism and Lutheranism. Those who could not conform to his choice were free to depart the land. Prince-bishops could not become Lutheran but must remain loyal to Rome. It was a settlement which did not concede toleration to the individual, but the principle of sovereignty through headship of the Church which it expressed, and which had already produced stable states in England and Spain gave Germany over 60 years of internal peace after almost 40 years of conflict.[5] No settlement clarifying the relationship of sovereignty and belief had been reached in France.

The subversion of Scotland and France

With the Treaty of Cateau-Cambrésis in 1559, Philip II of Spain and Henry II of France brought an end to the conflict of Habsburg and Valois. When Habsburg Spain next fought with France, it faced a new dynasty, that of Bourbon. After the sudden death of Henry II (above, p. 242), the realisation rapidly dawned that the new sovereign was a boy of 15, and that Protestantism in France had acquired a new and purposeful coherence by absorbing the doctrines which emanated from Geneva. In the maze of events which constitute the 8 civil wars which ensued, the most striking feature is the total breakdown of statehood as contemporaries understood it. Two 'revolutionary parties' faced each other. The Calvinists had their own organisation of colloquies and synods regional and national, and it was scarcely underground. The Catholic Guise moved to control the machinery of appointment to office as soon as Henry died. Both sides could mobilise private armies in the name of a religion which transcended the boundaries of France. Favour, faith and force were beyond royal control. The result was anarchy, the absence of statehood. Religion had brought the state into being, religion was poised to destroy it.

As in the case of Charles V's Germany, the monarchy faced three powerful houses of conflicting religious allegiances: Navarre, Montmorency and Guise. The House of Navarre came to the Protestant cause (though King Antoine died in 1562 from wounds received fighting for Catholicism), the Guise remained tenaciously Catholic,

284

Figure 12.1 The Houses of Valois, Orleans, Burgundy, Bourbon and Guise

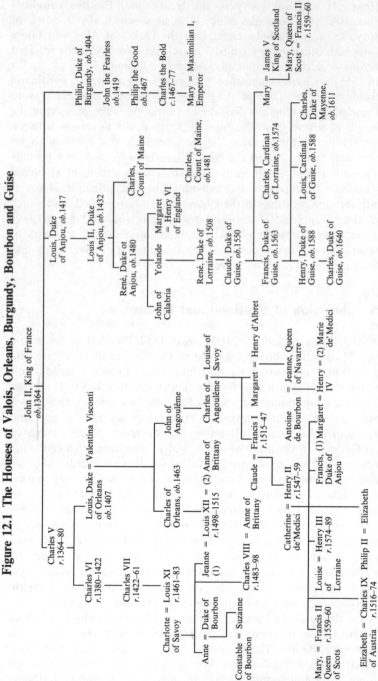

Source: A. G. Dickens, *The Age of Humanism and Reformation* (New York: Prentice-Hall International Inc., 1977), pp. 264–5.

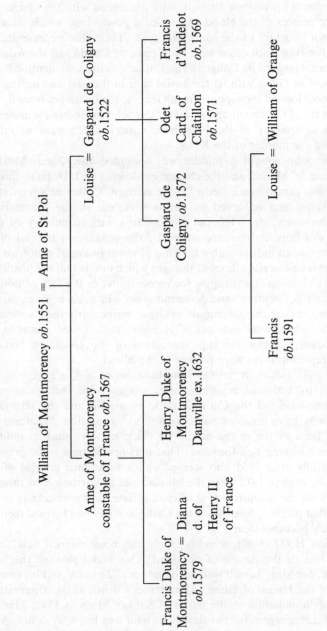

Figure 12.2 The Houses of Montmorency and Coligny

Source: J. H. Elliott, *Europe Divided, 1559–1598* (London: HarperCollins Ltd, 1968), p. 408.

and the House of Montmorency, led by the Constable of France, Anne, was first among the Catholic leadership, but became pro-Protestant in the person of his nephew Francis, who quarrelled with the Guise. The Navarre princes of the blood controlled a power base which included their own kingdom in the south and west. Their chief representatives within the Huguenot cause were the Prince de Condé and the Admiral of France, Gaspard de Coligny. The Catholic cause was identified with the House of Guise with its territorial base in the east and north. The Huguenots looked for support from Geneva, the Catholics from Spain. The agents of Calvinism and of Jesuit Catholicism showed a disregard for the sovereignty of the French monarchy which went as far as justifying the murder of the King.

Those who sought a middle way included the Queen Mother, Catherine de' Medici, and the chancellor, Michel de L'Hôpital, though neither has gained much credit for the attempt. Catherine's reputation is blackened and reddened by her involvement in the Massacre of St Bartholomew, de L'Hôpital's effort to create machinery of civil justice was hopelessly compromised by the venality of judicial office which remained indispensable because of royal financial problems.

There is a powerful school of thought which insists that the history of French Calvinism is a 'struggle for recognition', in the face of policies of 'savage persecution' and 'extermination'. In such a scenario, the prime movers are the unscrupulous Guise, particularly the Cardinal of Lorraine, who, at the moment of Henry's death, seized power in the royal council despite the superior claims of the House of Navarre whose representatives were princes of the blood.

However, events in Scotland in 1559, when a Guise regent was deposed by Calvinist revolutionaries suggest that there was more justification behind the Catholic sense of alarm, and the seizure of power may have involved panic as well as calculation. Whatever the reality, fears of the extent of the Calvinist network and its military capacity appeared well-founded. That network seemed to be growing purposefully after 1555 and seemed about to assume control of the monarchy itself in 1572 when the Massacre of St Bartholomew thrust it bloodily on the defensive. It is after that date, and particularly in the 1580s, that precisely how much the Catholic party had learned from its adversary becomes clear.

Francis II (1559–60), a sickly child, had been married in 1558 to Mary, heir to the throne of Scotland. This had tightened the 'auld alliance', for Mary herself was the daughter of James V and his consort Mary of the House of Guise. After James's death in the aftermath of the Scots humiliation at the battle of Solway Moss in 1542, Mary of Guise became regent for her daughter, who was but a week old. As in France, the first stirrings of the Reformation were brief awakenings from a troubled sleep. In both cases, Geneva was the stimulus to wakefulness and vision. Given the dynastic connection, what happened in Scotland, and particularly the speed with which it happened, had startling implications for France: a Catholic regent was suddenly deposed by a Calvinist revolution, justified by an ideology of lawful resistance to tyranny. With the clear rejection of Catholicism in England after the death of Mary Tudor and the accession of Elizabeth in 1558, Mary of Guise faced the possibility of a Protestant alliance which might cross the border. It is in this context that the return of Knox in May 1559 proved significant. After his inflammatory preaching, there was a riot in Perth and religious houses in the town were ransacked. It was only 22 May when the 'Congregation of Christ Jesus in Scotland', which had formed with suspicious rapidity, gave the regent a polite but unqualified warning about persecution :

> we are constrained, by unjust tyranny proposed against us . . . that except this cruelty be stayed by your wisdom, we will be compelled to take the sword of just defence against all that shall pursue us for the matter of religion and for conscience sake.

This appeared to be a very early instance of Calvin's doctrine actually being put into execution. Opponents of Calvinism could point to Scotland to show that such resistance had always been justified in Calvinist ideology, and indeed was natural to it. The 'Congregation' arrived in Edinburgh in July – the month of Henry II's death in France – and installed Knox as minister, and the provisional government, protesting its loyalty to the crown, deposed the regent in October. Mary of Guise did not receive much support from her cousins because they were mustering their strength for what would clearly be a much greater struggle in France itself.[6]

The formation of the Congregation in Scotland is in many ways paralleled on the grand scale by the activation of Calvinist cells in France, which had been forming since 1555. It would be a distortion to see the apparent mobilisation as the result of orchestration from Geneva. But there was a sense of momentum in their own numbers, and a threat perceived – though magnified – in the light of events in Scotland. Equally, therefore, it would be a distortion to isolate the Calvinist conspiracy of Amboise of 1560 – which clearly aimed to kill the Duke of Guise, seize the King and instal the Bourbon in control of government – and make it the work of the young nobleman, La Renaudie, as though he were some unauthorised hothead. One of its subsequent defenders was, after all, the entirely respectable theorist of resistance, François Hotman. After events in Scotland, one might credibly argue that Calvinism seemed poised to create its own state in France and that the Catholics had a lot of ground to make up in the matter of party organisation. This point is somewhat obscured by

Calvinism's notable failure to make any real headway in Paris, before its penetration by Catholic agitators. In 1559, the only sensible option in the defence of Catholic interests was to launch a preemptive strike which assured control of the structures of patronage in order to build up a network of their own clients, before such power fell into the hands of the House of Navarre.

Calvin, we should remember, was deeply committed to the evangelisation of his native land. His first recorded missionary went to Poitiers in 1555, we know of 22 who went to other destinations in 1558 and 32 in 1559. They had been carefully trained to give a clear exposition of passages from the Bible, they travelled under false names, and Calvin advised them to make particular efforts to convert members of the nobility. One estimate suggests that more than half the French nobility came to support the Huguenot cause, with aristocratic women – such as Jeanne d'Albret, Queen of Navarre – particularly prominent. The missionaries reached a wider audience, however. By 1562, it is reckoned that there were more than 200 Calvinist congregations in France and that as many as 1,800 other Protestant congregations had surfaced during toleration. French Calvinism's first national synod met in Paris in 1559, and there were to be ten more before the end of the century. The missionaries were armed with books from the presses of Geneva – which produced more than 27,000 copies of Béza's Psalms in 1561–2 – but they did not preach the word alone. They were fully aware that they would face charges of sedition, and rather than producing arguments to demonstrate that they were not, they proceeded as far as possible in secrecy. When discovered, they could be unrelenting. At his trial for sedition in Rouen, Augustine Marlorat openly admitted 'that if he preached war, it was as he had learned it in the word of God'. In Rouen in 1560, a Calvinist crowd of 20,000 had left a royal governor and his garrison powerless. Marlorat was executed in 1562 as 'one of the authors of the great assemblies which caused the rebellion and civil war'. Calvin pledged that if given the wood, he would provide the arrows, and there are records of arms shipments from Geneva, 'munitions of war . . . to take to the service of the churches of France', many of them destined for Lyon. Other weapons may have ended up in Agen, for in 1561, the colloquy there reported that the king's lieutenant had sought an order to enable him to 'seize the arms of the faithful'.

Such seizures were rarely successful, however, and what is apparent throughout the wars is the monarchy's impotence in the control of violence. As we have seen, after the death of Henry II, the Guise occupied the vacuum at the centre of power. Francis II died shortly after the failure of the Calvinist conspiracy of Amboise, to be succeeded by his brother, Charles IX, with Catherine as regent. The following year, 1561, Francis, Duke of Guise formed a Catholic triumvirate with

Anne de Montmorency – an old aristocratic rival – and Jean d'Albon, the Marshall Saint-André. Catherine sought to achieve compromise through the Colloquy of Poissy, which assembled in September 1561. Béza represented Protestant views – these were dismissed by that seasoned enemy of compromise, the Jesuit, Laynez, who insisted that the only council of any validity was the one in session at Trent. Inconveniently for the notion that the Guise always urged the cause of Catholic extremism, the Cardinal of Lorraine attracted criticism from the Catholics for his conciliatory attitude.

Persisting in the search for compromise, Catherine offered the Huguenots toleration through the Edict of Saint-Germain in 1562. The Catholics ignored it, most notably at Vassy where some 70 Protestants were slaughtered, and less notoriously in more massacres elsewhere. The battle of Dreux, inconclusive militarily, left Saint-André dead and both Condé and Montmorency prisoners in the camp of their enemies. A period of uncertain calm was shattered the next year with the assassination of the Duke of Guise as he laid siege to Orléans.

Catherine, meanwhile, strove to reassert the monarchy's prestige and authority by taking Charles on a spectacular series of progresses as he neared the age of majority. Unfortunately, the tour included in 1565 a meeting at Bayonne with none other than the Duke of Alba, that stern advocate of the destruction of heretics. The Protestants feared a reaffirmation of the terms of Cateau-Cambrésis which had committed the monarchs of France and Spain to the elimination of heterodox belief.

Condé sensed the threat and reminded the monarchy that it was 'limited from its origin by the authority of the nobility and the communities of the provinces and the great towns of the kingdom'. The monarchy scarcely needed reminders about its limitations. For the next 30 years, the forces of international religion worked in a relationship with their agents in France which was so direct that the sovereign power of the king did not appear to exist. After the meeting at Bayonne, Protestant fears of Spanish intervention grew in 1567 as the Duke of Alba took a glittering army of 10,000 along the 'Spanish Road' from north Italy to the Netherlands. Would he strike at Geneva or invade France en route? His arrival in the Netherlands (below, p. 302) led the Catholics to press for Spanish assistance while the Huguenots sought the support of the Dutch. Almost incidentally, the Huguenots attempted to seize the entire royal court at Meaux, before peace was nominally and briefly restored by the Treaty of Longjumeau.

The peace was rendered meaningless not least because the Protestants in La Rochelle, which had become their military headquarters after a purge of local Catholics in 1568, refused to accept many of its provisions. In the fighting which ensued, the Huguenots lost battles at Jarnac, after which Condé was murdered, and at Moncontour.

Condé's death served to bring greater clarity and religious commitment to the Protestant cause by elevating Gaspard de Coligny to the
leadership. There can be no doubt of his unshakeable religious
sincerity, and comparisons with Oliver Cromwell spring to mind. The
appalling tragedy which surrounds his murder in 1572, however, should
not blind us to the ascendancy which Calvinism seemed about to
achieve in France. Apparently ignoring any authority but its own,
the Calvinist party convened a national synod at Lyon in 1571. Béza –
Calvin's successor in Geneva – was elected as moderator; Louis of
Nassau, one of the leaders of the Dutch revolt, was also present in this
'Synod of Princes'. Coligny paid homage – a pledge of loyalty under
feudal law, undertaken in a magnificent ceremony – to Henry of
Navarre (above, p. 33). Henry's mother, the sovereign of Navarre,
asked the synod whether she might appoint Catholics to posts in her
household. The next year – that fateful year, 1572 – at the Synod held at
Nîmes, Coligny requested a formal expression of loyalty to the king,
which rather implies that such loyalty was in doubt.

Coligny had worked persuasively at court, urging war against Spain,
another example of 'social imperialism' which aimed to 'busy giddy
minds with foreign quarrels'. There was a flaw in this strategy,
however, for one might argue that Calvinism had so reduced the sense
of nationhood in France that such a war could only appear to be part
of Calvinism's international attack on Catholicism rather than the
defence of national interests. Such a view appeared to be confirmed by
the seizure of Brill by Calvinist rebels in the Netherlands in April 1572.
In August, the Protestant leadership met in Paris to celebrate the
wedding of Henry of Navarre and Margaret of Valois, the youngest
daughter of Henry II and Catherine de' Medici. The pressure on
Catherine herself was now enormous. The middle way which she had
sought to follow had reached a dead end. The dynastic stabilisation
which the marriage offered would be outweighed by the capitulation to
Protestantism, with all the implications which that held for the Catholic
party's reaction and the attitude of Philip II. The influence which
Coligny exerted over both Charles IX and one of his brothers, the Duke
of Alençon, was manifest. Catherine decided on his elimination. The
Guise were the obvious assassins, for they had made no secret of their
murderous intentions since the death of Duke Francis at Protestant
hands in 1563. Coligny was wounded, but not killed. To finish the job,
Catherine persuaded Charles to change his mind and to destroy all the
Protestant leaders. She had not bargained for the anti-Protestant
hatred of the Parisians: when Coligny met his death more than 2,000
Protestants perished at the hands of the mob, and the slaughter spread
to other cities.[7]

In some ways, the results of the massacre crystallised existing
tendencies rather than marking a turning-point. The King's complicity

was indisputable, and it would no longer be possible to argue that revolt was in the royal interest against his wicked advisers. This book has argued that it is less clear than historians sometimes suggest that such an argument was necessary to the Calvinist cause: after 1572, such an argument was no longer possible. That Calvinism implied violent revolution is suggested by the speed with which the ideology now appeared in full armour. Notions of passive disobedience and respect for civil authority were cast aside. This is strikingly the case in the *Francogallia* of François Hotman, which appeared in 1573, but which was probably started before its author's flight from Bourges to escape a massacre of Protestants in 1572 itself. This is a great statement of the opposition which Germanic feudalism provides for the Roman law: kingship in France was elective and therefore conditional. Béza, Calvin's successor as leader of Genevan Protestantism, contributed *The Right of Magistrates*, a work of startling clarity, again written before St Bartholomew but published once the massacre had settled doubts about the views which the author expresses. Béza sets out to answer the question whether 'subjects may curb manifest tyranny . . . by force of arms', and to do so 'I would begin by pointing out that peoples do not come from rulers.' There is a brilliantly lucid distinction between the person of the sovereign and the sovereignty of the office, and the obligation which the latter imposes upon the former, and a powerful identification of tyranny as a form of rebellion which is also heretical, for 'a people has as much power over a tyrant-king as a Council over a heretic pope'. In a chapter devoted to the subject of resistance to religious persecution, he concludes decisively that:

> we must honour as martyrs not only those who have conquered without resistance, and by patience only, against tyrants who have persecuted the truth, but those also who, authorised by law and by competent authorities, devoted their strength to the defence of true religion . . .

The *Vindiciae contra tyrannos*, most of which is probably the work of Philippe du Plessis-Mornay, goes further, pointing out that those who died on the cross merely did not object to death, while those who died in arms 'knowingly yet prudently assumed the risk'. Moreover, 'kings are not to think that they are of a higher nature than the rest of men and rule as men rule over cattle'. The state, he warns, is not a personal patrimony, but an elected office held in trust. Resistance against 'tyrants without title' is a positive duty against a criminal: 'if we do not resist, we are traitors to our country'. In the context of this chapter, it is highly significant that there is a deliberate breach of territorial sovereignty in the matter of religion which goes against all that had been achieved prior to 1555:

princes are not only to protect the Church but, as far as they are able, to provide for its extension. Therefore, if a prince should protect that part of the Church, say the German or the English, which is within his territory, but does not help another persecuted part; if he abandons and deserts it when he could send help, he must be judged to have abandoned the Church . . . if one prince transgresses the boundaries of religion and justice, a neighbouring prince may religiously and justly go beyond the boundaries of his territory, not to despoil the other of his lands, but to constrain him to his proper duty. And if the neighbour does not do so, he is himself irreligious and unjust.

The implications of such arguments spill into the next century in the build up to civil war in England. What would those of the 'true religion' think of a Stuart king if he did not intervene to protect Protestantism in Bohemia, where his own daughter was queen?[8] In the face of such powerful propaganda, the crown of France appeared a light thing on the wind of fortune. With the death of Charles IX in 1573 and the accession of the Duke of Anjou as Henry III in the following year, some rapprochement with the Huguenots was essential if the arguments expounded after the massacre of St Bartholomew were to be headed off. Henry III was not equal to the moment. He returned to France from Poland, where, as if to emphasise the triumph of consent, he had just been elected as king. At last, France had an adult male heir on the throne: and he proved useless. Effusive expressions of repentance and spiritual austerity punctuated a court routine of blatant decadence which polarised the court and the capital.

By 1576, Catholic party organisation had taken the form of a League in Picardy which was, to say the least, reserved in its recognition of royal authority. In 1578, some of the *mignons* were killed in sword-fights with members of the household of Henry, Duke of Guise. The King provided them with a marble tomb, a gesture which gave enormous impetus to the formation of a party under the leadership of the Guise in open defiance of the King:

> Such conduct, in truth unworthy of a great and magnanimous king such as he, was the cause of the gradual growth of contempt for this prince, and the increased hatred of the favourites who had taken possession of him. All this gave a great advantage to the House of Lorraine [Guise]. It enabled them to corrupt the people and slowly to build up their party, that is, the League, within the third estate, for which they had laid the foundations in the preceding year.

The attachment to the Protestant cause of the King's brother, the Duke of Alençon, who had taken on Henry's old title, Duke of Anjou,

seemed to confirm Catholic suspicions. He entered Mons as defender of
Dutch liberty in 1578, accepted sovereignty as leader against Spain in
1580, and the following year was betrothed to Elizabeth of England.

Map 12.2 France during the Catholic League

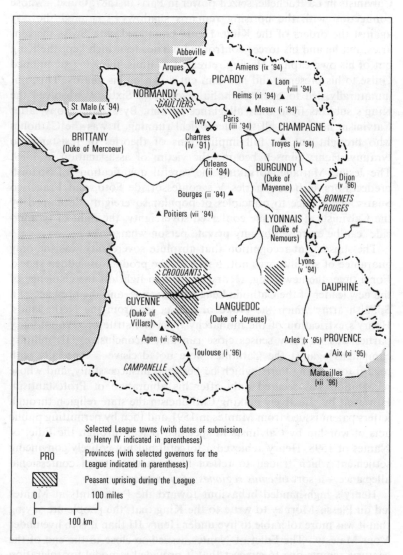

	Selected League towns (with dates of submission to Henry IV indicated in parentheses)
PRO	Provinces (with selected governors for the League indicated in parentheses)
	Peasant uprising during the League

0 — 100 miles

0 — 100 km

Source: Mark Greengrass, *France in the Age of Henri IV: The Struggle for
Stability* (London: Longman Group (UK), 1984), p. 229.

Worse still, when Anjou died in 1584, the succession passed to the Calvinist Henry of Navarre. There was open talk of Guise as the heir of Charlemagne. Crucially, Catholic agitators in the pulpit and in print, secured control of Paris, a city which had, in 1572, witnessed the grim lesson that heresy could be eliminated in a blood-bath. Catholic extremists known as 'the Sixteen', following the precedent set by the Calvinists in La Rochelle, seized power in Paris in 1587. Guise – whose connection with the uprising remains shadowy – entered the city against the orders of the King. Henry countered with Swiss mercenaries, but he and his forces confronted barricades which kept the King out of his own capital. Having retreated to Blois, the King summoned Guise to his presence and had him cut down by his guards. This, not unnaturally, led to open Catholic revolt, and Sixtus V absolved the King's subjects from their allegiance to him. By a bitter irony, after Calvinism had made all the ideological running, it was the Catholics who brought out the full implications of theories of resistance to tyranny. Henry himself became the victim of assassination in 1589. The Jesuit, Mariana, forsaking the careful qualifications of Spanish predecessors such as Charles V's confessor, de Soto, and Francisco Suarez, gave voice to principles of popular sovereignty developed by the Calvinists. The people conferred sovereignty, the right of tyrannicide 'can be exercised by any private person whatsoever'.

The subsequent recognition that absolute sovereignty was the only guarantee of stability was not, however, the product of sudden shock. For a time, the new King, Henry IV, had to fight off the challenge of the new leader of the Catholic League, Mayenne, and the presence of a Spanish army which the Duke of Parma led from the Netherlands. Henry's extrication of the monarchy from the strife of revolutionary parties was in many senses close run and inconclusive. His military campaigns against the Catholics were not decisive – especially with regard to securing Paris, which he besieged unsuccessfully, and whose recognition was secured only after his abjuration of Protestantism. However, by effectively making Catholicism the state religion through letters patent issued from Mantes in 1591 and then by permitting public acts of worship by Calvinists in specified places through the Edict of Nantes of 1598, Henry achieved a forceful but not entirely convincing settlement which tended to reflect his own changes of confessional allegiance – a sort of *cuius regiones, eius religiones*.

Henry's high-handed behaviour toward the Protestants at Mantes led du Plessis-Mornay to write to the King that 'the people are saying that it was more tolerable to live under Henry III than it is to live under Your Majesty'. The Edict of Nantes, issued so close to the end of the century, tempts one to suggest that it provided a model for toleration which was the way out of the Wars of Religion. It was not so conclusive. It was something of an interim measure, because it had 'not yet' pleased God to permit all France 'to be in one and the same form of religion', and rather than emphasising the positive value of toleration, it sought to 'take away the cause of mischief and trouble, which may happen from the actions of religion, which of all others are most prevalent and penetrating'. More significant perhaps, was the manner of the Edict's registration, which the King demanded from the parlement of Paris, the members of which 'would not be in their place but for me':

> I am aware that there have been intrigues in the Parlement, and preachers urged to talk sedition, but I shall take care of such people without expecting any help from you. That method led straight to the barricades and then by degrees to the late king's assassination. I shall certainly avoid all that kind of thing: I shall nip in the bud all factions and all attempts at seditious preaching; and I shall behead all those who encourage it. I have leapt onto the walls of towns; surely I can leap over barricades, which are not so high.

Even so, Henry himself was to die at the hand of a Jesuit assassin in 1610, becasuse his toleration of Huguenots suggested he was not a true Catholic. Whether the development of the absolutist state in France in the seventeenth century owed more to the example of Henry's reign or to the horrible prospect of the return of anarchy is beyond the scope of this study. What Henry had demonstrated was that the sovereign would determine the character of the religion practised by his subjects. While the king could grant toleration, he could also take it away. Perhaps the Reformation in France only reaches its end with the Revocation of the Edict of Nantes by Louis XIV in 1685.[9] The settling of the territorial relationship between political sovereignty and religious conformity was to prove far more complicated in the Netherlands.

Conclusion

Fin de siècle

The Spanish tragedy

The international character of the struggle between revolutionary parties in France and the Netherlands in the later sixteenth century is a measure of the threat which confessional conflict posed to the emergence of territorial states.[1] Yet the different theatres of struggle also offer a number of significant contrasts. Everyone knows that Paris was 'worth a mass' to Henry IV, while the idea of 'getting a pike to Flanders' remains proverbial in Spanish as a definition of the impossible. The problems of the French monarchy lay at the centre of the kingdom, those of Spain at the periphery of its domains. Moreover, while the confessional strife imperilled the principle of territorial sovereignty in France, it was dispute of that very principle which made the religious struggle so intense and so damaging in the Netherlands. Thus, while France was subverted from within and below – which can be allowed if we remember the directness with which Calvin aimed his version of the reform at his home country – the Netherlands faced the overthrow of their existing political system from outside and from above. While the monarchy – after Henry II – never provided a clear lead in France in the matter of religion, the intentions of the Spanish monarchy in the Netherlands were only too plain.

At first sight this may seem paradoxical, for the precocity of the Spanish monarchy in defining its relationship with the Church has provided one of the central themes of this book. The primacy of the Spanish monarchy in directing the affairs of the Church was in many ways established by royal leadership of the *Reconquista* – a religious war against the infidel which established Christian sovereignty coterminous with the borders of Spain. The successful completion of a frontier war and the monitoring of its aftermath by the Spanish Inquisition provided a model for the extirpation of heresy: and the determination not to tolerate heterodoxy seemed reinforced by the chaos which the French monarchy's 'middle way' rapidly created in France. Authoritarian repression was neither as illogical nor as doomed to failure as we might like to think. Yet the very combination of religion and nationhood which had created a Castilian identity was to blacken Spain's reputation abroad. And it was to break the power of Spain – not inevitably, and certainly not quickly – but eventually. Opponents of Spain became opponents of Catholicism, and opponents of Catholicism became opponents of Spain. Rebels were heretics and heretics were rebels. This identification was to create a coherence in the opposition to Spanish power in the Netherlands which otherwise it might not have acquired.

Here perhaps lies the real tragedy of the Wars of Religion, and it is above all a Spanish tragedy. It lies not in a general confusion of religion and politics but in a specific by-product of the assertion of territorial sovereignty in religious matters, a by-product which Calvinism's internationalism did not create, but which it had crystallised and hardened:

> These troubles must be ended by force of arms without any use of pardon, mildness, negotiations or talks until everything has been flattened. That will be the right time for negotiation.

The Duke of Alba's uncompromising advice to his successor as governor of the Netherlands, Dom Luis de Requesens, in 1573 is the stuff of the 'black legend', policies of terror and oppression identified with the Spanish presence. Who would wish to claim the Duke of Alba as one of the founding fathers of modern statehood? But once again, the influence of such thinking in the creation of the modern state may have proved uncomfortably strong. What is easily dismissed as intolerance or fanaticism had its own rationale, and indeed it was part of a general process rather than the product of 'ossified' or 'backward' Spain. Destroying the heretic as a rebel against God was an essential expression of sovereign power. And it made toleration an impossible option. One might risk a modern parallel by saying that no government could expect to hold on to power by advertising its encouragement of drug-peddling or terrorism, and that is what acceptance of heretical sects would have amounted to.

The necessity of this identification of heresy and rebellion is in many ways apparent in the work of Jean Bodin. Since he is often cited as the father of notions of secular statehood, it is puzzling to recall that he also displayed such animus and vigour in encouraging the persecution of witches. As we have already seen (above, ch. 9), the extension of territorial sovereignty under the sanction of religion found the witch or her counterparts, the Jew and the anabaptist, an easy opponent. What better way to define a state than to destroy or expel the stateless? The same sovereignty was nothing like as well-placed in terms of ideology or resources to take on Christian notions of freedom of conscience which enjoyed the protection of feudal law.

What brought this into sharp focus was the dubious nature of Spanish sovereignty. In the Spanish kingdoms in Iberia itself, the only unitary sovereignty lay in the person of the monarch. There was plenty of tension between the different constitutional traditions of Castile and Aragon (above, p. 34). Elsewhere in the monarchy the problems were still more complicated. With the Augsburg Interim of 1547, Charles V detached the rich Netherlands from his imperial inheritance in order to pass them with his Spanish kingdoms to his son, Philip. He allowed that taxes might be due to the empire in an emergency, but he returned his Flemish lands to their former status. The removal of imperial over-lordship was a poor preparation for the imposition of a new sover-eignty to be exercised through a governor appointed from Spain.

However, the Netherlands looked vulnerable to heresy which might seep in from outside: from Geneva itself, from France, from the Palatinate. For Philip II, who had made a great progress through the Low Countries in 1549, an obvious network of barriers could be established by increasing the number of dioceses. Given that only 4 dioceses existed for the 3 million inhabitants of the Netherlands, the decision to create another 14 need not be judged extreme – and it was certainly not sudden, for such proposals had been in the air since the 1520s, though the introduction of the Jesuits in 1556 seemed a dramatic initiative. The reaction to the labours of Philip's regent, his half-sister, Margaret of Parma, showed the disquiet of local nobles at the implications for their own positions in the structures of patronage of a new religious establishment appointed from afar. The new promi-nence of a member of Margaret's council, Antoine de Perrenot, Cardinal Granvelle, made him a focus of resentment, not least because the activities of a heavy-handed Inquisition were at their height during his ascendancy – some 600 prosecutions in 1562. Philip bowed to pressure at court and in the Netherlands and Granvelle bowed out. Philip's insistence on the promulgation of the decrees of the Council of Trent may have confirmed his worst fears by exposing the extent of infiltration – some of the Calvinists were of Jewish descent. Worse, it seemed that some of them were nobles.

In 1566, John Marnix, an overt Calvinist, Nicholas de Hames, herald of the Order of the Golden Fleece, and Louis of Nassau, brother of the most powerful nobleman in the Low Countries, William of Orange, formed a confederation. The agreement which it drew up under the nowadays misleading title of 'Compromise' openly opposed Philip's religious policies, especially the activities of the Inquisition, 'iniquitous and against all divine and human laws, surpassing the worst barbarism ever practised by tyrants'. They maintained that this was no act of rebellion, and presented their protest to Margaret, one of whose counsellors unwisely dismissed them as 'beggars'. The name ('*les gueux*') stuck. As Granvelle recorded, 'the style is borrowed from that of the League which the Huguenots have made in France and for the same ends'. The existence of a network of Calvinist power seemed confirmed by an outbreak of iconoclastic violence in 1566. As in France, the progress of Calvinism was slow and uneven, but once again, minds could turn to the disturbing precedent set in Scotland, and the body of the elect consistently demonstrated a conviction of their own international character. Sem Jansz of Monnikendam preached that 'those who attack images and shatter them are doing God's will'. In Kortrijk, Calvinist preachers:

> admonish the people that it is not enough to remove all idolatry from their hearts; they must also remove it from their sight . . . they are trying to impress upon their hearers the need to pillage the churches and abolish all images.

The destruction of the 'idols' began in Ghent, then hit Antwerp, Middelburg, 's Hertogenbosch, Breda, Michele, Amsterdam, Heusden, Tournai, Turnhout, Delft, Utrecht, Valenciennes, The Hague, Leyden, Eindhoven, Helmond, St Amand – within five days. Popular violence was not linked as closely to aristocratic opposition as Philip believed, but his reaction made them inseparable.

In 1567, that implacable foe of religious liberty, the Duke of Alba, was despatched to the Netherlands with an army of 10,000 troops to restore order and true religion – swiftly – prior to the arrival of Philip himself. This he did through his 'Council of Troubles' – 12,000 trials, 9,000 condemnations, 1,000 executions. Its victims included the prominent nobles, Egmont (who had actually executed iconoclasts) and Hoorn. Among Alba's other infamies was the imposition of a sales tax, the 'Tenth Penny' which sought in effect to make the Netherlands responsible for the upkeep of the Spanish army of occupation.

This policy of terror ended the first revolt. It drove Calvinism north and demoralised the aristocrats now grouped under the leadership of William of Orange. Even though it became increasingly clear that Philip himself would not come, for he was occupied first with the Moors of the Alpujarras and then with the Holy League, Alba seemed fleetingly to have stabilised the regency government's deteriorating finances. Operations in the Low Countries were self-financing in 1570 and 1571. In those two years, Alba extracted about 8 million florins from the Netherlands, while only 1 million were sent from Spain.

The achievement, such as it was, was wrecked in the 1570s. The seizure of Brill by the Sea Beggars in 1572 exposed the lack of Spanish power at sea. Court intrigue (above, p. 76) caused Alba's disgrace and recall. Perhaps the main lesson was that balancing the books and putting hard cash in the hands of the troops were not the same exercise. The stresses and strains showed in a series of mutinies in 1573–4. The new governor, Requesens, reported that some of the soldiers 'don't know what pay is (*no saben que cosa es paga*)'. One regiment received a full pay on enlistment in 1571 and nothing for the next 8 years. Alba's replacement sought to restore discipline by emphasising the religious mission of the troops. This pressed still more firmly together the

identification of all the Dutch as heretics, which had the welcome
effect of justifying extortion from the local inhabitants. Such feeble
expedients did not stave off Philip's bankruptcy in 1575. The discontent and the depredation culminated in general mutiny and the sack
of Antwerp and Aalst in 1576.[2]

The hideous brutality of the mutineers at Aalst alienated the
southern provinces which had been loyal after Alba's suppression of
the first revolt. The States-General began negotiations with the northern rebels in Holland and Zeeland. The sack of Antwerp merely
hastened confirmation of the terms of the common cause embodied
in the Pacification of Ghent of 1577. Spain's precocious nationhood
created a nation of its Dutch enemies. The signatories of the Pacification:

> oblige all inhabitants of the provinces to maintain, from now on a
> lasting and unbreakable friendship and peace and to assist each
> other at all times and in all events by words and deeds, with their
> lives and property, and to drive and keep out of the provinces the
> Spanish soldiers . . .

Don John had arrived to succeed Requesens in 1576, with instructions from the king that 'safeguarding religion and my authority as
much as may be . . . we shall have to concede everything necessary to
bring about a conclusion and save what we can'. The victor of Lepanto
was declared an enemy of the people, and even victory at Gembloux in
1578 could not halt a slide into utter humiliation and disgrace.

In 1579 Holland and Zeeland, Gelderland, Utrecht and the Omme-
landen of Gröningen forged the Union of Utrecht, standing overtly in
the name of individual religious freedom against any reconciliation
with Spain. 'The Spaniards . . . have sought and are still seeking by all
means in their power to bring these provinces wholly or partly into
subjection under their tyrannical government and slavery', the union
was to ensure that 'each individual enjoys freedom of religion and no
one is persecuted or questioned about his religion'.[3]

Thus the 'United Provinces' came into being. This was in no sense a
total defeat for Philip. The triumph of the Provinces and Spain's decline
were to be reversed in the 1580s. The strongest ideological weapon of
the rebels centred on the restraints which law, custom and title imposed
upon the king of Spain in the Low Countries. This was to prove double-
edged: if Philip did not rule, then who did? The demise of Spain's
military machine, which had seemed so complete at the death of Don
John in 1578, was forgotten amid the successes of Alessandro Farnese,
Duke of Parma, whom Don John on his death-bed had named as his
successor, an appointment confirmed with some reluctance by Philip II.
Philip's powers in the Low Countries were a vulnerable target. When

the King put a price on the head of William of Orange in 1584, the prince's 'Apology' raised serious questions about who was rebelling against whom. As William of Orange pointed out, Philip was not King of the Netherlands:

> this name of King is not allowed of by me. Let him be a King in Castille, in Arragon, at Naples, amongest the Indians, and in every place where he commaundeth at his pleasure: yea let him be a king if he will, in Ierusalem, and a peaceable governour in Asia and Africa, yet for all that I will not acknowledge him in this countrey for any more than a Duke and a Countie, whose power is limited according to our priviledges, which he sware to observe . . .

Spanish domination was a religious domination exemplified by the Inquisition – which Philip had no right to activate. William claimed that he had gone into voluntary exile in 1567 'because I would not consent, that the Spanish Inquisition, should be receaved into my governementes'. He warned that speaking ill of the Inquisition was 'the greatest crime that can be in Spayne'. It was the symbol not of Roman or Catholic dominion, but the tyranny of Spain, and he asked 'wherefore then, doth this cursed race of Spaniardes, go from countrey to countrey, to torment and to trouble all the world?'

However, if the King of Spain had no *regio* over which to extend his own *religio*, the question of where sovereignty resided remained open. Orange had acquired a dubious power over Holland and Zeeland in 1580 which at one point appeared as '*la souveraineté et gouvernement*' in French, but '*Hooge Overigheid en Regeringe*' in Dutch, the latter meaning something rather closer to overlordship. The Dutch Declaration of Independence of the following year carried similar ambiguities. The King of Spain it said, had lost his '*souveraineté*' – which appears successively as '*Heerschappye*' (lordship) and '*Hoogheyt*' (highness), which passed, after the resignation of the Archduke Matthias (a Catholic Habsburg) and in the absence of the Duke of Anjou, to the States-General – except in Holland and Zeeland, the largest provinces, which, until the establishment of a ruling council, would be self-governing – under the name of the Prince of Orange! The 'free and absolute' William of Orange, on the other hand, had earlier recognised the superiority of the States-General ('in this worlde, I acknowledge you only for my superiors'). Yet in 1586, after Orange's death, the States-General gave the Earl of Leicester, as Lieutenant-General 'full and absolute command (*volle macht en absolut*)' both 'in the matter of the war' and in 'civil government'. The subsequent tensions between the Orange *stadhouder* and the States-General in matters of political authority are a reflection of this awkward vagueness.

Among the events overshadowed by the Union of Utrecht in 1579 was an agreement (the Treaty of Arras) between Walloon Flanders, Hainaut and Artois with Spain – to prevent their being overrun by the armies of the States-General. Parma was appointed governor at the king's pleasure. He rapidly formed an army of nearly 60,000 men, many of them veterans of the Army of Flanders. In three years, this formidable force conducted some 30 successful sieges. Lier, Zutphen, Bergues, Aalst, Nijmegen . . . they fell through treachery and through lack of support from the States-General, but they fell, and Parma doubled the area obedient to the King of Spain (see Map C.1). American treasure had meanwhile heartened and strengthened the king himself, and he had cemented the Catholic cause in Iberia by taking the crown of Portugal after the death of young King Sebastian in a crusading campaign in 1578 – Alba was entrusted with making safe Philip's new Iberian domain. The Dutch rebels faced a crisis of leadership after the death of Anjou and the assassination of William of Orange in 1584. Although 7 provinces were lost, Farnese had regained 10 of the rebellious 17.[4] It is against this background that we must set the failure of the enterprise of England.

Map C.1 The conquests of the Prince of Parma, 1579–88

Source: A. W. Lovett, *Early Habsburg Spain, 1517–1598* (Oxford: Oxford University Press, 1986), p. 180.

What a masterful plan it was, and how narrowly it failed! The seizure of Brill had shown the Spaniards the necessity of some command of the sea. Pirates could, of course, trouble Spanish ships – but only as a fly could trouble a horse. However, for all the trouble which Drake could cause, the galleons were capable of using their numbers, weight and firepower to advantage in set-piece fights – as John Hawkins had experienced at San Juan de Ulúa in the Gulf of Mexico in 1568, when the English slaver fleet was almost annihilated, and as Richard Grenville was to find in the last fight of the *Revenge*. Queen Elizabeth's interventions in the Netherlands war were an irritation, but the inconsistency of her commitment suggested that she did not relish a confrontation with the power of Spain. If a Spanish fleet could secure the channel, it could protect Parma's army of invasion, and Elizabeth's troops would surely be no match for the *tercios*. The story of the campaign is so well-told elsewhere that here a few details will suffice.

Albeit there were many excellent and warlike ships in the English fleet, yet scarce were there 22 or 23 which matched 90 of the Spaniards in bigness, or could conveniently assault them. Wherefore the English ships using their prerogative of nimble steerage, whereby they could turn and wield themselves with the wind whichever way they listed, came often times very near upon the Spaniards, and charged them so sore, that now and then they were but a pike's length asunder: and so continually giving them one broad side after another, they discharged all their shot both great and small upon them, spending one whole day from morning till night in that violent kind of conflict, until such time as powder and bullets failed them.

The mobility and firepower of the English were to prove decisive by 8 August. The combination was not new: the Portuguese were already using such tactics by the beginning of the century (above, p. 10). Critical, however, was the four-wheeled gun-carriage, perhaps 'England's decisive secret weapon in 1588', because it ensured that the guns themselves were easily manoeuvrable and therefore could be reloaded at speed. Even then, it was a close fight. The prevailing winds on 9 August and for 3 days thereafter prevented the Spaniards from regrouping and trying once more to rendezvous with Parma – at a point when the English did not have the shot to stop them.[5]

The failure of the Armada did not mark the final defeat of Spain. It prepared the way for deadlock in the Netherlands, not defeat. It meant that the divisions among the leaders of the Dutch were balanced by the financial predicament of the Spanish monarchy. The balance had changed again by 1621, but it was to be 1640 before Spanish resources finally reached breaking-point.

Philip II had exhausted his own resources and those of his monarchy by 1598. With Henry IV an avowed Catholic, Philip could agree to respect the territorial sovereignty of France. Two days after the Edict of Nantes, the Spaniards and the French made peace at the Treaty of Vervins.[6] In 1598, our history of the sixteenth century reaches its natural end. By the year of Philip's final bankruptcy and death, Europe in general and Spain in particular seemed to have expended the energies – economic, intellectual and bellicose – which had seemed inexhaustible around 1500. For the first time, the *Reconquista* had been checked. The great Iberian crusade which had pressed unstoppably west, south and east around the globe had foundered in the north. Europe stood motionless. Only time itself seems to have proceeded to the next century.

Retrospect and prospect

After the compressed detail of changing strategic fortunes in the single theatre of the Netherlands, it is perhaps sensible to take a last look at the sixteenth century as a whole. What is its legacy to the Europe of the late twentieth? Perhaps this question is best answered in relation to the principal themes of this book, expansion and conflict. The Introduction identified a paradox: that Europe displayed an extraordinary unity in its approach to the non-European world at a time when the divisions in Europe itself had never been deeper. In the Conclusion, close examination of the end of the century in relation to the fortunes of Spain shows that the paradox is perhaps not so great. Europe's capacity for conflict was an essential part of the expansion itself. The continent impressed itself on the rest of the world by military and naval power, which it consistently tried and tested in its own domestic wars.

This has been rather obscured by the emergence of a mythology which threatens to become an ideology. The mythology is that Europe's first world empire – that of the Spaniards – provided a model which later European empires – most notably the Dutch and English – explicitly disowned and rejected. In an age when so much of the world seems to have embraced 'western' values – especially nationalism and capitalism – there is a danger that such a myth may become an ideology. The sixteenth century can easily be 'used' to show that resistance to the power of Spain gave birth to the notion of political liberty in the face of religious authoritarianism. Most specifically, the Dutch and the English were Protestant nations which succeeded in breaking the power of Spain and subsequently took European 'capitalism' around the globe: the forces of 'progress' had triumphed. Partly as a result of this misrepresentation of what happened in the sixteenth century, the history of so much of the world since then has been distortingly written in relation to the arrival of Europeans themselves. What do the social structures and political institutions of, say, Japan owe to indigenous development? Even China adopted an anti-capitalist ideology from Europe itself. Perhaps Islam's specific rejection of western values and its consciousness of its own past are what make it so disquieting to the European mind: as we saw at the very start of this book, Sir Edwyn Sandys defined 'the west' as those areas free of Islamic dominion (above, p. 12).

Since the sixteenth century, there has always been a danger that history might just be the unofficial ideology of the west, celebrating Europe's own capacity for change and implicitly downgrading the capacity of other civilisations to remain the same. As visions, rhetoric and complacency about Europe's future abound this is an appropriate time to be honest about Europe's past, especially since the greatest power on earth, the United States of America, seems to be suffering economic decline, despite its incomparable military power. That power helped to make Europe what it is by protecting it from forces which could easily have overrun it. That historic role cannot now be disowned or forgotten. In the sixteenth century, Spain helped to shape Europe, and its formative role cannot be denied. The late twentieth century is an appropriate time to recall the character of the Spanish monarchy and of Spanish culture in its age of greatness: pragmatic, unrhetorical, self-critical, above all honest about the role of military power in the maintenance of itself. This poses peculiar problems for the historian's self-esteem, as Don Quixote pointed out:

> Now to attain eminence in the learned professions costs a man time, nights of study, hunger, nakedness, indigestion and other such things, some of which I have mentioned already. But to reach the point of being a good soldier, requires all that it requires to be a good student, but to so much greater a degree that there is no comparison; for the soldier is in peril of losing his life at every step.[7]

The character of the Spanish monarchy was disowned and dis-claimed by the powers which superseded it. Yet – for better or worse – the Spanish imperial experience in the wider world and the Spanish protection of Europe against Islam were the foundations of the modern west. They were laid not merely with a view to gain but also at enormous cost: Cervantes, like so many of his countrymen, died 'old, a soldier, a gentleman, and poor'.

The need for a proper perspective on the place of the sixteenth century in the development of modern Europe is therefore particularly pressing as the twentieth draws to its close. Only by acknowledging the complexity of human experience in times past and refining our judgements on it accordingly can we begin to make sense of our own times. Without the constant reassessment of the past and without the debate which that must generate, there is a danger that history will lose its claims to be a science of the imagination and may instead become a factory of European mythology.

Abbreviations

The abbreviations used in the notes and bibliography are as follows:

CAWH   *The Collins Atlas of World History*, ed. Pierre Vidal-Naquet, trans. Chris Turner *et al.* (London, 1987).

CEHE   *Cambridge Economic History of Europe*, ed. E. E. Rich and C. H. Wilson, vol. 4, *The Economy of Expanding Europe in the Sixteenth and Seventeenth Centuries* (Cambridge, 1967); vol. 5, *The Economic Organisation of Early Modern Europe* (Cambridge, 1977).

NCMH   *New Cambridge Modern History*, vol. 1, *The Renaissance, 1493–1520*, ed. Denys Hay (Cambridge, 1975); vol. 2, *The Reformation, 1520–1559*, ed. G. R. Elton (Cambridge, 1975) 2nd edn, (Cambridge, 1990); vol. 3, *The Counter-Reformation and Price Revolution, 1559–1610*, ed. R. B. Wernham (Cambridge, 1968); vol. 13, *Companion Volume*, ed. Peter Burke (Cambridge, 1980).

RR   Ross, James Bruce and McLaughlin, Mary (eds) *The Portable Renaissance Reader*, rev. edn (Harmondsworth, 1968).

TAWE   *The Times Atlas of World Exploration*, ed. Felipe Fernandez-Armesto (London, 1991).

TAWH   *The Times Atlas of World History*, ed. Geoffrey Barraclough, rev. edn (London, 1979).

Notes

INTRODUCTION

1. Further reading will depend on individual interests and the availability of books. In this Introduction, I have chosen to cite the locations of specific quotations, but otherwise the reader is referred to the relevant section of the Bibliography. For this opening reference, see A. Marwick, *The Nature of History* (London, 1970) p. 170, discussing the comments of Denys Hay, *The Medieval Centuries* (London, 1964).
2. See Bibliography, section 6 (i)–(iv).
3. Kenneth Clark, *Civilisation* (London, 1969), p. 93.
4. Quoted in Walter Ullmann, *A Short History of the Papacy in the Middle Ages* (London, 1972), p. 275.
5. *The Prince*, ch. 24.
6. Such is the implication of Myron P. Gilmore, *The World of Humanism, 1453–1517* (New York, 1962).
7. Gordon Rupp, *Luther's Progress to the Diet of Worms* (New York, 1964).
8. See the grand perspective of J. M. Roberts, *The Triumph of the West* (London, 1985).
9. See Bibliography, sections 4 and 10 (vii).
10. See Bibliography, sections 2 and 4.
11. For regional surveys, see Bibliography, section 10.
12. See e.g., Caspar Vopelius Medebach, *Europae primae et potissime tertiae terrae partis recens descriptio* (Antwerp, 1572), endpaper of Jean-Baptiste Duroselle, *Europe: A History of its Peoples*, trans. Richard Mayne (London, 1990).
13. H. G. Koenigsberger, George L. Mosse, and G. Q. Bowler, *Europe in the Sixteenth Century*, 2nd edn (London, 1989).
14. G. V. Scamell, *The First Imperial Age: European Overseas Expansion, 1400–1715* (London, 1989), p. 49.
15. J. H. Hexter, *The Vision of Politics on the Eve of the Reformation* (London, 1973), pp. 150–78; Roland Mousnier 'The Exponents and Critics of Absolutism', *NCMH*, vol. 4, *The Decline of Spain and the Thirty Years' War, 1609–1648/59*, ed. J. P. Cooper (Cambridge, 1970), p. 117.
16. George Holmes, *The Florentine Enlightenment, 1400–1450* (London, 1969); Ralph Davis, *The Rise of the Atlantic Economies* (London, 1973), chs 11 and 12; Peter Kriedte, *Peasants, Landlords and Merchant Capitalists: Europe and the World Economy, 1500–1800*, trans. V. R. Berghahn (Leamington Spa, 1983) part 2.
17. Mia Rodríguez-Salgado, 'The Habsburg–Valois Wars' in *NCMH*, vol. 2, 2nd edn (1990) p. 385.
18. Quoted in Geoffrey Parker, *The Military Revolution: Military Innovation and the Rise of the West, 1500–1800* (Cambridge, 1986), p. 96.
19. For appropriate illustrations, see *Grosser Historischer Weltatlas, dritter Teil, Neuzeit* (Munich, 1962), pp. 112–13, 128–9 on the

discoveries; zu 115 and 115 on confessional divisions, and Bibliography, section 3.

20. From *Whether soldiers can also be in holy state*, quoted in G. H. Williams, *The Radical Reformation* (Philadelphia, 1962), pp. 437–8.
21. Sir Edwin Sandys, *A Relation of the State of Religion: and with what Hopes and Pollicies it hath been framed, and is maintained in the severall States of these Westerne partes of the world* (London, 1605), quotations from foll. S2r, Qv, Sv, P2v.
22. The concept can work superbly as the focus of a single study: see especially R. Po-chia Hsia, *Social Discipline in the Reformation: Central Europe, 1550–1750* (London, 1989).

1 THE POWER OF LORDS

1. On the social structure and changes within it, see for example, F. Braudel, *Civilisation and Capitalism, 15th–18th Centuries*, trans. S. Reynolds, 3 vols (London, 1981–85); Immanuel Wallerstein, *Capitalist Agriculture and the Origins of the European World Economy in the Sixteenth Century* (New York and London, 1974); Peter Kriedte, *Peasants, Landlords and Merchant Capitalists: Europe and the World Economy, 1500–1800*, trans. V. R. Berghahn (Leamington Spa, 1983); T. S. Aston and C. H. E. Philpin (eds) *The Brenner Debate: Agrarian Class Structure and Economic Development in Pre-Industrial Europe* (Cambridge, 1985); Roland Mousnier, *Social Hierarchies, 1450 to the Present*, trans. P. Evans (London, 1973), esp. pp. 23–4, 84–5.
2. See Thomas More, *Utopia*, trans. into English by Raphe Robinson (1551), (London, 1897), pp. 158, 18; on Jack of Newberry, see *RR*, pp. 183–4; on the Fuggers, Richard Ehrenberg, *Capital and Finance in the Age of the Renaissance: A Study of the Fuggers and their Connections*, trans. H. M. Lucas (London, 1928), p. 85 on rates of profit; Jakob Fugger is quoted in *RR*, pp. 180–1.
3. On the problems of the English aristocracy and the French nobility, see Lawrence Stone, *The Crisis of the Aristocracy, 1558–1641*, abridged edn (Oxford, 1967); Davis Bitton, *The French Nobility in Crisis* (Stanford, 1969). For the examples cited, see Philip Benedict, *Rouen during the Wars of Religion* (Cambridge, 1981), p. 15; David Kirby, *Northern Europe in the Early Modern Period: The Baltic World, 1492–1772* (London, 1990), p. 30. On the complexities of the society of orders, see Mousnier, *Social Hierarchies*; Perez Zagorin, *Rebels and Rulers, 1500–1660*, 2 vols (Cambridge, 1982), vol.1, ch. 3; Hermann Rebel, *Peasant Classes: The Bureaucratisation of Property and Family Relations under Early Habsburg Absolutism, 1511–1636* (Princeton, 1983), esp. p. 13; as an illustration of the durability of these structures, see Pierre Goubert, 'The French Peasantry in the 17th Century: A Regional Example', in Trevor Aston (ed.) *Crisis in Europe, 1560–1660* (London, 1965), pp. 141–66.
4. Sir Charles Oman, *A History of the Art of War in the Sixteenth Century* (Elstree, 1937), p. 66; Geoffrey Parker, *The Army of Flanders and the Spanish Road, 1557–1659* (Cambridge, 1972), pp. 187–8; Michael Knapton, 'City Wealth and State Wealth in North-East

Italy, 14th–17th Centuries', in Neithard Bulst and J.-Ph. Genet (eds) *La ville, la bourgeoisie et la genese de l'état moderne (xiie–xviiie siècles)* (Paris, 1988), p. 208; quotation from Felix Gilbert, *The Pope, his Banker and Venice* (Cambridge, Mass., 1980), p. 22.

5. E. Le Roy Ladurie, *The Peasants of Languedoc*, trans. John Day (Chicago and London, 1976), p. 136, the quotation is on p. 198; Richard Mackenney, *Tradesmen and Traders: The World of the Guilds in Venice and Europe, c.1250–c.1650* (London, 1987), pp. 97–101 on bread prices in Venice; Richard Gascon, *Grand commerce et vie urbaine au xvie siècle: Lyon et ses marchands, 1520–1580*, 2 vols (Paris, 1971), vol. 2, p. 541 on the seasonal rhythm of grain prices; W. G. Hoskins, *The Age of Plunder: The England of Henry VIII, 1500–1547* (London, 1976), p. 81 on material life and sheep; on 'science' and 'art', see Paolo Rossi, *Philosophy, Technology and the Arts in the Early Modern Era* (New York, 1970).

6. On the remoteness of certain regions, see Jean Delumeau, *Catholicism between Luther and Voltaire*, trans. J. Moiser (London, 1977), esp. ch. 3; Nigel Griffin, '"Un muro invisible": Moriscos and Cristianos Viejos in Granada', in F. W. Hodcroft, D. G. Pattison, R. D. F. Pring-Mill and R. W. Truman (eds) *Medieval and Renaissance Studies on Spain and Portugal in Honour of P. E. Russell* (Oxford, 1981), the quotation is on p. 135; on business letters, Richard Mackenney, 'Letters from the Venetian Archive', *Bulletin of the John Rylands University Library of Manchester*, 72 (1990), p. 135; on speeds of communication, F. Braudel, *The Mediterranean and the Mediterranean World in the Age of Philip II*, trans. S. Reynolds, 2 vols (London, 1975), vol. 1, pp. 362–3, 365–71; J. H. Elliott, *Imperial Spain, 1469–1716* (Harmondsworth, 1970), p. 175.

7. On the family in everyday life, see P. Ariès, *Centuries of Childhood*, trans. Robert Baldick (London, 1973), pp. 327–90; Peter Burke, *Popular Culture in Early Modern Europe, 1500–1800* (London, 1978); Peter Laslett, *The World We Have Lost*, 2nd edn (London, 1971); Michael Anderson, *Approaches to the Western Family, 1500–1914* (London, 1980), pp. 41–3; Steven Ozment, *When Fathers Ruled: Family Life in Reformation Europe* (Cambridge, Mass., 1984); Lyndal Roper, *The Holy Household: Women and Morals in Reformation Augsburg* (Oxford, 1989).

8. On the impact of the wars in France in general, see E. Le Roy Ladurie, *The French Peasantry, 1450–1660*, trans. Alan Sheridan (Aldershot, 1987), pp. 231–66. The quotations are in *RR*, pp. 214–16; J. H. M. Salmon, *Society in Crisis: France in the Sixteenth Century* (London, 1979), pp. 207–8, 284; J.-P. Gutton, *La société et les pauvres: l'exemple de la généralité de Lyon, 1534–1789* (Paris, 1970), p. 227.

9. H. J. Cohn, 'The Peasants of Swabia, 1525', *Journal of Peasant Studies*, 3 (1975), pp. 10–22; Jean-Noel Biraben, *Les hommes et la peste en France et dans les pays européens et méditerranéens*, 2 vols (Paris–The Hague, 1975), vol. 1, pp. 119–97; Keith Thomas, *Religion and the Decline of Magic* (Harmondsworth, 1973), ch. 1. Luther is quoted in E. G. Rupp, *The Righteousness of God: Luther Studies* (London, 1953), p. 309; Calvin in William J. Bouwsma, *John Calvin: A Sixteenth-Century Portrait* (Oxford, 1988), p. 34.

10. On this dangerous subject, see F. L. Ganshof, *Feudalism*, trans. Philip Grierson, 3rd edn (London, 1964); Marc Bloch, *Feudal Society*, 2 vols, trans. L. A. Manyon, 2nd edn (London, 1989); Georges Duby, *Rural Economy and Country Life in the Medieval West*, trans. Cynthia Postan (London, 1968), idem, *The Three Orders: Feudal Society Imagined*, trans. A. Goldhammer (Chicago, 1980); Michael Bush, *Noble Privilege* (Manchester, 1983), pp. 73, 141; B. H. Slicher van Bath, *The Agrarian History of Europe, A.D. 500–1850* (London, 1963), p. 39.

11. On conditions in eastern Europe and trading contacts with the west, see Kriedte, *Peasants*, part 1; Kirby, *Northern Europe*, ch. 1; Henry Kamen, *The Iron Century: Social Change in Europe, 1560–1660* (London, 1971), pp. 211–23; H. A. Miskimin, *The Economy of Later Renaissance Europe, 1460–1600* (Cambridge, 1977), pp. 56–64; O. Subtelny, *Domination of Eastern Europe: Native Nobilities and Foreign Absolutism, 1500–1715* (London, 1986), esp. pp. 4–11, 17, 48–9; M. Malowist, 'Poland, Russia and Western Trade in the Fifteenth and Sixteenth Centuries', *Past and Present*, 13 (1958), pp. 26–41; idem, 'The Economic and Social Development of the Baltic Countries from the Fifteenth to the Seventeenth Centuries', *Economic History Review*, 2 ser., 12 (1959–60), pp. 26–41; L. Makkai, 'Neo-Serfdom: Its Origin and Nature in East Central Europe', *Slavic Review*, 34 (1975), pp. 225–38, esp. p. 232 on the extension of lordly rights; H. Rosenberg, 'The Rise of the Junkers in Brandenburg–Prussia, 1410–1653', *American Historical Review*, 49 (1943–4), pp. 1–22, 228–42, esp. pp. 2, 16, 228–33; Robert Brenner, 'The Agrarian Roots of European Capitalism', in Aston and Philpin, *Brenner Debate*, pp. 213–327, esp. pp. 275–83; B. L. Kiraly, 'Neo-Serfdom in Hungary', *Slavic Review*, 34 (1975), pp. 269–78.

12. On the regional variations, see Brenner, 'Agrarian Roots', pp. 277–9; on social conditions, Peter Blickle, 'The Economic, Social and Political Background of the Twelve Articles of the Swabian Peasants of 1525', and David Sabean, 'German Agrarian Institutions at the Beginning of the 16th Century: Upper Swabia as an Example', both in *Journal of Peasant Studies*, 3 (1975), pp. 64–74 and 78–87 respectively. On the precedents for peasant unrest in a context of religious protest, see Norman Cohn, *The Pursuit of the Millennium* (London, 1970), ch. 12, esp. pp. 233–4.

13. For Franck's chronicle, see Gerald Strauss (ed.) *Manifestations of Discontent in Germany on the Eve of the Reformation* (Bloomington, Ind., 1971), pp. 166–9; the anti-noble slogan is quoted in Peter Blickle, *The Revolution of 1525* (Baltimore, 1981), p. 185; on Gaismair, see *RR*, pp. 236–41. For lists of peasant grievances, see Cohn, 'Peasants of Swabia', pp. 14–22; Strauss, *Manifestations*, pp. 154–66. On peasant violence, see Roland Bainton, *Here I Stand: A Life of Martin Luther* (New York and London, 1950), pp. 209–14; and, more generally, H. J. Cohn, 'Anti-clericalism in the German Peasants' War, 1525', *Past and Present*, 83 (1979), pp. 3–31; on Müntzer at Frankenhausen, Cohn, *Pursuit*, p. 250.

14. These quotations are from Bertram Lee Wolff (ed.) *Reformation Writings of Martin Luther*, 2 vols (London, 1952), vol. 1, pp. 113–16; E. G. Rupp and Benjamin Drewery (eds) *Martin Luther* (London, 1970), pp. 122–4.

15. For some general comments on southern Italy, see Miskimin, *Economy*, pp. 74–5. Campanella is quoted in Peter Burke, 'Southern Italy in the 1590s: Hard Times or Crisis?', in Peter Clark (ed.) *The European Crisis of the 1590s* (London, 1985), p. 188.

16. For French examples, see Ladurie, *Languedoc*, chs. 2–4; P. Tucoo-Chala, 'Un exemple d'essor urbain: Pau au 16e siècle' *Annales du Midi*, 78 (1966), pp. 345–62 and J. Russell Major, 'The Crown and the Aristocracy in Renaissance France', *American Historical Review*, 69 (1964), pp. 631–45; idem, 'Noble Income, Inflation and the Wars of Religion in France', *American Historical Review*, 86 (1981), pp. 21–48. For the controversial English situation, see Stone, *Crisis*; H. R. Trevor-Roper, 'The Elizabethan Aristocracy: An Anatomy Anatomized', *Economic History Review*, 2 ser., 3 (1951), pp. 279–98: the quotation is from p. 297; and on the long-term implications, D. C. Coleman, 'Gentlemen and Players', *Economic History Review*, 2 ser., 26 (1973), pp. 92–116.

17. On the aristocratic lifestyle and the urban milieu, see Gascon, *Grand commerce*, vol. 2, pp. 842–5; Grimaudet is quoted in Salmon, *Society in Crisis*, p. 110; N. B. Harte, 'State Control of Dress and Social Change in Pre-Industrial England', in D. C. Coleman and A. H. John (eds) *Trade, Government and Economy in Pre-Industrial England: Essays Presented to F. J. Fisher* (London, 1976), pp. 132–65; F. Redlich, 'European Aristocracy and Economic Development', *Explorations in Entrepreneurial History*, 6 (1953–4), pp. 78–91; Peter Burke, 'Conspicuous Consumption in 17th-Century Italy', in his collection of essays, *The Historical Anthropology of Early Modern Italy* (Cambridge, 1987), pp. 132–49; Marino Berengo, *Nobili e mercanti nella Lucca del '500* (Turin, 1965); F. J. Fisher, 'The Development of London as a Centre of Conspicuous Consumption in the Sixteenth and Seventeenth Centuries', in I. R. Christie (ed.) *Essays in Modern History* (London, 1968), pp. 75–90; Ruth Pike, *Aristocrats and Traders: Sevillian Society in the 16th Century* (London, 1972); James Amelang, *Honoured Citizens of Barcelona: Patrician Culture and Class Relations, 1490–1714* (Princeton, 1986). On the loan and the dagger, see Mary Elizabeth Perry, *Crime and Society in Early Modern Seville* (Hanover, New England, and London, 1980), p. 70; de Mercado is quoted in Stuart B. Schwartz, 'The New World Nobility: Social Aspiration and Mobility in the Conquest and Colonisation of Spanish America', in Miriam U. Chrisman and O. Gründler (eds) *Social Groups and Religious Ideas in the Sixteenth Century* (Kalamazoo, Mich., 1978), p. 24; Thomas A. Brady, 'Patricians, Nobles, Merchants: Internal Tensions and Solidarities in South German Ruling Classes at the Close of the Middle Ages', ibid, pp. 38–45; Champier is quoted in Elizabeth Teall, 'The Seigneur of Renaissance France: Advocate or Oppressor?', *Journal of Modern History*, 37 (1965), pp. 147–8.

18. Baldassare Castiglione, *The Book of the Courtier*, trans. Sir Thomas Hoby (1561) (London, 1928), p. 187. On the meeting at Utrecht, William S. Maltby, *Alba* (Los Angeles and London, 1983), p. 54; on the orders in Elizabethan diplomacy, see Roy Strong, *The Cult of Elizabeth* (London, 1977), pp. 176–7.

19. On the northern earls, see Anthony Fletcher (ed.) *Tudor Rebellions* (London, 1968), pp. 91–106; on France see Salmon, *Society in Crisis*, ch. 2, 'The End of Feudalism', and cf. Robert M. Kingdon, *Geneva and the Consolidation of the French Protestant Movement, 1564–1572* (Geneva, 1967), p. 196 on the Synod of La Rochelle. The Estates in the Netherlands are quoted in E. H. Kossmann and A. F. Mellink (eds) *Texts Concerning the Revolt of the Netherlands* (Cambridge, 1974), p. 119; the Aragonese in Elliott, *Imperial Spain*, p. 30.

20. Giles Fletcher, *Of the Rus Commonwealth*, ed. Albert J. Schmidt (New York, 1966), p. 69.

21. See A. Jouanna, 'Recherches sur la notion d'honneur au xvie siècle', *Revue d'Histoire Moderne et Contemporaine*, 15 (1968), pp. 597–623; Sydney Anglo, *The Courtier's Art: Systematic Immorality in the Renaissance* (Swansea, 1983), p. 7; the quotations are from Castiglione, *Courtier*, pp. 34, 35, 97, 98.

22. *Lazarillo de Tormes* (1554) in *Two Spanish Picaresque Novels* trans. Michael Alpert (Harmondsworth, 1969), p. 54; on Charles V, see M. J. Rodríguez-Salgado, *The Changing Face of Empire: Charles V, Philip II and Habsburg Authority, 1551–1559* (Cambridge, 1988), p. 48; Philip II is quoted in Geoffrey Parker, *Philip II* (London, 1979), p. 157; on Francis I, Francesco Guicciardini, *The Historie of Guicciardin conteining the Warres of Italie and other partes...*, trans. Geffray Fenton (London, 1579), p. 897; on the parvenu, see Guillaume des Autelz quoted in Salmon, *Society in Crisis*, p. 100.

2 THE SYMPTOMS OF EXPANSION

1. On the emergence of the Atlantic world, see Ralph Davis, *The Rise of the Atlantic Economies* (London, 1973); F. Braudel, *The Perspective of the World*, trans. S. Reynolds (London, 1984).

2. See *The Historie of Guicciardin conteining the Warres of Italie and other partes*... trans. Geffray Fenton (London, 1579), p. 329 on the significance of the discoveries; Bodin's remarks are in *La réponse de Jean Bodin à M. de Malestroit*, ed. Henri Hauser (Paris, 1932), p. 13; Gómara is quoted in J. H. Elliott, *The Old World and the New, 1492–1650* (Cambridge, 1972), p. 10.

3. On the uneven participation of European states, see G. V. Scammell, *The First Imperial Age: European Overseas Expansion, 1400–1715* (London, 1989), pp. 15, 17–18; on the Mediterranean revival, F. C. Lane, 'The Mediterranean Spice Trade: Further Evidence of its Revival in the Sixteenth Century', in Brian Pullan (ed.) *Crisis and Change in the Venetian Economy* (London, 1968), pp. 47–58.

4. In general, see C. R. Boxer, *The Portuguese Seaborne Empire, 1415–1825* (London, 1969); J. H. Parry, *The Spanish Seaborne Empire* (London, 1966); S. T. Bindoff, 'The Greatness of Antwerp', *NCMH*, vol. 2, pp. 50–69; the quotation is from Guicciardini, *Historie*, pp. 329–30; on the progress of discovery, see Scammell, *First Imperial Age*, and the superb maps and illustrations in *TAWE*, pp. 62–5 (west coast of Africa), 145–7 (Indian Ocean). Antonio Pigafetta, an Italian who sailed with Magellan, is quoted in J. H. Parry (ed.) *The European*

Reconnaissance (New York, 1968), p. 242; on Magellan, *TAWE*, pp. 164–7.

5. On fire-power, see Parry, *Reconnaissance*, pp. 22–3; Carlo M. Cipolla, *European Culture and Overseas Expansion* (Harmondsworth, 1970), quotations from pp. 94, 95; Cortés is quoted from Parry, *Reconnaissance*, pp. 198–207; the other quotations are from Bernal Díaz, *The Conquest of New Spain*, trans. J. M. Cohen (Harmondsworth, 1963), pp. 230, 228, 289, 78–80.

6. In general, see B. H. Diffie and G. D. Winius, *Foundations of the Portuguese Empire, 1415–1580* (Minneapolis, 1977); on the religious dimension, C. R. Boxer, *Race Relations in the Portuguese Colonial Empire, 1415–1825* (Oxford, 1963), esp. p. 42; idem, *Portuguese Seaborne Empire*, pp. 23, 229; on Sebastian, ibid, pp. 368–9; on the Muslim presence in north Africa, see Andrew C. Hess, *The Forgotten Frontier* (Chicago and London, 1978).

7. Angus MacKay, *Spain in the Middle Ages: From Frontier to Empire, 1000–1500* (London, 1977); E. Lourie, 'A Society Organised for War: Medieval Spain', *Past and Present*, 35 (1966), pp. 54–76; J. H. Elliott, 'The Mental World of Hernán Cortés', *Transactions of the Royal Historical Society*, 5th ser., 17 (1967), pp. 41–58; the quotations are from Díaz, *Conquest*, pp. 142, 159, 203, 241.

8. On the *encomienda*, see L. B. Simpson, *The Encomienda in New Spain: The Beginning of Spanish Mexico* (Berkeley, 1966). Quotations are from S. Zavala, *New Viewpoints on the Spanish Colonisation of America* (Philadelphia, 1943), p. 81; Stuart B. Schwartz, 'New World Nobility: Social Aspirations and Mobility in the Conquest and Colonisation of Spanish America', in M. U. Chrisman and O. Gründler (eds) *Social Groups and Religious Ideas in the Sixteenth Century* (Kalamazoo, Mich., 1978), p. 34; the Dominican view is quoted in Zavala, *New Viewpoints*, p. 71.

9. On the *audiencia*, see J. H. Parry, *The Audiencia of New Galicia in the Sixteenth Century* (Cambridge, 1948); on mining techniques and labour conditions, see Pierre Vilar, *A History of Gold and Money, 1450–1920*, trans. Judith White, (London, 1984), pp. 103–33; population figures from Scammell, *First Imperial Age*, p. 182; on the slave trade, H. A. Miskimin, *The Economy of Later Renaissance Europe, 1460–1600* (Cambridge, 1977), p. 134. Anchieta is quoted in C. R. Boxer, *The Church Militant and Iberian Expansion, 1440–1770* (Baltimore and London, 1978), p. 73; the unnamed Franciscan missionary in idem, *Portuguese Seaborne Empire*, p. 296.

10. On the new ethical dilemmas, see Lewis B. Hanke, *Aristotle and the American Indians* (London, 1959) and the important study by Anthony Pagden, *Spanish Imperialism and the Political Imagination* (New Haven, 1989); Bartolomé Las Casas, *The Spanish Colonie, OR Briefe Chronicle of the Acts and gestes of the Spaniardes in the West Indies, called the newe World, for the space of XI yeeres*, trans. 'M.M.S.' (London, 1583): these quotations are from foll. Iv, I2v, I3v.

11. On Spain's reputation, see W. S. Maltby, *The Black Legend in England: The Development of Anti-Spanish Sentiment, 1558–1660* (Durham, N.C., 1971); on Hawkins, Rayner Unwin, *The Defeat of John Hawkins* (Harmondsworth, 1962); on the English experiments in

Ireland, D. B. Quinn, 'Sir Thomas Smith (1513–1577) and the Beginnings of English Colonial Theory', *Proceedings of the American Philosophical Society*, 89 (1945), pp. 543–5; Edmund Spenser, *A View of the Present State of Ireland*, ed. W. L. Renwick, (London, 1934), pp. 17, 142; on Gilbert in Ireland, see Karl S. Bottigheimer, 'Kingdom and Colony: Ireland in the Westward Enterprise', in K. R. Andrews, N. P. Canny and P. E. H. Hair (eds) *The Westward Enterprise* (Liverpool, 1978), p. 50; Orange's words are from *The Apologie of Prince William of Orange*, ed. H. Wansink (Leyden, 1969), pp. 58–9; Sepúlveda is quoted in J. A. Fernandez-Santamaria, *The State, War and Peace: Spanish Political Thought in the Renaissance, 1516–1559* (Cambridge, 1977), p. 163. On the character of Dutch dominion, see C. R. Boxer, *The Dutch Seaborne Empire, 1600–1800* (London, 1965), p. 240; on the English in Ireland, Quinn, 'Sir Thomas Smith', p. 545; the quotation is in idem, *The Elizabethans and the Irish* (Ithaca, N.Y., 1966), p. 12; Eden is quoted in Maltby, *Black Legend*, pp. 23–4.

12. See *The Essayes of Michael Lord of Montaigne*, trans. John Florio (1603) (London, 1891), pp. 463–4; Purchas is quoted in Denys Hay, *Europe: the Emergence of an Idea* (Edinburgh, 1957), p. 110.

13. F. Braudel, *The Mediterranean and the Mediterranean World in the Age of Philip II*, trans. S. Reynolds, 2 vols, (London, 1975), vol. 1, pp. 394–7; Miskimin, *Economy*, pp. 21–4.

14. The statistics are drawn from the exhaustive study by J. de Vries, *European Urbanisation, 1500–1800* (London, 1984).

15. The quotations are in Brian Pullan, *Rich and Poor in Renaissance Venice* (Oxford, 1971), pp. 244 (Venice), 243 (Vicenza); Natalie Zemon Davis, 'Poor Relief, Humanism and Heresy', in her collection of essays, *Society and Culture in Early Modern France* (Cambridge, 1987), p. 27 (Lyon); *RR*, p. 348 (Vives).

16. On new public initiatives, see Paul Slack, *Poverty and Policy in Tudor and Stuart England* (London, 1988), pp. 8–14; on the situation in Lyon, Jean-Pierre Gutton, *La société et les pauvres: l'exemple de la généralité de Lyon, 1534–1789* (Paris, 1970), p. 226. The text of the Tudor Act is in John Pound (ed.) *Poverty and Vagrancy in Tudor England* (London, 1971), pp. 103–4; see also G. R. Elton, 'An Early Tudor Poor Law', *Economic History Review*, 2nd ser., 6 (1953), pp. 55–66; A. L. Beier, *Masterless Men: The Vagrancy Problem in England, 1560–1640* (London, 1985); on age ratios, Slack, *Poverty and Policy*, p. 44, and the quotation ibid, p. 28. On grain prices, Peter Kriedte, *Peasants, Landlords and Merchant Capitalists: Europe and the World Economy, 1500–1800*, trans. V. Berghahn (Leamington Spa, 1983), p. 48; Vilar, *Gold and Money*, pp. 176, 52, 70; on Venetian expedients, Richard Mackenney, *Tradesmen and Traders: The World of the Guilds in Venice and Europe, c.1250–c.1650* (London, 1987), pp. 97–9.

17. On precious metals and prices, see F. Braudel and F. Spooner, 'Prices in Europe from 1450 to 1750', *CEHE*, vol. 4, pp. 374–86; Vilar, *Gold and Money*, Kriedte, *Peasants*, and Miskimin, *Economy*, and the important collection, Peter H. Ramsey (ed.) *The Price Revolution in Sixteenth-Century England* (London, 1971).

18. *Advertisments from Parnassus*, trans. Henry, Earl of Monmouth (London, 1669), p. 337.

3 THE SHAPING OF STATEHOOD

1. I am indebted to Professor G. R. Elton for this orientation.
2. For a persuasive case history, see Howell A. Lloyd, *The State, France and the Sixteenth Century* (London, 1983). On central and eastern regions see William H. McNeill, *Europe's Steppe Frontier* (Chicago and London, 1964), esp. pp. 45–75; O. Subtelny, *Domination of Eastern Europe: Native Nobilities and Foreign Absolutism, 1500–1715* (London, 1986); R. J. W. Evans, *The Making of the Habsburg Monarchy, 1550–1700* (Oxford, 1979). On the narrowness of local horizons, see J. R. Hale, *Renaissance Europe, 1480–1520* (London, 1971), pp. 101–37, esp. p. 112. On the Netherlands, see A. C. Duke, 'From King and Country to King or Country? Loyalty and Treason in the Revolt of the Netherlands', in his collection of essays, *Reformation and Revolt in the Low Countries* (London, 1990), pp. 186–90; J. H. Elliott, *Europe Divided, 1559–1598* (London, 1968), pp. 293–4, 296–7. On Spain itself, see the many-sided discussion by H. G. Koenigsberger, 'National Consciousness in Early Modern Spain', in his collection of essays, *Politicians and Virtuosi* (London, 1986), pp. 121–48.
3. See in general Walter Ullmann, *A Short History of the Papacy in the Middle Ages* (London, 1972); for greater detail, see idem, *Medieval Papalism* (London, 1949); M. J. Wilks, *The Problem of Sovereignty in the Later Middle Ages* (Cambridge, 1963). The edited text of *Unam Sanctam* is in H. Bettenson (ed.) *Documents of the Christian Church* 2nd edn (Oxford, 1967), pp. 115–16. On the conciliar movement, see J. N. Figgis, *From Gerson to Grotius* (Cambridge, 1907), pp. 31–54. For a brilliant summary which demonstrates the relevance of these developments to the sixteenth century, see Steven Ozment, *The Age of Reform, 1250–1550* (New Haven, 1980), pp. 135–81.
4. On Charles's inheritance, see Francesco Guicciardini, *The Historie of Guicciardin conteining the Warres of Italie and other partes*, trans. Geffray Fenton (London, 1579), p. 762; his titles are quoted in Mia Rodríguez-Salgado, *The Changing Face of Empire: Charles V, Philip II and Habsburg Authority, 1551–1559* (Cambridge, 1988), p. 33.
5. On the idea of universal monarchy, see Bohdan Chudoba, *Spain and the Empire, 1519–1643* (Chicago, 1952), esp. p. 13; J. M. Headley, *The Emperor and his Chancellor: A Study of the Imperial Chancellery under Gattinara* (Cambridge, 1983), esp. pp. 4–7; G. R. Elton, '1555: A Political Retrospect', in Joel Hurstfield (ed.) *The Reformation Crisis* (London, 1965), p. 74. On the politics of the Empire, see G. R. Elton, *Reformation Europe, 1517–59* (London, 1963), pp. 35–85; H. G. Koenigsberger, 'The Empire of Charles V in Europe', *NCMH*, vol. 2, pp. 301–33; Rodríguez-Salgado, *Changing Face*; and the important remarks in G. Oestreich, *Neostoicism and the Early Modern State*, ed. by Brigitta Oestreich and H. G. Koenigsberger, trans. David McLintock (Cambridge, 1982), pp. 199–200, 212. On the survival of the universalist tradition, see R. J. W. Evans, *Rudolf II and his World* (Oxford, 1973), pp. 18–20.
6. Geoffrey Parker, *The Army of Flanders and the Spanish Road, 1567–1659* (Cambridge, 1972), esp. pp. 50–105; idem, 'Spain, her Enemies and the Revolt of the Netherlands' in his collection of essays *Spain and*

the Netherlands, 1559–1659 (London, 1979), pp. 18–44; H. G. Koenigsberger, 'Western Europe and the Power of Spain', *NCMH*, vol. 3, pp. 234–318.

7. On the fragility of the divide between representation and rebellion, see the brilliant collections of essays by H. G. Koenigsberger, *Estates and Revolutions* (Ithaca, N.Y., 1971), and *Politicians and Virtuosi*. For a general survey and helpful typology of estates, see A. R. Myers, *Parliaments and Estates in Europe to 1789* (London, 1975). On the Venetian Republic, see Richard Mackenney, *The City-State, 1500–1700* (London, 1989), pp. 43–52. On collective absolutism, see E. H. Kossmann, 'The Singularity of Absolutism', in R. Hatton (ed.) *Louis XIV and Absolutism* (London, 1976), pp. 13–17. On Sweden, see Michael Roberts, *The Early Vasas* (Cambridge, 1968); on central Europe, Evans, *Habsburg Monarchy*, Part Two; on England, see the works by G. R. Elton cited in the bibliography, but in particular, 'The Political Creed of Thomas Cromwell', in his collected papers, *Studies in Tudor and Stuart Politics and Government*, vol. 2 (Cambridge, 1974), esp. pp. 232–5.

8. For some cautious general comments and succinct case histories, see Perez Zagorin, *Rebels and Rulers, 1500–1660*, 2 vols, (Cambridge, 1982). See also Stephen Haliczer, *The Comuneros of Castile* (Madison, 1981); G. R. Elton, *Policy and Police* (Cambridge, 1972); Anthony Fletcher (ed.) *Tudor Rebellions*, 2nd edn (London, 1973); H. G. Koenigsberger, 'The Organisation of Revolutionary Parties in France and the Netherlands in the Sixteenth Century', in his *Estates and Revolutions*, pp. 224–52.

9. Francesco Zuccolo, quoted in Roland Mousnier, 'The Exponents and Critics of Absolutism', *NCMH*, vol. 4, *The Decline of Spain and the Thirty Years' War*, ed. J. P. Cooper (Cambridge, 1970), p. 117.

10. See especially Quentin Skinner, *The Foundations of Modern Political Thought*, 2 vols, (Cambridge, 1978).

11. *The Prince*, trans. George Bull (Harmondsworth, 1961), cap. xvii, p. 96.

12. *The Prince*, trans. Edward Dacres (London, 1640), cap. xvii, p. 130.

13. *The Prince*, trans. Dacres, cap. xi, pp. 85–7. It is possible that the papacy would have accepted this characterisation: see Paolo Prodi, *The Papal Prince*, trans. Susan Haskins, (Cambridge, 1987), p. 119.

14. *The Prince*, trans. Dacres, cap. vii, pp. 49–50.

15. *The Discourses*, trans. Leslie Walker, ed. Bernard Crick (Harmondsworth, 1970), p. 143.

16. See the important survey by Peter S. Donaldson, *Machiavelli and Mystery of State* (Cambridge, 1988). The quotations are from Giles Fletcher, *Of the Rus Commonwealth*, ed. Albert J. Schmidt (New York, 1966), p. 31; *Discourses*, p. 175. On '*dissimular*', see Chudoba, *Spain and the Empire*, pp. 5, 95. For a stimulating comparison of Machiavelli and More, see J. H. Hexter, *The Vision of Politics on the Eve of the Reformation* (London, 1973), pp. 179–202.

17. The quotations are from *The Six Bookes of a Commonweale*, Eng. trans. 1606, ed. Kenneth D. McRae (Cambridge, Mass., 1962), pp. 115–16, 137, 145, 137, 153, 159.

18. Among the works of G. R. Elton see *The Tudor Revolution in Government* (Cambridge, 1953); *The Tudor Constitution* (Cambridge,

1960); *Reform and Renewal: Thomas Cromwell and the Common Weal* (Cambridge, 1973). Critics of Professor Elton's ideas have had plenty of *Lebensraum* in print: the suggestion here is that his ideas gain a renewed persuasiveness in a comparative European context.

19. On these developments see J. R. Hale, 'International Relations in the West: Diplomacy and War', *NCMH*, vol. 1, pp. 259–91; idem, 'Armies, Navies and the Art of War', *NCMH*, vol. 2, pp. 481–509 and vol. 3, pp. 171–208; idem, *War and Society in Renaissance Europe, 1450–1620* (London, 1985), with a particularly informative chart of army size on pp. 62–3. On fortifications see Christopher Duffy, *Siege Warfare: The Fortress in the Early Modern World, 1494–1669* (London, 1979). On the significance of these changes in broader perspective, see André Corvisier, *Armies and Societies in Europe, 1494–1789*, trans. Abigail Siddall (Bloomington, Ind., 1979); Geoffrey Parker, 'Warfare', *NCMH*, vol. 13, pp. 201–19; idem, *The Military Revolution: Military Innovation and the Rise of the West, 1500–1800* (Cambridge, 1986), esp. p. 75 on supplies.

20. See Giovanni Botero, *The Reason of State*, trans. D. and P. Waley (London, 1956), pp. 182–3; on Siena, Judith Hook, 'Fortifications and the End of the Sienese State', *History*, 62 (1977), pp. 372–87; on Venice, M. E. Mallett and J. R. Hale, *The Military Organisation of a Renaissance State: Venice, c.1400–1617* (Cambridge, 1984), and on naval developments, John F. Guilmartin, *Gunpowder and Galleys* (Cambridge, 1974); Mackenney, *City-State*, p. 48; on England, Parker, *Military Revolution*, p. 62 and, with details of the political implications, G. R. Elton, *Reform and Reformation: England 1509–1558* (London, 1977), pp. 307–10; C. S. L. Davies, *Peace, Print and Protestantism, 1450–1558* (London, 1977), pp. 216–18; D. M. Loades, *Politics and the Nation, 1450–1660* (London, 1974), pp. 302–5.

21. Charles's remarks are in *The Autobiography of the Emperor Charles V*, trans. Leonard Simpson (London, 1862), pp. 21–2. On war costs and state finance, see Geoffrey Parker, 'The Emergence of Modern Finance in Europe, 1500–1730', in Carlo M. Cipolla (ed.) *The Fontana Economic History of Europe*, vol. 2 (London, 1974), pp. 527–94. On Charles V's finances, see Pierre Vilar, *A History of Gold and Money, 1450–1920*, trans. Judith White (London, 1984), pp. 148–9. On France, see R. J. Knecht (ed.) *French Renaissance Monarchy: Francis I and Henry II* (London, 1984), pp. 47–53. On *juros* and *rentes*, see Henry Kamen, *The Iron Century: Social Change in Europe, 1550–1660* (London, 1971), pp. 172–81. On sale of office in France, see J. H. M. Salmon, *Society in Crisis: France in the Sixteenth Century* (London, 1979), pp. 70–9, and on the contrasting situation in Spain, I. A. A. Thompson, 'The Purchase of Nobility in Castile, 1552–1700', *Journal of European Economic History*, 8 (1979), pp. 313–60. The quotations are from Pierre Goubert, *The Ancien Régime: French Society, 1600–1750*, trans. Steve Cox (London, 1969), p. 181.

22. Pierre de L'Estoile is quoted in Salmon, *Society in Crisis*, p. 200. There is a rich and exciting literature on the courts: see in general, A. G. Dickens (ed.), *The Courts of Europe, 1500–1800* (London, 1977); Sergio Bertelli (ed.) *Italian Renaissance Courts*, trans. Mary Fitton and Geoffrey Culverwell (London, 1986); Roy Strong, *Art and Power:*

Renaissance Festivals, 1450–1650 (London, 1984); Michael Levey, *Painting at Court* (London, 1971); Sydney Anglo (ed.) *Chivalry in the Renaissance* (Woodbridge, 1990); H. R. Trevor-Roper, *Princes and Artists: Patronage and Ideology at Four Habsburg Courts, 1517–1633* (New York, 1974); David Loades, *The Tudor Court* (London, 1986); David Starkey (ed.) *Henry VIII: A European Court in England* (London, 1991); Sydney Anglo, *Spectacle, Pageantry, and Early Tudor Policy* (Oxford, 1969). On Archduke Ernest, see *The Fugger News-Letters, 1568–1605*, ed. Viktor von Klarwill, trans. Pauline de Chary (London, 1924), pp. 177–8; on the court of Philip II, William S. Maltby, *Alba* (Los Angeles and London, 1983), pp. 74–5; on the *corps diplomatiques*, Garrett Mattingly, *Renaissance Diplomacy* (Harmondsworth, 1965), p. 168; on the 'shame' of opposition, S. J. Gunn, 'Chivalry and the Politics of the Early Tudor Court', in Anglo, *Chivalry*, p. 108. Machiavelli's remarks are in his *Florentine History*, trans. W. K. Marriott (London, 1909), p. 359. On material life at court David Chambers (ed.) *Splendours of the Gonzaga* (London, 1981); Richard Goldthwaite, '"The Empire of Things"', in F. W. Kent and Patricia Simons (eds) *Patronage, Art and Society in Renaissance Italy* (Oxford, 1987), pp. 153–76; for this aspect of Cellini's life and work, see *The Autobiography of Benvenuto Cellini*, trans. J. A. Symonds, ed. and abr. Charles Hope (Oxford, 1983); and the magnificent colour plates in John Pope-Hennesy, *Cellini* (London, 1985). On Leonardo in Milan, see J. Bronowski, 'Leonardo da Vinci', in J. H. Plumb (ed.) *The Penguin Book of the Renaissance* (Harmondsworth, 1964), pp. 178–9; on Rudolf II, Evans, *Rudolf II*, pp. 174, 164; on Charles V, Strong, *Art and Power*, p. 76; Paré is quoted in F. Braudel, *The Mediterranean and the Mediterranean World in the Age of Philip II*, trans. S. Reynolds, 2 vols (London, 1975), vol. 2, p. 752; on the importance of the Habsburg court, R. J. W. Evans, 'The Austrian Habsburgs: The Dynasty as a Political Institution', in Dickens, *Courts*, p. 145.

23.   On the papacy, see Peter Partner, 'The Papal State: 1417–1600', in Mark Greengrass (ed.) *Conquest and Coalescence: The Shaping of the State in Early Modern Europe* (London, 1991), pp. 25–47; Prodi, *Papal Prince*; and on what princes learned from popes, see the exhilarating article by Wolfgang Reinhard, 'Finanza pontificia, sistema beneficiale e finanza statale nell'età confessionale', in Hermann Kellenbenz and Paolo Prodi (eds) *Fisco, religione, Stato nell'età confessionale* (Bologna, 1989), pp. 459–504. Guicciardini's comments are from his *History of Florence*, trans. Mario Domandi (New York, 1970), p. 32. Savonarola is quoted in Pasquale Villari, *The Life and Times of Savonarola*, trans. Linda Villari (London, 1896), p. 23. The Concordat of Bologna is quoted in Knecht, *French Renaissance Monarchy*, p. 81. See also idem, 'The Concordat of 1516: A Reassessment', in Henry J. Cohn (ed.) *Government in Reformation Europe, 1520–1560* (London, 1971), pp. 91–112. Julius III is quoted in Prodi, *Papal Prince*, p. 168. For examples of appropriations by the state from the Church in France, see Salmon, *Society in Crisis*, pp. 82, 165. This section of the Act in Restraint of Annates appears in Elton, *Tudor Constitution*, p. 350. See also the powerful chapter 'The Royal Supremacy' in idem, *Reform and Reformation*, pp. 174–200. On the

Empire, see Hermann Tüchle, 'The Peace of Augsburg: New Order or Lull in the Fighting?', in Cohn, *Government*, esp. pp. 148, 164.

4 CITIES AND CITIZENS

1. See the general studies: Lewis Mumford, *The City in History* (Harmondsworth, 1966); Mark Girouard, *Cities and People: A Social and Architectural History* (New Haven, 1985); Gideon Sjoberg, *The Pre-Industrial City* (New York, 1960). On the particular features of the early modern period, see F. Braudel, *Civilisation and Capitalism, 15th–18th Centuries*, trans. S. Reynolds, 3 vols (London, 1982), vol. 1, *The Structures of Everyday Life*, vol. 2, *The Wheels of Commerce*, vol. 3, *The Perspective of the World*; Richard Mackenney, *The City-State* (London, 1989); and Peter Clark (ed.) *The Early Modern Town* (London, 1976).

2. The statistics are drawn from the meticulous work of Jan de Vries, *European Urbanisation, 1500–1800* (London, 1984), p. 76, which is splendidly informative on population levels and changes in them. For overviews of trade and manufactures, see Charles Wilson, 'Trade, Society and the State', *CEHE*, vol. 4, pp. 478–575; H. Kellenbenz, 'The Organisation of Production', *CEHE*, vol. 5, pp. 462–548; Carlo M. Cipolla, *Before the Industrial Revolution* (London, 1976), Part Two; idem (ed.) *The Fontana Economic History of Europe*, vol. 2 (London, 1976). On the character of urban production, see the penetrating remarks by J. R. Hale, *Renaissance Europe, 1480–1520* (London, 1971), pp. 149–51. On guild organisation, see Richard Mackenney, *Tradesmen and Traders: The World of the Guilds in Venice and Europe, c.1250–c.1650* (London, 1987). On particular enterprises, see Raymond de Roover, 'A Florentine Firm of Cloth Manufacturers', in his collection of essays, *Business, Banking and Economic Thought in Late Medieval and Early Modern Europe* (Chicago, 1974), pp. 85–119; on mining, John U. Nef, *Industry and Government in France and England, 1540–1640* (Ithaca, N.Y., 1964), ch. 3; F. C. Lane, *Venetian Ships and Shipbuilders of the Renaissance* (Baltimore, 1934); Richard Goldthwaite, *The Building of Renaissance Florence* (Baltimore, 1981). On the nature of demand, see F. J. Fisher, 'The Development of London as a Centre of Conspicuous Consumption in the Sixteenth and Seventeenth Centuries', in I. R. Christie (ed.) *Essays in Modern History* (London, 1968), pp. 75–90.

3. For this model of social structure, see Braudel, *Everyday Life*, pp. 479–558; Jean-Pierre Gutton, *La société et les pauvres: l'exemple de la généralité de Lyon, 1534–1789* (Paris, 1970), esp. pp. 213–88, and on the general vulnerability of the workers in the textile industry, pp. 38–50; C. Lis and H. Soly, *Poverty and Capitalism in Pre-Industrial Europe* (Brighton, 1982), pp. 54–96. On unemployment and vagrancy, see A. L. Beier, *Masterless Men: The Vagrancy Problem in England, 1560–1640* (London, 1985), p. 27. On grain reserves and social structure, see Cipolla, *Before the Industrial Revolution*, pp. 8–27, esp. the tables on pp. 11 and 18. On the queue of the poor in Lyon, see Richard Gascon, *Grand commerce et vie urbaine au xvie siècle: Lyon et ses marchands*, 2

vols (Paris, 1971), vol. 2, p. 797. On the impact of plague, R. Mols, 'Population in Europe, 1500–1700', in Carlo M. Cipolla (ed.) *Fontana Economic History of Europe*, vol. 2 (London, 1974), pp. 71–6; F. Braudel, *The Mediterranean and the Mediterranean World in the Age of Philip II*, trans. S. Reynolds, 2 vols (London, 1975), vol. 1, pp. 332–4; Jean-Noël Biraben, *Les hommes et la peste en France et dans les pays européens et méditerranéens*, 2 vols (Paris–The Hague, 1975), vol. 1, p. 197 on London.

4. For a pertinent summary of medieval urban development, see Braudel, *Perspective*, pp. 89–137. The population figures are from de Vries, *Urbanisation*. The commercial network of the Fuggers is shown in *TAWH*, p. 145.

5. For the value of a maritime perspective, see H. Kellenbenz, *The Rise of the European Economy*, rev. and ed. G. Benecke (London, 1976), p. 1. It is instructive to read three economic histories which use the sea rather than the land as their regional focus: Braudel, *Mediterranean*; David Kirby, *Northern Europe in the Early Modern Period: The Baltic World, 1492–1772* (London, 1990); Ralph Davis, *The Rise of the Atlantic Economies* (London, 1973).

6. On the international significance of Antwerp, see Braudel, *Perspective*, pp. 138–56; S. T. Bindoff, 'The Greatness of Antwerp', *NCMH*, vol. 2, pp. 50–69; H. van der Wee, *The Antwerp Market and the European Economy*, 3 vols, (The Hague, 1963); Jan A. van Houtte and Léon van Buyten, 'The Low Countries', in Charles Wilson and Geoffrey Parker (eds) *An Introduction to the Sources of European Economic History, 1500–1800* (London, 1977), pp. 81–114; G. D. Ramsay, *The City of London in International Politics at the Accession of Elizabeth Tudor* (Manchester, 1975), pp. 1–32. The part of Guicciardini's description quoted here is found in *RR*, pp. 187–8. On commodities, see the fascinating collection by V. Vasquez de Prada (ed.) *Lettres marchandes d'Anvers*, 4 vols, (Paris, 1959–62), vol. 1, pp. 67–70. On Zonca, Mackenney, *Tradesmen*, pp. 193–5. On the Sack, see Geoffrey Parker, *The Dutch Revolt* (Harmondsworth, 1979), pp. 214–15.

7. There are numerous references to Venice throughout Braudel, *Mediterranean*, and an important summary of the city's fortunes in idem, *Perspective*, pp. 116–37. Two important collections of essays on Venice are Brian Pullan (ed.) *Crisis and Change in the Venetian Economy* (London, 1969) and J. R. Hale (ed.) *Renaissance Venice* (London, 1973). On the metropolitan economy and manufactures, see Mackenney, *Tradesmen*; Richard T. Rapp, *Industry and Economic Decline in Seventeenth-Century Venice* (Cambridge, Mass., 1976); Robert C. Davis, *Shipbuilders of the Venetian Arsenal* (Baltimore, 1991). On the city's culture, see Richard Mackenney, 'Venice', in Roy Porter and Mikulas Teich (eds) *The Renaissance in National Context* (Cambridge, 1992), pp. 53–67.

8. On Genoa and the Genoese, see Braudel, *Perspective*, pp. 157–74; Jacques Heers, *Gênes au xve siècle* (Paris, 1961); Ruth Pike, *Enterprise and Adventure: The Genoese in Seville and the Opening of the New World* (Ithaca, N.Y., 1966), (de Mercado is quoted on p. 32). On Seville, idem, *Aristocrats and Traders: Sevillian Society in the Sixteenth Century* (London, 1972); Mary E. Perry, *Crime and Society in Early*

Modern Seville (Hanover, New Eng., and London, 1980), esp. pp. 6 and 35 on the city's ties to the monarchy.

9. On Lyon, see Gascon, *Grand commerce*; Gutton, *La société et les pauvres*; and the collection of essays by Natalie Zemon Davis, *Society and Culture in Early Modern France* (Cambridge, 1987). On the city's rivalry with Paris, Braudel, *Perspective*, pp. 326–30.

10. On Florence, see R. Burr Litchfield, *Emergence of a Bureaucracy: The Florentine Patriciate, 1530–1790* (Princeton, 1986); Samuel Berner, 'Florentine Society in the Late Sixteenth and Early Seventeenth Centuries', *Studies in the Renaissance*, 18 (1971), pp. 203–46. On the city's changing culture, see Eric Cochrane, *Florence in the Forgotten Centuries 1527–1800* (Chicago, 1973).

11. David Ringrose, 'The Impact of a New Capital City: Madrid, Toledo and New Castile, 1560–1660', *Journal of Economic History*, 33 (1973), 761–92. On the importance of the court, see Jonathan Brown and J. H. Elliott, *A Palace for a King: The Buen Retiro and the Court of Philip IV* (New Haven, 1980).

12. The quotation on the size and importance of London is in *Thomas Platter's Travels in England*, ed. C. Williams (London, 1937), p. 153. In general, see A. L. Beier and Roger Finlay (eds) *London 1500–1700: The Making of the Metropolis* (London, 1986), especially the editors' Introduction, pp. 1–34. On the economy and society, see Ramsey, *City of London*; Fisher, 'Conspicuous Consumption', idem, 'London as an "Engine of Economic Growth"', in Clark, *Early Modern Town*, pp. 205–15; George Unwin, *The Gilds and Companies of London*, 4th edn, (London, 1963); A. L. Beier, 'Social Problems in Elizabethan London', *Journal of Interdisciplinary History*, 9 (1978), pp. 203–21. There are also important remarks in Peter Clark and Paul Slack, *English Towns in Transition, 1500–1700* (Oxford, 1976), pp. 62–82. For a contemporary picture, see John Stow, *The Survey of London* (1598), ed. H. B. Wheatley (London, 1912): the passage quoted here is on p. 495.

13. F. Braudel, *The Character of France*, trans. S. Reynolds, 2 vols (London, 1988), vol. 1, pp. 251–9; N. M. Sutherland, 'Parisian Life in the Sixteenth Century', in Werner L. Gundersheimer (ed.) *French Humanism, 1470–1600* (London, 1969), pp. 51–64. The passages quoted are from R. J. Knecht (ed.) *French Renaissance Monarchy: Francis I and Henry II* (London, 1984), pp. 90–1 and *The Fugger News-Letters, 1568–1605*, ed. Viktor von Klarwill, trans. Pauline de Chary (London, 1924), p. 19.

14. See the important sociological comments of Sjoberg, *Pre-Industrial City*, pp. 256–84. On religion and the pattern of economic life, see Christopher Hill, *Society and Puritanism in Pre-Revolutionary England* (London, 1969), ch. 5, 'The Uses of Sabbatarianism', pp. 141–211; Steven Ozment, *The Reformation in the Cities* (New Haven and London, 1975), esp. pp. 97–8, 117, 157; R. Po-chia Hsia, *Social Discipline in the Reformation: Central Europe, 1550–1750* (London, 1989), p. 183.

15. The quotations are from *The Diary of Montaigne's Journey to Italy in 1580 and 1581*, trans. E. J. Trechmann (London, 1929), pp. 149–50. In general see the monumental work by Jean Delumeau, *Vie économique*

et sociale de Rome au xvie siècle, 2 vols (Paris, 1957–9), abridged as *Rome au xvie siècle* (Paris, 1975), in which pp. 1–24 cover communications. On the changing character of the city, see Peter Partner, *Renaissance Rome, 1500–1559* (Berkeley and Los Angeles, 1979); and for some helpful comments and illustrations of the changing townscape, see Girouard, *Cities and People*, pp. 115–36.

16. The link between the Protestant ethic and capitalism was rather a commonplace in Weber's own time. What he suggested was that Protestantism enabled and encouraged a rational organisation of work in the endless pursuit of profit. It was an extrapolation of this to connect the Reformation and the rise of capitalism. See the useful survey of this controversial subject by Pierre Besnard, *Protestantisme et capitalisme: la controverse post-Wéberienne* (Paris, 1970).

17. Montaigne mentions the absentee bishop in his *Diary*, p. 36. There is a vast literature on the urban Reformation. Much of it takes its inspiration from the classic work by Bernd Moeller, *Imperial Cities and the Reformation*, ed. and trans. H. C. Erik Midelfort and Mark U. Edwards (Durham, N.C., 1982). Of general studies, among the most lucid and accessible are R. W. Scribner, *The German Reformation* (London, 1986); Ozment, *Cities*; Thomas A. Brady, *Turning Swiss: Cities and Empire, 1450–1550* (Cambridge, 1985). The complexities of individual urban societies can be examined in R. W. Scribner, 'Civic Unity and the Reformation in Erfurt', *Past and Present*, 66 (1975); idem, 'Why was there no Reformation in Cologne?', *Bulletin of the Institute for Historical Research*, 49 (1976), pp. 217–41; Joachim C. Whaley, *Religious Toleration and Social Change in Hamburg, 1529–1819* (Cambridge, 1985); Lyndal Roper, *The Holy Household: Women and Morals in Reformation Augsburg* (Oxford, 1989); N. Birnbaum, 'The Zwinglian Reformation in Zurich', *Past and Present*, 15 (1959), pp. 27–47. It is possible to pursue many different paths of inquiry in relation to Strasbourg: see in particular Miriam U. Chrisman, *Strasbourg and the Reform* (New Haven and London, 1967); idem, *Lay Culture, Learned Culture: Books and Social Change in Strasbourg, 1480–1599* (New Haven, 1982); Lorna Jane Abray, *The People's Reformation: Magistrates, Clergy and Commons in Strasbourg, 1500–1518* (Oxford, 1985); Thomas A. Brady, *Ruling Class, Regime and Reformation at Strasbourg, 1520–55* (Leyden, 1978). It is also instructive to note that a centre of 'radical' Protestantism could become a Catholic stronghold: see R. Po-chia Hsia, *Society and Religion in Münster, 1535–1618* (New Haven, 1984).

5 NEW DIMENSIONS

1. On the character of humanism, see in particular, Paul O. Kristeller, *Renaissance Thought* (New York, 1961); John Stephens, *The Italian Renaissance* (London, 1990), Part One. On the diffusion of the Renaissance from Italy, see Peter Burke, *The Renaissance* (London, 1987); Sem Dresden, *Humanism in the Renaissance*, trans. Margaret King (London, 1968); Anthony Goodman and Angus MacKay (eds) *The Impact of Humanism on Western Europe* (London, 1990); Roy

Porter and Mikulas Teich (eds) *The Renaissance in National Context* (Cambridge, 1992). On the 'scientific' implications, see Allen Debus, *Man and Nature in the Renaissance* (Cambridge, 1978); on the religious implications, H. A. Enno van Gelder, *The Two Reformations in the Sixteenth Century* (The Hague, 1964).

2. See Quentin Skinner, *The Foundations of Modern Political Thought*, 2 vols (Cambridge, 1978), vol. 1, pp. 3–22; Richard Mackenney, *The City-State, 1500–1700* (London, 1989), pp. 3–4.

3. For a useful introduction, see A. G. Dickens, *The Age of Humanism and Reformation* (London, 1977), pp. 3–13. The quotation is in *Letters from Petrarch*, sel. and trans. Morris Bishop (Bloomington, Ind., 1966), p. 200. On the place of history in humanist thinking, see Peter Burke (ed.) *The Renaissance Sense of the Past* (London, 1969).

4. On civic humanism, see Skinner, *Foundations*, vol. 1, pp. 69–112, and the texts in Benjamin Kohl and Ronald Witt (eds) *The Earthly Republic* (Manchester, 1978); on neo-platonism, see H. R. Trevor-Roper, 'Sir Thomas More and Utopia' in his collection, *Renaissance Essays* (London, 1985), pp. 24–58, and the texts in Ernst Cassirer, Paul O. Kristeller and John H. Randall (eds) *The Renaissance Philosophy of Man* (Chicago, 1948). On mysticism and observation see Debus, *Man and Nature*, p. 53.

5. Valla is quoted in Burke, *Sense of Past*, p. 58; on Colet, see ibid, p. 60. On the different regional contexts, see Goodman and Mackay, *Humanism*; and Porter and Teich, *Renaissance*. The quotations from *The Handbook of the Militant Christian* are taken from *The Essential Erasmus*, sel. and trans. John P. Dolan (New York, 1964), pp. 59, 36–7, 68; that from *The Praise of Folly*, ibid, pp. 129–30. On the offers made to Erasmus, see H. R. Trevor-Roper, 'Erasmus and the Crisis of Christian Humanism', in his *Renaissance Essays*, pp. 59–60.

6. On humanism in France, see Dresden, *Humanism*, pp. 142–213; Enno van Gelder, *Two Reformations*, pp. 267–308; on Lefèvre, Eugene F. Rice, 'The Humanist Idea of Christian Antiquity: Lefèvre d'Étaples and his Circle', in Werner L. Gundersheimer (ed.) *French Humanism, 1470–1600* (London, 1969), pp. 163–80. When discussing Rabelais, it is a surprisingly fashionable convention to cite the very old book by Mikhail Bakhtin, *Rabelais and his World*, trans. Hélène Iswolsky (Boston, 1968), which, if consulted, should be read in conjunction with the review by Frances A. Yates, published as 'The Last Laugh' in *Ideas and Ideals in the Northern Renaissance* (London, 1984), vol. 3 of her collected essays, pp. 153–63, in which is quoted Rabelais's comment on Erasmus, pp. 156–7.

7. On Cisneros's offer, see Trevor-Roper, 'Erasmus', p. 60; on Erasmian influence in Spain, see Marcel Bataillon, *Erasme et l'Espagne* (Paris, 1937), and the comments in J. H. Elliott, *Imperial Spain, 1469–1716* (London, 1963), pp. 161–2, 215–16.

8. A highly readable selection exists as Giorgio Vasari, *Lives of the Artists*, trans. George Bull (London, 1965). There are two brilliant general introductions to the art of the Renaissance: Kenneth Clark, *Civilisation* (London, 1969), chs.4–7; E. H. Gombrich, *The Story of Art*, 13th edn, (London, 1978), chs.12–18. For more detail, see Peter and Linda Murray, *The Art of the Renaissance* (London, 1963);

Michael Levey, *Early Renaissance* (Harmondsworth, 1970) and *High Renaissance* (Harmondsworth, 1975); Erwin Panofsky, *Renaissance and Renascences in Western Art* (New York, 1972); Anthony Blunt, *Artistic Theory in Italy, 1450–1600* (Oxford, 1968).

9. On the diplomatic context of the Holbein commission, see J. D. Mackie, *The Earlier Tudors, 1485–1558* (Oxford, 1966), p. 404; Karl Brandi, *The Emperor Charles V*, trans. C. V. Wedgwood (London, 1965), p. 434; David Starkey (ed.) *Henry VIII: A European Court in England* (London, 1991), pp. 138–71; on Rudolf II, see R. J. W. Evans, *Rudolf II and his World* (Oxford, 1973), p. 182.

10. See Dresden, *Humanism*, pp. 94–107 on the quest for harmony; Debus, *Man and Nature*, pp. 35–47 on the understanding of botany; ibid, pp. 60–89 on Vesalius and Copernicus; Evans, *Rudolf II*, esp. p. 171 on the personnel at the Emperor's court. On the implications of a scientific notion of infinity, see Stephen Hawking, *A Brief History of Time* (London, 1987).

11. On Montaigne, see Dresden, *Humanism*, pp. 184–213; Enno van Gelder, *Two Reformations*, pp. 386–93; Peter Burke, *Montaigne* (Oxford, 1981). The quotations used here are from *The Essayes of Michael Lord of Montaigne*, trans. John Florio (1603) (London, 1891), pp. 61, 2, 26, 38, 43, 34.

12. The quotation from Leonardo's notebooks is in J. Bronowski, 'Leonardo da Vinci', in J. H. Plumb (ed.) *The Penguin Book of the Renaissance* (Harmondsworth, 1964), p. 188; see also Kenneth Clark, *Leonardo da Vinci* (Harmondsworth, 1959), esp. pp. 151–60. On Dürer, see the incomparable work by Erwin Panofsky, *The Life and Art of Albrecht Dürer*, 4th edn (Princeton, 1955), esp. pp. 156–71, 198–9. On the crisis among Italian painters, see the text of a lecture by Kenneth Clark, *A Failure of Nerve: Italian Painting, 1520–35* (Oxford, 1967), esp. pp. 13, 24–5. Michelangelo's sonnet is in *Complete Poems and Selected Letters of Michelangelo*, trans. Creighton Gilbert, ed. Robert N. Linscott (New York, 1970), p. 8; for the *Pietà*, see the complete edition by Ludwig Goldscheider, *Michelangelo: Paintings, Sculptures, Architecture*, 4th edn (London, 1964), Plates 262–3.

13. The text of Bebel's speech appears in Gerald Strauss (ed.) *Manifestations of Discontent in Germany on the Eve of the Reformation* (Bloomington, Ind., 1971), pp. 67–8; see also A. G. Dickens, *The German Nation and Martin Luther* (London, 1976), esp. pp. 21–48.

14. Luther's words are taken from, 'An Appeal to the Ruling Class of German Nationality', in Bertram Lee Woolf (ed.) *Reformation Writings of Martin Luther*, 2 vols, (London, 1952–56), vol. 1, pp. 127–8; the *Preface*, ibid, vol. 2, p. 278.

15. The passage from Vergerio, *De ingenuis moribus*, is in W. H. Woodward (ed.) *Vittorino da Feltre and Other Humanist Educators* (Cambridge, 1921), pp. 99–100; Erasmus's words are taken from *De ratione studii*, in *Desiderius Erasmus concerning the Aim and Method of Education*, ed. W. H. Woodward, intro. Craig R. Thompson (New York, 1964), p. 162 and *De pueris ... instituendis*, p. 181.

16. On the expansion of educational institutions, see Denys Hay, 'Schools and Universities', *NCMH*, vol. 2, pp. 414–37; Henry Kamen, *The Iron*

Century: *Social Change in Europe, 1550–1660* (London, 1971), pp. 284–97; R. Po-chia Hsia, *Social Discipline in the Reformation: Central Europe, 1550–1750* (London, 1989), esp. p. 15; Richard L. Kagan, 'Universities in Castile', *Past and Present*, 49 (1970), pp. 44–71; Lawrence Stone, 'The Educational Revolution in England, 1560–1640', *Past and Present*, 28 (1964), pp. 41–80.

17. On the spread of printing, see the abridged work by Elizabeth L. Eisenstein, *The Printing Revolution in Early Modern Europe* (Cambridge, 1983); on the diffusion of presses, *CAWH*, pp. 144–5; on printing techniques, see the splendid feature 'The Birth of Printing' in Edith Simon, *The Reformation* (Time-Life International, The Netherlands, 1967), pp. 133–41. On Erasmus and Froben, see Margaret Mann Phillips, *Erasmus and the Northern Renaissance* (London, 1949), esp. pp. 72–3; on Aldus, Martin Lowry, *The World of Aldus Manutius* (Oxford, 1979); on Luther's sales, Woolf, *Reformation Writings*, vol. 2, p. 274; on Luther's influence on Coverdale and Foxe, see E. G. Rupp, *The Righteousness of God: Luther Studies* (London, 1953), p. 37; on the price of a Bible in Strasbourg, Lorna Jane Abray, *The People's Reformation: Magistrates, Clergy and Commons in Strasbourg, 1500–1598* (Oxford, 1985), p. 23. The Henrician clergyman is quoted in E. G. Rupp, 'The Battle of the Books: The Ferment of Ideas and the Beginning of the Reformation', in P. Brooks (ed.) *Reformation Principle and Practice* (London, 1980), p. 11.

18. These examples of anti-academic attitudes are located as follows: Vergerio in Woodward, *Humanist Educators*, p. 110; Erasmus in Cambridge in Mann Philips, *Erasmus*, pp. 65–6; Luther in that key text, 'On Monastic Vows', in *Works*, ed. J. Pelikan and H. T. Lehmann, 55 vols, (St Louis and Philadelphia, 1955–75), vol. 44, *The Christian in Society*, ed. J. Atkinson (Philadelphia, 1966), p. 259; Montaigne, *Essays*, pp. 57, 58.

19. Montaigne is quoted in Burke, *Montaigne*, p. 22; see also J. H. Hexter, 'The Education of the Aristocracy in the Renaissance', in his collection of essays, *Reappraisals in History* (London, 1961), pp. 45–70.

20. See in particular, R. W. Scribner, *For the Sake of Simple Folk: Popular Propaganda for the German Reformation* (Cambridge, 1981); Miriam U. Chrisman, *Lay Culture, Learned Culture: Books and Social Change in Strasbourg, 1480–1599* (New Haven, 1982); Natalie Zemon Davis, *Society and Culture in Early Modern France* (Cambridge, 1987); Silvana Seidel Menchi, *Erasmo in Italia, 1520–1580* (Turin, 1987); Richard Mackenney, *Tradesmen and Traders: The World of the Guilds in Venice and Europe, c.1250–c.1650* (London, 1987), pp. 174–95: a part of Caravia's poem, in an uneven English version wrongly attributed to me, appears in B. S. Pullan and D. S. Chambers (eds) *Venice: A Documentary History* (Oxford, 1992), pp. 213–16.

6   THE DISSOLUTION OF MONASTICISM

1. On the development of this set of views, see A. G. Dickens and John Tonkin, *The Reformation in Historical Thought* (Oxford, 1985).

Among general surveys, see Euan Cameron, *The European Reformation* (Oxford, 1991); Pierre Chaunu (ed.) *The Reformation*, trans. Victoria Acland *et al.*, (London, 1989); A. G. Dickens, *Reformation and Society in Sixteenth-Century Europe* (London, 1966), esp. p. 13, for an illustration of Wyclif striking a spark, Hus holding a candle and Luther brandishing a torch; idem, *The English Reformation* (London, 1967), particularly penetrating on Lollardy, pp. 41–62; and on the antecedents K. B. McFarlane, *Wycliffe and English Non-Conformity* (Harmondsworth, 1972); Margaret Aston, *The Fifteenth Century: The Prospect of Europe* (London, 1969), esp. p. 129 for an illustration of a Hussite war waggon. On the intellectual traditions, see Alistair E. McGrath, *Reformation Thought: An Introduction* (Oxford, 1988); Steven Ozment, *The Age of Reform, 1250–1550* (New Haven, 1980); and the important collections, idem (ed.) *The Reformation in Medieval Perspective* (Chicago, 1972), and Charles Trinkaus and Heiko A. Oberman (eds) *The Pursuit of Holiness in Late Medieval and Renaissance Religion* (Leyden, 1974). Of the many other works of Heiko A. Oberman, see *The Harvest of Medieval Theology* (Cambridge, Mass., 1963); *Forerunners of the Reformation* (New York, 1966); *Masters of the Reformation*, trans. Denis Martin (Cambridge, 1981); and his collection of essays, *The Dawn of the Reformation* (Edinburgh, 1986).

2. On the link between the new learning and the reform, see A. G. Dickens, *The Age of Humanism and Reformation* (London, 1977); idem, *The German Nation and Martin Luther* (London, 1976), esp. pp. 21–71; H. A. Enno van Gelder, *The Two Reformations in the Sixteenth Century* (The Hague, 1964).

3. For these examples, see A. W. Haddan and W. Stubbs (eds) *Councils and Ecclesiastical Documents Relating to Great Britain and Ireland*, vol. 3, (Oxford, 1871), pp. 328–31, 361: my thanks to Dr Tom Brown for this reference. Liutprand of Cremona's account appears in Boyd Hill (ed.) *Medieval Monarchy in Action* (London, 1972), pp. 137–49; the fated lovers' passionate indiscretion is recorded in *The Letters of Abelard and Heloise*, trans. Betty Radice (Harmondsworth, 1974), p. 146. On the religious revival in Renaissance Italy, see Iris Origo, *The World of San Bernardino* (London, 1963); Brian Pullan, *A History of Early Renaissance Italy* (London, 1973), pp. 305–40.

4. See Paolo Prodi, *The Papal Prince*, trans. Susan Haskins (Cambridge, 1987), esp. pp. viii, 2–3; Peter Partner, 'The Papal State: 1417–1600', in Mark Greengrass (ed.) *Conquest and Coalescence: The Shaping of the State in Early Modern Europe* (London, 1991), pp. 25–47.

5. Among many citations, see Bertram Lee Woolf (ed.) *Reformation Writings of Martin Luther*, 2 vols (London, 1952–56), vol. 2, p. 130.

6. On the famous words of Luther at Worms, see Woolf, *Reformation Writings*, vol. 2, pp. 127–82: this quotation is from p. 157.

7. The literature *on* Luther is enormous, and it may be more helpful to concentrate on the literature *by* Luther. As E. G. Rupp has said, it is vital 'to listen to Luther himself', and Luther's own writings remain the best guide to the significance of what he thought. Their bulk makes selection difficult. There is a complete edition in translation, published as *Luther's Works*, ed. J. Pelikan and H. Lehman (St Louis, 1955–75). Browsing among these is always productive, for any smaller collection

is not necessarily representative. Of the collections, among the most manageable and accessible are the two volumes ed. Woolf and the masterly E. G. Rupp and Benjamin Drewery (eds) *Martin Luther* (London, 1970). Important individual works with full critical apparatus can be found in *The Library of Christian Classics* published in Philadelphia by the Westminster Press. Of the many biographical studies, see especially Heiko A. Oberman, *Luther: Man between God and the Devil* (London, 1985); the ones used here are Roland H. Bainton, *Here I Stand: A Life of Martin Luther* (New York, 1950), quotations from pp. 60 and 64; Michael Mullett, *Luther* (London, 1986); E. G. Rupp, *The Righteousness of God: Luther Studies* (London, 1953), with specific references drawn from pp. 3, 192–3. On the differences between Luther's earlier and later life, it is instructive to read E. G. Rupp, *Luther's Progress to the Diet of Worms* (New York, 1964) and then Mark U. Edwards, *Luther and the False Brethren* (Stanford, Cal., 1975). On specific intellectual influences, see McGrath, *Reformation Thought*; Stephen Ozment, *Mysticism and Dissent* (New Haven, 1973).

8. E. G. Rupp and Philip S. Watson (eds) *Luther and Erasmus: Free Will and Salvation* (Philadelphia and London, 1969), p. 344; see also Rupp, *Righteousness*, pp. 259–88.

9. The text is in Woolf, *Reformation Writings*, vol. 1, pp. 336–47: the quotations are from pp. 339, 340, 341, 346. It is vital to grasp that the papal supremacy rested on weak scriptural foundations and that it was founded on principles of Roman law which were strengthened by the canonists throughout the Middle Ages: see the fundamental statement by Walter Ullmann, *A Short History of the Papacy in the Middle Ages* (London, 1972), e.g. pp. 14, 22, 162; and in more detail, idem, *Principles of Government and Politics in the Middle Ages* (London, 1961), chs. 2–4.

10. The text is in Woolf, *Reformation Writings*, vol. 1, pp. 356–79; quotations from pp. 357, 358–9, 366, 370; on circulation, see Rupp, *Progress*, p. 54; Johan Huizinga, *Erasmus and the Age of Reformation*, trans. F. Hotman, (New York, 1957), p. 141.

11. For these examples, see Elizabeth Eisenstein, *The Printing Revolution in Early Modern Europe* (Cambridge, 1983), pp. 9–10 on a 'monastic revival', c.1350–1450; p. 89 on the *Germania*; G. R. Elton, *Reform and Reformation: England, 1509–1558* (London, 1977), p. 242; on the rejection of monasticism, see Cameron, *European Reformation*, pp. 33–4, 251.

12. The quotations are from *Gargantua and Pantagruel*, trans. Sir Thomas Urquhart and Peter Le Motteux (1653–94), 3 vols (Oxford, 1934), vol. 1, pp. 113–17, 153.

13. Luther, 'On Monastic Vows', in *Works*, ed. Pelikan and Lehman, vol. 44, *The Christian in Society*, ed. J. Atkinson (Philadelphia, 1966), pp. 245–400; quotations from pp. 266–7.

14. Urbanus Rhegius is quoted in Lyndal Roper, *The Holy Household: Women and Morals in Reformation Augsburg* (Oxford, 1989), p. 105; on Erasmus's parentage, Huizinga, *Erasmus*, p. 5; Erasmus on marriage is quoted from the *Colloquies*, trans. C. R. Thompson (Chicago, 1965), pp. 110, 354, 194.

15. The quotations on marriage are from Luther's *The Freedom of a Christian*, in Woolf, *Reformation Writings*, vol. 1, p. 363; and his *Letters of Spiritual Counsel*, ed. and trans. T. G. Tappert (London, 1955), p. 273; and from Zwingli's 'The Petition of Eleven Priests to be Allowed to Marry' in *Ulrich Zwingli (1484–1531): Selected Works*, ed. Samuel M. Jackson, intro. Edward Peters, (Philadelphia, 1972), pp. 33, 38.

16. On the famous syphilitics, see E. R. Chamberlin, *Cesare Borgia* (London, 1969), pp. 39, 71; Cellini, *Autobiography*, trans. G. Bull (Harmondsworth, 1956), pp. 111–12; von Hutten and Celtis, Dickens, *German Nation*, p. 34; Philip of Hesse, Luther, *Letters of Spiritual Counsel*, p. 288; on Henry VIII's ulcers, J. J. Scarisbrick, *Henry VIII* (Harmondsworth, 1971), p. 625; see also Dürer's grim woodcut in *The Complete Woodcuts of Albrecht Dürer*, ed. Willi Kurth (New York, 1963), no.92; on the hospital in Venice, Brian Pullan, *Rich and Poor in Renaissance Venice* (Oxford, 1971), p. 234. The examples from Erasmus are from the *Colloquies*, pp. 403–12; 156; Luther on whores is from *Letters of Spiritual Counsel*, pp. 293–4; on More, see G. R. Elton, 'The Real Thomas More?', in P. N. Brooks (ed.) *Reformation Principle and Practice* (London, 1980), pp. 23–31; on the monastic character of Calvin's Geneva, see Chaunu, *The Reformation*, p. 130. On the new importance of marriage in relation to religious changes, see Ozment, *Age of Reform*, pp. 381–96; Roper, *Holy Household*.

7   HOW THE WORD SPREAD

1. On 'confessionalisation', see the powerful work by R. Po-chia Hsia, *Social Discipline in the Reformation: Central Europe, 1550–1750* (London, 1989). As an illustration of the methodological problems of Reformation research, one might cite two books of quite different emphases by the same author: Steven Ozment, *The Reformation in the Cities* (New Haven, 1975) concentrates on the urban milieu, idem, *The Age of Reform, 1250–1550* (New Haven, 1980) concentrates on ideas and tends to treat them in isolation, to the detriment of popular culture or social forces. For a balanced assessment of the multiplicity of approaches and interpretations, see R. W. Scribner, *The German Reformation* (London, 1986); idem, 'The Reformation Movements in Germany' (note the plural), *NCMH*, vol. 2, 2nd ed.(1990), pp. 69–93, and 'Politics and the Institutionalisation of Reform in Germany', ibid, pp. 172–97.

2. Changes in the pattern of worship are lucidly presented in Euan Cameron, *The European Reformation* (Oxford, 1991), pp. 214–26, 80–1, 135–9. On Luther's *volte face* on communion, see G. H. Williams, *The Radical Reformation* (Philadelphia, 1962), p. 42. The quotations from Melanchthon are from his *Commonplaces*, in Wilhelm Pauck (ed.) *Melanchthon and Bucer*, (London, 1969), pp. 152 (on Scripture), 101–2, 105 (on justification). On the progress of the Reformation in the Baltic regions, see David Kirby, *Northern Europe in the Early Modern Period: The Baltic World, 1492–1772* (London, 1990), pp. 81–96. On the Tübingen circle, see Heiko A. Obermann,

Masters of the Reformation, trans. Dennis Martin (Cambridge, 1981). On Luther's tendency to treat even followers as opponents, see Mark U. Edwards, *Luther and the False Brethren* (Stanford, Cal., 1975), with the attack on Bucer quoted on p. 98. Karlstadt receives a measured appraisal from E. G. Rupp, *Patterns of Reformation* (London, 1969), pp. 59–151. On schooling, see Gerald Strauss, *Luther's House of Learning: Indoctrination of the Young in the German Reformation* (Baltimore, 1978): the quotation from the Leisnig constitution is on p. 4, the list of schools on p. 13.

3. But see Scribner, *German Reformation* and Gerald Strauss, 'Success and Failure in the German Reformation', *Past and Present*, 67 (1975), pp. 30–63.

4. The standard biography is G. R. Potter, *Zwingli* (Cambridge, 1976); see also R. C. Walton, *Zwingli's Theocracy* (Toronto, 1967); idem, 'Zwingli: Founding Father of the Reformation Churches', in Richard DeMolen (ed.), *Leaders of the Reformation* (London and Toronto, 1984), pp. 69–98. For the quotations, see G. R. Potter (ed.) *Huldrych Zwingli* (London, 1978), pp. 29–30 on scriptural inspiration; pp. 21–3 for his theses; pp. 62–3, 71 on schooling; p. 31 on the abolition of the mass; p. 34 on the real presence; p. 7 on mercenary service; p. 101 on Luther and p. 107 on Melanchthon. See also 'On the Lord's Supper', in G. W. Bromiley (ed.) *Zwingli and Bullinger* (London, 1953), pp. 188, 190, 204.

5. See the rather neglected work by Clyde L. Manschreck, *Melanchthon: The Quiet Reformer* (Nashville, 1957): the quotations are from pp. 294–5. For Zwingli on the elect, see B. M. G. Reardon, *Religious Thought in the Reformation* (London, 1981), p. 99. Bullinger's account of Zwingli's death is in Potter (ed.) *Huldrych Zwingli*, p. 144; ibid, p. 127 for the appeal to France. For views of his importance and achievements, see Walton, 'Founding Father', p. 83; Potter, *Zwingli*, p. 247.

6. Luther is quoted in Edwards, *False Brethren*, p. 98; Osiander's account of Marburg is in Potter (ed.) *Huldrych Zwingli*, the quotation used is from p. 104. The other quotations are taken from *The Common Places of Martin Bucer*, trans. and ed. David Wright (Abingdon, 1972), pp. 96, 111; and from *De Regno Christi* in Pauck (ed.) *Melanchthon and Bucer*, pp. 223, 226, 251, 252, 354.

7. On the economic contrasts between Zurich and Strasbourg, see Walton, 'Founding Father', p. 79; on Strasbourg itself, Thomas A. Brady, *Ruling Class, Regime and Reformation at Strasbourg, 1520–55* (Leiden, 1978); Miriam U. Chrisman, *Strasbourg and the Reform* (New Haven, 1967), esp. pp. 69–75 on literacy; pp. 83–6, 207–24 on the major reformers; p. 99 on Tilman von Lyn; pp. 201–2 on the rejection of the Augsburg Confession; pp. 260–83 on education and welfare; idem, *Lay Culture, Learned Culture: Books and Social Change in Strasbourg, 1480–1599* (New Haven, 1982), esp. pp. 50–3 on bookmen, p. 145 on the impact of the reform; Capito's letter to Zwingli is quoted on p. 147; Lorna Jane Abray, *The People's Reformation: Magistrates, Clergy and Commons in Strasbourg, 1500–1598* (Oxford, 1985), esp. pp. 70–6 on the progress of moral reform; on poor relief, see also Miriam U. Chrisman, 'Urban Poor in the Sixteenth Century:

The Case of Strasbourg', in M. U. Chrisman and O. Gründler (eds) *Social Groups and Religious Ideas in the Sixteenth Century* (Kalamazoo, Mich., 1978), pp. 59–68.

8. The quotations are from *De Regno Christi*, in Pauck (ed.), *Melanchthon and Bucer*, pp. 280, 277, 336, 306, 257, 308. On Bucer's impact on English puritanism, see Christopher Hill, *Society and Puritanism in Pre-Revolutionary England* (London, 1969), pp. 213, 272.

9. For an intriguing study of Calvin, see William J. Bouwsma, *John Calvin: A Sixteenth-Century Portrait* (Oxford, 1988), which may be supplemented with François Wendel, *Calvin: The Origins and Development of his Religious Thought*, trans. Philip Mairet (London, 1965), which is particularly helpful on the importance of predestination; and the excellent collection of documents, G. R. Potter and M. Greengrass (eds) *John Calvin* (London, 1983): see the editors' comments on Geneva on p. 43. Also on the Genevan context, see H. Höpfl, *The Christian Polity of John Calvin* (Cambridge, 1982), esp. p. 57; E. W. Monter, *Calvin's Geneva* (New York, 1967); Richard Stauffer, 'Calvin', in Menna Prestwich (ed.) *International Calvinism, 1541–1715* (Oxford, 1985), pp. 15–38; Gillian Lewis, 'Calvinism in Geneva in the Time of Calvin and Béza, 1541–1608', ibid, pp. 39–70; A. Dufour, 'Le mythe de Genève au temps de Calvin', *Schweizerische Zeitschrift für Geschichte*, n.s., 9 (1959), pp. 489–518.

10. See the important words of Höpfl, *Christian Polity*, pp. 1, 53, 57, 129, 109–10. On the opposition to Calvin in Geneva, see Potter and Greengrass, *Calvin*, pp. 85–96; for other contexts, see Michael Lynch, 'Calvinism in Scotland, 1559–1638', in Prestwich, *Calvinism*; pp. 225–56; Alastair Duke, 'The Ambivalent Face of Calvinism in the Netherlands, 1561–1618', ibid, pp. 109–34; Mark Greengrass, *The French Reformation* (Oxford, 1987), esp. pp. 39–43, 62.

11. For the character of Calvinist agencies in the city, see Höpfl, *Christian Polity*, esp. pp. 66, 94; Robert M. Kingdon, 'The Control of Morals in Calvin's Geneva', in L. P. Buck and J. W. Zophy (eds), *The Social History of the Reformation* (Columbus, Ohio, 1972), pp. 3–16. The quotations are taken from Potter and Greengrass, *Calvin*, p. 48 on the acceptance of reform; pp. 45–6 for Calvin's account of his arrival; p. 79 on marriage; p. 82 on visitations; pp. 79–81 on names, swearing and entertainment; p. 112 on relics; p. 116 on Calvin's intolerance.

12. On immigrant printers, see Paul F. Geisendorf, 'Lyon and Geneva in the Sixteenth Century: The Fairs and Printing', in Werner L. Gundersheimer (ed.) *French Humanism, 1470–1600* (London, 1969), pp. 146–59; J. Tedeschi and E. D. Willis, 'Two Italian Translations of Béza and Calvin', *Archiv für Reformationsgeschichte*, 55 (1963), pp. 70–4; Knox is quoted in Potter and Greengrass, *Calvin*, p. 124. For the 'Calvinist International', see the uncharacteristic conceptual extravagance of H. G. Koenigsberger, 'The European Civil War', in H. R. Trevor-Roper (ed.) *The Golden Age of Europe* (London, 1987), p. 136; it is also deployed by Hsia, *Social Discipline*, pp. 32–4; the other term derives from the challenging work by Michael Walzer, *The Revolution of the Saints: A Study in the Origins of Radical Politics* (New York, 1968).

13. To avoid a string of awkward notes, passages from the *Institutes* are referred to in square brackets in the text. The edition used is *Calvin:*

Institutes of the Christian Religion, ed. John T. McNeill, trans. Ford Lewis Battles, 2 vols, (Philadelphia, 1960).

14. On Calvin's doubts, see Bouwsma, *Calvin*, p. 213. The advice not to resist is from Potter and Greengrass, *Calvin*, p. 154; the aggressive words are quoted in Robert M. Kingdon, *Geneva and the Coming of the Wars of Religion in France, 1555–1563* (Geneva, 1956), p. i; and in the penetrating essay by David Foxgrover, 'Calvin as Reformer: Christ's Standard-Bearer', in DeMolen, *Leaders*, p. 186. On the speed of publication, see Tedeschi and Willis, 'Italian Translations'. Farel's emblem is illustrated in Pierre Chaunu (ed.) *The Reformation*, trans. Victoria Acland *et al.* (London, 1989), p. 125.

15. John Frederick is quoted in Gerald Strauss, 'The Mental World of a Saxon Pastor', in P. N. Brooks (ed.) *Reformation Principle and Practice* (London, 1981), p. 160; see also idem, 'Success and Failure', p. 53; on Bucer's problems, see Abray, *People's Reformation*, pp. 72–84; on Calvin's exile, Potter and Greengrass, *Calvin*, pp. 49–53; on Lyon, Richard Gascon, *Grand commerce et vie urbaine au xvie siècle: Lyon et ses marchands*, 2 vols (Paris, 1971), vol. 2, pp. 465–532; on Rouen, Philip Benedict, *Rouen and the Wars of Religion* (Cambridge, 1981), esp. pp. 97, 188–90; Michael Lynch, *Edinburgh and the Reformation* (Edinburgh, 1981), esp. p. v. The quotation from Calvin's ordinances is from Potter and Greengrass, *Calvin*, p. 72; on rural France, A. N. Galpern, *The Religions of the People in Sixteenth-Century Champagne* (Cambridge, Mass., 1977), e.g. p. 162; Greengrass, *French Reformation*, p. 62; on the Netherlands, Alistair Duke, 'Towards a Reformed Policy in Holland, 1572–78', in his *Reformation and Revolt in the Low Countries* (London and Ronceverte, 1990), pp. 199 and 219.

16. On the self-perpetuation of the clerical order, see Hsia, *Social Discipline*, pp. 14–15. For a superb quantification of princely sponsorship, see Cameron, *European Reformation*, p. 269. On the dangers for princes, see A. G. Dickens, *Reformation and Society in Sixteenth-Century Europe* (London, 1966), p. 75; on England, see G. R. Elton, *Reform and Reformation: England 1509–1558* (London, 1977), pp. 75–6, 177–9; J. J. Scarisbrick, *Henry VIII* (Harmondsworth, 1971), esp. chs.9 and 10; on France, R. J. Knecht, 'The Early Reformation in England and France: A Comparison', *History*, 57 (1972), pp. 4–6; on Denmark, G. R. Elton, *Reformation Europe, 1517–1559* (London, 1963), p. 128; on Sweden, there is a brilliant account in Michael Roberts, *The Early Vasas: A History of Sweden, 1523–1611* (Cambridge, 1968), pp. 107–43, esp. pp. 115, 141.

17. On these regions, see Hsia, *Social Discipline*, p. 26; Claus-Peter Clasen, *The Palatinate in European History, 1555–1618* (Oxford, 1966); Henry J. Cohn, 'The Territorial Princes in Germany's Second Reformation, 1559–1622', in Prestwich, *International Calvinism*, esp. p. 161; R. J. W. Evans, 'Calvinism in East Central Europe: Hungary and her Neighbours, 1540–1700', ibid, pp. 171, 177.

8 HOW THE IMAGE TRIUMPHED

1. On this very complicated subject there are so many laminations that the questions of emphasis and priority are critical. The problems are

neatly defined in N. S. Davidson, *The Counter-Reformation* (Oxford, 1987). For a lively and lucid view of Catholic reform and the reactions to Protestantism, see A. G. Dickens, *The Counter-Reformation* (London, 1968). For a measured appraisal of internal problems and Catholic reform, see Pierre Janelle, *The Catholic Reformation* (West Drayton, 1971). For a view which emphasises Catholicism's global impact, see A. D. Wright, *The Counter-Reformation: Catholic Europe and the Non-Christian World* (London, 1982). On the sources of religious inspiration, see H. Outram Evenett, *The Spirit of the Counter-Reformation*, ed. with a postscript by John Bossy (Notre Dame, Indiana, 1970); for the social translation of that spirit, see John Bossy, *Christianity in the West, 1400–1700* (Oxford, 1985). One of the most convincing interpretative syntheses is Jean Delumeau, *Catholicism between Luther and Voltaire: A New View of the Counter-Reformation*, trans. Jeremy Moiser (London, 1977).

2. On the tensions – spiritual and political – between Spanish and Roman Catholicism, see G. R. Elton, *Reformation Europe, 1517–1559* (London, 1963), pp. 207–8; Dermot Fenlon, *Heresy and Obedience in Tridentine Italy: Cardinal Pole and the Counter-Reformation* (Cambridge, 1972); A. D. Wright, 'The Borromean Ideal and the Spanish Church', in John M. Headley and John B. Tomaro (eds), *San Carlo Borromeo* (London and Toronto, 1988), pp. 188–207.

3. Christopher Hill, *Society and Puritanism in Pre-revolutionary England* (London, 1969), admits at the outset that 'I have not examined the extent to which the ideas of Puritans were shared with or derived from continental Protestantism', p. 9, and goes on to show the wide range of interpretations and usage even in the restricted context of seventeenth-century England, ibid, ch. 1, 'The Definition of a Puritan'. However, there is a case for saying that the term might be better understood in a broader perspective, see e.g. Michael Walzer, *The Revolution of the Saints: A Study in the Origins of Radical Politics* (New York, 1969). On the confrontation of the Calvinist and Jesuit strains of puritanism, see R. Po-chia Hsia, *Social Discipline in the Reformation: Central Europe, 1550–1750* (London, 1989), esp. p. 27. The revealing quotation from James VI and I is in James Brodrick, *Robert Bellarmine, 1542–1621*, 2 vols, (London, 1950), vol. 2, p. 221.

4. On San Bernardino, see Iris Origo, *The World of San Bernardino* (London, 1963), the quotations are from pp. 50 and 111; on Savonarola, Donald Weinstein, *Savonarola and Florence* (Princeton, 1970); the quotation is from *RR*, pp. 646–7; on the contrasting condition of the institutional church, see Denys Hay, *The Church in Italy in the Fifteenth Century* (Cambridge, 1977).

5. On the background, see Angus MacKay, *Spain in the Middle Ages: From Frontier to Empire, 1000–1500* (London, 1977); on the Spanish Church in our period, Ricardo Garcia-Villoslada (ed.) *Historia de la iglesia en Espana*, vol. 3, i, *La iglesia en la Espana de los siglos xv y xvi* (Madrid, 1980). For a concise revisionist overview, see Henry Kamen, *Golden Age Spain* (London, 1988). On Ferdinand, see Machiavelli, *The Prince*, trans. E. Dacres (London, 1640), ch. xxi, pp. 179–81.

6. On Cisneros, see Garcia-Villoslada, *iglesia*, pp. 268–90; see also the remarks of J. H. Elliott, *Imperial Spain, 1469–1716* (Harmondsworth,

1970), pp. 53–4, 104; on his enigmatic combination of puritan and Erasmian impulses, Henry Kamen, *Spain, 1469–1714: A Society of Conflict* (London, 1983), pp. 47–8. On the Inquisition, see idem, *The Spanish Inquisition* (New York, 1965): the quotations and figures are from pp. 85–6. On the proliferation of the Inquisition in the Spanish dependencies, see William Monter, *Ritual, Myth and Magic in Early Modern Europe* (Brighton, 1983), p. 62.

7. On the Roman Inquisition of the Middle Ages, see Walter Ullmann, *A Short History of the Papacy in the Middle Ages* (London, 1972), p. 253; the quotations relating to its revival in Italy in the sixteenth century are from L. von Ranke, *History of the Popes of Rome*, trans. E. Foster, 3 vols (London, 1866), vol. 1, pp. 85, 157, 159. On the tribunal's activities, see Monter, *Ritual*, pp. 60–77; and, in more detail, Stephen Haliczer (ed.) *Inquisition and Society in Early Modern Europe* (London, 1987); on Venice, Brian Pullan, *The Jews of Europe and the Inquisition of Venice, 1550–1670* (Oxford, 1983); Ruth Martin, *Witchcraft and the Inquisition in Venice, 1550–1650* (Oxford, 1989). The manual is available as Nicolau Eymeric, *Le manuel des inquisiteurs*, ed. and trans. L. Sala-Molins (Paris–The Hague, 1973): Peña's remarks are on p. 130. On the impact of the new Catholicism, see the majestic interpretation of H. R. Trevor-Roper, *Religion, the Reformation and Social Change*, 2nd edn (London, 1972), pp. 1–45; but on the modest scale of inquisitorial executions, Monter, *Ritual*, p. 62; Kamen, *Spain*, pp. 185–90; G. H. Williams, *The Radical Reformation* (Philadelphia, 1962), pp. 5–6.

8. On the uncertainties of the 'moderate' position, see Peter Matheson, *Cardinal Contarini at Regensburg* (Oxford, 1972), esp. p. 181. The quotations from Ignatius are found in James Brodrick, *The Origin of the Jesuits* (London, 1940), p. 67, n.1 on his rehabilitation; p. 107 on the mission to Ireland; *The Spiritual Exercises*, trans. W. H. Longridge, (London, 1919), pp. 198, 199; and in Ranke, *History of the Popes*, vol. 1, p. 147 on obedience to the papacy. On missionary activity, a roseate picture is available in J. Brodrick, *The Progress of the Jesuits* (London, 1946); more convincing are the examples of Jesuit influence discussed in R. J. W. Evans, *Rudolf II and his World* (Oxford, 1979), p. 158; Hsia, *Social Discipline*, pp. 39–110; the quotation concerning the Venetian hospital is from Brian Pullan, *Rich and Poor in Renaissance Venice* (Oxford, 1971), p. 265; on Borja, Michael Mallett, *The Borgias* (London, 1971), pp. 242–55.

9. Charles V recorded his frustrations in his autobiography: see *The Autobiography of the Emperor Charles V*, trans. Leonard Simpson (London, 1862), pp. 72–3, 74; on the tensions between Empire and papacy, see Fenlon, *Heresy and Obedience*, esp. p. 59; Elton, *Reformation Europe*, pp. 187–97. The Spanish grumble at Trent is quoted in Hubert Jedin, *Crisis and Closure of the Council of Trent*, trans. N. D. Smith (London, 1967), pp. 51–2.

10. The Bull of Convocation can be consulted in Eric Cochrane and Julius Kirshner (eds) *The Renaissance*, vol. 5 of *University of Chicago Readings in Western Civilization* (Chicago, 1986), pp. 387–95: this quotation is from p. 392; Pole's Appeal is in *RR*, pp. 665–72: this quotation is from p. 668. The quotations from Laynez are from *Jacobi*

Lainez Disputationes Tridentinae, ed. Hartmann Grisar, 2 vols (Innsbruck, 1886), vol. 2, pp. 165, 192; Salmerón is quoted in Hubert Jedin, *A History of the Council of Trent*, trans. Dom Ernest Graf, OSB, 2 vols (London, 1957–61), vol. 2, p. 257. The translation of Jedin's work remains incomplete: see Hubert Jedin, *Geschichte des Konzils von Trient*, 4 vols, (Freiburg, 1949–75).

11. The declaration on justification is quoted in Ranke, *History of the Popes*, vol. 1, p. 155. A concise version of the declarations – all the more powerful for its compression – is available in H. Bettenson (ed.) *Documents of the Christian Church* (Oxford, 1967), pp. 261–6: these quotations are taken from pp. 263, 264 and 266. Guise is quoted in Jedin, *Crisis and Closure*, p. 156; the Tridentine profession appears in Bettenson, *Documents*, pp. 266–8.

12. See *The Life of Saint Teresa of Avila by Herself*, trans. J. M. Cohen (Harmondsworth, 1957), p. 291; on the accommodation of rural traditions by the maintenance of universal authority at the local level, see William A. Christian, *Local Religion in Sixteenth-Century Spain* (Princeton, 1981), esp. p. 3; and more generally, Delumeau, *Catholicism*, pp. 175–202; Steven Ozment, *The Age of Reform, 1250–1550* (New Haven, 1980), pp. 397–418; John Bossy, 'The Counter-Reformation and the People of Catholic Europe', *Past and Present*, 47 (1970), pp. 51–70; idem, 'The Social History of Confession', *Transactions of the Royal Historical Society*, ser. 5, 25 (1975), pp. 21–38; Brian Pullan, 'Catholics and the Poor in Early Modern Europe', ibid, 26 (1976), pp. 15–34. On Italy, see Wright, 'Borromeo'; Paolo Prodi, 'The Application of the Tridentine Decrees: The Organisation of the Diocese of Bologna during the Episcopate of Cardinal Gabriele Paleotti', in Eric Cochrane (ed.) *The Late Italian Renaissance, 1525–1630* (London, 1970), pp. 226–43. Parts of Casale's diary are available in Cochrane and Kirshner, *Renaissance*, pp. 409–26: the quotations used here are from pp. 413, 419–20. On confraternities in a Counter-Reformation context, see Christopher Black, *Italian Confraternities in the Sixteenth Century* (Cambridge, 1989).

13. On cultural change in Italy, see Eric Cochrane, *Italy 1530–1630* (London, 1988), esp. chs. 6 and 7; for the decree on painting, Janelle, *Catholic Reformation*, p. 160; and in general, Emile Mâle, *L'art religieux après le Concile de Trente* (Paris, 1932) and – with a still stronger seventeenth-century emphasis – A. Asor Rosa, *La cultura della Controriforma* (Rome, 1979); on confraternities and 'propaganda', Black, *Italian Confraternities*, pp. 234–67 (p. 264 on Tintoretto).

14. On the ideological struggle at the social level, see Hsia, *Social Discipline*; Trevor-Roper's remarks are from his valedictory lecture at Oxford, 'History and Imagination', which is published in the collection of that title in his honour, Hugh Lloyd-Jones, Valerie Pearl and Blair Worden (eds) *History and Imagination* (London, 1981), p. 367.

9   VICTIMS

1. Machiavelli's opinions are found in *The Discourses*, trans. Leslie Walker, ed. Bernard Crick (Harmondsworth, 1970), pp. 300, 490.

On rebellion and the social world from which it rose, Perez Zagorin, *Rebels and Rulers, 1500–1660*, 2 vols (Cambridge, 1982); on the economic situation in the Netherlands, see J. H. Elliott, *Europe Divided, 1559–1598* (London, 1968), pp. 138–44; and on the spontaneity of riots, Phyllis Mack Crew, *Calvinist Preaching and Iconoclasm in the Netherlands, 1544–1569* (Cambridge, 1973), esp. p. 7. On ritual violence in Venice, see Robert C. Davis, *Shipbuilders of the Venetian Arsenal* (Baltimore, 1991), pp. 135–49; on lawlessness on the mainland, Gaetano Cozzi, 'Authority and the Law in Renaissance Venice', in J. R. Hale (ed.) *Renaissance Venice* (London, 1973), pp. 293–346; on piracy, F. Braudel, *The Mediterranean and the Mediterranean World in the Age of Philip II*, trans. S. Reynolds, 2 vols (London, 1972), vol. 2, pp. 734–56; Alberto Tenenti, *Piracy and the Decline of Venice, 1580–1615*, trans. Brian and Janet Pullan (London, 1967); Peter Earle, *Corsairs of Malta and Barbary* (London, 1970). On the violence of everyday life, Johan Huizinga, *The Waning of the Middle Ages*, trans. F. Hopman (Harmondsworth, 1955), pp. 9–30; E. Le Roy Ladurie, *Carnival: A People's Uprising in Romans, 1579–80*, trans. M. Feeney (Harmondsworth, 1981); Keith Thomas, *Religion and the Decline of Magic* (Harmondsworth, 1971), pp. 3–26. On ubiquitous crime, poor detection and terrifying deterrents, see Michael Weisser, *Crime and Punishment in Early Modern Europe* (Brighton, 1982); John H. Langbein, *Prosecuting Crime in the Renaissance* (Cambridge, Mass., 1974); Mary Elizabeth Perry, *Crime and Society in Early Modern Seville* (Hanover, New Eng., 1980); on the religious intolerance of whoever held the upper hand, see Conrad Russell, *The Crisis of Parliaments: English History, 1509–1660* (Oxford, 1971), p. 141.

2. On the papacy, see Denys Hay and John Law, *Italy in the Age of the Renaissance, 1380–1530* (London, 1989), p. 163; on the significance of the More trial, see E. G. Rupp, *Thomas More: The King's Good Servant* (London, 1978), pp. 59–60; on royal headship of the Church and its significance in Europe, see G. R. Elton, '1555: A Political Retrospect', in Joel Hurstfield (ed.) *The Reformation Crisis* (London, 1965), pp. 72–82; on the emergence of the confessional state, R. Po-chia Hsia, *Social Discipline in the Reformation: Central Europe, 1550–1750* (London, 1989), esp. p. 168; on the unusual conditions in Ireland, D. B. Quinn, *The Elizabethans and the Irish* (Ithaca, N.Y., 1966), pp. 83–7.

3. In general, see the important study by Henry Kamen, *The Rise of Toleration* (London, 1967). Castellio is quoted in John Edwards, *The Jews in Christian Europe, 1400–1700* (London, 1988), pp. 153–4; on the expulsions from Spain, see ibid, p. 34 and from the Empire, ibid, p. 104. On persecution as an index of changes in Christian feeling and the policies of Christian states, see Norman Cohn, *Europe's Inner Demons* (London, 1976), p. 262; Edwards, *Jews*, p. 98, referring to Jonathan Israel, *European Jewry in the Age of Mercantilism, 1550–1750* (Oxford, 1985).

4. On the Papal States, see Edwards, *Jews*, pp. 66, 68; on central and eastern Europe, ibid, pp. 109–23; on Venice, Brian Pullan, *The Jews of Europe and the Inquisition of Venice, 1550–1670* (Oxford, 1983); Riccardo Calimani, *The Ghetto of Venice*, trans. Katherine Silberblatt

Wolfthal (New York, 1987); the quotation is from Brian Pullan, *Rich and Poor in Renaissance Venice* (Oxford, 1971), p. 489; on the Jews in the United Provinces, see C. R. Boxer, *The Dutch Republic, 1600–1800* (London, 1965), pp. 129–31.

5. See the classic work of G. H. Williams, *The Radical Reformation* (Philadelphia, 1962); the imaginative thematic treatment, Michael Mullett, *Radical Religious Movements in Early Modern Europe* (London, 1980); and the recent summary of James M. Stayer, 'The Anabaptists and the Sects', *NCMH*, vol. 2, 2nd edn (1990), pp. 118–43 – of vital importance in that it takes the 'sects' away from the 'margins' of society. There are two other highly significant studies: Claus-Peter Clasen, *Anabaptism: A Social History, 1525–1618: Switzerland, Austria, Moravia, South and Central Germany* (Ithaca, N.Y., 1972): see pp. 1–14 on early developments and association with the peasant rebellion of 1525; and Peter Klassen, *The Economics of Anabaptism* (London–The Hague–Paris, 1964): see pp. 53–64 on the Hutterites in Moravia. Documents concerning the Servetus case are presented in G. R. Potter and M. Greengrass (eds) *John Calvin* (London, 1983), pp. 100–10: these quotations are from p. 105. Zwingli's opinions appear at length in *Ulrich Zwingli: Selected Works*, ed. Samuel M. Jackson, intro. by Edward Peters (Philadelphia, 1972), pp. 123–258: these quotations are from p. 128. Stadler's words are taken from G. H. Williams and Angela M. Mergal (eds) *Spiritual and Anabaptist Writers* (London and Philadelphia, 1967), p. 279.

6. The statistics are from Clasen, *Anabaptism*, pp. 26, 27, 31. For an exciting account of events in Münster, see Norman Cohn, *The Pursuit of the Millennium* (London, 1970), pp. 261–80; Williams, *Radical Reformation*, pp. 362–80; Müntzer's violent exhortation is in Williams and Mergal, *Spiritual and Anabaptist Writers*, p. 65; Blaurock's pacifism, ibid, p. 42; Philips's reservations about Hofmann, ibid, p. 209.

7. In the light of such problems, Stayer, 'Sects' is all the more important as a corrective. On the Dutch regions, see W. E. Keeney, *Dutch Anabaptist Thought and Practice, 1539–1564* (Nieuwkoop, 1968); and Cornelius Krahn, *Dutch Anabaptism* (The Hague, 1968). On baptism as a sacrament instituted by Christ, like the Eucharist, see Euan Cameron, *The European Reformation* (Oxford, 1991), p. 159, where, nevertheless, 'magisterial reformers' are distinguished from 'sectarian extremists'; and Alistair Duke, 'The Origins of Evangelical Dissent', in his collection *Reformation and Revolt in the Low Countries* (London and Ronceverte, 1990), p. 58, where he remarks that 'the passage from radical sacramentarianism to anabaptism was not difficult': the use of 'radical' here seems rather loaded, immmediately pushing anabaptism to an 'extreme'. These references are intended to highlight the problems of terminology, not to criticise the admirable works of the authors cited. Schlaffer is quoted in Williams, *Radical Reformation*, p. 173.

8. The quotations from Hofmann are from Williams and Mergal, *Spiritual and Anabaptist Writers*, pp. 191, 187–8, 190. On the influence of the Rhineland tradition, see Werner O. Packull, *Mysticism and the Early South German Anabaptist Movement, 1525–1531* (Scotdale, Pa., and Kitchener, Ontario, 1977), esp. pp. 176–84. On an

anabaptist community's organisation, see Klassen, *Economics*, pp. 34–5, 91: Hubmaier is quoted on p. 32. For a positive interpretation of work-sharing in Leyden, see R. C. Duplessis and M. C. Howell, 'Reconsidering the Early Modern Economy: The Cases of Leyden and Lille', *Past and Present*, 94 (1982), pp. 49–84. On *de facto* toleration in the Habsburg lands, see R. J. W. Evans, *The Making of the Habsburg Monarchy, 1550–1700* (Oxford, 1979), pp. 13, 15. Spittelmaier is quoted in Williams, *Radical Reformation*, p. 173.

9. On the 'revolution of the common man', see Peter Blickle, *The Revolution of 1525* (Baltimore, 1981); on communism, see Cohn, *Pursuit*, p. 265; cf. Klassen, *Economics*, p. 33. Grebel's words are from Williams and Mergal, *Spiritual and Anabaptist Writers*, p. 80. For an important set of revisions, see James M. Stayer, 'Christianity in One City: Anabaptist Münster, 1534–5', in H. J. Hillerbrand (ed.) *Radical Tendencies in the Reformation: Divergent Perspectives* (Kirksville, Miss., 1987), pp. 117–34. The details of the siege are assembled from G. Vogler, 'The Anabaptist Kingdom of Münster: The Tension between Anabaptism and Imperial Policy', ibid, p. 108 on the transition from elected council to kingdom; Williams, *Radical Reformation*, p. 371 on the death penalty and the strain of the siege; p. 373 on Charles V's negotiations with Rothmann; p. 763 for the impressive reminder that Calvinism in the Netherlands against Alba was 'no less disciplined and conventicular than the Münsterites, no less belligerent than the Münsterites'; on the grisly end of the leaders, see R. Po-chia Hsia, *Society and Religion in Münster, 1535–1618* (New Haven, 1984), p. 1; Kamen, *Toleration*, p. 73; Cohn, *Pursuit*, pp. 279–80.

10. Philips's comments are in Williams and Mergal, *Spiritual and Anabaptist Writers*, p. 219; Calvin on Simons is quoted in Klassen, *Economics*, p. 15; Manz's fate is mentioned in Williams, *Radical Reformation*, p. 145; Sattler's remarks on the Turks are in Williams and Mergal, *Spiritual and Anabaptist Writers*, p. 141, his *Gelassenheit* in preparation for execution in Klassen, *Economics*, p. 79; Hubmaier's death is described in Williams, *Radical Reformation*, p. 229; Hutter's ibid, p. 425. On toleration and economic advantage, see Klassen, *Economics*, pp. 107–12.

11. On local belief and formal Christianity, see William A. Christian, *Local Religion in Sixteenth-Century Spain* (Princeton, 1981), e.g. pp. 57, 102, 175; Euan Cameron, *The Reformation of the Heretics: The Waldenses of the Alps, 1480–1580* (Oxford, 1984); Carlo Ginzburg, *The Night Battles: Witchcraft and Agrarian Cults in the Sixteenth and Seventeenth Centuries*, trans. John and Anne Tedeschi (London, 1983): the quotations cited here are on pp. 3 and 6. On 'the reform of popular culture', see Peter Burke, *Popular Culture in Early Modern Europe* (London, 1978), pp. 207–22; Jean Delumeau, *Catholicism between Luther and Voltaire: A New View of the Counter-Reformation*, trans. Jeremy Moiser (London, 1977), pp. 175–202. For an important discussion of the attempt to 'colonise popular minds', see Stuart Clark, 'Protestant Demonology: Sin, Superstition and Cultural Reality (c.1525–c.1630)', in Bengt Ankarloo and Gustav Henningsen (eds) *Early Modern European Witchcraft: Centres and Peripheries* (Oxford, 1990), p. 46.

12. For comments and examples which narrow the divide between 'popular' and 'learned' culture, see Bengt Ankarloo and Gustav Henningsen, 'Introduction', in eidem (eds) *European Witchcraft*, p. 6; Eck is quoted in R. Po-chia Hsia, *The Myth of Ritual Murder: Jews and Magic in Reformation Germany* (New Haven, 1983), p. 127; on the fairy world, see Gustav Henningsen, '"The Ladies from Outside": An Archaic Pattern of the Witches' Sabbath', in Ankarloo and Henningsen, *European Witchcraft*, pp. 195–204; on the Faustus legend in popular culture, H. C. Erik Midelfort, *Witch Hunting in Southwestern Germany, 1562–1684* (Stanford, Cal., 1972), p. 69; on learned mumbo-jumbo, R. J. W. Evans, *Rudolf II and his World* (Oxford, 1979), pp. 153–278: pp. 163, 272 on Kepler; pp. 218–28 on Dee and Kelley; Frances Yates, *The Occult Philosophy in the Elizabethan Age* (London, 1983).

13. For an account of the campaign which began in 1487, see Cameron, *Heretics*; on the learned treatises, see H. R. Trevor-Roper, 'The European Witch-Craze of the Sixteenth and Seventeenth Centuries', in his collected essays, *Religion, the Reformation and Social Change*, 2nd edn (London, 1972), pp. 101, 151–3; on Bodin, Trevor-Roper significantly registers his astonishment on p. 122. Apart from Trevor-Roper, general surveys include Brian Easlea, *Witch-hunting, Magic and the New Philosophy* (Brighton, 1980); Brian P. Levack, *The Witch-Hunt in Early Modern Europe* (London, 1987); the regional examples are drawn from William Monter, *Ritual, Myth and Magic in Early Modern Europe* (Brighton, 1983), pp. 28–30 (Scandinavia), 30–1 (Bremen), 81–2 (Austria), 144–5 (Poland and Hungary). On the intensity of the hunt in central Europe, see Midelfort, *Witch Hunting*, esp. p. 71 on mass panics, p. 28 on Eichstätt and Quedlinburg; on von Schöneburg, Trevor-Roper, 'Witch-Craze', pp. 149–51; on Jesuit involvement in general, Hsia, *Social Discipline*, pp. 159–68; idem, *Münster*, pp. 75–6.

14. On Italy, see Ginzburg, *Night Battles*; Ruth Martin, *Witchcraft and the Inquisition in Venice, 1550–1650* (Oxford, 1989). Poor Walpurga's trial is recorded in *The Fugger Newsletters, 1568–1605*, ed. Viktor von Klarwill, trans. Pauline de Chary (London, 1924), pp. 107–14; the Friulian example is quoted in Ginzburg, *Night Battles*, pp. 123–4. On the sabbath as the creation of theologians, see Robert Muchembled, 'Satanic Myths and Cultural Reality', in Ankarloo and Henningsen, *European Witchcraft*, pp. 139–40; on the 'swoops' on anabaptist meetings, see Clasen, *Anabaptism*, p. 361. Calvin's views are quoted in Trevor-Roper, 'Witch-Craze', p. 137; on the pressure for conformity, see Hsia, *Social Discipline*, p. 168; Marvin Harris, *Cows, Pigs, Wars and Witches: The Riddles of Culture* (London, 1977), pp. 158–68, esp. p. 167: 'the poor came to believe that they were being victimised by witches and devils instead of by princes and popes'; on the chilling modern implications, see Thomas S. Szasz, *The Manufacture of Madness* (London, 1973).

10 HABSBURG AND VALOIS

1. While family ties among people outside the nobility may have strengthened since the Middle Ages, they were still much looser than in the industrial era: see the suggestive remarks of Philippe Ariès, *Centuries of Childhood*, trans. Robert Baldick (London, 1973), pp. 353–91; Peter Laslett, *The World We Have Lost*, 2nd edn (London, 1971), esp. pp. 47–8 on the contrasts between noble and non-noble households. On urban corporations, see Richard Mackenney, *Tradesmen and Traders: The World of the Guilds in Venice and Europe, c.1250–c.1650* (London, 1987); Brian Pullan, 'Support and Redeem: Charity and Poor Relief in Italian Cities from the Fourteenth to the Seventeenth Century', *Continuity and Change*, 3 (1988), pp. 177–208; idem, *Orphans and Foundlings in Early Modern Europe* (Reading, 1989); on vagabondage, A. L. Beier, *Masterless Men: The Vagrancy Problem in England, 1560–1640* (London, 1985); on patterns of inheritance in rural Europe, see E. Le Roy Ladurie, 'Peasants', *NCMH*, vol. 13, pp. 119–22; on dynastic politics, see the comprehensive study by Richard Bonney, *The European Dynastic States, 1494–1660* (Oxford, 1991).

2. See the classic study by Garrett Mattingly, *Renaissance Diplomacy* (Harmondsworth, 1965). A picture of consolidation in France and Spain and disunity in Italy is gleaned from four successive chapters of the *New Cambridge Modern History*, vol. 1: ch. ix, J. R. Hale, 'International Relations in the West: Diplomacy and War', pp. 259–91; ch. x, R. Doucet, 'France under Charles VIII and Louis XII', pp. 292–315; ch. xi, J. M. Batista I Roca, 'The Hispanic Kingdoms and the Catholic Kings', pp. 316–42; ch. xii, C. M. Ady, 'The Invasions of Italy', pp. 342–67. More recent work tends not to depart far from this format: see Bonney, *Dynastic States*, pp. 79–130; and the superior importance to the historian of diplomacy over fighting is reinforced by studies such as Felix Gilbert, *The Pope, his Banker and Venice* (Cambridge, Mass., 1980), p. 4; and Mia Rodríguez-Salgado, 'The Habsburg-Valois Wars', *NCMH*, vol. 2, 2nd edn (1990), p. 397.

3. On the general significance of the wars, see the trenchant assessment of Judith Hook, *The Sack of Rome, 1527* (London, 1972), pp. 15–36; Mattingly, *Diplomacy*, pp. 51–104; Denys Hay and John Law, *Italy in the Age of the Renaissance, 1380–1530* (London, 1989), pp. 158–69; on the changes in warfare, see Michael Mallett, *Mercenaries and their Masters* (Oxford, 1974), esp. pp. 231–60.

4. It seems entirely appropriate to base the account on one of the first works of truly modern historiography, Guicciardini's *Storia d'Italia*, the calibre and reputation of which are established in the brilliant study by Felix Gilbert, *Machiavelli and Guicciardini: Politics and History in Sixteenth-Century Florence* (Princeton, 1965). The version used in this book is *The Historie of Guicciardin conteining the Warres of Italie and other partes* . . . trans. Geffray Fenton (London, 1579). The military detail is given focus in Charles Oman, *A History of the Art of War in the Sixteenth Century* (Elstree, 1937), Books II–III, pp. 105–284. On Italian miscalculation, see Guicciardini, *Historie*, pp. 39–40; on Piero de' Medici's capitulation, p. 53; on Fornovo, pp. 103–4;

344 Notes to pp. 226–45

on the French success, p. 107 – see also the exciting account of the battle and an uninhibited view of its consequences, in Luigi Barzini, *The Italians* (London, 1966), pp. 283–98 – on the contraction of Lodovico il Moro's horizons, Guicciardini, *Historie*, p. 243.

5. On the 'libertie of warre', see Guicciardini, *Historie*, p. 405; on the sack of Ravenna, p. 589; on the death of Julius II, p. 631; on the accession of Francis I, pp. 684–5; the quotation on Francis's ambitions is from J. H. Hexter, *The Vision of Politics on the Eve of the Reformation* (London, 1973), p. 6; for the competition of Francis I and Charles V, see Guicciardini, *Historie*, p. 768.

6. On the general ferocity at Fornovo, see Guicciardini, *Historie*, p. 104; on the wastefulness of lives and manpower, William S. Maltby, *Alba* (Los Angeles, 1983), p. 55; on Charles VIII's artillery, Guicciardini, *Historie*, p. 45; on the destruction of cities, Eric Cochrane, *Italy 1530–1630* (London, 1988), p. 9.

7. Savonarola is quoted in John C. Olin (ed.) *The Catholic Reformation: Savonarola to Ignatius Loyola* (New York, 1969), p. 10; Egidio da Viterbo, ibid, p. 48. On the shadowy figure of Egidio, see also Christopher Black, *Italian Confraternities in the Sixteenth Century* (Cambridge, 1989), p. 96; John O'Malley, *Giles of Viterbo on Church and Reform* (Leyden, 1968). The number of Eucharistic confraternities in Venice is drawn from unpublished archival materials. The laments of the Venetians are quoted in Felix Gilbert, 'Venice in the Crisis of the League of Cambrai', in J. R. Hale (ed.) *Renaissance Venice* (London, 1973), pp. 277–8.

8. Guicciardini, *Historie*, pp. 1062–3 on the Sack of Rome; Melanchthon is quoted in André Chastel, *The Sack of Rome, 1527*, trans. Beth Archer (Princeton, 1983), p. 220; on the destruction of the papacy as a secular state, Hook, *Sack*, p. 157; on Venice as the new Rome, D. S. Chambers, *The Imperial Age of Venice, 1380–1580* (London, 1970), pp. 12–32.

9. Charles V records his preoccupations in his autobiography, *The Autobiography of the Emperor Charles V*, trans. Leonard Simpson (London, 1862), p. 29. On the increasing importance of sieges, see Christopher Duffy, *Siege Warfare: The Fortress in the Early Modern World, 1494–1660* (London, 1979), chs. 1–3; J. R. Hale, *Renaissance Fortification: Art or Engineering?* (London, 1977). On the painful changes in the Habsburg monarchy, Mia Rodríguez-Salgado, *The Changing Face of Empire: Charles V, Philip II and Habsburg Authority, 1551–1559* (Cambridge, 1988), esp. pp. 45–6 on the machinations of Henry II; on Henry's absolutism, and his accidental death, see R. J. Knecht (ed.) *French Renaissance Monarchy: Francis I and Henry II* (London, 1984), esp. pp. 30, 46, 66–7, 76.

11 CHRISTIANS AND TURKS

1. For Charles's problems, see *The Autobiography of the Emperor Charles V*, trans. Leonard Simpson, (London, 1862), pp. 13, 21–2, 24, 43, 50, 76, 94–5; Stephen A. Fischer-Galati, *Ottoman Imperialism and German Protestantism, 1521–1555* (Cambridge, Mass., 1959); C. Max Kortep-

eter, *Ottoman Imperialism during the Reformation: Europe and the Caucasus* (London and New York, 1972); Andrew C. Hess, 'The Moriscos: An Ottoman Fifth Column in Sixteenth-Century Spain?', *American Historical Review*, 74 (1968), pp. 1–25; Charles Petrie, *Don John of Austria* (London, 1967), ch. 4 on the Morisco rebellion. On the Ottoman recovery, see Andrew C. Hess, 'The Battle of Lepanto and its Place in Mediterranean History', *Past and Present*, 57 (1972), pp. 53–72: Sököllü is quoted on p. 53; on the 1573 expedition see p. 64.

2. For a concise introduction, see *TAWH*, pp. 170–1; an unusual and unusual prominence is given to the Turks in Myron P. Gilmore, *The World of Humanism, 1453–1517* (New York, 1962), pp. 6–21; more substantial are the chapters on 'The Ottoman Empire' by V. J. Parry, in *NCMH*, vol. 1, pp. 395–419 (1480–1520); vol. 2, pp. 510–33 (1520–66); vol. 3, pp. 347–76 (1566–1617); rather more lively are Robert Schwoebel, *The Shadow of the Crescent: The Renaissance Image of the Turk, 1453–1517* (Nieuwkoop, 1967), to which I am indebted for a sub-heading and a theme for this chapter; Paul Coles, *The Ottoman Impact on Europe* (London, 1968), which draws heavily on sections of William H. McNeill, *Europe's Steppe Frontier, 1500–1800* (Chicago, 1964). F. Braudel, *The Mediterranean and the Mediterranean World in the Age of Philip II*, trans. S. Reynolds, 2 vols (London, 1975), vol. 2, Part Three is concerned with the clash of empires, and vol. 1 has some valuable insights into the neglected but topical subject of Balkan history. However, it is essential to depart more completely from a western perspective, and this can be done through the magisterial work of Halil Inalcik, 'The Emergence of the Ottomans', in the *Cambridge History of Islam*, vol. 1A, (Cambridge, 1970), pp. 263–92; 'The Heyday and Decline of the Ottoman Empire', ibid, pp. 324–53; *The Ottoman Empire: the Classical Age, 1300–1600*, trans. Norman Itzkowitz and Colin Imber, (London, 1973). On kinship ties, see the contrasting case of Russia in Giles Fletcher, *Of the Rus Commonwealth*, ed. Albert J. Schmidt (New York, 1966), p. 36; and with the west, see the characteristically penetrating comments of Machiavelli in *The Prince*, trans. Edward Dacres (London, 1640), ch. iv, pp. 25–8; another contrasting western example is provided by the Netherlands nobility, see Geoffrey Parker, *The Dutch Revolt* (Harmondsworth, 1979), p. 49.

3. The quotations are from Ghiselin de Busbecq, *The Turkish Letters*, trans. E. S. Forster (Oxford, 1927): on meritocracy pp. 23, 59–60; on the advantages of slavery over poverty, pp. 100–1; on resistance to technological innovations, p. 135; on the lack of a historical sense, p. 20; on Istanbul, p. 34. On intrigue in the harem, see Kortepeter, *Ottoman Imperialism*, pp. 215–17. The Venetian observer of the two 'wings' of Ottoman power is quoted in Peter Earle, *Corsairs of Malta and Barbary* (London, 1970), p. 26.

4. For the course of expansion, see *TAWH*, pp. 134–5, 138–9, 170–1; 186–7; Inalcik, 'Emergence', idem, 'Heyday' and for valuable military detail, Charles Oman, *A History of the Art of War in the Sixteenth Century* (Elstree, 1937), Book VII, pp. 607–770; on the sieges, Christopher Duffy, *Siege Warfare: The Fortress in the Early Modern World, 1494–1660* (London, 1979), ch. 8, pp. 191–219; on Hungary,

G. R. Elton, *Reformation Europe, 1517–1559* (London, 1963), pp. 81–2, 133–6. On war at sea, see John F. Guilmartin, *Gunpowder and Galleys* (Cambridge, 1974), esp. p. 45 on the strategic importance of Corfu; the quotation on Prevesa is on p. 54; on the performance of the Great Galleon, p. 55. On Venetian defence policy, see F. C. Lane, 'Naval Actions and Fleet Organisation, 1499–1502', in J. R. Hale (ed.) *Renaissance Venice* (London, 1974), pp. 146–73; on policy and manpower, Richard Mackenney, *Tradesmen and Traders: The World of the Guilds in Venice and Europe, c.1250–c.1650* (London, 1987), pp. 216–21; and on the chronic problem of costs, Geoffrey Parker, 'Lepanto (1571): The Costs of Victory', in his collected essays, *Spain and the Netherlands, 1559–1659: Ten Studies* (London, 1979), pp. 122–34; on fortresses in the Venetian empire, see M. E. Mallett and J. R. Hale, *The Military Organisation of a Renaissance State: Venice, c.1400–1617* (Cambridge, 1984), pp. 429–60. Boccalini's comments are in his *Advertisements from Parnassus*, trans. Henry, Earl of Monmouth, (London, 1669), p. 10.

5. On the political repercussions of Charles V's retirement, see Mia Rodríguez-Salgado, *The Changing Face of Empire: Charles V, Philip II and Habsburg Authority, 1551–1559* (Cambridge, 1988), esp. pp. 220–1 on the disruptions of piracy; p. 302 on reputation; p. 342 on Philip's debt; pp. 46, 261 for important insights into the policies of Henry II; Bohdan Chudoba, *Spain and the Empire, 1519–1643* (Chicago, 1952), with important material on North Africa, pp. 60–88; on Djerba, Guilmartin, *Gunpowder*, pp. 123–34, and on the seriousness of Spanish losses, pp. 131–2.

6. For the siege of Malta, see Oman, *Art of War*, pp. 703–17 for the military narrative; and more interpretative accounts in Guilmartin, *Gunpowder*, pp. 176–93; Duffy, *Siege Warfare*, pp. 193–4. A full and exciting account is to be found in Ernle Bradford, *The Great Siege: Malta, 1565* (London, 1961); and for the views of one of the combattants, see Francisco Balbi di Correggio, *The Siege of Malta, 1565*, trans. Ernle Bradford (London, 1965), p. 13 on La Valette; p. 113 on incendiary devices and hand-to-hand fighting; p. 117 on 'a great deal of hashish' in the purses of the dead Turks.

7. On this phase of Turkish operations, see Oman, *Art of War*, pp. 718–37; on Cyprus, Duffy, *Siege Warfare*, pp. 194–6; Mallett and Hale, *Military Organisation*, pp. 439–43; on Bragadin's fate, Petrie, *Don John*, p. 139; Don John is quoted ibid, p. 144; on the damage wrought by the Venetian galleasses, see Geoffrey Parker, *The Military Revolution: Military Innovation and the Rise of the West, 1500–1800* (Cambridge, 1986), p. 87: there is an evocative visual representation of the two formations and then of their engagement in Giacomo Franco, *Habiti di huomeni e donne* (Venice, 1610); for accounts of the battle, see Petrie, *Don John*, pp. 161–87; Guilmartin, *Gunpowder*, 221–52.

8. On the aftermath and significance of Lepanto – subjects which are not necessarily closely connected – see Petrie, *Don John*, chs. 8 and 9; Hess, 'Lepanto'; Braudel, *Mediterranean*, vol. 2, pp. 1103–6; Gino Benzoni (ed.) *Il Mediterraneo nella seconda metà del '500 alla luce di Lepanto* (Florence, 1974); on Philip II's reaction to victory, see Petrie, *Don John*, p. 191, and on his let-down when Venice withdrew from the

Holy League, Mallett and Hale, *Military Organisation*, p. 241.
Botero's comment is in his *Della Ragion di stato* (Venice, 1589),
p. 219. Cervantes's contrasting opinion is quoted in Petrie, *Don
John*, p. 185: the climax of G. K. Chesterton's poem becomes irresistible:

> Cervantes in his galley sets the sword back in the sheath,
> (Don John of Austria rides homeward with a wreath,)
> And he sees across a weary land a straggling road in Spain,
> Up which a lean and foolish knight forever rides in vain
> And he smiles, but not as sultans smile, and settles back the blade
> (But Don John of Austria rides home from the crusade.)

9. On the general problem of distance, see Braudel, *Mediterranean*, vol.
   1, pp. 355–93; on the logistical difficulties for the Turks, see Coles,
   Ottoman Impact, p. 104; McNeill, *Steppe Frontier*, pp. 41–2; and on
   the maritime dimension, see the superb essay by Andrew C. Hess, 'The
   Evolution of the Ottoman Seaborne Empire in the Age of the Oceanic
   Discoveries, 1453–1525', *American Historical Review*, 75 (1970), pp.
   1892–1919; on the Portuguese victory at Chaul, Parker, *Military
   Revolution*, p. 131. On Cabot, Chancellor and the Muscovy Company, see K. R. Andrews, *Trade, Plunder and Settlement: Maritime
   Enterprise and the Genesis of the British Empire, 1480–1630* (Cambridge, 1984), pp. 68–9; on Archangel, M. Bushkovitch, *The Merchants of Moscow, 1580–1650* (Cambridge, 1980), pp. 168–9; on the
   importance of naval supplies to the west, see Richard Hakluyt,
   Voyages and Discoveries, ed. abr. and intro. Jack Beeching (Harmondsworth, 1972), pp. 75–6; on Jenkinson, ibid, pp. 77–90. For
   introductory discussions of mercantilism, see Charles Wilson, *Mercantilism* (London, 1958); Michael Howard, *War in European History*
   (Oxford, 1976), pp. 38–53.

12 CATHOLICS AND PROTESTANTS

1. The Venetian ambassador's views – at once complementary and
   contradictory – are quoted in J. H. Elliott, *Europe Divided, 1559–98*
   (London, 1968), p. 108; and in H. G. Koenigsberger, 'The Organisation of Revolutionary Parties in France and the Netherlands during
   the Sixteenth Century' in his collection of essays, *Estates and
   Revolutions* (New York, 1971), p. 226; Montaigne is quoted in
   J. H. M. Salmon, *Society in Crisis: France in the Sixteenth Century*
   (London, 1979), p. 127. On the significance of the wars in political
   thought, see Quentin Skinner, *The Foundations of Modern Political
   Thought*, 2 vols (Cambridge, 1978), vol. 2, Part Three; and the
   important study by Donald R. Kelley, *The Beginning of Ideology:
   Consciousness and Society in the French Reformation* (Cambridge,
   1981), which is particularly illuminating on the slow and subtle
   transition from theology to ideology. For a thoughtful study of the
   connections with the Thirty Years' War, see Theodore K. Rabb, *The
   Struggle for Stability in Early Modern Europe* (Oxford, 1975).

2. For the 'schollers of Machiavell', see *The Apologie of Prince William of Orange against the Proclamation of the King of Spaine*, ed. H. Wansink, (Leyden, 1969), p. 68; on the imperial claims of the Duke of Cleves and the King of England, G. H. Williams, *The Radical Reformation* (Philadelphia, 1962), p. 8; on the Diet of Speyer, Skinner, *Foundations*, vol. 2, pp. 194–5; on the medieval influences, not to be seen as 'background', Walter Ullmann, *Medieval Political Thought* (London, 1975); and, specifically, idem, *Principles of Government and Politics in the Middle Ages* (London, 1961), pp. 101, 288–9; idem, *Medieval Papalism* (London, 1949), p. 21; J. N. Figgis, *From Gerson to Grotius*, 2nd edn, (Cambridge, 1931), pp. 39–40; on changes in the nature of the imperial office, G. Oestreich, *Neostoicism and the Early Modern State*, ed. Brigitta Oestreich and H. G. Koenigsberger, trans. David McLintock (Cambridge, 1982), pp. 199–212; on patterns of confessional loyalty in the Empire, Euan Cameron, *The European Reformation* (Oxford, 1991), pp. 269–71. The quotation from Hotman is taken from Julian H. Franklin (ed.) *Constitutionalism and Resistance in the Sixteenth Century: Three Treatises by Hotman, Bèze and Mornay* (New York, 1969), p. 58.

3. Orange made his claim in his *Apologie*, p. 3; on the nature of papal power, see Paolo Prodi, *The Papal Prince*, trans. Susan Haskins, (Cambridge, 1987); the quotations on the royal supremacy in England are from G. R. Elton, 'The Political Creed of Thomas Cromwell', in his *Studies in Tudor and Stuart Politics and Government*, 2 vols, (Cambridge, 1974), vol. 2, pp. 230–1, 232, 233; on the Stuart failure to comprehend the principle, idem, 'A High Road to Civil War?', ibid, pp. 164–82; on the adoption of the Reformation, see the lucid presentations in *TAWH*, p. 183; Cameron, *European Reformation*, p. 269; on the risks which princes faced, A. G. Dickens, *Reformation and Society in Sixteenth-Century Europe* (London, 1966), p. 75; on the Peace of Augsburg, see Hermann Tüchle, 'The Peace of Augsburg: New Order or Lull in the Fighting?', in Henry J. Cohn (ed.) *Government in Reformation Europe, 1520–1560* (London, 1971), pp. 145–65; G. R. Elton, '1555: A Political Retrospect', in Joel Hurstfield (ed.) *The Reformation Crisis* (London, 1965), pp. 72–82.

4. On the urban Reformation, see Bernd Moeller, *Imperial Cities and the Reformation*, trans. and ed. H. C. Erik Midelfort and Mark U. Edwards (Durham, N.C., 1982), pp. 41–115; A. G. Dickens, *The German Nation and Martin Luther* (London, 1976); R. W. Scribner, *The German Reformation* (London, 1986); Thomas A. Brady, *Turning Swiss: Cities and Empire, 1450–1550* (Cambridge, 1985); and on Nuremberg, Gerald Strauss, *Nuremberg in the Sixteenth Century* (Bloomington, Ind., 1976), esp. pp. 154–86.

5. On the national grievances, see Dickens, *German Nation*, chs.1 and 2; and the revealing primary sources in Gerald Strauss (ed.) *Manifestations of Discontent in Germany on the Eve of the Reformation* (Bloomington, Ind., 1971), pp. 35–63; on the dynastic intricacies, Richard Bonney, *The European Dynastic States, 1494–1660* (Oxford, 1991), pp. 116–24; Frederick the Wise is quoted in Roland H. Bainton, *Here I Stand: A Life of Martin Luther* (New York, 1950), pp. 77–8; G. R. Elton, *Reformation Europe, 1517–1559* (London, 1963), pp. 53–

65, esp. p. 63 on Albrecht of Hohenzollern; E. G. Rupp, 'Luther and the German Reformation to 1529', *NCMH*, vol. 2, pp. 70–95, esp. p. 92 on the League of Torgau. On the changing theoretical position, Skinner, *Foundations*, vol. 2, p. 197: Luther's views are quoted ibid, pp. 200, 201. On the changing fortunes of Charles V, see Elton, *Reformation Europe*, pp. 35–52, 75–85, 141–75, 239–73; Karl Brandi, *The Emperor Charles V*, trans. C. V. Wedgwood, (London, 1965), pp. 292–332, 435–52, 523–636; Mia Rodríguez-Salgado, *The Changing Face of Empire: Charles V, Philip II and Habsburg Authority, 1551–1559* (Cambridge, 1988), esp. pp. 45–6. My account of the German situation owes much to the detail available in an old and old-fashioned book, A. H. Johnson, *Europe in the Sixteenth Century, 1494–1598*, 7th edn (London, 1941), chs.III-V, in particular the chart on p. 166, n. 1 and the superb map, 'Germany in 1547' which appears in the endpapers.

6. On the French Wars, see Elliott, *Europe Divided*, pp. 107–25, 215–27; Robin Briggs, *Early Modern France, 1560–1715* (Oxford, 1977), ch. 1; Salmon, *Society in Crisis*, Part Two; Koenigsberger, 'Revolutionary Parties'. On Catholic aggression, see the work of N. M. Sutherland, *The Huguenot Struggle for Recognition* (New Haven, 1980), e.g. pp. 2, 5, 41–3, 212–15; and her collection of essays, *Princes, Politics and Religion, 1559–1589* (London, 1984), e.g. p. 8. She says very little about Scotland, on which see Jenny Wormald, *Court, Kirk and Community: Scotland, 1470–1625* (London, 1981), esp. pp. 149–50, 192–4: the Congregation is quoted on p. 115; Michael Lynch, 'Calvinism in Scotland, 1559–1638', in Menna Prestwich (ed.) *International Calvinism, 1541–1715* (Oxford, 1985), pp. 225–56: p. 227 on Knox's arrival.

7. On the sense of common purpose among Calvinists in France, see Mark Greengrass, *The French Reformation* (Oxford, 1987), pp. 39–41; and on the struggle for control of patronage, pp. 72–8; on Hotman's attitude to the conspiracy of Amboise, see Salmon, *Society in Crisis*, p. 125: cf. the account of N. M. Sutherland, 'Calvinism and the Conspiracy of Amboise', *History*, 47 (1962), pp. 111–38. On Calvinist subversion, see R. M. Kingdon, *Geneva and the Coming of the Wars of Religion in France, 1555–1563* (Geneva, 1956): although the case may be overstated, the examples are persuasive, see p. 2 on Calvin's mission and the number of missionaries; p. 6 on noble support; pp. 111 and 127 on Marlorat; p. 121 on arms shipments; p. 87 on the cache in Bordeaux. On Poissy, see Elliott, *Europe Divided*, p. 104; Condé is quoted in Salmon, *Society in Crisis*, p. 170; the Synod of Nîmes is discussed in R. M. Kingdon, *Geneva and the Consolidation of the French Protestant Movement, 1566–1572* (Geneva, 1957), pp. 196–7; on Coligny's 'social imperialism', see J. Shimizu, *Conflict of Loyalties: Politics and Religion in the Career of Gaspard de Coligny* (Geneva, 1970), p. 182.

8. On the massacre, Elliott, *Europe Divided*, pp. 215–27; Salmon, *Society in Crisis*, ch. 8; N. M. Sutherland, *The Massacre of St Bartholomew and the European Conflict, 1559–72* (London, 1973); on the theoretical implications, Skinner, *Foundations*, vol. 2, pp. 304–5, 307–9. The quotations cited here are from the selections published in Franklin, *Constitutionalism*, pp. 90–6 (*Francogallia*); pp. 119, 129, 135 (*Right of*

Magistrates); pp. 156–7, 188, 198 (*Vindiciae*). On the implications for England, see Michael Walzer, *The Revolution of the Saints: A Study in the Origins of Radical Politics* (New York, 1968); J. V. Polisensky, *War and Society in Europe, 1618–1648* (Cambridge, 1978), pp. 163–79.

9. On the agony of France in the late sixteenth century, see Briggs, *France*, pp. 24–34; Salmon, *Society in Crisis*, chs. 9–11: Pierre de L'Estoile's comments on Henry III are quoted on p. 203. On Mariana, see Skinner, *Foundations*, vol. 2, pp. 346–7; Bernice Hamilton, *Political Thought in Sixteenth-Century Spain* (Oxford, 1963), pp. 60–3; on the transition to the absolutist order, see Mark Greengrass, *France in the Age of Henri IV: The Struggle for Stability* (London, 1984), chs. 1–3: du Plessis-Mornay is quoted on p. 74; Roland Mousnier, *The Assassination of Henry IV: The Tyrannicide Problem and the Consolidation of the French Absolute Monarchy in the Early Seventeenth Century*, trans. Joan Spencer (London, 1973): the quotation from the Edict of Nantes is taken from the text which Mousnier includes as an appendix, p. 317; the passage from Henry's speech requesting registration is from p. 365; for the extension of the French Reformation to 1685, see Pierre Chaunu (ed.) *The Reformation*, trans. Victoria Acland *et al.* (London, 1989), p. 232.

CONCLUSION

1. On the common European context of the wars, see J. H. Elliott, *Europe Divided, 1559–1598* (London, 1968), esp. pp. 107–44, 201–27, 250–64, 301–65; H. G. Koenigsberger, 'The Organisation of Revolutionary Parties in France and the Netherlands during the Sixteenth Century', in his collection of essays, *Estates and Revolutions* (New York, 1971), pp. 224–52. On the particular characteristics of the Dutch Revolt, see Pieter Geyl, *The Revolt of the Netherlands, 1555–1609*, 2nd edn (London, 1958); idem, 'The National State and the Writers of Netherlands History', in his collection *Debates with Historians* (London, 1962), pp. 211–33; Gordon Griffiths, 'The Revolutionary Character of the Revolt of the Netherlands', *Comparative Studies in Society and History*, 2 (1959–60), pp. 452–72; J. W. Smit, 'The Netherlands Revolution', in Robert Forster and Jack P. Greene (eds) *Preconditions of Revolution in Early Modern Europe* (Baltimore, 1972), pp. 19–54. Much has been learned from the research findings of Geoffrey Parker, *The Army of Flanders and the Spanish Road, 1567–1659* (Cambridge, 1972); idem, *The Dutch Revolt* (Harmondsworth, 1979); idem, *Spain and the Netherlands, 1559–1659: Ten Studies* (London, 1979). Other aspects have been clarified by Phyllis Mack Crew, *Calvinist Preaching and Iconoclasm in the Netherlands, 1544–1569* (Cambridge, 1978); and by the essays of Alistair Duke, *Reformation and Revolt in the Low Countries* (London and Ronceverte, 1990). For a fresh and lucid approach to Spanish government in the Netherlands, see A. W. Lovett, *Early Habsburg Spain, 1517–1598* (Oxford, 1986), ch. 10.

2. Alba's letter to Requesens in 1573 is quoted in Parker, *Dutch Revolt*, p. 161; on diocesan reform, see Elliott, *Europe Divided*, p. 131; on *les*

gueux, ibid, p. 136; Jansz is quoted encouraging iconoclasm in Alistair Duke, 'The Time of Troubles in the County of Holland, 1566–67', in his *Reformation and Revolt*, p. 137; the comments on Calvinist preachers in Kortrijk are quoted in Parker, *Dutch Revolt*, p. 75; the list of iconoclastic riots is ibid, p. 78; on the way in which oppression cemented opposition, see Alistair Duke, 'Salvation by Coercion: The Controversy surrounding the "Inquisition" in the Low Countries on the Eve of the Revolt', in his *Reformation and Revolt*, pp. 153–4. On Alba's regime, see William S. Maltby, *Alba* (Los Angeles, 1983), pp. 131–276; on his finances, Parker, *Army of Flanders*, p. 141; on non-payment of troops, ibid, pp. 159–60 and n.1; on the extortions on the grounds of religion, ibid, pp. 178–9. On the mutinies of the Spaniards, see Geoffrey Parker, 'Mutiny and Discontent in the Spanish Army of Flanders, 1572–1607', in his *Spain and the Netherlands*, pp. 106–21 (pp. 118–19 on Antwerp and Aalst).

3.　The Pacification appears in E. H. Kossmann and A. F. Mellink (eds) *Texts Concerning the Revolt of the Netherlands* (Cambridge, 1974), pp. 126–32, this passage is from p. 127; Philip's desperation as expressed to Don John is quoted in Parker, *Dutch Revolt*, p. 177; on the deterioration of Don John's position, Lovett, *Early Habsburg Spain*, pp. 166–8. The Union of Utrecht appears in Kossmann and Mellink, *Texts*, pp. 165–72, these passages are from pp. 165 and 170.

4.　For a lively account of the Spanish recovery and its implications, see Lovett, *Early Habsburg Spain*, ch. 12; and on Parma's sieges, Parker, *Dutch Revolt*, pp. 208–16. William of Orange's defence is contained in *The Apologie of William of Orange against the Proclamation of the King of Spaine*, ed. H. Wansink (Leyden, 1969), p. 48; on the Inquisition, ibid, pp. 70, 138; on the Spaniards as a 'cursed race', ibid, p. 132. On the ambiguities of power in the United Provinces, see Gordon Griffiths (ed.) *Representative Government in Western Europe in the Sixteenth Century* (Oxford, 1968), pp. 526–8, 528–31; Orange's acknowledgement of the authority of the Estates is in the *Apologie*, p. 7. On the implications of such confusion, see Herbert H. Rowen, *The Princes of Orange: The Stadholders in the Dutch Republic* (Cambridge, 1988), esp. p. 55.

5.　On the international situation, see Geoffrey Parker, 'Spain, her Enemies and the Revolt of the Netherlands, 1559–1648', in his *Spain and the Netherlands*, pp. 18–44; see also his brilliantly evocative piece on the narrowness of Spanish failure, 'If the Armada had landed', ibid, pp. 135–48. On the complexities and anxieties of the English position, see N. M. Sutherland, 'The Foreign Policy of Queen Elizabeth, the Sea Beggars, and the Capture of Brill, 1572', in her collection of essays, *Princes, Politics and Religion, 1547–1589* (London, 1984), pp. 186–206; R. B. Wernham, *The Making of Elizabethan Foreign Policy, 1558–1603* (London, 1980); Charles Wilson, *Queen Elizabeth and the Revolt of the Netherlands* (London, 1970). On successful Spanish naval actions, see Rayner Unwin, *The Defeat of John Hawkins* (Harmondsworth, 1962); Peter Earle, *The Last Fight of the Revenge* (London, 1991). On the Armada see the incomparable work by Colin Martin and Geoffrey Parker, *The Spanish Armada* (London, 1988): the English gun carriages are discussed on p. 208; the exhaustion of English ammunition, p. 213; the account of the English tactics is from Emanuel van Meteren, *History of the Low Countries*, which is quoted in Richard Hakluyt, *Voyages and Discoveries*, ed. abr. and intro. Jack Beeching (Harmondsworth, 1972), pp. 322–3.

6. On the treaties, see Elliott, *Europe Divided*, pp. 357–66; for assessments of Philip II, see Geoffrey Parker, *Philip II* (London, 1979); H. G. Koenigsberger, 'The Statecraft of Philip II', in his collection of essays, *Politicians and Virtuosi* (London and Ronceverte, 1986), pp. 77–96.

7. *Don Quixote*, trans. J. M. Cohen (Harmondsworth, 1950), p. 343.

Bibliography

Any list of books on so vast a subject is of necessity selective. Precise references for passages of the text and comment on the particular value of individual works are provided in the Notes. A very few items of detail used in passing are not listed here. Correspondingly, there are some works which have not been specifically cited in the text to which the reader's attention should all the same be drawn. My debt to the books listed is so great that comment here seems superfluous.

This list is intended to provide supplementary information to teachers and students on a range of subjects. As far as possible, I have encouraged a comparative approach, though a few works of obvious importance for certain countries are listed according to national context.

The sections are as follows:

1. *The sixteenth century in European history*: general accounts which give a sense of the importance of the sixteenth century in modern European history as a whole.
2. *The sixteenth century in the early modern period*: works which set the sixteenth century in the context of the period c.1400–c.1800.
3. *Atlases*: these provide a helpful introductory text as well as the maps which add so much to an understanding of historical events.
4. *Reference*: these are works which may provide greater detail or alternative interpretations on various topics.
5. *Sources*: there are many available collections of documents and many texts in translation, and the primary materials of historical research and understanding are much more accessible than is often thought.
6. *Themes*: these are works which cover the themes conventionally identified with the sixteenth century: Renaissance, Reformation, Counter-Reformation and Overseas Expansion. Some or all of these terms may be dispensed with, but the reader is likely to encounter them so frequently that it is important to establish a set of working definitions, the strength of which may then be judged against further research.
7. *Economies and societies*: since so many works on specific regions or topics have general conceptual and methodological implications for Europe as a whole, I have compiled a list which will encourage a comparative approach. Whether an interpretative synthesis is possible will be for the reader to determine.
8. *Urban history*: the vast literature which has now developed reflects the importance of towns in the economic, social, religious and political life of sixteenth century Europe, and studies of the urban Reformation are included here.
9. *States and wars*: this is another compilation which seeks to stimulate comparisons, in this case comparisons of different aspects of statehood across the European regions.

10. *Regional studies*: these are mostly general books on particular countries in the period, but there are also items which provide greater detail on chiefly political matters.
11. *Essays*: it is curious that students are often asked to write history essays without reading essays by historians. These collections are intended to provide a stimulus to creative browsing and models for style and structure.

It should be emphasised that these categories are only loosely defined. In the interests of publisher's space and reader's patience, I have sought to avoid duplicating entries and the listing of every essay from every collection. It is to be hoped that clear alphabetical listing in each category of reading - supplementing the information in the notes - will make it relatively easy to find any particular item.

1.   The sixteenth century in European history

Bronowski, J., *The Ascent of Man* (London, 1973).
Clark, Kenneth, *Civilisation* (London, 1969).
Duroselle, Jean-Baptiste, *Europe: A History of its Peoples*, trans. Richard Mayne (London, 1990).
Gombrich, E. H., *The Story of Art* (London, 1978).
Hay, Denys, *Europe: The Emergence of an Idea* (Edinburgh, 1957).
Roberts, J. M., *The Triumph of the West* (London, 1985).

2.   The sixteenth century in the early modern period

Here are some general studies which take in all or part of the sixteenth century. There are many more books which do so in relation to a particular theme or region, and these should be sought under the appropriate headings.

Braudel, F., *Civilisation and Capitalism, 15th–18th Centuries*, trans. S. Reynolds, 3 vols: vol. 1, *The Structures of Everyday Life* (London, 1981); vol. 2, *The Wheels of Commerce* (London, 1982); vol. 3, *The Perspective of the World* (London, 1984).
Cipolla, Carlo M., *Before the Industrial Revolution: European Society and Economy, 1000–1700* (London, 1976).
Clark, George, *Early Modern Europe: From about 1450 to about 1720*, 2nd edn (Oxford,1966).
Dickens, A. G., *The Age of Humanism and Reformation* (New York, 1977).
Green, V. H. H., *Renaissance and Reformation* (London, 1952).
Kellenbenz, H., *The Rise of the European Economy: An Economic History of Continental Europe from the Fifteenth to the Eighteenth Century*, rev. and ed. G. Benecke (London, 1976).
Koenigsberger, H. G., *Early Modern Europe, 1500–1789* (London, 1987).
Kriedte, Peter, *Peasants, Landlords and Merchant Capitalists: Europe and the World Economy, 1500–1800*, trans. Volker Berghahn (Leamington Spa, 1983).

Parker, Geoffrey, *The Military Revolution: Military Innovation and the Rise of the West, 1500–1800* (Cambridge, 1986).
Rabb, Theodore K., *The Struggle for Stability in Early Modern Europe* (Oxford, 1975).

3. Atlases

Grosser Historischer Weltatlas, dritter teil, Neuzeit, ed. Josef Engel, 2nd edn (Munich, 1962).
The Collins Atlas of World History, ed. Pierre Vidal-Naquet, trans. Chris Turner *et al.* (London, 1987).
The Times Atlas of World Exploration, ed. Felipe Fernandez-Armesto (London, 1991).
The Times Atlas of World History, ed. Geoffrey Barraclough, rev. edn (London, 1979).

4. Reference

Bonney, Richard, *The European Dynastic States, 1494–1660* (Oxford, 1991).
Braudel, F., *The Mediterranean and the Mediterranean World in the Age of Philip II*, trans. S. Reynolds, 2 vols (London, 1975).
Cipolla, Carlo M. (ed.) *The Fontana Economic History of Europe*, vol. 2, *The Sixteenth and Seventeenth Centuries* (London, 1974).
Davis, Ralph, *The Rise of the Atlantic Economies* (London, 1973).
Dunn, Richard S., *The Age of Religious Wars, 1559–1689* (London, 1971).
Elliott, J. H., *Europe Divided, 1559–1598* (London, 1968).
Elton, G. R., *Reformation Europe, 1517–1559* (London, 1963).
Gilmore, Myron P., *The World of Humanism, 1453–1517* (New York, 1952).
Hale, J. R., *Renaissance Europe, 1480–1520* (London, 1971).
Johnson, A. H., *Europe in the Sixteenth Century, 1494–1598*, 7th edn (London, 1941).
Kamen, Henry, *The Iron Century: Social Change in Europe, 1550–1660* (London, 1971).
Kelly, J. N. D., *The Oxford Dictionary of Popes* (Oxford, 1986).
Kiernan, Victor, *State and Society in Europe, 1550–1650* (Oxford, 1980).
Koenigsberger, H. G., Mosse, George L., and Bowler, G. Q., *Europe in the Sixteenth Century*, 2nd edn (London, 1989).
Mandrou, Robert, *From Humanism to Science, 1480–1700*, trans. Brian Pierce (Harmondsworth, 1978).
Miskimin, H. A., *The Economy of Later Renaissance Europe, 1460–1600* (Cambridge, 1977).
Murray, Peter and Linda, *A Dictionary of Art and Artists* (Harmondsworth, 1968).
New Cambridge Modern History, vol. 1, *The Renaissance, 1493–1520*, ed. Denys Hay (Cambridge, 1975); vol. 2, *The Reformation, 1520–1559*, ed. G. R. Elton (Cambridge, 1975), 2nd edn (Cambridge, 1990); vol. 3, *The Counter-Reformation and Price Revolution, 1559–1610*, ed. R. B. Wern-

ham (Cambridge, 1968); vol. 13, *Companion Volume*, ed. Peter Burke (Cambridge, 1980).

Rice, Eugene F., *The Foundations of Early Modern Europe, 1460–1559* (London, 1971).

Stuppereich, Robert, *Reformatorenlexicon* (Gütersloh, 1984).

Trevor-Roper, H. R. (ed.) *The Golden Age of Europe* (London, 1986).

Wilson, Charles, *The Transformation of Europe, 1558–1648* (London, 1976).

Zagorin, Perez, *Rebels and Rulers, 1500–1660*, 2 vols (Cambridge, 1982).

5. Sources

(i)　Collections of documents

Bettenson, Henry (ed.) *Documents of the Christian Church*, 2nd edn (Oxford, 1967).

Burke, Peter (ed.) *The Renaissance Sense of the Past* (London, 1969).

Cochrane, Eric, and Kirshner, Julius (eds) *The Renaissance, University of Chicago Readings in Western Civilisation*, vol. 5 (Chicago, 1986).

Cross, Claire (ed.) *The Royal Supremacy in the Elizabethan Church* (London, 1969).

Dickens, A. G. and Carr, Dorothy (eds) *The Reformation in England to the Accession of Elizabeth I* (London, 1967).

Elton, G. R. (ed.) *The Tudor Constitution* (Cambridge, 1972).

Fletcher, Anthony (ed.) *Tudor Rebellions*, 2nd edn (London, 1973).

Fugger Newsletters, 1568–1605, ed. Viktor von Klarwill, trans. Pauline de Chary (London, 1924).

Hakluyt, Richard, *Voyages and Discoveries*, ed., abr. and intro. Jack Beeching (Harmondsworth, 1972).

Knecht, R. J. (ed.) *French Renaissance Monarchy: Francis I and Henry II* (London, 1984).

Kossmann, E. H., and Mellink, A. F. (eds) *Texts Concerning the Revolt of the Netherlands* (Cambridge, 1974).

Olin, John C. (ed.) *The Catholic Reformation: Savonarola to Ignatius Loyola. Reform in the Church, 1495–1540* (New York, 1969).

Parry, J. H. (ed.) *The European Reconnaissance* (New York, 1968).

Potter, G. R. (ed.) *Huldrych Zwingli* (London, 1978).

Potter, G. R., and Greengrass, M. (eds) *John Calvin* (London, 1982).

Pound, J. F. (ed.) *Poverty and Vagrancy in Tudor England* (London, 1971).

Ross, James Bruce and McLaughlin, Mary (eds) *The Portable Renaissance Reader*, rev. edn (Harmondsworth, 1968).

Rowen, Herbert H. (ed.) *The Low Countries in Early Modern Times* (London, 1972).

Rupp, E. G. and Drewery, Benjamin (eds) *Martin Luther* (London, 1970).

Shennan, J. H. (ed.) *Government and Society in France, 1461–1661* (London, 1969).

Strauss, Gerald (ed.) *Manifestations of Discontent in Germany on the Eve of the Reformation* (Bloomington, Ind., 1971).

(ii)   Texts

Balbi di Correggio, Francisco, *The Siege of Malta, 1565*, trans. Ernle Bradford (London, 1965).

Bodin, Jean, *The Six Books of a Commonweale*, Eng. trans. 1606, ed. Kenneth D. McRae (Cambridge, Mass., 1962).

Bromiley, G. W. (ed.) *Zwingli and Bullinger* (London, 1953).

Bucer, Martin, *The Common Places of Martin Bucer*, trans. and ed. D. F. Wright (Appleford, 1972).

Busbecq, Ogier Ghiselin de, *The Turkish Letters*, trans. E.S. Forster (Oxford, 1927).

Calvin, John, *Institutes of the Christian Religion*, ed. J. T. McNeill, trans. Ford Lewis Battles (London, 1960).

Casas, Bartolomé de Las, *The Spanish Colonie OR Briefe Chronicle of the Acts and gestes of the Spaniardes in the West Indies*, trans. M.M.S. (London, 1583).

Cassirer, Ernst, Kristeller, Paul, and Randall, John H. (eds) *The Renaissance Philosophy of Man* (Chicago, 1948).

Castiglione, Baldassare, *The Courtier*, trans. Sir Thomas Hoby (1561) (London, 1928).

Castiglione, Baldassare, *The Book of the Courtier*, trans. George Bull (Harmondsworth, 1967).

Cellini, Benvenuto, *Autobiography*, trans. George Bull (Harmondsworth, 1956).

Cervantes Saavedra, Miguel de, *Don Quixote*, trans. J. M. Cohen (Harmondsworth, 1950).

Charles V, *The Autobiography of the Emperor Charles V*, trans. Leonard Simpson (London, 1862).

Díaz, Bernal, *The Conquest of New Spain*, trans. J. M. Cohen (Harmondsworth, 1963).

Elyot, Sir Thomas, *The Boke Named the Governour* (1531) (London, 1907).

Erasmus, Desiderius, *Concerning the Aim and Method of Education*, ed. W.H. Woodward, intro. Craig R. Thompson (New York, 1964).

Erasmus, Desiderius, *The Essential Erasmus*, ed. and trans. John P. Dolan (New York, 1964).

Erasmus, Desiderius, *The Colloquies of Erasmus*, trans. Craig R. Thompson (Chicago, 1965).

Eymerich, N., *Le manuel des inquisiteurs*, ed. L. Sala-Molins (Paris–The Hague, 1973).

Fletcher, Giles, *Of the Rus Commonwealth*, ed. Albert J. Schmidt (New York, 1966).

Franklin, Julian H. (ed.) *Consitutionalism and Resistance in the Sixteenth Century: Three Treatises by Hotman, Bèze and Mornay* (New York, 1969).

Guicciardini, Francesco, *The Historie of Guicciardin conteining the Warres of Italie and other partes...*, trans. Geffray Fenton (London, 1579).

Guicciardini, Francesco, *The History of Italy*, trans. S. Alexander, intro. J. R. Hale (New York 1970).

Kohl, Benjamin G., and Witt, Ronald G. (eds) *The Earthly Republic: Italian Humanists on Government and Society* (Manchester, 1978).

Lazarillo de Tormes in *Two Spanish Picaresque Novels*, trans. Michael Alpert (Harmondsworth, 1969).
Ley, Charles (ed.) *Portuguese Voyages, 1498–1663* (London, 1947).
Loyola, Ignatius, *The Spiritual Exercises*, trans. W. H. Longridge (London, 1919).
Luther, Martin, *Works*, ed. J. Pelikan and H. T. Lehmann, 55 vols (St Louis and Philadelphia, 1955–75).
Luther, Martin, *Letters of Spiritual Counsel*, ed. and trans. G. Tappert (London, 1955).
Machiavelli, Niccolo, *The Prince*, trans. Edward Dacres (London, 1640).
Machiavelli, Niccolo, *The Prince*, trans. George Bull (Harmondsworth, 1961).
Machiavelli, Niccolo, *The Discourses*, trans. Leslie Walker, SJ, ed. Bernard Crick (Harmondsworth, 1970).
Michelangelo, *Complete Poems and Selected Letters*, trans. Creighton Gilbert, ed. Robert Linscott (New York, 1970).
Montaigne, Michel de, *The Essayes of Michael Lord of Montaigne*, trans. John Florio (1603) (London, 1891).
Montaigne, Michel de, *The Diary of Montaigne's Journey to Italy in 1580 and 1581*, trans. E. J. Trechmann (London, 1929).
More, Thomas, *Utopia*, trans. Raphe Robinson (1551) (London, 1899).
Pauck, Wilhelm (ed.) *Melanchthon and Bucer* (London, 1969).
Platter, Thomas, *Thomas Platter's Travels in England*, ed. C. Williams (London, 1937).
Rupp, E. G., and Watson, P. S. (eds) *Luther and Erasmus: Free Will and Salvation* (Philadelphia, 1969).
Sandys, Sir Edwin, *A Relation of the State of Religion: and with what Hopes and Pollicies it hath been framed and is maintained in the severall States of these Westerne partes of the world* (London, 1605).
Santa Teresa, *The Life of Saint Teresa of Avila by herself*, trans. J. M. Cohen (Harmondsworth, 1957).
Seyssel, Claude de, *The Monarchy of France*, trans. J. H. Hexter, ed. Donald R. Kelley (New Haven, 1981).
Spenser, Edmund, *A View of the Present State of Ireland*, ed. W. L. Renwick (London, 1934).
Vasari, Giorgio, *The Lives of the Artists*, sel. and trans. George Bull (Harmondsworth, 1965).
William of Orange, *The Apologie of Prince William of Orange against the Proclamation of the King of Spaine*, ed. H. Wansink (Leyden, 1969).
Williams, G. H. and Mergal, Angela M. (eds) *Spiritual and Anabaptist Writers* (London, 1957).
Woodward, W. H. (ed.) *Vittorino da Feltre and Other Humanist Educators* (Cambridge, 1921).
Woolf, Bertram Lee (ed.) *Reformation Writings of Martin Luther*, 2 vols (London, 1952–6).
Zwingli, Ulrich, *Selected Works*, trans. Samuel Jackson, intro. Edward Peters (Philadelphia, 1972).

6. Themes

(i) Renaissance

To keep this list within manageable proportions, the works listed emphasise the long-term implications of Italian achievements for Europe as a whole, especially with reference to the Scientific Revolution.

Anglo, Sydney, *The Courtier's Art: Systematic Immorality in the Renaissance* (Swansea, 1983).
Bataillon, Marcel, *Erasme et l'Espagne* (Paris, 1937).
Blunt, Anthony, *Artistic Theory in Italy, 1450–1600* (Oxford, 1968).
Burke, Peter, *Montaigne* (Oxford, 1981).
Burke, Peter, *The Renaissance* (London, 1987).
Chabod, Federico, *Machiavelli and the Renaissance*, trans. David Moore, intro. A. P. d'Entrèves (New York, 1965).
Clark, Kenneth, *Leonardo da Vinci: An Account of his Development as an Artist* (Harmondsworth, 1959).
Clark, Kenneth, *A Failure of Nerve: Italian Painting, 1520–1535* (Oxford, 1967).
Debus, Allen, *Man and Nature in the Renaissance* (Cambridge, 1978).
Drake, Stillman, *Galileo* (Oxford, 1980).
Dresden, Sem, *Humanism in the Renaissance*, trans. Margaret King (London, 1968).
Eisenstein, Elizabeth L., *The Printing Revolution in Early Modern Europe* (Cambridge, 1983).
Evans, R. J. W., *Rudolf II and his World* (Oxford, 1973).
Goodman, Anthony, and MacKay, Angus (eds) *The Impact of Humanism on Western Europe* (London, 1990).
Hale, J. R., *Renaissance* (Time-Life, The Netherlands, 1966).
Hay, Denys (ed.) *The Age of the Renaissance* (London, 1986).
Kagan, R. L., 'Universities in Castile, 1500–1700', *Past and Present*, 49 (1970), 44–71.
Kearney, Hugh, *Science and Change, 1500–1700* (London, 1971).
Kemp, Martin, *The Science of Art* (New Haven, 1990).
Levey, Michael, *Early Renaissance* (Harmondsworth, 1967).
Levey, Michael, *High Renaissance* (Harmondsworth, 1975).
Lowry, Martin, *The World of Aldus Manutius* (Oxford, 1979).
Mann Phillips, Margaret, *Erasmus and the Northern Renaissance* (London, 1949).
Panofsky, Erwin, *The Life and Art of Albrecht Dürer*, 4th edn (Princeton, 1971).
Panofsky, Erwin, *Renaissance and Renascences in Western Art* (New York, 1972).
Porter, Roy, and Teich, Mikulas (eds) *The Renaissance in National Context* (Cambridge, 1992).
Rossi, Paolo, *Philosophy, Technology and the Arts in the Early Modern Era* (New York, 1970).
Seidel Menchi, Silvana, *Erasmo in Italia, 1520–1580* (Turin, 1987).
Skinner, Quentin, *Machiavelli* (Oxford, 1981).
Smith, A. G. R., *Science and Society in the Sixteenth and Seventeenth Centuries* (London, 1972).

Stephens, John, *The Italian Renaissance: The Origins of Intellectual and Artistic Change before the Reformation* (London, 1990).
Stone, Lawrence, 'The Educational Revolution in England, 1560–1640', *Past and Present*, 28 (1964), 41–80.
Weiss, Roberto, *The Spread of Italian Humanism* (London, 1964).
Wind, Edgar, *Pagan Mysteries in the Renaissance* (Oxford, 1980).
Yates, Frances A., *The Occult Philosophy in the Elizabethan Age* (London, 1979).

(ii)   Reformation

This section includes books on the concept of the Reformation, and on the thought of the reformers. Materials pertinent to popular religion and culture are listed under 'Economies and Societies', the numerous studies of the Reformation in the cities are found under the sub-heading 'Urban History'.

Bainton, Roland H., *Here I Stand: A Life of Martin Luther* (New York, 1950).
Besnard, P., *Protestantisme et capitalisme: la controverse post-Wéberienne* (Paris, 1970).
Birnbaum, N., 'The Zwinglian Reformation in Zurich', *Past and Present*, 15 (1959), 27–47.
Bouwsma, William J., *John Calvin: A Sixteenth-Century Portrait* (Oxford, 1988).
Cameron, Euan, *The European Reformation* (Oxford, 1991).
Chadwick, Owen, *The Reformation* (Harmondsworth, 1964).
Chaunu, Pierre (ed.) *The Reformation*, trans. Victoria Acland *et al.* (London, 1989).
Clasen, Claus-Peter, *Anabaptism: A Social History, 1525–1618: Switzerland, Austria, Moravia, South and Central Germany* (Ithaca, N.Y., 1972).
Cohn, Norman, *The Pursuit of the Millennium* (London, 1970).
Cohn, Norman, *Europe's Inner Demons* (London, 1976).
Collinson, Patrick, *The Elizabethan Puritan Movement* (London, 1967).
Cowan, Ian B., *Regional Aspects of the Scottish Reformation* (H.A. pamphlet, London, 1978).
Crew, Phyllis Mack, *Calvinist Preaching and Iconoclasm in the Netherlands, 1544–1569* (Cambridge, 1978).
DeMolen, Richard (ed.) *Leaders of the Reformation* (London and Toronto, 1984).
Dickens, A. G., *Thomas Cromwell and the English Reformation* (London, 1959).
Dickens, A. G., *Reformation and Society in Sixteenth-Century Europe* (London, 1966).
Dickens, A. G., *Martin Luther and the Reformation* (London, 1967).
Dickens, A. G., *The English Reformation* (London, 1967).
Dickens, A. G., *The German Nation and Martin Luther* (London, 1976).
Dufour, A., 'Le mythe de Genève au temps de Calvin', *Schweizerische Zeitschrift für Geschichte*, n.s. 9 (1959), 489–518.
Edwards, Mark U., *Luther and the False Brethren* (Stanford, Cal., 1975).
Elton, G. R., 'The Real Thomas More?', in Brooks (ed), *Principle and Practice*, 23–31 (see section 11, Essays).

Enno van Gelder, H. A., *The Two Reformations in the Sixteenth Century* (The Hague, 1964).

Foxgrover, David, 'Calvin as Reformer: Christ's Standard-Bearer', in DeMolen, *Leaders*, 178–210 (see above or section 11, Essays).

Hendrix, Scott H., 'Luther's Communities' in DeMolen, *Leaders*, 43–68 (see above or section 11, Essays).

Hill, Christopher, *Society and Puritanism in Pre-Revolutionary England* (London, 1969).

Höpfl, Haro, *The Christian Polity of John Calvin* (Cambridge, 1982).

Höss, Irmgard, 'The Lutheran Church of the Reformation: Problems of its Formation and Organisation in the Middle and North German Territories', in Buck and Zophy, *Social History*, 317–39 (see section 11, Essays).

Hsia, R. Po-chia, *Social Discipline in the Reformation: Central Europe, 1550–1750* (London, 1989).

Huizinga, Johan, *Erasmus and the Age of Reformation*, trans. F. Hopman (New York, 1957).

Hurstfield, Joel (ed.) *The Reformation Crisis* (London, 1965).

Hyma, A., 'Calvinism and Capitalism in the Netherlands, 1555–1700', *Journal of Modern History*, 10 (1938), 321–43.

Kamen, Henry, *The Rise of Toleration* (London, 1967).

Keeney, W. E., *Dutch Anabaptist Thought and Practice, 1539–1564* (Nieuwkoop, 1968).

Kingdon, Robert M., 'The Control of Morals in Calvin's Geneva', in Buck and Zophy, *Social History*, 3–16 (see section 11, Essays).

Kirchner, Walther, 'State and Anabaptists in the Sixteenth Century: An Economic Approach', *Journal of Modern History*, 46 (1974), 1–25.

Klassen, Peter, *The Economics of Anabaptism* (London–The Hague–Paris, 1964).

Knecht, R. J., 'The Early Reformation in England and France: A Comparison', *History*, 57 (1972), 1–16.

Knowles, David, *The Religious Orders in England*, vol. 3, *The Tudor Age* (Cambridge, 1959).

Krahn, Cornelius, *Dutch Anabaptism: Origin, Spread, Life and Thought (1450–1600)* (The Hague, 1968).

Lewis, Gillian, 'Calvinism in Geneva in the Time of Calvin and of Bèze (1541–1605)', in Prestwich, *Calvinism*, 41–65 (see section 11, Essays).

Manschreck, Clyde L., *Melanchthon: The Quiet Reformer* (Nashville, Tenn., 1957).

Marius, Richard, *Luther* (London, 1975).

McGrath, Alister E., *Reformation Thought: An Introduction* (Oxford, 1988).

Midelfort, H. C. Erik, 'Protestant Monastery? A Reformed Hospital in Hesse', in Brooks, *Principle and Practice*, 71–94 (see section 11, Essays).

Mullett, Michael, *Radical Religious Movements in Early Modern Europe* (London, 1980).

Mullett, Michael, *Luther* (London, 1986).

Oberman, Heiko A., *The Harvest of Medieval Theology* (Cambridge, Mass., 1963).

Oberman, Heiko A., *Forerunners of the Reformation* (New York, 1966).

Oberman, Heiko A., *Masters of the Reformation: The Emergence of a New Intellectual Climate in Europe*, trans. Dennis Martin (Cambridge, 1981).

Oberman, Heiko A., *Luther: Man between God and Devil* (London, 1985).
Oberman, Heiko A., *The Dawn of the Reformation* (Edinburgh, 1986).
Ozment, Steven, *Mysticism and Dissent* (New Haven, 1973).
Ozment, Steven, *The Age of Reform, 1250–1550* (New Haven, 1980).
Packull, Werner O., *Mysticism and the Early South German Anabaptist Movement, 1525–1531* (Scottdale, Pa. and Kitchener, Ontario, 1977).
Parker, T. M., *The English Reformation to 1558*, 2nd edn (Oxford, 1966).
Potter, G. R., *Zwingli* (Cambridge, 1976).
Potter, G. R., *Zwingli* (H.A. pamphlet, London, 1977).
Prestwich, Menna, 'The Changing Face of Calvinism', in Prestwich, *Calvinism*, 1–10 (see section 11, Essays).
Reardon, B. M. G., *Religious Thought in the Reformation* (London, 1981).
Rupp, E. G., *The Righteousness of God: Luther Studies* (London, 1953).
Rupp, E. G., *Luther's Progress to the Diet of Worms* (New York, 1964).
Rupp, E. G., *Patterns of Reformation* (London, 1969).
Rupp, E. G., 'Protestant Spirituality in the First Age of the Reformation', in G. J. Cumming and Derek Baker (eds), *Popular Belief and Practice* (Cambridge, 1972), 155–70.
Rupp, E. G., *Thomas More: The King's Good Servant* (London, 1978).
Rupp, E. G., 'The Battle of the Books: The Ferment of Ideas and the Beginning of the Reformation', in Brooks, *Principle and Practice*, 1– 20 (see section 11, Essays).
Scribner, R. W., 'Practice and Principle in the German Towns: Preachers and People', in Brooks, *Principle and Practice*, 95–117 (see section 11, Essays).
Scribner, R. W., *For the Sake of Simple Folk: Popular Propaganda for the German Reformation* (Cambridge, 1981).
Scribner, R. W., *The German Reformation* (London, 1986).
Scribner, R. W., 'The Reformation Movements in Germany', *NCMH*, vol. 2, 2nd edn, 69–93.
Scribner, R. W., 'Politics and the Institutionalisation of Reform in Germany', *NCMH*, vol. 2, 2nd edn, 172–97.
Stayer, James M., 'Christianity in One City: Anabaptist Münster, 1534–35', in Hillerbrand, *Radical Tendencies*, 117–34 (see section 11, Essays).
Stayer, James M., 'The Anabaptists and the Sects', *NCMH*, vol. 2, 2nd edn, 118–43.
Strauss, Gerald, 'Success and Failure in the German Reformation', *Past and Present*, 67 (1975), 30–63.
Strauss, Gerald, 'The Mental World of a Saxon Pastor', in Brooks, *Principle and Practice*, 157–70 (see section 11, Essays).
Strauss, Gerald, *Luther's House of Learning: Indoctrination of the Young in the German Reformation* (Baltimore, 1978).
Tedeschi, John, and Willis, E. D., 'Two Italian Translations of Beza and Calvin', *Archiv für Reformationsgeschichte*, 55 (1964), 70–4.
Tentler, Thomas N., *Sin and Confession on the Eve of the Reformation* (Princeton, 1977).
Vogler, G., 'The Anabaptist Kingdom of Münster: The Tension between Anabaptism and Imperial Policy', in Hillerbrand, *Radical Tendencies*, 99–116 (see section 11, Essays).
Walton, R. C., *Zwingli's Theocracy* (Toronto, 1967).

Walton, R. C., 'Zwingli: Founding Father of the Reformed Churches', in DeMolen, *Leaders*, 69–98 (see above or section 11, Essays).

Walzer, Michael, *The Revolution of the Saints: A Study in the Origins of Radical Politics* (New York, 1968).

Wendel, François, *Calvin: The Origins and Development of his Religious Thought*, trans. Philip Mairet (London, 1965).

Williams, G. H., *The Radical Reformation* (Philadelphia, 1962).

Williams, G. H., 'The Two Social Strands in Italian Anabaptism, c.1526–c.1565', in Buck and Zophy, *Social History*, 156–207 (see section 11, Essays).

(iii) Counter-Reformation

Asor Rosa, Alberto, *La cultura della Controriforma* (Rome, 1979).

Black, Christopher, *Italian Confraternities in the Sixteenth Century* (Cambridge, 1989).

Bossy, John, 'The Counter-Reformation and the People of Catholic Europe', *Past and Present*, 47 (1970), 51–70.

Bossy, John, 'The Social History of Confession', *Transactions of the Royal Historical Society*, ser. 5, 25 (1975), 21–38.

Bossy, John, *Christianity in the West, 1400–1700* (Oxford, 1985).

Brodrick, James, SJ, *Robert Bellarmine, 1542–1621*, 2 vols (London, 1950).

Brodrick, James, SJ, *The Origin of the Jesuits* (London, 1940).

Brodrick, James, SJ, *The Progress of the Jesuits* (London, 1946).

Davidson, N. S., *The Counter-Reformation* (Oxford, 1987).

Delumeau, Jean, *Catholicism between Luther and Voltaire: A New View of the Counter-Reformation*, trans. Jeremy Moiser (London, 1977).

Dickens, A. G., *The Counter-Reformation* (London, 1968).

Evenett, H. O., *The Spirit of the Counter-Reformation*, ed. with a postscript by John Bossy (Notre Dame, Ind., 1970).

Fenlon, Dermot, *Heresy and Obedience in Tridentine Italy: Cardinal Pole and the Counter-Reformation* (Cambridge, 1972).

Janelle, Pierre, *The Catholic Reformation* (West Drayton, 1971).

Jedin, Hubert, *Geschichte des Konzils von Trient*, 4 vols (Freiburg, 1949–75); first two vols translated as *A History of the Council of Trent*, trans. Dom Ernest Graf, OSB, 2 vols (London, 1957–61).

Jedin, Hubert, *Crisis and Closure of the Council of Trent*, trans. N. D. Smith (London, 1967).

Mâle, E., *L'art religieux après le Concile de Trente*, 2nd edn (Paris, 1951).

Matheson, Peter, *Cardinal Contarini at Regensburg* (Oxford, 1972).

Prodi, 'The Application of the Tridentine Decrees: The Organisation of the Diocese of Bologna during the Episcopate of Cardinal Gabriele Paleotti', in Cochrane, *Late Italian Renaissance*, 226–43 (see section 11, Essays).

Quinn, Peter A., 'Ignatius Loyola and Gian Pietro Carafa: Catholic Reformers at Odds', *Catholic Historical Review*, 67 (1981), 386–400.

Ranke, L. von, *The History of the Popes*, trans. E. Foster, 3 vols (London, 1866).

Szasz, Thomas S., *The Manufacture of Madness* (London, 1973).

Tedeschi, John A., *The Prosecution of Heresy: Collected Studies on the Inquisition in Early Modern Italy* (Binghampton, N.Y., 1991).

Wright, A. D., *The Counter-Reformation: Catholic Europe and the Non-Christian World* (London, 1982).

Wright, A. D., 'The Borromean Ideal and the Spanish Church', in John M. Headley and John B. Tomaro (eds), *San Carlo Borromeo* (London and Toronto, 1988), 188–207.

(iv)   Overseas expansion

Andrews, K. R., *Drake's Voyages* (London, 1970).

Andrews, K. R., *Trade, Plunder and Settlement: Maritime Enterprise and the Genesis of the British Empire, 1480–1630* (Cambridge, 1984).

Andrews, K. R., Canny, N. P. and Hair, P. E. H. (eds) *The Westward Enterprise: English Activities in Ireland, the Atlantic, and America, 1480–1650* (Liverpool, 1978).

Boxer, C. R., *Race Relations in the Portuguese Colonial Empire, 1415–1825* (Oxford, 1963).

Boxer, C. R., *The Portuguese Seaborne Empire, 1415–1825* (London, 1969).

Boxer, C. R., *The Dutch Seaborne Empire, 1600–1800* (London, 1977).

Boxer, C. R., *The Church Militant and Iberian Expansion, 1440–1770* (Baltimore, 1978).

Cipolla, Carlo M., *European Culture and Overseas Expansion* (Harmondsworth, 1970).

Diffie, B. W., and Winius, G. D., *Foundations of the Portuguese Empire, 1415–1580* (Minneapolis, 1977).

Elliott, J. H., *The Old World and the New, 1492–1650* (Cambridge, 1970).

Elliott, J. H., 'The Mental World of Hernán Cortés', *Transactions of the Royal Historical Society*, 5 ser., 17 (1967), 41–58, or in his essays, *Spain and its World* (see section 11, Essays).

Hale, J. R., *Age of Exploration* (Time-Life, The Netherlands, 1966).

Hale, J. R., *Renaissance Exploration* (London, 1968).

Hanke, Lewis, *Aristotle and the American Indians* (London, 1959).

Lang, James, *Portuguese Brazil: The King's Plantation* (New York, 1979).

Pagden, A. R., *Spanish Imperialism and the Political Imagination* (New Haven, 1989).

Parry, J. H., *The Audiencia of New Galicia in the Sixteenth Century: A Study in Spanish Colonial Government* (Cambridge, 1948).

Parry, J. H., *Europe and a Wider World, 1415–1715* (London, 1949).

Parry, J. H., *The Age of Reconnaissance* (New York, 1963).

Quinn, D. B., 'Sir Thomas Smith (1513–1577) and the Beginnings of English Colonial Theory', *Proceedings of the American Philosophical Society*, 89 (1945), 543–60.

Quinn, D. B., *The Elizabethans and the Irish* (Ithaca, N.Y., 1966).

Scammell, G. V., *The First Imperial Age: European Overseas Expansion, 1400–1715* (London, 1989).

Simpson, L. B., *The Encomienda in New Spain: The Beginning of Spanish Mexico* (Los Angeles, 1966).

Unwin, Rayner, *The Defeat of John Hawkins* (Harmondsworth, 1962).

Zavala, S., *New Viewpoints on the Spanish Colonisation of America* (Philadelphia, 1943).

7. Economies and societies

Anderson, Michael, *Approaches to the History of the Western Family, 1500–1914* (London, 1980).

Ankarloo, Bengt, and Henningsen, Gustav (eds) *Early Modern European Witchcraft* (Oxford, 1990).

Ariès, Philippe, *Centuries of Childhood*, trans. Robert Baldick (London, 1973).

Backus, O. P., 'The Problem of Feudalism in Lithuania, 1506–1548', *Slavic Review*, 21 (1962), 639–59.

Bakhtin, M., *Rabelais and his World*, trans. Hélène Iswolsky (Boston, 1968).

Beier, A. L., *Masterless Men: The Vagrancy Problem in England, 1560–1640* (London, 1985).

Biraben, Jean-Noël, *Les hommes et la peste en France et dans les pays européens et méditerranéens*, 2 vols (Paris–The Hague, 1975).

Bitton, Davis, *The French Nobility in Crisis* (Stanford, Cal., 1969).

Blickle, Peter, 'The Economic, Political and Social Background of the Twelve Articles', *Journal of Peasant Studies*, 3 (1975), 64–74.

Blickle, Peter, 'Peasant Revolts in the German Empire in the Late Middle Ages', *Social History*, 4 (1979), 223–39.

Blickle, Peter, *The Revolution of 1525* (Baltimore, 1981).

Blickle, Peter, Rublack, H.-C., and Schulze, W., *Religion, Politics and Social Protest: Three Studies on Early Modern Germany* (London, 1984).

Blum, Jerome, *Lord and Peasant in Russia from the Ninth to the Nineteenth Century* (Princeton, 1961).

Braudel, F. and Spooner, F., 'Prices in Europe from 1450 to 1750', *CEHE*, vol. 4, 374–486.

Brenner, Robert, 'Agrarian Class Structure and Economic Development in Pre-Industrial Europe', in Aston and Philpin, *Brenner Debate*, 10–63 (see section 11, Essays).

Burke, Peter, *Popular Culture in Early Modern Europe* (London, 1978).

Burke, Peter, 'Popular Piety', in J. O'Malley (ed.) *Catholicism in Early Modern Europe* (St Louis, 1988), 113–31.

Bush, M. L., *Noble Privilege* (Manchester, 1983).

Cameron, Euan, *The Reformation of the Heretics: The Waldenses of the Alps, 1480–1580* (Oxford, 1984).

Christian, William A., *Local Religion in Sixteenth-Century Spain* (Princeton, 1981).

Cohn, Henry J., 'The Peasants of Swabia, 1525', *Journal of Peasant Studies*, 3 (1975), 10–22.

Cohn, Henry J., 'Anticlericalism in the German Peasants' War, 1525', *Past and Present*, 83 (1979), 3–31.

Cohn, Norman, *Europe's Inner Demons* (London, 1976).

Coleman, D. C., 'Gentlemen and Players', *Economic History Review*, 2 ser., 26 (1973), 92–116.

Edwards, John, *The Jews in Christian Europe, 1400–1700* (London, 1988).

Ehrenberg, Richard, *Capital and Finance in the Age of the Renaissance: A Study of the Fuggers and their Connections*, trans. H. M. Lucas (London, 1928).

Estèbe, J., 'La bourgeoisie marchande et la terre à Toulouse au xvie siècle', *Annales du Midi*, 76 (1964), 457–67.

Fischer, W., 'Rural Industry and Population Change', *Comparative Studies in Society and History*, 15 (1973), 158–70.

Galpern, A. N., *The Religions of the People in Sixteenth-Century Champagne* (Cambridge, Mass., 1977).

Ginzburg, Carlo, *The Cheese and the Worms: The Cosmos of a Sixteenth-Century Miller*, trans. John and Anne Tedeschi (London, 1980).

Ginzburg, Carlo, *The Night Battles: Witchcraft and Agrarian Cults in the Sixteenth and Seventeenth Centuries*, trans. John and Anne Tedeschi (London, 1983).

Gutmann, M., *War and Rural Life in the Early Modern Low Countries* (Princeton, 1980).

Gutton, Jean-Pierre, *La société et les pauvres: l'exemple de la généralité de Lyon, 1534–1789* (Paris, 1970).

Harris, Marvin, *Cows, Pigs, Wars and Witches: The Riddles of Culture* (London, 1977).

Harte, N. B., 'State Control of Dress and Social Change in Pre-Industrial England', in D. C. Coleman and A. H. John (eds) *Trade, Government and Economy in Pre-Industrial England* (London, 1976), 132–65.

Hillerbrand, Hans J., 'The German Reformation and the Peasants' War', in Buck and Zophy, *Social History*, 106–36 (see section 11, Essays).

Hsia, R. Po-chia, *The Myth of Ritual Murder: Jews and Magic in Reformation Germany* (New Haven, 1983).

Israel, Jonathan, *European Jewry in the Age of Mercantilism, 1550–1750* (Oxford, 1985).

Jeannin, Pierre, *Les marchands au xvie siècle* (Paris, 1957).

Jouanna, A., 'Recherches sur la notion d'honneur au xvie siècle', *Revue d'Histoire Moderne et Contemporaine*, 15 (1968), 597–623.

Kaminsky, A., 'Neo-Serfdom in Poland-Lithuania', *Slavic Review*, 34 (1975), 253–68.

Kellenbenz, H., 'The Organisation of Production', *CEHE*, vol. 5, 462–548.

Kellenbenz, H., 'German Aristocratic Entrepreneurship: Economic Activities of the Holstein Nobility in the Sixteenth and Seventeenth Centuries', *Explorations in Entrepreneurial History*, 6 (1953–4), 103–12.

Kiraly, B. K., 'Neo-Serfdom in Hungary', *Slavic Review*, 34 (1975), 269–78.

Kirilly, Z., and Kiss, I. N., 'Production de céréales et exploitations paysannes en Hongrie aux xvie et xviie siècles', *Annales*, 23 (1968), 1211–36.

Larner, Christina, *Witchcraft and Religion: The Politics of Popular Belief* (Oxford, 1984).

Laslett, Peter, *The World We Have Lost*, 2nd edn (London, 1971).

Le Roy Ladurie, E., *The Peasants of Languedoc*, trans. John Day (Urbana, Ill., 1974).

Le Roy Ladurie, E., *Carnival: A People's Uprising at Romans, 1579–80*, trans. M. Feeney (Harmondsworth, 1981).

Le Roy Ladurie, E., *The French Peasantry, 1450–1660*, trans. A. Sheridan (Aldershot, 1987).

Levack, Brian P., *The Witch-Hunt in Early Modern Europe* (London, 1987).

Lis, C. and Soly, H., *Poverty and Capitalism in Pre-Industrial Europe*, trans. James Coonan (Brighton, 1979).

Lütge, Friedrich, 'The Fourteenth and Fifteenth Centuries in Social and Economic History', in Strauss, *Pre-Reformation Germany*, 316–79 (see section 11, Essays).

Makkai, L., 'Neo-Serfdom: Its Origin and Nature in East Central Europe', *Slavic Review*, 34 (1975), 225–38.

Malowist, M., 'Poland, Russia and Western Trade in the Fifteenth and Sixteenth Centuries', *Past and Present*, 13 (1958), 26–41.

Malowist, M., 'The Economic and Social Development of the Baltic Countries from the Fifteenth to the Seventeenth Centuries', *Economic History Review*, 2 ser., 12 (1959–60), 177–89.

Marshall, S., *The Dutch Gentry, 1500–1650: Family, Faith and Fortune* (New York, 1987).

Martin, Ruth, *Witchcraft and the Inquisition in Venice, 1550–1650* (Oxford, 1989).

Midelfort, H. C. Erik, *Witch-Hunting in Southwestern Germany, 1562–1684: The Social and Intellectual Foundations* (Stanford, Cal., 1972).

Monter, E. W., *Ritual, Myth and Magic in Early Modern Europe* (Brighton, 1983).

Mousnier, Roland, *Social Hierarchies: 1450 to the Present*, trans. P. Evans, ed. M. Clarke (London, 1973).

Nader, H., 'Noble Income in Sixteenth-Century Castile', *Economic History Review*, 2 ser., 30 (1977), 411–28.

Nef, John U., *Industry and Government in France and England, 1540–1640* (Ithaca, N.Y., 1964).

Outhwaite, R. B., *Inflation in Tudor and Early Stuart England* (London, 1969).

Ozment, Steven, *When Fathers Ruled: Family Life in Reformation Europe* (Cambridge, Mass., 1983).

Pach, Z. P., 'En Hongrie au xvie siècle: l'activité commerciale des seigneurs et leur production marchande', *Annales*, 21 (1966), 1212–31.

Phythian-Adams, Charles, *Local History and Folklore: A New Framework* (London, 1975).

Powis, Jonathan, *Aristocracy* (Oxford, 1983).

Pullan, Brian, 'Catholics and the Poor in Early Modern Europe', *Transactions of the Royal Historical Society*, ser. 5, 26 (1976), 15–34.

Pullan, Brian, *The Jews of Europe and the Inquisition of Venice, 1550–1670* (Oxford, 1983).

Pullan, Brian, *Orphans and Foundlings in Early Modern Europe* (Reading, 1989).

Ramsey, Peter H. (ed.) *The Price Revolution in Sixteenth-Century England* (London, 1971).

Rebel, Hermann, *Peasant Classes. The Bureaucratisation of Property and Family Relations under Early Habsburg Absolutism, 1511–1636* (Princeton, 1983).

Redlich, F., 'European Aristocracy and Economic Development', *Explorations in Entrepreneurial History*, 6 (1953–4), 78–91.

Rosenberg, H., 'The Rise of the Junkers in Brandenburg-Prussia, 1410–1653', *American Historical Review*, 49 (1943–4), 1–22.

Schalk, E., 'The Appearance and Reality of Nobility in France during the Wars of Religion', *Journal of Modern History*, 48 (1976), 19–31.

Slack, Paul, *Poverty and Policy in Tudor and Stuart England* (London, 1988).
Slicher van Bath, B. H., *The Agrarian History of Western Europe, AD 500–1850*, trans. O. Ordish (London, 1963).
Stone, Lawrence, *The Crisis of the Aristocracy, 1558–1641*, abr. edn (Oxford, 1967).
Teall, E. S., 'The Seigneur of Renaissance France: Advocate or Oppressor?', *Journal of Modern History*, 37 (1965), 131–50.
Thomas, Keith, 'Work and Leisure in Pre-Industrial Society', *Past and Present*, 29 (1964), 50–66.
Thomas, Keith, *Religion and the Decline of Magic* (Harmondsworth, 1973).
Thompson, I. A. A., 'The Purchase of Nobility in Castile, 1552–1700', *Journal of European Economic History*, 8 (1979), 313–60.
Trevor-Roper, H. R., 'The Elizabethan Aristocracy: An Anatomy Anatomised', *Economic History Review*, 2 ser., 3 (1951), 279–98.
Tucoo-Chala, P., 'Un exemple d'essor urbain: Pau au xvie siècle', *Annales du Midi*, 78 (1966), 345–62.
Unger, W. S., 'Trade through the Sound', *Economic History Review*, 2 ser., 12 (1959–60), 206–21.
Vilar, Pierre, *A History of Gold and Money, 1450–1920*, trans. Judith White (London, 1984).
Wallerstein, I., *Capitalist Agriculture and the Origins of the European World Economy in the Sixteenth Century* (New York, 1974).
Wiley, W. L., *The Gentleman of Renaissance France* (Cambridge, Mass., 1954).
Wilson, Charles, and Parker, Geoffrey (eds) *An Introduction to the Sources of European Economic History, 1500–1800* (London, 1977).
Wood, J. B., *The Nobility of the Election of Bayeux, 1463–1666* (Princeton, 1980).
Wright, W. E., 'Neo-Serfdom in Bohemia', *Slavic Review*, 34 (1975), 239–52.

8.   Urban History

Abray, Lorna Jane, *The People's Reformation: Magistrates, Commons and Clergy in Strasbourg, 1500–1598* (Oxford, 1985).
Amelang, James, *Honoured Citizens of Barcelona: Patrician Culture and Class Relations, 1490–1714* (Princeton, 1986).
Baron, Hans, 'Religion and Politics in the German Imperial Cities during the Reformation', *English Historical Review*, 52 (1937), 405–27, 614–33.
Beier, A. L., 'Social Problems in Elizabethan London', *Journal of Interdisciplinary History*, 9 (1978), 203–21.
Beier, A. L. and Finlay, Roger (eds) *London 1500–1700: The Making of the Metropolis* (London, 1986).
Benedict, Philip, *Rouen and the Wars of Religion* (Cambridge, 1981).
Berengo, Marino, *Nobili e mercanti nella Lucca del '500* (Turin, 1965).
Berner, Samuel, 'Florentine Society in the late Sixteenth and early Seventeenth Centuries', *Studies in the Renaissance*, 18 (1971), 203–46.
Bindoff, S. T., 'The Greatness of Antwerp', *NCMH*, vol. 2, 50–69.
Birnbaum, N., 'The Zwinglian Reformation in Zurich', *Past and Present*, 15 (1959), 27–47.

Brady, Thomas A., *Ruling Class, Regime and Reformation at Strasbourg, 1520–1555* (Leyden, 1978).

Brady, Thomas A., 'Patricians, Nobles, Merchants: Internal Tensions and Solidarities in South German Urban Ruling Classes at the Close of the Middle Ages', in Chrisman and Gründler, *Social Groups*, 38–45 (see section 11, Essays).

Brady, Thomas, *Turning Swiss: Cities and Empire, 1450–1550* (Cambridge, 1985).

Broadhead, Philip, 'Politics and Expediency in the Augsburg Reformation', in Brooks, *Principle and Practice*, 53–70 (see section 11, Essays).

Brulez, Wilfred, 'Bruges and Antwerp in the Fifteenth and Sixteenth Centuries: An Antithesis?', *Acta Historica Neerlandica*, 6 (1973), 1–26.

Bushkovitch, M., *The Merchants of Moscow, 1580–1650* (Cambridge, 1980).

Chrisman, Miriam U., *Strasbourg and the Reform* (Newark, N.J., 1967).

Chrisman, Miriam U., *Lay Culture, Learned Culture: Books and Social Change in Strasbourg, 1480–1599* (New Haven, 1982).

Chrisman, Miriam U., 'Urban Poor in the Sixteenth Century: The Case of Strasbourg', in Chrisman and Gründler, *Social Groups*, 59–68 (see section 11, Essays).

Clark, Peter and Slack, Paul, *English Towns in Transition, 1500–1700* (Oxford, 1976).

Delumeau, Jean, *Rome au xvie siècle* (Paris, 1975).

De Vries, Jan, *European Urbanisation, 1500–1800* (London, 1984).

Dollinger, Philipp, *The German Hansa*, trans. D.S. Ault and S.H. Steinberg (London, 1970).

Duplessis, R.C., and Howell, M.C., 'Reconsidering the Early Modern Economy: The Cases of Leyden and Lille', *Past and Present*, 94 (1982), 49–84.

Fisher, F.J., 'The Development of London as a Centre of Conspicuous Consumption in the Sixteenth and Seventeenth Centuries', in I.R. Christie (ed.) *Essays in Modern History* (London, 1968), 75–90.

Fisher, F.J., 'London as an "Engine of Economic Growth"', in Clark, *Early Modern Town*, 205–15 (see section 11, Essays).

Friedrichs, Christopher R., 'Citizens or Subjects? Urban Conflict in Early Modern Germany', in Chrisman and Gründler, *Social Groups*, 46–58 (see section 11, Essays).

Gascon, Richard, *Grand commerce et vie urbaine au xvie siècle: Lyon et ses marchands*, 2 vols (Paris, 1971).

Hsia, R. Po-chia, *Society and Religion in Münster, 1535–1618* (New Haven, 1984).

Kingdon, R.M., 'Social Welfare in Calvin's Geneva', *American Historical Review*, 76 (1971), 50–69.

Lynch, Michael, *Edinburgh and the Reformation* (Edinburgh, 1981).

Mackenney, Richard, *Tradesmen and Traders: The World of the Guilds in Venice and Europe, c.1250–c.1650* (London, 1987).

Mackenney, Richard, *The City-State, 1500–1700* (London, 1989).

Martz, Linda, *Poverty and Welfare in Habsburg Spain: The Example of Toledo* (Cambridge, 1983).

Moeller, Bernd, *Imperial Cities and the Reformation*, ed. and trans. H.C. Erik Midelfort and Mark U. Edwards (Durham, N.C., 1982).

Monter, E. W., *Studies in Genevan Government* (Geneva, 1964).

Monter, E. W., *Calvin's Geneva* (New York, 1967).

Ozment, Steven, *The Reformation in the Cities* (New Haven, 1975).

Partner, Peter, *Renaissance Rome, 1500–1559: Portrait of a Society* (Los Angeles, 1976).

Perry, Mary Elizabeth, *Crime and Society in Early Modern Seville* (Hanover, New Eng., 1980).

Pike, Ruth, *Enterprise and Adventure: The Genoese in Seville and the Opening of the New World* (Ithaca, N.Y., 1966).

Pike, Ruth, *Aristocrats and Traders: Sevillian Society in the Sixteenth Century* (London, 1972).

Pullan, Brian, *Rich and Poor in Renaissance Venice* (Oxford, 1971).

Pullan, Brian, 'Support and Redeem: Charity and Poor Relief in Italian Cities from the Fourteenth to the Seventeenth Century', *Continuity and Change*, 3 (1988), 177–208.

Ramsay, G. D., 'Industrial Discontent in Early Elizabethan London: Clothworkers and Merchants Adventurer in Conflict', *London Journal*, 1 (1975), 227–39.

Ringrose, D., 'The Impact of a New Capital City: Madrid, Toldeo and New Castile, 1560–1660', *Journal of Economic History*, 33 (1973), 761– 92.

Roper, Lyndal, *The Holy Household: Women and Morals in Reformation Augsburg* (Oxford, 1989).

Scribner, R. W., 'Civic Unity and the Reformation in Erfurt', *Past and Present*, 66 (1975), 29–60.

Scribner, R. W., 'Why was there no Reformation in Cologne?', *Bulletin of the Institute for Historical Research*, 49 (1976), 217–41.

Seebass, Gottfried, 'The Reformation in Nürnberg', in Buck and Zophy, *Social History*, 17–40 (see section 11, Essays).

Sjoberg, Gideon, *The Preindustrial City: Past and Present* (New York, 1960).

Strauss, Gerald, *Nuremberg in the Sixteenth Century* (Bloomington, Ind., 1976).

van der Wee, H., *The Antwerp Market and the European Economy*, 3 vols (The Hague, 1963).

van Houtte, J. A., 'Anvers au xve et xvie siècles: expansion et apogée', *Annales*, 16 (1961), 248–78.

van Houtte, J. A., 'Déclin et survivance d'Anvers', in *Studi in onore di Amintore Fanfani*, 5 vols (Milan, 1962), vol. 5, 703–26.

Whaley, Joachim C., *Religious Toleration and Social Change in Hamburg, 1529–1819* (Cambridge, 1985).

9. States and wars

Anglo, Sydney, *Spectacle, Pageantry and Early Tudor Policy* (Oxford, 1969).

Anglo, Sydney, *Machiavelli* (London, 1971).

Aylmer, G. E., 'Bureaucracy', *NCMH*, vol. 13. 164–200.

Bertelli, Sergio (ed.) *Italian Renaissance Courts*, trans. Mary Fitton and Geoffrey Culverwell (London, 1986).

Chabod, F., 'Was there a Renaissance State?', in H. Lubasz (ed.) *The Development of the Modern State* (New York, 1964), 26–42.

Corvisier, André, *Armies and Societies in Europe, 1494–1789*, trans. Abigail Siddall (Bloomington, Ind., 1979).

Dickens, A. G. (ed.) *The Courts of Europe* (London, 1977).

Donaldson, Peter S., *Machiavelli and Mystery of State* (Cambridge, 1988).

Duffy, Christopher, *Siege Warfare: The Fortress in the Early Modern World, 1494–1660* (London, 1970).

Elton, G. R., *Policy and Police: The Enforcement of the Reformation in the Age of Thomas Cromwell* (Cambridge, 1972).

Elton, G. R., *Reform and Renewal: Thomas Cromwell and the Common Weal* (Cambridge, 1973).

Fernandez-Santamaria, J. A., *The State, War and Peace: Spanish Political Thought in the Renaissance, 1516–1559* (Cambridge, 1977).

Figgis, J. N., *From Gerson to Grotius*, 2nd edn (Cambridge, 1916).

Goodman, Anthony, *The New Monarchy: England, 1471–1534* (Oxford, 1988).

Hale, J. R., *War and Society in Renaissance Europe, 1450–1620* (London, 1985).

Hamilton, Bernice, *Political Thought in Sixteenth-Century Spain* (Oxford, 1963).

Hexter, J. H., *The Vision of Politics on the Eve of the Reformation* (London, 1973).

Hurstfield, Joel, 'Social Structure, Office-Holding and Politics, chiefly in Western Europe', *NCMH*, vol. 3, 126–49.

Langbein, John H., *Prosecuting Crime in the Renaissance: England, Germany, France* (Cambridge, Mass., 1974).

Levey, Michael, *Painting at Court* (London, 1971).

Litchfield, R. Burr, *Emergence of a Bureaucracy: The Florentine Patriciate, 1530–1790* (Princeton, 1986).

Lloyd, Howell A., *The State, France, and the Sixteenth Century* (London, 1983).

Loades, D. M., *The Tudor Court* (London, 1986).

Mallett, Michael, *Mercenaries and their Masters: Warfare in Renaissance Italy* (London, 1974).

Mallett, M. E., and Hale, J. R., *The Military Organisation of a Renaissance State: Venice, c.1400–1617* (Cambridge, 1984).

Maravall, J. A., 'The Origins of the Modern State', *Journal of World History*, 4 (1961), 789–808.

Martin, Colin, and Parker, Geoffrey, *The Spanish Armada* (London, 1988).

Mattingly, Garrett, *Renaissance Diplomacy* (Harmondsworth, 1965).

Morris, Christopher, *Political Thought in England: Tyndale to Hooker* (Oxford, 1953).

Myers, A. R., *Parliaments and Estates in Europe to 1789* (London, 1975).

Oestreich, G., *Neostoicism and the Early Modern State*, ed. Brigitta Oestreich and H. G. Koenigsberger, trans. David McLintock (Cambridge, 1982).

Oman, Charles, *A History of the Art of War in the Sixteenth Century* (Elstree, 1937).

Owens, J. B., 'The Conception of Absolute Royal Power in Sixteenth-Century Castile', *Pensiero Politico*, 3 (1977), 349–61.

Petrie, Charles, *Don John of Austria* (London, 1967).

Prodi, Paolo, *The Papal Prince*, trans. Susan Haskins (Cambridge, 1987).

Ranke, L. von, *The History of the Popes*, trans. E. Foster, 3 vols (London, 1866).

Reinhard, Wolfgang, 'Finanza pontificia, sistema beneficiale e finanza statale nell'età confessionale', in Hermann Kellenbenz and Paolo Prodi (eds) *Fisco, religione, Stato nell'età confessionale* (Bologna, 1989), 489–504.

Rodríguez-Salgado, M., 'The Habsburg-Valois Wars', *NCMH*, vol. 2, 2nd edn, 377–400.

Shennan, J. H., *The Origins of the Modern European State, 1450–1725* (London, 1974).

Skinner, Quentin, *The Foundations of Modern Political Thought*, 2 vols (Cambridge, 1978).

Smith, A. G. R., *The Government of Elizabethan England* (London, 1967).

Starkey, David (ed.) *Henry VIII: A European Court in England* (London, 1991).

Strong, Roy, *The Cult of Elizabeth* (London, 1977).

Strong, Roy, *Art and Power: Renaissance Festivals, 1450–1650* (Woodbridge, 1984).

Thompson, I. A. A., *War and Government in Habsburg Spain, 1560–1620* (London, 1976).

Thompson, I. A. A., 'The Purchase of Nobility in Castile, 1552–1700', *Journal of European Economic History*, 8 (1977), 313–60.

Trevor-Roper, H. R., *Princes and Artists: Patronage and Ideology at Four Habsburg Courts, 1517–1633* (New York, 1976).

Ullmann, Walter, *A Short History of the Papacy in the Middle Ages* (London, 1972).

Ullmann, Walter, *Medieval Political Thought* (Harmondsworth, 1975).

Wernham, R. B., *The Making of Elizabethan Foreign Policy, 1558–1603* (Los Angeles, 1980).

Wilks, Michael, *The Problem of Sovereignty in the Later Middle Ages* (Cambridge, 1963).

Wilson, Charles, *Mercantilism* (H.A. pamphlet, London, 1958).

Wilson, Charles, *Queen Elizabeth and the Revolt of the Netherlands* (London, 1970).

Yates, Frances, *Astraea: The Imperial theme in the Sixteenth Century* (Harmondsworth, 1977).

10.   Regional Studies

(i)   Spain

Elliott, J. H., *Imperial Spain, 1469–1716* (Harmondsworth, 1970).

Garcia-Villoslada, Ricardo (ed.) *La Iglesia en la Espana de los siglos xv y xvi*, vol. 3–1 of *Historia de la Iglesia en Espana* (Madrid, 1980).

Haliczer, Stephen, *The Comuneros of Castile: The Forging of a Revolution, 1475–1521* (Madison, 1981).

Kamen, Henry, *The Spanish Inquisition* (New York, 1975).

Kamen, Henry, *Spain, 1469–1714: A Society of Conflict* (London, 1983).

Kamen, Henry, *Golden Age Spain* (London, 1988).
Lourie, E., 'A Society Organised for War: Medieval Spain', *Past and Present*, 35 (1966), 54–76.
Koenigsberger, H. G., 'Western Europe and the Power of Spain', *NCMH*, vol. 3, 234–318.
Lovett, A. W., *Early Habsburg Spain, 1517–1598* (Oxford, 1986).
Lynch, John, *Spain under the Habsburgs*, 2 vols (Oxford, 1964).
MacKay, Angus, *Spain in the Middle Ages: From Frontier to Empire, 1000–1500* (London, 1977).
Maltby, William S., *The Black Legend in England: The Development of Anti-Spanish Sentiment, 1558–1660* (Durham, N.C., 1971).
Maltby, William S., *Alba* (Los Angeles, 1983).
Parker, Geoffrey, *The Army of Flanders and the Spanish Road, 1567–1659* (Cambridge, 1972).
Parker, Geoffrey, *Philip II* (London, 1979).
Rodríguez-Salgado, M. J., *The Changing Face of Empire: Charles V, Philip II and Habsburg Authority, 1551–1559* (Cambridge, 1988).
Vilar, Pierre, 'The Age of Don Quixote', in Peter Earle (ed.) *Essays in European Economic History, 1500–1800* (Oxford, 1974), 100–13.
Wright, L. P., 'The Military Orders in Sixteenth and Seventeenth-Century Spanish Society', *Past and Present*, 43 (1969), 34–70.

(ii)   The Low Countries

Geyl, Pieter, *The Revolt of the Netherlands, 1555–1609*, 2nd edn (London, 1958).
Geyl, Pieter, 'The National State and the Writers of Netherlands History', in his *Debates with Historians* (London, 1962), 211–33.
Griffiths, Gordon, 'The Revolutionary Character of the Revolt of the Netherlands', *Comparative Studies in Society and History*, 2 (1959–60), 452–72.
Parker, Geoffrey, *The Dutch Revolt* (Harmondsworth, 1979).
Schöffer, I, '"The Dutch Revolt Anatomised": Some Comments', *Comparative Studies in Society and History*, 3 (1960–1), 470–77.
Smit, J. W., 'The Netherlands Revolution', in Robert Forster and Jack P. Greene (eds) *Preconditions of Revolution in Early Modern Europe* (Baltimore, 1970), 19–54.
Swart, K. W., *William the Silent and the Revolt of the Netherlands* (H.A. pamphlet, London, 1978).

(iii)   France

Briggs, Robin, *Early Modern France, 1560–1715* (Oxford, 1977).
Greengrass, Mark, *France in the Age of Henri IV: The Struggle for Stability* (London, 1984).
Greengrass, Mark, *The French Reformation* (Oxford, 1987).
Kelley, Donald R., *The Beginning of Ideology: Consciousness and Society in the French Reformation* (Cambridge, 1981).
Kingdon, R. M., *Geneva and the Coming of the Wars of Religion in France, 1555–1563* (Geneva, 1956).

Kingdon, R. M., *Geneva and the Consolidation of the French Protestant Movement, 1564–1572* (Geneva, 1967).

Major, J. Russell, *The Estates General of 1560* (Princeton, 1951).

Major, J. Russell, 'The Crown and the Aristocracy in Renaissance France', *American Historical Review*, 69 (1964), 631–45.

Major, J. Russell, *Representative Government in Early Modern France* (New Haven, 1980).

Major, J. Russell, 'Noble Income, Inflation and the Wars of Religion in France', *American Historical Review*, 86 (1981), 21–48.

Neale, J. E., *The Age of Catherine de Medici* (London, 1953).

Parker, David, *The Making of French Absolutism* (London, 1983).

Prestwich, Menna, 'Calvinism in France, 1559–1629', in Prestwich, *Calvinism*, 71–89 (see section 11, Essays).

Salmon, J. H. M., *Society in Crisis: France in the Sixteenth Century* (London, 1979).

Shimizu, J., *Conflict of Loyalties: Politics and Religion in the Career of Gaspard de Coligny* (Geneva, 1970).

Sutherland, N. M., 'Calvinism and the Conspiracy of Amboise', *History*, 47 (1962), 111–38.

Sutherland, N. M., *Catherine de Medici and the Ancien Régime* (H.A. pamphlet, London, 1966).

Sutherland, N. M., 'Parisian Life in the Sixteenth Century', in Gundersheimer, *French Humanism*, 51–64 (see section 11, Essays).

Sutherland, N. M., *The Massacre of St Bartholomew and the European Conflict, 1559–1572* (London, 1973).

Sutherland, N. M., *The Huguenot Struggle for Recognition* (New Haven, 1980).

(iv) Italy

Chambers, D. S., *The Imperial Age of Venice, 1380–1580* (London, 1970).

Chastel, André, *The Sack of Rome, 1527*, trans. Beth Archer (Princeton, 1983).

Cochrane, Eric, *Italy, 1530–1630* (London, 1988).

Gilbert, Felix, *Machiavelli and Guicciardini: Politics and History in Sixteenth-Century Florence* (Princeton, 1965).

Gilbert, Felix, *The Pope, his Banker, and Venice* (Cambridge, Mass., 1980).

Hale, J. R. (ed.) *Renaissance Venice* (London, 1973).

Hay, Denys and Law, John, *Italy in the Age of the Renaissance, 1380–1530* (London, 1989).

Hook, Judith, *The Sack of Rome, 1527* (London, 1972).

Koenigsberger, H. G., *The Government of Sicily under Philip II* (London, 1951).

Mallett, Michael, *The Borgias* (London, 1971).

Martines, Lauro, 'The Gentleman in Renaissance Italy: Strains of Isolation in the Body Politic', in Kinsman, *Darker Vision*, 77–94 (see section 11, Essays).

Martines, Lauro, *Power and Imagination: City-States in Renaissance Italy* (New York, 1980).

Partner, Peter, 'The Papal State: 1417–1600', in Mark Greengrass (ed.) *Conquest and Coalescence: The Shaping of the State in Early Modern Europe* (London, 1991), 25–47.

Pullan, Brian (ed.) *Crisis and Change in the Venetian Economy* (London, 1969).

Stephens, J. N., *The Fall of the Florentine Republic, 1512–1530* (Oxford, 1983).

Tenenti, Alberto, *Piracy and the Decline of Venice, 1580–1615*, trans. Brian and Janet Pullan (London, 1967).

Villari, Rosario, 'The Insurrection in Naples of 1585', in Cochrane, *Late Italian Renaissance*, 305–30 (see section 11, Essays).

Weinstein, Donald, *Savonarola and Florence: Prophecy and Patriotism in the Renaissance* (Princeton, 1970).

(v) Germany and the Empire

Barraclough, Geoffrey, *The Origins of Modern Germany* (Oxford, 1979).

Benecke, G., *Society and Politics in Germany, 1500–1750* (London, 1974).

Brady, Thomas A., *Turning Swiss: Cities and Empire, 1450–1550* (Cambridge, 1985).

Brandi, Karl, *The Emperor Charles V*, trans. C. V. Wedgwood (London, 1965).

Carsten, F. L., *The Origins of Prussia* (Oxford, 1954).

Carsten, F. L., *Princes and Parliaments in Germany from the Fifteenth to the Eighteenth Century* (Oxford, 1959).

Chudoba, Bohdan, *Spain and the Empire, 1519–1643* (Chicago, 1952).

Clasen, Claus-Peter, *The Palatinate in European History, 1555–1618* (Oxford, 1966).

Evans, R. J. W., *The Making of the Habsburg Monarchy, 1550–1700* (Oxford, 1979).

Headley, John M., *The Emperor and his Chancellor: A Study of the Imperial Chancellery under Gattinara* (Cambridge, 1983).

Holborn, Hajo, *A History of Modern Germany: The Reformation* (New York, 1959).

Hsia, R. Po-chia, *Social Discipline in the Reformation: Central Europe, 1550–1750* (London, 1989).

(vi) The Frontiers: Northern, Central and Eastern Europe

Benzoni, Gino (ed.) *Il Mediterraneo nella seconda metà del '500 alla luce di Lepanto* (Florence, 1974).

Bradford, Ernle, *The Great Siege* (London, 1961).

Chejne, Anwar, *Islam and the West: The Moriscos. A Cultural and Social History* (Albany, New York, 1983).

Coles, P. H., *The Ottoman Impact on Europe* (London, 1968).

Crummey, R. O., *The Formation of Muscovy, 1304–1614* (London, 1987).

Earle, Peter, *Corsairs of Malta and Barbary* (London, 1970).

Fischer-Galati, Stephen A., *Ottoman Imperialism and German Protestantism, 1521–1555* (Cambridge, Mass., 1959).

Guilmartin, John F., *Gunpowder and Galleys* (Cambridge, 1974).

Hess, Andrew C., 'The Moriscos: An Ottoman Fifth Column in Sixteenth-Century Spain?', *American Historical Review*, 74 (1968), 1–25.

Hess, Andrew C., 'The Evolution of the Ottoman Seaborne Empire in the Age of the Oceanic Discoveries, 1453–1525', *American Historical Review*, 75 (1970), 1892–1919.

Hess, Andrew C., 'The Battle of Lepanto and its Place in Mediterranean History', *Past and Present*, 57 (1972), 53–73.

Hess, Andrew C., *The Forgotten Frontier: A History of the Sixteenth-Century Ibero-African Frontier* (Chicago, 1978).

Inalcik, Halil, 'The Emergence of the Ottomans', *Cambridge History of Islam*, vol. 1A (Cambridge, 1970), 263–323.

Inalcik, Halil, 'The Heyday and Decline of the Ottoman Empire', *Cambridge History of Islam*, vol. 1A (Cambridge, 1970), 324–53.

Inalcik, Halil, *The Ottoman Empire: The Classical Age, 1300–1600*, trans. Norman Itzkowitz and Colin Imber (London, 1973).

Kirby, David, *Northern Europe in the Early Modern Period: The Baltic World, 1492–1772* (London, 1990).

Kortepeter, C. Max, *Ottoman Imperialism during the Reformation: Europe and the Caucasus* (London and New York, 1972).

McNeill, William H., *Europe's Steppe Frontier, 1500–1800* (Chicago, 1964).

Roberts, Michael, *The Early Vasas: A History of Sweden, 1523–1611* (Cambridge, 1968).

Schwoebel, Robert, *The Shadow of the Crescent: The Renaissance Image of the Turk, 1453–1517* (Nieuwkoop, 1967).

Subtelny, O., *Domination of Eastern Europe: Native Nobilities and Foreign Absolutism, 1500–1715* (London, 1986).

Willetts, Henry, 'Slav Nations: Poland and the Evolution of Russia', in Trevor-Roper, *Golden Age*, 204–30 (see section 4, Reference).

(vii)   The British Isles

Bottigheimer, Karl S., 'Kingdom and Colony: Ireland in the Westward Enterprise, 1536–1660', in Andrews, Canny and Hair, *Westward Enterprise*, 45–65 (see section 11, Essays).

Bradshaw, Brendan, *The Irish Constitutional Revolution of the Sixteenth Century* (Cambridge, 1979).

Canney, Nicholas, 'Early Modern Ireland, c.1500–1700', in R. F. Foster (ed.) *The Oxford Illustrated History of Ireland* (Oxford, 1989), 108–30.

Cross, Clare, *Church and People, 1450–1660* (London, 1976).

Davies, C. S. L., *Peace, Print and Protestantism, 1450–1558* (London, 1977).

Elton, G. R., *Reform and Reformation: England, 1509–1558* (London, 1977).

Guy, John, *Tudor England* (Oxford, 1988).

Hoskins, W. G., *The Age of Plunder: The England of Henry VIII, 1500–1547* (London, 1976).

Hurstfield, Joel, *Elizabeth I and the Unity of England* (Harmondsworth, 1971).

Loades, D. M., *Politics and the Nation, 1450–1660: Obedience, Resistance and Public Order* (London, 1974).
Lynch, Michael, 'Calvinism in Scotland, 1559–1638', in Prestwich, *Calvinism*, 225–55 (see section 11, Essays).
Russell, Conrad, *The Crisis of Parliaments: English History, 1509–1660* (Oxford, 1971).
Scarisbrick, J. J., *Henry VIII* (Harmondsworth, 1968).
Williams, Penry, *The Tudor Regime* (Oxford, 1979).
Wormald, Jenny, *Court, Kirk and Community: Scotland, 1470–1625* (London, 1981).
Zeefeld, W. Gordon, *Foundations of Tudor Policy* (London, 1969).

11. Collections of Essays

A training in history has always laid great emphasis on writing essays, but the importance of reading essays is rarely given equal stress. The following collections show how the historian identifies a problem, constructs and qualifies an argument and moves from the particular to the general or the general to the particular, drawing balanced conclusions in the light of the strengths and weaknesses of available evidence. Attention is drawn to some individual essays in the preceding parts of this list.

Andrews, K. R., Canny, N. P. and Hair, P. E. H. (eds) *The Westward Enterprise: English Activities in Ireland, the Atlantic and America, 1480–1650* (Liverpool, 1979).
Anglo, Sydney (ed.) *Chivalry in the Renaissance* (Woodbridge, 1990).
Aston, T. S. and Philpin, C. S. E. (eds) *The Brenner Debate: Agrarian Class Structure and Economic Development in Pre-Industrial Europe* (Cambridge, 1985).
Brooks, P. N. (ed.) *Reformation Principle and Practice* (London, 1981).
Buck, L. P., and Zophy, J. W. (eds) *The Social History of the Reformation* (Columbus, Ohio, 1972).
Burke, Peter, *The Historical Anthropology of Early Modern Italy* (Cambridge, 1987).
Chrisman, Miriam U., and Gründler, O. (eds) *Social Groups and Religious Ideas in the Sixteenth Century* (Kalamazoo, Mich., 1978).
Clark, Peter (ed.) *The Early Modern Town: A Reader* (London, 1976).
Clark, Peter (ed.) *The European Crisis of the 1590s* (London, 1985).
Cochrane, Eric (ed.) *The Late Italian Renaissance, 1525–1630* (London, 1970).
Cohn, Henry J. (ed.) *Government in Reformation Europe, 1520–1560* (London, 1971).
Davis, Natalie Zemon, *Society and Culture in Early Modern France* (Cambridge, 1987).
DeMolen, Richard (ed.) *Leaders of the Reformation* (London and Toronto, 1987).
Duke, Alistair, *Reformation and Revolt in the Low Countries* (London and Ronceverte, 1990).
Elliott, J. H., *Spain and its World, 1500–1700* (New Haven, 1989).

Elton, G. R., *Studies in Tudor and Stuart Politics and Government*, 2 vols (Cambridge, 1974).

Grendler, Paul, *Culture and Censorship in Late Renaissance Italy and France* (London, 1981).

Gundersheimer, W. L. (ed.) *French Humanism, 1470–1600* (London, 1969).

Hexter, J. H., *Reappraisals in History* (London, 1961).

Hillerbrand, H. J. (ed.) *Radical Tendencies in the Reformation: Divergent Perspectives* (Kirksville, Miss., 1987).

Hurstfield, Joel (ed.) *The Reformation Crisis* (London, 1965).

Kingdon, Robert M. (ed.) *Transition and Revolution: Problems and Issues of European Renaissance and Reformation History* (Minneapolis, 1974).

Kinsman, Robert S. (ed.) *The Darker Vision of the Renaissance: Beyond the Fields of Reason* (Los Angeles, 1974).

Koenigsberger, H. G., *Estates and Revolutions* (Ithaca, N.Y., 1971).

Koenigsberger, H. G., *Politicians and Virtuosi* (London and Ronceverte, 1986).

Ozment, Steven (ed.) *The Reformation in Medieval Perspective* (Chicago, 1971).

Parker, Geoffrey, *Spain and the Netherlands, 1559–1659: Ten Studies* (London, 1979).

Prestwich, Menna (ed.) *International Calvinism, 1541–1715* (Oxford, 1985).

Scribner, R. W. and Benecke, G. (eds) *The German Peasant War, 1525: New Viewpoints* (London, 1979).

Strauss, Gerald (ed.) *Pre-Reformation Germany* (London, 1972).

Sutherland, N. M., *Princes, Politics and Religion, 1559–1589* (London, 1984).

Trevor-Roper, H. R., *Religion, the Reformation and Social Change*, 2nd edn (London, 1972).

Trevor-Roper, H. R., *Renaissance Essays* (London, 1985).

Yates, Frances A., *Collected Essays*, 3 vols, vol. 1 *Lull and Bruno*; vol. 2 *Renaissance and Reform: The Italian Contribution*; vol. 3 *Ideas and Ideals in the North European Renaissance* (London, 1982–4).

Index